Social Marketin

Social marketing involves the application of marketing techniques (usually associated with promoting consumption) to social ends. As a socially conscious marketing student this new edition will arm you with:

- case studies from across the globe
- accessible exercises
- engaging stories, and
- online support with an expanded and enhanced companion website

which will all enable you to think critically about the individual and systemic drivers of both harm and progress, and provide you with the tools to act.

This popular introductory textbook has been thoroughly updated to enable students to challenge the bad, champion the good and become rebels with a cause. Now including more on systems thinking, evaluation and apps, Hastings and Domegan also introduce the influential new 3Cs model (Containment, Counter-Marketing, Critical Capacity Building).

This book is essential reading for all social marketing, marketing ethics, and marketing and society courses.

Gerard Hastings is Professor of Social Marketing at Stirling University, UK, the Open University, UK, and L'École des Hautes Etudes en Santé Publique, Rennes, France. He is currently a Commissioner on the Lancet Obesity Commission, and a member of the Board of Alcohol Focus Scotland and of the British Medical Association Board of Science.

Christine Domegan is Head of Marketing at NUI Galway, Ireland, and European Editor of the *Journal of Social Marketing*. Christine is also Honorary Associate Professor, ISM, University of Stirling, UK, Adjunct Professor, Social Marketing, Griffith University, Brisbane, Australia, and Visiting Professor, Florida Prevention Research Center Fellow, Associate of the World Health Organization Collaborating Center on Social Marketing and Social Change at the University of South Florida, USA.

Social Marketing
Rebels with a Cause

Third Edition

Gerard Hastings and
Christine Domegan

Routledge
Taylor & Francis Group

LONDON AND NEW YORK

Third edition published 2018
by Routledge
2 Park Square, Milton Park, Abingdon, Oxon OX14 4RN

and by Routledge
711 Third Avenue, New York, NY 10017

Routledge is an imprint of the Taylor & Francis Group, an informa business

First edition published by Butterworth-Heinemann 2007

British Library Cataloguing-in-Publication Data
A catalogue record for this book is available from the British Library

Library of Congress Cataloging-in-Publication Data
Names: Hastings, Gerard (Professor), author. | Domegan, Christine, author.
Title: Social marketing / Gerard Hastings and Christine Domegan.
Description: Third edition. | Abingdon, Oxon ; New York, NY :
    Routledge, 2018. | Includes bibliographical references and index. |
    Description based on print version record and CIP data provided
    by publisher; resource not viewed.
Identifiers: LCCN 2017019699 (print) | LCCN 2017033058 (ebook) |
    ISBN 9781315648590 (eBook) | ISBN 9781138123823
    (hardback : alk. paper) | ISBN 9781138123830 (pbk. : alk. paper)
Subjects: LCSH: Social marketing—Handbooks, manuals, etc. |
    Behavior modification.
Classification: LCC HF5414 (ebook) | LCC HF5414 .H37 2018 (print) |
    DDC 658.8—dc23
LC record available at https://lccn.loc.gov/2017019699

ISBN: 978-1-138-12382-3 (hbk)
ISBN: 978-1-138-12383-0 (pbk)
ISBN: 978-1-315-64859-0 (ebk)

Typeset in Iowan Old Style
by Swales & Willis Ltd, Exeter, Devon, UK
Printed and bound by CPI Group (UK) Ltd, Croydon, CR0 4YY

Visit the companion website: www.routledge.com/cw/hastings

For Peter

Contents

List of figures   *xi*
List of tables   *xiii*
Case study contributors   *xv*
Foreword: a book to make you stop and think   *xxxi*
Preface: rebels with a cause   *xxxiii*

1. Harnessing the power of marketing   1

2. Social marketing principles   26

3. The shoulders of giants   52

4. Making it happen – the toolbox   83

5. Research and the teller of tales   119

6. Compelling content   152

7. Competitive analysis   187

8. Critical marketing   214

9. Spiritual dimensions   250

10. Ethical issues   276

11. Systems social marketing   291

Case studies   310

1. A wicked problem and the SIMPle solution   310
    Sinead Duane, Christine Domegan, Aoife Callan, Sandra Galvin,
    Martin Cormican, Kathleen Bennett, Andrew W. Murphy
    and Akke Vellinga

2. Seas of energy: using a systems research approach for a
    wicked problem   329
    Patricia McHugh, Christine Domegan, Marzia Mazzonetto,
    Sinead Duane, John Joyce, Michelle Devaney, Michael Hogan,
    Benjamin J. Broome and Joanna Piwowarczyk

3. Meals on Wheels: a community-led approach and stakeholder
    analysis   339
    Christine Fitzgerald, Christine Domegan and Tom Scharf

4. Reduce Your Juice: a digital social marketing programme for
    reducing residential electricity use   346
    Rebekah Russell-Bennett, Rory Mulcahy, Ryan McAndrew,
    Tim Swinton, Jo-Anne Little and Neil Horrocks

5. Innovative youth engagement: empowerment, co-production
    and health optimisation (tobacco-free generation 2034:
    the Fife Project)   357
    Marisa de Andrade, Karen Cooper and Kay Samson

6. The Porto Tap Water programme   381
    Ana Sofia Dias and Sara Balonas

7. Development of strategies to promote solid waste management
    in Bourj Hammoud, Lebanon   390
    Amena El Harakeh, Farah Madi and Marco Bardus

8. "I know what I'm doing": communicating a safety message
    to change the attitudes and behaviours of older men   406
    Linda Brennan, Glen Donnar, Lukas Parker and Natalia Alessi

9. Walk to School 2014   420
    Krzysztof Kubacki, Kellye Hartman, Annemarie Wright,
    Haruka Fujihira and Sharyn Rundle-Thiele

10. Cycle Against Suicide: the creation of a community-based
    social marketing programme to promote mental health in Ireland   432
    Amy Cannon, Olivia Freeman and Patrick Kenny

11. Moi(s) sans tabac: the first collective challenge for smoking
    cessation launched by Santé publique France   444
    Karine Gallopel-Morvan, Olivier Smadja, Anna Mercier, Elodie Safta,
    Jennifer Davies, Romain Guignard, Pierre Arwidson and Viêt Nguyen Thanh

12. Food waste in higher education institutions: 'Smaller Eyes than
    Belly Movement'   453
    Sara Balonas and Susana Marques

13. Civil society monitoring of tobacco industry point-of-sale
    marketing in Colombia   462
    Juan Miguel Rey-Pino, Liliana Andrea Ávila-García,
    Jaime Arcila Sierra and Marian Lorena Ibarra Ávila

14. Reducing the negative environmental impact of SMEs in
    Pakistan's leather and tanning industry   468
    Anne M. Smith and Aqueel Imtiaz Wahga

15. Changing population salt intake behaviour: lessons from the
    UK salt reduction strategy   478
    Michael Barry and Maurice Murphy

16. The Act-Belong-Commit mental health promotion campaign   482
    Rob J. Donovan and Julia Anwar McHenry

17. From concept to action: integration of systems thinking and
    social marketing for health disparities elimination   492
    Brian J. Biroscak, Carol A. Bryant, Claudia X. Aguado Loi,
    Dinorah Martinez Tyson, Tali Schneider, Laura Baum, Aldenise Ewing
    and Peter S. Hovmand

18. Fast fashion: a wicked problem for macro-social
    marketing   502
    Ann-Marie Kennedy, Sommer Kapitan, Neha Bajaj,
    Angelina Bakonyi and Sean Sands

19. Whale sharks, Ningaloo Reef, Western Australia   509
    Sarah Duffy and Roger A. Layton

20. Wheels, Skills and Thrills   525
    Alan Tapp

21. An evaluation of Sea for Society using system
    indicators   534
    Patricia McHugh and Christine Domegan

22. The Taj Must Smile   542
    Sanjeev Vyas

23. Identification of behavioural change strategies to prevent cervical
    cancer among Malay women in Malaysia   555
    *Julinawati Suanda, Desmond Cawley, Maria Brenner, Christine Domegan
    and Neil Rowan*

24. Making India open-defecation-free: lessons from the Swachh
    Bharat Mission – Gramin process evaluation   567
    Anurudra Bhanot, Vinti Agarwal, Ashutosh Awasthi and Animesh Sharma

    Index   580

Figures

1.1   The exchange process in marketing   9
1.2   The domain of social marketing   14
2.1   A strategic vision of social marketing   44
3.1   Assessing people's stage of change   56
3.2   The 'Spiral' model   58
3.3   Stages of change Mark 2   59
3.4   The wider determinants of health behaviour   60
3.5   A social ecological model   65
3.6   Social marketing's value triad   69
3.7   Social marketing's interacting value-driven exchanges and
      value action fields.   72
3.8   A nurses' flu vaccination triple triad value-driven exchanges
      and value action fields   73
4.1   A social marketing plan   86
4.2   The marketing environment   87
5.1   Action research   122
5.2   Branding prescription drugs   128
5.3   The social marketing research process   141
5.4   Reflective evaluation research   145
6.1   Report of a radio broadcast of *The War of the Worlds* from *The
      Guardian*, 1 November 1938   155
6.2   The medium is the message   161
6.3   Safefood's folic acid campaign   163
6.4   The hazards of using sign language   164
6.5   Images have many levels of meaning   165
7.1   The delights of quitting   196
7.2   Promoting obesity?   203

8.1	How power distorts marketing relationships	225
8.2	Graffiti	227
8.3	Facebook and you	237
9.1	The 3Cs Model	272
10.1	Ethical dilemmas in social marketing planning	280
11.1	Systems social marketing – practice, planning and implementation	303
11.2	Indicators for systems social marketing	306

Tables

1.1 The case studies in this book   18
4.1 Stakeholder characteristics   91
4.2 The social marketing intervention mix   104
6.1 Examples of social marketing utilising social and digital marketing   183
11.1 Dominant community social marketing models   297

Case study contributors

Vinti K. Agarwal holds a specialisation in economics, finance and data analytics, with almost two decades of experience working primarily in an academic environment while often taking up appointments within the developmental and tertiary education sector, such as the Nirma Institute of Management, the ICFAI Business School, and the last with the National Institute of Financial Management. She is now currently working as Sr. Research Manager, BBC Media Action, handling quantitative research, knowledge management activities and academic publications. Prior to this, she carried out research projects in areas such as usage of private and public health facilities among women users, the effectiveness of microfinance in empowering women, health financing in India, enrolment, attendance and infrastructure in Indian primary education, and the workings of central autonomous bodies of the Government of India. She holds a doctorate in economics from Meerut University, a Chartered Financial Analyst designation from the Institute of Chartered Financial Analysts of India, and a Master's in government analytics from Johns Hopkins University. She has several national and international academic publications and conference presentations to her credit. She also actively contributes pro-bono to many research and data analysis initiatives for nonprofits, spiritual organisations and society organisations.

Claudia X. Aguado Loi, PhD, MPH, CPH, CHES is Assistant Professor in Health Science and Human Performance at the University of Tampa. She specialises in research methodology in public health education and promotion, programme planning and evaluation, community-engaged research, and epidemiology. She brings extensive experience working with Latino populations in cancer survivorship (e.g., quality of life of Latina breast cancer survivors), chronic disease self-management, and cancer health disparities.

Natalia Alessi is a graphic designer and PhD candidate in the School of Media and Communications at RMIT University in Melbourne, Australia. Her design areas are visual communication, book design and info-graphics. Her research interests include branding, place branding, stereotypes and Latin America.

Julia Anwar McHenry is the Evaluation Officer for Mentally Healthy WA based at Curtin University's School of Public Health. She has previously worked on a number of diverse research projects in the areas of mental health and wellbeing, health promotion, the arts and health, indigenous communities, and regional development.

Jaime Arcila Sierra has been the Latin America Organiser with Corporate Accountability International since 2009. An effective communicator with the ability to implement and advance innovative campaigns, he has wide experience in strategic marketing and global tobacco control.

Pierre Arwidson studied at the Tours Faculty of Medicine in France. He was initially involved in medical education and the development of problem-based learning. He then worked at a regional level in health education and the prevention of cardiovascular diseases and thereafter was in charge of the scientific department at the French Institute of Health Promotion and Health Education. He is now deputy of the Prevention and Health Promotion department of the newly created agency called Public Health France.

Liliana Andrea Ávila-García is the legal advisor for Educar Consumidores (Colombia) and responsible for undertaking strategic litigation at both national and local levels, as well as developing the legal component of the project orientated towards enforcing the national policy on tobacco control through advocacy actions that bring about changes in the legislation regarding packaging and labelling, monitoring tobacco industry interferences to the tobacco control measures embodied in Law 1339/2009, and strengthening civil society actions to support and demand the adequate implementation of that law.

Ashutosh Awasthi works as Research Manager at BBC Media Action (India). His current role involves advising and guiding different communication interventions on a wide array of social issues like maternal and child health, gender, sanitation, child labour and disaster management. It also involves the design and execution of monitoring, evaluation and learning strategies on different social and behavioural change communication outputs on these issues across different geographies of India. This current role has also given him an opportunity to closely interact of various international donors and government agencies like the Bill and Melinda Gates Foundation, USAID, the Ministry of Drinking Water and Sanitation, and the Ministry of Health and Family Welfare. He has a Master's degree in Rural Management from the Xavier Institute of Management, Bhubaneswar.

Neha Bajaj has been lecturing and tutoring at RMIT University Melbourne since 2012. Her research projects include the wicked problems of fast fashion, household obesity and Drinking Related Lifestyles for VIC Health, International CRM, Meaning of Cool and Consumer Service Encounters. Her minor thesis was based on why consumers buy counterfeit products and she has published two competitive papers at the Australia and New Zealand Marketing Association conference. She is currently completing her PhD in marketing at RMIT University Melbourne, Australia. Her present research is on peer-to-peer exchange economies, looking at the role that networks play in the growth of peer-to-peer platforms and understanding consumer motivations. Neha has been a visiting lecturer in Singapore.

Angelina Bakonyi is a Masters of Marketing student at RMIT. Her research interests are in social marketing and social issues.

Sara Balonas is Assistant Professor at the University of Minho and Researcher at the Communication and Society Research Centre. She has a PhD degree in Communication Sciences – Advertising in the Social Sphere, and teaches strategic communication and advertising. Her research work is focused on the reconfiguration of advertising, its role in society beyond consumption and as a contribution to a better citizenship practice. Areas of study include advertising in the social sphere, behavioural advertising, non-profit communication strategies, and corporate social responsibility. Other study themes are communication and public health, territorial communication, political communication, and the relationship between communication and religion. She is also CEO of B+ Communication, an advertising company created in 2002, and founder of the Be True Programme for social responsibility (2010), as well as a member of the board of a non-profit association and of ADDICT (an agency for creative industries). She has been a columnist in a national newspaper (2012–2015) and an ambassador of entrepreneurship, nominated by the European Commission (2010–2013).

Marco Bardus is Assistant Professor in Health Promotion and Community Health at the Faculty of Health Sciences at the American University of Beirut (AUB), where he teaches Social Marketing, Health Communication and other related subjects, both at the graduate and undergraduate level. With a background in corporate communication and marketing, acquired in over fifteen years' experience in the public relations and journalism industries, his research aims to understand how persuasive communication strategies, combined with mobile and web technologies, can be used to address public health issues, such as noncommunicable diseases and chronic conditions. His research focuses on the use of smartphone and mobile apps, social media and wearable devices as delivery modes for health promotion and behaviour change interventions. Marco aims to expand his investigations to include a broader spectrum of health and pro-environmental and sustainable behaviours (e.g., recycling, reusing), as well as disease management and prevention.

Michael Barry was a Master's of Business student at the Cork Institute of Technology, Cork, Ireland. His case study represents the work he did as part of his thesis.

Laura Baum, CPH, MA, MPH, is a research associate conducting and analysing qualitative research at USF's Florida Prevention Research Center. She works on the Center is Community-Based Prevention Marketing for Systems Change project, as well as a mobile health study on teen asthma. With an MPH in community health and MA in applied anthropology from USF, her research topics include community and environmental health, health disparities, human rights, and social determinants of health, with a focus on the southern United States.

Professor Kathleen Bennett is a biostatistician and epidemiologist in RCSI, and is currently funded as an HRB research leader in statistical epidemiology and investigator on the Irish Cancer Society-funded Breast-Predict collaborative cancer research centre, leading a work-package related to population health. She has over twenty-five years' experience conducting research in chronic disease, including cardiovascular disease, diabetes and cancer, and use of medicines in the population. She has published over 200 peer review articles and supervised several PhD and post-doctoral projects. She also works collaboratively with multi-disciplinary groups to achieve the research goals.

Anurudra Bhanot is a communications researcher and social marketing expert with three decades of experience in the development and private sectors. For over a decade he has been responsible for providing leadership to the knowledge management function, and research-based strategic inputs for the development, management and impact evaluation of social behaviour change communication (SBCC) programmes. These programmes have covered a range of themes from Public Health, Governance and Gender Development to Poverty Alleviation, Environment and WASH (Water, Sanitation and Hygiene). Prior to this he handled marketing, consumer research and general management functions in leading corporate organisations in Asia and Africa, and in his early career looked after sales, product and marketing management functions in a dairy products company which was part of the world's largest farmer co-operative network. He has worked and travelled extensively and presented research papers in international conferences, published in international journals, and contributed case studies to books by prominent authors.

Brian J. Biroscak, PhD, MS, MA, is Assistant Professor as well as Research Director in the Department of Emergency Medicine at Yale University School of Medicine. Currently, he is applying system dynamics modelling to the research and development of Community-Based Prevention Marketing for Systems Change – a framework for community coalitions to create 'upstream' change that reduces health disparities. His research experience sits at the intersection of violence and injury prevention, social marketing, and systems science.

Linda Brennan, PhD, is based in the School of Media and Communication at RMIT University in Melbourne. In the lead-up to becoming a full-time academic, she had an active consulting practice in marketing and strategic research. Her clients include government, not for profit and educational institutions. Her research interests are social and government marketing and especially the influence of marketing communications and advertising on behaviour.

Maria Brenner is Associate Professor in Children's Nursing in the School of Nursing and Midwifery, Trinity College Dublin. She obtained her PhD, MSc and BSc from University College Dublin, and is on the nursing register of the Nursing and Midwifery Board of Ireland for Children's Nurses, General Nurses and Nurse Tutors. Her clinical background is in intensive care nursing. Her current research is focused on the care of children with complex needs and their families, their transition to home, and the management of children with complex care needs at the acute/community interface. She is leading an international team exploring this area, as part of a three and a half year programme, Models of Child Health Appraised (MOCHA), funded by the EU Horizon 2020 programme.

Benjamin J. Broome is a professor in the Hugh Downs School of Human Communication at Arizona State University, where he teaches courses in intercultural communication, group facilitation and conflict resolution. His research focuses on the third-party role in facilitating dialogue in intercultural conflicts. He has been involved with peace-building efforts in Cyprus since 1994, working closely with groups of Greek Cypriots and Turkish Cypriots in conflict resolution, problem solving and interactive design. In addition to his work in Cyprus, he has facilitated workshops with a number of government agencies, business organisations, professional associations, educational institutions, Native American tribes and community groups in the United States, Mexico and Europe, including Sea for Society.

Carol A. Bryant, PhD, MS, is a Founding Director of the University of South Florida's (USF) World Health Organization Collaborating Center in Social Marketing, and former Director of the Florida Prevention Research Center. She has directed social marketing research on a wide variety of public health and environmental protection projects. With colleagues at the Florida Prevention Research Center, she helped develop the framework, *Community-Based Prevention Marketing*, for designing and tailoring behavior-change interventions, policy development, and systems-level change.

Aoife Callan, PhD, was a postdoctoral researcher in health economics at the National University of Ireland, Galway, at the time of her research. She is currently team leader of the HE&OR Manager Team at Novartis Global Services Centre, Dublin, Ireland.

Amy Cannon, BSc, MSc, is a PhD candidate at the Dublin Institute of Technology. She was granted the Dean of Graduate Research School Award to carry out research in the area of marketing. Her research is generally driven by an interest in the broader consequences of marketing communications, and their impact upon the construction of complex social issues. As a marketing communications practitioner, she has worked with a number of national and international household-name brands. She is co-founder of Far From Avocados, a content marketing agency based in Dublin. She lives in Dublin with her partner Aidan and new baby Arthur.

Desmond Cawley is a lecturer in the Department of Nursing at the Athlone Institute of Technology with research expertise in nurse education and men's health. He obtained his PhD in nursing from the University of Ulster (UK). He has published extensively in these areas and supervised numerous MSc work by research and PhD students. He is on the management committee of the EU Cost action for men's health and conducts significant humanitarian work in Africa.

Karen Cooper is a post-doctoral researcher in clinical psychology at the University of Edinburgh and has a background in Criminological and Sociological research. She has previously worked in the Scottish Government's Justice Analytical Services and at the Centre for Criminology, University of Oxford. Her work explores the role of communication technology on adolescent risk taking, online child exploitation, and deterrents to online offending. She has also worked on a portfolio of health policy projects linked to adolescent behaviours and the reintegration of young offenders with education and learning.

Martin Cormican graduated medical school at NUI Galway in 1986. He trained in Ireland, the UK and the USA prior to his appointment as Professor of Bacteriology at NUI Galway and Consultant Microbiologist at Galway University Hospital in 1999. His work includes clinical service at GUH and surrounding community and teaching and research at NUI Galway.

Jennifer Davies graduated from the London School of Economics and Sciences-Po in Paris and then took up a post at the OECD Development Centre on women's health and education. She moved to the French Institute of Health Promotion and Health Education in 2005, where she was in charge of European and international relations. At Public Health France, she works on tobacco cessation issues and is responsible for partnerships, networks, and the regional implementation of *Moi(s) sans tabac*.

Marisa de Andrade is a lecturer in Health, Science & Society at the University of Edinburgh's School of Health in Social Science. She is also Associate Director for the Centre for Creative-Relational Inquiry. Alongside research on corporate-sector involvement in public health policy and work with Professor Gerard Hastings on a number of projects in tobacco, alcohol and pharmaceutical regulation, she is passionate about arts-informed methodologies and co-producing knowledge with marginalised groups. Her current project, 'Measuring Humanity', is changing the way health and inequalities in community settings is understood and 'measured'; informing policies on equality, community empowerment; poverty and sustainability; increasing understanding of how solidarity is linked to health and equity; and changing attitudes about 'what is evidence?' when humanistic approaches are advocated in policy and practice.

Michelle Devaney has a BA, HDBS and MSc in marketing from NUI Galway, and is Projects and Operations Manager with MANA Digital in Galway. Prior to that, she was the lead research assistant for the EU-funded Sea for Society and Sea Change projects.

Ana Sofia Dias is account manager at B+ Communication, an advertising company created in 2002, with a Master's degree in Communication Sciences (Advertising and PR) under the theme 'Social Marketing: Symbolic as a strategy for behavioral change: the Águas do Porto case'. In 2013–2014, Ana was responsible for the institutional communication of SOPRO – *Solidariedade e Promoção*, a portuguese NGO.

Christine Domegan, PhD, MBS, is Head of Marketing and Senior Lecturer at the National University of Ireland, Galway, and a Visiting Professor, Florida Prevention Research Center Fellow and Associate of the World Health Organization Collaborating Center on Social Marketing and Social Change at the University of South Florida. Her current funded EU and national research work embraces H2020 Sea Change; EPA/HSE NearHealth, IRC and Safefood's Operation Transformation. She teaches social marketing at undergraduate and postgraduate level, including extensive PhD supervision. Recent social marketing publications, among others, appeared in the *Canadian Medical Association Journal, BMJ open, Marketing Theory* and the *Journal of Applied Science Research*. She is also European Editor for the *Journal of Social Marketing*.

Glen Donnar is a lecturer in the School of Media and Communication at RMIT University in Melbourne, Australia. His research focuses on popular cultural representations of masculinity, and male lives in crisis or extreme situations. He has published diversely on masculinities in periods of turmoil, including 9/11, Vietnam and the Great Recession, and also on male action film stardom, the mediation of terror in news media, and the ethics of news viewership.

Rob Donovan is Adjunct Professor in the School of Sport Science Exercise & Health at the University of Western Australia where he was previously Principal Senior Research Fellow. He has an international reputation in health promotion and social marketing across a broad variety of social issues and physical and mental health areas. He also chairs the World Anti-Doping Agency's Social Science Research Sub-Committee. He is the founder of the Act-Belong-Commit campaign and remains very much involved.

Sinead Duane was the social marketing post-doctoral researcher on the SIMPle study, funded by the Health Research Board through their Interdisciplinary Capacity Enhancement (ICE) award. She specialises in social marketing intervention design for wicked problems, and has a special interest in trial methodology and using novel techniques such as text messaging and app development to evaluate social marketing interventions.

Sarah Duffy has a PhD in marketing from the University of New South Wales and is a lecturer at the School of Business at Western Sydney University. She has worked as a marketing professional and consultant with a strong practical background in relationship management, product and brand marketing. Her professional work has informed her focus areas of research and teaching, including tackling the fundamental issue of how marketing impacts on society through strategy, policy and practice. This has led to research and publishing that concerns marketing systems theory, how marketing practice impacts on society, fairness and sustainability.

Amena B. El Harakeh is an MPH student in the Department of Health Management and Policy at the Faculty of Health Sciences at AUB. In 2015 she completed her BSc in environmental health as a scholar of the MasterCard Foundation, and was the recipient of the Penrose Award for the best combination of scholarship, character, leadership, and contribution to the university as a whole. She has been involved in research activities which revolve around occupational health, chronic diseases, palliative care and shared decision-making in healthcare. She also assisted in research activities for the Global Health Initiative at AUB and the Lancet Commission on Syria.

Aldenise Ewing, MPH, is a doctoral student in the Department of Community and Family Health at the University of South Florida, College of Public Health. While pursuing her degree, she has been involved with numerous research projects related to colorectal cancer prevention and screening interventions at the Florida Prevention Research Center. Her research interests also include addressing the social determinants of health and health inequities through utilising community-based system dynamics and social marketing. She received her MPH from Emory University's Rollins School of Public Health in Behavioral Science and Health Education.

Christine Fitzgerald is an Atlantic Fellow with the Global Brain Health Institute at Trinity College Dublin, and a visiting Fellow at the Centre for Economic and Social Research on Dementia at the National University of Ireland, Galway. Her doctoral research examined behaviour change from the perspective of a community, encompassing the environment in which behaviours occur. This research, undertaken in the Irish Meals on Wheels community, addressed key stakeholders' behaviours through the application of a community social marketing model: the Community Readiness Model. With research interests stemming from a background in health, her current role reflects the influential role that community plays on the impact and prevention of dementia.

Olivia Freeman is a lecturer in the School of Marketing, Dublin Institute of Technology. Her teaching areas include consumer behaviour and communications. Having completed her PhD in sociology, her research interests are now focused on the use of discourse analytical approaches across a range of substantive contexts from the wider sphere of business and society. She has a particular interest in children's consumption, media literacy, and the wellbeing of children and youth.

Haruka Fujihira is a PhD candidate in Social Marketing @ Griffith, Griffith University. Her current PhD study focuses on the investigation of modifiable factors of self-efficacy in sedentary behaviour reduction and physical activity advocacy in the workplace. She holds a BA in comparative cultural studies and completed her honours' dissertation on children's active school travel. She has worked on several social marketing research projects across a variety of contexts such as organ donation, healthy eating, physical activity, environmental conservation, and alcohol consumption. She has also worked in commercial marketing in Japan and Australia.

Karine Gallopel-Morvan, PhD, is Professor in Social Marketing at the EHESP School of Public Health in France (Rennes). She teaches social marketing and marketing for health organisations to MBA students and health managers. Her research activities deal with social marketing in the context of tobacco and alcohol control and look at the effects of public health prevention tools (e.g., warnings, tobacco plain packaging, advertising regulations) on people. She has contributed several research papers to academic journals as well as book chapters, and a book on *Marketing and Communication of the NGOs* (2nd edn, 2013, Dunod). She is regularly involved in expert committees for the WHO, the European Union, the French Health Ministry, the Haut Conseil de la Santé Publique, among others, and is regularly invited to national and international conferences.

Sandra Galvin holds a BSc in Microbiology (UCC) and a PhD in Bacteriology (NUI Galway). In 2012 she joined the Discipline of General Practice, NUI Galway, as a research fellow working on the SIMPle Study to improve antimicrobial prescribing by GPs in the community. She is now the Coordinator of the Health Research Board's Trials Methodology Research Network, which is an all-Ireland support network for trialists where she oversees the national development of trial methodology research and the strategic development and management of the HRB-TMRN.

Romain Guignard is in charge of the evaluation of smoking prevention programmes at Public Health France. He has a Master's degree in statistical engineering from the National School for Statistics and Information Analysis (ENSAI) in France. His areas of interest refer to the measure and the analysis of health behaviours, attitudes and their changes, in particular concerning addiction and mental health issues, and related to social inequalities. He has contributed several research papers to academic journals and book chapters.

Kellye Hartman is a communications professional with a strong drive to deliver positive change within the community. Holding a postgraduate diploma in editing and communications, and with experience across a range of marketing and communications roles within government organisations, Kellye specialises in social marketing, research and evaluation, editing, and print and online publishing, and as a senior campaigns advisor at VicHealth is responsible for campaign development, delivery and evaluation across a range of social marketing interventions, with a particular focus on physical activity and healthy eating. Kellye has successfully developed and delivered VicHealth's Walk to School campaign over several years, achieving significant campaign growth and positive behaviour change outcomes among Victorian primary students.

Michael Hogan is a senior lecturer and researcher in the Psychology Department at NUI Galway. His research foci include individual, social and technology factors contributing to child and adult learning, motivation, and collaborative performance. A key designer of the collective intelligence methodology in the EU-funded Sea for Society project (2012–2014), in the EU's ROUTE-TO-PA project (2015–2017) and in projects applying innovative technology in classrooms, he is an active member in international networks and is currently working on four EU projects.

Neil Horrocks is the CEO of CitySmart and has experience in the energy markets of electricity, natural gas and LPG. He has held executive roles with oversight responsibilities for retail, distribution, asset management, administration and safety management functions.

Peter S. Hovmand, PhD, MSW, is the Founding Director of the Social System Design Lab at the Brown School at Washington University in St Louis, where he uses system dynamics modelling to understand and evaluate community-level interventions. He has a background in electrical engineering, mathematics, and philosophy, and received his doctorate in social work and community psychology from Michigan State University. His research focuses on developing and using participatory group model building (GMB) techniques to involve community members in the creation of models to understand the role of social determinants of health, scale-up of health innovations, and the design of community prevention strategies.

Aqueel Imtiaz Wahga is a doctoral researcher in the Department for Public Leadership and Social Enterprise in The Open University Business School with a background in organisational research, education and training. His research interests include entrepreneurship, enterprise development, environmental sustainability and SMEs. Previously, he has examined the growth challenges of SMEs in Pakistan and the dynamics of nascent entrepreneurship in entrepreneurially active and passive economies. Presently, he is investigating the environmental engagement of SMEs in Pakistan's leather industry.

Marian Lorena Ibarra Ávila is a physiotherapist with a Master's degree in Health Promotion at Deakin University (Australia). She has worked in the social determinants of heath and health promotion approach with special attention on advocacy strategies for policy change in the realms of tobacco control and food nutrition.

John Joyce, having obtained his PhD while working at the Fisheries Laboratory at Lowestoft in the UK, moved to Dublin to join BIM (the Irish Sea Fisheries Board) in the development of the Irish aquaculture industry. He left BIM to become the CEO of the Irish Salmon Growers Association and is a former President of the European Aquaculture Society. He founded the trade magazine *Aquaculture Ireland* and is a recipient of a number of awards, including the Glaxo Fellowship for EU Science Writers for Ireland and the Public Relations Institute of Ireland's Gladys McNevin Award. As Communications Manager of the Marine Institute, he led a team that set up the 'Explorers' national primary school marine education programme. He is a keen cartoonist, writer and the author of five novels, three screenplays and four marine-themed books for children, including *Black John the Bogus Pirate – Cartoon Workbook of Marine Beasts*. John was Senior Scientific Project Manager with Aquatt for Sea for Society.

Sommer Kapitan is a senior lecturer in marketing at the Auckland University of Technology. Her research centres on sustainability, consumer wellbeing, persuasion and advertising effectiveness. She earned her PhD in 2014 from the University of Texas at San Antonio.

Ann-Marie Kennedy (PhD) is a senior lecturer in marketing at the University of Canterbury. Her research interests include macromarketing, social marketing, ethics and sustainability. She is an associate editor for the *Journal of Macromarketing* and on the editorial policy review board for the *Journal of Social Marketing*. She has published in journals such as the *European Journal of Marketing, Journal of Macromarketing, Journal of Business Research* and *Journal of Social Marketing*. Her most recent research focuses on macro-social marketing and social marketing ethics, and also on authentic sustainability as a business strategy.

Patrick Kenny is senior lecturer in the School of Marketing in the Dublin Institute of Technology. He teaches marketing strategy and strategic management on MBA and executive education programmes. His research interests revolve around critical and social marketing and the interface between marketing and public policy. He is a frequent media commentator on issues relating to business and society and has been an expert court witness on marketing regulatory issues. He completed a PhD in the Institute for Social Marketing in the University of Stirling where he examined the impact of alcohol marketing on both social norms and drinking behaviour among Irish students.

Krzysztof Kubacki is an associate professor, a VicHealth's Social Marketing Research Practice Fellow and Higher Degree by Research Director in the Griffith Business School. He has published over 80 books, book chapters, journal articles and industry reports. Krzysztof has lead a review of the effectiveness of social marketing, including for example campaigns targeting children, which remains one of the most comprehensive overviews of the current state of social marketing practice. In his latest work, published in the *Journal of Business Ethics*, he proposes a human rights-based approach to the social good in social marketing.

Roger Layton was appointed Professor of Marketing in 1967, filling a newly established chair that had been funded by a group of leading Sydney business people, and is currently Emeritus Professor and continues as Professor of Marketing. He was elected a Fellow of ANZMAC in 2010, a Fellow of the Royal Society of New South Wales in 2016, and is a Fellow of the Australian Institute of Management, the Australian Marketing Institute, the Australian Market and Social Research Society, and an Honorary Fellow of UNSW. He is the joint author of several books including *Fundamentals of Marketing* and *Contemporary Hospitality Marketing: A Service Management Approach*. His research in macromarketing has been recognised through the award of the Charles Slater Memorial Award in 1990, 2008, 2011 and 2017; the George Fisk best paper awards in 2006, 2007, 2008, 2011 and 2017; the Shelby Hunt Award in 2011; and the Robert Nason Award for extraordinary and sustained contribution in 2013.

Jo-Anne Little is the Marketing Project Manager for the Reduce Your Juice project at CitySmart. She is a marketing professional with over fifteen years' industry experience across a variety of brands and organisations. Specialising in digital and social marketing, she has an interest in the application of digital marketing and gamification techniques for social good.

Farah Madi is a graduate student with a Master's in public health concentrating on health management and policy at the Faculty of Health Sciences at the American University of Beirut (AUB) with an educational background in environmental health.

She is a subcommittee member in the National Public Health Campaign, a member of the University Student-Faculty Committee (USFC) at AUB, and co-founder and former secretary of the Arab Youth Climate Movement NGO. Her work experience includes research assistance at the department of Health Management and Policy at AUB and trainings at the Evidence-based Health Management Unit (EHMU) at AUBMC and at Bellevue Medical Center.

Susana Marques is Assistant Professor at the High Institute of Accounting and Administration, University of Aveiro, where she has been teaching services marketing, strategic management and marketing and sustainability. She received her PhD in marketing from the University of Stirling, Scotland, in 2008, and her research work is focused on the transference of relationship marketing to social marketing multifaceted and complex programmes, especially in terms of organisational implications and the redesign of process evaluation frameworks. Further research interests include the reconfiguration of marketing for an intersection of business and social value creation.

Dinorah Martinez Tyson, PhD, MPH, MA, is Assistant Professor in the Department of Community and Family Health in the College of Public Health at the University of South Florida and also a courtesy professor in Anthropology. She has extensive experience in qualitative methods and community-engaged research. She has worked closely with various community organisations to address health disparities among ethnic minorities and underserved populations in the Tampa Bay area and Spanish-speaking Caribbean.

Marzia Mazzonetto is completing a PhD at the Athena Institute for Research on Innovation and Communication in Health and Life Sciences of the VU University of Amsterdam. Prior to that, Marzia was the project manager at Ecsite (the European network of science centres and museums), coordinating projects financed by the European Commission, such as VOICES and Sea for Society. She holds a degree in communication studies and a Master's in Science Communication. Her main fields of interest are science communication and social innovation processes, such as citizens' and stakeholders' participation in scientific research and policy-making (Responsible Research and Innovation, RRI).

Ryan McAndrew holds a PhD in social marketing and is a senior research assistant at the Queensland University of Technology. His research involves examining group-level motives for excessive alcohol consumption in friendship groups. He has previously worked on social marketing projects in the areas of healthcare, tertiary education, and alcohol reduction. He has presented his research at Australian and international conferences.

Patricia McHugh is a postdoctoral researcher with the Whitaker Institute at NUI Galway. Patricia holds a PhD on the development and measurement of process indicators for science communication using social marketing and innovation theory. Her current work involves designing, training, and implementing Social Innovation Participation Processes (SIPPs) within an ocean literacy context for *Sea Change*, an

EU H2020-funded project. In *Sea Change*, she is also responsible for the design and coordination of a collective impact assessment framework to monitor and track the progress of the project over its lifetime.

Anna Mercier is a campaign manager at Public Health France where she is in charge of 360 national campaigns on tobacco cessation. She devised the strategy and coordinated the production of the *Moi(s) sans tabac* campaign. Prior to working on tobacco cessation, she supervised national campaigns on sexual health. Before joining Public Health France, she served as a project manager at the French Environment and Energy Management Agency. She holds a Master's degree in political philosophy and communications of public institutions, and a BA in modern literature.

Rory Mulcahy is a lecturer of marketing at the University of the Sunshine Coast. He recently completed his PhD in 2015 and has published articles and conference papers in the *Journal of Social Marketing*, ANZMAC, the World Social Marketing Conference and the International Social Marketing Conference. His research interests include serious games, digital marketing and micro-celebrity endorsement.

Andrew W. Murphy is the Foundation Professor of General Practice at NUI Galway, a principal in a semi-rural practice at Turloughmore, County Galway, and director of the Health Research Board Clinical Trials Network Primary Care Ireland.

Maurice Murphy is a senior lecturer in business at the Cork Institute of Technology, Cork, Ireland. He lectures on marketing and management to undergraduate and postgraduate students and his research areas are in social marketing and health communication.

Viêt Nguyen Thanh holds a Master's degree in engineering from AgroParistech, a French *Grande école*. Viêt began her career in 2004 at the French Institute of Health Promotion and Health Education as the manager of the French quitline 'Tabac Info service'. In 2008 she became the Head of Studies in charge of the strategic conception and evaluation of preventive interventions dedicated to smoking cessation, reduction in alcohol consumption, skin cancer prevention, and environmental risks. In 2014 she was appointed to head up the 'Lifestyles Unit' within the scientific department, and in 2016 was appointed head of the 'Addictions' Unit of Public Health France. She has participated in several research papers in academic journals and also teaches at university level.

Lukas Parker is a lecturer in the School of Media and Communication at RMIT University in Melbourne, Australia. His research interests are in social marketing, digital advertising and marketing communications. Lukas has published widely in the field of social marketing, particularly within the domains of road safety, alcohol consumption behaviours and fostering green behaviours. He has extensive experience working with various nonprofit organisations and development projects in Ho Chi Minh City and rural Vietnam.

Joanna Piwowarczyk is a research assistant in the Department of Ecology at the Institute of Oceanology, Polish Academy of Sciences. She is an economist by training and graduated in 2002 from the Faculty of Management, University of Gdansk. Her research focuses on the ecosystem approach to marine spatial planning, societal governance and marine ecosystem services, their indicators and valuation methodologies. She has been involved in many EU-funded projects, including Sea for Society, and has co-authored several scientific papers on biological valorisation, use of the sea space, and the perception of climate change.

Juan Miguel Rey-Pino is Associate Professor in marketing management and market research at the Universidad de Granada (Spain). His PhD was in economics at the Universidad de Cadiz (Spain). Juan has specialised in social and critical marketing, working on different topics related to tobacco and food control.

Neil Rowan is director of the Bioscience Research Institute at the Athlone Institute of Technology, Ireland, and Adjunct Professor in the School of Medicine at NUI Galway, Ireland. He lectures in the areas of infection control, epidemiology, sexually-transmitted diseases and risk assessment and modelling. He has supervised PhD and MSc by Research students and mentored postdoctoral research fellows in these and other disease mitigation areas. He also has expertise in host-pathogen interactions and is national representation on EU Cost Action for Food-borne parasites.

Sharyn Rundle-Thiele is director of Social Marketing @ Griffith, and editor-in-chief for the *Journal of Social Marketing*. Drawing on her commercial marketing background her research focuses on applying marketing tools and techniques to change behaviour for the better. She is currently working on projects delivering changes to the environment, people's health and for the greater social good. Selected current projects include changing adolescent attitudes towards drinking alcohol (see www.blurredminds.com.au/students), increasing healthy eating and physical activity to combat obesity, reducing food waste, and delivering change in a wide variety of settings. Research partners in 2017 include the Defence Science and Technology Organisation, the Australian Defence Force, the Queensland Catholic Education Commission, Redland City Council, VicHealth and more. Her research has been published in more than 100 books, book chapters and journal papers.

Rebekah Russell-Bennett is a professor in the QUT Business School and the immediate past president of the Australian Association of Social Marketing. She undertakes research in social marketing with a technology or services focus, has published more than 150 peer-reviewed articles, and is considered an international leader in the field of social marketing. She is also co-editor of the *Journal of Services Marketing*, an A-ranked journal in the ABDC list.

Elodie Safta holds a Master's degree in global communications from Cesacom, a French professional school. Elodie served at BBDO Paris, an advertising agency, as a junior web project manager, and thereafter as a freelance graphic designer and communications consultant for small businesses and associations. Now at Public Health France, she is the communications officer for *Moi(s) sans tabac*.

Kay Samson has twenty years' experience in tobacco control in the NHS supporting local and national policy. In particular, she is part of the steering group for the development of the Scottish Government's tobacco strategy, 'Creating a Tobacco-Free Generation 2013'.

Sean Sands is Associate Professor and Managing Director of the Australian Consumer, Retail, and Services (ACRS) Research Unit at Monash University, and focuses on creating alignment between service experiences and brand promises to deliver meaningful customer interactions. Sean has over fifteen years of academic and commercial research experience and works with some of the greatest brands globally. His research expertise spans a wide range of qualitative and quantitative methodologies, with a particular interest in advanced methodologies to understand consumer behaviour and aid business decision-making.

Tom Scharf is Professor of Social Gerontology at the Institute of Health and Society, Newcastle University, having previously been Director of the Irish Centre for Social Gerontology, NUI Galway. Tom is a Fellow of the UK Academy of Social Sciences and sits on the advisory board of the German Ageing Survey. His research addresses issues relating to social inclusion and exclusion in later life, often with a focus on the spaces and places in which inclusion and exclusion arise and on the policy responses to forms of exclusion.

Tali Schneider, MPH, CHES, is the Centre Programme Administrator at the Florida Prevention Research Center (FPRC), University of South Florida. Her areas of interest include social marketing, chronic disease, and adolescent health with an emphasis on qualitative research methods. In the past seven years she has served as a research associate at the FPRC addressing issues related to adolescents' asthma, teen pregnancy, mHealth, colorectal cancer screening, and obesity prevention. She received her MPH in health education and a social marketing graduate certificate from the University of South Florida.

Animesh Sharma has over six years' experience in the monitoring and evaluation of programmes focusing on gender, sanitation and public health. His functional area of expertise is in conducting impact assessments and evaluations, specifically on social behaviour change communication interventions, and he has worked on multiple interventions addressing gender, maternal and child health, and water WASH as thematic areas, using different formats of communication. At NR Management Consultants, he is currently engaged in the monitoring and evaluation of a communication-oriented behavioural change programme, 'Empowering Adolescents', across seven districts in Uttar Pradesh, and also working on a study aimed at evaluating the role of m-learning and Wireless Reach in managing TB patients' care and their adherence to treatment regimens. As a senior research officer (specialising in social behaviour change communication) at the BBC Media Action, Research and Learning unit, he was involved in the conceptualisation and development of a mobile phone game addressing gender stereotypes among adolescents. He graduated with a degree in commerce from the University of Delhi, and completed his postgrad in management at the Lal Bahadur Shastri Institute of Management in Delhi.

Olivier Smadja holds a Master's degree in psychology and tobacology and was the manager of the Regional Information Centre on Drugs for Île-de France for five years. He then moved to the French Institute of Health Promotion and Health Education in 2009, where he first was the manager of the French quitline 'Tabac info service', consisting of a website and an app, as well as the French version of Stoptober. Now at Public Health France, Olivier is the project leader of tobacco prevention, and teaches smoking cessation at university level. He is, among other things, the leader of *Moi(s) sans tabac*, and interacts with all public actors working on tobacco cessation in France.

Anne Smith is Reader in Marketing at the Open University Business School. She has previously held full-time posts at the universities of Glasgow, the West Indies, Sheffield and Manchester. Her main research interests focus on services marketing and management and the principles and practice of social marketing. Studies have examined how consumers evaluate services, the ways in which service design and service quality impact on evaluation and behaviour and how this differs across cultures. Further research focuses on the nature and determinants of environmentally responsible behaviour and how an internal marketing approach can promote such behaviour within organisations. Her work has been published in a number of international journals including the *European Management Journal, the European Journal of Marketing*, the *Journal of Business Research*, the *International Marketing Review*, the *Journal of Marketing Management, Journal of Service Research*, the *Service Industries Journal* and *Long Range Planning*.

Julinawati Suanda is a PhD student and lecturer in the Faculty of Technoeconomics, University of Malaysia Perlis. Her research interests include social marketing, cancer research, epidemiology and health promotion. As part of a transdisciplinary study, Julinawati received doctoral training in Ireland in the areas of social marketing, mixed research methodologies, health promotion, nurse education, physiology and medicine.

Tim Swinton is the Commercial Projects Manager at CitySmart. He has delivered a range of innovative energy efficiency programmes producing tangible environmental, social and commercial outcomes across the residential and business sectors. Tim is a graduate of the QUT Business School and completed a Graduate Certificate in Built Environment and Engineering.

Alan Tapp is Professor of Marketing at Bristol Business School. Formerly the founder and director of the Bristol Social Marketing Centre, he has recently stepped down from this role in order to concentrate on specific research interests, including behaviour changes relating to physical activity, everyday sport, road safety, promoting cycling and public health.

Akke Vellinga is a senior lecturer at the Department of General Practice and Bacteriology of the National University of Ireland, Galway. The focus of her research is to support appropriate prescribing of antibiotics through education and feedback for prescribers, patients and public. She has extensive experience in the development and management of research projects as well as interventions. She has more than 70 peer-reviewed publications, most as first or senior author, on topics ranging from antimicrobial resistance and prescribing, infectious diseases, asthma and allergies, out-of-hospital cardiac arrest and statistical modelling applications, reflecting her research activity in these areas. Akke holds a PhD in Medicine, a Master in Epidemiology, diplomas in health economics, teaching, education and a Master and Bachelor in Science (Biology).

Sanjeev Vyas, BSc, MBA, has over 26 years' experience in marketing and communications, of which the last twelve years have been in public health. His last assignment was with USAID/India as Senior Private Health Sector Solutions and Health Systems Specialist. Prior to this he worked with FHI 360 (Senior Private Sector Specialist, Improving Healthy Behaviours Program) and with Abt Associates Inc. as Program Director and Communications Advisor on the USAID-funded Market-based Partnerships for Health (MBPH) and the Private Sector Partnerships-*One* (PSP-*One*) Projects. He has set up and led several large networks of private providers for reproductive health and child health. His areas of interest include health partnerships with the private sector, social and behaviour change communication, and developing innovative health networks for the base of the pyramid population. Having begun his career in advertising he was given the AAP's prestigious 'Leaders of Tomorrow' award in 1997.

Annemarie Wright is the Manager of Knowledge and Health Equity at the Victorian Health Promotion Foundation (VicHealth). She completed her PhD in public health and mental health at the University of Melbourne, which was supported by scholarships from the National Health and Medical Research Council (NHMRC) and the Sidney Myer Health Fund. She has an undergraduate degree in occupational therapy and a Master's degree in medical science (health promotion). She has worked as a clinician, clinical trainer, health promotion programme manager and population health researcher. Her research has been published in a range of highly cited journals.

Foreword

A book to make you stop and think

I'm honoured to be asked to write the foreword to *Social Marketing: Rebels with a Cause,* the new edition of Gerard and Christine's textbook on social marketing. Gerard Hastings and Christine Domegan remain at the top of their game in producing innovative research and insightful commentaries on social marketing and its related subjects. Picking up this book you will want a clear explanation of what social marketing is and what its relevance is in this period of history; you will also hope for a lively style, and interesting stories that illustrate how the principles and theories are applied in practice. This book offers all this and much more: in short, not only the capacity to surprise, but also the priceless ability to make you stop and think.

One of my 'stop and think' moments came in reading their brand new Chapter 9, 'Spiritual Dimensions'. You might expect a title like this in a philosophy text, but less so in marketing! As I read the chapter my first thought was what a courageous idea it was to write a chapter encouraging us to think about our own place in the world and our personal capacity to change things. This is daunting and at the same time potentially exhilarating. It certainly challenged my worldview: I have been a strong advocate of the idea that most of the behavioural challenges we face are inherently structural in nature, that is, that they are primarily due to large-scale ecological or social determinants (industrial marketing, government policies, social norms and so on) that are outside our immediate control. That may still be so, but it does not mean we should not reflect on our own choices, our own behaviours, what drives these, and whether there is a better way to live.

Of course, each of us on our own can do relatively little to change things. Should we get together? One of the points that Gerard and Christine make throughout the book, taking us 'back to the future' is the role of social marketing in influencing ideas. In my own work on trying to influence policy changes to encourage the move away from a car-dominant society, I wonder about the capacity of social marketing to create social movements, even protests and civil activism. I found this chapter food for thought – to put it mildly.

Lastly, I return to the book in its entirety and marvel at its scope and scale. The world of social marketing – and how it fits into the multi-disciplinary arena that is behaviour change – has become more complex in recent times. You need a strong hand on the tiller to navigate through the deeper waters of how best to fit together the jigsaw of behaviour change techniques – and the role of social marketing within this puzzle. Of course, social marketing is now truly international as well, with its US home base long since expanded into Europe, Australasia, South America and Asia. These multinational perspectives need to be taken on board as part of the development of the subject – here you will find not just case studies from all corners of the globe, but also Hastings and Domegan's trademark lessons from history, fables and poems that are carefully chosen, once again, to make us stop and think.

Hastings and Domegan's years of experience belie their youthful exuberance in continuing to drive forward the field of social marketing with this passionately written book. They truly are rebels with a cause.

Alan Tapp
July 2017

Preface

Rebels with a cause

Welcome to the third edition.

As the Chinese saying has it, we are living in interesting times: times of momentous change; often disturbing and disruptive change.

Communications are merging with Orwell's Newspeak: the word 'post-truth' has entered the dictionary, and phrases like 'alternative fact' and 'fake news' are commonplace. Social media are becoming not just a dominant channel for social interaction, but also a major marketing channel, a means of mass surveillance and even an arm of government. Expertise has become suspect, and what seemed to be unshakable verities are being challenged, rejected or overturned. The popular voice has bearded the establishment, in what might be a refreshing demonstration of grassroots power were it not linked to nationalism and xenophobia with unsettling historical undertones. The word refugee has become divisive, as likely to trigger intolerance and hatred as it is humanity and compassion. The walls emerging in Palestine and being mooted in Mexico, less than twenty years after the fall of the one in Berlin was thought to have ended history, present both an alarming prospect and a powerful metaphor. Where once they were dismissed as hyperbole, comparisons with the 1930s are now being given serious attention.

For social marketing – a discipline that aims to systematise, not just behaviour change, but social change – these developments raise difficult questions. We have always known that our discipline is in essence an amoral technology that can be used for good or ill. Indeed, we pride ourselves on replicating many of the consumer marketing techniques used by the tobacco, alcohol and junk food multinationals that are causing the public health problems we seek to mitigate. We also work upstream and match their (disparaged) lobbying with our own (praiseworthy) advocacy. We have noted uneasily that basic social marketing precepts, such as listening to your clients, recognising the power of emotion, and targeting campaigns to key groups, are techniques that will further a cause whether it be good or bad. Populism, which has driven the recent political turbulence, is defined as "politics or political ideology based on the perceived interests of ordinary people, as opposed to those of a privileged elite"[1] – which is, at least in part, what social marketing aims to do. This underlines the need for caution in our work and the vital importance of considering values and ethics, and using research and co-production to think through the full implications of our activities.

That turbulence has also been driven by inequalities, which continue to deteriorate. The first edition of this book appeared in 2007, a year before the financial crisis which led to a decade of divisive austerity. The second edition came seven years later, noting that "burgeoning inequalities" were a cause for continuing concern, and reducing them "a vital global priority" if worsening divisions were not to precipitate "social fracture and conflict".[2] The threat of such dislocation feels even more apparent today.

The yawning gap between rich and poor is shocking in absolute terms. Whether it is Oxfam's 2017 analysis showing that "eight men own the same wealth as the 3.6 billion people who make up the poorest half of humanity",[3] the astronomical salaries of CEOs, or the growth of zero hours contracts and the coining of a more ominous new term 'the precariat', the picture is grim. More alarming though is the direction of travel – the gulf between those at the top and the rest of us has been growing remorselessly for three decades. The Stiglitz 1% has become the 1% of the 1%, the ratio between CEO and employee has grown tenfold since 1980, and the 'gig economy' is flourishing by employing the 'precariat' on 'zero hours' contracts. Wealth for the few built on insecurity for the many. It is shocking to reflect that a country the size of the UK – the fifth biggest economy in the world – has become more divided than it was when Charles Dickens wrote *Hard Times*.[4]

These divisions transcend national boundaries. Incidents like the collapse of the Rana Plaza factory in Bangladesh which killed over a thousand garment workers, the iPhone suicides and recurrent concerns about conflict minerals remind us that ours is a small, interconnected world. From a global perspective, our shopping habits have painful repercussions and our materialistic lifestyles set a dangerously unsustainable lead. When a source as conservative as the Vatican reminds us that "twenty percent of the world's population consumes resources at a rate that robs the poor nations and future generations of what they need to survive",[5] we really do need to start paying attention.

Nowhere is our mutual dependence more apparent – or vital – than with the problem of climate change. Here there has been progress since the last edition: the dominant narrative is now that action is urgently needed and the Paris Accord has begun to put these sentiments into effect. But there have also been setbacks: we are still wedded to the idea of perpetual economic growth, the consumption behaviour of the 20% in the developed world is out of control, and a climate sceptic has just been elected to the most powerful office on earth. Furthermore, the climate data continue to worsen: 16 of the 17 hottest years have occurred since the millennium, the polar ice is retreating further each year, and 2016 was the hottest year ever recorded. Inevitably this is causing very real harm: a quarter of the Great Barrier Reef has died, low-lying land from Miami to Mumbai has gone underwater, and extreme weather events are proliferating.

This daunting trinity of populism, inequalities and climate change has stimulated the production of this new edition. It has put our discipline under extraordinary scrutiny – all three problems are intimately linked to our economic system, and the engine of that system is marketing. Our consumption behaviour lies at the heart of the current crisis and those who can influence this behaviour have immense power. It is more important than ever that we look critically at this system, learn more about how marketing works, and devise robust regulatory and personal defence mechanisms. There is vital need for us to question, resist and rebel against the interests that would have us merely buy and sell. The critical marketing agenda is more pressing than ever.

The positive side of this coin is social marketing. If marketing has driven us to the brink of catastrophe it clearly has the power to bring about the profound changes that are needed to avert this same catastrophe. Moreover, there is now ample evidence to show that, just as commercial marketing has an acute effect on our shopping habits even when these threaten our health and our planet, so social marketing can make our behaviour more responsible. The power of the tobacco MNCs over our young people was successfully challenged and subverted by the Truth Campaign, and this lesson is eminently generalisable. We all have the capacity to rebel.

The daunting trinity has also informed the content of the new edition. As well as the necessary updating which any textbook needs with the passage of time, we have made some significant additions:

1. Chapter 11 on systems social marketing has undergone major revision to reflect both the importance of such thinking in our shrinking world and recent advances in the area. In particular we have given more space to the idea of social movements.

2. To balance this emphasis on the collective, we have also developed a new chapter looking at individual responsibility (Chapter 9). It seems to us that a discipline that can be used to bring about both desirable and undesirable change needs to be grounded in an understanding of the human condition, moral agency and human rights. Our capacity to fight back needs to be guided by appropriate humanitarian values – we can become not just rebels, but rebels with a cause. In this way we can ensure that social marketing is used to fulfil the goal Dante Alighieri ascribed to we humans: "to follow after wisdom and virtue".[6] With some trepidation we have called this new chapter 'Spiritual Dimensions'.

3. Digital developments have also made themselves felt, and we have introduced more material across a number of chapters assessing the pros and cons of the online world.

In addition, we are delighted to add that we have a fresh crop of case studies which will help to explore these new areas and reinforce the learning in more established ones. We are deeply grateful to our colleagues around the world who have provided these invaluable insights into their – and all our – work.

So yes, we do live in interesting times and face uniquely daunting challenges, but we can and will respond to them. As teachers and students we know that the most effective tools for doing so are critical analysis, learning and skills development; that the most powerful intervention of all is education. We also know that social marketing has an important and honourable role to play in this pedagogy. We hope that this third edition, with the help of our colleagues across the globe, will energise and extend our discipline, enabling us not just to respond to the pressing challenges we face, but proactively build a healthier, more progressive and, above all, sustainable world.

Gerald Hastings
Christine Domegan

Notes

1 Encarta. http://encarta.msn.com:80/dictionary_1861737909/populism.html (accessed 19 January 2008).
2 Hastings and Domegan, 2014, *Social Marketing; From Tunes to symphonies*. Routledge UK.
3 www.oxfam.org/en/pressroom/pressreleases/2017-01-16/just-8-men-own-same-wealth-half-world.
4 Dorling, D. (2010) 'Are the times changing back? There are painful similarities between life lived in London now and the unjust inequalities of Victorian times', *New London Review*, 2 July, 16–17.
5 Laudato Si (2015) http://w2.vatican.va/content/francesco/en/encyclicals/documents/papa-francesco_2050524_enciclica-laudato-si.html.
6 Dante Alighieri, *The Divine Comedy*, Canto 26.

Chapter **1**

Harnessing the power of marketing

OF MEMORY AND MARKETING

Let us start with a question. Where were you when the Larsen B ice shelf broke up and melted into the Weddell Sea? If Amitav Ghosh (2016) is right, you, like us, will have no idea. And yet this was a momentous event, arguably more significant than the fall of the Berlin Wall or the birth of social media.

The NASA website[1] explains that in the Antarctic summer of 2002 scientists "watched in amazement" as an ice shelf that had existed for at least 11,000 years disintegrated in just over a month. An area of ice measuring over 3,000 square kilometres and reaching a thickness of 500 metres simply melted into the sea. NASA confirms that along with the immediate effect, Larson B's demise has also had long-term consequences for sea levels as the glaciers it previously held back accelerate. Research since has confirmed an eightfold acceleration – "comparable to a car accelerating from 55 to 440 mph". In a NASA scientist's words, "it is certainly a warning; the conclusion is inescapable".

But most of us have escaped it. We don't even know about it.

In contrast, when it comes to shopping our memory is first class. Consider another question: what is the best-known word in the world? . . . Sex? . . . Life? . . . Death? . . . Jesus? . . . No. It's Coca-Cola. In essence, Coke (notice we even have a pet name for it) is just fizzy brown sugar water, but it has a turnover approaching $10 billion in some 200 countries[2] and its familiar bottle, font and red and white

(continued)

(continued)

livery are symbols of fun, freedom and the American way of life across vastly different cultures. And Coke is not alone: Google, McDonald's, Nike, Marlboro and countless other brands each provide commonplace products with distinctive values and personalities. In the process they have become an intimate part of our daily lives, influencing our ideas, emotions, behaviour and lifestyles.

Meanwhile NASA has just announced that the (even bigger) Larson C ice shelf has started to disintegrate.[3]

Amitav Ghosh calls our purblindness to the obvious signs of climate change "the Great Derangement"; given that we are causing it, our ignorance seems to him to be a form of mental illness. That climate change is our own doing has recently been underlined by the announcement from the International Geological Conference that we have just entered the Anthropocene, a new, human-influenced geological epoch, "based on overwhelming global evidence that atmospheric, geologic, hydrologic, biospheric and other earth system processes are now altered by humans."[4] And yet we know little about it, and do less, causing Ghosh (2016, p. 129) to plead: "will our future generations, standing in a rising pool of swirling waters, not beseech us with this question – 'Why didn't you do something?'"

Paradoxically, comfort comes from Coca-Cola. Central to the human influence on our planet is our consumption behaviour – something about which we are immensely well informed and in which we participate with great enthusiasm. The soft drinks giant, along with its many commercial rivals, demonstrates the enormous potential power of marketing.

This book builds on the premise that this insight has two sets of implications for anyone interested in behaviour change. First, we should look and learn. If Coke and its commercial marketing colleagues are so good at getting close to us and influencing the way we live our lives, we should study what they are doing and find out what lessons it holds for us. That which has caused us to melt the Larson ice shelves, can also encourage us to behave sustainably.

Second, we should be critical. Such power is daunting and needs checks and balances. The success of companies like Coke in getting people to consume increasing quantities of what nutritionists call 'empty calories' holds important lessons for those who feel our economic system needs better regulation. Specifically, if our concern is with obesity driven by poor diets, perhaps we should seek to put constraints on the fast-food industry; more broadly, if we are anxious about global warming, we should be examining the impact that the marketing of *all* corporate bodies is having on our consumption levels and thereby the planet. As the Global South struggles to replicate the materialism of the North it is surely time to recall Gandhi's warning: "God forbid that India should ever take to industrialism after the manner of the west . . . If [our nation] took to similar economic exploitation, it would strip the world bare like locusts."

This combination of critically examining commercial marketing so as to *learn from its successes*, on the one hand, and *curb its excesses*, on the other, is the essence of *social marketing*. This book will explain its principles and provide detailed guidance on their practical application to real-life problems. This first chapter discusses the nature of social marketing in more detail, and also explains how to get the most from the rest of the book.

Learning outcomes

By the end of this chapter, you should be able to:

- ✓ Discuss and explain the power of commercial marketing
- ✓ Understand the connections between marketing and behaviour
- ✓ Explain the importance of behaviour change
- ✓ Outline the linkage between marketing and society
- ✓ Present the positive and negative effects of marketing
- ✓ Describe the evolution of social marketing
- ✓ Define social marketing
- ✓ Distinguish between social advertising, social media and social marketing.

Key words

Marketing – commercial marketing – consumption – corporation – exchange – human behaviour – behavioural change – marketing system – marketplace – critical analysis – social marketing.

The power of marketing

We will start by looking more closely at how marketing works. Have a go at Exercise 1.1.

EXERCISE 1.1 SHOPPING MATTERS

Consider something you have bought recently – an item of clothing perhaps or a takeaway coffee – or something as big as a car. Anything. Think through why and how you bought it. What made you think of it in the first place? What encouraged or discouraged you? What did you like/dislike about it and the process of buying it? Would you buy it again?

Take a few minutes to do this and jot down some notes.

The exercise demonstrates some of the basic principles of marketing. First, it shows that the process starts not with the marketer, but with you; specifically, with something you need or want. This might be for something major, such as a house or food to feed your family; or it could be utterly trivial, such as an impulse to buy a hot drink when a moment previously you had no such desire. Both extremes, though, illustrate a core insight: the customer has to be at the centre of the marketing process. The key lesson from Exercise 1.1 is that when we shop we are seeking satisfaction. The first job of the marketer, then, is to understand us and what we want.

Their second job is to deliver to these needs in the most attractive way possible (or at least in a more attractive way than that of the competition). What constitutes 'attractive' will vary for different people and needs. An impulse purchaser of a takeaway coffee will prioritise ease of access, and, if they pride themselves on their sophisticated palate, put an emphasis on the quality of the bean and the brewing process. A moderately high price might help to reinforce this high-end positioning. A bit of Italian iconography and American have-a-nice-daying will likely increase the appeal.

A house, by contrast, will involve a much more considered and bespoke purchasing process. But the same four elements will be manipulated to make the process as pleasant as possible: price (perhaps through a financing deal), place (both in the sense of the image and accessibility of the sales agent and the location of the property), promotion (think of the effort that goes into estate agents' property descriptions) and, of course, the product itself – the house has to be the right size, layout and design.

We consumers are also good at learning from experience. If coffee chain X under-performs on any of these dimensions – if the coffee is cold or the service sullen – they will soon lose our custom. Similarly, if the real estate company gets caught cheating, the damage to its good name will make us leery of any future transactions. So, reputation matters, and good ones take time to develop.

Exercise 1.1 then teaches us that consumer orientation is central to good marketing; that the 4Ps of product, price, place and promotion are used to deliver on this promise; that competition in the marketplace hones this process; and that time and experience make it strategic as well as tactical.

Having used this exercise in classes over many years, we can also suggest another lesson: it works. The exercise invariably triggers lots of animated discussion; everyone has a story to tell and they can typically tell it at some length. Marketers have succeeded in making shopping a central and much valued part of our lives. They are, then, masters at getting us to do things – buy their products, visit their shops, attend to their messages, buy their products again . . . They can even get us to do their marketing for them: count how many company names and logos are on the clothing you are wearing; think of the concerns that have been expressed about young people being recruited as 'brand ambassadors' (CAP 2012); remember that the massive recent increases in viral and social networking marketing completely depend on us 'passing on' digital messages or 'liking' particular brands.

What is more, we cooperate with marketers' behaviour change schemes on a voluntary basis. We visit their shops, attend their messages and promote their brands because we want to. We will now explore why this capacity to deliver voluntary behaviour change is such a vital skill in our complex, modern world.

Why behaviour change matters

> ### EXERCISE 1.2   WHY DOES BEHAVIOUR CHANGE MATTER?
>
> Make a list of what you think are the most pressing problems facing society. Think about the things that have the biggest impact on people's happiness and welfare. Illness and premature death or crime and criminal justice may come to mind, along with conflict and oppression, prejudice and intolerance, and climate change.
>
> Now consider how important human behaviour is to each of these. How in each case these complex and multifaceted problems have our decisions, actions and lifestyles at their heart.

The sense from Exercise 1.2, that how we behave and live our lives has a big impact on both our individual and collective welfare, is amply supported by the evidence. We are now well into an era where chronic, lifestyle-related illnesses are a much greater risk to life and limb than the more familiar communicable killers of yesteryear. Two decades ago, a landmark paper in the *Journal of the American Medical Association* concluded that more than half of premature deaths, at that time, were attributable to lifestyle diseases such as smoking-related cancer and alcohol-driven cirrhosis (McGinnis and Foege 1993). Since then, the problem of obesity has reached epidemic levels with a combination of poor diet and inactivity bringing an explosion in type 2 diabetes, high blood pressure and heart disease. World Health Organization (WHO) data[5] show that, worldwide, obesity has more than doubled in the last three decades. In 2014, more than 1.9 billion adults were overweight, and of these over 600 million were obese. Children have not escaped: the data showed that 41 million under-5-year-olds were overweight or obese.

The far-reaching impact of tobacco use is an equally alarming threat to public health; as Exercise 1.4 at the end of this chapter states, by 2030, up to 10 million people are likely to be killed by tobacco every year unless we can encourage significant numbers of smokers to quit or youngsters not to start. Meanwhile alcohol is already killing nearly three and half million people a year despite the fact that half the world's population is teetotal.

These health behaviours also have a big collateral impact. In Europe, for example, before the implementation of legislation to make public places smoke-free, it was estimated that some 19,000 *non*-smokers were dying from 'second-hand' smoke every year. Alcohol consumption also causes massive damage beyond the individual drinker – think about drunk driving for example, and remember that domestic violence and other crime are strongly correlated with inebriation. We are only just beginning to understand and document the full range of harms that one person's drinking can cause to others – be they children, spouses, neighbours or complete strangers who just happen to be in the wrong place at the wrong time (see for example Gell *et al.* 2015).

Putting these harms together, the WHO's European office recently concluded that no fewer than 88% deaths in its region are now attributable to the lifestyle illnesses implicated in McGinnis and Foege's (1993) paper.

Then there is our *environmental* behaviour. Think back the Larsen ice shelves that opened the chapter. We seem all too ready to ignore the link between our consumption patterns and environmental degradation (Connolly and Prothero 2003: 289). This goes beyond the purchase of notoriously unsustainable products such as plastic water bottles and diesel-driven cruise liners and takes in the collective impact of our shopping habits. As Geels *et al.* point out, "the lower environmental impact of a single product may actually be accompanied by higher environmental impact at a more systemic level due to increases in consumption" (2008: 8). This is having an inevitable impact on natural resources: "Human numbers are growing, forests are shrinking, species are dying, farmland is eroding, freshwater supplies are dwindling, fisheries are collapsing, rivers are constricting, greenhouse gases are accumulating, soot is contaminating the air and lead is contaminating our blood" (Hardin 1968). It is also changing our climate and degrading our planet. As we noted above, these disturbing realities have led the International Geological Conference to conclude that we have now entered a new geological epoch which they have christened the Anthropocene: "the period during which human activity has been the dominant influence on climate and the environment".

Thinking more broadly still, the smooth running of any democratic society depends on people living their lives in a way that serves both individual and collective needs. The criminal justice system, international diplomacy, the democratic process itself all depend on voluntary, cooperative behaviour (Quelch and Jocz 2007).

The capacity to bring about behaviour change, then, is far too valuable to be limited to the marketplace; the wider application of marketing insights has the potential not only to benefit public health but also to make all our lives better, improve social cohesion and even save the planet. This book is all about how to do this. Before proceeding, however, it is also necessary to recognise some less pleasant truths about marketing.

The dark side of marketing

At first glance, the implications of Exercise 1.1 and the consumer-centred nature of marketing are very agreeable: marketing, it seems, is ensuring that the economic system is run entirely for our benefit. Whatever we want will be provided for us as efficiently and enjoyably as possible. It is as if we had all migrated to the Sugar Rock Candy Mountain.

The reality, of course, is much less prepossessing: marketers do what they do not for our benefit, but for their own. The perfect Americano in London or condo in Hawaii is provided because the seller can make a profit out of it. And this profit motive will ultimately supersede our wishes. If you have any doubts about this, try telling your local coffee shop that you are a bit short of money today so could they let you have your daily coffee for nothing, or try buying that Hawaiian condo if you are an out-of-work Nicaraguan immigrant. The profit motive effectively excludes the poor from the market.

In this way, marketing, while purporting to meet all our needs, actually both creates and fuels different guises of inequality. This is what Andreasen (2006) calls "the dark side of the marketplace". There are inequalities between those who have and those who don't; between rich and poor; young and old; male and female; the marginalised, disadvantaged and ethnic minority groups; and the economic and social needs of our societies. Ronald Paul Hill (2011) picks up the vital concern of inequalities: "Hill adopts a profoundly ethnographic approach, enabling the poor to tell their own stories and arguing that only when these stories are accorded at least equal value with other narratives will serious progress be made" (Hastings 2011: 11).

These inequalities are particularly marked on an international front. A FTSE-100 CEO earns as much in a year as 10,000 people working in garment factories in Bangladesh (World Bank 2015), and so "some are mired in desperate and degrading poverty, with no way out, while others have not the faintest idea of what to do with their possessions, vainly showing off their supposed superiority and leaving behind them so much waste which, if it were the case everywhere, would destroy the planet."

Whatever form it takes, inequality in any society is harmful to everyone – rich and poor alike (Wilkinson and Pickett 2010). It also fundamentally undermines collective living; as Barack Obama pointed out in his 2016 address to the 71st Session of the United Nations General Assembly, "A world in which 1% of humanity controls as much wealth as the other 99% will never be stable." And the divisions continue to increase; a recent analysis by Oxfam concluded that:

- Since 2015, the richest 1% has owned more wealth than all the rest of humanity together.

- Eight men now have as much wealth as the poorest half of the world.

- Over the next twenty years, 500 people will pass $2.1 trillion on to their heirs – a sum larger than the GDP of India, a country of 1.3 billion people.

- The incomes of the poorest 10% of people increased by less than $3 a year between 1988 and 2011, while the incomes of the richest 1% increased 182 times as much.

Ironically, though, for the haves, the blessings of being included in the market can also be distinctly mixed. Commercial marketing is implicated in promoting many of the individually and communally harmful behaviours discussed above. It has now been established, for example, that alcohol, tobacco and food marketing all have a significant impact on our smoking (Lovato *et al.* 2003), drinking (Anderson and Cavanagh 2000) and unhealthy eating behaviour (Hastings *et al.* 2003; McGinnis *et al.* 2006), and this unholy trinity lies at the heart of public ill health. At a wider level, Layard (2005) reminds us that consumption does not bring satisfaction and material possessions do not deliver happiness – something we all know even without the countless studies proving it to be so.

Thinking more broadly still, excess consumption has obvious implications for the sustainability of our lifestyles: the FTSE-100 CEO is just as much dependent on the planet as the Bangladeshi garment worker.

Corporate power

The contradiction at the heart of commercial marketing – the profit motive disguised as consumer focus – is most apparent in big business. This is dominated by the corporation, for which the prioritising of profits is enshrined in law through what is called the 'fiduciary imperative' (see Box 1.1 and refer to Chapter 8 for a detailed discussion).

BOX 1.1   THE CORPORATION EXPLAINED

The essence of the corporation is that executive decision making is separated from ownership: CEOs spend other people's – shareholders' – money. Because of this, very strict rules are put in place by government to make sure that shareholders' interests (and therefore profits) always come first. This 'fiduciary imperative' ensures that the focus never leaves the bottom line. Even the excessive levels of bonuses and executive pay that we have witnessed in recent years are justified in terms of shareholder returns: "it's the only way we can get and keep the best people."

(*Source*: Hastings 2012: 4)

This single-mindedness has certainly borne fruit. In 2014 Lou Pingeot, using data from the World Bank and *Fortune Magazine*, showed that 110 of the 175 largest global economic entities in the world were corporations not countries. Furthermore, he argued that mere size understated the problem. Network analysis makes it clear that interconnections between transnational corporations further concentrate power to the extent that fewer than 150 companies control 40% of this corporate wealth, and 737 control 80% of it. Since Pingeot's (2014) analysis, big businesses have continued to grow: by 2016, 69 of the 100 largest economic entities in the world were corporations and only 31 were countries. According to Oxfam this means that the combined revenue of the ten biggest corporations exceeded that of 180 countries put together. Quite simply, marketing and businesses govern the way we live and preside over our societies and planet to an unprecedented extent.

Thus, the consequences of marketing's power to frame and shape our behaviour go far beyond the individual's consumption of a bottle of Coke or cup of coffee. While commercial marketing can and has contributed to an improved quality of life for individuals (Drucker 1957), it just as often creates new and difficult challenges for society. The true and full extent of marketing's power lies in the often invisible, ignored links our individual consumption behaviours have with our health, environmental, social and societal behaviours. Marketing is a societal process, tightly woven into the fabric of our lives and that of our communities, societies and, in an era of globalisation, our planet.

This state of affairs should alarm you. It has brought about a culture of individualism, with all the tensions, power struggles and value differences this produces. It also depends on untrammelled growth and raises unavoidable questions about the extent of consumption in a finite world, and the power and accountability of corporations. However, it cannot be ignored. The critical analysis of our current marketing systems is an essential dimension of any attempt to make the world a better place.

Enter social marketing

Social marketing pulls these behaviour changes and critical threads together. It is not a new idea. More than fifty years ago, the American academic G.D. Wiebe started people thinking in this way when he analysed contemporaneous social advertising campaigns and argued that the best ones were those that mimicked their commercial counterparts. He concluded that it is possible to "sell brotherhood like you sell soap" (1951: 179). In 1971, Kotler and Zaltman used the term 'social marketing' for the first time in the *Journal of Marketing*, and defined it as "the design, implementation, and control of programs calculated to influence the acceptability of social ideas and involving considerations of product planning, pricing, communication, distribution, and marketing research" (1971: 5). Prior to the 1970s, 'marketing' was synonymous with economic activities by companies in commercial market settings. Many argued this 'broadening' of marketing from commercial firms into the management of non-profits and social issues was a step too far (Luck 1969).

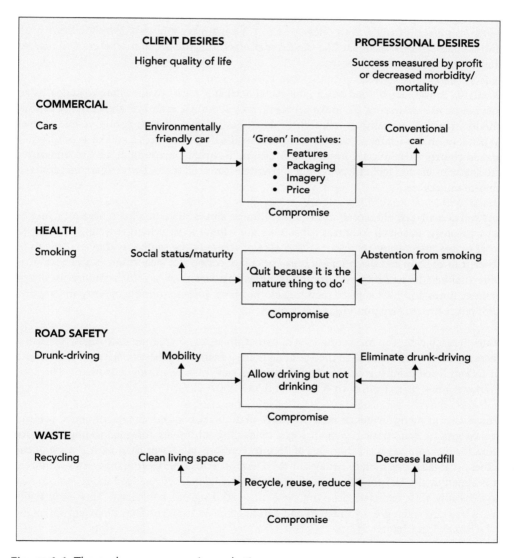

Figure 1.1 The exchange process in marketing

(*Source*: based on Hastings and Elliott 1993)

Bagozzi (1975) brought clarity to the debate, explaining that marketing was about exchanges and there are different types of marketing exchanges. These range from the restricted exchange of economic goods associated with commercial firms to the more complex, often symbolic, transfer of values seen in social marketing. Figure 1.1 illustrates this process with examples from the commercial, health, safety and waste sectors.

In the health example, the social marketer wants to sell life, living healthier, happier and longer lives that includes 'non-smoking'. To do this, they too must attempt to satisfy their target group's needs. In the case of young smokers, there may be a need for social status and sophistication, which cigarette smoking is felt to offer. In response, the social marketers can change their offerings from ones that, for example, emphasise the carcinogenic properties of tobacco to ones stressing the maturity and strong-mindedness of the non-smoker. In this way, just like the car manufacturer, the social marketers will increase their chances of a sale, of success.

Similarly, in the case of road safety, the social marketer wants to eliminate road deaths and focuses on drunk driving. To make progress, they too must examine, and respond to, their clients' needs. For example, research in Australia has shown that young people are very dependent on their cars for mobility. This led road-safety advocates to make a compromise, and to change their initial intention of imposing a curfew on young drivers to one of promoting zero blood alcohol levels. This movement towards their clients again increases the chance of success.

For waste management, social marketers' ultimate aim is sustainability where recycling has a part to play. Research indicates consumers are willing to recycle, if recycling facilities are local – consumers want convenience and ease of access in the same way they are able to nip to their local shop and buy a loaf of bread or cup of coffee. So, local councils and authorities offer mobile Christmas-tree-shredding facilities that travel around to communities at convenient times and NGOs place recycling clothes bins dotted around a country in car parks, shopping centres, playgrounds and schools.

Thus, in each case, the marketing idea of compromise, of co-creating exchanges, leads to an increased chance of success. In the social marketing exchange process, "the consumer in each of us can learn from the citizen, and the citizen can learn from the consumer". The social marketer must learn from both (Quelch and Jocz 2007: 227).

There is a growing evidence base to show that social marketing can influence multiple behaviours. A systematic review of social marketing initiatives designed to improve nutrition, for instance, showed that, out of 25 interventions, no fewer than 21 had a significant effect on at least one dietary behaviour (McDermott *et al.* 2005). Similar reviews were commissioned by the UK government and show that social marketing ideas and techniques can successfully shift exercise, drinking, smoking and drug-use behaviour. This early review work has now been greatly updated and extended by Sharyn Rundle-Thiele and colleagues (see Box 5.5 in Chapter 5).

Chapters 2 to 6 discuss the main principles and practices of this core element of social marketing.

Length and breadth

Social marketers, then, argue that, in essence, marketing is about human behaviour and that this behaviour can be seen in terms of exchange. We human beings cooperate by doing deals. This raises the question of power; any deal-doing is going to be underpinned by the relative power of the parties involved. In commercial marketing, we have already touched on financial inequalities and the problems these create for the have-nots in the short term and all of us in the long term. Social marketers have to deal with a wider concept of power; we are none of us in complete control of our own lives – our social circumstances, the availability of choices, the behaviour of siblings and parents will all constrain our decision making. This problem was recognised centuries ago by John Donne when he pointed at out that "no man is an island". For social marketers, it means we have to consider not just *which* behaviour to change, but *whose*.

Take the problem of alcohol misuse. This might address the behaviour of the teen who chooses to binge drink; the neglectful parent who fails to intervene; the bar worker who sells her the booze despite being underage; the drink producer who develops alcopops that appeal to juvenile palates; or the politician who fails to control such irresponsibility. This process of analysing the influences on our decision making was dubbed 'moving upstream' by Lawrence Wallack. Have a go at Exercise 1.3.

EXERCISE 1.3   LAWRENCE WALLACK'S RIVER

A man out walking happens across a river in which people are being swept along and in danger of drowning. His immediate desire is to help them, and he considers various options – throwing in lifebelts, diving in himself and pulling some to shore or even shouting out instructions on how to swim. And each of these certainly has the potential to help; but it is equally clear that some people will drown – he hasn't got the time or resources to reach them all. He begins to question why this calamity has arisen; why are so many people in the river in the first place? To find out he has to go upstream. When he does so, he finds that a few hundred metres further on there are huge and evocative billboards extolling the virtues of the river – how clean and refreshing it is – and calling on people to "jump on in; the water's lovely". A beautiful new diving board has been provided to make the prospect even more enticing, and it costs only 10 cents a go. Kids are daring each other to give it a try.

The man shakes his head and carries on upstream.

After he walks for a few more minutes, the bank begins getting wet, muddy and treacherous. He becomes anxious about falling in the river himself. Then he sees houses built on these poor foundations. They are cheap and dilapidated, more like shacks than houses, and some are clearly in danger of collapse. As he is watching, a small child slips down the bank and only just manages to save itself from falling in the river.

(continued)

> *(continued)*
>
> The man is left pondering about how he can best do something about the drowning people: should he help the people who have already fallen in, stop advertisers encouraging others to jump in or move right upstream and change macroeconomic policy so that the poor can afford better housing?
>
> Whose behaviour does he need to change: that of the individual, the marketer or the minister of finance?
>
> (*Source*: based on Wallack *et al.* 1993)

The answer is that to be truly successful, a social marketer will need to address the behaviour of all these people. Wallack is compelling us to remember that time and again our individual behaviours are actually intimately related to the system in which we live. Indeed, he is rightly uneasy about approaches that do not recognise this – ones that, in his words, put too much emphasis on the loose threads of the individual, and ignore problems with the fabric of society. Such thinking is not just ineffective, but also unethical.

The idea of systems also introduces the dimension of time to our thinking. As we noted when discussing Exercise 1.1, our behaviour is rarely ad hoc; in particular, we learn from experience. Commercial marketers have recognised this in recent decades and developed the concept of 'relationship marketing' – which has spawned a plethora of reward schemes, loyalty cards and strategic branding efforts – to get and keep our attention. Social marketers have to adopt similar long-term approaches, as we discuss in Chapter 2.

Why it's critical to be critical

The broader systemic implications of upstream and relational thinking also remind us of the importance of competitive and critical analysis, which we will discuss in detail in Chapters 7 and 8.

The business sector accords great importance to competition, which greatly influences market behaviour – as Exercise 1.1 illustrated. So McDonald's and Burger King keep a very careful eye on each other, as do Philip Morris and Japan Tobacco. This not only helps them to out-do each other, it also provides a valuable insight into their customers' behaviour. McDonald's can learn a lot about what people gain from going to a rival fast food outlet, or indeed the broader options they may select in preference to eating a Big Mac, such as having a picnic or eating at home then going to the cinema. Specifically, it tells them more about the needs they are satisfying, and that these can go beyond the obvious one of hunger. This, in turn, helps them hone the service they offer.

All four companies will also be watching those working in public health, nutrition, obesity management and tobacco control – including us in social marketing – closely. We may offer opportunities for collaboration and partnership, or threats to their operation in the form of unwelcome criticism or calls for regulation.

Not surprisingly, then, competitive analysis is also very important to social marketers. To start with, we too need to remember that our clients have a choice. Remember, as we've already noted, our interest is in involuntary behaviour change: our clients can choose to go on eating burgers despite their weight problem, or smoking even though their breath is beginning to go. If we cannot compel, we need to take the time and trouble to understand these competing behaviours and learn to outbid them. This approach is sometimes referred to as tackling the 'passive' competition.

There is also 'active' competition in social marketing: we are frequently at odds with parts of the commercial sector. For example, those working in public health want to reduce the consumption of the products marketed by the tobacco, fast food and alcohol industries. Social marketers should therefore use their marketing expertise to deconstruct these activities.

Harking back to Exercise 1.1, for example, it is important to emphasise that advertising and promotion are only part of the picture; we need to think about all the ways that marketers attract customers, including packaging, branding, new product development, price, promotions and distribution. In addition, this analysis needs to be backed with careful research to help develop an evidence base that will enable policy makers to act and, where necessary, constrain the activities of commercial marketers. Guiding the development of socially beneficial regulatory systems is a crucial task for social marketers.

Moving beyond the transgressions of individual industries, social marketing can and should contribute to the wider debate about the role and values of commercial marketing in a modern democracy. In a finite world, is a system that works ceaselessly to encourage consumption a desirable one? Should we be concerned about the rise of 'stakeholder marketing' (National Cancer Institute 2008) by the corporate sector, which aims to influence the behaviour of policy makers and politicians just as conventional marketing does that of consumers? Are we comfortable to learn that the American Beverage Association spent at least $67 million between 2009 and 2016, to lobby against government initiatives to reduce sugary drink consumption? And how do we feel about corporate social responsibility (CSR), which, as business texts emphasise, is not driven by philanthropic intent, but commercial interest?

This re-emphasises the systems thinking we touched on above and locates social marketing in the broader social economy. Following the European tradition of social change, transformation and innovation, social marketing can realign market structures with wider societal values, rather than just applying business models to the day-to-day management of social problems. In this way, it is possible to address the profound question raised by US academics Wilkie and Moore of how to "facilitate the maximal operations of the system *for the benefit of the host society*" (2003: 118, emphasis added). We discuss this thinking in more detail in Chapter 11.

To balance this emphasis on the collective, we have developed a new chapter (Chapter 9, 'Spiritual dimensions') looking at individual responsibility. Every system is, in the final analysis, made up of individuals and it is therefore important to examine what it is to be human. This takes us into profound issues of morality, agency and accountability. We all have a responsibility to think through the full implications of our own actions, to question injustice and, where necessary, to rebel against unfair systems. This is not easy; it brings with it the need for continuous effort: it is 'up to us'. However, it is essential that we take on this introspective task, not just because it is our duty to do so, but also because it is what defines us as human beings. Human rights legislation recognises this essential dimension to our humanity and enshrines in international law not just the right to protection, but also *the right to equal participation in the process of change, of creating a better world*. An essential dimension of social marketing, then, is to move beyond mere behaviour change and start thinking about people, always remembering that at the core of social progress lies the well-rounded human being – in body, mind and spirit.

Reflecting these ambitious aims, Figure 1.2 presents a view of the domain of social marketing, which recognises that the citizen is at the centre of any successful society, and that their empowerment is vital. They need to have the knowledge and skills to make constructive decisions about their lifestyles. Figure 1.2 also recognises that, as we have noted, this empowerment will be constrained by social context. Building on the work of Bloom and Gundlach concerning the "paths through which marketing affects societal welfare" (2001: xv), it acknowledges the role of three key sets of influences:

- public policy decisions;
- corporate marketing decisions; and
- civil society.

This is undoubtedly a big agenda. However, before we get too daunted we should remember the power of our commercial cousins. The Coca-Cola Corporation has not only developed into one of the most successful economic organisations on the planet, but also arguably

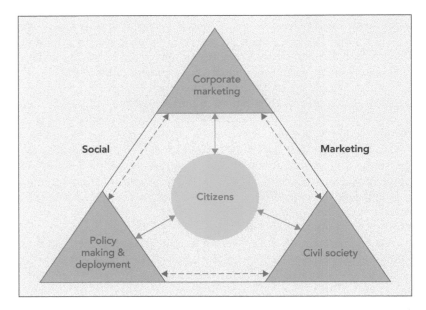

Figure 1.2 The domain of social marketing

(*Source*: Hastings 2011)

did more to open up China than Richard Nixon. More ominously, the 2008 banking crisis, which brought the world economic system to its knees, was largely driven by bright young marketing-literate MBAs. And the same skill sets have enabled corporations to vastly out-grow many countries. If commercial marketing can do all this, social marketing can foster equitable democratic societies around the world for the betterment of all.

Furthermore, ambitious or not, social marketing has to address these societal issues if it is to continue to be a force to be reckoned with. The alternative is to be relegated to the cleaner-up of other people's messes – whether this be the cancer sufferers created by the tobacco industry or the new poor of a deeply flawed financial sector.

These systemic issues and their ramifications for both society and social marketing are discussed in detail in Chapters 10 and 11.

A definition

In summary, then, social marketing takes insights from the commercial marketer's efforts to influence our consumption behaviour and applies same to health and social behaviours; it also looks critically at business in order to reduce the potential harms being done at both an individual and systemic level. This twin approach was recognised by Lazer and Kelley four decades ago when they stated "social marketing is concerned with the application of marketing knowledge, concepts and techniques to enhance social as well as economic ends. It is also concerned with analysis of the social consequence of marketing policies, decisions and activities" (1973: ix).

More recently, in 2013, three social marketing associations – the International Social Marketing Association (iSMA), the European Social Marketing Association (ESMA) and the Australian Association of Social Marketing (AASM) – agreed that "Social Marketing seeks to develop and integrate marketing concepts with other approaches to influence behaviours that benefit individuals and communities for the greater social good.

Our briefer version is:

Social marketing critically examines commercial marketing so as to learn from its successes and curb its excesses.

Box 1.2 expands this definition into eight key social marketing precepts.

BOX 1.2   KEY CHARACTERISTICS OF SOCIAL MARKETING

Good social marketing:

1. Sets behavioural goals

2. Creates attractive motivational exchanges with target groups

3. Makes judicious use of theory

(continued)

(continued)

4. Pays attention to what people value and don't value

5. Thinks beyond communications

6. Thinks beyond the individual

7. Pays careful attention to the competition

8. Looks critically at commercial marketing

9. Thinks systemically and

10. Empowers people to participate

Three common fallacies

Having laid out what social marketing *is*, it is now worth emphasising what it is *not*.

The word 'marketing' causes perennial problems and considerable confusion. First, it is very familiar to all of us both as a term and a phenomenon in our daily lives, and the form of marketing with which we are most familiar is advertising – which is unsurprising given that its principal function is to attract attention. This perhaps explains why the literature is full of studies and interventions that are labelled social marketing but turn out to be no more than communications initiatives. Indeed, when Laura McDermott and her colleagues carried out the review on social marketing discussed above, they had to make a deliberate effort to move beyond labels and evaluate interventions that genuinely applied social marketing precepts rather than ones that were simply called social marketing (McDermott *et al.* 2005). So let's deal with our first fallacy: *social marketing is not social advertising*.

Social marketers may make use of communications, or not, depending upon the problem being addressed and, in particular, the needs of the people they are trying to influence. To equate social marketing and social advertising is as misguided as assuming that Coke's dominance of the soft drinks industry has been delivered purely by their advertising campaigns. In reality, advertising is a tiny part of their effort, which also includes getting the right product in the right place at the right price, as well as addressing the needs of key stakeholders, such as suppliers, franchisees and policy makers.

The word 'marketing' also causes emotional problems. For many, it smacks of manipulation. People see it is a twentieth-century invention by business schools simply designed to get us to consume more. It is, in fact, as old as humankind; its core principles of mutually beneficial exchange and doing strategic deals that benefit all those concerned underpin the cooperation at the heart of any successful society. This puts paid to fallacy number 2: while some campaigns are deceitful and misleading, *marketing need not be manipulative*.

Finally, search online for the term 'social marketing' and it is easy to conclude that it is a synonym for marketing using social media such as Facebook and Twitter. In reality, as with other forms of communication, social marketing makes use of these channels but it is much more than this. For example, take a look at Case Study 1 where SIMPle – a prescription intervention in the west of Ireland – used not only a variety of digital tools and online methods including an award-winning app with mini-games, emails, social media and SMS, but also personalised cards, cupcakes and stickers.

So, to slay our final fallacy: *social marketing is not social media marketing.*

Coming of age

Social marketing has now gained currency around the globe. Many business schools and universities offer courses in it: the idea that skills learned to push fast-moving consumer goods or financial services can also be used to address pressing social problems such as HIV/AIDS or sustainability is extremely appealing to students.

In addition, the clear need to improve the functioning of our socio-economic system adds to the attraction of a discipline that has insights to share on topics as wide ranging as inequalities, international development and corporate malpractice. In the process, they demonstrate that the discipline has a valuable part to play, not just in tackling micro behavioural problems, such as binge drinking or teen pregnancy, but also in the biggest debates of our time, such as poverty, obesity and climate change (Kotler and Lee 2010).

The case studies featured in the book (see Table 1.1), from experienced and respected social marketers from across the world that have been kind enough to allow their work to be included, demonstrate the real-world impact of social marketing. From road safety in the UK (Case Study 20), drinking water in Portugal (Case Study 6), energy saving in Australia (Case Study 4) and mental health and suicide prevention in Ireland and Australia (Case Studies 10 and 16), to tobacco regulation in Colombia (Case Study 13), health communication outreach in India (Case Study 22) and sustainable whale shark tourism in Australia (Case Study 19), it is clear that social marketing is making a difference at both the individual and systemic level around the world.

The case studies also provide tangible evidence of how sophisticated social marketing concepts, tools and techniques have become. A discipline that in the 1980s and 1990s (what Andreasen calls its 'childhood years') focused on ad hoc and individual behaviour change using a limited number of fairly basic tools has developed into a mature and complex one intent on delivering strategic social change.

For example, look at value-based exchanges with hard to reach audiences in Case Study 20 or see recent developments in systems thinking, system mapping and modelling at work in Case Studies 2, 17 and 19. Case Study 14 presents behavioural change in a B2B context, while Case Study 7 illustrates the importance of networks and partnerships in the environmental field. Partnerships and participation are central to Case Studies 22, 23 and 24. We see message communication and resistance throughout the social system in Case Study 8, while branding is key to water management (Case Study 6), waste campaigns (Case Studies 8 and 12) and tobacco (Case Study 11).

Critical marketing in health and sustainability issues can be found in Case Studies 11, 13, 15 and 18. For a detailed insight into the online and offline world and integrated communications, using extensive partnerships across the profit and non-profit divide, go to Case Study 22. In Case Study 9 you'll also see paid, earned and owned media at work. In Case Study 21 online and offline promotion is discussed as well as the role of research and partnerships.

Community social marketing and participatory action research are evident in Case Studies 3, 5 and 16, while process evaluation and indicators go to the core of Case Study 21. To conclude, there's extensive qualitative research undertaken in Case Study 23, while the final Case Study 24 covers topics such as research, partnerships, community social marketing and participation. All in all, an exciting collection of new and highly informative case studies from social marketing experts around the world, joining those from the second edition which is now on the accompanying website, with stimulating and challenging questions for serious consideration.

Table 1.1 The case studies in this book

No.	Topic	Authors	Key Issues	Country
1	Antimicrobial resistance 'SIMPle'	Sinead Duane, Christine Domegan, Aoife Callan, Sandra Galvin, Martin Cormican, Kathleen Bennett, Andrew W. Murphy and Akke Vellinga	Exchange; technology; social media; games and gamification	Ireland
2	Marine environment 'Sea for energy'	Patricia McHugh, Christine Domegan, Sinead Duane, John Joyce, Michelle Devaney, Michael Hogan, Benjamin J. Broome, Marzia Mazzonetto and Joanna Piwowarczyk	Stakeholder engagement; participatory action research; systems mapping	EU
3	Healthy lifestyles 'Meals on Wheels'	Christine Fitzgerald, Christine Domegan and Tom Scharf	Community Readiness Model; ethics; services	Ireland
4	Energy consumption 'Reduce Your Juice'	Rebekah Russell-Bennett, Rory Mulcahy, Ryan McAndrew, Tim Swinton, Jo-Anne Little and Neil Horrocks	Technology; games and gamification; digital marketing	Australia
5	Tobacco endgame 'Fife'	Marisa de Andrade, Karen Cooper and Kay Samson	Co-creation; participatory action research; community social marketing	UK

6	Drinking water 'Porto Tap Water'	Ana Sofia Dias and Sara Balonas	Public branding; targeting; marketing mix	Portugal
7	Solid waste management 'Reduce and reuse'	Amena El Harakeh Farah Madi and Marco Bardus	Formative research; marketing mix; partnerships	Lebanon
8	Drowning prevention 'I know what I'm doing'	Linda Brennan, Glen Donnar, Lukas Parker and Natalia Alessi	Communication; messaging; stakeholder mapping	Australia
9	Physical activity 'Walk to School'	Krzysztof Kubacki, Kellye Hartman, Annemarie Wright, Haruka Fujihira and Sharyn Rundle-Thiele	Digital marketing; evaluation; competition	Australia
10	Mental health 'Cycle Against Suicide'	Amy Cannon, Olivia Freeman and Patrick Kenny	Community-based social marketing; intervention; competition	Ireland
11	Tobacco endgame 'Moi(s) sans tabac'	Karine Gallopel-Morvan, Olivier Smadja, Anna Mercier, Elodie Safta, Jennifer Davies, Romain Guignard, Pierre Arwidson and Viêt Nguyen Tanh	Branding; partnerships	France
12	Food waste 'Less Eyes than Belly Movement'	Sara Balonas and Susana Marques	Branding; social movements; communication	Portugal
13	Tobacco control 'Point of sale'	Juan Miguel Rey-Pino, Liliana Andrea Ávila-García, Jaime Arcila Sierra and Marian Lorena Ibarra Ávila	Point of sale; critical marketing	Colombia
14	Pro-environment behaviour 'SMEs'	Anne Smith and Aqueel Imtiaz Wahga	CSR critical marketing	Pakistan
15	Healthy lifestyles 'Changing population salt intake behaviour'	Michael Barry and Maurice Murphy	Critical marketing; ethics; upstream social marketing	UK and Ireland
16	Mental health 'ABC Act-Belong-Commit'	Rob Donovan and Julia Anwar McHenry	Community social marketing; theory; values	Australia

(continued)

Table 1.1 *(continued)*

No.	Topic	Authors	Key Issues	Country
17	Colorectal cancer 'CBPM for systems change'	Brian J. Biroscak, Carol A. Bryant, Claudia X. Aguado Loi, Dinorah Martinez Tyson, Tali Schneider, Laura Baum, Aldenise Ewing and Peter S. Hovmand	Systems change; system dynamics modelling	USA
18	Sustainability 'Fast fashion'	Ann-Marie Kennedy Sommer Kapitan, Neha Bajaj, Angelina Bakonyi and Sean Sands	Wicked problems; ethics	Global
19	Sustainable tourism 'Ningaloo Reef'	Sarah Duffy and Roger A. Layton	Commons problems; marketing systems ethics	Australia
20	Road safety 'Wheels, Skills and Thrills'	Alan Tapp	Community social marketing	UK
21	Marine environment 'Sea for Society'	Patricia McHugh and Christine Domegan	Evaluation; indicators	EU
22	Health communication 'The Taj Must Smile'	Sanjeev Vyas	Promotion; online and offline partnerships; research	India
23	Healthy lifestyles 'Pap Smears'	Julinawati Suanda, Desmond Cawley, Maria Brenner, Christine Domegan and Neil Rowan	Research; qualitative sampling	Malaysia
24	Healthy lifestyles 'Making India open-defecation-free'	Anurudra Bhanot, Vinti Agarwal, Ashutosh Awasthi and Animesh Sharma	Evaluation; research; promotion; partnerships; CSM	India

Note: The full cases, with accompanying questions, are presented in the Case Studies section.

Wrap-up

This first chapter has introduced you to the basic precepts of social marketing. It used the example of Coca-Cola to emphasise the power and ubiquity of commercial marketing, which has – time and again – proved its capacity to influence our consumption behaviour. We then explored how important behaviour is to our welfare – whether it be our eating habits, our driving patterns or the sustainability of our lifestyles. Social marketing combines and applies the tools used by commerce to affect our consumption behaviour to address our social and health behaviours. These tools include the need for strategic vision and a recognition of the important influence that social context can have on our behaviour.

In addition, the chapter emphasised the importance of competitive analysis to social marketers. Thinking more broadly, social marketers need to look critically at the wider economic system to ensure that it too is contributing to welfare of the many. This critical engagement is not only desirable; it is also an essential part of what makes us human.

This led us to define social marketing as a discipline that *critically examines commercial marketing so as to learn from its successes and curb its excesses.* You can remind yourself of its basic precepts by looking again at Box 1.2.

Now try putting the lessons you have learned into practice by doing Exercise 1.4.

EXERCISE 1.4   SOCIAL MARKETING AND TOBACCO

The problem

One in two long-term smokers dies as a result of their habit. Of these, half will die in middle age. This translates to 6.3 million people in the UK since 1950 (Peto *et al.* 2005). Or, in global terms, given the present trends in global tobacco consumption, the projected number of deaths by tobacco will grow to 10 million per year by 2030. If prevalence remains unchanged and children start smoking at the expected rates, in 2025 there will be almost 1.9 billion smokers consuming more than 9 trillion cigarettes (Guindon and Boisclair 2003).

The demographics of smoking

The uptake of smoking is a paediatric phenomenon: as we noted in the preface, almost 90 per cent of smokers start as children. Acquiring the habit demands a degree of perseverance and the principal reasons both for trying it and sticking at it are to do with personal image: to look older, more sophisticated and cool. A limited repertoire of premium brands provides the cigarette of choice. Adult smoking is quite different. Most (66 per cent) want to give up (Office for National Statistics 2004), but cannot. The principal driver of continued consumption is addiction. Nicotine is now known to be as addictive as heroin and cocaine (Royal College of Physicians 2000). Thus, image takes second place to nicotine delivery.

The other principal social demographic at play in tobacco consumption is social class. The further down the social scale you are, the more likely you are to smoke. Only 14 per cent of those in higher professional occupation households smoke

(continued)

(continued)

compared with 32 per cent of those in semi-routine occupation households (Goddard and Green 2005). Studies of deprived and disadvantaged groups have shown smoking levels among lone parents in receipt of social security benefits in excess of 75 per cent (Marsh and McKay 1994).

The tobacco industry

Until recently, the UK tobacco industry spent around £100 million a year on advertising and promotion. This has now been banned, but the rest of their marketing effort remains: product innovation, distribution, packaging and pricing strategies all play a big part in their effort. Research has shown that this both encourages uptake and discourages cessation.

The economics of smoking

Tobacco is a profitable business. Cigarettes cost pennies to make, particularly with modern production methods, and generate long-term profits. The average UK smoker will smoke a pack a day for twenty-five years and, at today's prices, spend about £36,000 on tobacco. Governments also do well out of tobacco. In the UK, 80 per cent of the cost of a pack of cigarettes is tax; the Revenue netted £8,093 million in 2003–2004 (excluding VAT) (HM Customs & Excise 2005).

Increasing tobacco prices through taxation also has public health benefits. There is a direct, inverse correlation between the price of tobacco and the number of smokers. The one exception to this rule is among the poor, who seem immune to price increases and will carry on smoking regardless, cutting down on essentials in the process.

How would you as a social marketer respond to this problem?

Reflective questions

1. What is marketing?

2. Why is marketing powerful?

3. Describe the three public health problems that have arisen from our consumption behaviours.

4. Explain the relationship between commercial marketing and social marketing.

5. Discuss social marketing's societal role.

6. Bloom and Gundlach maintain social marketers are concerned with three of the "paths through which marketing affects societal welfare" (2001: xv). Elaborate with illustrations.

7. Delineate the key precepts of social marketing.

8. Differentiate between the concepts of social media, social advertising and social marketing.

9. Elaborate upon Lazer and Kelley's definition: "Social marketing is concerned with the application of marketing knowledge, concepts and techniques to enhance social as well as economic ends. It is also concerned with analysis of the social consequence of marketing policies, decisions and activities" (1973: ix).

10. Compare and contrast Lazer and Kelley's definition of social marketing with iSMA's one.

Reflective assignments

1. Conduct an Internet search on social marketing interventions or campaigns.

2. Locate and critique three papers that discuss the characteristics of social marketing.

3. Locate and examine three case studies that display the characteristics of social marketing.

4. Make sure you are comfortable with the content of this chapter by writing a concise paragraph, in your own words, about each of the key words listed at the start of the chapter.

5. You are a social marketer with responsibility for increasing volunteer numbers by 5 per cent for a local meals-on-wheels service. How might you use social marketing to guide your actions and decision making?

6. Your local renewable energy (RE) co-op has employed you to increase the usage of RE within the local area. What role could social marketing fulfil? What other approaches would you consider?

7. Consult the *Journal of Social Marketing* and/or *Social Marketing Quarterly* to read a classic or contemporary article, or more, on what social marketing is and is not to advance your understanding of the topic.

8. 'Rebels with a cause' – reflect upon the consumption patterns of your close friends and family. What would you change, alter, modify? What ignites your passion for change? Who else feels the same way as you? A sister, brother, best friend or college buddy? How might you, as rebels with a cause, use social marketing thinking to bring about these changes?

9. Make your own 'Rebels with a cause' checklist of salient points from this chapter.

Notes

1 www.nasa.gov/press-release/nasa-study-shows-antarctica-s-larsen-b-ice-shelf-nearing-its-final-act and http://earthobservatory.nasa.gov/Features/WorldOfChange/larsenb.php.
2 www.statista.com/statistics/264423/revenue-and-financial-results-of-coca-cola.
3 www.nasa.gov/image-feature/rift-in-antarcticas-larsen-c-ice-shelf.
4 http://anthropocene.info.
5 www.who.int/mediacentre/factsheets/fs311/en.

References

Anderson, S. and Cavanagh, J. (2000) *Top 200: The Rise of Corporate Global Power*. Washington, DC: Institute for Policy Studies.

Andreasen, A.R. (2006) *Social Marketing in the 21st Century*. Thousand Oaks, CA: Sage Publications.

Bagozzi, R. (1975) 'Marketing and exchange', *Journal of Marketing*, 39(October): 32–39.

Bendell, J. (2011) *Evolving Partnerships: A Guide to Working with Business for Greater Social Change*. Sheffield: Greenleaf Publishing.

Bloom, P.N. and Gundlach, G.T. (2001) *Handbook of Marketing and Society*. Thousand Oaks, CA: Sage Publications.

Cairns, G., Mackay, B. and MacDonald, L. (2011) 'Social marketing and international development', in G. Hastings, K. Angus and C. Bryant (eds) *The SAGE Handbook of Social Marketing*. London: Sage Publications, ch. 22.

CAP (2012) *CAP Review of the Use of Children as Brand Ambassadors and in Peer-to-Peer Marketing*. London: Committee of Advertising Practice. Online: www.cap.org.uk/Media-Centre/2012/~/media/Files/CAP/Misc/CAP%20Review%20document%20- %20brand%20ambassadors%20%282%29.ashx/ (last accessed March 2016).

Casswell, S., You, R.Q. and Huckle T. (2011) 'Alcohol's harm to others: Reduced wellbeing and health status for those with heavy drinkers in their lives', *Addiction*, 106(6): 1087–1094.

Connolly, J. and Prothero, A. (2003) 'Sustainable consumption', *Consumption, Consumers and the Commodity Discourse*, 6(4): 275–291.

Drucker, P. (1957) *Landmarks of Tomorrow*. New York: Harper & Row.

Geels, F.W., Hekkert, M.P. and Jacobsson, S. (2008) 'The dynamics of sustainable innovation journeys', *Technology Analysis & Strategic Management*, 20(5): 521–536.

Gell, L. *et al.* (2015) *Alcohol's Harm to Others*. Online: www.ias.org.uk/uploads/pdf/IAS%20reports/rp18072015.pdf (accessed March 2016).

Ghosh, A. (2016) *the The Great Derrangement:. Climate Change and the Unthinkable*. Chicago: University of Chicago Press.

Goddard, E. and Green, H. (2005) *Smoking and Drinking Among Adults, 2004*. London: Office for National Statistics, December.

Guindon, G.E. and Boisclair D. (2003) *Past, Current and Future Trends in Tobacco Use*. Health, Nutrition and Population (HNP) Discussion Paper: Economics of Tobacco Control Paper No. 6. Washington, DC: The World Bank, March.

Hardin, G. (1968) 'The tragedy of the commons', *Science*, 162(3859): 1243–1248.

Hastings, G. (2011) 'Introduction: A movement in social marketing', in G. Hastings, K. Angus and C. Bryant (eds) *The SAGE Handbook of Social Marketing*. London: Sage Publications.

Hastings, G. (2012) *The Marketing Matrix*. London: Routledge.

Hastings, G. and Elliott, B. (1993) 'Social marketing practice in traffic safety', in *Marketing of Traffic Safety*. Paris: OECD, pp. 35–53, ch. 3.

Hastings, G.B., Stead, M., McDermott, L. and Forsyth, A., MacKintosh, A.M., Rayner, M., Godfrey, G., Carahar, M. and Angus, K. (2003) *Review of Research on the Effects of Food Promotion to Children – Final Report and Appendices*. Prepared for the Food Standards Agency, UK. Online: www.food.gov.uk/healthiereating/advertisingtochildren/promotion/readreview/ (last accessed March 2016).

Hill, R.P. (2011) 'Impoverished consumers and social marketing', in G. Hastings, K. Angus and C. Bryant (eds) *The SAGE Handbook of Social Marketing*. London: Sage Publications, ch. 21.

HM Customs & Excise (2005) *Tobacco Factsheet (February)*. London: HMCE.

Kotler, P. and Lee, N.R. (2010) *Social Marketing: Influencing Behaviors for Good*. Newbury Park, CA: Sage Publications.

Kotler, P. and Zaltman, G. (1971) 'Social marketing: An approach to planned social change', *Journal of Marketing*, 35(3): 3–12.

Layard, R. (2005) *Happiness: Lessons from a New Science*. London: Allen Lane.

Lazer, W. and Kelley, E. (1973) *Social Marketing: Perspectives and Viewpoints*. Homewood, IL: Richard D. Irwin, Inc.

Lovato, C., Linn, G., Stead, L.F. and Best, A. (2003) 'Impact of tobacco advertising and promotion on increasing adolescent smoking behaviours', *Cochrane Database of Systematic Reviews*, (4): CD003439.

Luck, D.J. (1969) 'Broadening the concept of marketing – too far', *Journal of Marketing*, 33 (July), 53–55.

McDermott, L., Stead, M. and Hastings, G. (2005) 'What is and what is not social marketing: The challenge of reviewing the evidence', *Journal of Marketing Management*, 21(5–6): 545–553.

McGinnis, J.M. and Foege, W.H. (1993) 'Actual causes of death in the United States', *Journal of the American Medical Association*, 270(18): 2207–2212.

McGinnis, J.M., Gootman, J.A. and Kraak, V.I. (eds) (2006) *Food Marketing to Children and Youth: Threat or Opportunity?* Committee on Food Marketing and the Diets of Children and Youth; Food and Nutrition Board; Board on Children, Youth, and Families; Institute of Medicine of The National Academies. Washington, DC: The National Academies Press.

Marsh, A. and McKay, S. (1994) *Poor Smokers*. London: Policy Studies Institute.

National Cancer Institute (2008) *The Role of the Media in Promoting and Reducing Tobacco Use*. Tobacco Control Monograph No. 19. Vol. NIH Pub. No. 07-6242. Bethesda, MD: U.S. Department of Health and Human Services, National Institutes of Health, National Cancer Institute.

Office for National Statistics (2004) *Proportion of smokers who would like to give up smoking altogether, by sex and number of cigarettes smoked per day: 1992 to 2003: GHS 2003*. London: ONS.

Olshansky, S.J., Passaro, D.J., Hershow, R.C., Layden, J., Carnes, B.A., Brody, J., Hayflick, L., Butler, R.N., Allison, D.B. and Ludwig, D.S. (2005) 'A potential decline in life expectancy in the United States in the 21st century', *New England Journal of Medicine*, 352(11): 1138–1145.

Peto, R., Lopez, A.D., Boreham, J. and Thun, M. (2005) *Mortality from Smoking in Developed Countries 1950–2000*, 2nd edn. Oxford: Oxford Medical Publications.

Pingeot, L. (2014) corporate influence in the post-2015 process. Online: http://dnb.d-nb.de. ISBN 978-3-943126-12-9. Aachen/Berlin/Bonn/New York, January.

Quelch, J.A. and Jocz, K.E. (2007) *Greater Good: How Good Marketing Makes for Better Democracy*. Watertown, MA: Harvard Business Press.

Royal College of Physicians (2000) *Nicotine Addiction in Britain*. Report of the Tobacco Advisory Group of the Royal College of Physicians. London: Royal College of Physicians.

Wallack, L., Dorfman, L., Jernigan, D. and Themba, M. (1993) *Media Advocacy and Public Health*. Thousand Oaks, CA: Sage Publications.

Wiebe, G.D. (1951) 'Merchandising commodities and citizenship in television', *Public Opinion Quarterly*, 15(4): 679–691.

Wilkie, W.L. and Moore, E.S. (2003) 'Scholarly research in marketing: Exploring the "four eras" of thought development', *Journal of Public Policy & Marketing*, 22(2): 116–146.

Wilkinson, R. and Pickett, K. (2010) *The Spirit Level: Why Equality is Better for Everyone*. London: Penguin Books UK.

World Bank (2015) 'A Measured Approach to Ending Poverty and Boosting Shared Prosperity: Concepts, Data, and the Twin Goals'. Policy Research Report. Washington, DC: World Bank. Online: www.worldbank.org/en/research/publication/a-measured-approach-to-ending-poverty-and-boosting-shared-prosperity https://doi.org/10.1596/978-1-4648-0361-1 (accessed March 2016).

Chapter 2

Social marketing principles

IN-SIGHT

Three old friends had gone to the golf club to have a beer. One, Fred, was an anti-tobacco advocate with many years' experience. The second, Joe, was a successful advertiser, famous for several social campaigns. The third guy, Bill, was a social marketer who had worked on infant mortality in developing countries for many years.

As they drank their beers, they heard a commotion on the golf course and noticed that there was a real fight brewing on the second green. They asked the waiter, "What's going on?"

"Oh, this happens every Wednesday," said the waiter. "The golf course owner's son is blind and he loves to play golf, so the owner opens the course to him and a bunch of his friends to play on Wednesdays. But as you can imagine they are a lot slower than the other players and the sighted guys get angry and often belligerent at the blind guys. We've actually had fist fights, and the blind guys don't always lose."

Fred said, "This is easy to fix. Those sighted guys have got to learn to obey the policy. It has got to be clear and then they need to lose their rights to play if they violate the policy which allows these blind guys to play. Somebody's got to stand up for their rights."

Joe responded, "You are always looking for bad guys to hurt. I think the sighted guys don't know what the blind guys are going through. I can imagine a campaign with some fabulous images showing how these blind guys navigate the course. Develop some empathy – use emotion to make the sighted guys aware of the blind guys' needs. Empathy and awareness are the deeper answer."

The debate between Joe and Fred raged for an hour and finally Fred turned to Bill and said, "You've been awful quiet? Don't you have any ideas at all about how to solve this problem?"

"Oh, sorry," said Bill, "I've been making notes about a new service the club could offer: night-time golf. Let the blind guys have the whole course when the sun goes down. No electric bill needed. I'd offer a limo to pick them up, but first I'd want to talk to them about what else we could do for them, for a small fee, of course, to cover costs."

We are indebted to Bill Smith for this story which tells us a lot about social marketing. Specifically, it shows how social marketers see the world (their orientation) and the principal lever (mutually beneficial exchange) that they bring to the challenge of changing the world for the better.

There are four dimensions to a social marketing orientation (see Box 2.1).

BOX 2.1   FOUR SOCIAL MARKETING ORIENTATIONS

Client orientation	Identify people's needs, aspirations, values and priorities
Creative orientation	Find imaginative ways to engage them
Collective orientation	Recognise that the social context matters
Competitive orientation	Reduce the price; critically address the competition

The first is already familiar to us through commercial marketing – the concept of **client orientation** – and is a quintessentially marketing idea. This client orientation is the prime directive for social marketers as successful behaviour change is built through a well-grounded understanding of current behaviour and the people engaged in it. The aim of this understanding is to identify the grail of social marketing, the mutually beneficial exchange.

Social marketing, like commercial marketing, needs to start with a clearly defined behaviour and target group: *what* do you want *who* to do? To deliver effectively to their needs, we have to understand them and their current behaviour very well and this requires a solid grounding in behaviour change and exchange theory (Chapter 3) and sophisticated research (Chapter 5). Good social marketing starts by appraising the situation, understanding the problem and assessing the competing forces, and only then begins to deduce possible solutions. This process needs to go beyond mere data collection, and incorporate a genuine empathy for the client group. As the Chinese proverb has it, we need to walk a mile in the other person's shoes.

To these insights need to be added vital elements of imagination and innovation to make our approaches as attractive and motivating as possible, always remembering that marketers, whether commercial or social, deal in voluntary behaviour. We cannot compel people to do business with us. Bill Smith's story brilliantly illustrates the value of what Edward De Bono would call lateral thinking – and we use the term **creative orientation** to encapsulate this.

However deep we dig, though, in our bid to understand people, we won't get a full picture unless we also recognise the importance of the *social* determinants of behaviour. All of us are influenced by the circumstances in which we find ourselves: a young person's inclination to smoke is partly a matter of personal volition, but also a function of their local environment (e.g., whether friends smoke and tobacco is readily available in neighbourhood shops) and wider social norms (e.g., whether tobacco advertising or smoking in public places is permitted). Similarly, road accidents are not just a matter of driver and pedestrian behaviour, but also car design (manufacturer behaviour) and road infrastructure (government behaviour).

By the same token, social marketing solutions also have to be multifaceted; often it is as important to think about wider-scale social change as individual behaviours. Effective social marketing therefore has to incorporate a **collective orientation**.

This complex social picture also means we all have lots of choice. Think about obesity, for instance, and the myriad ways a person can tackle losing weight: buying gym membership to exercise; WeightWatchers dinners to limit calorie intake; lifestyle intervention programmes to rebalance work/life; surgery to shrink the stomach. The individual also has the freedom to choose *not* to deal with obesity, despite what experts might say. The terrain becomes even more contested, because there are other actors – the fast food and soft drinks industries for instance – who have a vested interest in pushing against many obesity interventions.

These multiple choices or decision points for the individual represent competition for the social marketer. By adopting a **competitive orientation**, we can ensure that, as the airlines have taken to saying, we never forget our clients have a choice. They also remind us that sometimes the best thing we can do for the individual is to protect them from unscrupulous competition. Notwithstanding Bill Smith's story, there are some bad guys out there. Maybe the overweight adult would have avoided becoming fat in the first place if there had been statutory nutritional standards when they were at school – or effective controls on the marketing of energy-dense food.

These four orientations become even more powerful when applied strategically, not just to change ad hoc behaviours, but also to build ongoing relationships. The final part of the chapter discusses how commerce has embraced relationship marketing, and discusses the enormous benefits that can result when social marketers do likewise.

Learning outcomes

By the end of this chapter, you should be able to:

✓ Understand the four key orientations of social marketing and why each is important

✓ Recognise that client orientation, seeing the world as our customers see and value it, is the starting point for good social marketing

✓ Discuss the importance of insight and creativity in ensuring client engagement

✓ Outline the various types of competition faced by the social marketer

✓ Understand the need to address the collective influences on our behaviour

✓ Explain that exchange means both the target population and the social marketer gain something – and why this matters

✓ Understand the value of relationship marketing.

Key words

Client orientation – collective orientation – competitive orientation – creative orientation – external and active competition – flexible offerings – internal and passive competition – mutually beneficial exchange – relationship marketing – social context.

Client orientation

Arguably the single most important proposition that marketing has brought to the business process in the last one hundred years is that of consumer orientation. It is the simple and unobtrusive idea of putting us at the heart of the business process. As noted in the introductory chapter, this deceptively simple change approach has revolutionised how companies work and helped create the enormous corporations that now dominate the globe. This dominance has come about for many reasons, but at its heart is the idea of *putting the customer first*.

Consumer orientation works because, paradoxically, listening to someone and taking care to understand their point of view make it easier to influence their behaviour. So, in commercial terms, it makes much more sense to work out what people need and want and then to set about producing this, rather than developing a product and putting resources into trying to push people into buying it. This principle is so fundamental to marketing it has been used to define the discipline as 'producing what you can sell', instead of 'selling what you can produce'. Remember, though, that the marketer's interest in understanding the customer and world is not driven by altruism. As noted before, commercial marketers take an interest in us because listening to us and taking care to understand our point of view make it easier to sell us things.

Social marketers share the commercial sector's commitment to 'consumer-oriented' thinking and argue that attempts to influence social and health behaviour should also start from an understanding of the people we want to do the changing. The task is to work out why they do what they do at present, their values and motivations, and then use this understanding to develop an offering that is equally appealing but with positive personal and/or social outcomes. Given social marketing's focus on voluntary behaviour change, client orientation can be seen as the most important of the four orientations.

The most immediate benefit of this approach is that it allows for the fact that, time and again, the picture is much more complex than mere ignorance of the facts. In public health, for example, most people know that smoking is dangerous or how their diet could be improved. They continue to behave 'badly' because they see some other benefit in doing so – relaxation perhaps or a treat. The secret for the social marketer is to devise a way of enabling them to get the same benefit more healthily. In this sense, social marketing has a great deal in common with good, patient-centred healthcare. The proficiency of experts and other professionals is much more effectively deployed when combined with empathy for the client. Ultimately, better health, a better environment and a better-functioning society has to be a joint endeavour. This process is sometimes referred to as the 'joint creation of value', and we will return to it in Chapter 3.

Social marketers also embrace the idea of mutually beneficial exchange. This brings us to exchange theory, which we will also discuss in the next chapter. For the moment, though, it raises two contentious issues:

i) Motivation – not just on the part of the client group but also the social marketer. The idea that social marketers are just like their commercial counterparts, and looking for some kind of payback, has ruffled a few feathers.

ii) Compromise – which is at the heart of any mutually beneficial exchange. But can social marketers adjust their offering; aren't they fixed by the evidence base – smoking kills, therefore our non-smoking product is surely set in stone?

We will look at both of these in more detail.

The power of payback

More fundamentally, some commentators have strong reservations about the assumption in exchange theory that the social marketer (safety worker/probation officer/health promoter) as well as the target group are getting something out of the behaviour change process. Buchanan *et al.* (1994) argue, for example, that such an analysis fundamentally undermines the essentially altruistic basis of health promotion. Exercise 2.1 explores their views in more detail; do you agree with them?

EXERCISE 2.1   IS EXCHANGE UNACCEPTABLE?

We have two concerns with importing the notions of exchange and related concepts into the field of health promotion. By promoting an exchange mentality, social marketing concepts propagate radical transformations in: (i) the types of motivations thought to characterise the health promoter's work, and (ii) the ways in which health promoters relate to the public. We wish to explore the implications of such a transformation. To anticipate, our concern is that such a transformation will both undermine the health promoter's commitment to the field and lead to a more antagonistic relationship to the public.

In marketing, the nature of the relationship between the two parties is characterised by the strategic pursuit of self-interest. It is an adversarial bargaining relationship. There is mutual antagonism that is captured in the primordial marketing principle: *caveat emptor* ('buyer beware'). The two parties are drawn together by a cost–benefit calculus, and as soon as the costs are perceived to be too high by one or the other, the relationship is terminated.

In contrast, people have traditionally entered the health field out of a sense of caring for others, not to satisfy self-interests. The vast majority of health professionals still feel that to be a health professional means to have a vocation, a sense of calling. They strive to create a healthy society in which no one will be handicapped from participating due to unnecessary illness and suffering. The yardstick by which their work is measured is the realisation of a collective good that flows from the elimination of disease, pollution, hunger, poverty and oppression.

A shift to the idea that it would be better to think of the purpose of health promotion in terms of exchange would mark a major transformation. If enough people can be talked around into thinking that the reason for doing health promotion is gains for the health promoter themselves, we believe the field will be sapped of a major source of strength [. . .] We believe the field is better off now, while health promoters draw on inspiration from role models who give freely of themselves without self-regard. Under the logic of exchange such people can only be considered suckers.

Finally, if health promoters conceive of their work in marketing terms, then the ways they think about their relationships with the public will also be transformed. The uneasiness many people feel about social marketing is that it constantly threatens to slip into a manipulative relationship.

(Buchanan *et al.* 1994)

How would you respond to Buchanan *et al.*?

- Are the target groups for social marketing inevitably passive?
- Do marketers always seek to manipulate?
- Are all health professionals philanthropists who are answering a vocation?

From a social marketing perspective, there are a number of major problems with Buchanan *et al.*'s view. First, the rejection of exchange seems to suggest that people have nothing of value to offer and health workers can learn nothing from them. But it is only by listening to our clients that we can understand the limitations of our initiatives and the narrowness of our own views. We need their help.

Second, Buchanan *et al.* see exchange as inevitably involving one party trying to get the better of another. They cannot envisage a mutually beneficial system or Lefebvre's 'win–win' situation (1992). For them, marketing exchange is in reality based on "mutual antagonism" and "constantly threatens to collapse into a manipulative relationship". Of course, there is deceit and manipulation in some marketing exchanges, but this is the exception rather than the rule even in the commercial sector – otherwise, there could be no such thing as repeat purchase, brand loyalty or customer satisfaction.

Third, Buchanan *et al.*'s view of the motivations of health professionals being "altruism, self-sacrifice and concern for the common welfare" carries with it connotations of superiority: "we know what's best for you and because we are such good people we are prepared to give you the benefit of our wisdom". It is a short step from here to imposing our view on the client and condemning their (almost inevitable) ingratitude.

Flexible offerings

However, there is another potential snag: client orientation, the mutual benefit it entails and the notion of meaningful relationships raises the thorny issue of flexible offerings. Can social marketers really vary their offerings like their commercial counterparts? Can we really produce what will sell, rather than selling a predetermined offering? Exercise 2.2 presents the views of two commentators who think not.

EXERCISE 2.2   CAN YOU CHANGE THE PRODUCT IN SOCIAL MARKETING?

If a commercial marketer's customers do not like their product, it will be changed. Can a social marketer do the same?

Barry Elliott (1995) argues not. He takes the view that the social marketer's product, often conceived 'outside the marketplace', is typically an unalterable given, driving the programme manager largely into the business of selling or advocacy. Keith Tones has similar concerns contending that "(i) in general, people do not actually want to be healthy . . . and (ii) health education cannot abandon its product and diversify its interests just because its main product may not be very popular" (1996: 32).

Do you agree with Elliott and Tones? Jot down your thoughts before continuing.

Now consider the following two questions:

1. Does the commercial sector really change its products on a regular basis, even when faced with sustained negative reactions? The tobacco industry (TI) provides an example of one that certainly has not. Despite knowing for over fifty years that cigarettes are carcinogenic (Doll *et al.* 2004) and coming under immense political and social pressure as a result, it has steadfastly stuck with its product. On the other hand, it has tried to respond to market concerns by *adjusting* their products – low-tar cigarettes and filters are two examples – but these are relatively minor alterations on the periphery of the product, rather than the full-scale abandonment of it. Neither, for example, made their products any safer. VW addressed the pollution from its diesel engine in much the same way. In both cases faults with the product were disguised rather than corrected, because to do otherwise was too expensive and hence would threaten the all-important bottom line.

Interestingly, the TI is treating the arrival of electronic cigarettes, which probably are much safer tobacco cigarettes ('combustibles'), in the same way. The new products were an innovation from outside the TI – a Chinese entrepreneur called Hon Lik is credited with their invention[1] – to which the TI was compelled to respond because, as an alternative to combustibles, they posed a commercial threat. However, they have not abandoned their existing products, they have just incorporated ecigarettes into their product portfolios. This enables them to present a range of options to their customers: the risk averse (some of whom might otherwise have quit) can go for the safer new products, the more reckless can carry on smoking the old hazardous ones – and the undecided can 'dual-use' smoking or vaping as the mood or the regulatory environment takes them. Furthermore, these choices are presented in a transparent way – the TI talks openly of 'harm reduction' – so it is now the customer who is taking the chances, enabling the TI to avoid responsibility (and litigation) for tobacco related illness. In this way ecigarettes have been turned from a threat into an opportunity.

So commercial marketers are nearly as ready to change their offering as marketing's client orientation might suggest they would be. However, make no mistake the TI and VW do not want to kill people. If they can change their product to avoid such collateral, they surely will – as long as doing so does not reduce profitability.

2. Second, is not social marketing capable of similar flexibility? In HIV/AIDS education, for example, it has been widely accepted that messages of *absolute* safety and behaviours such as celibacy and complete abstinence from injecting drugs simply will not sell to many potential customers. They have been replaced by offerings of *relative* safety – safer sex and safer drug use.

Similarly, many in tobacco control have embraced ecigarettes as a means of reducing tobacco-related harm. Given the TI industry's business planning it remains to be seen whether this proves to be a wise decision.

More fundamentally, keep in mind that an absence of flexibility or the lack of compromise strikes at the heart of social marketing. If social marketers cannot alter or modify their offerings, how meaningful are the core marketing concepts of consumer orientation and exchange? Walsh and colleagues encapsulated this point when they concluded their overview of the field with:

> *social marketing . . . challenges health specialists to think in new ways about consumers and product design. Entering the marketing world requires abandoning the expert's mind-set that the product is intrinsically good, so that if it fails to sell, the defect must reside in uninformed or unmotivated consumers who need shrewder instruction or louder exhortation.*
>
> *(Walsh et al. 1993: 117–118)*

More fundamentally still, if social marketers cannot modify their product or service, how can there be mutually beneficial exchanges? At the end of the day, even the tobacco industry will stop producing cigarettes if no one buys them. Saying that products cannot be varied ignores this ultimate pressure and condemns social marketers to stagnation. They will cease to be valuable and become extinct.

But remember, this is a mutual process. The social marketer needs to be flexible in their offering, but the other side of the coin is that the client is more open to change because of the compromise. The Scottish folk musician Hamish Imlach once walked off halfway through a gig because 'the audience werenae up to it' (i.e. were not good enough!).

Creative orientation

Client orientation will not deliver a great deal without insight and innovation. Bill Smith's story beautifully illustrates how an original (but deceptively simple) idea can completely transform our view of a behavioural problem and provide a solution that satisfies everyone. It is surely apocryphal, but the following incident really happened. We know because one of us witnessed it.

Bethany was waiting for her husband, Steve, in my neighbourhood pub and he was late for their rendezvous. As time passed with no sign of her man, Bethany began to get cross. A further half-hour went by and steam began emerging from her ears. When Steve eventually rushed in, he looked hunted; any man reading this who has ever let down his partner will understand precisely how he felt. He knew he was in trouble, and was preparing to take his punishment.

But he had forgotten Mary, the pub landlady, and her acute marketing skills. She had seen what was unfolding and when Steve arrived she drew him across to her at the bar before he could go across the room to Bethany. He was anxious to make his domestic peace, but somehow Mary insisted. She then said one simple phrase to him: "Remember, Bethany has had her hair done." Steve's face relaxed and his eyes smiled in gratitude: Mary had provided his 'get-out-of-jail-free' card. He floated across to Bethany and swept aside her irritation with an unanswerable: "Darling, your hair looks lovely."

Mary is a consummate marketer. Not only has she worked out what her customers need and provided it just in time, but also her solution is abundantly creative. As a publican, you might expect her offering to be some variation on food or drink – a pint of beer perhaps or a bowl of soup. However, she recognised the need for quick and original thinking and provided a much more valuable alternative: marital harmony. She also recognised that good marketing has an emotion dimension – it appeals to our hearts as well as our heads. She knew that her adroit mo   d make Bethany and Steve feel good.

Not that she has forgotten her beer sales; these will surely follow. Her sensitivity and customer focus will result in deep loyalty from Steve (with Bethany also acquiring pleasant associations with the King's Head); as a result, he won't buy her beer just tonight but for weeks and probably years to come. Mary is good not just at marketing but also at relationship marketing, which we will return to later in the chapter.

In social marketing as well, the answer is often not the obvious one as Case Study 34, 'Wheels, Skills and Thrills', shows. In this the lack of success in recruiting young participants based on the attractiveness of a 'free advanced driving course' highlights the difficulties of gaining the trust of a hard-to-reach audience from a traditional working-class area, despite the youths being social media savvy. Instead, the team have had to rely on the personal touch of a community worker who lived locally and was known and trusted by potential participants. Furthermore, the attractiveness of the 'Wheels, Skills and Thrills' intervention had to be bolstered by offering free monthly karting sessions at a local indoor facility in order to appeal to the target audience.

Social marketers, then, have to put great efforts into understanding and indeed empathising with clients' behaviour. A very clear fix is needed; not just *what* they do and *why* they do it, but also what they value and don't value, what motivates and drives them. And in both the commercial and social sectors this is as much about emotion as rationality. Behaviour is not always the perfect product of rational-deductive reasoning; if it were, no one would smoke, drunk driving would be a distant memory and mindful consumption would be the order of the day. This is why commercial marketers put such an effort into developing evocative brands. It is also why social marketers put a particular premium on ethnographic, qualitative research and data for good decision making (see Chapter 5).

To illustrate, in the early 1990s, the Institute for Social Marketing conducted a survey of 16–24-year-olds in Dundee. At the time, HIV/AIDS had emerged as a major threat to public health, and sexual transmission by young people was a particular concern – as indeed it still is. The survey therefore concerned sexual habits. The key findings made perplexing reading. Virtually everyone knew that HIV could be passed on during heterosexual encounters; virtually everyone knew this could be prevented by using a condom – *but around a third were continuing to practise unprotected sex.*

Many similar surveys, before and since, have repeated the findings, which beg the question: why is there such a gap between knowledge and behaviour? Social marketers adopt what Taleb (2010) calls the black swan logic: what you don't know is oftentimes more pertinent than what you do. Detailed qualitative research is needed to unpick this riddle, as Box 2.2 notes.

BOX 2.2   THE VALUE OF ETHNOGRAPHY

Marketing is the art of ensuring your offering fits with the needs, emotions and lifestyles of your customer. Quantitative research can only go so far in providing the insights you need. In addition, ethnographic techniques are needed to dig below the surface of socio-demographic statistics and help explain why people behave as they do. There is a need to explain apparent irrationalities, like taking up smoking despite the threat of lung cancer or risking unprotected sex with a stranger. As the psychologist Dick Eiser points out, "just because people do stupid things, it doesn't mean they are stupid". Ultimately, the social marketer needs to learn to see things from the perspective of their customer – then, and only then, will their world make sense.

Ethnographic or qualitative research typically uses smaller samples than its quantitative cousin and in-depth questioning procedures that enable the researcher to probe deeply and explore the reasons behind people's attitudes and behaviour.

Chapter 5 underlines the value of this sort of research to decision making and explains how it can be done, but in the meantime Exercise 2.3 will help to get you thinking.

EXERCISE 2.3   AN EMBARASSING ASSIGNMENT

First, remind yourself that using condoms involves talking to your partner about sex before engaging in it, raising issues of previous sexual encounters and the protective steps you did (or did not) take. Then, next time you meet with a friend of the opposite sex, try telling them when you last had sex, whether you used a condom and why you did or did not do so. If your friend has not fled from your presence, ask them to do the same.

Note: In the interests of your mental health and social life, we will keep this exercise hypothetical.

Recall again that the simple injunction to 'use a condom' (how many adverts and posters have you seen this on in the last decade?) demands exactly this behaviour from all its readers. Suddenly, the actions of the young Dundonians do not seem so difficult to understand and the real benefit of empathy becomes clear.

An innovative social marketing research example is seen in operation in Case Study 3, 'Meals on Wheels'. The participatory mixed research methods included regular reflective sessions with MOW service providers, management and staff workers in the development phase to elicit emerging issues and developments. Focus groups were conducted with community residents, stakeholders and local partners to discover their experiences and views of referring individuals to the service while key informant interviews (KII) were undertaken with past, current and potential service users to uncover their needs, wants, desires, motivations, concerns and worries. Unstructured observation of several project activities and anecdotal feedback were recorded throughout as well. Then, the community readiness model quantified issues such as leadership, knowledge sharing and culture to augment the qualitative findings.

Ultimately, these two threads of marketing – the client and creative orientations – come together in the idea of partnership working and joint stakeholder endeavours. It was Mary's detailed and empathetic insights into her customers' needs that enabled her to come up with such a creative solution – but it would have come to nothing if Steve hadn't immediately grasped her meaning and delivered the cleverly provided compliment to Bethany, who in turn had to accept it with good grace. It was a team effort built on mutual understanding and creative insight.

Collective orientation

Such empowered behaviour, however, is not always possible.

The American author David Foster Wallace (2008) tells the story of two young fish who are swimming along, and they happen to meet an older fish swimming the other way, who nods at them and says, "Morning, boys, how's the water?" And the two young fish reply, "It is lovely, thank you." They swim on for a bit, and then eventually one of them looks over at the other and asks, "What the heck is water?" Wallace goes on to explain that the point of the story is that the most ubiquitous and powerful influences on our behaviour are those closest to us – the ones we take for granted, do not even realise are there and cannot discuss and describe. Our immediate environment is to us as the water is to the young fish, and has an equally powerful impact on our lives whether we realise it or not. Have a go at Exercise 2.4.

> **EXERCISE 2.4   TESTING THE WATER**
>
> Think about some facet of your own behaviour – your drinking perhaps, or eating habits. Write down all the different influences you can think of that make you behave as you do. These may range from full-on pressure, such as your friend urging you to have another drink because it's your round, to background nudges like a tempting bottle of lager on a supermarket cold shelf. When you have thought of every possible trigger, ask your friends what influences them – and add these to the list.

The exercise typically results in an extensive list.

Recognising these broader determinants of how we live our lives is important to social marketers for three key reasons:

1. It provides us with a fuller understanding of why our clients behave as they do, so it enhances our client orientation and hence all the benefits of this that are discussed above. In short, it makes our attempts to change behaviour more effective.

2. It avoids the danger of 'victim blaming': pushing someone to change a behaviour that is not – or not entirely – of their own making. This is not only ineffective, but also potentially unethical. The dilemma is most apparent when we consider vulnerable groups: there are obvious problems with a media campaign telling poor sub-Saharan villagers to feed their children better when they can't access food because there has been a drought, their government is corrupt and the world economic system is dysfunctional. The problems are less obvious when people do have good access to food and live in a working democracy. Nonetheless, as the Foster Wallace fish emphasise, it is still necessary to ask how much power any given individual or population has over its own fate.

Sociologists refer to such power as 'agency', which has to be balanced against the structures of society that simultaneously constrain and facilitate it. The notion of structuration theory has been conceived to explain the dynamic relationship between agency and structure and social marketers have to be continually aware of this dynamism. Rebekah Russell-Bennett and colleagues from Queensland University capture agency and structure in Case Study 4. They talk of a participant-focused experience and digital engagement, design thinking and co-creating digital games with rewards for low income adult renters to make better decisions about energy use. We will discuss the idea of agency in greater detail in Chapter 9.

3. Finally, a collective orientation helps us think properly about genuinely strategic goals. If we consider all the causes of our behaviour, we are compelled to raise our eyes above the detail of individual coping strategies and look at the system. This has fundamental implications for our social marketing efforts because it helps us determine how we can best use the inevitably limited resources at our disposal. In our sub-Saharan example above, it may be that the best thing we can do is to advocate the UN to alter the terms of aid programmes or provide agricultural training for locals so that they can improve crop yield in a dry climate. In social marketing terms, it enables us to make intelligent decisions about *whose* behaviour needs to change and *how* it needs to change.

In essence, then, a collective orientation again puts an emphasis on thinking about the systems we live in, the marketplace and space, how things are connected, or not, and the bigger picture.

Competitive orientation

This bigger picture has to include the competition, which for social marketers comes in two forms.

First, there is passive competition. Social marketing recognises that clients, whether government ministers or teenage tearaways, have choices. They can, and often do, continue with their current behaviour. There are internal barriers to change, which could be in the form of beliefs, feelings, attitudes or intentions. As we have just discussed, such blockages also come from family, friends and the immediate environment.

It is therefore very important to look closely at this 'competition' in order to understand what benefits it is perceived to bring and how alternative behaviour can be made more attractive for a fruitful exchange. For example, it is clear that for some teenagers smoking is felt to hold a range of benefits, including rebellion, weight control and sophistication, which can outstrip health concerns such as lung and heart disease in years to come. Social marketers need to take these perspectives into account if there is to be any hope of winning over young people. The Truth Campaign, a US anti-smoking campaign of many years standing, does precisely this by adopting the theme of rebellion – not against society but against the manipulative practices of the tobacco industry. It has proven to be one of the most successful youth prevention campaigns ever run (Farrelly *et al.* 2002).

Mention of the tobacco industry brings us to the second sense in which social marketers need to address the competition. As well as current behaviours and social systems, there are organisations actively pushing in the opposite direction. What social marketers see as a problem, the competition see as their opportunity and goldmine. This is direct or active competition. Thus, in the case of tobacco, one of the reasons so many young people continue to take up smoking is that the tobacco companies use their marketing to encourage them to do so. And extensive research shows that their efforts are successful, as are those of the alcohol and fast food companies. Box 2.3 discusses why this additional competitive dimension to social marketing, sometimes termed 'critical marketing', is so important.

BOX 2.3   ACTIVE COMPETITION AND CRITICAL MARKETING – THREE REASONS WHY IT MATTERS

- Understanding the efforts of Philip Morris or Diageo, and the consumer response to these, provides us with invaluable intelligence. As advertising guru David Ogilvy once remarked, ignoring this would be like an army general ignoring decodes of enemy signals.

- Commercial activity is a crucial aspect of the environment that we have already accepted is itself an important determinant of behaviour. Ignoring the impact of commercial marketing would open up the discipline to the same criticisms as if it only focused on individual behaviour: ineffectiveness and immorality.

- The success of the tobacco, alcohol and food industries provides a rich seam of evidence that marketing works. If marketing can get us to buy a Ferrari, it can also encourage us to drive it safely.

Most social marketing scenarios face strong 'active' competition and the temptation is to ignore it because of its complexity. Don't forget Andreasen's (2006: 104) words, "often behavioural influence is about beating the competition": social marketers must craft a strategy, i.e. an intervention which will hold its own against the competition's and ideally develop a competitive edge. In the face of active and critical competition, McArdle (2016) tells us we can get a handle on a competitive orientation by thinking about competition from four different angles: brand competition; product competition; enterprise competition; and generic competition. We'll pick up on these in more detail in Chapter 7 with examples, exercises and Case Study 9.

Collective and competitive orientations come together when we accept that societal progress depends on movement, not just by the individual citizen mobilisation but also by community groups and civil society movements, as Case Study 2 demonstrates. Patricia McHugh and colleagues show that, even if individuals wanted to adopt pro-environmental behaviours – e.g. protect our seas and ocean – a combination of social, economic, political and physical environmental forces at country and EU levels are blocking them. The issues of passive and active competition are also examined in Case Study 9 'Walk to School'.

This takes us back to the domain of social marketing (Box 1.2) and reminds us that successful social transformation is also influenced by the wider social and system context and specifically by the actions of other stakeholders, as well as individual citizens. As Marques and Domegan (2011) point out, "social marketers' legitimacy is greater if social marketers are critical about themselves: their own processes and outcomes but especially about their assumptions or taken for granted 'truths'. From a critical perspective, the challenge is to make those assumptions explicit so they can be contested on other grounds than are provided for by the prevailing paradigm." This last sentiment captures the important role of critical thinking – and indeed this book – to uncover the taken-for-granted barriers and test them in the courtroom of academic and public debate. And, as

Jones (2011), Hoek (2011) and Dewhirst and Lee (2011) make clear, an open and frank debate about the role of commercial marketing is an essential part of this rigour. This book is testament to the power of marketing and its potential to do good if used by the right people in the right way. It would be derelict, and profoundly damaging to social marketing, if we did not also recognise and point out its capacity to do harm. Speaking truth to power is a crucial part of the social marketer's role.

We will continue this discussion of competitive and critical thinking in Chapters 7 and 8 respectively.

The orientations combined

The mandating of smoke-free public places was one of the great success stories of Scottish public health. Scotland moved on this ahead of all its UK and European neighbours, with the exception of Ireland, and the success of the measure perfectly illustrates the importance of all four social marketing dimensions:

- **Client orientation.** Smoke-free legislation typifies this first orientation; the measure was almost (see competitive orientation below) universally welcomed. Press speculation about mass disobedience by smokers proved completely groundless. A public opinion survey just a few days after the law's introduction showed that no fewer than 84 per cent of 16–24-year-olds not only approved of the measure, but also thought it one "that Scotland could be proud of" (Cancer Research UK 2006) – a massive endorsement for a patriotic country like Scotland. Realising smoke-free public places was probably the single most popular achievement of the then McConnell government.

  However, the success was by no means a solo effort by the authorities; the public also played an important role. Their experiences of smoky pubs told them that going smoke-free was a good idea, not so much because it would save them from illness as the ad campaigns maintained, but because it was so unpleasant. The need to wash your hair and clothes after every night out was as influential as the threat of second-hand lung cancer. This policy measure worked because *both* the authorities *and* the public wanted it to. This is a good example of what is sometimes termed bottom-up, top-down 'co-created value' (see Chapters 4 and 6).

- **Creative orientation.** Smoke-free was an immensely innovative move. Prior to the legislation Scotland had long been caricatured as the 'sick man of Europe', and Glasgow pubs were a by-word for hard-drinking, unhealthy lifestyles. To make these semi-shebeens the spearhead of a pioneering public health measure was extremely bold. It also presented a perfect opportunity to steal a march on Scotland's proverbial rival England, which took another 18 months to put its smoke-free house in order.

- **Collective orientation.** This success depended on the engagement of multiple stakeholders. The attention of politicians was captured with a carefully marshalled evidence base showing that: (a) second-hand smoke is extremely toxic; and (b) making hospitality venues smoke-free does not harm business. This attention turned to commitment when the Scottish First Minister met with the Irish Minister for Health, Micheál Martin, who had already brought in similar legislation. Reputedly, when asked by Jack McConnell what he would do differently if he had his time over, Martin replied simply "I would have done more sooner." McConnell was won over: he had gone over to Ireland on the Friday night set against going smoke-free and he returned on the Monday all in favour, one of the clearest examples of source effect (see Chapter 6) ever recorded. Other key stakeholders in the social system, including the hospitality trade unions, the health and safety professionals and, of course, the medics were recruited to the cause, discussing the benefits both through their professional bodies (more helpful source effects) and concerted press and PR activity.

- **Competitive orientation.** There was, however, also loud and very active competition. Extreme opposition came from the tobacco companies. As persona non grata, they stirred things up from afar. Perhaps the most well-documented evidence of their hostility was revealed in a paper published in the journal *Tobacco Control* (Scollo *et al.* 2003). Of the 97 studies on the economic impact of smoke-free ordinances, 35 showed it had a bad effect on bars and restaurants. However, 31 of the 35 studies had two things in common. First, they were generally of poor quality, e.g. they lacked control groups or objective outcome measures, and second, every single one was supported in some way by the tobacco industry. (The funding sources for the other four studies were unknown.) The higher-quality independent studies all showed that going smoke-free had no negative commercial impact. Despite the revelation of this and other trickery, however, most of the hospitality sector remained adamantly opposed to going smoke-free and an excellent public health intervention had to proceed in spite of their opposition.

Turn again to Case Study 1 'SIMPle' to see all four orientations in action. Client orientation is captured in numerous ways: focusing on what the GPs and clients were already doing 'right' and validating good prescription behaviours of community members were central to community members' needs, as was the stimulus to 'code' the UTI consultation and GP workshops. The collective perspective is seen in the variety of resources considered: the AMR game for the kids in the doctor's waiting room and the audit report for GPs. Competitive orientation plays out in the perceptual and practical barriers identified: many participants didn't see the value in 'delayed' prescriptions and wanted an antibiotic to get better for the weekend and social events planned. Finally, the case study's tagline 'SIMPle' reflects its creative orientations where 'Supporting the Improvement and Management of Prescribing for UTIs' was facilitated by a range of award-winning digital and offline tools. For example, see a public awareness video at www.youtube.com/watch?v=wecthQ7Md-Q as part of the EU's AMR Awareness Day, or try out the award-winning Bug Run School Days game at www.youtube.com/watch?v=wecthQ7Md-Q.

Now have a try at Exercise 2.5 to contemplate further the four social marketing orientations in action. The following is an extract from an interview with Kate, a young single mum.

EXERCISE 2.5   KATE

"Well I just live up the road really. Eh . . . I've already got two kids, this is ma third. Em I've got a brother, a sister, and a mum . . . em never really knew ma dad. Eh . . . basically a bottle-fed 'em . . . the two before and I'm not dead against breastfeeding,

(continued)

(continued)

I just . . . I can't really be doing wi' people like pushing stuff on me so I . . . like breast-feeding's something that . . . it's not really a done thing to do around here . . . I'm not . . . like ma friends just . . . I know none of ma friends do it and a don't really wanna be like gettin', you know, ma boobs out in public an' that, like, I don't wanna have the physical changes and . . . but the main thing is that I just really can't be doing wi' people talking down to me.

"I didn't really do well at school, I left school when I was 14, so I really couldn't have, like, a tolerance for people in authority, so you know, an', I've decided that it's just easier if a try make ma mind up myself but you know . . . and speak to midwives and stuff like that . . . they just forcing it an' it's making me like a bit apprehensive and a little bit anxious an' a just can't be doing wi' it to be honest . . . so it's something that I'm a little bit like indecisive about. Eh, Bradley's four and Louise is 18 months now. A don't know whether she's doing her job properly or not to be honest because all the information she gives me I just dun't even listen to her because it's the way she says it, it's the . . . she's not asking . . . well she's not advising me, she's like telling me and it's more of a . . . she's saying stuff that . . . what's on her form what she needs to fill out and a don't . . . I just don't like the attitude, so it's probably my own fault really for switching off, but I automatically do cos I don't like somebody talking down to me about something that I feel that is totally my decision an' it makes me a little bit . . . well, not bothered really, so a can't even be bothered. So if, you know, like a say I'm not even against breastfeeding, a just don't like everything that comes with it an' the pressure of being told that breastfeeding is best an' a know that it's best, but you know it's a big responsibility an' . . . bottles just ten times easier and I have got a big social life . . . an' you know, midwives like, 'yeah well you can express and stuff', but I've heard that hurts so . . . she talks down to me a little bit, a just don't like her attitude so I tend to switch off."

What implications do Kate's views on breastfeeding have for the four orientations of social marketing?

Kate's dislike of authority, having stuff pushed on her, being talked down to and being told what to do all seriously detract from any sense of agency and empowerment she might have around breastfeeding. Kate is clearly telling the social marketer there is no client orientation in operation. She is 'switched off' and not open to behaviour change. A collective orientation reinforces this lack of mutuality and compounds her stance, as breastfeeding is not the 'done thing' where she lives or among her friends. Competition-wise, expressing milk is associated with pain, while bottle-feeding is easier, more acceptable with her peers and fits with her social life. So far, three out of the four social marketing orientations are negative from Kate's perspective and she is highly unlikely to engage in any intervention. The fourth and final orientation, a creative dimension, tells the social marketer a significant degree of innovation, empathy, understanding, reform and redesign of numerous issues with many stakeholders would have to occur for Kate to feel empowered to give up bottle-feeding and adopt breastfeeding. The implications arising from Kate's views for the four social marketing orientations call for a strategic and empowered view of behavioural and social change.

Relationship marketing

The smoke-free success of Scotland is impressive, but on its own it only addresses one element of the smoking epidemic. How much more effective would it be if we were able to build on this success, along with the positive experience of the public and (most of) the stakeholders? How many other problems could be solved? Maybe Scotland could become an international leader not just in the elimination of second-hand smoke, but also in public health more widely – or indeed the fight against climate change and for sustainable living. Given what we have already said about the gravity and complexity of these challenges, and of the need to empower people and build their agency to engage in transformation, perhaps this positive energy should be harnessed.

The commercial sector has been thinking along similar lines for several decades and, as a result, has deliberately introduced continuity into the frame. They have progressed from seeking to define and satisfy our needs once, or on an ad hoc basis, to doing so continuously. Their aim is not just to create a one-off transaction, but also to build ongoing *relationships* with us. Tesco and Walmart, for example, do not want us to do our shopping online or at their stores just once, they want us to shop every week – so if we do, they reward each of us with a loyalty card and discounts and regularly send us texts and emails, vouchers, updates on new products and 'special' offers, tailored to our unique preferences, personality, lifestyle and past purchases. They try to build a relationship with us. And all the evidence is that, despite the obvious mercenary motivations of their charm offensive, it works: we respond by joining their loyalty schemes, adopting their brands and paying them regular visits. We will revisit this phenomenon in Chapter 9.

This thinking has much to offer social marketing, not least because, just like Tesco, Walmart, Apple and Coca-Cola (see Chapter 1), we too want to move beyond the ad hoc. We do not want people to wear a seatbelt once, refrain from hitting their partner every now and then or eat five portions of fruit and vegetables occasionally. We want them to do these things again and again – indeed forever more. Actually our interest is very often in lifestyles rather than isolated behaviours.

Even when target behaviours are apparently ad hoc, such as with one-off immunisations during a sudden outbreak of infectious disease or temporary speed restrictions following a road traffic accident, relationship issues such as source credibility (we will discuss the idea of source credibility in more detail when we consider communications in Chapter 6) and trust are going to be crucial. The scare over the MMR (measles, mumps, rubella) vaccine in the UK, for example, which has bedevilled childhood immunisation efforts over the last decade, is driven by a lack of trust in the health authorities among parents (Evans *et al.* 2001). Theory strongly supports this strategic perspective. As we will discuss in Chapter 3, stages of change theory will tell us that changes do not, for the most part, occur overnight. They involve a series of steps from initial contemplation through to reinforcement after the fact, a process that is both dynamic and precarious: the individual can regress or change heart at any point.

Relational thinking also compels us to prioritise client satisfaction and value co-creation, which has fundamental implications for social marketing. It means that Andreasen's (1994) injunction to focus on behaviour change needs to be matched with an equal commitment to service quality. Otherwise, promising programmes that do not result in rapid behaviour change are liable to be written off as failures.

Figure 2.1 A strategic vision of social marketing

All this suggests that social marketers should combine the four orientations with relational thinking as in Figure 2.1.

Try Exercise 2.6.

EXERCISE 2.6   NE CHOICES – FAILED BEHAVIOUR CHANGE OR INCOMPLETE RELATIONSHIP MARKETING?

NE Choices was a three-year drugs prevention intervention built around a high school drama initiative, with additional community, school governor and parent components. It had four behavioural objectives:

1. To reduce the prevalence of drug use.
2. To delay the age of onset of drug use.
3. To reduce the frequency of drug use among those who use drugs.
4. To reduce mixing of drugs (including with alcohol) by those who use drugs.

The programme adopted a social influences approach, backed by social marketing, and was thoroughly researched with all the stakeholder groups using a design that incorporated a two-year pilot, along with formative, process, impact and outcome evaluations. The last comprised a rigorous experimental design.

An action-research model meant that the pilot and formative research informed the initial programme design, and ongoing process and impact findings guided its development. The result was, therefore, extremely consumer oriented, and the young people – as well as other stakeholders – strongly endorsed it. The impact evaluation showed, for example, that the vast majority of children felt the programme was enjoyable (89 per cent), thought-provoking (88 per cent) and credible (84 per cent), and that the drama was realistic (79 per cent) and non-didactic (e.g. 88 per cent agreed that "it encouraged us to speak our own minds"). In addition, the young people trusted the programme and its brand. For example, the last stage of research had to be conducted by mail, as a proportion of the young people had, by then, left school. The vast majority were prepared to provide contact details, and 70 per cent completed the sensitive and complex (40-minute) questionnaire. However, despite three annual follow-ups, the outcome research showed no changes on any of the four behavioural objectives.

According to social marketing lore, and the programme's own objectives, NE Choices had failed.

From a relationship marketing perspective, is such a judgement justified?

(*Source:* MacFadyen *et al.* 2002)

NE Choices delivered excellent customer service and built up a marked degree of trust with the young people, as well as other stakeholders, as was demonstrated by the success of the final survey. A valuable database of a vulnerable and normally elusive group was also developed, providing a unique opportunity to develop these putative relationships further. (Indeed, the programme delivery team was approached by more than one commercial operator wanting to buy the database.)

Furthermore, three of NE Choices' impact evaluation successes – reaching a range of stakeholders and settings as well as the core customers (Fortmann *et al.* 1995; Pentz *et al.* 1997; King 1998); the successful use of drama in education to engage the audience (Blakey and Pullen 1991; Denman *et al.* 1995; Bouman *et al.* 1998; Orme and Starkey 1998); and being non-didactic (Blakey and Pullen 1991; ACMD 1993; JRF 1997; Allott *et al.* 1999; Orme and Starkey 1999) – are known to be linked to effective knowledge, attitude and behaviour change. This does suggest that, as well as good relationships being established, the first signs of behaviour change were also emerging.

Arguably, therefore, from a relationship marketing perspective, NE Choices offered a great deal of promise, but transactional thinking cut it off in its prime. As Morgan and Hunt (1994) express it in their analysis of relationship marketing in the commercial sector: "Understanding relationship marketing requires distinguishing between the discrete transaction, which has a 'distinct beginning, short duration, and sharp ending by performance', and relational exchange, which 'traces to previous agreements [and] . . . is longer in duration, reflecting an ongoing process'." NE Choices was judged by the former school of thought, but had the potential to deliver the latter (Hastings *et al.* 2002).

Morgan and Hunt's work also identifies two key relational constructs: trust and commitment, both of which have been shown to have particular relevance to social marketing.

Trust

In an extensive social marketing partnership study, Duane (2012) defines *trust* as the willingness and confidence to depend upon exchange partners. It is this confidence that allows the citizen to assess the dangers of engaging in exchange when the benefits of doing so are often intangible and not immediate; trust then is closely linked to the credibility of the social marketer. In social marketing scenarios where risk and uncertainty are present, for example with infant immunisation as we noted above, trust becomes particularly important. Trust, Duane says, can, however, become problematic when concern arises about the motivations of and benefits for the exchange parties. Any perceived conflict of interest, for example, can corrode trust. This happened with MMR in the UK where local doctors were felt to be too closely linked to what some saw as a manipulative government and medical establishment agenda – anxieties that were exacerbated when the then Prime Minister Tony Blair refused to declare whether his own son had been given the vaccine. Note Mr Blair, as most parents would agree, was well within his rights to insist on privacy for his child; the fact that his exercising of this right caused such alarm and despondency is an indicator of how badly damaged trust had become. The effects of this breakdown in trust were very serious: immunisations dropped to dangerously low levels, herd immunity was undermined, and children and parents were badly harmed as a result. And, as history has proved, the concerns about the vaccine were utterly unfounded – the one study raising questions about it has been completely discredited and withdrawn from publication. The problem was not a faulty vaccine, but a faulty relationship.

Commitment

Trust is a precursor of commitment as a party will not commit unless they trust; it is the presence of 'time' that turns trust into commitment (Hastings *et al.* 2003; Donovan and Henley 2010). Duane (2012) explains that commitment in social marketing can manifest itself in different forms, for example, a pledge to undertake and maintain a positive behaviour; a formal contract (Lagarde *et al.* 2005; Donovan and Henley 2010) or access to necessary resources. For example, *safe*food, the promotional body responsible for food safety and healthy eating on the island of Ireland, integrated pledges into their social media strategy whereby citizens could publicly commit to adopting one behaviour into their lifestyles (Duane 2012). Other forms of commitment such as a memorandum of agreement between parties in a social marketing partnership assist in the maintenance of both commitment and trust as the roles and responsibilities of all parties involved are understood and therefore expectations are managed. Once a commitment has been pledged between all parties, it can continue to manifest itself over time: "after committing oneself to a position, one should be more willing to comply with requests for behaviours that are consistent with that position" (Donovan and Henley 2010: 106). Unfortunately, characteristics such as management styles, loss of ownership and control can cause partners to lose motivation, which can show itself in tension and dilution of the commitment.

Complex relational exchanges

Marques and Domegan (2011) point out that "relationship marketing is based on cooperation with customers, other stakeholders and network partners. This means firms will not view one another from a win-lose perspective but will rather benefit from a win-win situation, where the parties work as partners." Such relationship building in social marketing is demanding. There is rarely one single entity involved. Consider the typical social marketing scenario – interventions are funded, developed and delivered by different organisations. The delivery, in particular, tends to make use of the existing infrastructures ranging from commercial retail outlets to health and educational pathways, for example, schools, doctors or community partners. Furthermore, conflict and tensions often occur. For instance, delivery agents may not approve or have any allegiance to the funder or the developer, which poses challenges such as the need to define who is responsible for the relationship and for developing the consistency and integration of the 'collective'.

The point is that complex relational exchanges demand innovative ways of thinking about social issues. As put by Marques and Domegan (2011):

> [T]he main contributions of relationship marketing is that it helps to uncover fundamental contradictions in, and challenges to, current social marketing thinking. First and foremost, the collaboration is with the client as a co-creator of value. The organisation starts with the client and where their behaviour is and not where the organisation wants their behaviour to be.

Case Study 19 illustrates how relationship marketing is central to commons issues such as whale sharks and sustainable tourism in the World Heritage Area, Ningaloo Reef, Western Australia. Ningaloo Marine Park has to offer low-impact commercial tourism activities which add to the Marine Park users' experiences while also ensuring whale shark tour operators, recreational fishing facilities, photographers and local businesses don't deplete or impact on the ecological or cultural heritage values. But relationship marketing is 'a tricky balancing act' as tension and conflict can develop in the absence of fairness, trust and a commitment to shared values for one and all.

Therefore, projects had to be appreciated as a joint or co-learning process allowing all parties and stakeholders to become enthusiastic and willing to go on further with the learning and activities. This further learning "points to the power of dialogue and co-learning to re-contextualise specific problems in wider social issues" (Marques and Domegan 2011). Thus, the benefits of relational thinking – satisfaction, sustainability, trust and commitment – raise the potential for more profound concepts of change; ones that take in the idea of partnership working, social movements and wide-scale social or 'systemic' change. This type of 'bigger picture' thinking is of vital importance if we are to tackle complex, multifaceted and highly contended problems such as climate change. We will return to this discussion in Chapter 11.

Wrap-up

In this chapter, we have examined four social marketing orientations:

1. **Client orientation** – puts a premium on understanding the relevant people and genuinely catering for their needs.

2. **Creative orientation** – emphasises the need for meaningful insights, innovative thinking and imaginative solutions to problems.

3. **Collective orientation** – a client's behaviour is shaped, moulded and influenced by those around them, such as family and friends, together with the structures and policies of the society they live in. Effective social marketing has to be equally multifaceted.

4. **Competitive orientation** – social marketing is all about voluntary behaviour change: clients have choices – they can ignore, subvert or reject our overtures. The challenge for the social marketer is to understand this 'passive' competition and whenever possible transform it into cooperation. There is also the need to recognise and address more 'active' competition – the marketing of tobacco companies, for example.

These orientations build on the concept of mutually beneficial, complex exchanges and become strategic drivers when combined with relational thinking and recognition of the need to engage with multiple stakeholders.

Ultimately, these ideas make most sense when we see social marketing as a *process* for engaging *with* people in social change, rather than just a means to the end of getting or telling them to behave in a certain way. Wicked social problems (highly complex and dynamic problems such as obesity, ocean acidification, climate change and sustainability) can only be tackled when we *all* feel empowered to address them and live in social structures and systems that enable us to do so. In this sense, social marketing is as much about power, agency and social movements as it is about smoking cessation services or recycling initiatives.

Reflective questions

1. What are the four orientations of social marketing?
2. Discuss what being client oriented means to the social marketer.
3. 'Behaviours have context' – a core premise of social marketing's collective orientation. Elaborate with examples.
4. The concept of Exchange underlies the client, creative, collective and competitive orientations of social marketing. What does exchange mean to you? How do marketers use client, creative, collective and competitive orientations to achieve successful and repeated exchange with you as a customer?
5. How might exchange be relevant to social, environmental and welfare issues?
6. What does relationship marketing offer the social marketer?
7. What are the roles of trust and commitment in relationship marketing?

Reflective assignments

1. Locate three social marketing case studies or papers that demonstrate client orientation, creative orientation, competitive orientation and collective orientation.
2. Make sure you are comfortable with the four orientations of social marketing by writing a concise paragraph about each.
3. Based upon the organisation you work in, or an organisation of your choice, map out its client and competitive orientation.

4. You are social marketing manager with Alcol, a non-profit entity focused on young teenagers in inner cities around the country. You have been tasked with designing an ID card for underage teenagers. How could you use the idea of exchange in your job?

5. How, where and why do the four orientations – client, creative, collective and competitive – integrate with our discussions of social marketing in Chapter 1?

6. Debate with friends or colleagues whether or not social marketers are really just out to satisfy their own ends like commercial marketers, or are they more altruistic? What impact does it have on your argument if we define social marketing outcomes as about engagement, inclusion, and agency rather than just behaviour change?

7. Consult the *Journal of Social Marketing* and/or *Social Marketing Quarterly* to read a classic or contemporary article, or more, on social marketing's philosophy to advance your understanding of its client, creative, collective and competitive foundational pillars.

8. Complete your 'Rebels with a cause' agenda using relevant social marketing thinking from this chapter.

Note

1 See for example www.scmp.com/news/china/article/1322857/chinas-electronic-cigarette-inventor-fights-financial-rewards.

References

ACMD (Advisory Council on the Misuse of Drugs) (1993) *Drug Education in Schools: The Need for a New Impetus.* London: HMSO.

Allott, R., Paxton, R. and Leonard, R. (1999) 'Drug education: A review of British Government policy and evidence on effectiveness', *Health Education Research Theory and Practice*, 14(4): 491–505.

Andreasen, A.R. (1994) 'Social marketing: Its definition and domain', *Journal of Public Policy & Marketing*, 13(1): 108–114.

Andreasen, A.R. (ed.) (2006) *Social Marketing in the 21st Century.* Thousand Oaks, CA: Sage Publications.

Blakey, V. and Pullen, E. (1991) '"You don't have to say you love me": An evaluation of a drama-based sex education project for schools', *Health Education Journal*, 50(4): 161–165.

Bouman, M., Maas, L. and Kok, G. (1998) 'Health education in television entertainment – "Medisch Centrum West": A Dutch drama serial', *Health Education Research Theory and Practice*, 13(4): 503–518.

Buchanan, D.R., Reddy, S. and Hossain, H. (1994) 'Social marketing: A critical appraisal', *Health Promotion International*, 9(1): 49–57.

Cancer Research UK (2006) 'Young Scots "most proud" to be smoke-free as iconic image unveiled'. Online: www.cancerresearchuk.org/cancer-info/news/archive/pressrelease/2006-03-14-young-scots-most-proud-to-be-smokefree-as-iconic-image-unveiled (accessed 16 May 2013).

Denman, S., Pearson, J., Moody, D., Davis, P. and Madeley, R. (1995) 'Theatre in education on HIV and AIDS: A controlled study of schoolchildren's knowledge and attitudes', *Health Education Journal*, 54(1): 3–17.

Dewhirst, T. and Lee, W.B. (2011) 'Social marketing and tobacco control', Ch. 26 in G. Hastings, K. Angus and C. Bryant (eds) *The SAGE Handbook of Social Marketing.* London: Sage Publications.

Doll, R., Peto, R., Boreham, J. and Sutherland, I. (2004) 'Mortality in relation to smoking: 50 years' observations on male British doctors', *British Medical Journal*, 328: 1519.

Donovan, R. and Henley, N. (2010) *Principles and Practice of Social Marketing*. Cambridge: Cambridge University Press, UK.

Duane, S. (2012) *A Social Marketing Partnership Framework: An Extension of Morgan and Hunt's (1994) Commitment – Trust Key Mediating Variable Model*. PhD thesis, National University of Ireland, Galway, Ireland.

Elliott, B.J. (1995) *Marketing's Potential for Traffic Safety: Under or Over Stated?* Presented at the 13th International Conference on Alcohol, Drugs and Traffic Safety (T'95), 13–18 August, Adelaide, Australia. Online: http://casr.adelaide.edu.au/T95/paper/s19p2.html (accessed March 2016).

Evans, M., Stoddart, H., Condon, L., Freeman, E., Grizzell, M. and Mullen R. (2001) 'Parents' perspectives on the MMR immunization: A focus group study', *British Journal of General Practice*, 51: 904–910.

Farrelly, M.C., Healton, C.G, Davis, K.C., Messeri, P., Hersey, J.C. and Haviland, M.L. (2002) 'Getting to the truth: Evaluating national tobacco countermarketing campaigns', *American Journal of Public Health*, 92(6): 901–907.

Fortmann, S.P., Flora, J.A., Winkleby, M.A., Schooler, C., Taylor, C.B. and Farquhar, J.W. (1995) 'Community intervention trials: Reflections on the Stanford Five-City Project experience', *American Journal of Epidemiology*, 142(6): 576–586.

Hastings, G. and Haywood, A. (1991) 'Social marketing and communication in health promotion', *Health Promotion International*, 6: 135–145.

Hastings, G. and Haywood, A.J. (1994) 'Social marketing: A critical response', *Health Promotion International*, 9(1): 59–63.

Hastings G., Stead M. and MacKintosh A.M. (2002) 'Rethinking drugs prevention: Radical thoughts from social marketing', *Health Education Journal*, 61(4): 347–364.

Hastings, G., Stead, M., McDermott, L., Forsyth, A., MacKintosh, A.M., Rayner, M., Godfrey, C., Caraher, M. and Angus, K. (2003) *Review of Research on the Effects of Food Promotion to Children*. Prepared for the Food Standard Agency, 22 September. Stirling: Institute for Social Marketing, University of Stirling.

Hoek, J. (2011) 'Critical marketing: Applications', Ch. 22 in G. Hastings, K. Angus and C. Bryant (eds) *The SAGE Handbook of Social Marketing*. London: Sage Publications.

Jones, S. (2011) 'Social marketing's response to the alcohol problem: Who's conducting the orchestra?', Ch. 17 in G. Hastings, K. Angus and C. Bryant (eds) *The SAGE Handbook of Social Marketing*. London: Sage Publications.

JRF (Joseph Rowntree Foundation) (1997) *Young People and Drugs – Findings*. *Social Policy Research*, 133. Online: www.jrf.org.uk/knowledge/findings/socialpolicy/sp133.asp (accessed March 2016).

King, A.C. (1998) 'How to promote physical activity in a community: Research experiences from the US highlighting different community approaches', *Patient Education and Counselling*, 33(1 Suppl): S3–S12.

Lagarde, F., Doner, L., Donovan, R.J., Charney, S. and Grieser, M. (2005) 'Partnerships from the downstream perspective: The role strategic alliances play in implementing social marketing programs', *Social Marketing Quarterly*, 11(3–4), 38–45.

Lefebvre, C. (1992) 'Social Marketing and health promotion'. Ch. 8 in R. Bunton and G. MacDonald (eds) *Health Promotion: Disciplines and Diversity*. London: Routledge.

MacFadyen, L., Stead, M. and Hastings, G.B. (2002) 'Social marketing', Ch. 27 in M.J. Baker (ed.) *The Marketing Book*, 5th edition. Oxford: Butterworth-Heinemann.

McArdle, M. (2016) 'Closing the loop – values and reasons in the value-action gap for recycled consumer paper products'. Doctoral Colloquium, 42nd Macromarketing conference, Dublin, Ireland, 13 July.

Marques, S. and Domegan, C. (2011) 'Relationship marketing and social marketing', Ch. 3 in G. Hastings, K. Angus and C. Bryant (eds) *The SAGE Handbook of Social Marketing*. London: Sage Publications.

Morgan, R.M. and Hunt, S.D. (1994) 'The commitment-trust theory of relationship marketing', *Journal of Marketing*, 58(3): 20–38.

Orme, J. and Starkey, F. (1998) *Evaluation of HPS/Bristol Old Vic Primary Drug Drama Project 1997/98. Full report.* Bristol: Faculty of Health and Social Care, UWE.

Orme, J. and Starkey, F. (1999) 'Young people's views on drug education in schools: Implications for health promotion and health education', *Health Education*, 4(July): 142–152.

Pentz, M.A., Mihalic, S.F. and Grotpeter, J.K. (1997) *Blueprints for Violence Prevention: Book One – The Midwestern Prevention Project.* Series editor D.S. Elliott. Boulder, CO: University of Colorado.

Scollo, M., Lal, A., Hyland, A. and Glantz, S. (2003) 'Review of the quality of studies on the economic effects of smoke-free policies on the hospitality industry', *Tobacco Control*, 12(1): 13–20.

Taleb, N.N. (2010) *The Black Swan: The Impact of the Highly Improbable.* London: Penguin UK.

Tones, K. (1996) 'Models of mass media: Hypodermic, aerosol or agent provocateur?', *Drugs: Education, Prevention and Policy*, 3(1): 29–37.

Wallace, D.F. (2008) 'Plain old untrendy troubles and emotions', *The Guardian*, 20 September. Online: www.guardian.co.uk/books/2008/sep/20/fiction/ (accessed March 2016).

Walsh, D.C., Rudd, R.E., Moeykens, B.A. and Moloney, T.W. (1993) 'Social marketing for public health', *Health Affairs*, 12(2): 104–109.

Chapter **3**

The shoulders
of giants

THEORY: ALWAYS A GOOD BET

Harry likes a flutter on the horses (or, as he puts it, the gee-gees). He has just driven his invalid trike four miles (eight miles there and back) to the next village because the local bookie is closed on a Tuesday. After much pondering, he put 10 euros on Agamemnon to win in the 3.30 at Wincanton. The odds were 10 to 1, so he stands to make 100 euros.

He decided on Agamemnon because the filly comes from good stock – her sire (father) won the Grand National in his youth and her dam (mother) was also a well-regarded racer. He also took into account Agamemnon's form to date – one win, and three times placed in the first three. Finally, he thought about 'the going' (the condition of the race course, which is typically rated on a six-point scale: heavy – soft – good to soft – good – good to firm – firm) and calculated that Wincanton's firm all-weather track would suit the young filly.

Harry was now back home with the telly on and waiting eagerly for the outside broadcast from Wincanton to begin.

Harry is an experienced punter and well versed in horse-racing lore. He is rightly proud of his skills. But he would be astonished to discover that he is also an accomplished user of theory. Indeed, his Wincanton punt harnessed three theories: that lineage will influence a horse's performance; that past performance is predictive of future outcomes; and that different horses are suited to different conditions. These theories have emerged because generations of race-goers have observed, recorded and analysed results to try to work out how they can anticipate winners. In short, a legion of past experience has been neatly and economically turned into three predictive models, three theories, with which Harry has been able to improve his chances of winning.

We social marketers do the same thing to improve our chances of changing behaviour. As we've already discovered, this is challenging territory: many things influence how we behave – from individual knowledge, attitudes and agency through collective attributes such as community coherence and family structures to systemic geopolitical factors. With these multiple variables and levels of behavioural influence, where does the social marketer start?

Newton famously remarked that he had achieved so much, not on his own, but by "standing on the shoulders of giants", a reference to all the hard work done by fellow scientists that formed the basis for his ideas about gravity. So, regardless of whether the behaviour change is sought in the area of health, the environment or safety; whether it is in a conurbation in a wealthy northern country or an impoverished village of sub-Saharan Africa, the starting point for all social marketing is with previous thinking – or what we call theory.

Theory is the distillation of previous endeavours in a particular field. Simply put, it is a way of learning from other people's work. It enables us to follow suit and codify past efforts so that we too can build on solid foundations. It also helps us avoid the duplication of error and the reinvention of solutions. In addition, theories aim to simplify the world in order to explain it better. Theories model, or provide a systematic generalised framework, of what are typically much more complex phenomena in the real world, and thereby help us to get a grip on them. And it works: "interventions that are based on social and behavioural science theories are more effective than those lacking a theoretical base" (Glanz and Bishop 2010).

Behavioural scientists have listened and the result is a vast array of theories that can become almost as daunting as the problems to be tackled. In this chapter, we want to introduce you to some of the key theories and look at how they might help solve social marketing problems. In essence, as we have already noted, all social marketers seek to do three things: understand their clients' current behaviour, identify what factors influence this and find a motivational means of triggering change. We will look at how theory can help with all three tasks. In the process, we will discuss seven different theories (see Box 3.1) but even then we will only be scratching the surface.

BOX 3.1   SEVEN USEFUL THEORIES

Theory	Key principles
Stages of change theory	Behaviour change is a gradual multi-stage process
Social cognitive theory	Social context matters
Social norms theory	What other people do around us matters
Social epistemology theory	Knowledge has a social as well as a personal dimension
Social ecological theory	Everything is connected so the smallest act can have massive repercussions
Social capital theory	A sense of belonging to and trust in our communities is vital
Exchange theory	We look for values and benefits when considering change

Our aim is not to advocate for particular theories, but to make the more general point that, for social marketers, theory is a valuable tool that is easy to understand and straightforward to use. It will enable you to get to know the principles underlying specific theories and see how helpful they can be, but ultimately we would echo Donovan's (2011) call for "an eclectic approach to theory, suggesting social marketers should be prepared to trawl a wide selection of models and constructs to select ones that best suit their field of endeavour, always combining this thinking with ethical vigilance." We are also very cognisant of the Kurt Lewin maxim, "there is nothing so practical as a good theory" (1951: 169), so the chapter concludes by going beyond principle, and providing an opportunity to put theories to work on a tangible case.

Before we begin, however, a word of caution. Social marketers need to respect theory – but they should also recognise its limitations. Human behaviour is ineffably complex, and almost as difficult to predict as the winner at Wincanton. This means that, on the one hand, we need all the theories and models we can get to help us make sense of it. On the other, we have to recognise that all these theories and models will, inevitably, be gross over-simplifications that will ultimately be found wanting if we set too much store by them. A mathematician friend pointed out that if she were to try to model a cow she would start by assuming it to be spherical; the variability and complexity of a real cow shape are just too much to handle. Her ungulate model might well have been of some help to animal husbandry, but it would fall a long way short of enabling a Martian to recognise a Friesian. Hence, social marketers also adopt a pragmatic perspective on theory, with a keen eye for what works rather than searching for the all-encompassing and unalloyed – but inevitably elusive – perfect theory.

Learning outcomes

By the end of this chapter, you should be able to:

✓ Explain why and how theory is important in social marketing

✓ Analyse three theories of behaviour change: stages of change theory, social cognitive theory and exchange theory – while recognising that there are many other useful ones as well

✓ Introduce values and their vital role in Exchange for behaviour change

✓ Demonstrate how these can help social marketers answer three key questions: where their customers are in relation to a particular behaviour, what factors influence this positioning and how it might be changed

✓ Apply the theory to a given social marketing situation

✓ List important theoretical considerations in social marketing.

Key words

Exchange theory – values – restricted and complex exchanges – social capital theory – social cognitive theory – social ecology theory – social epistemology theory – social norms theory – stages of change theory – value exchange fields – value action fields – self-interest – mutuality – morality.

Three questions to get you started

In essence, a social marketer's focus on behaviour change begs three questions:

1. Where are people in relation to a particular behaviour?
2. What factors cause this positioning?
3. How can they be moved in the desired direction?

Theory can help answer these questions. The first and third are relatively straightforward and we discuss just two theories under these headings. Stages of change (or the transtheoretical model) helps us examine people's proximity to a particular behaviour, and recognise that this varies between individuals, behaviours and over time. Exchange theory, a quintessentially marketing contribution, addresses the third question and brings dynamism to the process. As Kurt Lewin advises, it focuses our attention on the practicalities of change.

The second question, what factors influence our relationship to change, is more complex. It picks up all the issues we have already acknowledged about the social and systemic drivers of behaviour. We start by discussing social cognitive theory, a sort of catch-all that maps out this social space, but then pick up on the four other theories that populate it with specific ideas about the forces at play. The full complexity, detail and dynamics of change or the bigger picture using systems thinking is discussed in Chapter 11.

Just to emphasise what we said above, this is not to suggest that these are the only theories that social marketers should use. There are also many other useful ones you can call upon. The important point is that theory is a valuable tool for social marketers.

Stages of change theory

The stages of change theory is more formally known as the transtheoretical model of behaviour change. This rather clunky name belies the beautiful simplicity underlying Prochaska and DiClemente's (1983) basic idea: that we do not make and carry through decisions, especially complex behavioural ones, in a simple binary fashion. So the smoker does not just wake up one morning and think, 'OK, I'll quit', then do so and sit down to breakfast as a non-smoker. It is much more likely they will spend a long time considering the possibility of giving up, think about ways of doing it, give quitting a go and then spend weeks or months adjusting to the change. Indeed, the accepted definition of a non-smoker is someone who has been smoke-free for at least 12 months.

Prochaska and DiClemente noticed this foot-dragging phenomenon and began to study it in detail. It occurs not just with smoking but also with a whole series of addiction-related and other health behaviours. Prochaska and DiClemente suggest that we move through five stages, from ignorance of or indifference towards the idea of changing through trial to becoming committed to the new behaviour:

- **Precontemplation**: you may be aware of the new behaviour (e.g. quitting smoking or obeying the speed limit) but are not interested in it, at least at this point in your life.
- **Contemplation**: you are consciously evaluating the personal relevance of the new behaviour.

- **Preparation**: you have decided to act and are trying to put in place the measures needed to carry out the new behaviour.

- **Action**: you give it a go.

- **Confirmation (or maintenance)**: you are committed to the behaviour and have no desire or intention to regress.

The Transtheoretical Model has undergone considerable field testing. Since 1983, Prochaska and his colleagues have validated it for 12 types of behaviour, including smoking cessation, condom use, quitting cocaine, using sunscreen and weight control (Prochaska and Velicer 1997).

Alan Andreasen (1995) argues that, from a social marketing standpoint, three features of this model are significant. First, Prochaska and DiClemente have been able to show that it is relatively straightforward to separate consumers into these five stages by asking them a few simple questions. Figure 3.1 shows a questionnaire based on their work, which was used in Scotland to map low-income smokers across the stages, along with definitions of how respondents should be allocated to the various stages.

Current smokers	Precontemplation:
Q1 During the **past 12 months** have you, **on purpose**, given up smoking for one day or more? (Please tick one box only) Yes ☐ No ☐ I'm not sure ☐	'No' to Qs 1, 2 & 3.
	Contemplation:
Q2 Do you plan to give up smoking in the next 30 days? (Please tick one box only) Yes ☐ No ☐ I'm not sure ☐	'No' to Q1 & 'Yes' to Q2. *Or*
	'No' to Q2 & 'Yes' to Q3.
IF 'YES' GO TO Q4 **OTHERWISE CONTINUE WITH Q3**	**Preparation:**
	'Yes' to both Qs 1 & 2.
Q3 Do you think you will **try to give up smoking** in the next 6 months? (Please tick one box only) Yes ☐ No ☐ I'm not sure ☐	**Action:**
	Abstinent for less than 6 months [Answers 4 (a) – (c)].
Past smokers	
Q4 When did you give up smoking cigarettes? (Please tick one box only) (a) Within the last week ☐ (b) Within the last month ☐ (c) Within the last 6 months ☐ (d) Within the last year ☐ (e) Within the last 3 years ☐ (f) Within the last 5 years ☐ (g) Within the last 10 years ☐ (h) More than 10 years ago ☐ (i) I'm not sure ☐	**Maintenance:** Abstinent for 6 months or more [Answers 4 (d) – (h)]

Figure 3.1 Assessing people's stage of change

Second, they found that the appropriate intervention strategy depends on position in the process. For example, it is important to emphasise benefits in the early stages and costs in later stages. Finally, they recognised that a social marketer's goal should not be to propel the client to the Confirmation Stage in one step, but to move that client to the next stage. Only through a series of steps will they reach the social marketer's goal of sustained behaviour change (Andreasen 1995). Have a try at Exercise 3.1.

EXERCISE 3.1   MEASURING STAGE OF CHANGE

Try out the questionnaire in Figure 3.1 on your colleagues. If you wish, you can adjust it to deal with another behaviour such as speeding or diet.

Does it work? Are you convinced by the idea that decisions to change these behaviours are indeed multi-stage?

This all seems very plausible and agreeably practical: the social marketing practitioner has a nice simple rubric for enacting behaviour change. At which point, we should beware – as we have already noted, nothing is that simple with human behaviour. The UK Smoking Cessation Service (SCS) adopted stages of change with great gusto and applied it much as Andreasen recommends. The result was that precontemplators were ignored and only those in the action stage were referred to the service. This assumes that the model is spot on (and we know no model ever is) and that our measurement procedures are perfect (which, as we will discuss in Chapter 5, they never are).

Predictably, therefore, the model has come under criticism on a number of fronts. First, it has been challenged for assuming people move in a linear fashion through the stages (Davidson 1992). Although it was initially proposed that people would progress linearly, behaviour change is now recognised as a 'spiral' where the individual may relapse back to a previous stage, but through experiential learning may eventually reach maintenance (Basler 1995).

Second, the model has been criticised for not considering those who change their behaviour without consciously going through all five predefined stages (Davidson 1992). This point is refuted by the authors who suggest that consumers may pass through some stages more rapidly than others (Prochaska *et al.* 1992). Later versions of the model recognise these dynamics and variations (see Figure 3.2).

These refinements of the model (seen in Figure 3.3), however, still fall a long way short of providing a complete representation of our behaviour. To muddy the waters further, for instance, complex and challenging behaviours typically take several attempts to change – as the anonymous wit pointed out, "Giving up smoking is easy – I've done it hundreds of times." Some of these attempts will, undoubtedly, be spur of the moment. Heavy drinkers will spontaneously forswear booze and dieters cake on a regular basis. Indeed, Robert West (2005) points out that the evidence suggests *most* smokers kick the habit in this apparently instantaneous manner. This seemingly damning failing – West goes on to argue that the model should be laid to rest – does not fatally undermine the theory, however;

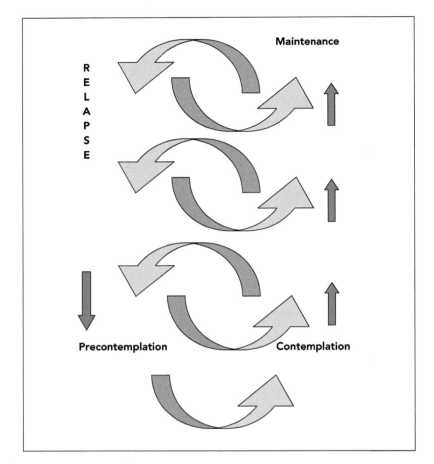

Figure 3.2 The 'spiral' model

(*Source:* adapted from Buxton *et al.* 1996)

spur of the moment quitters may well have gone through all the stages of change in their previous attempts.

The theoreticians will go on arguing about the validity of this model. From a social marketer's point of view, however, the discussion becomes increasingly redundant. Theories will never model human behaviour perfectly, but they can help us think about it more systematically. Stages of change brings a useful and plausible idea to the table: that *behaviour change is a process* rather than an on/off switch, and it is a good idea for those interested in enacting change to start by finding out how far people have progressed along this process.

Such a 'process' in fact consists of *ten* processes, each of which corresponds with a stage of change. These change processes drive movement through the stages of change and provide social marketers with a systematic method of facilitating movement through the stages framework. The processes of change ultimately explain how and to what extent

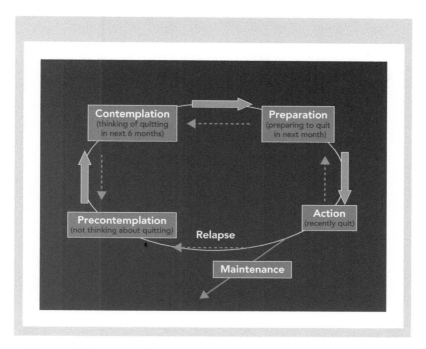

Figure 3.3 Stages of change mark 2

behaviour change occurs, and once applied to a social marketing intervention, the successes and pitfalls of the intervention in achieving behaviour change become clear. One such application of the processes to the Facebook page of 'Operation Transformation' – an Irish lifestyle change programme – revealed that while the Facebook page did facilitate movement from behavioural intention to behavioural commitment, it did so to different extents for the followers due to the processes of change (Gately 2015). While some processes were a natural fit for behaviour change in the context of a social medium (e.g. self-liberation and helping relationships), other processes proved less suitable for the context of Facebook (e.g. stimulus control).

The problems that Robert West identified are real enough, but they stem more from how the theory is being applied than from flaws in its basic precept. It does not provide a rigid manual on how to proceed; nor should it be used in the inflexible way it was by the UK Smoking Cessation Service. As DiClemente (2005) himself recently put it, it is a mistake to treat "the model as a religion and not a heuristic to explore the change process." The model simply provides an intelligent way of thinking about how close our clients are to a particular behaviour.

We need to turn elsewhere to understand why people arrive at a particular stage and what moves them on to the next (Buxton *et al.* 1996).

Social cognitive theory

Social cognitive theory postulates that human behaviour is reciprocally determined by internal personal factors (such as knowledge and self-efficacy) and environmental factors

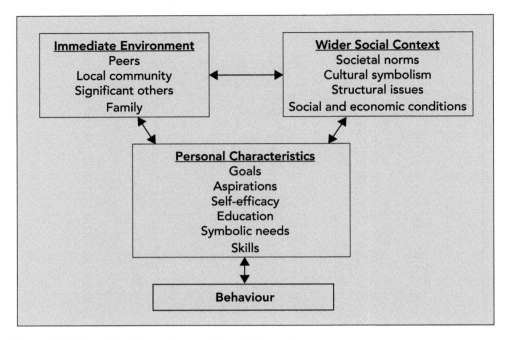

Figure 3.4 The wider determinants of health behaviour

(*Source:* adapted from MacFadyen *et al.* 1998)

(such as levels of deprivation or availability of facilities in the local community) (Bandura 1986; Maibach and Cotton 1995). As social marketers, then, our view of behaviour should take into account the influence not only of the individual, but also of their environment. The latter can be further divided into two domains. First, there is the relatively direct influence of friends, family and the local community, which has been termed the 'immediate environment'. Second, there is the more indirect influence of social mores, economic conditions and cultural norms, which we have called the 'wider social context' (i.e. the structures and systems surrounding their lives). Figure 3.4 illustrates how these different influences interact.

In this way, social cognitive theory recognises the two-way relationship that exists between personal and environmental factors: environments shape people and their behaviours, who in turn shape their environments through their behaviour and expectations (Maibach and Cotton 1995). Try applying this thinking by doing Exercise 3.2.

EXERCISE 3.2 EXTERNAL INFLUENCES ON OUR BEHAVIOUR

Think of a social problem with which you are familiar – maybe youth smoking, obesity or some aspect of non-ecological behaviour. Try to complete your own version of Figure 3.4 using this as an example.

In the case of youth smoking, for instance, the immediate environment might include shops that sell age-limited goods to minors, the wider social context, ubiquitous tobacco advertising, personal characteristics and extensive ignorance of the dangers of smoking.

The people/structure nature of social cognitive theory echoes our discussion of structuration and agency in Chapter 2 and underlines the need for social marketers to address both dimensions or risk failure. Simply telling people in poor communities to eat more fruit and vegetables if none are available in local shops is going to do little for public health. Arguably, as we noted in Chapter 2, it is also an unethical case of victim blaming – putting an unfair degree of responsibility for their own predicament on people who are already suffering and disempowered.

This thinking also underpins the idea of 'denormalisation' – that if we can adjust people's perceptions of how common and normal a particular behaviour is we will also be able to influence their inclination to engage in this behaviour (Sussman 1989; Hansen 1990). For example, young people's perceptions of the prevalence and acceptability of smoking in both their immediate peer and family group, and in society as a whole, are key predictors of their tendency to take up smoking. Accordingly, smoking uptake will be reduced if pro-smoking norms are challenged and anti-smoking norms strengthened. Normative education, or denormalisation programmes, therefore correct "erroneous perceptions of the prevalence and acceptability of drug and alcohol use and establish conservative group norms . . . [they] are postulated to operate through lowering expectations about prevalence and acceptability of use and the reduced availability of substances in peer-oriented social settings" (Hansen 1992). Evidence reviews suggest this is a useful insight and that normative education is a valuable ingredient of effective substance use prevention (e.g. MacKinnon *et al.* 1991; Donaldson *et al.* 1994; Coggans *et al.* 2003).

Social norms, social epistemology, social ecology and social capital theories can help social marketers to unpick and respond to this phenomenon.

Social norms theory

Social norms theory builds on the established phenomenon that our behaviour is partly derived from what other people do or say (descriptive norms), and what are approved behaviours (injunctive norms). This is the herd instinct at work – conforming to and wanting to be accepted by others in one's group, such as family members, friends, work and society. Rewards (e.g. acceptance, status, power) are provided for conformity, while punishments (e.g. exclusion, fines and jail) can occur for non-compliance. Social norms are pervasive: Kenny and Hastings (2011) list social norms studies in areas as varied as smoking; littering and environmental protection; sexual behaviour; gambling; tax compliance; eating and dieting behaviours; video pirating; opinion formation in childhood; pre-marital counselling; voting intentions; workplace health and safety; the purchase of luxury products; subject enrolment choices in schools; and parenting approaches.

The 'lead by example' principle lies at the core of descriptive norms. We are influenced by our perceptions of what others do because those who are similar to us provide behavioural cues and triggers. This is particularly important in new situations such as a first-year college student in the university student bar or a child arriving at her new secondary school. In contrast, a trans-situational effect defines injunctive norms as they reflect societal values. That's to say injunctive norms "communicate generalized values and indicate what is generally socially acceptable within a particular culture", whereas "descriptive norms seem to communicate effective behaviour in a particular setting" (Kenny and Hastings 2011: 66).

Social norm campaigns work (Hastings *et al.* 2010). Enacting strong regulations (i.e. clean indoor air regulations and laws prohibiting sales to youths) in Massachusetts significantly affected adults' and youths' perceived community norms to be more anti-smoking (Hamilton *et al.* 2008). In Scotland and the rest of the UK, support for smoke-free legislation pre-ban significantly increased perceptions of non-smoking norms (Brown *et al.* 2009). Now have a go at Exercise 3.3.

EXERCISE 3.3   SOCIAL NORMS APPROACH TO PREVENTING BINGE DRINKING

You are employed as a social marketer by a non-governmental organisation to design a social marketing campaign to discourage first-year university students from binge drinking. Consider how you could use a social norms approach to plan an intervention to decrease binge drinking on campus.

What are the limitations of this approach to your campaign?

(*Source:* Brown et al. 2009)

As the success of most social norms campaigns is grounded in a sound understanding of the majority attitudes and/or behaviours, you could start by doing a survey to gather reliable data about first-year students. This would need to establish how many students actually drink and to what extent, as well as their perceptions of their peers' drinking habits. Any tendency for the latter to be exaggerated would suggest a need for a campaign correcting these misperceptions. The evidence suggests that repeated exposure to a variety of positive, credible data-based norms messages can correct misperceptions and assist in reducing binge drinking.

Although social norms campaigns hold great promise for behaviour change, some campaigns have failed, as shown in Box 3.2.

BOX 3.2   A FAILED NORMS SOCIAL MARKETING CAMPAIGN

Clapp *et al.* (2003) tested the efficacy of an intensive norms social marketing campaign to reduce heavy drinking among college students living in a residence hall. They employed a pre-test/post-test non-equivalent comparison group design, conducted in two (experimental and comparison) comparable residence halls located in a large urban public university. The campaign successfully corrected students' misperceptions of drinking norms but had no effects on actual drinking behaviours. They concluded that, despite the popularity of such norms interventions, universities would be prudent to proceed with care before adopting social norms wholesale.

(*Source:* Clapp *et al.* 2003)

This last point, to proceed with care when utilising social norms, is reinforced by social epistemology.

Social epistemology theory

Social epistemology (Hastings *et al.* 2010) focuses on the social aspects of knowledge – how groups acquire and justify knowledge and not just knowledge as a personal, individual concern. For example, social marketers involved in campaigns to inform smokers in the pre-contemplation stage about the health consequences of smoking would benefit from having an informed idea about how their target group – as a group – acquire and justify knowledge. If the informational campaign does not take account of how the target group thinks, reasons and puts emphasis on knowledge, it is unlikely to succeed. Social epistemology is useful because it shifts the social cognitive theory focus on knowledge as an internal, personal phenomenon to an external, contextual one. Social epistemology asks 'how did the client arrive at and justify their beliefs?', while social cognitive theory asks 'what does the client know?' (Hastings *et al.* 2010). Exercise 3.4 explores how useful this distinction is.

EXERCISE 3.4   SOCIAL EPISTEMOLOGY AND INFORMATIONAL CAMPAIGNS

You are a social marketer faced with developing an informational campaign to improve the dietary choices of a group of people that (a) are predominantly vegan, (b) distrust official public advice on health and rely heavily on 'alternative, non-scientific, spiritual experts', (c) frequently take yoga classes and (d) are subject to malnutrition, because their diet contains too few proteins.

Social epistemology emphasises how social groups acquire knowledge and whom they trust as reliable sources of information.

Why is this perspective important to your campaign?

To design an effective campaign, it is crucial for the social marketer to understand how the target group acquires knowledge, and what sources of knowledge it particularly values. If your target group, for instance teenagers, distrust public experts, an informational campaign that quite clearly originates from a public health department is going to be a significant disadvantage. To get your message across, you will need to tap into a knowledge source that the target group respects and trusts – a celebrity perhaps, or community leader. In Exercise 3.4, a partnership with yoga instructors might be an effective way to support and strengthen your social marketing communications. In this way, social epistemology strengthens the marketer's power of persuasion through encouraging an exploration and analysis of the target group's idea of reliable knowledge and harnessing the power of source effect (a point picked up again in Chapter 6).

Social ecological theory

Social ecological theory adopts an even wider perspective on change, looking at whole social systems. It recognises what is called 'the butterfly effect', a phrase coined by meteorologist Edward Lorenz to convey how tiny seemingly unrelated events, such as butterfly wings flapping in Brazil, could become magnified by the world's essential interconnectedness and have potentially huge effects on the other side of the world – causing, for instance, tornado weather in Texas. In essence, the butterfly effect describes *co-ordinated* and *interactive* links; individuals and groups are loosely bonded in the system, permitting it to operate as a whole, while at the same time allowing for alterations and modifications in parts by some of those individuals or groups (Alderson 1957). It explains individual/environment interactions as dynamic and active processes.

To this end, McHugh (2013) in her work demonstrates how social ecological theory moves us towards an understanding of multiple group behaviours from a networked stance. Whole network behaviour integrates *multi-structural, multi-factorial* and *multi-institutional* influences and co-ordinates the cross-level interrelationships in a system. Applied to obesity, for example, this challenges us to think not just about the child's eating behaviour, but also about parents' cooking skills, as well as school lunch policies, food advertising and production methods, in addition to government regulations and how they all affect the child. Advocating more fruit and vegetable consumption may be meaningless until our highly processed and sugary food production methods are dramatically transformed.

Another pressing example of these effects in action is global warming: the tiny butterfly-wing consumption acts of the individual in Paris are linked with the activities of multinationals, the decisions of governments and the degradation of the planet – and across the world in Bangladesh fishing villages are disappearing under the sea. Figure 3.5 provides a graphic illustration of social ecological theory.

We will return to these complex, interconnected problems and how to deal with them in later chapters. For the moment, let us just note that they need equally sophisticated and far-reaching solutions – social cognitive theory and social ecological theory help us to appreciate the dynamics and detail of this complexity.

Social capital theory

Social capital theory addresses the patterns and configurations of connections between people. The World Bank defines social capital as the relationships that shape societal interactions, while organisations such as the Organisation for Economic Co-operation and Development (OECD) and the WHO acknowledge that social capital influences education, social justice, health, civic engagement and hence the quality of life in a society.

Importantly for social marketing, social capital highlights the importance of *structural* and *relational* embeddedness within and among individuals in a society, i.e. our sense of belonging

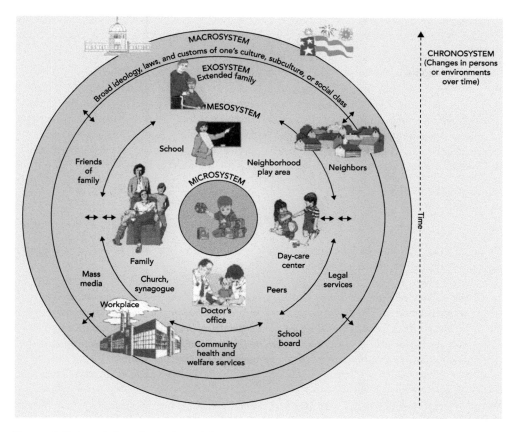

Figure 3.5 A social ecological model

(*Source:* Bronfenbrenner 1988)

to and trust in our communities. The structural aspect looks at networks and their ties; their connectivity; density and form. The relational element concerns values, trust, norms, identity and expectations, reflected in shared narratives, meanings and language. Together, these shape the quantity and quality of a society's social interactions.

There are three different kinds of social capital: bonding, bridging and linking as captured by Jones (2011) in Box 3.3.

BOX 3.3   BONDING, BRIDGING AND LINKING

"Bonding, bridging and linking have to be carefully balanced if society is to function effectively. Bonding refers to the networks that exist among 'people like us' or people who share the same values . . . In extreme cases bonding can lead to terrorism

(continued)

(continued)

. . . The OECD refers to this as the 'ties that bind turning into ties that blind'. Bridging social capital is the relationships with 'people not like us' such as those from different faith or ethnic groups . . . the vertical links that go up and down the social ladder . . . Linking social capital refers to the networks people use to leverage resources from powerful institutions . . . I suspect bonding has increased considerably whereas bridging and linking social capital has decreased because of the growing mistrust of citizens . . . Broken societies can result unless all types of social capital are present in roughly equal amounts."

(Source: Jones 2011)

The core insight is that social capital is about relationships. Increased social capital encourages cooperative behaviour, which is vital. In fact:

> *the quality of these networks can help explain variations in key policy outcomes between communities in areas such as crime, education and health. In general, higher levels of social capital result in communities, and individuals within them, that are better able to act and take responsibility for themselves. Social capital can also assist in spreading behavioural change amongst the community.*
> *(Hyndman et al. 2007: 25)*

We can turn to Lefebvre (2011: 37) for further social marketing insights:

> *One of the implications is that people learn about and choose among behavioural options not only based on directly observing how others in their social circle engage in behaviours and the consequences they experience, but also by who their friends and associates also connect with outside that proximal network and then transmit that information or those practices back to the immediate network.*

We return to this last point again in Chapter 6 and in discussions about engagement, communication and participatory media. But Lefebvre also warns us, as with all theory, that while social ecological theory has become popular in social science and public health it's not without its detractors. In particular, there are concerns that it does not deal adequately with issues of power and conflict – and yet these are inherent to relationships. This concern about relative power will re-emerge when we discuss exchange theory.

In summary, it is helpful to have a social perspective to the understanding of behaviour change. Social norms, social epistemology, social ecology and social capital make it easier for social marketers to apply this insight. Specifically, they shed light on why people have a given positioning with regard to a particular behaviour. Check out Case Study 4 for its discussion of behavioural learning theory and instrumental (operant) conditioning with its positive reinforcement and reward and the experiential learning hierarchy (learning by doing) for digital engagement selected as fit-for-purpose with the target audience of low-income adult renters. Go to Case Study 11 and a life without tobacco movement, and look at Case Study 12, generating a movement away from food waste among university students and staff, both making use of social contagion theory to fuel change (we pick up on this movement idea again in Chapter 11). The theories also begin to identify possible social marketing interventions that might alter this positioning.

Exchange theory can also help here.

Exchange theory

Exchange theory is central to social marketing, which is why we have already touched on it in the two previous chapters. To recapitulate, the theory posits that, given behavioural options, people will ascribe values to the alternatives and select the one that offers greatest benefit – or enhancement – to themselves. This process assumes we are need-directed beings with a built-in inclination to try to improve our lot. Richard Layard takes this thinking way back to the origins of our species, arguing that cooperation and mutually beneficial exchange were key to our success on the African savannah:

> *If human beings had not been able to co-operate in this way they would probably not have survived the rigours of the savannah – or subsequently of regions much colder. At best our lives would have been, as Thomas Hobbes put it, solitary, poor, nasty, brutish and short. We survived because our genes gave us the ability to co-operate.*
>
> *(Layard 2005: 98)*

He goes on to point out that "the result of this co-operation is not a zero sum game; it is a win-win activity." Zak (2011: 222) explains that "exchange is necessarily other regarding" – we interact with strangers on a routine basis, gauging our own and others' behaviours against our expectations and manifesting shared values. Crucially, Craig Lefebvre (1992) argues that social marketing is in essence this same process of seeking win–wins.

In order to increase client readiness to change and exchange, therefore, social marketers must provide them with something beneficial in return. In this sense, exchange and the notion of value co-creation (where the client and social marketer jointly determine what values matter) involves the transfer of tangible or intangible items between two or more social actors (Bagozzi 1979). Kotler (2000) suggests five prerequisites are required for exchange to take place:

1. There are at least two parties.

2. Each party has something that might be of value to the other party.

3. Each party is capable of communication and delivery.

4. Each party is free to accept or reject the offer.

5. Each party believes it is appropriate or desirable to deal with the other party.

Central to these assumptions is the notion that the exchange must be mutually beneficial. There must be something of value for each party or an exchange won't happen. Exchange theory postulates that, if social marketers can "demonstrate that the perceived bene-fits . . . outweigh the perceived costs of its purchase, voluntary adoption by the consumer is most likely" (Maibach 1993). A tobacco advertiser put the same point more baldly when he pointed out that "If a brand of cigarettes does not convey much in the way of image values, there may well be little reason for a young adult smoker to persist with or adopt the brand" (Rothmans UK 1998, cited in Hastings and MacFadyen 2000: 12).

Clearly, no discussion of what makes for a winning exchange is complete without some insights into what we value and don't value.

Value is in the eye of the beholder

We know value is individualised and subjective, based upon experiences, actual and perceived. When talking about value, we equate value with money, price, quality and cost. In the plural, 'values' take in high-minded principles – as in 'the values of a civi-lised society'. As Hastings and Lowry (2010: 279) remind us "values ascribed to the marketer's offering during an exchange may be tangible (e.g. monetary) or psychological (e.g. status), immediate (e.g. nicotine now) or deferred (e.g. better health later), but they will always be subjective." For example, the subjective nature of value is reflected when social marketers talk about physical activity as fun for young children, exercise for the 30+s, fitness for the 40+s and wellness for the 50+s. Value cannot and does not have a single meaning. Value also presents complexity for the social marketer because clients, policy makers, stakeholders and funders all have different values. Moreover, these diverse outlooks can seem like chalk and cheese. Think of the doctor who sees non-smoking as a valuable health advantage and the teenager who uses smoking to control weight, to impress, to be accepted and to 'be cool' or as a way to rebel against the establishment and parents. This highlights one last important aspect of value— its collective generation within families, friendship groups, communities and societies (Alderson 1967).

The take-away message is that values signal what is important to people in their lives; values determine our needs, wants, beliefs, motivations and goals. Importantly, **values drive our choices and exchange behaviours** (McHugh *et al.* 2015). With values *that* central to suc-cessful exchanges, it is helpful to understand the main features of values (Schwartz 2012: 3–4) and Crompton (2010):

1. Values are *beliefs* . . . tied inextricably to emotion, not objective, cold ideas.

2. Values *motivate action*. They refer to the desirable goals which people strive to attain.

3. Values *transcend specific actions and situations*.

Values can be divided into the value triad of (a) self-interest values, e.g. I want to have a good time; (b) mutuality values, e.g. I want to have a good time with my friends also having a good time; and (c) moral values, e.g. I want to have a good time while not hurting or harm-ing anyone. Any blend of this self-interest, mutuality and morality values triad, as captured in Figure 3.6, will be context driven (Layton 2009, 2015).

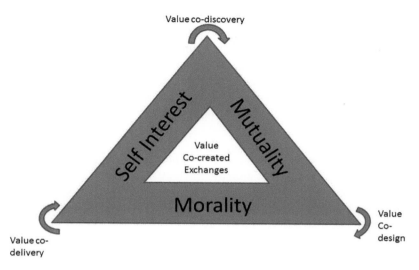

Figure 3.6 Social marketing's value triad

(*Source:* Layton and Domegan 2016: 4)

Now try Exercise 3.5.

EXERCISE 3.5   VALUES AT WORK AND PLAY

Take any of the lovely summer days you cast your mind back to in the middle of a cold and blustery winter . . . the sun is shining, blue skies roll out as far as the eye can see and the odd white cloud gently floats by. It's hot, so hot you can almost smell the heat, but there's a gentle breeze blowing that refreshingly cools you down. Schools are closed. Families and friends are on the beach for a day of fun and laughter, swimming, sandcastles, picnics and the all-important ice-creams.

At the end of a fabulous day, as the sun sets, people head home. Some put their rubbish in the bin while others leave the evidence of their beach day behind on the sand.

What values do you see at work?

For most individuals, a day at the seaside with family and friends represents having a good time and enjoying life. This is the hedonism value at work. Those who went sailing or on a banana boat ride were adding excitement and adventure to their day, which is stimulation value in operation. For others the day at the beach could represent tradition; the family custom is for everyone to go swimming and build sandcastles, followed by a homemade picnic, where there is great chat, laughter and stories told and shared for all to enjoy. These are mutuality values where the individuals consider the **outcomes of their actions** and reflect the **common interests of the group**. The individual is concerned with themselves and with others. The individuals who put their rubbish in the bins provided by the local authority were following the rules and acting according to their conformity values (high mutuality). On the other hand, those who ignored the signs saying "Put you rubbish in the Bins provided" "Don't leave your Litter Behind" and "Leave no Trace" and left evidence of their behaviours that day on the sand – bottles, cans and other packaging which would probably be washed out to sea – may have been non-conformists (high self-interest values) or persons with little concern or low appreciation for nature (low universalism mutuality value). Alternatively, perhaps there were no bins provided by the local authority in the first place to activate pro-environmental values!

Also in operation on the beach were moral values. Morality represents the broad acceptance or prohibition of behaviours within a society (Zak 2011). In many situations we tend not to be conscious of moral values until they are broken, such as the taking of another's life – unacceptable in everyday life in most societies but tolerated in wartime. In keeping with this moral value, no one was attacked or killed that summer's day. We'll follow up on human rights and moral agency in Chapters 9 and 10.

This brings us to three important and final characteristics that social marketers have to contend with when thinking about the values triad:

1. "Values are ordered by importance relative to one another" (Schwartz 2012: 4). Self-interest values such as the attainment of wealth, personal status and success are opposed to or can suppress mutuality values such as the wellbeing of others or wellbeing of the environment.

2. "The relative importance of multiple values guides action" (Schwartz 2012: 4). Recall what Richard Layard said above about improving our lot and cooperation. We all have self-interest values and mutuality values underpinning our daily lives. What's important is the relative importance and balance behind these different values.

3. The mixtures of different value triads for diverse individuals, families and friends (e.g. the self-interest of hedonism and stimulation or the mutuality of tradition, conformity and universalism and morality), in the same setting or context, give rise to a range of behaviours or 'value action fields' (VAFs; Layton and Domegan 2016).

In effect, each family or tight-knit group of friends represents a 'value action field', where unique interactions, co-operation and relationships, based on blends of self-interest and reciprocity, trust and commitment, were at play on the beach that hot summer's day. On any given beach (or visitor attraction, community centre, shopping centre, restaurant, pub, school, doctor's surgery, park . . .) on any given day, in any given country, you'll see value action fields in operation and you'll also notice and experience how some of these value action fields are similar and dissimilar to others. The mutuality and morality or greater-than-self values tend not to be fully articulated in economic terms whereas self-interest values are normally expressed in economic terms.

Value action fields are akin to the saying "different folks, different strokes" while echoing our client and collective orientations from the previous chapter. Linking value action fields to our competition orientation and active competition in particular, we can begin to see how commercial marketing products and services can push behaviours in the opposite direction from social marketing offerings – some cars are marketed based on power, status, achievement, all self-interest values and not benevolence or universalism mutuality values. Keeping an eye on the competition is as much about *value destruction* as *value creation* for social marketers! In their book *Freakonomics*, Levitt and Dubner (2005) show value destruction and creation at work in unusual and unexpected ways as schoolteachers were motivated to defy years of training and professionalism and cheat in school tests in order to gain financial rewards for good results. In the same book, the authors point out that inadequate rewards or penalties can actually be counter-productive. They tell the story of a nursery that instituted a system of fines for parents who were late picking up their offspring. The fines were set so low that parents saw it as a cheap form of additional child minding! (You'll find more about this when we discuss competition in Chapter 7, spirituality in Chapter 9 and ethics in Chapter 10.)

Back to exchange theory

Tie the notion of our *values triad* to *exchange* and it will come as no surprise that the ebb and flow of self-interest, mutuality and morality value action fields generates a vast kaleidoscope of simple and complex relational exchanges for social marketers.

Wood (2012) pondered "who is exchanging what value with whom?" Bagozzi (1975, p.38) explains, "there is most definitely an [mutually beneficial] exchange in social marketing relationships" and that "the exchange is not the simple quid pro quo notion characteristic of most economic exchanges." Individuals and stakeholders in different contexts are participants in complex networks and webs of value exchanges, which do not occur in isolation. From this new vantage point, we can see a broader view of all values (the individual, the family, the banana boat operator, the ice-cream vendor, the lifeguards, the local authority . . .), the perception of different values and their interconnections at work.

Any value action field or value exchange field (VEF) within a particular setting and context is driven by (1) a person's self-interest, mutuality and moral values; (2) their perceptions of others' self-interest, mutuality and moral values; (3) others' self-interest, mutuality and moral values; (4) others' perception of a person's self-interest, mutuality and moral values; (5) the self-interest, mutuality and moral values framed and amplified by the organisations and social institutions; (6) the person's perception of self-interest, mutuality and moral values framed and amplified by the organisations and social institutions; together with (7) the perception of the organisations and social institutions of the person's self-interest, mutuality and moral values; and finally, (8) others' perception of the institution self-interest, mutuality and moral values; and (9) vice versa!

In summary, exchanges aren't just about values *but also the relationship between what people value*. Exchanges do not happen in isolation; clients, stakeholders and competitors have values that shape and influence the exchanges social marketers need to co-create for behavioural change. This is captured by our VEFs and VAFs diagram in Figure 3.7.

For example, consider how autumn and winter usher in endless months of coughing and sneezing – the all too familiar signs of the contagious flu. The flu is a mild illness for many, yet it contributes to increased hospitalisation and medical costs, higher workforce absenteeism and decreases in productivity each year. Economic, medical and social

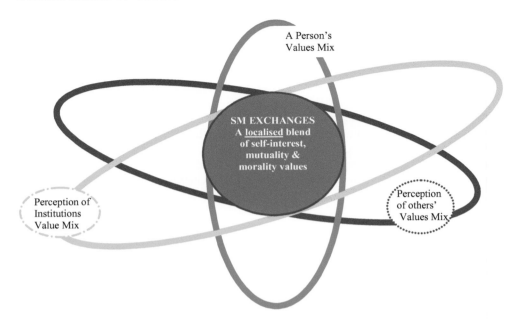

Figure 3.7 Social marketing's interacting value-driven exchanges and value action fields

(*Source:* Layton and Domegan 2016: 4)

costs mount as more vulnerable people, at higher risk of seasonal influenza, risk the exacerbation of existing medical conditions, severe pneumonia and multi-organ failure. The pathway to vaccination decision making and flu jab exchanges for target audiences is complex to say the least!

Personal factors are linked to flu awareness, knowledge, beliefs, attitudes and the person's motivation to get vaccinated or not. The individual's social networks, family, friends and workplace also play their part in the decision. Communications and the social norms, the personnel and professional relationships alongside media habits within a person's social networks, culminate in influences on each individual's factual and experiential practices around the flu and vaccination injections. In turn, wrapped around the diversity and variety of individuals social networks are environmental, societal, cultural, political and technological forces that shape and frame values, choice mechanisms, delivery methods and desired norms. Considering all these triple triad components (self-interest, mutuality and moral values among nurse, friends and hospital) to an individual's vaccination behaviour, it is clear there is nothing simplistic about a flu jab exchange (WHO 2015). In a real-life example, social marketing's triple triad value-driven exchange is mapped in Figure 3.8, showing the actual operation of value action fields and value-driven exchanges for flu vaccinations, or not, among nurses in a hospital setting.

In a similar manner, Kennedy looks at sustainability and ethical consumption in Case Study 18. She highlights how value exchanges are complex and far from fair trade for all – consumers, buyers, retailers, suppliers, workers – involved in triple triad value exchange chains and webs. In the world of fast fashion, deal-conscious consumers experience the purchase of

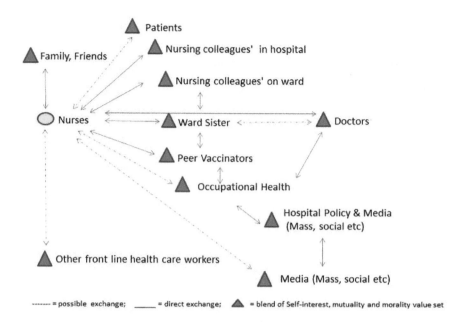

Figure 3.8 A nurses' flu vaccination triple triad value-driven exchanges and value action fields

(*Source:* adapted from Layton and Domegan 2016)

inexpensive clothing as "a symbol of consumer democracy", delivering the ability to "culti-vate a distinctive personality" relative to those of others. H&M facilitate these value-driven exchanges by selling their fast fashion as clothing "for everyone, not just the elite", while the workers – mainly invisible and distant females – face long unpredictable hours, low wages, non-existent maternity protection and life-threatening safety concerns.

The job of the social marketer – forever selling unseen benefits and appealing to multiple high-minded values, while suppressing or disrupting other less noble ones – is particularly challenging. In Wiebe's words (see Chapter 1) selling brotherhood seems to be far harder than selling soap. However, further consideration reveals that commercial marketers also spend a great deal of their time selling complex value-driven exchanges, as we outlined in Chapter 2. They offer us services such as restaurant meals, the enjoyment of which depends on much more than the simple quality of the food or the satisfaction of hunger; insurance from which (for the most part) we hope never to get any tangible return; and lifestyle benefits such as weight control. We happily pay more for branded goods because we trust them, feel more fashionable consuming them time and time again, or want to be seen to belong to a particular social group. Capturing this, Charles Revlon (arguably the doyen of soap sellers!) famously argued that, while his factories made cosmetics, the shops sold hope!

Some criticisms have been directed at exchange theory and its applicability to social marketing. The first concerns the suitability of the idea of mutual benefit for a discipline focused on doing good and was discussed in Chapter 2. The second is more profound and echoes our discussion of social cognitive theory. It concerns Kotler's third and fourth prerequisites: social marketers face problems in ensuring that people are capable of communication and delivery and also have the ability to accept or reject the offer. It assumes a balance of power that is often no more than a chimera; many groups in society lack the knowledge, articulacy and power to ensure a genuine compromise is reached. For example, those living in disadvantaged communities may not have either the money or the access necessary to eat fresh fruit and vegetables. This re-emphasises the need to maintain a collective as well as an individual perspective in social marketing; there is a continuous need to be cognisant of both the individual and social determinants of behaviour – and all the theories about this discussed above. It also underlines the importance of thinking critically about how people's lives are constrained by those with power. We will return to this theme in Chapter 7 onwards.

From theory to practice

At the beginning of this chapter, we noted the adage that 'there is nothing so practical as a good theory', so we will now have a go at using the theories we have explored.

EXERCISE 3.6   THE CASE OF GREENVILLE

Greenville is a town of 100,000 people with awful dental health. Children as young as five years old have significant caries and are in need of fillings. By the age of ten, 50 per cent have fillings, and many also have had to have teeth extracted. Because their teeth are associated with so much pain and discomfort, many of these extractions take place under general anaesthetic with, inevitably, a small risk of serious side effects – and even death. Widespread dental disease progresses into adulthood and, by the age of 40, a third of the population have lost all their natural teeth, a proportion that rises to two-thirds by the age of 60.

You are a social marketing consultant who has been retained by the local health authority to tackle this problem. What additional information would you seek about the people of Greenville in order to guide your efforts? Jot down your thoughts before continuing.

The theories suggest that three additional types of information would be helpful to address Greenville's problems.

Where are Greenville's people with regard to dental health? (Stages of change)

The people of Greenville know little about the principles of dental health, and do not feel it to be a very important issue. Toothbrushes and toothpaste are familiar items to them but they are considered to be expensive and non-essential. Other oral health products, such as floss and fluoride drops, are unfamiliar to them. Fillings, extractions and false teeth are seen as a normal and acceptable part of everyday life. Indeed, false teeth are felt to have many advantages over natural ones – not least the absence of pain and discomfort. Sugary food is also very popular in Greenville: it provides a cheap and tasty way of getting calories into the diet.

This suggests that they are very early on in the process of improving their own dental health. They are what Prochaska and DiClemente would term 'precontemplators', and this has obvious implications for any direct approaches you might make. It also begs questions about why the people of Greenville are so distant from the ideas of dental health.

Why are they in this position? (Social cognitive theory plus social norms theory, social ecological theory, social epistemological theory and social capital theory)

The people of Greenville are very poor, and dental health inevitably has a low priority compared with basics such as food, clothing and housing. The local health professionals are concerned about oral hygiene in Greenville, but feel they are fighting a losing battle. Their bosses in the nearby city are more concerned with issues of community safety and crime, which have a greater political priority. The oral hygiene product manufacturers see Greenville as a lost cause with little demand for their products, so take no interest in it. Their products are not promoted or widely distributed in Greenville. The sugar industry, on the other hand, sees it as a lucrative market opportunity. High-sugar products, such as candy, cakes and cookies, are relatively cheap, readily available and heavily promoted as nutritious and fun. After all, it is well known by all in Greenville that children love sweets and good parents regularly give treats to reward good behaviour. Journalists, doctors and scientists are seen as authoritarian and mistrusted, while friends and family are more reliable and dependable.

This insight forces us to think beyond the individual and recognise the social determinants of health, reinforcing the importance of the broader perspectives encapsulated in the social sciences school of thought. However, it leaves you wondering about how things might be improved.

How can change be encouraged? (Exchange theory)

There are some shafts of light. The young people of Greenville put a priority value on their appearance and a good smile, with clean white teeth, is an important part of this. There are also centrally funded welfare schemes that could allow community activity at no cost to the people of Greenville. Competition in the oral hygiene market is fierce and new markets are badly needed. At the same time, the sugar industry is coming under increasing scrutiny for its marketing practices.

The mists are now beginning to clear and a series of mutually beneficial exchanges can be planned with both people and stakeholders alike. Only the sugar industry looks like it may remain an obstacle to progress – but any marketer worthy of the name has to learn to best the competition.

Choosing your theory

As we explained at the outset, the aim in this chapter is not to present an exhaustive list of the 60-plus models discussed in the social marketing literature (Jackson 2005; Darnton 2008;

French *et al.* 2010). Instead, we simply wanted to demonstrate that theory is helpful – and will continually become more so: theory is constantly being tested and amended, giving the ability to explain more. With more explanatory and diagnostic power comes a greater capability and capacity to achieve innovation and transformation. So, having established that theory matters, the key skill is that of selecting the particular theory that will help you with your social marketing challenge. To this end, we suggest the following six rules:

1. **Theory is essential**

   There has to be a theoretical basis to any social marketing strategy. Without theory, there is no reliable basis upon which to explain or predict human behaviour. Without theory, there's no building on past experience or past knowledge.

2. **Exchange is at the core of social marketing**

   Exchange theory lies at the heart of social marketing. Exchange theory does not replace or supersede other behavioural theories, but its premise of mutually beneficial rewards is central to social marketing's change agenda. Without exchange theory, there is no social marketing.

3. **Combine theories**

   Behavioural theories that explain human actions/inactions together with theories of behaviour change are utilised to complement exchange theory in social marketing. As Brennan *et al.* explain in their overview of behaviour change models, theories and applications, "integrated approaches and synthesis of multiple theories may be more effective in promoting behaviour change than the use of an individual guiding theory" (2008: 1). Donovan (2011) agrees and points out there are now some generally agreed principles of behaviour change (see Box 3.4).

4. **Include social perspectives**

   Horses are renowned for their herd instincts. Survival in the wild for an individual horse is exceptionally rare. As a result, all horses have strong instincts to be with other horses. There is safety in numbers and horses are, inherently, social animals. In a similar manner, people don't live their lives in isolation (OK, except for hermits – but how many can you name?); the importance in our lives of exchange, values, networks and relationships testifies to this. That is why models like social cognitive theory and so many others recognise this collective dimension, and why this chapter has given it so much emphasis.

5. **Think about the change domain**

   In examining social marketing principles and exchange, there's been much discussion about changing the individual. Social marketing also considers altering the environment or situation to free or unblock the person to change their behaviour – think of the point of sale (POS) ban on cigarettes. Would-be non-smokers are reporting that the lack of POS helps them in their fight to give up cigarettes (Galvin 2011). The point is people behaviours are often situational behaviours. Therefore, choose the theory domain according to the appropriate level, be that downstream, midstream, upstream – or all three together, as we will see when we revisit systems thinking later on.

6. **Recognise the limits of theory**

Remember what we said at the beginning of the chapter. Theory is an attempt to model the complexities of the real world and will inevitably fall short in this task. It pays, therefore, to be sceptical and to question. As for other aspects of social marketing, theories are no substitute for critical thinking.

Now have a read of Box 3.4, which describes how theories from other sciences can be combined with exchange theory for behavioural change, and think about how the different theories and rules we have discussed in this chapter apply.

BOX 3.4   DONOVAN'S CONSENSUS

Social marketer Rob Donovan argues that "behavioural scientists have now generally come to the following set of principles with respect to an individual performing a recommended behaviour:

1. There are no physical or structural environmental constraints that prevent the behaviour being performed.

2. The individual has the skills and equipment necessary to perform the behaviour.

3. The individual perceives themselves to be capable of performing the behaviour.

4. The individual considers that the rewards/benefits of performing the behaviour outweigh the costs/disbenefits.

5. Social normative pressure to perform the behaviour is perceived to be greater than social normative pressure not to perform the behaviour.

6. The individual perceives the behaviour to be consistent with their self-image and internalised values (i.e., morally acceptable).

7. The individual perceives the behaviour to be consistent with their social roles and

8. The individual's emotional reaction (or expectation) in performing the behaviour is more positive than negative."

(*Source:* Donovan 2011)

BOX 3.5   CHOOSING THEORIES FOR BEHAVIOURAL CHANGE

The Food Dudes Programme combined taste acquisition theory (repeatedly tasting different foods) with reinforcement theory (rewards and positive role models) and exchange theory (behaviour change) for increased consumption of fruit and

(continued)

(continued)

vegetables among school-age children in the UK, Ireland, Italy, and now the USA (Food Dudes 2012).

Similarly behavioural reasoning theory is useful in pro-environmental behaviours, acting as the missing link to close the gap between our attitudes and beliefs and our behaviours; in urban bicycle commuting behavioural reasoning theory (BRT) explains the most cited reasons for cycling to work concern cost and time savings and well-being, while the reasons against focus on weather, inconvenience and danger (Claudy and Peterson 2014). McArdle (2016), examining buying recycled products using BRT, identifies the lack of engagement, price and availability as reasons against while feeling good and 'doing your bit' are mentioned as reasons for buying recycled.

Wrap-up

Ultimately, social marketers are interested in people – in understanding and responding to their needs. Theories are one important way of helping us think about them and how we might engage in the co-creation of value. They do this by explaining some of the behaviour we see or don't see. They also direct us to possible change options. Theories are guides but that is all they are. Theories don't design programmes or interventions. Theories don't do the co-listening or co-learning needed for mutually beneficial exchanges. Theories are no substitute for research and planning, critical reflection or creative thinking. They can inform our decision making about the needed exchange processes – about the plans we devise and the activities we engage in – but as we will see in the remaining chapters, so do other tools and techniques.

Against this background and by way of example, this chapter introduced you to the more popular theories of behaviour change that are of potential value to social marketers:

1. Stages of change, which shows that decisions about complex behaviour are often protracted, ranging from first beginning to considering the possibility of change through to trying to reinforce permanent change.

2. Social cognitive theory, which emphasises the social as well as the individual causes of behaviour, particularly when extended by social norms, social epistemology, social ecology and social capital theories.

3. Exchange theory (combined with values and relational thinking), which helps us think about how people can be encouraged to change.

This chapter is not – nor is it intended to be – an exhaustive list of theories. Its primary goal is to illustrate the enormous potential for theory to help, and hopefully in the process has removed some of the negative connotations the word can have. Finally, remember theory is only as useful as it is practical; in the next few chapters, we turn to these more applied considerations, starting with the social marketing planning process and toolbox.

Reflective questions

1. What is theory? What are its strengths and weaknesses?
2. How and why is theory relevant and useful to the social marketer?
3. Model and explain the stages of change theory.
4. "Social cognitive theory postulates that human behaviour is reciprocally determined by internal personal factors and environmental factors." Discuss with examples.
5. Social cognitive theory has a number of limitations with which social norms, social epistemology, social ecology and social capital theory can assist. Explain.
6. Define social capital theory, its components and relationships to health, education and quality of life.
7. Explain how exchange theory is foundational to social marketing.
8. How are values defined? What role do values play in marketing exchanges?
9. "What's more poignant and theoretically illuminating for the social marketer is the aptitude to select and use theories, rather than an in-depth descriptive knowledge of numerous models." Discuss with examples.

Reflective assignments

1. Visit www.peecworks.org/PEEC/PEEC_Gen/S01796129-01796169 and read about the uses of theory in social marketing. In particular, work your way through the appendices where behaviour is matched to theories and areas of application are mapped to models.
2. Locate and critique a social marketing intervention or programme that includes a theory section.
3. Download scholarly papers in relation to the Food Dudes case study. Describe how exchange theory is combined with theories from other fields, such as taste acquisition theory, to change children's behaviour about trying new fruits and vegetables.
4. Identify one behavioural theory and one behaviour change theory that could be applied to an issue facing an organisation of your choice. Outline the behaviour change implications of these theories for that organisation.
5. You are the social marketing manager for the WHO's Healthy Cities in your area. Choose one aspect of Healthy Cities, such as gardening, cycling, waste management or drunk driving, and develop a theory grid to identify relevant behavioural and behaviour change theories that could potentially underlie a social marketing initiative. The more specific you can be about the particular intervention, the better to guide the selection of theories.
6. Visit www.globalactionplan.ie/education/water-explorer/ to see how values, and their measurement, are used in a practical way with teachers and students, to underpin a water conservation programme.
7. Write a short essay on value action fields and value exchange as the basis for exchange, evolution and revolution for social marketing.
8. Consult the *Journal of Social Marketing* and/or *Social Marketing Quarterly* to read a classic or contemporary article, or more, on social marketing's use of theories, especially exchange, to advance your understanding of this key principle.
9. Update your 'Rebels with a cause' checklist to incorporate the benefits of using theories in behavioural change work and social marketing.

References

Alderson, W. (1957) *Marketing Behaviour and Executive Action: A Functionalist Approach to Marketing Theory*. Homewood, IL: Richard D. Irwin Inc.

Andreasen, A.R. (1995) *Marketing Social Change: Changing Behavior to Promote Health, Social Development, and the Environment*. San Francisco, CA: Jossey-Bass.

Bagozzi, R. (1975) 'Marketing and exchange', *Journal of Marketing*, October 39(4): 32–39.

Bagozzi, R. (1979) 'Toward a formal theory of marketing exchanges', in O.C. Ferrell, S.W. Brown and C.W. Lamb Jr (eds) *Conceptual and Theoretical Developments in Marketing*. Chicago, IL: American Marketing Association, pp. 431–447.

Bandura, A. (1986) *Social Foundations of Thought and Action: A Social Cognitive Approach*. Englewood Cliffs, NJ: Prentice Hall.

Basler, H.D. (1995) 'Patient education with reference to the process of behavioral change', *Patient Education and Counseling*, 26: 93–98.

Brennan, L., Binney, W., Parker L., Aleti, T. and Nguyen, D. (eds) (2008) *Behaviour Change Models: Theory and Application for Social Marketing*. Cheltenham: Edward Elgar.

Bronfenbrenner, U. (1988) 'Interacting systems in human development', in N. Bolger, C. Caspi, G. Downey and M. Moorehouse (eds) *Persons in Context: Developmental Processes*. Cambridge, UK: Cambridge University Press, pp. 25–30. Also see www.des.emory.edu/mfp/302/302bron.PDF (accessed March 2016).

Brown, A., Moodie, C. and Hastings, G. (2009) 'A longitudinal study of policy effect (smoke-free legislation) on smoking norms: ITC Scotland/United Kingdom', *Nicotine and Tobacco Research*, 11(8): 924–932.

Buxton, K., Wyse, J. and Mercer, T. (1996) 'How applicable is the stages of change model to exercise behaviour?', *Health Education Journal*, 55: 239–257.

Clapp, J.D., Lange, J.E., Russell, C., Shillington, A. and Voas, R. (2003) 'A failed norms social marketing campaign', *Journal of Study of Alcohol*, 64: 409–414.

Claudy, M and Peterson, M. (2014) 'Understanding the underutilization of urban bicycle commuting: a behavioral reasoning perspective', *Journal of Public Policy & Marketing*, 33(2): 173–187.

Coggans, N., Cheyne, B. and McKellar, S. (2003) *The Life Skills Training Drug Education Programme: A Review of Research*. Edinburgh: Scottish Executive Drug Misuse Research Programme, Effective Interventions Unit.

Crompton, T. (2010) *Common Cause: The Case for Working with our Cultural Values*. Online: http://valuesandframes.org/ (accessed May 2016).

Darnton, A. (2008) *GSR Behaviour Change Knowledge Review. Reference Report: An overview of behaviour change models and their uses*. London: Government Social Research (GSR). Online: www.civilservice.gov.uk/wp-content/uploads/2011/09/Behaviour_change_reference_report_tcm6-9697.pdf (accessed May 2016).

Davidson, R. (1992) 'Prochaska and DiClemente's model of change: A case study (Editorial)', *British Journal of Addiction*, 87(6): 821–822.

DiClemente, C.C. (2005) 'A premature obituary for the transtheoretical model: A response to West (2005)', *Addiction*, 100(8): 1046–1048.

Donaldson, S.I., Graham, J.W. and Hansen, W.B. (1994) 'Testing the generalizability of intervening mechanism theories: Understanding the effects of adolescent drug use prevention interventions', *Journal of Behavioral Medicine*, 17(2): 195–216.

Donovan, R. (2011) 'Theoretical models of behaviour change', Ch. 1 in G. Hastings, K. Angus and C. Bryant (eds) *The SAGE Handbook of Social Marketing*. London: Sage Publications.

Food Dudes (2012) *Food Dudes Around the World*. Online: www.fooddudes.co.uk/en/fda-around-the-world/ (accessed May 2016).

French, J., Blair-Stevens, C., McVey, D. and Merritt, R. (2010) *Social Marketing and Public Health: Theory and Practice*. Oxford: Oxford University Press.

Galvin, C. (2011) *The Ban on the Display and Promotion of Tobacco at Point of Sale in Ireland*. MSc thesis, National University of Ireland, Galway.

Gately, N. (2015) *Operation Transformation: Facebook's role in shifting lifestyle change from behavioural intention to behavioural commitment*. MComm thesis, National University of Ireland, Galway.

Glanz, K. and Bishop, D.B. (2010) 'The role of behavioral science theory in development and implementation of public health interventions', *Public Health*, 31: 399.

Hamilton, W., Biener, L. and Brennan, R. (2008) 'Do local tobacco regulations influence perceived smoking norms? Evidence from adult and youth surveys in Massachusetts', *Health Education Research*, 3(4): 709–722.

Hansen, W.B. (1990) 'Theory and implementation of the social influence model of primary prevention', in K. Rey, C. Faegre and P. Lowery (eds) *Prevention Research Findings: 1988, OSAP Prevention Monograph Number 3*. Rockville, MD: OSAP.

Hansen, W.B. (1992) 'School-based substance abuse prevention: A review of the state of the art in curriculum', *Health Education Research*, 7(3): 411.

Hastings, G., Brown, A.K. and Anker, T. (2010) 'Theory in social marketing', in M.J. Baker and M. Saren (eds) *Marketing Theory: A Student Text,* 2nd edition. London: Sage Publications, pp. 330–344. ISBN 9781849204651.

Hastings, G. and Lowry, R. (2010) 'Social marketing: A tale of beer, marriage and public health', in A.E.A. Steptoe (ed.) *Handbook of Behavioral Medicine*. New York: Springer Science & Business Media.

Hastings, G. B. and MacFadyen, L. (2000) *Keep Smiling: No one's going to die. An analysis of internal documents from the tobacco industry's main UK advertising agencies*. The Centre for Tobacco Control Research and the Tobacco Control Resource Centre. London: British Medical Association.

Hyndman, D., Hodges, A. and Goldie, N. (2007) *National Landcare Programme Evaluation 2003–06*, p. 25

Jackson, T. (2005) *Motivating Sustainable Consumption: A Review of Evidence on Consumer Behaviour and Behaviour Change*. London: Sustainable Development Research Network (SDRN). Online: www.sd-research.org.uk/wp-content/uploads/motivatingscfinal_000.pdf (accessed May 2016).

Jones, J. (2011) 'Lessons learned from the London riots', *The Irish Times*, Tuesday, 30 August, p. 20.

Kenny, P. and Hastings, G. (2011) 'Understanding social norms: Upstream and downstream applications for social marketers', Ch. 4 in G. Hastings, K. Angus and C. Bryant (eds) *The SAGE Handbook of Social Marketing*. London: Sage Publications.

Kotler, P. (2000) *Marketing Management – Analysis, Planning, Implementation and Control,* 10th edition. London: Prentice Hall International.

Layard, R. (2005) *Happiness: Lessons from a New Science*. London: Allen Lane.

Layton, R.A. (2009) 'On economic growth, marketing systems, and the quality of life', *Journal of Macromarketing*, 29(4): 349–362.

Layton, R. A. (2015) 'Formation, growth and adaptive change in marketing systems', *Journal of Macromarketing*, 35(3): 302–319.

Layton, R.A. and Domegan, C.T. (2016) *Initiating and Managing Disruptive Social Marketing – A Systems Approach*, ISMC Wollongong, Australia, September 26.

Lefebvre, C. (1992) 'Social marketing and health promotion', Ch. 8 in R. Bunton and G. MacDonald (eds) *Health Promotion: Disciplines and Diversity*. London: Routledge.

Lefebvre, C. (2011) 'Social models for social marketing', Ch. 2 in G. Hastings, K. Angus and C. Bryant (eds) *The SAGE Handbook of Social Marketing*. London: Sage Publications.

Levitt, S. and Dubner, S.J. (2005) *Freakonomics: A Rogue Economist Explores the Hidden Side of Everything*. London: Allen Lane.

Lewin, K. (1951) *Field Theory in Social Science; Selected Theoretical Papers*. Edited by D. Cartwright. New York: Harper & Row.

McArdle, M. (2016) 'Closing the loop – values and reasons in the value-action gap for recycled consumer paper products'. Doctoral Colloquium, 42nd Macromarketing conference, Dublin, Ireland, 13 July.

MacFadyen, L., Hastings, G.B., MacKintosh, A.M. and Lowry, R.J. (1998) 'Tobacco marketing and children's smoking: moving the debate beyond advertising and sponsorship'. Paper presented at the 27th EMAC Conference, Stockholm, Sweden, 20—23 May. In *Track 3 'Marketing Strategy and Organization': Proceedings, 27th EMAC Conference – Marketing Research and Practice*, pp. 431–456. Stockholm: European Marketing Academy.

McHugh, P. (2013) *The Use of Social Marketing and Innovation Theory for the Development of Process Indicators for Science Communication*. PhD thesis, National University of Ireland, Galway, Ireland.

McHugh, P. and Domegan, C. (2013) 'From reductionism to holism: How social marketing captures the bigger picture through system indicators', in K. Kubacki and S. Rundle-Thiele (eds) *Contemporary Issues in Social Marketing*. Newcastle, UK: Cambridge Scholars Publishing.

McHugh, P., Domegan, C., Devaney, M. and Hastings, G. (2015) A Set of *Sea Change Guiding Principles and Protocols*. EU Sea Change Project.

MacKinnon, D.P., Johnson, C.A., Pentz, M., and Dwyer, J.H. (1991) 'Mediating mechanisms in a school-based drug prevention program: First year effects of the Midwestern Prevention Project', *Health Psychology*, 10(3): 164–172.

Maibach, E.W. (1993) 'Social marketing for the environment: Using information campaigns to promote environmental awareness and behavior change', *Health Promotion International*, 3(8): 211.

Maibach, E.W. and Cotton, D. (1995) 'Moving people to behaviour change: A staged social cognitive approach to message design', Ch. 3 in E.W. Maibach and R.L. Parrott (eds) *Designing Health Messages: Approaches From Communication Theory and Public Health Practice*. Newbury Park, CA: Sage Publications, pp. 41–64.

Prochaska, J.O., and DiClemente, C.C. (1983) 'Stages and processes of self-change of smoking: Toward an integrative model of change', *Journal of Consulting and Clinical Psychology*, 51(3): 390–395.

Prochaska, J.O. and Velicer, W.F. (1997) 'The transtheoretical model of health behavior change', *American Journal of Health Promotion*, 12(1): 38–48.

Prochaska, J.O., DiClemente, C.C. and Norcross, J.C. (1992) 'In search of how people change', *American Psychologist*, 47: 1102–1114.

Rothmans UK (1998) 'Young Adult Smokers', *Smoking Behaviour and Lifestyles 1994–1997*. The Rothmans (UK) Marketing Services, October.

Schwartz, S.H. (2012) 'An Overview of the Schwartz Theory of Basic Values'. *Online Readings in Psychology and Culture*, 2(1).

Sussman, S. (1989) 'Two social influence perspectives of tobacco use development and prevention', *Health Education Research*, 4: 213–223.

West, R. (2005) 'Time for a change: putting the Transtheoretical (Stages of Change) Model to rest', *Addiction*, 100(8): 1036–1039.

WHO (2015) 'Tailoring Immunization Programmes for Seasonal Influenza (TIP FLU)', A guide for increasing health care workers' uptake of seasonal influenza vaccination, Division of Communicable Diseases, Health Security and Environment of the WHO Regional Office for Europe, Denmark.

Wood, M. (2012) 'Marketing social marketing', *Journal of Social Marketing*, 2(2): 94

Zak, Paul, (2011) 'Moral Markets', *Journal of Economic Behaviour & Organization*, 77: 212–233.

Chapter **4**

Making it happen – the toolbox

THE IMPORTANCE OF VISION

I say to you today, my friends, so even though we face the difficulties of today and tomorrow, I still have a dream. It is a dream deeply rooted in the American dream.

I have a dream that one day this nation will rise up and live out the true meaning of its creed: "We hold these truths to be self-evident: that all men are created equal."

I have a dream that one day on the red hills of Georgia the sons of former slaves and the sons of former slave owners will be able to sit down together at the table of brotherhood.

I have a dream that one day even the state of Mississippi, a state sweltering with the heat of injustice, sweltering with the heat of oppression, will be transformed into an oasis of freedom and justice.

I have a dream that my four little children will one day live in a nation where they will not be judged by the color of their skin but by the content of their character.

I have a dream today.

I have a dream that one day, down in Alabama, with its vicious racists, with its governor having his lips dripping with the words of interposition and nullification; one day right there in Alabama, little black boys and black girls will be able to join hands with little white boys and white girls as sisters and brothers.

I have a dream today.

(Martin Luther King Jr, August 28, 1963)

Martin Luther King's ringing words remind us that any enterprise needs a vision; a clear declaration of what its authors seek to achieve. King calls it a dream rather than a vision, perhaps reflecting the obvious challenges that stood in the way of racial harmony at that point in US history, but spelling out his destination – however distant – in this way laid the foundations for success. First, it put all his followers and colleagues on the same page: they could agree, argue or even leave the movement – but they knew where they stood. Second, it expressed the vision in a deeply engaging way: a perfect example of the creative orientation we discussed in Chapter 2. King connected with his listeners' hearts as well as their minds. Third, and most importantly, he laid the basis for action. Having identified the destination, the journey could now be planned.

In this chapter, we take up his cue and move on from theories and principles to examine the practicalities of changing behaviour. Like him, we need a vision; like him, we must remember that our efforts depend on voluntary cooperation; like him, we need to think long term. Tactics have to be bedded in strategy, transactions built into relationships.

We begin with the vital importance of strategic planning, which helps map out a route towards our equivalent of King's dream. The social marketing planning process (see Figure 4.1) starts by appraising the situation, defining the problem and assessing the competing forces. This avoids the danger of making assumptions about the challenge at hand or how we should consider addressing it. Specifically, it helps answer the three crucial strategic questions that lie at the heart of any social marketing endeavour: *who* we would like to do *what*, and how we can *best encourage them to do it*.

King's speech suggests there were multiple possible answers to these questions for the civil rights movement in 1963. The *who* could have been the ancestors of both sides of the slave trade; state and federal political leaders or the next generation. The *what* could, respectively, have been to come together in mutual understanding; to pass enlightened race relations policies or to carry on the struggle. The third strand, encouragement, comes from his inspirational presentation. The job of the social marketing planner is to assess these alternatives and chart them against the current situation to decide which show most promise and how they can best be implemented.

More specifically, the *who* question leads us to 'segmentation and targeting', which helps improve our understanding of our clients, and lays the ground work for helping to meet their needs more effectively. Similarly, the *what* question makes us think about our objectives – the milestones en route to our vision – a crucial first step in both identifying our direction of travel and, later on, determining whether or not we have arrived.

These preparations bring us to the crux of the matter: how do we devise an offering that will encourage the target group to engage in an exchange with us not just once but repeatedly? What is our equivalent of Martin Luther King's inspiration? To approach this task, marketers like to think about getting the right product to the right people in the right place at the right price – 'right' being that which best satisfies their customers. Social marketing adopts a similar mix of tools, recognising that in the arena of voluntary behaviour change it is vital to make your offerings as appealing, accessible, available and appreciated as possible.

Finally, to cement in the strategic progress being made, marketers pull this thinking together with the idea of positioning. King made sure his followers understood the full power and potential of his offer – nothing short of a new dawn. Social marketers need to be equally far-sighted – and indeed equally ambitious.

This chapter will provide a detailed explanation of all these concepts and processes.

Learning outcomes

By the end of this chapter, you should be able to:

✓ Explain that planning guides strategic as well as tactical decision making, and ensures that our efforts take account of the social context

✓ Undertake a stakeholder and problem boundary analysis

✓ Discuss why segmentation and targeting are important, and how to do them

✓ Outline the importance of setting measurable and realistic objectives

✓ Use the social marketing mix as a tool for devising appealing, accessible, available and appreciated (the 4As) offerings

✓ Demonstrate the practical application of positioning in social marketing.

Key words

Strategic planning – intervention mix – objectives – place – positioning – price – product – promotion – participation – segmentation – situation analysis – stakeholder analysis – strategic planning – targeting.

Strategic planning

Constructing a successful programme to change behaviour is like climbing a Himalayan peak. You need to acquire or devise a map, take careful compass bearings, check your equipment and ensure you have the skills and resources to reach the top. Marketing therefore puts great emphasis on planning and any marketing enterprise worthy of the name begins with a marketing plan. Figure 4.1 presents a typical schema for one.

As can be seen, it comprises a number of standard steps that guide the marketer through accepted best practice from an analysis of the operating environment through to outcome evaluation. Before discussing the detail of these steps, three general points should be noted.

The first reflects what might be called the gestalt of marketing planning. Seen as a whole, the plan becomes more than the sum of its parts. It provides a progressive process of learning about the market and its particular exchanges. This learning takes place within particular initiatives. For example, a systematically produced and carefully researched cycling proficiency initiative for schoolchildren will enable social marketers to improve their understanding of schoolchildren and their desires, and thereby to enhance the initiative.

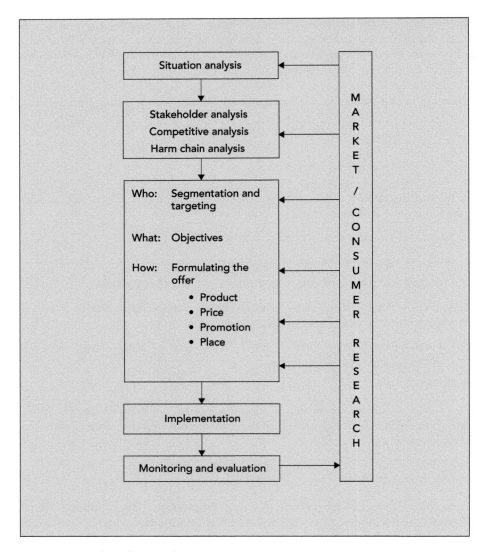

Figure 4.1 A social marketing plan

(*Source:* adapted from Hastings and Elliott 1993)

Second, the learning process also takes place between initiatives. The social marketer will be able to use the lessons learned from one initiative as a basis for future projects. Thus, the process is not just progressive but also cyclical; hence, the 'return arrow' in Figure 4.1. Furthermore, the development of understanding is not restricted to repeated cycling proficiency initiatives; social marketing efforts in quite different areas, such as pedestrian safety or sexual health, may well provide useful insights. The link between cycling and sex may seem tenuous, but both are social behaviours that are heavily influenced by perceptions and imagery. Both also have to address the competing interests of safety and social acceptability. Condoms and cycling helmets, in fact, have a lot in common: adolescent behaviour.

In this way, when marketing planning is seen as a whole and also an ongoing process, it can maximise the chance of success both for a particular initiative and, more importantly in the longer term, for health, safety and the environment in general. Thus, as well as providing the tactical support through various marketing tools, planning also guides strategic thinking. This idea of *progressive and continuous learning* is absolutely fundamental to social marketing. We've seen it in exchange theory alongside relationship marketing in Chapter 3 and we will return to it when we discuss research in Chapter 5, communications in Chapter 6 and systems thinking in Chapter 11.

A situation analysis

Strategic vision requires breadth as well as length, and the third general lesson we should draw from marketing planning concerns the importance of setting our actions within a broader context. To return to our Himalayan metaphor, before choosing your mountaineers and getting them equipped, you need to check out some bigger issues: has the mountain been climbed before? What are the weather conditions at different times of the year? Do you have to get permission from the necessary authorities to undertake the expedition? Without this advance thinking, you are not only less likely to succeed, you will also put your sponsor's resources and the lives of your team in unnecessary jeopardy – you will be behaving unethically as well as unprofessionally.

The business community has long recognised that economic success is dependent not only on their own 'micro-level' marketing, but also on the macro political and economic environment within which the company operates. Standard marketing texts (Jobber 2004; Kotler and Armstrong 2004; Wilson and Gilligan 2005) typically divide this macro environment into six forces: political, economic, social, technological, environmental and legal (PESTEL) (see Figure 4.2).

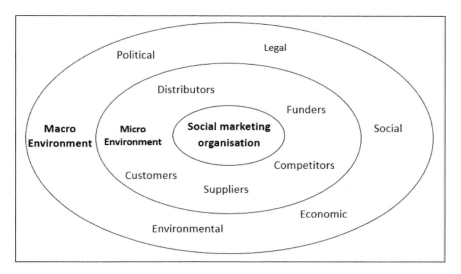

Figure 4.2 The marketing environment

Effective business planning includes careful monitoring of these forces. In many instances – such as the weather conditions on our Himalayan peak – they are largely uncontrollable. Technological developments, for example, or social mores cannot typically be manipulated at will. However, companies still need to know about them so that they can respond to the threats and opportunities they present. And these forces can have a fundamental impact on decisions about marketing strategies. For example, in the United States in the early 1970s, tobacco companies were required to fund health promotion messages at a similar level to their own expenditure on television advertising. After just a few years of this, they elected to withdraw from television altogether, transferring their promotional budgets to other, unfettered media (US Department of Health and Human Services 1989). Similarly, in the UK, television advertising for cigarettes was banned in 1965, but the decade saw a steady increase in advertising spend reflecting the move to other media (ASH 2006).

In other instances, however, there is at least the potential for business to exert influence. Thus, the tightening of tobacco control policy in Europe over the last twenty years has greatly influenced the tobacco industry's marketing to both consumers and stakeholders – in the latter case spawning numerous campaigns to stave off legislation in such areas as smoke-free provisions and advertising bans (Hastings and Angus 2004).

This can include marketing to the final consumer, or it may not. For example, a UK brewer conducting a situation analysis in the late 1980s would have identified a major threat to their business in the form of the Government Monopolies and Mergers Commission undertaking a review of the industry. This ultimately forced brewers to sell off their retail outlets, but careful and sustained marketing to politicians (rather than consumers) mitigated the extent of the changes (Stokes 1997).

Exactly the same thinking applies in social marketing. Sticking with the same sector, anyone trying to respond intelligently to the UK problem of binge drinking would need to undertake a careful assessment of licensing laws, which have made alcohol more available than at any time since the First World War, taxation policy, which has brought prices to their lowest level in thirty years, and technologies that have delivered a range of new products onto the market – before considering consumer-directed efforts.

Decisions about how to respond to environmental forces are made by mapping the analysis against the strengths and weaknesses of the marketing organisation. This is often referred to as a SWOT analysis – the strengths and weaknesses of the organisations are laid alongside the opportunities and threats of the environment. In this way, thinking is influenced not just by what is out there, but also by the marketer's capacity to respond. To stick with our Himalayan metaphor, the weather conditions, physical environment and sheer scale of the peaks have been tackled in two distinct ways over the years. Some have chosen to invest enormous funds in very large parties of climbers and porters who effectively lay siege to the mountain. They succeed almost by a process of attrition. Others, who lack – or disapprove of using – such extensive resources opt for a much quicker in-and-out approach with a small, lightly equipped team. It is not that either is intrinsically wrong or right, just that two sets of factors – the external and the internal – need to be taken into account as some aspects will be helpful to our climb and some will be harmful.

In the case of binge drinking, the social marketer needs to think about their capacity to influence policy makers or the market. This may well be considerable, and an 'upstream' approach can be contemplated. Alternatively, they may conclude that their power in this domain is actually very limited and the only thing they can do is produce downstream efforts targeting teenagers, however challenging this might be in an unsympathetic environment.

Furthermore, many social marketers are faced with a 'done deal'; they respond to a tender to do a specific task, to reduce binge drinking or some other behaviour in a particular population, and the approach is already defined – perhaps specifying a public education campaign or schools-based initiative. They have to take on trust that someone else has done the necessary strategic analysis.

In both instances, it still makes sense to do some of this thinking themselves: at the very least, it will give them a realistic idea of the task they face, as well as potentially useful insights into any shortfalls in their performance. It will also enable them to engage constructively with the funder and help them to think more carefully in the future. Gradually, the result will be a very desirable increase in the strategic emphasis of all our work. Exercise 4.1 illustrates the point.

EXERCISE 4.1   SOCIAL MARKETING AND TOBACCO CONTROL IN COLOMBIA

Go to Case Study 13, where you will read about tobacco industry point of sale and civil societies monitoring activities in Colombia. You are a social marketing consultant working for a major NGO and have been charged with developing a five-year marketing plan which will help Colombia move towards an 'endgame for tobacco'. What will your SWOT (strengths, weaknesses, opportunities and threats) analysis look like? Scotland is one of several countries around the world that has declared a date (2034) for its tobacco endgame. You can consult their five-year strategy online.[1]

If you are daunted by this task (and you should be), just imagine what it would be like trying to tackle the tobacco problems of Colombia without these insights.

A stakeholder analysis

The planning process continues by assessing what is currently happening in the marketplace (or the macro environment in Figure 4.2). We need to establish who the key stakeholders are and what they are doing or might do. Stakeholders are 'all of those groups and individuals that can affect, or are affected by' the social marketer's behaviour change proposal (Freeman 1984). They may control assets, information, communications, networks and markets, as will be seen in Chapters 6 and 10. In many cases, their support is needed to implement behaviour change in Case Study 14, and occasionally they are the problem, the dark side of the marketplace. In other cases, as we discussed in Chapter 2, they can represent direct opposition to change, as Rey-Pino and colleagues show in Case Study 13.

It is clear from these examples, that a stakeholder analysis takes a very inclusive and collective approach. Bryson (2004) argues that stakeholder analysis has never been more important due to the increasingly interconnected nature of the world. Many complex, wicked and commons problems, including an 'ocean-literate' society, as Patricia McHugh *et al.* show in Case Study 21, "encompasses or affects numerous people, groups and organizations . . . no one is fully in charge . . . instead many individuals, groups and organizations are involved or affected or have some partial responsibility to act" (Bryson 2004).

Stakeholder analysis is the systematic mapping of these potentially influential actors, which might include suppliers, trade unions, charities, policy makers, commercial firms, special interest groups, governments, banks, the media and many others. Translating this into practice, the Australian Red Cross Blood Service (ARCBS) identified 11 key (or primary) stakeholder groups for its work as shown in Box 4.1.

BOX 4.1   KEY STAKEHOLDER GROUPS FOR THE ARCBS

1. The Commonwealth Government of Australia

2. The parent non-profit organisation

3. State and territory governments

4. Union representatives (including some ARCBS employees)

5. The health sector (including end users in hospitals)

6. Regulators

7. Suppliers

8. Major commercial stakeholders

9. Blood donors

10. R&D institutions

11. The media

(*Source:* Fletcher *et al.* 2003: 513)

Stakeholders can be divided into three broad groups – incumbents, challengers and regulating agencies. Incumbents are the dominant organisations; they are happy with the way things are and wish to preserve the status quo. Challengers are less privileged than the incumbents.

Table 4.1 Stakeholder characteristics

Incumbents	Challengers	Regulating agencies
Dominant in your system	Entrepreneurial or innovative groups and individuals	Responsible for overseeing compliance with system rules
Highly influential and powerful in your system	Have very little influence and power over the operation of your system	Facilitate the smooth running of the system
Interests and views are heavily reflected in your system	Less privileged than the incumbents	Internal to your system and distinct from external state structures
Have claims to a large proportion of resources within your system	Recognise the dominant logic of incumbents	They are there to reinforce the dominant logic and safeguard the interests of incumbents
The rules and regulations favour them	Can often describe another vision for the system and their position in it	Defenders of the status quo
They have a privileged position in your system	Not in open revolt or aggressive purveyors of oppositional logics	Form in response to pressures by incumbents or challengers
Benefit from the current situation	Often conform to the prevailing order (possibly grudgingly)	
Wish to preserve stability	Awaiting new opportunities to challenge the structure of your system	
	May strive for a crisis or shift, opening up the incumbents to entrepreneurial and innovative initiatives	
	Will work to bring external and internal changes to the point where stability is in danger	

(*Sources*: Fligstein 2001; Fligstein and McAdam 2011; Layton 2014)

They often conform to the prevailing order, but are awaiting new opportunities to challenge the structure of the existing system. Regulating agencies are in the system to defend the status quo and facilitate its smooth running.

This classification helps to recognise that different stakeholders have different levels and types of interest. The key consideration is how power is dispersed among the stakeholders. Does power reside within a few stakeholders (making them more influential) or is power spread out (making them less influential)? The ARCBS deemed all 11 stakeholders to be powerful and highly influential to their performance.

The ARCBS used stakeholder identification and analysis to identify the Key Performance Areas they needed to pay attention to for strategic deployment and management of their resources (human, structural and relational). They achieved this through stakeholder workshops and interviews where product safety and sufficiency emerged as the top two priorities (see Box 4.2) for ARCBS to deliver a valued public service and fulfil their *raison d'être*.

BOX 4.2   STAKEHOLDER ANALYSIS AND KEY PERFORMANCE AREAS

1. **Safe product**   All matters relating to the safety of products

2. **Product sufficiency**   Availability of products as and where required

3. **R&D and other services**   Provision of specialist services and R&D initiatives

4. **External management** All aspects of governance and compliance

(*Source:* Fletcher *et al.* 2003: 525)

Stakeholder analysis then leads to a scrutiny of possible behaviour change strategies, if any, with each stakeholder. Stakeholders can be helpful in changing behaviours, such as schools, or they can hinder change, causing harm. If helpful, there is an opportunity for social marketers to collaborate with them in the social marketing exchange, through a greater co-ordination, interaction and integration of efforts. This normally happens when there are many stakeholders with dispersed power and a win-win is possible for all.

If stakeholders are quintessentially harm-causing, such as tobacco firms, the only option for the social marketer is a *competitive strategy*, where the social marketing norm of a win–win can become a win–lose. We will discuss this dimension of social marketing in greater detail in Chapter 7.

This analysis can take on a much broader system-wide form if we think about complex, multifactorial issues such as inequalities, conflict resolution or climate change – a point we come back to in Chapter 11. The extent of change needed in these instances can generate opposition from stakeholders who have a vested interest in the status quo. As we will discuss in Chapters 7 and 8, this is especially true of the corporate sector, which – because of past marketing investments (especially in brand-building), along with its commitment to growth and increasing shareholder value – is at best going to consider only minor *improvements or redesigns* to an imperfect system. Radical, disruptive change, however necessary, is simply too threatening.

To recap, stakeholder analysis involves three broad steps:

1. Identify, map and prioritise stakeholders.

2. Establish stakeholder propensity to be helpful or harmful.

3. Choose your stakeholder strategy: collaborate or compete.

For examples of stakeholder analysis in action, look at Case Study 15, as well as Case Studies 8, 9 and 19. From a practical perspective, try Exercise 4.2.

EXERCISE 4.2   CONDUCT A STAKEHOLDER ANALYSIS

Take the three steps to stakeholder analysis and apply to a behaviour change option of your choice. When you have done this, take a look at Case Studies 8 and 19 and use them to reassess your work.

When stakeholders matter, Case Studies 8 and 10 illustrate how useful stakeholder mapping is to the social marketer to address the social ill at hand. This will also suggest the relevant strategies (cooperate and partnerships or compete) for the social marketer to pursue when designing their offering.

In summary, a stakeholder analysis reveals two powerful ideas: malign systems (harmful exchanges) and benign systems (hale and hearty exchanges), which social marketing should both map and then respond to using the rest of the planning process.

The rest of the planning process

Once these macro and micro environments have been examined and factored in, social marketing planning focuses on the nitty-gritty of *who* needs to do *what*, and *how* they can be encouraged to do it. Or more formally, segmentation and targeting, setting objectives and devising an offering – each of which is discussed next. The notion of 'positioning', i.e. how their offering sits in a client's mind and with competing offerings, which helps social marketers to think through these decisions, is also considered here.

Segmentation and targeting

Marketers recognise that we are all unique: we all have different make ups and experiences and live in varied circumstances. This means we will also have diverse needs, and because marketing is all about meeting these needs as well as possible, the ideal marketer would offer a bespoke service – a unique offering for each and every one of us. This is clearly impractical in most instances. A few (typically expensive) operators – such as tailors and architects – can offer this level of customisation, but in most cases a compromise is necessary. This involves dividing the population into reasonably homogeneous segments and then choosing particular target groups to approach with an offering that better matches their needs than would one designed for the population as a whole.

There are a number of criteria which a commercial marketer can use to segment the population into potential target markets (see Box 4.3). Personal characteristics – typically subdivided into demographic, psychographic and geo-demographic variables – present an obvious option. Life stage, personality and where we live can all have a fairly apparent impact on the sort of products and services we consume. For example, a car manufacturer might consider offering people carriers to families, small runabouts to single women and sports cars to testosterone-charged men.

BOX 4.3   THREE COMMONLY USED SEGMENTATION CRITERIA

1. *Personal characteristics*: demographic, psychographic and geo-demographic variables can all have an important link to behaviour.

2. *Past behaviour*: in commercial terms, for example, previous purchasing can provide important insights; in social marketing, proximity to the desired behaviour (perhaps measured using Stages of Change) can be useful.

3. *Benefits sought*: why people do as they do at present – and how these motives vary – can be a sensible way of subdividing the population.

Previous purchase behaviour – usage of a particular product category, loyalty to a brand and related attitudes – also provides a helpful tool for sorting potential customers. Someone who has bought a BMW before is a likely prospect for another one – and a better prospect for a Mercedes than, say, a Ford customer. The benefits different customer groups are seeking can also help with categorisation. As we have already alluded to, cars actually offer far more than a means of transportation: they can represent modern family living, independence or machismo.

From a social marketing perspective, all these segmentation approaches offer potential, but they often need extending and developing. Try Exercise 4.3 before proceeding.

EXERCISE 4.3   DIETARY SEGMENTATION

You have been charged with developing a strategy for improving the dietary health of the Scottish population. As a first step, you are considering the task of segmentation. How might the three approaches we have discussed here – personal, behavioural and benefit – help? Can you see ways in which they should be developed or extended for use in a social marketing context?

Demographic characteristics have obvious implications for health. Gender, for example, provides a sensible starting point for many screening programmes; age and ethnicity are related to specific conditions such as Alzheimer's disease and sickle cell anaemia; and in Exercise 4.3 schoolchildren have particular dietary needs, as do the elderly and nursing mothers. Health status itself provides a useful extension to the personal characteristics we might consider – you might want to target specific efforts at people who are obese or have type 2 diabetes.

Psychographic methods also show potential, particularly if we think back to social cognitive theory (Chapter 3), which shows that characteristics such as self-efficacy are an important determinant of behaviour.

In both Chapters 1 and 3, we noted that inequalities are linked to damaging health, social and environmental behaviours, such as smoking, unhealthy diet, crime and recycling rates. Perhaps not surprisingly, they are also linked to greater illness and earlier death. In the UK, for example, men in the deprived inner-city area of Glasgow have a life expectancy of just under 73 years, while their peers in Dorset live on average more than a decade longer.[2] This suggests that degree of disadvantage/inequality is a very useful extension to geo-demographic segmentation, particularly because it does tend to cluster in well-defined localities such as inner-city housing schemes.

Social marketing's focus on behaviour also suggests that **behavioural** segmentation has potential. Furthermore, again thinking back to Chapter 3, it can be linked with stages of change and social norms theories. Populations can be segmented according to their proximity to a particular behaviour or perceptions thereof – with precontemplators being approached differently from contemplators for instance. In our exercise, this might involve plotting the population in terms of their readiness to change their eating habits.

Pause and go to Case Study 17 'From concept to action' for an excellent and cutting-edge example of segmentation in action. Using segmentation tools from commercial marketing, the Florida Prevention Research Center (FPRC) staff conducted a classification tree analysis called CHAID which examines correlates of several health-related risk factors or behaviours. One of its major advantages is that the tree-like display to summarise results makes it easy for community groups to identify and compare audience segments. Figure 4 in Case Study 17 shows the first three levels of the CHAID analyses where 'up-to-date screening status' was the dependent variable and served as the seed structure for segmentation. Through an iterative CHAID process, mutually exclusive and exhaustive segments were identified based on the independent variables considered (e.g. race/ethnicity, age, insurance coverage, access to a regular health provider, BMI, education, health status, gender). In the end, two priority populations were selected as the segmentation focus of the to-be-developed social marketing strategy: (a) Florida residents aged 50–64 years without health insurance but with a provider; and (b) Florida residents aged 50–64 years with health insurance.

A final approach to segmentation addresses the *benefit* different customer groups are seeking, based on their values, that might also help with improving diet. Food is much more than fuel and provides many psycho-social benefits, which could generate useful segmentation variables. For example, people who are more inclined than most to use food as a means of treating themselves might need to be approached with different offerings than other segments of the population. Box 4.4 shows how benefit segmentation worked for social marketers who were trying to encourage more active lifestyles.

BOX 4.4   THE BENEFITS OF EXERCISE

A comparative study into younger and older people's perceptions of exercise found that different sub-groups perceived different benefits in the product 'physical activity': some, typically younger men, wanted to compete against an opponent, while others aimed to better their own personal targets – to run faster or swim further for example. A third group was most concerned with body image and a fourth enjoyed the prospect of meeting new people, maintaining friendships and just 'getting out'.

These benefit segments formed the basis of a targeted strategy to encourage physical activity.

(*Source:* Stead *et al.* 1997)

Obstacles to segmentation and targeting

Two potential problems with segmentation and targeting may have already occurred to you.

First, there is an assumption in the process that our potential clients want what we are offering, and we just have to split them into groups who will want it even more. But as Tones (1996) pointed out (refer back to Exercise 2.2), this is not always the case in social marketing. Exercise 4.4 describes such a situation, where the key target is actually least likely to take up the offering. Before proceeding, consider how this impacts on our discussion so far.

EXERCISE 4.4   RELUCTANCE TO ATTEND FOR CERVICAL SCREENING

A public health department wishes to encourage women within a certain age range in the health authority area to attend for cervical screening. There are a number of possible ways in which this population can be segmented, including:

- Personal – for example, socio-demographic (social class, education, income, employment) or psychographic (beliefs about preventive health, fatalism, attitudes towards health services).
- Behavioural – health behaviour (smokers/non-smokers, etc.); previous usage behaviour (attendance for screening).
- Benefits – health protection; reassurance.

From available secondary research into the characteristics of attenders and non-attenders for cervical and other screening (Austoker *et al.* 1997; Skinner *et al.* 1994;

Thorogood *et al.* 1993), the public health department could make certain assumptions about the women most likely to respond positively to the programme: they will be ABC1, well educated, in work, have positive beliefs about their ability to protect themselves from cancer, favourable attitudes towards health services, and so on. If the screening programme were to be run as a profit-making service, this would be the segment to target. The screening agency could develop messages consonant with these women's beliefs, deliver them through workplaces at which the women are most likely to be employed, utilise media most likely to be consumed by them, and so forth. However, the health authority's objective is not to run the most profitable screening service but to make the biggest possible impact on public health by reducing the incidence of cervical cancer. To do this, the screening programme needs to reach those groups with the highest risk of cancer – the groups who, the same research shows, are the least likely to attend for screening.

How does this impact on our discussion of segmentation? Specifically:

- How practical is it when our clients do not want our offerings?
- How acceptable is it when our offerings are life-saving?

Despite initial appearances, this does not undermine the principles of segmentation and targeting – indeed, it presents a nice example of how all the variables we discussed above can be used in concert – but it does suggest that, as well as benefits, social marketers should look to perceived *barriers* as a differentiating tool. The research is not just telling us that there will be problems in reaching our target, but also how we can overcome them. As we will discuss below, making our approach more appealing is not just a matter of increasing its perceived benefits, but also of reducing its costs.

The second potential obstacle is philosophical, and focuses on the fact that social marketers are typically addressing more serious issues, such as cervical screening services, clean water or needle exchanges, than people in commerce. Making segmentation and targeting decisions can be especially fraught as a result. Deciding which group will get life-saving services (and, by extension, which will not) is much more contentious than who will get a new brand of chocolate bar.

How would you respond to this concern? Jot down your ideas before you continue; thinking about inequalities might help. You can remain focused on cervical screening or pick another example.

Lefebvre *et al.* (Box 4.5) argue that, because people vary, they will, in any case, respond differently to generalised offers. Segmentation and targeting, they point out, is an inevitable product of human diversity. If our behaviour change efforts omit to manage it, they will simply fall victim to it.

> ### BOX 4.5   THE INEVITABILITY OF SEGMENTATION
>
> This [segmentation and targeting] often raises the concern among some public health professionals that by focusing so narrowly on certain segments of the population, others will be missed. The reality, however, is that – depending on how the health message is executed and distributed – certain groups will always be reached and others will not. The only issue is whether the targeting is done based on research and strategic analysis or by happenstance and default.
>
> (*Source:* Lefebvre *et al.* 1995: 222)

Although they are talking specifically about communications, their view dovetails with the inequalities literature. This shows, as we have already noted, that health behaviours and outcomes are strongly linked to relative wealth. In the UK, for instance, these differentials have emerged and remain despite decades of population-wide health promotion and a universally available, free health service. The most highly resourced, educated and motivated sections of society – and the least in need – seem to be best able to avail themselves of standardised provision. Thus it seems that an egalitarian, level playing field might make the provider feel morally satisfied but does relatively little for those most in need.

The inequalities experience also suggests that past efforts have, albeit inadvertently, actually been of most benefit to the better-off, and thereby have **increased** social divisions. Arguably, segmentation and targeting can help us do a bit of systematic and overdue positive discrimination.

Choosing the target audience(s)

Having chosen the segmentation variables and divided the population into groups, the next task is to decide which segments will become targets. Three principles guide this decision. First, the target should be big enough to warrant attention – it should be **viable**. In commercial terms, it must be capable of generating sufficient profit; in a social context, it must have the potential to make an impact on the problem being tackled. This will be determined by the size of the group and their level of need. Picking up the example of disadvantaged groups, these are likely to score highly on this criterion. Second, it must be **accessible**. Usable channels of communication and service delivery must exist. Again, low-income groups are likely to meet this condition – as noted above, they are frequently geographically clustered, and if we focused down further to women or teenagers then community groups and schools would offer obvious channels to access them.

Third, the target should be one that the marketer is capable of serving; it should be, at least potentially, **responsive** to their efforts. There is no point in having a big and accessible target if there is nothing to offer them or they are likely to be impervious to any initiatives. Past research and the statistics of inequality suggest that low-income groups are typically unresponsive, at least in the public health arena. Arguably, however, this just emphasises the crucial need, which we will discuss later on in this chapter, to design an offering that genuinely meets the need of the target group. Certainly, Box 4.6 shows how targeting was successfully used to improve cancer screening rates among disadvantaged groups in the west of Scotland.

BOX 4.6   REACHING DISADVANTAGED GROUPS

There had traditionally been low awareness of both bowel (24 per cent) and mouth (6 per cent) cancer in the west of Scotland, particularly among working-class groups. Knowledge of the signs and symptoms of these cancers is also poor despite the fact that presenting early to the NHS can greatly improve survival outcomes and quality of life. The West of Scotland Cancer Awareness Project aimed to tackle this. The segmentation was geo-demographic, and the key target working-class, over-50 year olds of both sexes. These were both numerous enough and sufficiently reluctant to present to the NHS to comprise a *viable* target group. *Accessing* them was also straightforward: this group are more likely than most to watch television (ITC data show that in 2001 C2DEs watched an average of four hours of TV per day compared with three hours among ABC1s). Focusing on the correct age group was done by ensuring that the messages were delivered by people in their fifties. Furthermore, local services could be geared up to ensure that it was easy for people to act on the messages. And they were *responsive*: a high proportion of patients that were aware of the campaigns admitted that seeing these had encouraged them to seek advice more quickly (62 per cent for bowel cancer and 68 per cent for mouth cancer), and those who attended were genuinely symptomatic.

(*Source:* ITC 2002; WoSCAP 2005)

Thinking beyond the final client

The tendency in discussing segmentation and targeting is to assume we are concerned only with grouping our end clients. But in many instances, as we have already seen, social marketers are thinking about stakeholders as well – or even instead, as we outlined above. Remember what social cognitive and social ecology theory tells us about the impact that social context (and structure) has on people's behaviour. Remember, therefore, that we should always ask ourselves which stakeholder groups can have an impact on the relevant parts of this social context.

As we discussed in Chapter 1, Wallack *et al.* (1993) described this as a process of moving 'upstream'. Case Study 15 provides a neat illustration of how this type of thinking might assist with salt consumption and reduction. If you go to the world of fast fashion and sustainability in Case Study 18 from Ann-Marie Kennedy and colleagues in Australia, you'll see the upstream or macro social-marketing as it is sometimes dubbed, in action in a different setting.

Objectives: Measurability and realism

Once the target(s) has (have) been determined, the next step is to clarify exactly what we would like them to do: to set our behavioural objectives. These objectives can be to avoid, modify or adopt behaviours. There can be a primary objective – an overarching main behavioural goal supported by secondary objectives or aims, which break the primary goal into more manageable aims, or a management number of main objectives. This thinking should, of course, be informed by the strategic planning process.

Setting clear objectives brings two important benefits (see Box 4.7). First, they ensure that a clear understanding and consensus about the intent of the intervention are developed by all those involved which will include people both within the organisation and outside it. For example, if an advertising agency is being used, well-defined and agreed objectives can ensure that they are absolutely clear about what their advertising has to achieve from the outset. Similarly good objectives facilitate communication with superiors and controlling bodies. This can be particularly important in social marketing where funding agencies or politicians may have to be convinced of the value of an intervention.

Second, objectives provide an excellent measurement tool. They give a clear focus to intervention design and make it possible to monitor progress and ultimately assess effectiveness.

BOX 4.7   GOOD OBJECTIVES

Clear objectives bring two benefits:

- *Improved communications* between the stakeholders in the initiative. Everyone knows what they are trying to do.
- *Enhanced evaluation*: if you know exactly where you are trying to reach, it is much easier to confirm whether or not you have arrived.
- To provide these benefits, objectives need two qualities:
- *Measurability*: there must be an agreed way of calibrating whether or not they have been achieved – or at least a suitable proxy.
- *Achievability*: you need a realistic hope of success.

It follows, therefore, that good objectives are **measurable**. It may be very desirable, for instance, to run an initiative with the objective of making people happier, as Richard Layard (2005) suggests, but actually calibrating this will present great challenges. Measurability is also a function of resources. As we will discuss in Chapter 6, determining whether a particular programme has brought about a change in a population demands a complex and expensive research design that would probably swamp the budget of most small interventions. This raises the challenging question of whether or not we should set objectives – however desirable – that cannot be measured. One solution is to do so, but only if you can agree reasonable proxy measures to mark progress. Have a try at Exercise 4.5.

EXERCISE 4.5   PROMOTING SAFER SEX

You have been awarded a contract to improve the sexual health of Brownton's teenagers. You have six months, a modest budget and a large supply of free condoms. What objectives might you set for the programme?

Direct, attributable measures of changes in the sexual health of Brownton's teen sexual health are going to be beyond your means, so setting this as an objective will not be very helpful. Indeed measuring any change in the population is going to be very challenging, unless there just happen to be existing surveys going on from which you can benefit. Assuming not, it makes much more sense to set more modest but measurable objectives – such as encouraging a specified minimum proportion of Brownton's teenagers to access the free condoms, and to do so in a way they find empowering and acceptable.

The need for measurability leads naturally to the second key attribute of good objectives – that they are *achievable*, i.e. they should be within the capability of the organisation and the programme budget. Again, the strategic planning process helps here, especially the process of matching external threats and opportunities with internal strengths and weaknesses. The temptation in social marketing is to be overambitious. This may be because the jobs we are trying to do are so obviously desirable and worthy. Giving people the support they need to quit smoking or have their baby immunised is quite literally a matter of life and death, and the rewards for success are truly mind blowing. If we really could get all of the UK's 10 million smokers to give up overnight, Doll *et al.*'s (2004) work shows we would save around *five million* lives.

However, as we noted in Chapter 3 when discussing theories of human behaviour, changes are usually hard won. This is particularly true of the sort of engrained lifestyle behaviours we tend to focus on, which often have an element of addiction thrown in for good measure, and so it beholds us to cut our cloth accordingly. In time this may also help, as we noted in our discussion of strategic planning, to educate funders and policy makers about the long-term and systemic work that is usually needed to generate real improvements in health and environmental status.

The ultimate arbiter

Ultimately, objectives, as with all aspects of effective marketing, depend on the target group. They have crucial insights into a particular behaviour and can be studied to uncover valuable antecedents. Research published in the *Harvard Business Review* shows that consumer satisfaction is an absolutely vital measure of both current and future success in the business sector (Reichheld 2003). This only emerged through research with customers. To complete the circle, Reichheld also produced a reliable and straightforward way of measuring his construct: Would you recommend this product/service to a friend? Furthermore, not only does this reveal how well you are doing now, it also predicts how fast you will grow by identifying not just satisfied but 'delighted customers'. These *will* recommend the service to a friend. Indeed, Reichheld suggests that, on average, they will tell four other people of their pleasure, effectively becoming the company's marketing department.

This takes us back to our discussions of relationship marketing in Chapter 2. Box 4.8 shows how this thinking might be applied to the smoking cessation services, which enable some 15 per cent of their clients to give up smoking successfully. (If you are not convinced that giving up smoking is an extremely positive experience flick forward to Box 7.3 on p.202.)

BOX 4.8   RELATIONAL THINKING IN SMOKING CESSATION

Let us think for a moment about the 15 per cent of users who quit successfully. They will be delighted with both themselves and the service. Just suppose we did not lose interest in these people, but, like Tesco, gave them a loyalty card, kept in touch, and built relationships with them. They would persuade friends and family to use cessation services (they are living, breathing testimonials) and could be encouraged to think about their other health behaviours. From a marketing point of view, there is an obvious opportunity to build on success. It comes back to the basic point of marketing – and indeed medicine – that progress is made by co-operation and partnership. The doctor has the medical expertise, but it is the patient's behaviour.

(*Source:* Hastings and McDermott 2006)

Formulating the offer

In this section, we will get down to the nitty-gritty of how a marketer goes about designing and deploying an offering to a particular target segment to meet the agreed objectives. The starting point has to be the client. We need to understand why they are currently behaving as they are (e.g. speeding or binge drinking or not recycling), the perceived attractiveness of behaving differently (e.g. driving safely or drinking sensibly or recycling) and how the latter might be enhanced.

The audiences themselves will undoubtedly have valuable insights on all these areas. For example, teenagers will be able to shed light on the challenges of practising safer sex, and will have ideas about how these might be overcome. They will also be able to tell you how it feels to be faced with the task of discussing safer sex with a potential partner or how empowered they feel by a poster simply telling them to use a condom. However, there are also very real limitations to their insights into their behaviour. A smoker might not really know why they took up smoking, or whether addiction, peer pressure or tobacco advertising is playing a role in reinforcing the habit. This is no surprise – they are smokers not social scientists, and answering such questions requires more complex research procedures.

Similarly, your client group may know the answers to some of your questions, but be unwilling to divulge them. To take an upstream example, a politician may be reluctant to let on that their disinclination to legislate on smoking in public places is caused by a fear of electoral harm because many of their constituents smoke – that they are, in effect, putting their own interests ahead of the public's health.

So yes, the offering is designed around the needs of the client, but the task of divining these must be approached in a subtle and sophisticated way. We will return to this topic in Chapter 5 when we talk about research.

The intervention mix

Marketers do not just think about the customer with respect to their core offering; consumer perceptions also influence decisions about what the offer will cost, where it will be made available and how they should talk about it. As Cannon succinctly puts it, "commercial marketing is essentially about getting the right product, at the right time, in the right place, with the right price and presented in the right way that succeeds in satisfying buyer needs" (1992: 46). These four variables – **p**roduct, **p**rice, **p**romotion and **p**lace – are, for some, the core tools of marketing that need to be manipulated carefully to produce the most effective 'mix'. Social marketing can also use the 4P mix, but in recognition of the complexity of behavioural change often involved, it is usefully augmented with participation, partnerships and positioning to make a 7P intervention mix.

The marketing mix (whether 4Ps or 7Ps) has been criticised in marketing literature over the last ten years for being too mechanistic and naive to handle complex marketing situations, such as service provision, business-to-business networking – or, indeed, the challenging behaviours typically being addressed by social marketers (Tapp and Spotswood 2013).

The criticism of the marketing mix has some validity, but does not mean that it should be completely abandoned. As with behavioural theory (see Chapter 3), it just needs to be used with care and subtlety. It offers a way of thinking about a behaviour change challenge and how resources should be allocated to maximise the potential for success. It is not a pastry cutter, forcing every social marketing effort into the shape of the 4Ps or 7Ps.

The marketer is seeking the best combination of variables to offer their consumers (Kotler *et al.* 1999) and this is the one that comes closest to satisfying their needs – i.e. what Cannon means by the term 'right' in the quote above. Hence it is essential to monitor the marketing mix continually so it can be designed and developed to meet these needs. For example, research may show that a particular population is unaware of the benefits of safer sex, and so the promotional element of the mix may be given greatest emphasis. However, as the campaign proceeds, awareness may become widespread and the main problem will change to one of condom availability. This is likely to increase the importance of the product and place (online and offline) elements of the mix.

In essence, therefore, the intervention mix is a multifaceted and flexible means of responding to client needs. Table 4.2 gives some illustrations of the mix and Exercise 4.6 gives you a chance to try it out for yourself. While doing this, it will help to take a look at Ana Sofia Dias and Sara Balonas's work in Portugal, where the marketing mix helped inform their Porto Tap Water programme (see Case Study 6). The Porto Tap Water programme was designed with a pricing strategy that positioned tap water as cheaper than bottled water, and a product strategy that transformed a perceived simple commodity into an offering with its own personality and attributes – high quality, distinctive taste, reliable, convenient healthy, cool and trendy. The creation of bottles with access to existing water supply points in the city, and the creation of new public water access points, constituted the 'place' component, while an integrated promotional plan, built on a strong branding platform of "as good as it gets," made use of online and offline communications including events, PR, stickers and water ambassadors.

In Case Study 5, informed by an asset-based approach, co-production and co-design, the 'Pop-Up Radio Project' sought to engage creatively with pupils in Fife's secondary schools in order to explore the impact of two tobacco-education school interventions.

The acid test for the much poked and prodded marketing mix is whether or not you find it useful. If you do, use it. If not, find another way of thinking through how you will make your offer as appealing, accessible, available and appreciated as possible. The strength of the Ps approach is that it provides us with a systematic process for thinking about what we are doing from the perspective of our clients. We will now look at it P by P.

Product

Product refers to the offering, activity, event, service, or product to facilitate the desired behaviour. As you can see from this description, social marketing products are frequently intangible and complex behaviours, which makes it difficult to formulate simple, meaningful product concepts (MacFadyen *et al.* 2002). To take an example, 'reducing one's fat intake' involves a change in food choice, menu design, shopping behaviour, food preparation, personal habits, family routines, wider social values and so on. Furthermore, it is a behaviour which needs to be practised not just once but repeated and sustained over a long period of time.

Table 4.2 The social marketing intervention mix

Tool	Definition	Examples	Key change questions
Product	The desired **offering** made to the target group. Can be a service or an experience.	Adoption of idea (belief, attitude, value) Adoption of offering (one-off), sustained) Distance from current offering Non-adoptions of future offerings	How appealing is the offer? Or What behaviour does the product/service enable?
Price	The **costs** that target groups have to bear and the barriers they have to overcome	Psychological, Emotional, Cultural, Social, Behavioural, Temporal, Practical, Physical, Financial Costs	How affordable is it? Or On what basis is the target group empowered?

Place	The **channels** by which the change is promoted and **places** in which the change is supported and encouraged	Media channels Distribution channels Interpersonal channels Physical places Non-physical places (e.g. social and cultural climate)	How readily available is it? Or Where does engagement occur?
Promotion	The means by which the change is **communicated and positioned** to the target group	Advertising, flyers Public relations Media Advocacy Direct Mail Websites Branding Social media	How well known and appreciated is it? Or How is the desired offering exemplified?
Participation	Engaging in **dialogue, interaction and mutual learning**	Collaboration Value co-discovery Value co-design Value co-delivery	How accessible is the offering? What degree of empowerment and co-creation is required by the target audience for your offering?
Partnerships	**Building partnerships** in order to help bring about the desired Sea Change offering	Shared Values Mutually Beneficial Communication Trust Commitment	What alliances are best? What potential enterprises could be part of your offering?
Positioning	**Framing** a behaviour in the client's mind relative to the competition	Framing Relativity	How does the target audience arrange the product, service, offering in their mind and how does it measure up to the competition?

EXERCISE 4.6   USING THE MIX

Your task: choose a behaviour change challenge – speeding in your town for instance, or teen antisocial behaviour – and design a marketing mix for it. Consider how useful the various Ps, As and Es are and how they might vary given another project or the same project at a different stage. Consider the digital component of the various Ps.

As a first step towards formulating product concepts, social marketers need to identify and clarify their product attributes. In commercial marketing, these range from the tangible (colour, taste, shape, size, packaging, performance, technology) to the intangible (brand, image, status, perceived ease of use). Social marketing product attributes are largely situated at the intangible end of this continuum. Some potential classifications of product attributes are suggested in Box 4.9.

BOX 4.9   SOCIAL MARKETING PRODUCT ATTRIBUTES

Trialability:	Can the behaviour be tried out beforehand before permanent or full adoption (wearing a cycling helmet or using an app)?
Ease:	How easy or difficult is it to adopt the behaviour (wearing a seatbelt versus giving up smoking)?
Risks:	What are the risks of adopting the behaviour?
Image:	Is the behaviour attractive or unattractive?
Acceptability:	Is the behaviour socially acceptable?
Duration:	Is the behaviour to be practised once or repeatedly? Is it to be sustained over the short or long term?
Cost:	Does the behaviour have a financial cost or not (eating a healthier diet may involve more expense; drinking less alcohol does not)?

(*Source*: MacFadyen et al. 2002)

Analysing product attributes in this way helps social marketers to formulate meaningful and communicable offerings. For example, in addressing teen smoking, research may suggest that image is a key issue, rather than the avoidance of health risks. (Go to Case Study 6 to see product attributes in action in the Porto Tap Water campaign.) The social marketer can then put a particular emphasis on producing non-smoking options that are cool and trendy (as Porto Tap Water did, such as self-empowerment and independence) rather than ones that major on the health benefits of quitting.

Kotler *et al.* (1999) provided another way for social marketers to think about their products when he distinguished the *actual* product (the behaviour change), the *core* product (the benefits it brings) and the *augmented* product (tangible objects and services to support the behaviour change). Again, it helps us think coherently about what we are offering from the perspective of our clients. For example, if your behavioural change job is to create more ocean-literate citizens, the **core product** or service is intangible; it is the **benefit** that target group will get from engaging with the desired offering, e.g. providing a better education for your children. The **actual product** is the physical product or service, e.g. a book of sea stories and songs. The **augmented product** is everything that is associated with the product that **adds value** to it, e.g. a website that provides downloadable sheet music as additional information and support.

Before we leave the 'Product' concept, one final comment goes to the product development process. Just as commercial marketing, product development and prototyping are important as part of the social marketing planning process and intervention mix – recall our conversations about flexible offerings and the ability to compromise with clients – read Box 4.10 to see product development in the field.

BOX 4.10   LEAN PRODUCT DEVELOPMENT AT THE UNIVERSITY OF SOUTH FLORIDA

'Lean product development' is where products are built in short, repeated cycles with frequent customer/client input and an eye towards improving the chances of success by "failing fast and continually learning" (Blank 2013: 66). In the commercial sector, lean product development has been reported to increase both innovation effectiveness and efficiency (e.g. Ward 2007) – benefits that may be even more important for social marketers who often work with modest budgets and in resource-constrained settings (e.g. developing countries).

The Florida Prevention Research Center at the University of South Florida has been funded by the U.S. Centers for Disease Control and Prevention (CDC) since 1998. Most recently, and drawing on lessons learned from their previous demonstration projects – *Community-Based Prevention Marketing (CBPM)*, to teach community coalitions how to design behavior change programs, and *CBPM for Policy Development*, to provide guidance for policy making – they are partnering with a new community committee to combine elements of the previous iterations of *CBPM* into a version better suited to address complex, dynamic problems that require a whole-systems perspective (Kessler and Glasgow 2011; Lyn *et al.* 2013).

This work, entitled *CBPM for Systems Change*, incorporates social marketing and community-based system dynamics, "a participatory method for involving communities in the process of understanding and changing systems from the endogenous or feedback perspective of system dynamics." The work of developing the *CBPM for Systems Change* framework as a product to be used by other community coalitions is guided by 'developmental evaluation', which supports the development of innovations and adaptation of interventions in dynamic environments. One niche for developmental evaluation is where evaluation is intended to support exploration and innovation *before* there is an intervention model to summatively test. Thus, the developmental evaluation perspective dovetails nicely with that of 'lean product development'.

Social marketers at the Florida Prevention Research Center have used one lean-development approach: 'human centered design'. Human-centered design is a creative approach to problem solving – one that starts with people and ends with innovative solutions (e.g. products, services, systems) tailored to meet their needs. It has been applied in a number of contexts including, for example, health

(continued)

(continued)

care innovation (Salmon *et al.* 2015), quality improvement initiatives (Trail-Mahan *et al.* 2016), and public health innovation (Vechakul *et al.* 2015).

Through a lean-product development lens, social marketers at the Florida Prevention Research Center employed Steps 3–7 from IDEO's human-centered design toolkit:

3. Identify patterns

4. Create opportunity areas

5. Brainstorm new solutions

6. Make ideas real

7. Gather feedback

These social marketers found the toolkit useful for identifying additional product features to be added to their *CBPM* framework as well as engaging potential customers to gather feedback. Positioned as a methodology that can reduce the risk of failure, lean product development favours "experimentation over elaborate planning, customer feedback over intuition, and iterative design over traditional 'big design up front' development."

(Source: Biroscak *et al.* 2017.)

Price

Only a few of social marketing's products have a monetary price, and given all we have said about inequalities, this might seem to be a good thing. If the poor are in most need of our products, it seems crazy to start charging for them; this will surely be regressive. However, marketers remind us that price and value are closely interrelated: the value of a Rolls-Royce is reinforced by its exclusive price tag, and at the other extreme, freebies are often – figuratively as well as literally – taken for granted. Condom social marketing in developing countries provides instructive lessons here. Initial efforts to encourage contraception in India involved shipping out large quantities of free condoms. However, because they were free, neither the distributors nor the would-be users treated them with much respect. The product ended up mouldering in warehouses, sell-by and storage instructions were not respected and the products acquired a poor public reputation.

By contrast, it was very apparent that commercial products such as soft drinks were doing much better. They were well distributed (even the poorest village seemed to have a Coke machine), properly stored and readily consumed. Brand value was also very much in evidence. Success was due to commercialisation: everyone in the supply chain stood to make money out of effective distribution. Even the final customer gained because the product offering had added brand value, to which price contributed. The condom social marketers decided to follow suit and charge (a very modest) amount for their products. The result has been vastly increased condom usage and much wider availability (Dahl *et al.* 1997; Harvey 1997).

This does not suggest that we should rush to commercialise all social marketing efforts. But it does warn us to think carefully about what 'free' actually means – and ensure that it does not just result in second-rate product or service offerings.

Price also has a wider meaning in social marketing; there are almost always costs associated with behaviour change. These may be to do with time, embarrassment, effort, inertia, pain and perceived social stigma, among other variables. Thus the speeding driver thinks he is going to be late if he obeys the speed limit, the teenager has to overcome embarrassment to acquire a condom. These costs are balanced against the benefits of engaging in the behaviour – and both costs and benefits vary for different behaviours. Exercise 4.7 suggests a systematic way of thinking about these variations.

EXERCISE 4.7   THINKING SYSTEMATICALLY ABOUT PRICE

	Tangible	Intangible
Low cost	Personal benefits e.g. Wearing seatbelts	Societal benefits e.g. Recycling programmes
High cost	Personal benefits e.g. Smoking cessation	Societal benefits e.g. Avoiding use of cars

Which combination will be the toughest for social marketing to address? Which the easiest? What are the strategic implications of your answers?

(*Source:* based on Rangun *et al.* 1996)

i) *Low cost and tangible, personal benefits*, e.g. seatbelt wearing.

In this case, the target perceives clear, direct benefits to themselves, and change is easy (assuming reliable seatbelts are fitted as standard) relative to the four other types of initiative. Communication is likely to be a key element of the social marketing strategy.

ii) *Low cost and intangible, societal benefits*, e.g. recycling programmes.

Here the behaviour change is relatively easy to adopt, but the benefits are not perceived to be as relevant to the individual. Kash Rangun and colleagues (1996) argue that convenience is the key to this type of programme and the ultimate benefit to the recycler and society should be stressed.

iii) *High cost and tangible, personal benefits*, e.g. smoking cessation programmes.

In this case, there is a very clear personal benefit to adopting the suggested behaviour, but the costs associated with doing so are high. Here the authors advocate the adoption of what they call 'push marketing' approaches: providing support services and augmented products that will reduce the cost.

iv) *High cost and intangible, societal benefits*, e.g. avoiding car use.

> This is the hardest type of behaviour change to induce as the costs are high and the benefits are hard to personalise and quantify. In this case, it may be necessary to adopt de-marketing approaches, and use moral persuasion or social influence. In addition, increasing the cost of the current behaviour (e.g. by increasing the fuel tax) may help.

Place

Kotler and Zaltman suggest that place in social marketing covers both distribution and response channels, and "clear action outlets for those motivated to acquire the product" (1971: 9). Thus where there is a communications element to a social marketing initiative, place applies to the media channels through which messages are to be delivered, but it can also apply to the distribution or delivery channels for tangible products or services, such as clean needles or online smoking cessation groups.

In both instances, place variables such as channel, coverage, cost, timing (Kotler and Roberto 1989), location, transport (Woodruffe 1995) accessibility (Cowell 1994) and online-offline are all relevant. For example, an initiative to increase the uptake of cervical screening could reduce the costs of attending by manipulating the place variables of distance, time and convenience (offering screening at flexible times and in varied locations).

In Case Study 6, place is a challenging force for behavioural change as the competition was with portable bottled water products that were accessible and available inside and outside the home. The solution? To make tap water more accessible by (1) having more physical taps around the city and (2) providing bottles to put the tap water in!

In addition, many social marketing initiatives depend on intermediaries, such as health professionals, pharmacists, teachers, and community workers, to act as distribution channels for media materials or as retailers for a particular behaviour change product. For example, GPs are often given responsibility for changing smoking and drinking behaviour. Where intermediaries are to act primarily as distribution agents for media products, key variables such as accessibility and appropriateness should be considered. When these intermediaries have a more complex role (e.g. youth workers and teachers delivering a sex education curriculum), place variables such as source visibility, credibility, attractiveness and power (Percy 1983; Hastings and Stead 1999) should guide the selection of appropriate agents and inform the sort of support and training that is offered to them. For example, the drugs prevention literature has examined the relative merits of teachers, youth workers, police and peers as delivery channels for drugs prevention messages (Bandy and President 1983; Shiner and Newburn 1996).

Social marketers are often dependent on the goodwill and co-operation of intermediaries for access to their end targets. This is particularly the case when dealing with sensitive health issues or with vulnerable groups such as young people, where there is usually a need to communicate not only with the young people themselves but also with key groups such as parents, teachers and politicians. These groups may act as gatekeepers, controlling or influencing the distribution of a message to a target group, or as stakeholders, taking an interest in and scrutinising the activities of the prevention agency (McGrath 1995). If an initiative is to be effective, it needs to satisfy the information and other needs of these two groups and maintain their support.

To see how product (core and augmented) works together with place and price, take, for example, Marsha Smith's Super Kitchens (www.superkitchen.org). Realising there was a lack of 'hang-out spaces' (place) where people can eat good food (product) affordably (price) and in ways that are convenient and suitable for modern-day lifestyles (product, place and price), Marsha set up a 'public eating service', a network of members who run social eating spaces and are cooking for their communities with love. Social eating spaces feed the whole person – belly and heart (feeding the belly and heart represents the core product while setting up a Super Kitchen social eating space, including, food delivery, training, signage and publicity and monthly members meetings, represents an augmented product).

Promotion

The fourth P is promotion, including branding, digital marketing, online and offline communications. This is discussed in Chapter 6.

Participation

Linked closely to communication, co-operation and shared values is participation. Participation provides the necessary dialogue, interaction and mutual learning to manage highly complex exchanges. Participation is about collaboration, empowerment and direct active engagement with your target audience(s) through *all* stages of your planning and implementation work. Participation is about speaking and listening to people on their own terms. Participation goes significantly beyond just asking people for their opinions or what might be called 'participation by consultation'. It gives your target audience(s) a voice about the barriers to change and ownership and responsibility for solutions to influence their welfare (Saunders *et al.* 2015).

Active participation to define the problem, the barriers and enablers to change and potential solutions is more empowering because it reflects the blend of values important to the individual and increases control (Domegan *et al.* 2016). Recall our VATs and VETs from Chapter 3. To uncover the blend of values at work for any exchange cluster, value co-discovery (revisit Figure 3.6) is about genuine in-depth relationships with your target audience(s). The target audience(s) and change stakeholders become dynamic and equal in developing a deep understanding of experiences. Value co-discovery's essence lies in building relationships as outlined in Chapter 2. Value co-design takes this full and intensely deep understanding of your target audience(s), worked out in partnership with them, and captures it in jointly designed offerings, products, services, solutions and interventions. With value co-delivery, the co-ordinating system around shared values, product, service or offering comes into operation, which means front-line people are important at this point. In its simplest form value co-delivery is about optimising the systems factors beyond the control of the target group that block or facilitate the rest of the intervention mix.

> ### BOX 4.11 'WAVES OF FREEDOM'
>
> 'Waves of Freedom' utilises participation in surfing to empower and transform women and girls into "self-advocates and empowered change-makers in their community and beyond." When Easkey Britton and Marion Poizeau travelled to Iran to surf, they wanted to explore how women in Iran could get to the water and surf. They connected with pioneering Iranian sportswomen and co-created, co-designed and co-delivered an initiative to empower women through surfing (see http://wavesoffreedom.org/#about-us).

Participation is a recurrent theme in social marketing and hence this book. We'll come back to it in Chapter 5, when we note that giving your target audience(s) a clear and loud voice means research has to be interactive; it's conducted *with* and not *on* your clients (McHugh *et al.* 2015). Likewise, in Chapter 9 we'll discuss how this participation has been deemed so important it has been written into international human rights law. Finally, in Chapter 11 we will examine how participation is the defining quality of the social movement. For now, flick through any of the 24 case studies and you'll see multiple examples of participation in action.

Partnerships

Partnerships are widely accepted as the 6th 'P' in the social marketing intervention mix – just take a look at any of the case studies from our colleagues around the world, and you'll see how important partnerships are to the social marketer's toolkit, simply because it can be difficult for one organisation to bring about behaviour change and desired offerings on their own. When organisations with similar goals and shared values come together, they can target their audience(s) more effectively. We'll come back to this point in Chapter 7 when we look at co-operative strategies. For now, note partnerships as the 6th P in our toolbox.

Positioning

Before we wrap up, there's one more P in our toolbox – positioning. This chapter has introduced us to the marketing toolbox, but the danger with toolboxes is that they get us too focused on the minutiae and in the process crowd out the big picture – not being able to see the woods for the trees. Commercial marketers help to avoid this with the idea of 'positioning' their products. Mullins *et al.* (2004), for example, in their textbook *Marketing Management*, describe how French wine was successfully repositioned in the US market from an elitist option for the cognoscente to something you can quaff at your barbecue. A combination of well-targeted, down-to-earth advertising, accessible point of sale material, a pocket guide with supporting website and a helpline all succeeded in achieving their objective of making the product less exclusive and thereby widening its appeal.

Positioning is guided by two things: how the consumer sees the product and how it measures up to the competition. Positioning is about how we mentally frame products in our minds relative to other things and stuff: "Frames are the mental structures that allow human beings to understand reality – and sometimes to create what we take to be reality . . . They structure our ideas and concepts, they shape how we reason, and they even impact how we perceive and how we act. For the most part, our use of frames is unconscious and automatic – we use them without realising it" (Darnton and Kirk 2011: 67). In the case of French wine, it was seen as high quality, but too exclusive for ordinary occasions. In terms of the competition, it was losing out to more mundane alternatives such as a can of beer; indeed, the effort to reposition it was characterised as "trying to make Americans as comfortable with Fumé Blanc as they are with a Bud". Turn your attention to Exercise 4.8.

EXERCISE 4.8   POSITIONING AND FRAMES

Take a few minutes out to watch Harrison Ford and David Attenborough talk about our oceans and planet at www.youtube.com/watch?v=rM6txLtaoc and www.youtube.com/embed/auSo1MyWf8g?rel=0 respectively.

Which one is an example of 'strict parenting' framing? Which one is an example of 'nurturing parent' framing?

(*Source:* McHugh *et al.* 2015)

No doubt you'll have picked up on the tone of voice, mood, colours, music and compelling content which identify Ford's clip positioned as 'strict parenting' while Attenborough's clip is positioned as the 'nurturing parent'. We come back to positioning and framing in Chapter 6 when looking at communication and Chapter 11 when talking about Community Social Marketing and social movements.

Social marketers do likewise. It simply provides a reminder that, in using the tools we have examined in this chapter, we have to retain a strategic view of where we want to be in our client's mind and relative to the competition. Rob Donovan and colleagues give a great illustration of how this can work in their review of the 'Act-Belong-Commit' Mentally Healthy Campaign in Western Australia (Donovan *et al.* 2006). In this instance, the aim was to reposition mental health from its current focus on illness and symptoms to a much more positive one – or as they express it, "to reframe people's perceptions of mental health away from the absence of mental illness, to the belief that people can (and should) act proactively to protect and strengthen their mental health." Careful market research was used to understand how people currently framed mental illness, and how this related to more positive concepts of mental health. For the latest updates on 'Act-Belong-Commit', turn to Case Study 16, where the broader societal and positioning implications of the campaign beyond mental health promotion is described.

As Box 4.12 illustrates, being active, socially engaged and feeling in control of your circumstances were widely accepted prerequisites for good mental health. The 'Act-Belong-Commit' Campaign shows how Donovan and colleagues used the social marketing toolbox both to reinforce this positive construction and deliver to the resulting needs.

BOX 4.12   REPOSITIONING MENTAL HEALTH

"There was near universal support for the concepts that remaining active (physically, socially and mentally), having good friends, being a member of various groups in the community, and feeling in control of one's circumstances were necessary for good mental health."

(*Source:* Donovan *et al.* 2006)

The social marketing planning process and associated tools can be observed in action in Case Study 20. It describes how the intervention was positioned on skills of interest to the cohort (cornering, smooth driving) as part of an 'advanced status' skills workshop rather than telling the young men what to do as part of a free advanced driving course because the men found the skills approach with its demonstration drive more appealing. Note, however, this does not mean that all road safety aspects were ignored, just that they were covered within this male-oriented framing – just as Lucozade is positioned as a sports drink but its contents remain unchanged. The intervention's tagline, which also came from the young male drivers, 'Wheels, Skills and Thrills', reinforced this positioning for the men.

Wrap-up

This chapter began by evoking one of the twentieth-century's greatest exponents of social change, Martin Luther King. From his lead, we examined how a clear strategic vision enables us to put together an effective strategic plan. We then examined how environmental and competitive analysis set the context for the deployment of three key marketing tools: segmentation and targeting help us to get a better fix on whose behaviour we want to change; objective setting helps us pin down precisely what we want them to do; and the marketing mix provides a systematic way of thinking about how we will encourage people to engage with the idea of empowered change. Specifically, we want to make our offer appealing, accessible, available, affordable and appreciated. This tactical activity is guided by the strategic idea of positioning.

We will continue this practical theme in the next chapter when we discuss the use of research and storytelling in social marketing.

Reflective questions

1. What is strategic planning? What are the steps in strategic social marketing planning?
2. Critically discuss how the principles of social marketing are reflected in the social marketing planning process.
3. "We run to awareness and education like an alcoholic runs towards his next drink. We have got to 'get on the wagon', and identify those interventions that really do determine behaviour" (Newton-Ward 2011, personal communication). Discuss with examples.
4. Define a situation analysis. Explain its role and function in the strategic social marketing planning process.

5. A SWOT analysis is about the internal and external helpful and harmful forces regarding the issue on hand. Elaborate.
6. Outline what a stakeholder analysis is and is not. How might you classify stakeholders?
7. What should a social marketer consider when setting objectives?
8. Segmentation is central to the strategic social marketing planning process. Discuss with examples.
9. Explain how the marketing mix (4Ps or 7Ps) helps the social marketer respond to their client's needs.
10. Partnerships are often considered the 6th P of the social marketer's marketing mix. How so? Why? Answer with real world examples from the selection of case studies available to you.
11. "Positioning is guided by two things: how the consumer sees the product and how it measures up to the competition." Detail with examples.

Reflective assignments

1. Conduct an Internet search on social marketing planning.
2. Locate and review a strategic social marketing plan.
3. Model a SWOT and stakeholder analysis for one of the following: drug addiction, caffeine addiction, a drink addiction or a sugar addiction.
4. A renowned university in the top 100 has approached you to use your behaviour change skills in tackling campus student binge drinking which is now considered out of control. How might you use a strategic focus and social marketing planning process?
5. Devise a strategic plan for a local community who wish to increase the number of community members who harvest rainwater.
6. Develop a one-page summary of a segmentation and targeting strategy you would recommend for a social marketing topic of your choice.
7. Examine your experiences and document where you have experienced passive participation and active participation. What have been your co-creation (co-discovery, co-design, co-delivery) experiences?
8. Take the partnership model in this chapter and utilise it to analyse a social marketing partnership you are interested in.
9. Apply the theory about positioning to a behaviour change strategy of your choice.
10. Consult the *Journal of Social Marketing* and/or *Social Marketing Quarterly* and read a classic or contemporary article(s) on the social marketing planning process, the social marketing mix or one aspect of the mix such as product or place to advance your understanding of the theory and practice in this area.
11. Complete your 'Rebels with a cause' checklist for (a) the social marketing planning process and (b) the toolkit to undertake such planning.

Notes

1 www.gov.scot/Resource/0041/00417331.pdf.
2 www.ons.gov.uk/peoplepopulationandcommunity/birthsdeathsandmarriages/life expectancies/bulletins/lifeexpectancyatbirthandatage65bylocalareasintheunitedkingdom/ 2014-04-16.

References

ASH (2006) *Tobacco Advertising and Promotion, Factsheet No: 19*. London: Action on Smoking and Health (ASH). Online: www.ash.org.uk/files/documents/ASH_temp_7160.pdf/ (accessed May 2016).

Austoker, J., Davey, C. and Jansen, C. (1997) *Improving the quality of the written information sent to women about cervical screening. NHS Cervical Screening Programme Publication No 6.* London: NHSCSP Publications.

Bandy, P. and President, P.A. (1983) 'Recent literature on drug abuse prevention and mass media: Focusing on youth, parents and the elderly', *Journal of Drug Education*, 13(3): 255–271.

Biroscak, B.J., Schneider, T., Martinez Tyson, D., Aguado Loi, C.X. and Bryant, C.A. (2017) *Social Marketing and Social Innovation: Tools for Human Centered Design*. Unpublished manuscript, Florida Prevention Research Center, University of South Florida, Tampa, Florida, USA.

Bryson, J. (2004) 'What to do when stakeholders matter; Stakeholder identification and analysis techniques', *Public Management Review*,; 6(1): 21–53.

Cannon, T. (1992) *Basic Marketing: Principles and Practice,* 3rd edn. London: Cassell.

Cowell, D.W. (1994) 'Marketing of Services', Ch. 29 in M. Baker (ed) *The Marketing Book*, 3rd edn. Oxford: Butterworth Heinemann.

Dahl, D.W., Gorn, G.J. and Weinberg, C.B. (1997) 'Marketing, Safer Sex and Condom Acquisition', Ch. 11 in M.E. Goldberg, M. Fishbein and S.E. Middlestadt (eds) *Social Marketing: Theoretical and Practical Perspectives*. Mahwah, NJ: Lawrence Erlbaum Associates.

Darnton, A. and Kirk, M. (2011) *Finding Frames: New Ways to Engage the UK Public in Global Poverty*. Online: www.findingframes.org/Finding%20Frames%20New%20ways%20to%20engage%20the%20UK%20public%20in%20global%20poverty%20Bond%202011.pdf p 67 (accessed 16 June 2017).

Doll, R., Peto, R., Boreham, J. and Sutherland, I. (2004) 'Mortality in relation to smoking: 50 years' observations on male British doctors', *British Medical Journal*, 328: 1519.

Domegan, C., McHugh, P., Devaney, M, Duane, S., Hogan, M., Broome, B., Layton, R., Joyce, J., Mazzonetto, M., and Piwowarczyk, J. (2016) 'Systems-thinking Social Marketing; Conceptual Extensions and Empirical Investigations' *Journal of Marketing Management*, 32(11–12): 1123–1144

Donovan, R.J., James, R., Jalleh, G. and Sidebottom, C. (2006) 'Implementing mental health promotion: The "Act-Belong-Commit" Mentally Healthy WA campaign in Western Australia', *International Journal of Mental Health Promotion*, 8(1): 29–38.

Fletcher, A., Guthrie, J., Steane, P., Roos, G and Pike, S. (2003) 'Mapping stakeholder perceptions for a third sector organisation', *Journal of Intellectual Capital*, 4(4): 513.

Fligstein, D. (2001) 'Social skill and the theory of fields', *Sociological Theory*, 19(2): 105–125.

Fligstein, N. and McAdam, D. (2011) 'Toward a general theory of strategic action fields', *Sociological Theory*, 29(1): 1–26.

Freeman, R.E. (1984) *Strategic Management: A Stakeholder Approach*. Boston, MA: Pitman.

Gillan, A. (2006) 'In Iraq, life expectancy is 67. Minutes from Glasgow city centre, it's 54', *The Guardian*, 21 January.

Harvey, P.D. (1997) 'Advertising Affordable Contraceptives: The Social Marketing Experience', Ch. 10 in M.E. Goldberg, M. Fishbein and S.E. Middlestadt (eds) *Social Marketing: Theoretical and Practical Perspectives*. Mahwah, NJ: Lawrence Erlbaum Associates.

Hastings, G. and Angus, K. (2004) 'The influence of the tobacco industry on European tobacco-control policy', in The ASPECT Consortium (ed.) *Tobacco or Health in the European Union Past, Present and Future*. Prepared with financing from the EC Directorate-General for Health and Consumer Protection. Luxembourg: Office for Official Publications of the European Communities.

Hastings, G. and Elliott, B. (1993) 'Social Marketing Practice in Traffic Safety', Ch. III in *Marketing of Traffic Safety*. Paris: OECD, pp.35–53.

Hastings, G. and McDermott, L. (2006) 'Putting social marketing into practice', *British Medical Journal*, 332: 1210–1121.

Hastings, G.B. and Stead, M. (1999) *Using the media in drugs prevention*. Drugs Prevention Initiative Green Paper. London: Home Office Central Drugs Prevention Initiative, Paper 19.

ITC (2002) *Developments in the UK Television Market*. London: Independent Television Commission (ITC). Online: www.ofcom.org.uk/static/archive/itc/research/industry_info_march02.pdf (accessed May 2016).

Jobber, D. (2004) *Principles and Practice of Marketing*, 4th edn. Maidenhead: McGraw-Hill International.

King Jr., M.L. (1963) *Address at March on Washington for Jobs and Freedom*, 28 August, Lincoln Memorial, Washington, DC.

Kotler, P. and Armstrong, G. (2004) *Principles of Marketing*, 10th edn (International Edition). London: Pearson/Prentice Hall.

Kotler, P. and Roberto, E.L. (1989) *Social Marketing: Strategies for Changing Public Behaviour*. New York, NY: The Free Press.

Kotler, P. and Zaltman, G. (1971) 'Social marketing: An approach to planned social change', *Journal of Marketing*, 35(3): 3–12.

Kotler, P., Armstrong, G., Saunders, J. and Wong, V. (1999) *Principles of Marketing*, 2nd European Edition. Prentice Hall Europe.

Layard, R. (2005) *Happiness: Lessons from a New Science*. London: Allen Lane.

Layton, R. A. (2014) 'Formation, growth and adaptive change in marketing systems', *Journal of Marcomarketing*, 35(3): 302–319.

Lefebvre, R.C., Doner, L., Johnston, C., Loughrey, K., Balch, G.I. and Sutton, S.M. (1995) 'Use of database marketing and consumer-based health communication in message design: An example from the office of cancer communications': "5 A Day for Better Health" program', in E. Maibach and R.L. Parrott (eds) *Designing Health Messages: Approaches From Communication Theory and Public Health Practice*. Thousand Oaks, CA: Sage Publications.

MacFadyen, L., Stead, M. and Hastings, G.B. (2002) 'Social Marketing', Ch. 27 in M.J. Baker (ed.) *The Marketing Book*, 5th edn. Oxford: Butterworth-Heinemann.

McGrath, J. (1995) 'The Gatekeeping Process: The Right Combinations to Unlock the Gates', Ch. 11 in E. Maibach and R.C. Parrott (eds) *Designing Health Messages: Approaches From Communication Theory and Public Health Practice*. Thousand Oaks, CA: Sage Publications.

McHugh, P., Domegan, C., Devaney, M. and Hastings, G. (2015) A Set of *Sea Change Guiding Principles and Protocols*. EU Sea Change Project, Whitaker Institute, NUI Galway, Ireland.

Mullins, J.W., Boyd, H.W., Walker, O.C. and Larreche, J.-C. (2004) *Marketing Management* (Intl Edition). London: McGraw-Hill.

Noble, G. (2006) 'Maintaining Social Marketing's Relevance: A Dualistic Approach', ANZMAC Conference, Brisbane, Australia.

Percy, L. (1983) 'A review of the effect of specific advertising elements upon overall communication response', *Current Issues and Research in Advertising*, University of Michigan.

Polonsky, M.J., Carlson, L. and Fry, M.-L. (2003) 'The harm chain: A public policy development and stakeholder perspective', *Marketing Theory*, 3 (3): 345–364.

Rangun, V.K., Karim, S. and Sandberg, S.K. (1996) 'Do better at doing good', *Harvard Business Review*, 74(3): 42–54.

Reichheld, F.F. (2003) 'The one number you need to grow', *Harvard Business Review*, 81(12): 46–54.

Saunders, S.G., Barrington D.J. and Sridharan, S. (2015) 'Redefining social marketing: beyond behavioural change', *Journal of Social Marketing*, 5(2): 160–168. doi: 10.1108/JSOCM-03-2014-0021.

Shiner, M. and Newburn, T. (1996) *Young People, Drugs and Peer Education: An Evaluation of the Youth Awareness Programme (YAP)*. London: DPI, Home Office.

Skinner, S.C., Strecher, V.J. and Hospers, H. (1994) 'Physicians' recommendations for mammography: Do tailored messages make a difference?', *American Journal of Public Health*, 84(1): 43–49.

Stead, M., Wimbush, E., Eadie, D.R. and Teer, P. (1997) 'A qualitative study of older people's perceptions of ageing and exercise: The implications for health promotion', *Health Education Journal*, 56(1): 3–16.

Stokes, D.R. (ed.) (1997) *Marketing: A Case Study Approach*, 2nd edn. London: Letts Educational.

Tapp, A. and Spotswood, F. (2013) 'From the 4Ps to COM-SM: reconfiguring the social marketing mix',*Journal of Social Marketing*, 3(3: 206–222). doi: 10.1108/JSOCM-01-2013-0011.

Thorogood, M., Coulter, A., Jones, L., Yudkin, P., Muir, J. and Mant, D. (1993) 'Factors affecting response to an invitation to attend for a health check', *Journal of Epidemiology and Community Health*, 47(3): 224–228.

Tones, K. (1996) 'Models of mass media: Hypodermic, aerosol or agent provocateur?', *Drugs: Education, Prevention and Policy*, 3(1): 29–37.

US Department of Health and Human Services (1989) 'Reducing the Health Consequences of Smoking', Report of the Surgeon General.

Wallack, L., Dorfman, L., Jernigan, D. and Themba, M. (1993) *Media Advocacy and Public Health*. Newbury Park, CA: Sage Publications.

Walsh, A., Domegan, C. and Fleming, D. (2012) 'Marketing response to environmental decline and the call for sustainability', *Social Business*, 2(2): 121–143.

Wilson, R.M.S. and Gilligan, C. (2005) *Strategic Marketing Management: Planning, Implementation and Control*, 3rd edn. Oxford: Elsevier Butterworth-Heinemann.

Woodruffe, H. (1995) *Services Marketing*. London: M&E Pitman.

WoSCAP (2005) West of Scotland Cancer Awareness Project 2002–2005. Final Report. UK Institute for Social Marketing.

5

Research and the teller of tales

Anita's dilemma of needing to trim Christmas fantasies without damaging her children's evolving sense of self stands in stark contrast to Coca-Cola's images of a joy-filled, warm family home, where an abundance of toys and food and ensuring happiness are the holiday narrative. However, they have in common an important quality: they both illustrate the power of the story. The Coke Christmas has been carefully crafted by ad agency creatives to evoke feelings of comfort and plenty, and link these with a commercial product. However synthetic it is, it has been immensely powerful, moulding our values, understanding and appreciation of one of humankind's most important festivals. A festival, incidentally, that is supposed to be about moral values, new beginnings and renewal, and not the consumption of sugary drinks.

Anita's story brings us down to earth with a bump by reminding us that many people will never have a 'Coke Christmas', just a painful awareness of its unaffordability. Again, it evokes emotions, but very different ones: sadness perhaps, or anger about injustice. Together, the stories tell us a great deal about our society: about the extent of materialism, about inequalities, about vulnerability. They connect individual behaviour to a social context and give each of us an identity; we all have our own story to tell. As a result, stories resonate and offer insight and wisdom that facts and figures alone cannot provide. This makes them invaluable to social marketing: they are the bedrock of our core social marketing orientations – client, creative, collective and competitive – that we discussed in Chapter 2.

At the same time, however, while stories take us beyond the data, they must emerge from and be grounded in these. Anita's story depends for its power on detailed facts and figures about the extent of inequalities in our society. This is how we know that her family's predicament is not an aberration or even an exception – it is commonplace. Likewise, the glitzy and seductive image of Coke is put in its proper perspective by the same data showing that many people are excluded by a system that depends on money for participation. And carefully conducted public health studies remind us that the much-lauded product actually makes you fat and rots your teeth (a dentist friend refers to all such sugary sodas as 'liquid chainsaws').

Stories, then, depend on the science of research, while research becomes the art of story-telling. For these reasons, social marketing has an "abiding and very adult relationship with research – which recognises that it should act as neither an overbearing judge nor a blunt substitute for decision making, but as a facilitator of intelligent action" (Hastings 2011: 5).

Against this background, we examine research in this chapter. The intention is to look at research through a social marketing lens: the thinking that underpins it; the purpose it serves; the potential and pitfalls it presents. In the process, we discuss methodology, but only insofar as it serves our main purpose. We start by arguing that research should be seen as (a) a navigational aid, to guide progress and aid decision making; and (b) a way of learning about people and empathising with them. We then consider what decisions we, as social marketers, have to make and examine the qualitative and quantitative research methodologies that can be used to inform them.

The chapter concludes by warning about the potential downsides of research if it is misused or overused. It can, for example, become a way of avoiding hard choices or smothering intuitive thinking. It can also encourage what might be termed the 'intervention mentality', which focuses its efforts on perfecting materials and mechanisms for intervening, rather than the more important task of improving our understanding of people, their lifestyles, and how they make sense of the world.

This brings us full circle. Arguably, the job of social marketing research is to uncover and map the development of people's individual and collective stories so that social marketers can then work with these to enable progressive and empowered change.

Learning outcomes

By the end of this chapter, you should be able to:

✓   Discuss the importance of research in social marketing

✓   Explain the navigational and empathic roles of research

✓   Discuss the role of the story in social marketing research

✓   Outline the research decisions social marketers have to make

✓   Model the research steps and methodologies that can help guide them

✓   Outline the dangers of an over-reliance on research, stultifying decision making and hindering progress.

Key words

Decision making – empathy – evaluation – formative research – individual/group interviews – Internet research – navigational aid – problem definition – qualitative research – quantitative methods – research – research methodology – secondary data – storytelling.

The purpose of learning in social marketing

In social marketing, research is a strategic tool: it guides the planning process (Chapter 4) and helps maintain the creative, competitive, collective and (all-important) client orientations (Chapter 2).

Strategic planning, building successful behaviour change programmes as we discussed in Chapter 4, is like climbing a Himalayan peak – with a resulting need for maps, compasses and careful route planning. Research fulfils the role of these **navigational aids**. It helps us get our bearings; establish achievable objectives and staging posts towards these; check our progress; adjust our route; and determine when we have reached the summit. Furthermore, because our ultimate goal is relative rather than absolute (improved, rather than perfect health; a better society, not an idyll), our Everest is infinitely high and our planning has to be continuous. This may sound grandiose, but it merely reflects what happens in commercial marketing: Coke has been realigning our conceptions of Christmas for the best part of a century.

This long-term perspective emphasises the need for progressive learning, not just within but also between initiatives, and ties in with our discussion of social marketing planning

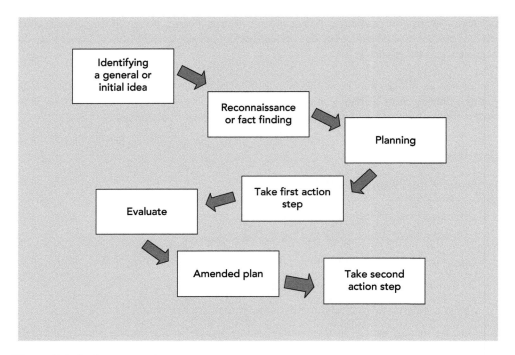

Figure 5.1 Action research

(*Source:* adapted from Lewin 1951)

in Chapter 4, communications in Chapter 6, and systems thinking in Chapter 11. The implications for methodology feedback to the work of Kurt Lewin coined the term 'action research', and emphasised the need for empirical research to go beyond the production of books and articles, and help us to take action and make decisions on social phenomena. This is the same man whose much-quoted aphorism 'there is nothing so practical as a good theory' we noted in Chapter 3. Lewin highlighted the notion of incremental learning using a range of methodologies and expressed this as a **cyclical** research process (see Figure 5.1).

This feeds into a plan of action that defines ultimate goals/objectives as well as immediate and intermediate steps, all of which are honed and adapted as the plan is implemented. At the same time, however, the sequential model should not be applied too rigidly; because social phenomena are complex and subtle, the researcher has to be both flexible and sensitive. All these lessons transfer neatly into social marketing thinking, which sees research as a process that provides progressive learning – not just about how we should intervene, but also about the people with whom we want to intervene, or, more properly, work.

Client orientation. This brings us to the primary of social marketing (refer back to Chapter 2), the drive to see the world through the eyes of our clients and stakeholders. As we have already noted, clients, stakeholders and even competitors are all free to choose whether or not they do business with us. The decisions we make about constructing our marketing plan, therefore, have to be driven by an understanding of these actors, their motives and lifestyles. This is sometimes referred to as adopting an *experiential* view and *value co-creation*, taking in the thinking, feeling and doing or the head, heart and hands of potential exchanges.

In *To Kill a Mockingbird* (see Box 5.1) Harper Lee suggests that in order to really understand why people behave as they do you have to 'get inside their skin'; she is making the point that you need to be able to empathise with them.

BOX 5.1   EMPATHY – A SIMPLE BUT CRUCIAL SKILL

Atticus (the father) is explaining to his daughter (Scout) how she can get on better with her new teacher:

Atticus stood up and walked to the end of the porch. When he completed his examination of the wistaria vine he strolled back to me.

"First of all," he said, "if you can learn a simple trick, Scout, you'll get along a lot better with all kinds of folks. You never really understand a person until you consider things from his point of view – "

"Sir?"

"– until you climb into his skin and walk around in it."

Atticus said I had learned many things today, and Miss Caroline had learned several things herself. She had learned not to hand something to a Cunningham, for one thing, but if Walter and I had put ourselves in her shoes we'd have seen it was an honest mistake on her part. We could not expect her to learn all Maycomb's ways in one day, and we could not hold her responsible when she knew no better.

(*Source:* Harper Lee, *To Kill a Mockingbird*, 1960)

One powerful way to empathize with others is to listen to their story and connect with their emotions. At the beginning of this chapter, hearing about Anita, her family and their lives makes it easier for us to empathise with their circumstances and begin to understand how welfare is altering her behaviour, thinking and feelings.

Exercise 5.1 explores how Nelson Mandela used a similar approach to connect with young African men.

EXERCISE 5.1   NELSON MANDELA AND TOBACCO CONTROL

When Nelson Mandela was serving his sentence in the prison on Robben Island, he took on the task of briefing each new intake of prisoners. These were young men whose lives had been turned upside down; a few weeks previously they had been fighting the hated apartheid regime with Molotov cocktails and stones, now they were prisoners of this same brutal system. They were angry and frustrated. Mandela's talk was designed to help them adjust and survive in what were very difficult circumstances.

(continued)

(continued)

Perhaps surprisingly, he found time to touch on tobacco. However, he was far too wise to wag the finger or invoke horror stories about premature death. Instead, he simply remarked that he had noticed some of the new prisoners were smoking, and reminded them that tobacco was dependence-inducing. He also noted that the guards were well aware of this and would on occasion supply prisoners with tobacco. In return, of course, they would ask favours of the prisoners. Sometimes, he continued, the inmate's need for tobacco would be small, and the favours small; but sometimes the need would be big and the favour would grow accordingly . . .

That is all Mandela said; he left his audience to complete the story.

Put yourself in the shoes of one of these the young men. How would you react? How would it make you feel about your smoking? What would you do?

Now think about how you would have reacted if Mandela had taken a more traditional approach, telling you that smoking causes lung cancer – and anyway was prohibited by the prison's new smoke-free ordinances.

Mandela used the power of the story both to connect with these angry young prisoners, and provide them with a constructive way forward. He knew they were united by a hatred of the apartheid regime and he aligned tobacco use with this regime – an indictment that easily surpassed its carcinogenic properties. He then presented the rejection of tobacco as an act of rebellion against the regime, as a means of undermining the guards. Thus tobacco becomes part of their political struggle, their fight for justice, freedom and status, of their story – and quitting smoking enables them to become heroes in their own story.

But the lesson here is not that we all have to become Nelson Mandelas – it is that **we all have a story to tell**, a narrative that encapsulates what we think is important in our lives, past, present and future. Harnessing these stories is a potentially invaluable social marketing tool, but doing so requires careful research and systematic methods. Even Mandela's efforts were in a sense research based. Not that he had done surveys of the young prisoners or interviewed them, but that he listened to them and got to know them, their values and their aspirations intimately, and these insights were vital.

Richard Krueger (2010) reminds us that there are three key steps in storytelling research. Having identified the practice or behaviour of concern you have to (a) capture the story of those engaged in it using pictures, words and dialogue; (b) present that story by identifying themes, patterns or contradictions; and (c) uncover a lesson or moral. These correspond perfectly with the three core stages of any research project: data collection, data analysis and data presentation.

Try this for yourself with Exercise 5.2.

EXERCISE 5.2   TELLING A POLISHED STORY

From your experience or reading, choose a behaviour that is known to be risky and needs to change, and a target group which is involved with it. It might be binge drinking among teenage girls or football hooliganism by young men. Now follow Krueger's three steps:

1. Capture the story (through quotes, pictures, words, dialogue).
2. Present the story (as told or re-scripted?). What are the main themes, patterns and differences?
3. End with the message (the moral, point being made, lesson).

(*Source:* Krueger 2010)

Krueger goes on to present a beautiful example of how insightful this can be (see Box 5.2).

BOX 5.2   STORY EXAMPLE – MEDICAL MISTAKES

We were conducting an evaluation of patient safety in a large medical system. Our goal was to uncover the barriers that deterred the hospital staff from disclosing mistakes. It was a sensitive topic. With some frequency, frontline staff contended that hospital management sent mixed signals. One participant told this story:

"I enjoy hang gliding. We've got some terrific places to hang glide in this area. When we do it, we do it as a group. We gather at the top of a mountain and then one person sails off alone while the others watch. We call this person the 'wind dummy'. Everyone's eyes are on this first person. We watch how the updrafts and crosswinds affect the glide. We are attentive to the turbulence and watch for any difficulties encountered by the wind dummy. When this first person has completed the sail, then the rest of us take off, incorporating the lessons we learned from watching the wind dummy. The same is true here at the hospital. We watch what happens when someone reports a medical mistake. If they crash and burn, then the rest of us change our behaviour accordingly."

(*Source:* Krueger 2010)

Stories then have huge potential to enrich all social marketing research.

A mix of methodologies

This strategic purpose, combining long-term planning with empathy for people's stories, encourages social marketers to draw on both *positivist* and *humanist* research traditions.

The first builds on the notion that there is an objective reality out there that we are trying to measure and influence. This pushes us towards quantitative methods, theory to build on previous insights, establishing cause and effect and hypothesis testing. The second recognises that the world – or at least the social and behavioural bits of it in which we are interested – is actually much messier than this, and will not succumb to scientific analysis, however rigorous and highly powered. As a result, social marketers, like their commercial cousins, adopt a pragmatic mix of methodologies that they feel will best aid decision making and help them get a better (though always imperfect) understanding of what makes people do what they do.

A large selection of the case studies provide good illustrations of action-oriented, empathetic social marketing research. Check these out to see which is your favourite.

Testing or learning?

All too often with behaviour change, however, the focus is on testing the *intervention*, which pushes things towards a more positivist research approach. In public health, for example, such thinking is exemplified in the randomised controlled trial (RCT). The RCT adopts the classic experimental design, randomly ascribing subjects to either an experimental or a matched control group. The first group is exposed to the intervention and both are monitored before and after the trial. Inferential statistics are then used to determine whether or not the intervention had any effect. The overriding aim is to separate out the effects of the intervention from any other possible change agents – most notably there is a need to discount the impact of the characteristics of the different populations.

This makes very good sense when the problem at hand is to determine whether or not a new drug therapy is effective. In these circumstances, it is vital that we determine what impact a new substance has, not least – as thalidomide (see Box 5.3) will always remind us – because it can do all too apparent harm as well as good. As the UK's Medical Research Council (MRC) makes clear, the great virtue of the RCT is that it helps to separate out the 'active ingredients' in an intervention. We can find out precisely what the drug is doing by using placebos and double-blind procedures to factor out any contribution from the human beings involved (MRC 2000).

BOX 5.3   THE THALIDOMIDE DISASTER

Thalidomide was developed in the 1950s by the West German pharmaceutical company Chemie Grünenthal GmbH to expand the company's product range beyond antibiotics. It was an anticonvulsive drug, but instead it made users sleepy and relaxed. It seemed a perfect example of newly fashionable tranquilisers.

Animal tests did not include tests looking at the effects of the drug during pregnancy. The apparently harmless thalidomide was licensed in July 1956 for prescription-free, over-the-counter sale in Germany and most European countries. The drug also reduced morning sickness, so it became popular with pregnant women.

There was an increase in births of thalidomide-impaired children in Germany and elsewhere. However, no link with thalidomide was made until 1961. The drug was only taken off the market after the German Widukind Lenz and the Australian William McBride independently suggested the link. Over 10,000 children were born with thalidomide-related disabilities worldwide.

There was a long criminal trial in Germany and a British newspaper campaign. They forced Grünenthal and its British licensee, the Distillers Company, to give financial support to victims of the drug. Thalidomide led to tougher testing and drug approval procedures in many countries, including the United States and the United Kingdom.

(*Source:* Science Museum undated)

However, social marketers, as is the case with many people in health promotion, get uneasy when the same methods are advocated as the 'optimal study design' for 'complex interventions to improve health', which includes 'media-delivered health promotion campaigns' (MRC 2000: 2). In a similar vein, the US Department of Education argues that "well-designed and implemented randomized controlled trials are considered the 'gold standard' for evaluating an intervention's effectiveness, in fields such as medicine, welfare and employment policy, and psychology" (2003: 1).

It is not that we can be less cautious about our offerings than a surgeon or pharmacist. A badly conceived drug prevention programme that hectors and patronises might actually increase the attractiveness of illicit substances. In addition, the programme will typically use public money, so it is important to know this is being well spent. Furthermore, as we will discuss in Chapter 10, there are serious ethical issues to consider in behaviour change. All of this demands that we treat our offerings with great care.

On the other hand, the Hippocratic principle, advising us first and foremost to do no harm, can be too limiting a guide when inactivity is also dangerous.

We should also recognise that caution and precision are not the same thing. Focusing in on testing the intervention before we proceed underrates the importance of the target group in the behaviour change process. Think back for a moment to our discussion of relationship marketing in Chapter 2 and pick up on the idea that satisfaction, trust and commitment are key outcomes. How people feel about what we are doing will help determine what behaviour change results. Add to this the idea that our clients are not just recipients, but also co-designers of improved health or community safety. From these perspectives, limiting our studies to the isolated influence of the intervention seems perverse to the social marketer. Or, as Stead *et al.* put it, "the traditional biomedical approach to evaluation, with the randomised controlled trial as its gold standard, has limited relevance for the analysis of complex health promotion interventions" (2002: 354).

The story, with its practicality, tells us about people. (Think back to our discussion of client and creative orientations of social marketing in Chapter 2.) The danger with an overly positivist approach, as an RCT can be, is that the people we want to persuade, influence and build relationships with become marginalised, which both limits our effectiveness and causes alienation. As the songwriter Jez Lowe expresses it:

So you people in power and position I tell you beware
I tell you beware
Of your facts and your figures to tell you what, when and where
'Cos your facts and your figures are the likes of me
And don't try and tell me how me life should be
– or you won't make old bones.

(J. Lowe/Lowe Life Music 1985)

The lyrics have a sweet symmetry about them, as the last line turns the threat, so beloved of public health and safety campaigns, back on us. We will discuss the pros and cons of fear messaging again in Chapter 6.

Lessons from commerce

A myopic focus on the intervention also undermines the great opportunity to learn on the hoof. The dominant brands in our lives – Marlboro, Coca-Cola, Nike, McDonald's – have an enormous impact on our behaviour. We know, for example, that tobacco and alcohol brands are among the key drivers of youth smoking (Greenland 2016) and drinking (Harris et al. 2015), and a study in California among 3- to 5-year-olds showed that children's food preferences are being moulded by McDonald's branding even before they have learned to tie their shoelaces (Robinson *et al.* 2007). Brands come from a mixture

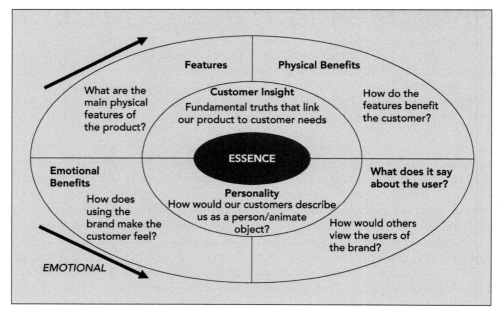

Figure 5.2 Branding prescription drugs

(*Source:* Devlin *et al.* 2007)

of happenstance, intuition and bright ideas, which are guided by a variety of different research exercises and traditions, ranging from the ethnographic to the heavily quantitative simulated modeling.

Figure 5.2, for example, shows how, having used RCTs to develop them, pharmaceutical companies go about selling their new drugs in the UK. This gives us a useful glimpse of how a marketer sees the task of behaviour change. Bear in mind that, as this document concerns prescription medicines in the UK, the marketing is aimed at doctors, not patients.[1] It seems that even when trying to influence the behaviour of highly trained professionals, whom it might be thought would be susceptible to hard-nosed, positivist arguments, softer, more flexible appeals are needed. They want to engage 'emotional' as well as 'rational drivers' and determine how 'using the brand makes the customer feel' and 'how others would see the users of the brand'. This is one of a number of internal documents that go on to talk about the need to make doctors feel 'reassured', 'fashionable' and even 'sexy' about prescribing particular drugs.

RCTs are unlikely to help here. They might be able to disentangle cause and effect, but they will say little about the personality of a brand. More flexible methods are needed to do this.

Figure 5.2 also illustrates a more basic truth: human behaviour is just too complex to succumb to the RCT. The MRC's comments extolling their virtues for public health researchers overlook a crucial point for social marketers – that when it comes to behaviour change, the most important 'active ingredients' are people. Or as Jez Lowe puts it, "your facts and your figures are the likes of me."

Research methodology

Social marketers then will do all sorts of research at every juncture of the social marketing planning process. The point is to get the best possible grip on the client's perspective (both rational and emotional) so that we can make intelligent decisions about how to build and maintain good relationships with them. The trick is to work out *what* sort of information we need *when, from whom and why* to guide our decision making and actions.

Before looking at these issues in detail, however, we need to know more about methodology. This section will touch briefly on secondary research (the use of existing research data), and then qualitative and quantitative interviewing. It is not intended to provide a comprehensive discussion of methodology or a do-it-yourself guide; there are other sources for this (e.g. Malhotra 2016). Rather, we just want to demonstrate that there are a range of techniques available, each of which has its strengths and weaknesses – and that the best social marketing uses these in conjunction with one another.

Secondary research

Any research exercise should begin by seeking out and analysing existing relevant studies. This can be done with great rigour and precision using the systematic review (SR) procedures or more flexibly using more conventional narrative reviews (NR) (see Box 5.4).

BOX 5.4   SYSTEMATIC AND NARRATIVE REVIEWS

A review of a clearly formulated question that uses systematic and explicit methods to identify, select, and critically appraise relevant research, and to collect and analyse data from the studies that are included in the review. Statistical methods (meta-analysis) may or may not be used to analyse and summarise the results of the included studies.

(*Source:* Cochrane Collaboration 2005)

The rigour and precision SR provides are invaluable when we need to resolve specific issues of cause and effect (e.g. does tobacco advertising encourage teen smoking?) which are likely to be hotly contested – and can even finish up in the courtroom. The same qualities are also useful when trying to establish whether a particular behaviour change approach produces results. For example, some years ago the Institute for Social Marketing undertook a series of SRs looking at whether social marketing works in three specific fields: nutrition, exercise and substance misuse. Because the reviews were systematic, the (positive) results are much more credible than they would have been had we conducted standard reviews. This work has recently been updated and greatly extended by Sharyn Rundle-Thiele and colleagues (see Box 5.5). The principal aim in all these reviews is to disentangle cause and effect, so SR is again one of the best approaches.

BOX 5.5   SYSTEMATIC REVIEWS OF SOCIAL MARKETING EFFECTIVENESS

Almestihiri, R., Rundle-Thiele, S.R., Parkinson, J. and Arli, D. (forthcoming) 'Extent of benchmark criteria use in social marketing tobacco cessation programs: a systematic review', *Social Marketing Quarterly* [accepted 16 March 2017].

Almosa, Y., Parkinson, Y. and Rundle-Thiele, S. (2017) 'Littering reduction: a systematic review of research 1995–2015', *Social Marketing Quarterly*, 16: 71–96. Buyucek, N., Kubacki, K., Rundle-Thiele, S. and Pang, B. (2016) 'A systematic review of stakeholder involvement in social marketing interventions', *Australasian Marketing Journal*, 24(1): 8–19.

Carins, J.E. and Rundle-Thiele, S.R. (2014) 'Eating for the better: a social marketing review (2000–2012)', *Public Health Nutrition*, 17(7): 1628–1639.

Dietrich, T., Rundle-Thiele, S., Schuster, L., and Connor, J.P. (2016) 'A systematic literature review of alcohol education programmes in middle and high school settings (2000–2014)', *Health Education*, 116(1): 50–68.

Fujihira, H., Kubacki, K., Ronto, R., Pang, B. and Rundle-Thiele, S. (2015) 'Social marketing physical activity interventions among adults sixty years old and older: a systematic review', *Social Marketing Quarterly*, 21(4): 214–229.

Knox, K., Pang, B., Fujihira, H., David, P., Parkinson, J. and Rundle-Thiele, S.R. (forthcoming) 'Organ donation decision communication: a systematic literature review and research agenda', *Transplantation* [accepted 13 January 2017].

Kubacki, K., Ronto, R., Lahtinen, V., Pang, B. and Rundle-Thiele, S. (2017) 'Social marketing interventions aiming to increase physical activity among adults: a systematic review', *Health Education*, 117(1): 69–89.

Kubacki, K., Rundle-Thiele, S., Lahtinen, V. and Parkinson, J. (2015) 'A systematic review assessing the extent of social marketing principle use in interventions targeting children (2000-2014)', *Young Consumers*, 16(2): 141–158.

Kubacki, K., Rundle-Thiele, S., Pang, B. and Buyucek, N. (2015) 'Minimising alcohol harm: a systematic social marketing review (2000–2014)', *Journal of Business Research*, 68(10): 2214–2222.

Kubacki, K., Rundle-Thiele, S., Pang, B., Carins, J., Parkinson, J., Fujihira, H. and Ronto, R. (2017) 'Segmentation in social marketing: An umbrella review', in T. Dietrich, S. Rundle-Thiele, and K. Kubacki (eds) *Segmentation in Social Marketing*. Heidelberg: Springer.

Kubacki, K., Rundle-Thiele, S., Schuster, L., Wessels, C. and Gruneklee, N. (2015) 'Digital innovation in social marketing: A systematic literature of interventions using digital channels for engagement', in W. Wymer (ed.) *Innovations in Social Marketing and Public Health Communication: Improving the Quality of Life for Individuals and Communities*. Heidelberg: Springer.

However, SR can be less helpful when we are trying to answer broader questions of not just what works, but in what circumstances, how and why. Like RCTs, they can be too inflexible for the task. This is perhaps not surprising: the rigorous quality controls that SR applies mean that they frequently limit inclusion to RCTs.

For this remit, a conventional narrative review is a more flexible and practical option. The focus can move beyond identifying which previous efforts have worked, and towards helping us define the problem and identify potential solutions. Thus, secondary sources can help answer crucial questions about the prevalence and prominence of a particular social or health problem. They can shed light on the extent of the drugs or youth disorder problems in a particular locality, for instance, and show how these stack up against other issues. They may show that drugs are indeed a problem, but that alcohol is much more of one, suggesting that funders are less comfortable with addressing this issue head on (perhaps because of industry interests).

Using a narrative review, secondary sources can also reveal how previous campaigns and initiatives have fared, providing valuable clues about the best way forward. Note we are not now talking simply about whether previous interventions worked, but the broader questions we identified above about how they were received and why.

Thus both systematic and narrative reviews have a role to play in social marketing research: the rigour of the first helps identify cause and effect; the flexibility and pragmatism of the latter helps us move forward. Furthermore, it is wasteful and risky to start on primary research until existing secondary sources have been exhausted. However, primary research is usually essential once we need to know about how today's target group will respond to a specific intervention, the objectives it can realistically fulfil and how it should set about doing so.

Broadly speaking, primary research comes in two forms: qualitative and quantitative.

Qualitative methods

Qualitative methods can cover a range of techniques such as ethnography, grounded theory, case studies and participatory research, as highlighted in Box 5.6.

BOX 5.6   PARTICIPATORY RESEARCH

What makes participatory research participatory? Typically, participatory research involves a process of learning and reflection, followed by action, and then by more learning and reflection, and so on. Crucially, though, the research is carried out *with* people rather than *on* them; ordinary people who would normally be 'subjects' of research are given the power to help define the research problem, collect and analyse the data, interpret its meaning and communicate it to others. They – not the research team or the funder – own the findings and the goal is to take action, rather than simply to create knowledge (Dietrich *et al.* 2016).

Paulo Freire maintained that "the silenced are not just incidental to the curiosity of the researcher but are the masters of inquiry into the underlying causes of the events in their world" (1982: 30–31). This illustrates the core principle of participatory research: that people who wouldn't usually have a great deal of power or influence are empowered, through research, to change things for themselves and their communities. So, the participatory researcher becomes a catalyst and facilitator of the process, rather than the sole seeker, interpreter and owner of knowledge.

This section now concentrates on the ever-popular observational and interviewing qualitative procedures. (For a detailed discussion of ethnography, grounded theory and case studies, see Pettigrew and Roberts 2011. If you want to know more about observation and other methods, consult with standard market research textbooks.)

Qualitative interviewing is typically done in-depth with small samples that have been selected through non-random procedures; it can take various forms including individual in-depth interviews, paired interviews, small group interviews, key informant interviews and focus groups. Detailed questionnaires are not used, although interviews may be guided by a schedule of 'points to be covered' or 'questions to be asked' or a 'script'. Respondents can be interviewed individually or in 'focus' groups of 4–12 people. Case Study 3 combined Key Informant Interviews (KII) with focus groups to document service users' preferences, likes and dislikes. A similar KII approach is being used in brain health where KII regarding cognitive training and potential intervention participation (Panizzutti *et al.* 2017), while Case Study 1 used in-depth interviews and focus groups in designing a complex social marketing intervention as well as its recruitment and retention strategies. The research explored the culture of antibiotic prescribing and consumption in the community for urinary tract infections (UTIs) from the perspective of both the GPs (N = 15) and community members (N = 6 community focus groups with 42 participants). It identified key barriers and facilitators to change.

The main advantage of qualitative interviewing comes from the depth or quality of the data it provides. It enables the researcher to approach a subject in a completely open-ended manner, starting from the perspective of the respondent; using their language and concepts to develop the discussion and relying on their experiences to illustrate it. Thus, in contrast to questionnaire-based research, there is no need to make assumptions about what the important issues are, how to label these or the type of responses that might be expected.

Qualitative interviewing procedures also allow a range of responses to be examined. For example, when checking reactions to media materials, fairly straightforward matters such as understanding of the language used, or its ability to communicate clearly, can be assessed, as well as more complex issues, such as likes and dislikes, audience identification and other emotional responses (see Chapter 6). The subtlety and flexibility of qualitative methods also help when researching intense or potentially threatening issues such as sexual health or life-threatening illness (Hastings *et al.* 1990). Similarly exploring and building brand imagery would be very difficult without the flexibility of these methods.

Thinking back to the pharmaceutical marketing discussed in Figure 5.2, how would we go about exploring brand image, and how prescribing particular medicines would make a doctor feel? What is the best way to approach elusive phenomena such as reassurance, fashion and sexiness? Try Exercise 5.3.

EXERCISE 5.3   MEASURING HOPES AND DREAMS

In Figure 5.2, we saw the complex and subtle ways in which pharmaceutical companies promote their prescription medicines to doctors. We noted that branding, and the capacity of a particular product to make a GP feel reassured, fashionable and even sexy, introduce elusive constructs and ideas that are not susceptible to rigorous positive methodologies such as the RCT. Indeed, even qualitative methodologies struggle to plumb these depths. How could you go about doing research to provide these insights? What questions might you ask and how? What obstacles could you meet?

One option would be to address the issues directly and simply ask GPs how they feel about prescribing different medicines, and how this varies depending on whether it is a branded or generic product. The problem you will face, however, is that GPs may be reluctant to admit their prescribing is influenced by anything other than the best science. It is also possible, of course, that this behaviour is unconscious; that they do not realise their prescribing is affected by something as subjective as brand image. You would likely meet the same problem if you asked most men why they bought a particular car. They would tell you about engine size and performance, not the feeling of superiority they get from piloting a four-wheel-drive BMW, which is perfectly capable of crossing the Serengeti, to the local supermarket.

We therefore have to approach our GPs in a more indirect way, probably using some sort of 'projective' technique, where the answer is projected away from the respondent to a third party. This makes it both safer and easier to answer. So you might like to ask a GP, 'What sort of doctor would prescribe medicine A?' or 'How would they feel in doing so?' Taking it a step further, you might try showing them pictures of doctors who just happen to be prescribing generic or branded versions of a particular drug, and ask them to describe the scene. Box 5.7 presents some other examples of projective techniques.

BOX 5.7   FIVE USEFUL PROJECTIVE TECHNIQUES

1. *Personification*: e.g. if the product (image/slogan) were a person, how would you describe him or her/what kind of life would they lead/how would they be different from each other, etc. (adaptable and easy to use)?

2. *Choice ordering*: e.g. place these products (images/slogans) in order from the one you like best to the one you like least (provides a way of understanding the factors that differentiate subjects or items – straightforward to use).

3. *Mapping*: e.g. position each product (image/slogan) on the two-dimensional grid to indicate how much you like each product and how popular each one is (more sophisticated version of choice ordering, allows you to explore the relationship between different attributes – more difficult to administer).

4. *Clustering*: e.g. position the products (images/slogans) according to how closely related they are to each other (useful way of understanding the dimensions people use to judge products – can be difficult to administer).

5. *Completion*: e.g. so . . . ?/what springs to mind . . . ?/what about that one . . . ? (useful way of understanding the factors that shape a person's view about a subject (product/image/slogan) – naturalistic form of enquiry, simple and extremely adaptable).

(*Source*: Douglas Eadie, Institute for Social Marketing)

The quality of the data produced by these methods is also enhanced by the fact that they enable the interviewer to delve into the motivations and reasons underlying responses. They make it possible to ask 'why' questions. This point is illustrated by a Scottish anti-smoking campaign which was misinterpreted by its 10–14-year-old target audience (see Box 5.8). They assumed that bogus products such as a hairspray called 'Ashtré' and an aftershave called 'Stub', which were intended to highlight the drawbacks of smoking, were actually real. Focus group research revealed that this was not because they lacked intelligence or were unsophisticated, but because they could see real benefits in the bogus products. In particular they seemed to be offering a good means of smoking surreptitiously. From the audience's perspective, this was the *sensible way* to interpret the ads. It is difficult to imagine quantitative procedures uncovering this explanation.

BOX 5.8   STUB AND ASHTRÉ

A television advertising campaign targeting 10–14-year-olds aimed to emphasise the benefits of not smoking by promoting a number of bogus products, including an aftershave called 'Stub' and a hairspray called 'Ashtré', both of which made the user smell of cigarettes and thereby much less attractive to the opposite sex. Qualitative research with 10–14-year-olds revealed problems. When they saw the commercials, the anti-smoking message was lost. They believed the products would be real and available in shops.

To understand why they reacted in this way, it was necessary to understand what it is like to be an underage smoker. The research showed that, for them, smoking is forbidden by parents, teachers and other adults, expensive, and a difficult habit to acquire. Initially, it is unpleasant – youngsters complained that their first cigarettes had caused sore throats and sickness – and only after considerable perseverance does it become enjoyable. The bogus products in the anti-smoking commercials would overcome these problems. For the respondents, the products offered obvious benefits that justified their existence; and the strap-line for the ads, "*all the fun of cigarettes, without the drag of smoking*", inadvertently confirmed this.

(*Source:* Hastings 1990)

Qualitative procedures also improve the quality of the data collected by enabling the researcher to monitor *how* things are said. Tone of voice, context and non-verbal cues can all be important here. For example, when researching the potential for using the female condom as a contraceptive among Glasgow women, their hilarity at the idea spoke very articulately about how awkward the product made them feel and how unlikely they were to use it without a considerable amount of persuasion. Again, it is difficult for quantitative methods to provide this kind of insight.

Finally, as we noted above, qualitative procedures permit the examination of delicate and embarrassing topics because they enable the researcher to build a rapport with the respondent. This makes it possible to discuss subjects that are socially unacceptable – or even criminal – such as shoplifting or vandalism, as well as very personal ones such as sexual behaviour. Go to Case Study 23, 'Prevent cervical cancer among Malay women' to read about the sensitive intricacies of cervical cancer screening. It is difficult to delve into areas like these without the trust that in-depth interviewing can generate. It is important to note, though, as we will discuss in Chapter 10, the licence these methods give also raises serious ethical issues.

Julinawati Suanda *et al.*'s case study also shows us how translation and back-translation were used, together with field notes, written inclusive of the facial expressions or body language of the participants and assisted drawings to illustrate more detail about the situation – all to ensure data quality. Read further into the case study to identify other data quality activities of interest.

As well as the quality of the data it provides, qualitative interviewing also has at least three important practical advantages. First, because it is flexible, a range of unfinished materials can be researched. Everything, from rough drawings and concept boards through to polished television commercials, from product designs to product prototypes, can be used to stimulate a response. This makes qualitative interviewing particularly suitable for developmental research on new initiatives. For example, focus groups to guide the development of an initiative to promote fruit and vegetable consumption in a major Scottish city (Anderson *et al.* 2005) tested out the idea of distributing these through primary schools. Initial reactions were favourable. It was only when a storyboard appeared depicting a small child carrying the fruit and veg home that the parents hit on the sheer impracticality of the idea: visions quickly emerged of veggies being thrown around the school bus, bananas getting squashed and tomatoes sat on! Second, qualitative research projects can be conducted quickly – within a week if necessary. Third, because small samples are involved, qualitative research is often relatively cheap.

The main disadvantages of qualitative research concern its statistical validity. In statistical terms, both the sampling and interviewing procedures are flawed. The former is typically too small and selected incorrectly to be representative and the latter is not standardised, thereby precluding the summation of responses. Consequently, it is not possible to use qualitative methods to produce estimates of population prevalence to any calculable degree of accuracy.

Qualitative procedures are also criticised because they put respondents in an artificial situation. For example, in asking them to respond in great detail to a particular leaflet or service, you are probably asking them to do something they would not normally do in everyday life. However, this criticism is true of any research procedure – qualitative or quantitative – that examines the response to an initiative by prompting the subject with examples. It does not invalidate such methods; it just means findings have to be interpreted with caution.

A final criticism commonly levelled at qualitative interviewing is that it is very dependent on the researcher conducting the interview well and analysing the data correctly. All too often, it is argued, excessive subjectivity contaminates the process. In the case of data analysis, for example, the fact that qualitative researchers rely on their own selection and interpretation of the findings is contrasted with the quantitative researchers' production of apparently independent and hard statistics (see below). These problems are most apparent with projective techniques. How do we interpret people's responses to the pictures? How reliable is word association as a means of revealing underlying and unconscious associations? And how do we begin to calibrate the influence of such associations on decision making?

Two points can be made in response to this criticism. First, the objectivity of statistical data is often more illusory than real. Just as with qualitative data, they are greatly influenced by the researcher – they design the questions, attribute meanings to the answers and numbers to the meanings. Second, it is questionable whether researcher influence is a bad thing. Researchers are typically highly qualified, skilled and theoretically informed – a bit like extreme positivism, we end up so distrusting the subjectivity of humankind that we overlook its benefits.

However, the main point to note here is not that there is an overall conclusion to be drawn for or against qualitative research. It is that qualitative procedures have both strengths and weaknesses. The former make them a valuable tool for certain research tasks, but the latter should always be kept in mind.

Individual versus group interviews

Exactly the same 'horses for courses' point applies when choosing between individual and group interviewing. Both approaches have strengths and weaknesses. Individual in-depth interviews provide a clear and longitudinal view of each person's perspective, avoid the problems of peer and group pressure, and permit the discussion of extremely intimate issues.

The strengths of focus groups, on the other hand, stem from the interaction that takes place between respondents. This can take many forms. Respondents can question each other's claims. A group member might remind a fellow respondent that, although he claims to have given up smoking, he accepted a cigarette immediately prior to the group. Respondents might also seek information and guidance from each other – 'What is that new doctor like?' and 'How do you find using condoms?' are both questions that were asked by one respondent of another in groups we have moderated.

They can also provide reassurance and group identity that facilitates the discussion of otherwise difficult topics. For example, groups on drunk driving only came to life when one respondent admitted committing a serious drunk-driving offence. The other members of the group then felt able to admit to similar behaviour. In these instances, the respondents are essentially interviewing each other. It is this dynamic process that contributes to the 'gestalt' of group discussions – the tendency for the whole to amount to more than the sum of the parts. It has a number of benefits – for example, it generates data, avoids respondent intimidation, and makes it possible to exploit differences in opinion and examine peer interaction.

So, again, individual and group interviews each have strengths and should be used as appropriate. Indeed, in many instances, a combination of the two approaches may be the best option. Exactly the same points apply when considering quantitative methods.

Quantitative methods

Quantitative methods put a great emphasis on descriptive and numeric data (e.g. 45% of people eat fruit and veg 5 times a day; 24% of all nurses had a flu vaccination within the past year; 1 in 2 will die from tobacco-related smoke). Quantitative research is dependent upon *sample selection* and *questioning procedures*.

Sample selection – Samples have to be collected in a way that ensures they are representative of a particular population. Ideally, random selection procedures should be used, because this ensures that each potential respondent has an equal chance of being included in the study. Quota sampling methods sidestep this issue by identifying the key variables (e.g. gender or ethnic origin) and ensuring that these are adequately represented in the final sample. As a result, they lack a certain degree of statistical rigour, but provide a pragmatic way through. As with RCTs, social marketers tend to veer towards the pragmatic end of the argument and will readily use quota sampling methods.

Representative sampling also usually requires large numbers. Whereas a qualitative study might typically measure its sample in dozens, a quantitative one will do so in hundreds or thousands.

This can be a complex and expensive process; at the very least, it assumes you have an accurate 'sampling frame' or list of the population in question – which may not be too difficult to find if your interest is in all adults or schoolchildren, but if you want to sample sex workers and their clients, or illegal immigrants, it becomes much more difficult. Fiona Harris (2011) explains that, as well as accessing sampling frames, the process can be difficult when we need to engage with vulnerable (e.g. young children, older people) or under-represented groups (e.g. religious or ethnic minorities), recruit around sensitive issues (e.g. underage drinking, teenage pregnancy, drug usage) and, if we are conducting longitudinal research, find replenishment samples (i.e. respondents to replace any dropouts between research stages). Try Exercise 5.4.

EXERCISE 5.4   SOCIAL MARKETING SAMPLING CHALLENGES

You are working as part of a Healthy Cities initiative to improve mental health among young adults in your city. You need a sample of individuals to interview.

How would you define your population of interest? What list, if any, will you use as your sampling frame? What sampling method will you use and why? How many individuals will you recruit? How will you ensure full representation from young adults? How will you incentivise young adults to participate in your research?

You could begin by defining your population as all 18–24-year-olds within the geographical area of your city. For a sample list, you could use the local registrar of electors. This is a direct sample frame. You could use quota sampling to reflect the mixture of 18–24-year-old male and females, from lower and higher social classes, employed and unemployed, who had or are experiencing mental health difficulties for full representation. This will need a large sample size (100+) to ensure all quota categories (male/female, etc.) are filled. These people could be incentivised, depending on budgets, with USBs, phone credit or other music, clothes and festival vouchers.

Questioning procedures – The second key quantitative challenge is with the standardisation of questioning. It is vital that each respondent is asked exactly the same set of questions, in the same order and, as far as possible, in the same way. Hence, we move from the free-flowing interview sequences of focus groups and depth interviews designed to gather unique data, to carefully constructed and piloted questionnaires, combined with detailed interviewer instructions, to collect common data. Standardisation is so important because answers will be summed. If we want to know how many people use a particular service, or exactly how pleased they are with it, we have to be able to add up the answers to our questions. The questions and answers therefore have to mean the same thing – otherwise, we are adding up apples and oranges.

Again, it is worth emphasising that the purpose here is just to give a flavour of quantitative research that will enable our discussions about the purpose of social marketing research. Readers who want to go into more depth on quantitative research and sampling should consult Harris's (2011) comprehensive discussion of measurement in quantitative methods. Other questionnaire design or sampling dimensions can be consulted in standard market research texts (e.g. Churchill and Iacobucci 2010; Malhotra 2016).

At this point, go to Case Study 24, on 'Making India open-defecation-free', to see how these issues were managed with a mixed-research methods approach using both qualitative and quantitative data for assessment purposes, consisting of:

1. A quantitative survey of 1,700 households that had constructed latrines under the SBM–G programme. (100 households were surveyed in each of the 17 districts.)

2. An audit (physical inspection) of the latrines that had been constructed by the households surveyed.

3. A total of 85 in-depth interviews with key programme implementation staff. (Five interviews were conducted in each of the 17 districts, three with the officers at the district/block level, and two with the functionaries at the village level.)

4. A total of 47 focus group discussions with community members in 85 villages. Discussions were conducted among males, females and community opinion leaders in villages that had been declared ODF by the district administration. A small sample of villages that had not yet become ODF was also included to understand the problems and barriers faced in eliminating open defecation.

Online research

Jones *et al.* (2017) found that that "social media use was frequently, and often spontaneously, discussed when talking about drinking behaviours, illustrating the extent to which alcohol and social media use have become conjoined in young adults' lives, and suggesting efforts to reduce alcohol-related harms in this age group will need to appreciate and accommodate the relationship between these two pastimes." With both a dynamic and synergistic relationship between our consumption behaviours and digital marketing, online research, whether it is social network sites, blogs, texting or app usage, features high on the social marketer's agenda throughout the entire strategic planning process (recall Chapter 4) to capture our experiences as they happen (Burton and Nesbit, 2015).

Facebook, Twitter, Instagram, Snapchat, LinkedIn, social networking sites, apps, gamification and other digital platforms contain massive quantities of information across almost limitless topics, exposing researchers to the array of issues associated with the desired behavioural change including many of the colloquial terms used by the target audience. We'll revisit this point and more in the next chapter on communication, promotion and participation. Tools such as Google's Campaign planner, Google Trends and Keyword Planners are examples of digital place analysis possibilities to identify client segments, partners, key online influencers and channels, and understand the client's journeys. Such interactions can be a valuable source of data relating to issues that are inappropriate to raise directly with certain populations. For example, discussing alcohol perceptions and positioning with young teens in a research context may unintentionally normalise drinking behaviour (Jones *et al.* 2017).

The advantages of online research are self-evident; for example, the task of data entry, a costly and time consuming process involved in traditional offline research, is avoided as data are collected automatically, saving time and money while eliminating coding errors and interviewer bias. But online research has its own pitfalls; some groups, such as over-65s, do not use the Internet, Twitter, Facebook etc. to the same degree as others. Countries have varying degrees of broadband coverage affecting the social marketer's ability to utilise the internet, particularly in primary research. Furthermore, there are ethical issues of trust and privacy to consider (discussed in Chapter 10). Remember, online research is another case of horses for courses.

'Of clocks and clouds'

Most of our research and storytelling so far has been about what Karl Popper (1966) dubbed 'clock problems' – predictable, controllable and finite problems, lending themselves to linear scientific research. Linear research, using tools such as systematic reviews and RCTs, is based on the assumption that a change in one variable, all other factors being constant, brings about a predictable change in another variable, all supported by advanced data analysis tools such as regression (which accounts for interactions between variables) and structural equation modelling (which acknowledges the interaction between factors).

But turn to Case Study 2, or Case Study 17, "From concept to action', CBPM Systems for change. They are both examples of what Popper called 'cloud problems' – challenges and social issues that are unpredictable, out of control and infinite. They are "ill-formulated, where the information is confusing, where there are many clients and decision-makers with conflicting values, and where the ramifications in the whole system are thoroughly confusing" (Churchman 1967: 141) and are called 'wicked problems'. As a result, multi-causality research lies at the heart of these stories and is done through systems mapping, modelling and simulation studies.

When to do what sort of research

Social marketers, then, have a range of methodologies from which to choose. To select the right one – or more likely the right combination – is going to depend on the decisions we have to make. Exercise 5.5 will help you think through what those decisions might be.

EXERCISE 5.5   SOCIAL MARKETING RESEARCH QUESTIONS

You are a consultant who has been commissioned to use social marketing to try to reverse the rise in antisocial behaviour among the adolescent boys of Brownesville, a small industrial town in a deprived part of the country. You will be working with the local social work department and an advertising agency. The initial proposal is to use a combination of youth outreach, mass media activity and police liaison, but as yet nothing has been firmly agreed.

How will you use research to guide your decision making? Specifically: WHEN during the campaign will you want to answer WHICH QUESTIONS, and WHAT METHODOLOGIES will provide the best insights?

Figure 5.3 presents the answer to Exercise 5.5 as a diagram, which we will now explore step by step.

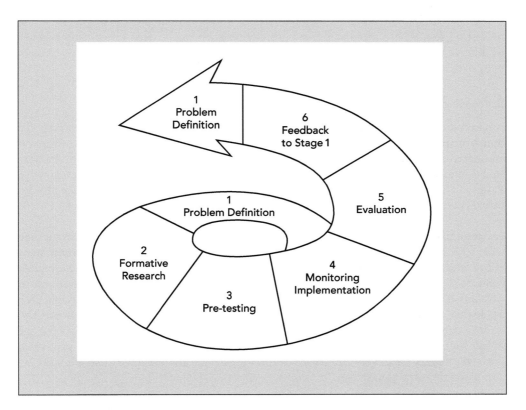

Figure 5.3 The social marketing research process

Problem definition

In the first place, research can help define the problem (see stage 1 in Figure 5.3) from the target group's perspective, exploring their perceptions of the particular issues being considered, such as smoking, sex or cancer – or in this case, antisocial behaviour. More specifically, it examines what role, if any, a particular intervention might perform, and assuming it has a role, campaign objectives can then be clarified and a precise brief given to the production and delivery teams.

Problem definition research can also clarify who the key target and stakeholder groups are. In Exercise 5.5, for instance, the latter may include parents, youth workers, civic leaders and neighbours of the proposed youth centre, all of whom may have useful insights to offer at each decision-making stage.

Methodologically, the first stop here is with secondary research (see above) to check what is already known from past studies and official statistics about the problem. For example, in our case, it might tell us something about the extent of the problem, the age and demographic background of offenders and whether previous research tells us anything about their motives or patterns of behaviour. Equally, it might inform us about past efforts to tackle the problem, and how the target groups responded.

If existing sources are inadequate new primary research might need to be commissioned: qualitative to give us ideas about the target group's perceptions and quantitative to reveal more statistical data, such as the prevalence of particular behaviours.

Formative and pre-testing research

Assuming this problem definition research suggests the need for an intervention, further primary research can guide its development. Figure 5.3 divides this into formative and decision-making research, but this is perhaps overly neat and tidy. In reality, several stages of research – typically qualitative – may be needed to perfect and hone the campaign. Essentially, the need is to identify key intervention ideas and work out how they can best be executed.

For example, qualitative research could be used to compare the potential of two different ideas for a youth outreach service, on the one hand, or a more conventional communications effort designed to encourage young people to be more considerate, on the other. These methods would enable you to show examples of materials and visuals of potential services. They would also make it possible to assess complex emotional reactions. A youth club might seem a plausible option, and make sense on a rational level – if the kids are playing five-a-side, they are not fighting in the town square – but it may be more valuable to determine what sort of youngster would actually use the service. Would they be middle-class 'goody-goodies' or those with street cred? This type of issue typically calls for not just qualitative methods, but also projective techniques.

This same research approach can be used to guide decisions about both the nature of the initiative (youth service or media effort) and how it should be executed. Thus, if the youth service shows most potential, it can help us determine what form it should take, where it should be located and how it should be promoted. There may also be some demand for quantitative research at this stage to determine the extent of demand or the prevalence of opinions.

We will revisit these formative and decision-making stages of research in the next chapter when we discuss communications.

Monitoring implementation

During implementation (see stage 4 in Figure 5.3), our questions concern *what* is being delivered (how many training courses were run or leaflets handed out) and the extent to which it matches the programme objectives and expectations (Flora *et al.* 1993). It also assesses the extent to which implementation is internally consistent across different sites and over the duration of the intervention period, and identifies the factors that can aid or hinder delivery. This is particularly important where there are many contextual and other factors that can affect how a programme is run – and, in turn, how effective it is. Box 5.9 illustrates some of the benefits of what is also called 'process evaluation', using a drugs prevention initiative as an example. It also illustrates how the monitoring of implementation fits in with both formative and evaluation research.

BOX 5.9   THE BENEFITS OF MONITORING

Think, for example, about a drug education package designed to be taught by classroom teachers in 20 different schools by 50 different teachers. Even if the teachers are supplied with exactly the same package, the same written instructions on how to use it and the same training in its methods, how they teach the package is likely to vary widely depending on how confident they feel about drug education, whether they agree philosophically with the approach taken in the package, whether they volunteered to teach the package or are doing it unwillingly, whether their classroom space is suitable for the activities, whether their head teacher values drug education and makes them feel it is worthwhile, whether parents support or oppose teaching their children about drugs, and many other factors.

Process evaluation of programme implementation is an essential part of any social marketing research study, not only because it yields valuable learning in itself (for example, about the challenges of doing drug education in schools) but also because it can help explain the final results of a research study. Supposing our drug education research study finds that the package does not seem to have produced any changes in pupils' attitudes towards drugs: without process evaluation, we cannot know whether this is because the package was a bad package or whether it was just poorly implemented.

(*Source:* Stead *et al.* 2002)

All the points made in the figure apply to our youth initiative. Monitoring implementation will, for instance, help us establish whether the youth centre has been successfully set up, is being used and matching the requirements established in the formative research. It can also give feedback on the sort of young people using the club and their experiences of doing so.

In terms of methodology, both qualitative and quantitative research can be used. In addition, a technique we mentioned briefly under methodology, observation, can also be useful. For example, the process evaluation in Box 5.9 included systematic classroom observation of lessons taking place.

Evaluation

Evaluation research occurs before, during and after a programme. Stead and McDermott (2011) explain how evaluation "shapes programme content and quality; examines the delivery process and the immediate outcomes and subsequent long-term impact. In short, it tells one whether the programme has made a difference." The starting point for any evaluation of effectiveness must be our objectives, as the social marketing planning process teaches us (Chapter 4). It is not possible to measure achievements without clear original intentions. This reinforces the importance of clearly defining objectives at the problem definition stage.

There are essentially two kinds of objectives. First, there are those concerned with the target's reactions to an initiative – whether they are aware of it, have participated in it, understood it and so on. Second, there are objectives concerned with changes in the target population – whether, for example, there are fewer accidents as a result of an initiative, or whether, following a seatbelt promotion campaign, the target population has become more aware of the value of seatbelts, more in favour of them or more likely to use them. These two types of objectives require different evaluation procedures.

Measuring reactions to an initiative is fairly straightforward. Once the initiative is complete, the target audience simply has to be asked the relevant questions (e.g. have they seen the relevant advertising, or visited the youth club?). Provided that the research methodology is sound, reliable data will result. However, it may be argued that objectives and evaluations that are restricted purely to response are too limited. Furthermore, if social marketing aims to bring about social change, then, arguably, change is what should be measured when evaluating its effectiveness. Surely we need to know whether antisocial behaviour has reduced? Turn to Case Study 10 to read about participation and engagement outcomes, or Case Study 16 for process and impact evaluations of the campaign, conducted annually among the general population together with their partner questionnaire measuring the extent to which organisations have benefited from the partnership in terms of staff capacity, organisation awareness, promotion of events, and obtaining funds for specific activities.

In reality, the evaluation of effectiveness should, as in Figure 5.3, be seen as only one part of a research function that takes place throughout the development and implementation of a given programme of change. As we saw in Chapters 2 and 3, relationships and value co-creation take time – time to be established, time to be built and time to be maintained. We'll see later on, in Chapters 8, 9 and 11, this involves ongoing continuous critical

Developmental Research	Co-discovery – Your intervention is in development.
What's happening?	• Partners are assembling the core elements of their offerings and interventions, developing action plans and exploring different strategies and activities. • There is a degree of uncertainty as to what will work and how. • New questions, challenges, and opportunities are emerging.
Reflective Question	What needs to happen?
Formative Research	Co-design – Your intervention is evolving and being refined.
What's happening?	• The core elements of your intervention are in place and partners are implementing agreed upon strategies and activities. • Outcomes are becoming more predictable. • The context of your intervention is increasingly well-known and understood.
Reflective Question	How well is your intervention working?
Summative Research	Co-delivery – Your intervention is stable and established.
What's happening?	• Your intervention is well-established. • Implementers have significant experience and increasing certainty about "what works". • Your intervention is ready for a determination of impact, merit, value, or significance.
Reflective Question	What differences did your intervention make?

Figure 5.4 Reflective evaluation research

(*Source:* adapted from McHugh *et al.* 2015)

thinking, mutuality and morality monitoring with constant adjustments, modifications and alternations. Nothing stands still. Patricia McHugh *et al.* and the EU Sea for Society team capture the notion of this constant changing through a continuous mindful evaluation in Figure 5.4.

As we noted at the beginning of this chapter, social marketing should look beyond these one-off judgements in research, and adopt a strategic perspective combining *long-term planning* with *empathy* for the client. To this we have now added the idea of the *integrated research model*, which, like the strategic planning process described in Chapter 4, is action oriented and progressive.

The Swiss response to the challenge of HIV/AIDS provides a good example of the value of this type of integrative, strategic research model. In 1987, they were faced with an urgent problem of having the highest prevalence of HIV/AIDS in Europe. A wide-ranging prevention programme was instigated, and after an initial assessment of the first wave of publicity a comprehensive and ongoing evaluation approach was adopted. They describe this as a "comprehensive, utilization-focused evaluation" that "seeks to produce results of immediate value to the development of the prevention strategy, and includes a continual process of questioning and feedback between the strategy makers and other potential users of the findings and the evaluators" (Dubois-Arber *et al.* 1999: 2573). They conclude that this approach to research "allows for a 'real world' verification of strategic choices that in turn can guide further resource allocation and, last but not least, can help to maintain a high level of commitment of the different stakeholders" (1999: 2580).

Social marketing suggests that this thinking can be applied not just to HIV/AIDS prevention programmes as in Switzerland, but also to behaviour change more generally. However, to do so we need to engage all four social marketing orientations – client, creative, collective and competitive (see Chapter 2). The stories we have examined in this chapter reinforce the need for this comprehensive approach.

Think of the power of Anita's tale with which we began this chapter, or Mandela's intervention on Robben Island. These stories help us to see through the eyes of others and recognise that agency and empowerment are essential precursors to any significant change offering. Mandela's young men seemed to be in an utterly parlous situation, but his creative approach gave them the power to walk away from tobacco. The stories also remind us of the value of a collective orientation. Ultimately, the young Africans' lives were transformed not by tobacco control but by wholesale political changes in South Africa: the apartheid system was swept away. Anita needs a similar systems transformation if her place at the bottom of the heap is to be improved. Such change will undoubtedly encounter both passive and active competition, which will need to be addressed (refer back to Chapter 2 and on to Chapters 7 and 8).

In this way, ad hoc behaviour change can develop into comprehensive social change. We will develop this thinking in Chapter 11.

The dangers of overdoing it

Given what we have agreed about the importance of doing plenty of research in social marketing, it is perhaps surprising to have a section warning against becoming too dependent on it. But there are such dangers, and they stem from misunderstanding about: (a) how research and decision making fit together; and (b) the strategic purpose of research.

Research for decision making and intervention strategies

As we have seen, a mix of research methodologies is used to guide decision making and intervention strategies in social marketing. However, it is important to recognise that research does not make decisions for us; it is not a matter of delegating the tough choices to a focus group or a survey. The target group's expertise is in responding, not social marketing or intervention design. For example, as we will discuss in Chapter 6, fear campaigns are frequently justified on the grounds that target audiences ask for them, opting for some variant on the blackened, cancerous lung or bloody car smash – the gorier the better. This misses the point of pre-testing. Smokers and drivers have a great deal to tell us about what it is like to be on the receiving end of our interventions, but they do not know which ones are most effective. They are clients, *not* consultants.

In other closely related spheres, we readily accept this argument. We recognise, for instance, that most people are not experts in human behaviour, not even their own. So we would not simply ask smokers why they smoke, and take their answers at face value. Indeed, in the 1980s, when the tobacco industry did precisely this to try to show that advertising had no effect on children's smoking (Jenkins 1988), their research was rightly dismissed.

Indeed, there are times when decisions have to be made without any research. Good marketing has to cope when there are no data available and good marketers leave space for imagination, lateral thinking and educated guesses. For the truth is all research can do is lessen the risk that we get things wrong. It can reduce uncertainty; it cannot produce certainty.

Malcolm Gladwell, in his book *Blink* (2005), reminds us of the power of intuition. He tells the story of a Kuoros, an ancient Cretan statue that was offered to the John Paul Getty Museum in California. The museum subjected the potential exhibit to 14 months of very careful and high-powered scientific analysis to try to ascertain whether it was genuine. Their research provided reassurance, and they were on the verge of buying the Kuoros when a visiting expert looked at it and immediately warned against the purchase. He had done no research, no science, but just felt the statue was dubious. Other experts then responded in a similar negative way, again on the basis of intuition.

The statue was a fake.

Gladwell does not conclude that we should therefore abandon science and go back to guess-work. Indeed, he points out that gut feelings can be just as misleading, and in any case the experts will have educated their instincts with years of scientific rigour. He simply argues that we should leave space for intuition in our decision making. Marketers agree.

Wrap-up

In this chapter, we have examined the two key roles of research in social marketing:

i) **As a navigational aid in the strategic planning**. Here, its job is to guide our decision making from project inception through to completion, and illuminate the strategic fit between initiatives. We have also looked at the strengths and weaknesses of qualitative and quantitative methods, and how they complement each other. Both have a role in guiding social marketing decision making. We also acknowledged the dangers of being over-dependent on research. It guides but does not replace decision making, and should not preclude intuition.

ii) **As an experiential tool**. Here the challenge is to provide an empathetic perspective on our clients' lives. The Chinese proverb argues that to understand a person you have to first walk a mile in their shoes; only when we use research to do the same thing can we hope to really understand why people behave as they do – and have any hope of negotiating change. More profoundly, these insights enable us to start building relationships that make the ideas of co-creation we will discuss in Chapter 10 a realistic possibility.

Pulling these ideas together we concluded that systematic research acting as the servant of social marketing helps to improve our understanding not just of our marketing tools and techniques, but also of our target groups and their behaviours. Like good carpenters, we come to understand the wood as well as the chisels. In this way, it can move us beyond the stop-start of interventions and towards a process of continuous health, environmental and systems improvement.

Or, in the language of storytelling: the function of research is to uncover and examine the stories we all have to tell so that social marketing can enable us to become heroes in those stories. When we can begin to develop coherent collective stories, we will be able to tackle not just behaviour change but also systemic change; the sort of change that will make Anita's story, with which we began this chapter, a historical curiosity; the sort of transformation we need to address complex, 'wicked' (see Chapter 11) problems such as obesity, inequalities and climate change.

Reflective questions

1. What is the purpose of research in social marketing?
2. Secondary research lends itself to systematic or narrative review. Explain.
3. Discuss the two types of primary research, qualitative and quantitative, and when they might be used in research.
4. Discuss the navigational and empathetic benefits of research.
5. Quantitative research is concerned with sampling and questioning in a way qualitative research is not. Discuss.
6. Explain evaluation research.
7. Online research is influencing social marketing research. In what ways? Why?
8. "Research is the art of storytelling." Discuss with examples.
9. What are the research pitfalls for the social marketer?
10. The 'best' social marketing research combines rigour with pragmatic flexibility. Discuss with short illustrations.

Reflective assignments

1. Conduct an Internet search on storytelling tips and suggestions.
2. Locate and critique a social marketing example that includes a story.
3. Locate and review a social marketing systematic review study.
4. Locate and evaluate a social marketing RCT.
5. Select secondary research about a behaviour change topic of your choice and locate a story that supports the data.
6. Locate and present a story of a behaviour change experience in the health or environmental field.
7. Locate a large-scale social marketing survey and develop three success stories around the data.
8. You are a team comprising of (a) social marketing consultants, (b) a local city council, and (c) a PR agency. You have been charged with developing and running an initiative to encourage rainwater collection. How will you use research to help you develop and evaluate your initiative? What research methods would you use?

9. Reconsider how your answers to question 8 above might change if you were just using online research?

10. Reconsider how your answers to questions 8 and 9 above might change if you were conducting multi-causal wicked problem research?

11. Go to the *Journal of Social Marketing* or *Social Marketing Quarterly*, and then download and read an article on qualitative or quantitative research to challenge your thinking on this topic.

12. Complete your 'Rebels with a cause' arsenal for social marketing research and storytelling.

Note

1 In the UK, prescription medicines cannot be promoted directly to the public.

References

ACMD (2005) Pathways to Problems. Online: www.drugs.gov.uk/publication-search/acmd/pathways-to-problems/Pathwaystoproblems.pdf (accessed May 2016).

Anderson, A.S., Porteous, L.E.G., Foster, E., Higgins, C., Stead, M., Hetherington, M., Ha, M.-A. and Adamson, A.J. (2005) 'The impact of a school-based nutrition education intervention on dietary intake and cognitive and attitudinal variables relating to fruits and vegetables', *Public Health Nutrition*, 8(6): 650–656.

Burton, S. and Nesbit, P. (2015) 'Capturing experiences as they happen: Diary data collection for social marketing', *Journal of Social Marketing*, 5(4): 307–323. doi: 10.1108/JSOCM-09-2014-0061.

Churchill, G.A. and Iacobucci, D. (2010) *Marketing Research: Methodological Foundations*. Ohio, USA: Cengage Learning.

Churchill, G.A., Brown, T.J. and Suter, T. (2009) *Basic Marketing Research*. Ohio, USA: Cengage Learning.

Churchman, C. W. (1967) Guest Editorial, "Wicked Problems", *Management Science*, 14 (4): B141–B142.

Cochrane Collaboration (2005) *Glossary of Terms in The Cochrane Collaboration*. Version 4.2.5. Online: www.cochrane.org/sites/default/files/uploads/glossary.pdf (accessed May 2016).

Devlin, E., Hastings, G., Smith A., McDermott, L. and Noble, G. (2007) 'Pharmaceutical marketing: a question of regulation', *Journal of Public Affairs*, 7(2): 135–147.

Dietrich, T., Rundle-Thiele, S., Schuster, L. and Connor, J. (2016) 'Co-designing social marketing programs', *Journal of Social Marketing*, 6(1): 41–61. doi: 10.1108/JSOCM-01-2015-0004.

Domegan, C. and Fleming, D. (2007) *Marketing Research in Ireland: Theory and Practice*. Dublin, Ireland: Gill and Macmillan.

Dubois-Arber, F., Jeannin, A. and Spencer, B. (1999) 'Long-term global evaluation of a national AIDS prevention strategy: The case of Switzerland', *AIDS*, 13(18): 2571–2582.

Flora, J.A., Lefebvre, R.C., Murray, D.M., Stone, E.J. and Assaf, A. (1993) 'A community education monitoring system: Methods from the Stanford Five-City Project, the Minnesota Heart Health Program and the Pawtucket Heart Health Program', *Health Education Research Theory and Practice*, 8(1): 81–95.

Freire, P. (1982) 'Creating alternative research methods: Learning to do it by doing it', in B. Hall, A. Gillette and R. Tandon (eds) *Creating Knowledge: A Monopoly*. New Delhi: Society for Participatory Research in Asia, pp. 30–31.

Gladwell, M. (2005) *Blink: The Power of Thinking Without Thinking*. London: Allen Lane

Grant, I.C., Hassan, L., Hastings, G., MacKintosh, A.M. and Eadie, D. (2008) 'The influence of branding on adolescent smoking behaviour: Exploring the mediating role of image and attitudes', *International Journal of Nonprofit and Voluntary Sector Marketing*, 13(3): 275–285.

Greenland, S.J. (2016) 'The Australian experience following plain packaging: The impact on tobacco branding', *Addiction*, 111 (12): 2248–2258.

Grindle, M. (2004) 'At what stage is our understanding of the interactive entertainment development industry in Scotland?', paper presented at *The Scottish Media and Communication Association Annual Conference*, 3 December, Dundee, University of Abertay.

Harris, F. (2011) 'Measurement in quantitative methods', Ch. 15 in G. Hastings, K. Angus and C. Bryant (eds) *The SAGE Handbook of Social Marketing*. London: Sage Publications.

Harris, F., Gordon, R., MacKintosh, A.M. and Hastings, G. (2015) 'Consumer socialization and the role of branding in hazardous adolescent drinking', *Psychology & Marketing*, 32(12): 1175–1190.

Hastings, G.B. (1990) 'Qualitative research in health education', *Journal of the Institute of Health Education*, 28(4): 118–127.

Hastings, G. (2011) 'Introduction: A movement in social marketing', in G. Hastings, K. Angus and C. Bryant (eds) *The SAGE Handbook of Social Marketing*. London: Sage Publications.

Hastings, G., Brooks, O., Stead, M., Angus K., Anker, T. and Farrell, T. (2010) 'Alcohol advertising: The last chance saloon', *British Medical Journal*, 340: b5550, doi: 10.1135/bmj.b5550.

Hastings, G.B., Eadie, D.R. and Scott, A.C. (1990) 'Two years of AIDS publicity: A review of progress', *Health Education Research*, 5(1): 17–25.

Henderson, M. (2006) *School Effects on Adolescent Pupils' Health Behaviours and School Processes Associated With These Effects*. Glasgow: MRC Social & Public Health Sciences Unit, University of Glasgow.

Hill, R.P. (2011) 'Impoverished consumers and social marketing', Ch. 21 in G. Hastings, K. Angus and C. Bryant (eds) *The SAGE Handbook of Social Marketing*. London: Sage Publications.

Jenkins, J. (1988) 'Tobacco advertising and children: Some Canadian findings', *International Journal of Advertising*, 7(4): 357–357.

Jones, S., Pettigrew, S., Biagioni, N., Daube, M., Chikritzhs, T. and Stafford, J. (2017) 'Young adults, alcohol and Facebook: A synergistic relationship', *Journal of Social Marketing*, 7(2): 172–187.

Kent, R. (2007) *Marketing Research: Approaches, Methods and Applications*. London: Thomson Learning.

Krueger, R.A. (2010) 'Using stories in evaluation,' in J.S. Wholey, H.P. Hatry and K.E. Newcomer (eds) *Handbook of Practical Program Evaluation*. San Francisco, CA: Jossey-Bass, pp. 404–424.

Lee, H. (1960) *To Kill a Mockingbird*. New York: HarperCollins.

Lewin, K. (1951) *Field Theory in Social Science: Selected Theoretical Papers*, D. Cartwright (ed). New York: Harper & Row.

Lowe, J. (1985) Extract from the song 'Old Bones', published by Lowe Life Music.

Malhotra, N. (2016) *Marketing Research: An Applied Orientation, 6th edn*. Upper Saddle River, NJ: Pearson Education.

McHugh, P., Domegan, C., Devaney, M. and Hastings, G. (2015) *A Set of Sea Change Guiding Principles and Protocols*. EU Sea Change Project, Whitaker Institute, NUI Galway, Ireland.

MRC (2000, April) *A Framework for Development and Evaluation of RCTs for Complex Interventions to Improve Health*. London: Medical Research Council.

Panizzutti, R., Fitzgerald, C., Gillan, C. and Lawler, B. (2017) 'Cognitive Training to Promote Brain Health: Implementation and Engagement', Global Brain Health Conference, Barcelona Spain, April 19–22.

Pettigrew, S. and Roberts, M. (2011) 'Qualitative research methods in social marketing', Ch. 14 in G. Hastings, K. Angus and C. Bryant (eds) *The SAGE Handbook of Social Marketing*. London: Sage Publications.

Popper, K. (1965) Arthur Holly Compton lecture, *Of Clouds and Clocks*, delivered at Washington University in St Louis, USA, April.

Robinson, T.N., Borzekowski, D.L., Matheson, D.M. and Kraemer, H.C. (2007) 'Effects of fast food branding on young children's taste preferences', *Archives of Pediatrics & Adolescent Medicine*, 161(8): 792–797.

Science Museum (undated) 'Thalidomide'. Online: www.sciencemuseum.org.uk/broughttolife/
themes/controversies/thalidomide.aspx.

Stead, M., Hastings, G. and Eadie, D. (2002) 'The challenge of evaluating complex interventions:
A framework for evaluating media advocacy', *Health Education Research Theory and Practice*, 17(3):
351–364.

Stead, M. and McDermott, R. (2011) 'Evaluation in social marketing', Ch. 13 in G. Hastings,
K. Angus and C. Bryant (eds) *The SAGE Handbook of Social Marketing*. London: Sage Publications.

US Department of Education (2003) *Identifying and Implementing Educational Practices Supported
by Rigorous Evidence: A User Friendly Guide*. Prepared for the Institute of Education Sciences,
Washington DC, Coalition for Evidence-Based Policy, December.

West, R. (2004) *Stop Smoking Service Quality and Delivery Indicators and Targets*. A briefing for the
Healthcare Commission, July. Online: www.ash.org.uk/html/cessation/smqtargetsbrief.pdf
(accessed May 2016).

Chapter **6**

Compelling content

Four score and seven years ago our fathers brought forth on this continent a new nation, conceived in liberty, and dedicated to the proposition that all men are created equal.

Now we are engaged in a great civil war, testing whether that nation, or any nation, so conceived and so dedicated, can long endure. We are met on a great battle-field of that war. We have come to dedicate a portion of that field, as a final resting place for those who here gave their lives that that nation might live. It is altogether fitting and proper that we should do this.

But, in a larger sense, we cannot dedicate . . . we cannot consecrate . . . we cannot hallow this ground. The brave men, living and dead, who struggled here, have consecrated it, far above our poor power to add or detract. The world will little note, nor long remember what we say here, but it can never forget what they did here. It is for us the living, rather, to be dedicated here to the unfinished work which they who fought here have thus far so nobly advanced. It is rather for us to be here dedicated to the great task remaining before us – that from these honored dead we take increased devotion to that cause for which they gave the last full measure of devotion – that we here highly resolve that these dead shall not have died in vain – that this nation, under God, shall have a new birth of freedom – and that government of the people, by the people, for the people, shall not perish from the earth.

(*Source:* Abraham Lincoln, *The Gettysburg Address*, 1863)[1]

Lincoln's speech on the battlefield of Gettysburg is a brilliant piece of oration, and 150 years after its delivery it can still teach us much about how to communicate. First, he had a clear **aim**: he very much needed to steady a wavering public in the northern states to ensure their continuing support for what was proving to be a very costly war against the South. More specifically, he needed to keep the electorate's vote in the upcoming presidential elections. Second, he **understood his audience**. Speaking as he was on the remnants of a battlefield, with half the dead still unburied, he was careful to invoke the heroism of the soldier, and he used this powerful symbolism to reframe the war as an historic struggle for freedom and emancipation (refer back to the discussion of positioning in Chapter 4). In the process, he took a third step and aligned his need to be re-elected with his audience's need for an enlightened and responsive political system – government of the people, by the people, for the people. He was putting them in charge and beautifully illustrates the principle of **participation and moral agency** (Chapter 9) and **co-creation** (Chapter 11). Fourth, he was **focused** on the job in hand: the iconic address took less than two minutes to deliver.

Fifth, he took his chance. You may be surprised to learn that Lincoln was not the main presenter at the Gettysburg dedication; that honour went to Edward Everett, another eminent politician and renowned public speaker. Everett spoke for over two hours, but few now remember him or what he said. He was humble enough to acknowledge Lincoln's accomplishment: "I should be glad if I could flatter myself that I came as near to the central idea of the occasion, in two hours, as you did in two minutes."[2]

Clear aims, understanding your audience, co-creation, focus and pragmatic opportunism: all characteristics of great social marketing communications. In the century and a half since Gettysburg, our understanding of how mass communications work has been honed through decades of academic and applied research – and this understanding reinforces the same social marketing insights manifested in the Gettysburg Address. In particular, it is now clear that the audience is actively involved in the communication process: what we understand from and how we react to a particular message or content is as much a function of us and our experiences as it is of the characteristics of the message. It is therefore crucial for would-be communicators to use careful audience research to guide the development and monitor the impact of their efforts whether this is online or offline. We will discuss these research challenges in this chapter.

Looking more carefully at communications also shows that Lincoln was right to get **emotional**. Much public health and social change activity adopts a positivist perspective, assuming that if we are told that behaviour A has negative consequences we will respond by changing to behaviour B; that we will logically weigh up the pros and cons and do the sensible, healthy and safe thing. In reality, life is more complex than this; I will continue to eat chocolate and drink beer despite the health risks because they make me feel good – and for me feeling good is an important part of being healthy. Similarly, my friend has bought himself a gas-guzzling SUV despite the damage he knows it is doing to the planet because it makes him feel successful and rugged, and he will speed in it on his way to work because, even though this will not get him there much faster (all the other SUVs on the road will see to that), it gives him the reassuring illusion of being in control. Life is imperfect and emotion plays a big part in the strategies we deploy to cope with it. Attempts to encourage us to change our behaviour for the better must take this into account.

If we think about road safety or public health campaigns, however, where emotion is considered at all, they tend to revolve around one sentiment – fear. And yet the evidence supporting the use of fear is chequered at best. Over-reliance on it also means that we miss out on opportunities to engage with our clients using other, more positive, emotions and puts serious limitations on our long-term efforts at behaviour, lifestyle and social change. The commercial sector is not so self-limiting. It uses **branding** to get across a sustained array of attractive and reassuring associations and images. Lincoln was equally positive, evoking powerful emotions of validation and empowerment.

Social networking sites, blogs, microblogging, apps, email, video, feed-based platforms and other mobile and social media innovations might seem like revolutionary developments, but in reality digital marketing just confirms not only the lessons from the Gettysburg Address, i.e. that active audience involvement, positive emotion and empowerment matter, but also the ensuing communications research matters – and indeed the discussions we have had throughout this book about the importance of relational thinking and partnership working. Social marketers need to think beyond hackneyed ideas of doing things *to* people and instead start conceiving of ways of doing things *with* people. One phenomenon of the digital era – **user-generated content** – neatly demonstrates the impossibility of any other course of action.

This focus on people also reminds us that this chapter is about communications, not media. The Gettysburg Address was delivered in person, and face-to-face engagement is also important in social marketing. This is most apparent when we think about what might be termed the 'social marketing sales force': the staff in the clinic, classroom or on the street who have direct contact with the target group. The commercial sector invests heavily in front-line staff selection and their training, and so should social marketers. Refer to Case Study 24, which highlights the importance of training and empowerment to trigger demand for sanitary latrines at the village level. Districts that had received training and orientation seemed convinced in its effectiveness and also seemed to be practising it more vigorously.

Before we jump in, though, let us return to Abraham Lincoln and the final crucial lesson he provides. His speech reminds us that communication – however well crafted – is but a small part of what is needed to bring about social change. Remember, as well as making a great oration, he also had to get re-elected, win a war and abolish slavery! And so it is with social marketing. Communications can form an important part of our work, but as we noted in Chapter 4, they are only one element of the intervention mix – which, in turn, is but one step in the strategic planning process. More importantly, Lincoln reminds us that social change will only be achieved when people are fully engaged in the process: government of the people, by the people, for the people. By the same token, we need social marketing of the people, by the people, for the people – a point we pick up again in Chapters 9 and 11.

Learning outcomes

By the end of this chapter, you should be able to:

✓ Explain that social marketers have to recognise that the message content sent is not necessarily the same as the message content received – and that it is the latter that matters

✓ Recognise that this underpins the need for careful developmental, process and outcome research to guide and monitor campaigns

✓   Critique fear-based messages from a marketing perspective

✓   Understand the potential of positive emotion and branding in social marketing

✓   Discuss the role of digital marketing in social marketing

✓   Explain that communications are only part of the social marketing process.

Key words

Communication – two-step communication model – opinion leaders – research – problem definition – medium – content – images – links – fear-based messages – branding – social media – digital marketing – promotion.

How communication works

When Orson Welles broadcast his radio production of *The War of the Worlds* in 1938 (*Guardian* 1938) (see Figure 6.1), the effect was dramatic. Around a million Americans actually believed that the science-fiction story was true, and little green men from Mars were invading Earth and about to march on New York. The result was extensive public panic, people actually getting killed in the ensuing rush to avoid the invaders and the US rules of public broadcasting being changed forever.

A wireless dramatisation of Mr. H. G. Wells's fantasy, *The War of the Worlds* – a work that was written at the end of last century – caused a remarkable wave of panic in the United States during and immediately after its broadcast last night at eight o'clock. Listeners throughout the country believed that it ˙ was an account of an actual invasion of the earth by warriors from Mars. The play, presented by Mr. Orson Welles, a successful theatrical producer and actor, gave a vivid account of the Martian invasion just as the wireless would if Mr. Wells's dream came true.	The programme began with music by a New York City hotel dance band, which was interrupted suddenly by a news announcer who reported that violent flashes on Mars had been observed by Princeton University astronomers. The music was soon interrupted again for a report that a meteor had struck New Jersey. Then there was an account of how the meteor opened and Martian warriors emerged and began killing local citizens with mysterious death-rays. Martians were also observed moving towards New York with the intention of destroying the city.	Many people tuning in to the middle of the broadcast jumped to the conclusion that there was a real invasion. Thousands of telephone calls poured into the wireless station and police headquarters. Residents of New Jersey covered their faces with wet cloths as a protection against poisonous gases and fled from their homes. Roads leading to a village where a Martian ship was supposed to have landed were jammed with motorists prepared to repel attackers. Panic evacuations were also reported around the New York area. In some cases people told the police and newspapers that they had seen the 'invasion'.	Mr. Jacques Chambrun, Mr. H.G. Wells's representative, stated today that Mr Wells was 'deeply concerned' that last night's wireless dramatisation should have caused such alarm. Mr. Wells added that the dramatisation was made 'with a liberty that amounts to complete rewriting and made the novel an entirely different story'. Today nerves are steadier and it is recalled that in England some years ago there was a similar reaction to the famous 'spoof broadcast' by Father Ronald Knox. Many listeners took his parodied description of a riot in London seriously.

Figure 6.1 Report of a radio broadcast of *The War of the Worlds* from *The Guardian*, 1 November 1938

(*Source: The Guardian*: copyright Guardian News and Media Limited 2002)

From our perspective, the events also had a more subtle impact: they engrained a perception that the mass media are extremely powerful, and that all that is needed to get people to do as you want is to design a suitably clever message. The contemporaneous rise of the Nazi party in Germany, and the central role played by Goebbels's infamous Ministry of Propaganda, served to reinforce this omnipotent reputation.

However, the seven decades of research done since Goebbels's demise suggest that this picture is actually very misleading. Early models in communication theory did characterise the process as a one-way phenomenon, involving an active message sender and a completely passive recipient. Analogies are often drawn between this model and a hypodermic syringe: just as the doctor injects the drug into the patient so the communicator injects the message and content into the audience. In both cases, the effects are both predictable and easily measured.

This analysis presents the communicator as powerful and directly manipulative, with dramatic effects being relatively easy to achieve. Traditional media, television and radio, as channels of mass communication, came to be seen as a means of controlling the population. These ideas were given added credibility when commentators like Vance Packard (2007) applied them to commercial advertising, the influence of which he exaggerated and over-simplified.

The limitations on the manipulative power of advertising can be illustrated by a couple of examples. It is estimated that 80–90 per cent of new food products fail within one year of introduction (Rudolph 1995). If advertising were as powerful as Packard suggests, this could never be. Similarly, given the frequency of mass media efforts to dissuade people from taking up smoking (and in many countries a complete ban on pro-tobacco advertising), one would have expected an all-powerful media to have resolved the problem – and yet thousands of young people still take up smoking every year in Europe alone.

It is not that advertising lacks influence – it is immensely powerful – it is just that more complex explanations were needed and these duly emerged. They included the two-, or more, step model initially proposed by Katz and Lazarsfeld (1955), involving opinion leaders in the process of communication; the use and gratification approaches (McQuail *et al.* 1962; Rosengren and Windahl 1962), which depict the consumer as deliberately using the media rather than vice versa; and, more recently, cultural effects models, which place the media in a cultural context and see the effects as indirect and long term (Tudor 1996).

Interestingly, thinking in communication theory matches that in advertising. Early models of advertising conceptualised the process as a hierarchy of effects on consumers – typically cognitive (e.g. product awareness), affective (e.g. product liking) and then conative (e.g. product purchase). However, these 'linear sequential models' have also been heavily criticised (Barry and Howard 1990). As with early communication theory, they assume a passive audience, ignore the effects of significant others and present an overly tidy picture of how communication actually works. Indeed, it has become increasingly apparent that it is at least as relevant to ask 'What do people do to advertising?' as 'What does advertising do to people?' (Hedges 1982). English health promoters have been all too aware of this since the mid-1980s, when teenagers were found to be stealing supposedly off-putting 'Heroin Screws You Up' posters and hanging them on their bedroom walls (see Box 6.1).

BOX 6.1   HEROIN SCREWS YOU UP

In the mid-1980s, the government responded to a surge in heroin use with a television and poster campaign featuring a wasted youth with the caption: "Heroin Screws You Up." Dozens of posters went missing as the boy in them became a teenage pin-up. Within months "heroin chic" appeared on the catwalks.

(*Source:* Burke and Thompson 2002)

Linear sequential models also overlook all the thinking that has emerged from postmodernism and what it tells us about the importance of symbolism and cultural meaning to consumption, whether of products or messages (Elliott and Wattanasuwan 1998). We now know that audiences, especially young ones, are extremely sophisticated consumers of digital and social media and that meaning and content have to be negotiated, not imposed (Dahl *et al.* 2015). This interactive social environment, where participation is king, has far-reaching ripple effects beyond promotion and communication. In this converged world of paid, earned and owned media and communication, the product becomes user-driven; the brand social; place can be online and offline while promotion focuses on integrating mobile, social and digital to more traditional communication ways and means (Kaufman and Horton 2015).

Positioning, as always, is based on a blend of value proposition(s) and how they are framed relative to that of the competition, except now it's more complicated – digital marketing can be deployed as an advertising medium; a direct-response mechanism; a platform for transactions and exchanges; a distribution channel, a client service tool or a relationship building mechanism (Chaffey and Ellis-Chadwick 2016).

At this point, go to Case Studies 1, 4, 9 and 22 to see communications, digital marketing, participation, online and offline strategies at work.

Thus many plausible theories of how the mass media, advertising, communication and promotion work have emerged. Much as with behaviour change theory (Chapter 3), social marketing does not get too hung up about which of these theories is right (they are probably all a bit right). Rather, it uses the insights that result to progress campaigns, and the key insight that links all these theories is that **the audience is actively engaged in the entire communications process**, from design to delivery.

Exercise 6.1 is a chance to explore the two-way nature of communication in advertising.

> ### EXERCISE 6.1   ADVERTISING AND WHAT IT DOES
>
> Next time you are watching an ad online or offline, ask yourself the following questions:
>
> 1. What factual information do the ads provide?
> 2. What other messages are communicated?
> 3. Do any appeal to you? Why/Why not?
> 4. How do the ads compare or contrast with others you have seen in the past day or so?
> 5. What might you do as a result of seeing them?

It will illustrate that adverts – traditional or digital – communicate a vast array of messages and content, many of them emotional rather than factual; that some work for you (most likely the online ones as they are more targeted at you) but some do not. If you are watching with other people, as is often the case with TV ads, preferences will vary from person to person who will each bring different experiences and priorities to the communication process. This variation in response will also be accentuated if you engage with content at different times of the day.

We see this clearly in Case Study 24, where all districts reported using a variety of promotional methods to create awareness about sanitation and the SBM-G programme. Nearly all used processions and sloganeering by school children, *swachhta saptaha* [sanitation week] celebrations in schools and villages, the distribution of pamphlets, as well as posters/wall-paintings, *nukkad natak* [street plays], and cultural programmes around sanitation. Some districts also reported using video films and radio jingles. Importantly, in most, communications were tailored to the local situations. For instance, most districts created sub-campaigns within the umbrella SBM–G campaign with themes that resonated well with local issues and culture. Udaipur, for example, launched its 'Garvilo Mewar' campaign to invoke the Rajputana pride, while Indore launched its 'Lota Jalao' campaign to motivate people to reject the practice of open defecation. The Angul district organised ministerial visits to villages that achieved ODF status, while Mandya organised 'Autorickshaw Campaigns' and half-marathons by inviting sports celebrities to villages to promote latrine use.

The crucial role of research

Exercise 6.1 and the conclusions we have drawn about the two-way nature of communication demonstrate that the only certain way of knowing what is being communicated by a particular media effort is to ask the intended audience. The more obvious manifestations of this conclusion are unlikely to be disputed. Thus the need to check that an audience understands the language in a leaflet, or that the images on a website are decipherable, needs little justification.

However, the implications are more fundamental than this. An active, engaged and participating audience means more than testing their understanding of particular words or passing
verdicts on completed posters. It implies a need to design communications, from inception
to dissemination and beyond, with the intended audience's needs and perspectives clearly
in mind. To do this, social marketers must maintain continuous contact with the target
audience – ideally through formal consumer research as *safe*food did in Box 6.2. This contact
will provide invaluable insights at every stage and on all aspects of a campaign.

BOX 6.2 *SAFEFOOD'S* CHILDHOOD OBESITY CAMPAIGN

Continuous contact and engagement through consumer research were paramount
to Safefoods childhood obesity campaign which ran from 2013 to 2016. It included
TV, outdoor and radio advertisements as well as stakeholder engagement, partnerships and social and digital media marketing.

Formative research pre-campaign indicated there was a demand among parents for
practical solutions which they could put in place. Thus the campaign focuses on six
core actions for parents, phased over the three years. However, consumer research
at different phases during the campaign found that some of the messages were not
cutting through the noise with parents, as their needs and understanding of the
messages had changed. This resulted in *safe*food reevaluating some of their creative content and producing content which was in line with suggestions made by the
target audience during the campaign research.

(*Source:* Flaherty 2017)

This need for continuous research is fundamental to the whole social marketing process, as
Chapter 5 demonstrated, discussing its whys and hows. At this point, focusing on communications, we will look at the sort of pitfalls research can help us avoid. This naturally leads
us first to formative research which can help us decide whether the media, digital and/or
traditional, can help resolve a particular social marketing problem, and, if so, what task it
can perform, as well as guiding decision making about all aspects of message design and the
rest of the 7P intervention mix. These include problem definition, medium, content, images,
links, and compelling content discussed below.

Problem definition

At the very beginning of a project, research with the target group can help define the nature of
the problem to be tackled, determine what media have a role to play and, if so, what objectives
they might fulfil. Let's assume we are considering the possibility of developing a campaign for
15–16-year-olds to tell them about the dangers of STDs. As a first step, research could examine
teenagers' perceptions about sexual health and explore what, if any, information they feel they
need. This might show that teenagers know of the risks and that condoms afford the best protection, but that they feel extremely disempowered about using them – suggesting that the campaign
needs to focus on safer sexual skills development rather than simply warning about the dangers.

Arguably, in the process, it might suggest that this is not principally a communication problem and hence a media campaign is only a part of solution. In fact something more engaging and better able to develop skills is needed – maybe a combination of school-curriculum development, outreach work and condom distribution with some YouTube videos and Snapchat content. Thus audience research can help to define not only communication and advertising objectives, but also which media activity is needed for promotion, and possibly place, price, product and participation.

Assuming initial contact with the client does define a role for mass or digital media, further research can help determine the relative merits of the different creative ideas or approaches on which to base a campaign. For instance, the sexual health campaign could approach the subject with a conventionally negative emphasis on the drawbacks of *not* practising safer sex – unwanted pregnancy and disease. Alternatively, it could be more positive, emphasising the benefits of safer sex in terms of enjoying more adult and fulfilled relationships. Interestingly, when these alternative ideas were presented to young people and their views sought, an initial preference for the more familiar, negative approach rapidly changed to a preference for the positive one. In particular, teenage girls were much more able and willing to associate themselves with the benefits of using contraception than the drawbacks of not doing so (Hastings and Leathar 1986).

Research with the client can also provide invaluable feedback on all aspects of campaign and intervention design, including the choice of medium, content and language, images and links with non-media intervention mix elements as signalled in Chapter 5, 'Research and the Teller of Tales'.

Medium

Judge Dredd is a cartoon character (see Figure 6.2) in the comic *2000AD*, which is read by teenagers. A few years ago, it was proposed to use him and his comic as a vehicle for drug education material, but the idea had to be abandoned when teenagers were consulted. Many had never read the comic and saw it as puerile, assuming it to be for young children. Those who did read it rejected its use as a vehicle for such a serious topic. Judge Dredd was, for them, a fantasy character whose rather ridiculous escapades were not intended to be taken literally. He had no basis in reality, no existence off the page or outside the reader's mind.

Using him as a way of transmitting a very serious and literal message about drugs completely contradicts this. It suggests that they believe Judge Dredd to be real, much as a child might believe in Superman. It implies that they defer to him and are likely to do as he tells them. As a result, it is grossly patronising.

A similar instance of the medium being the message – or at least greatly influencing the effectiveness of it – is provided by 'advertorials'. These are jointly written and produced by the social marketer and the producer of the host publication. When a Scottish health agency was looking for a more reliable means of delivering information-rich messages capable of engaging its audience, research showed that people were far more likely to

Figure 6.2 The medium is the message

(*Source: 2000AD* 1998)

read and attend to content that was endorsed by and written in the style of their favourite magazine. The agency went on to use this approach to deliver health messages requiring detailed information to groups who were regular readers of news and entertainment magazines – dietary advice emerged as just one area to benefit from this approach.

Sanjeev Vyas in Case Study 22 makes a similar point in his work to encourage healthy behaviours for reproductive, maternal, and child health in India, showing how the choice of communication channels – in this case, both online and offline – was a key dimension of their success in the multi-stakeholder campaign involving the private sector, civil society, celebrities and key opinion leaders, and media.

Content

The content and language used in media material must be compelling and understandable to the intended audience. Reading-age tests can help in this respect, but the only certain check is to expose the material to your audience and ask for their reactions. This assesses not only comprehension, but also equally important issues such as acceptability. For example, draft material on the safer sex campaign discussed above used the term 'bonking' for making love, in an attempt to be fashionable. Teenagers took great exception to this. They felt it implied a totally amoral and cynical attitude to sex that they rejected and found insulting. Similar patterns can be seen in Case Study 20 'Wheel, Skills and Thrills'.

The Foolsspeed road safety campaign illustrates a similar point. A pre-test using storyboards and narrative audiotapes helped avoid the inappropriate use of language and gesture. In one version of the proposed ads, road users were portrayed tapping their heads to show their disapproval of the (speeding) central character, and to encourage him to 'use his head' and slow down (see Figure 6.4). Unfortunately, the gesture was interpreted as an act of aggression more likely to elicit a violent response than to encourage more responsible driving, or as one male respondent put it, *"it doesnae mean 'use your head' it means 'you're a nutter!' – it's a threatening gesture."* This problem was subsequently resolved by focusing the storyline exclusively on the driver where he was challenged to drive more slowly by his alter ego, talking to him in his rear-view mirror (see Figure 6.4).

Read Case Study 8, 'I know what I'm doing'. Fifteen- and thirty-second spot ads, as part of the 2014 nationally as a community service announcement campaign, *"The Talk" – Reducing Drowning in People over 55*, depict an adult son trying to talk to his aged father about water safety. The ad shows an awkward start to a conversation as the son attempts to engage his father while they fish on a pier, declaring, "Dad, we need to have the talk." The father humorously misconstrues the intent, responding with "What, you're going to talk to me about the birds and the bees?" This permits a light-hearted segue into broaching the main issue, i.e. that over-55 year olds are more vulnerable in and around water than they think.

Images

Similar strictures apply to the visual elements of media materials. They must be decipherable and acceptable. In 2005, as part of a sexual health initiative targeting young people in deprived communities in the east of Scotland, the Scottish Government funded[3] a campaign promoting respect for others and acceptance of difference.

One approach tested was to superimpose the wigs worn by court judges onto young people to signify inappropriate judgemental behaviour (see Figure 6.5). While the target audience understood the imagery and could relate this to their behaviour, the creative approach was ultimately rejected because it was seen as childish and failed to deliver a credible challenge. A different creative route was therefore adopted, which set out to challenge young people in public spaces (such as at bus stops and on board public transport) where they might be encouraged to make inappropriate judgements about people based on appearance alone (see Figure 6.5).

In passing, it is worth noting that the quality of the graphics in Figure 6.5 is quite low. This is because we are not looking at finished material, but an image produced

Figure 6.3 Safefood's folic acid campaign

purely for research purposes. Another example pertains to Safefood's folic acid campaign. Given the sensitive nature of the topic which was being addressed as part of the campaign, *safe*food needed creative materials which would grab the target audiences' attention, where the core messages could then be disseminated. The creative content for this campaign combined babies, the most sharable content on digital and social media, with mammisms, your quintessential Irish mammy who is full of wisdom and knowledge – akin to the trending Mrs Brown mammy. Figure 6.3 is an example of the images used for this campaign. However, it is also worth noting here that had this creative not been tested on the target audience the tone, messages and overarching campaign could have been rejected.

Links

As we have noted numerous times, social marketing thinking suggests that media, traditional or digital, are most likely to work if used in conjunction with other initiatives. Target group opinion can help determine the nature of these other elements and how they should be linked to the communication activity. This takes us on naturally to wider social marketing research, which was discussed in Chapter 5. Issues of campaign evaluation are also discussed in this chapter.

In addition, these examples illustrate another point that we already noted during our discussion of planning in Chapter 4 and research in Chapter 5. Target audience research does

Figure 6.4 The hazards of using sign language

(*Source:* The Foolsspeed Road Safety Campaign from the Scottish Road Safety Campaign)

not just help improve individual media campaigns; because it requires continuous contact between communicator and audience throughout and between initiatives, it also enables us to increase our understanding of our clients and build relationships with them. Some of the examples quoted above illustrate this point. The research on Judge Dredd revealed as much about teenagers and how they read comics as it did about the actual material. Similarly, young people's reaction to the word 'bonking' provides a valuable insight into their sexual feelings and attitudes. This type of target audience understanding is fundamental to effective communication and clearly seen in Case Study 4, about a digital social marketing programme for reducing residential electricity use. The communication strategy, recognising that young low income earners have high electricity bills, also managed for a low care factor, short attention span and hyperconnected clients. Specifically, learning components of the intervention were designed to address the barrier of information failure to help participants change their energy consumption behaviour and were delivered using a range of digital channels, including an app with mini-games and a supporting suite of integrated digital communications (email, social media and SMS).

We also have noted a number of times now that social marketing is, in essence, a process of exchanging values. Likewise, communication is a form of exchange – it requires shared

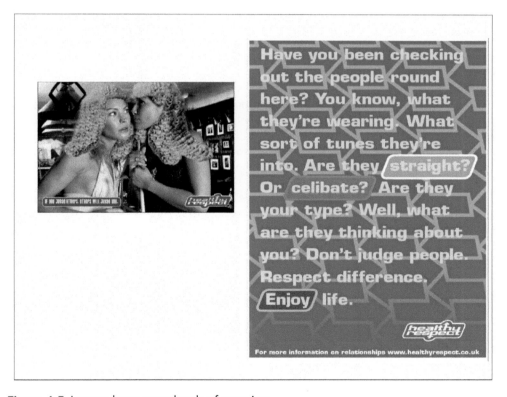

Figure 6.5 Images have many levels of meaning

(*Source:* Campaign promoting respect for others. Reproduced with permission from 1576 Ltd and Healthy Respect, a Scottish Executive funded national health demonstration project for young people and sexual health, 2001–2008, www.healthyrespect.co.uk.)

experiences, mutual understanding, empathy, and as we've seen, active participation. If, as social marketers, we do not take the trouble to try to understand our clients, to take their ideas seriously and, at least to some extent, accept their view of the world, how can we expect them to accept ours?

Fear messages in marketing

Given what we have agreed about the two-way nature of communication and the need for empathy and shared understanding, it seems inappropriate to ask generic questions about whether certain sorts of content work better than others. The answer is bound to be 'it depends' – on circumstances, past communications, available channels and so on. Above all, it depends on the audience. And yet precisely this question has been asked again and again about fear messages.

Thus, several attempts have been made to develop a theory to explain and predict how fear works, but the results are inconclusive. Three alternative models have emerged. First, the curvilinear model posits that fear *can* persuade up to a threshold of tolerance, beyond which it becomes counter-productive.

Second, Leventhal's (1960)`parallel response model proposes that emotional and cognitive factors act independently to mediate behaviour, with emotional factors affecting internal attempts to cope with the threat (e.g. by rationalising or rejecting it), while cognitive factors will determine the behaviour change.

Finally, Rogers's (1965) expectancy-valence model states that the effectiveness of a fear-arousing communication is a function of three variables: the magnitude of the threat; the probability of its occurrence; and the efficacy of the advocated protective response. It is proposed that these three variables will interact to produce a level of 'protection motivation' within an individual and that this will determine the level of change.

The research into the effectiveness of fear appeal is inconclusive, but the majority of studies show a positive relationship between fear arousal and persuasion (Higbee 1969). More specifically, the following conclusions have been drawn:

- Fear appeals can raise awareness of an issue and bring it to the forefront of people's thoughts.

- Fear appeals can make people re-evaluate and change their attitudes.

- Fear may be successful in stimulating an intention to change behaviour sometime in the future.

- In some cases, *immediate* behaviour change takes place shortly after exposure to a fear communication.

In summary, therefore, the findings do vary considerably between studies. The problem, however, is that the research has been very narrowly focused, typically using experiments in laboratory settings, to ask very specific and short-term questions. As we have seen, the resulting answers can, with some difficulty, be resolved into a coherent picture, but many other questions are left begging. Most importantly, it is not clear what happens outside the laboratory where there is much less control, nor what the long-term and wider effects of fear appeals are.

Marketing provides a rubric for asking these bigger questions. Have a try at Exercise 6.2.

EXERCISE 6.2   FEAR IN TRAFFIC SAFETY

You have just been appointed as Head of Communications at the Transport Accident Commission in Victoria, Australia. They have used fear messages consistently for the last fifteen years. Log on to their website (www.tacsafety.com.au) and click on CAMPAIGNS followed by any of the campaign topics to view some of the road safety ads. As a social marketer, what questions does their approach raise?

You might, for example, like to consider the following:

a. What will our customers do with these messages?

b. What benefits will they get from them?

c. How will it affect our brand?

d. How will it affect their feelings for our other products?

e. What about our non-targets who will also see the message?

f. What are our competitors doing?

g. Where do we go from here?

h. What about alternative approaches?

i. Are our messages ethically acceptable?

---

a. *What will our clients do with the message?*

Outside the laboratory, audiences can choose whether or not to accept our messages; they cannot be compelled to pay attention any more than they can be compelled to drive safely or give up smoking. This creates several potential barriers: the audience may not look at the message at all; they may look at it, but ignore it; they may look at it, accept it, but misunderstand it; or they may look at it, understand it, but rationalise it (e.g. "that couldn't happen to me", "there are other greater risks" or simply "life is risky"). All of these barriers – especially the last – can be accentuated by fear appeals – look at point 1 in Box 6.3. In a world where media messages are an optional extra, it may make more sense to use subtlety and compromise than brute force.

At a more fundamental level, it is arguable that campaigns employing extreme fear appeals, such as those used in Victoria by the Road Safety Commission (Exercise 6.2), undermine the whole notion of voluntary behaviour. The ads literally say accept our message or *"you're a bloody idiot."* The danger is that people will reject such uncompromising approaches, or, like characters in the movie *Crash*, even do the opposite of what is proposed. This latter response is not as far-fetched as it may sound. Focus groups suggested that certain young men enjoy gory road safety ads in the same way as horror movies: *"that was a cracker that one"*, *"that's brilliant that, when you saw her face get smashed up'"* *"really clever"*, *"and you hear it go bang, crack!"*. Social change practitioners would no doubt be appalled to discover they are competing with violent pornographers!

b. *What benefits will they get from them?*

Voluntary behaviour is benefit driven, so paying attention to message content, just like buying Coke or driving safely, must provide the target with something they want. As Barry Day, vice-chairman of McCann-Erickson Worldwide, expressed it, "I believe an ad should be a reward" (Foote 1981). The question then is "What reward does a fear appeal offer?", and by extension, is being upset, scared and/or discomfited much of a reward?

c. *How will it affect our brand?*

Coca-Cola, Nike and Marlboro will all be very careful to ensure that any ads they produce online and offline not only work effectively in their own right, but also enhance or (at the very least) do no damage to the company and the product's good name – typically encapsulated in the brand. Most successful brands are the result of decades of careful effort and design.

Social marketing organisations have their equivalents of brands; they have an image and reputation with the public. The question then is how do fear appeals affect this reputation? Do claims that are felt to be exaggerated, or at least not to reflect people's everyday experience, discredit the communicator? Does content that causes short-term offence, but which might be justified by high awareness figures, do long-term damage to the sender's good name? Interestingly, none of the 24 case studies from colleagues around the world used fear. In fact, quite the opposite with IPA's effectiveness award-winning From Anti-smoking to Pro-Quitting as part of the national Smoking Control 2011 strategy by the Health Promotion Board of Singapore.

d. *How will it affect their feelings for our other products?*

Fear messages say something about the absolute risk of the behaviour being addressed, but also imply things about the relative risk of other behaviours. Take traffic safety as an example: a very fearful anti-drink campaign may lead audiences to assume that other driving behaviours, such as speeding, are less dangerous. Focus groups with young drivers conducted at the University of Wollongong in New South Wales (see Box 6.3) showed that, while drunk driving and speeding were recognised as risky behaviours, others, such as driving at night and driving while under the influence of marijuana, were not. Indeed, some respondents interpreted the constant messaging on drunk driving as implicitly endorsing the alternative of marijuana use. The option of extending the traffic topics addressed by fear messages to cover all potential risks is equally problematic. It would likely lead to overload and rationalisation: *"I know the roads are dangerous, but I have to get on with my life."*

It is also worth remembering that road use is only one source of danger in people's life (and danger is only one source of problems). For example, tobacco use kills more people in Europe than traffic, crime and accidents in the home and workplace combined.

Fear messages need to reflect this reality, if only for ethical reasons.

BOX 6.3   YOUNG AUSTRALIAN DRIVERS AND THE USE OF FEAR

Focus groups with young (18–24-year-old) drivers conducted recently at the University of Wollongong in New South Wales revealed worrying tendencies in their response to fear-based messages. The discussions examined responses to ads they had seen on television in the last few months and years, which had been dominated by hard-hitting messages on drunk driving and speeding. Three findings stand out:

1. The young drivers were becoming inured to fear messages and numerous comments were made about being tired of being told what to do and that speeding and drunk driving are dangerous.

   "the ads are all the same, can't speed, can't drink and drive or you will crash – so what? Everyone knows that . . . they don't stop me" (Eric, 18)

   "ever since I can remember the ads have been about what happens when you speed . . . I stopped taking any notice of them ages ago" (Jenny, 21)

   "the ads are silly, the latest ad shows a guy crashing this big powerful car after speeding and killing people, then right after is an ad for the same car showing these young guys enjoying themselves in it . . . I just turn off from the anti-speeding ads now" (Dean, 23)

2. Other risky driving behaviours such as driving at night or with lots of friends in the car were not even on their radar. As long as they did not speed or drink they felt they were OK.

   "I guess other things are dangerous but not as bad as speeding and drink driving" (Tim, 16)

   "I don't think there is a problem if you have four or five of your mates in the car with you" (Michael, 18)

   "No one has said that driving at night is more dangerous than driving at daytime . . . have they?" (Samantha, 22)

3. Dysfunctional solutions emerged from the narrow focus on alcohol; most notably the less well educated of the young people were inclined to see no problem with marijuana use and driving. The broader idea of mind-altering substances in general impairing driving had been lost.

   "smoking some weed then driving home isn't as dangerous as having a heap of beers at a party" (Tiffany, 16)

   "when I go out and if I'm driving and I had a choice between dope and alcohol then it's a no brainer . . . you're safer with the dope" (Adam, 20)

   "I have a friend and he thinks his driving improves when he has had some herb" (Sam, 24)

(*Source:* Noble et al. 2006)

e. *What about our non-targets who will also see the message?*

Targeting is an important aspect of social marketing (recall our conversations in Chapter 4): only well-targeted products and messages can really satisfy client needs. However, content transmitted in the media will inevitably reach other people as well as the intended target, more so for mass and traditional sources than digital. Sticking with road safety, TV ads aimed at 18–24 year old 'boy racers' will also reach older drivers. The use of fear in these circumstances can have two untoward effects. First, it may breed complacency among older speeding drivers by implying that deaths on the roads are the fault of other inexperienced and unskilled drivers. Second, it may cause unwarranted anxiety among other road users, perhaps discouraging parents from letting their children play outside or walk to school.

f. *What are our competitors doing?*

As we will discuss in Chapters 7 and 11, social marketers frequently have to compete with commerce and the market system. Tobacco, alcohol, fast food, car producers – among others – frequently push in the opposite direction. Even a cursory look at their advertising and digital marketing shows that they make relatively little use of fear.

g. *Where do we go from here?*

Fear appeals present both creative and strategic problems. On the creative front, once fear has been used, there is a need to increase it on each subsequent occasion to have the same impact. At what point does this cross the threshold of acceptability? On the other hand, is there a point at which people become inured? (Have another look at Box 6.3.) On this point, Henley and Donovan remind us of "an unintended consequence of the frequent use of fear-arousal in social marketing may be the creation of a sense of helplessness both in the target market and in unintended markets" (1999: 1).

Turning to strategy, if marketing tells us that success is dependent on building long-term relationships with the client, the strategic question becomes: is fear a good basis for a relationship? Does the client participate, or not, with fear-based content?

h. *What about alternative approaches?*

It is clear then that fear approaches present considerable costs to social marketers. The main benefit it offers is high profile: strong emotional messages attract a lot of attention. But other approaches can also have a strong emotional pull – love, excitement, sex, hope, humour and sophistication are all used successfully by commercial advertisers. The key issue therefore is not "Should fear appeals be used?" but "Will they do the job better and more efficiently than alternative approaches?" For any interesting 'alternative' approach see how art and social marketing come together in the face of the rising problem of ocean plastics at http://ideastations.org/radio/news/art-and-social-marketing-address-rising-problem-ocean-plastics.

i. *Are our messages ethically acceptable?*

The final question a social marketer will ask (or be compelled to ask by the relevant regulatory authorities) is: "Do our messages meet normal ethical standards? Will people be hurt or damaged by them?" For example, Awagu and Basil (2016: 361) found "threat orientation impacts individuals' responses to fear appeals. Control-oriented individuals respond in a more adaptive manner, heightened-sensitivity-oriented individuals are a 'mixed-bag' and denial-oriented individuals respond in a more maladaptive manner." The fact that we social marketers tend to fight on the side of the angels does not absolve us from this responsibility.

Check out Case Study 8 again to read about the ethical stance taken in 'The Talk' ads. 'The Talk' is not really shown; a voice-over talks over it. The 30-second ad declares, "Don't be shy about talking to your parents about the facts of life," but itself exhibits this shyness. This potentially positions reverse socialisation as slightly embarrassing and possibly stigmatises the act of talking about water safety.

Emotion and branding

From a social marketer's perspective, then, fear messages leave many questions unanswered. However, the one thing they do confirm for us is that our behaviour is driven by both rational and emotional factors (the head and heart concept again). As Joan Bakewell put it, "for many people reasoned argument is not the final arbiter of how they choose to live their lives. They are swayed by feelings, moved by loyalties, willing to set logic aside for the sake of psychic comfort" (2006: 7). Their recognition of this encourages commercial marketers to produce lots of content that focuses on feelings, promotes a product's or a company's image, generates positive associations and generally makes the potential customer feel good.

Research suggests that three other factors make emotional messages particularly persuasive:

* They are better able to gain clients' attention than factual messages. Audiences are under pressure from the increasing clutter of advertising and promotional content, and it becomes impossible to process this. They therefore attend selectively to that content and those messages which are relevant, comprehendible and congruent with their *values* (Hawkins and Mothersbaugh 2010).

* They encourage deeper processing of the content and as a result tend to be remembered better.

* People buy products (and engage in behaviours) to satisfy not only objective, functional needs, but also symbolic and emotional ones, such as self-enhancement and group identification. The most obvious example of this is cigarette smoking. When they first take up the habit, the prospective smoker does not have an objective need for nicotine, but rather a symbolic need to display independence or rebellion (Barton *et al.* 1982).

Lefebvre *et al.* (1995) also remind us that all social marketing communications have an emotional dimension – a 'personality' or 'tonality' – whether the sender intends this or not. They caution that we, just like our commercial counterparts, must use research, design and careful targeting to ensure that the tonality matches the needs of our target audience(s). Leathar (1980) and Monahan (1995) go a step further and argue that we should actively promote positive images about health: "Positive affect can be used to stress the benefits of healthy behaviour, to give individuals a sense of control, and to reduce anxiety or fear. All of these tactics are likely to enhance the success of a communication campaign" (Monahan 1995).

On a more specific level, qualitative research conducted by the Health Education Authority in England with pregnant women (Bolling and Owen 1996) also emphasises the importance of emotional communication, concluding that messages have to be sympathetic, supportive and non-judgemental. The primary need, the research suggested, is to establish a sense of trust. This resonates with the discussions of relationship marketing in Chapters 2 and 4 and value co-creation in Chapter 4.

Branding

The brand is the marketers' most advanced emotional tool. It combines and reinforces the functional and emotional benefits of the offering (Murphy 1986; de Chernatony 1993) and so adds value, encouraging consumption and loyalty. In essence, a good marque facilitates recognition, makes a promise and, provided the full marketing back-up is in place, delivers satisfaction. This last point is vital: promise without delivery is extremely damaging and brings us into value destruction territory. To paraphrase Wally Olins, a world leading practitioner of branding and identity, it is like painting the toilet door when the cistern is broken.[4] Inevitably, therefore, the brand and its persona are developed using not just communications, but the whole intervention mix (see Chapter 4).

The process also needs care and time, and to be driven by client needs – which will be both individual and social. At an individual level, a brand will be chosen because it is liked and matches the person's self-image. At a social level, brands can be used by clients to tell other people more about themselves, particularly with conspicuously consumed products. Moreover brands can also provide very practical benefits, making consumption easier. They can act as guarantees of quality or reduce risks by confirming that "this product is for you." For example, for young people, quick and clear brand identification can make both the buying and smoking of forbidden products such as cigarettes much less risky.

Over time, brands become a fast and powerful way of confirming the synergy – the relationship – between buyer and seller. Indeed, it can be argued that successful brands are only part-owned by the company; the customer and stakeholders also have a share. When Coca-Cola changed their formulation a few years ago, its ultimate failure and the need to scurry back to Coca-Cola Classic were partly put down to consumer displeasure at *their* brand being adulterated.

There is also evidence that branding may be a particularly effective way to reach people in deprived communities. Research into how working-class populations use cultural symbols in advertising found that these groups are often poorly informed about the objective merits of different products, and therefore tend to rely more heavily than other groups on 'implicit meanings' – context, price, image – to judge products (Durgee 1986). Similarly, de Chernatony (1993) and Cacioppo and Petty (1989) found that people in deprived communities are less likely to evaluate products on a rational, objective basis, and instead look for clues as to the product's value in terms of its price or its image. They argued that the symbolic appeal of brands is particularly effective in targeting those individuals who do not have the time, skills or motivation to evaluate the objective attributes and benefits of a particular campaign.

The use of such a powerful emotional tool by commercial operators, and its particular influence over vulnerable groups, raises obvious concerns. We touched on these in Chapter 1, when we noted that branding is implicated in the uptake of smoking, drinking and unhealthy diets in young people, and will give them a full airing in the next two chapters. For the moment, though, let us focus on the more positive implication – that branding is a useful tool for social marketers.

EXERCISE 6.3   BRANDING IN SOCIAL MARKETING

The Scottish Health Education group (SHEG) was the government body responsible for health education in Scotland in the 1980s and early 1990s. Over a number of years, they commissioned a full range of research on their mass media activity, from basic problem definition work, through concept and pre-testing to evaluation. This began to reveal a number of recurrent problems, including a tendency for the advertising to be:

- Negative rather than positive. Smoking campaigns emphasised the dangers of smoking, not the benefits of non-smoking; contraception advice threatened people with unwanted pregnancies, rather than stressing the advantages of safer sex.
- Authoritarian rather than empathetic. Material seemed to be telling people what to do and how to run their lives, rather than enabling and encouraging them to make their own informed health decisions.
- Long-term rather than short-term focused. Anti-smoking material emphasised the health risks of cigarettes, many of which are very long term and probabilistic.
- Fragmented from other non-media activity. It did not connect with other types of intervention such as local services or policy changes – there was only one P in the marketing mix.
- Topic-based rather than whole-person orientated. Separate campaigns were run on drinking, smoking and contraception, seemingly ignoring the fact that these activities can overlap and often reflect the individual's overall lifestyle.

How might branding help resolve these problems?

(*Source:* Hastings and Leathar 1986)

While some of the weaknesses highlighted by SHEG's research could be removed during pre-testing of individual campaigns, it is branding that can communicate a general lifestyle message of empowerment – "promoting good health in much the same way as a marketing company would promote its corporate identity" (Hastings and Leathar 1986). Branding links positive imagery to clear solutions and real health problems by, for instance, providing branded health products.

Ana Sofia Dias and Sara Balonas in Case Study 6 about the Porto Tap Water programme talk to the importance of branding. The strategy included necessarily a symbolic perspective of the brand: the creation of a connotation between an essential good, the water, and the 'quality' and 'vitality' perceived about the city of Porto. In fact, Porto is recognised as a city of strong emotions, the centre of a 'northerner' pride which goes from people to culture, history, heritage and products. In addition, the brand provided an opportunity to explore the potential of the sense of belonging, of 'a common thing', i.e. water as a unifying element for Porto citizens.

Moreover, the brand made it easier to create a personality which was associated with a functional benefit rather than simply saying it; the creative line led to the signature "*É boa todos os dias!*" ["As good as it gets"] – a typical expression of the oral speech of Porto people. In a very familiar and customised way, this signature summarises the key-argument that crosses the whole programme: trust and quality. The brand has a confident and assertive tone, but one that is also trendy and positive, which refers to the perception and attitude change and adoption of a social behaviour underrated.

For more brand insights, go to Case Study 12, and read how branding can be embedded throughout the intervention. The notion of movement was communicated through a visual brand logo and a statement referring to a popular expression that was easily recognised and altered in order to generate humour and surprise!

Box 6.4 explores the birth and development of a social marketing brand to address problem gambling. It provides a fascinating insight into the complexities, pitfalls and potential of branding in social marketing. Read it through and then have a try at Exercise 6.4.

BOX 6.4   DEVELOPING A 'COMMUNITY BRAND' – 'CHOICE NOT CHANCE'

In 2006 the Health Sponsorship Council (HSC) was tasked with developing a national social marketing strategy to address gambling harms. The strategy included significant national communications activities and HSC decided that a brand would assist positioning, collective action and coherence.

Part of HSC's operating philosophy is that social brands need to be community brands. By this we mean that instead of operating to commercial brand management practice which sees brands centrally and rigidly managed to maintain their identity and integrity, the brand is designed for the community and is 'given away'. The identity and integrity of the brand grows and develops because it is used by the communities that want to act on the issue being addressed – social marketing and community development blend. Control is not required, permission isn't needed (though some friendly advice and usable tools help with consistency). Success is measured by how often it is used by others as well as to what extent it is embraced and understood by the intended audiences. This had been a very successful approach with other HSC brands such as 'Smokefree' and 'SunSmart'.

In considering how to provide what was hoped would be an enduring brand to carry many years of messages and themes, the HSC analysed existing terms and names used by the gambling harm minimisation sector. 'Problem Gambling' was the almost universally used descriptor by the key organisations and for communications activities, etc. HSC also considered a number of other possibilities but none worked well and therefore a 'Problem Gambling' brand was launched with phase one of the campaign.

Over the first few years of the programme concerns were raised by the problem gambling sector about the brand – primarily that it focused on the problem, not the solution. Many within the sector commented that it was difficult to adopt the brand usefully as part of their public health work because the public immediately turned away from it. Unlike other HSC community brands, the sector was not actively utilising the brand as part of its work and therefore the ideal of having a single image being used to carry messages and themes nationally was not being achieved.

At the implementation level it failed the 'tee-shirt test'. Would you want to wear a tee-shirt that boldly proclaimed 'Problem Gambling'? Would you visit a marquee at a community event that was branded 'Problem Gambling' – might as well put up a sign – herpes sufferers line up here! It was not engaging, it was not offering a solution.

So, HSC undertook an extensive exercise with the sector to identify the values that they believed were inherent in their work and therefore that a brand should reflect. A creative process was then entered into – and not surprisingly it proved very difficult to find a solution. However – out of a very exhausting process emerged the thought – 'Choice Not Chance'. The sector believed that it met their needs – empowering, speaks to individuals, families and communities, and can be related to various campaign messages over time. At a community level, this could mean making a choice to end harmful gambling, rather than leaving the effects of gambling in your community to chance. On a personal level, it might mean making a choice to reach out and help someone or as a gambler to choose more positive and certain options rather than the chance associated with gambling.

A question mark was whether the name would be immediately understood as it could be about any number of things. However, it was agreed that the visuals and core messages provided alongside it would provide the context. In addition, a strapline such as 'let's choose to end harmful gambling' would be added to help support the brand, particularly in the first few years.

The 'Choice Not Chance' brand has been a success in that it has been embraced by the sector and is enthusiastically used and displayed as part of the many community-based activities undertaken by people interested in minimising gambling harms. It passed the 'tee-shirt test' and is being used to promote individual behaviour change, help seeking and societal change. It has assisted collective effort and coherence.

Iain Potter
August 2012

EXERCISE 6.4   BUILDING A WINNING BRAND

When you have read through the story, try to answer Iain Potter's three questions:

1. Why wasn't the 'Problem Gambling' brand working?
2. What traits should a brand carry?
3. How could a community brand be supported and encouraged?

Iain answered his own questions for us. The brand failed, he explains, because "the people who should be using it – the community – did not feel comfortable with it, it was problem oriented not solution focused, it did not represent the values the sector believed were inherent in their work. As a result they didn't like it and it didn't encourage public engagement." Turning to key characteristics, he argues that "a brand should carry the personality traits that you believe are central to your offering – in this case these included empowerment, community, caring, aspiration." Finally, addressing the issue of support, he emphasises the key notion of involvement, collaboration and co-creation: "the development process could include sector involvement, it should be used on all national promotional materials, an offering of branded resources could be made available to the sector, merchandise could be offered to sector workers – meeting the 'tee-shirt test' – sector personnel could be invited to suggest resources that could be developed".

Ultimately, the case illustrates beautifully how branding can help us think collectively and coherently about the problems we are trying to tackle, making sure that the needs of all stakeholders are being met. It also provides a refreshing illustration of social marketers being prepared to talk about and learn from their mistakes (e.g. Evans and Hastings 2008).

The potential of branding in social marketing is unsurprising. It sits comfortably with ideas of active engagement, participation, relationship building and partnership working. Digital marketing takes things to a new level: blogs, Twitter and Facebook, emails and texts, videos and platforms have made the theory of co-created content and meaning a practical reality. They also provide a whole new arena for research.

Digital marketing

Social marketing has clearly embraced digital, mobile and social media possibilities. Arguably it is the active, empowered engagement in digital marketing that provides an electronic and ubiquitous platform for the grassroots activism of social change and community engagement (see Chapter 11). This has the power to transform ordinary people and community groups from passive content recipients into fellow storytellers, network builders and co-creators of value. They are now able to search for, or 'pull', the information they want, instead of waiting for it to be 'pushed' to them. An example of effective use of digital marketing for positive behaviour change was evident in Safefood's folic acid campaign. *safe*food, an all-island implementation body in Ireland, launched a campaign in 2015 solely on digital and social media to highlight the importance for all sexually active women to take a folic acid supplement irrespective of whether they were planning a pregnancy or not. As a result of this campaign there was an increase, from 7% to 14%, among women who reported that they now routinely take a folic acid supplement although they are not planning a pregnancy. Furthermore, folic acid sales increased by 26% on average from the same period in 2014 (*safe*food 2015).

So, digital marketing affords social marketers with greater prospects for segmentation and targeting. Upon signing up for social media or social networking sites, users enter personal information such as demographic details, location and likes. Consequently, the social marketer is provided with automatic, readily-available segmentation information leading to greater targeting possibilities. For example, *safe*food use Facebook for live chats where Facebook users can log on and ask questions based on the topic that is being discussed and they will receive an instant answer. This was used for the portion size phase of the childhood obesity campaign and also as part of the Christmas series where all turkey and cooking related questions were answered. Furthermore, for the majority of Safefood's campaigns, digital display advertising is utilised. Taking the childhood obesity campaign as an example the core messages were advertised online across a range of high-traffic websites through display advertising (independent.ie, her.ie) and through various 'partner sites' (including Mummy Pages, Rollercoaster, EUMom, Mykidstime and Family Friendly HQ), all giving the social marketer greater profile data about the target audience.

And it's not just the younger generation. All segments of society – rich, poor, young and old – are adopting mobile and social media, though admittedly at different rates. Those in lower socio-economic groups are harder to reach on social media as the level of adoption is lower among these groups due to access to internet, smartphones etc. (Corcoran 2017). Resonating with Grindle (2004), Mays *et al.* (2011: 188) also demonstrate that digital media change "the ways consumers communicate, share, and seek information, facilitating more active participation in the information exchange process" and "understanding their potential for content interactivity and constant connectivity with large, diverse populations is critically important" for the social marketer.

Digital marketing helps make value co-creation and relationship marketing possible as 'individuals can actively acquire, prioritize, and interpret information when, where, how, and from whom they want' (ibid.: 183). The dialogue and interactions needed for partnership working can occur and be shared in real-time two-way conversations and engagements through connected storytelling of experiences and lived lives. Pictures, videos, games, words, music, sounds, events – a collage of communication tools and channels can be simultaneously shared between the client, partners, stakeholders and social marketers. Interestingly, though, this progress is dependent on traditional constructs such as trust, likeability, language, source reputation and source credibility (see Mays *et al.* 2011, and refer back to our discussion of relationship marketing in Chapter 2).

In this way, digital media can again be seen as an extension to current thinking. In particular, echoing our discussions of planning in Chapter 4, they raise a series of strategic and operational questions about the target audience, the organisational resources and the social marketing strategy/intervention

The commercial sector has also embraced Twitter, Facebook, Linkedin, Snapchat, Instagram and YouTube, having learnt lessons about the rules of engagement – in particular, that the agency of digital participants has to be given due respect. People use mobile and social media for their own purposes – to meet like-minded people, help each other, develop themselves and gain status (Gossieaux and Moran 2010). They adopt a healthy and critical distance from commerce and its products, even if it's simply at the level of pointing their peers towards better deals – and/or behaviours elsewhere. Moreover, significant rewards are made available in the form of peer approval and social status to those who do. Business has learned quickly that digital marketing grows and speaks from the bottom up; it allows marketers to come alongside customers, listen to them, understand *their* motives and desires – and then helps *them* to co-create *their own* new products, processes, behaviours and lifestyles. In the digital space, we move from the traditional AIDA model (awareness – interest – desire and action) to AIICLAC (awareness – interest – involvement – commitment – loyalty – advocacy and champion). Clients are no longer linear but iterative in their search for information and content and in their decision-making processes, incrementally building upon all inputs (digital, internet, social, mobile and traditional) (Kaufman and Horton 2015).

The prospects of digital marketing for social marketers are indeed exciting, and the greatest potential comes, Grindle (2010) argues, when we move beyond a focus on technological wands towards the wizard and begin to absorb some of the storytelling skills of traditional media (perhaps best exemplified by commercial cinema). Interactive storytelling allows people not just to participate but also to perform in a journey of their own making. Cinematic storytelling has the ability to structure and evoke powerful emotions – pride, self-worth, identity, belonging, status and validation: it will make it possible for people to experiment with whole new lifestyles in safe and self-asserting, life-affirming contexts. Refusing a cigarette from your mate can be very challenging in real life – and it is unlikely to deliver any greater status or rewards – but as an avatar such possibilities can be tried out, tested and rewarded. Tips for a Twitter avatar are outlined in Box 6.5, while other trending examples of digital marketing and social media uses in social marketing are outlined in Box 6.6.

BOX 6.5   TIPS FROM THE TWEETING GODDESS

A Twitter avatar (Twitter pic), according to the tweeting goddess, Samantha Kelly, is commonly a photo of the team. It is the portal to a Tweet which must **stand out** from the rest if you want to succeed on Twitter. This is very easy to do:

Be kind – How you make someone feel is really important. Don't put others down, or bitch or complain about things we have no control over, e.g. the weather!

Assist others – This could be by simply re-tweeting a start-up (sharing what they are saying).

Share your knowledge – Obviously don't share everything! But let people into your world also. Let them know what works and what doesn't. Be friendly and willing to help others who are just starting out. Content and storytelling are an opportunity for you to show you are the expert in what you do. Give tips, share knowledge

Be consistent – Blog about what your area of expertise is. Give tips for others who might now know. The more you write articles about what you do, and the more you will share other tips from people in the area you are the expert in, the more people will see that you are the 'Go to' person.

(*Source:* http://tweetinggoddess.com/how-twitter-can-create-awesome-opportunities)

BOX 6.6   TOP 10 TRENDING DIGITAL INNOVATIONS FOR SOCIAL MARKETING

In a landmark systematic review study from Kubacki *et al.* 2015, examining Digital Innovation in Social Marketing, the key finding shows social marketers continue to learn from commercial marketing trends by adopting new, more interactive digital media to improve quality of life interventions. Their relatively low cost per contact and significant creative opportunities to engage audiences in behaviour change offer important benefits to social marketers. The top 10 trending issues include the following:

1. Digital channels formed a major component of successful interventions.

2. A range of traditional offline and online media was employed.

3. The most commonly used digital channels included intervention websites, social media and online advertisements, and the majority of interventions used more than one channel to increase their effectiveness and engage audiences in behaviour change.

4. Mobile phones are used to inform, notify and/or encourage target audience(s).

5. Video-sharing involving posting videos on popular video-sharing sites is also evident.

6. Blogs and/or discussion boards, webisodes, and online games are also in use.

7. Online advertising (i.e. Google AdWords, Yahoo! Search Ads, banner advertisements and advertisements on other websites) is employed to promote and/or redirect users to the intervention websites.

8. YouTube, Yahoo and Daily Motions, as well as five interventions used this digital strategy.

9. Stronger Interventions use four or more digital components (in conjunction with exchange, segmentation, competition, other marketing mix elements etc.).

10. Digital channels offer interactivity and anonymity to audiences that would not be accessible by, or willing to engage with, more traditional media.

(*Source:* Kubacki et al. 2015)

By combining participation, interactivity and reward structures – as evolved by the computer games industry – with storytelling and emotional structuring – as evolved by commercial cinema – this is exactly what we see accounting for success in Case Studies 1, 4 and 9.

> Social marketing can help clients to experiment outside of their local, real world familial and peer group milieu – as many young people around the world do and enjoy. By embracing digital marketing and emergent storytelling forms, social marketers can collaborate with and help to co-create identities, environments, behaviours and lifestyles. It can help participants rehearse real-life challenges, take on real-life antagonists and experience rewards and emotions unavailable anywhere else. We can be heroes. (Grindle 2004, quoted in Hastings 2011: 11).

The last sentiment was recognised fully by game designer Jane McGonigal, who in collaboration with World Bank ran an initiative last year called *Evoke: A crash course in changing the world* (Hawkins 2010).[5] Participants were given the opportunity to take on the role of hero and experiment with the challenges of real-world development scenarios played out online. Real-world financial rewards and opportunities were given to those who were able to empower others and collaborate to collect real-world evidence. No formal evaluation has been released at the time of writing, but the weblogs are certainly very positive. It's also seen in *Operation Transformation* – an Irish lifestyle behaviour change programme. The television show, created by VIP Productions and airing on RTÉ (Ireland's national TV broadcaster), challenges five overweight or obese individuals – or 'leaders' as they are called on the show – to change their weight, health and lifestyle in general. They receive assistance from a fitness instructor, nutritionist and psychologist. The general public are encouraged to adopt and follow one of the leaders in order to achieve the same behaviour change goals. The *Operation Transformation* Facebook page has over 185,221 fans who participate and co-create stories with one another, offering support, motivation, tips and camaraderie for those trying to reach their behaviour change goals, while the *Operation Transformation Twitter* has 10.6k followers.[6]

Digital downsides

However, before we get carried away, the digital domain is not a magic bullet. Nor is it revolutionary – it just extends and reinforces what good social marketing should already be doing: listening, empowering and partnering to bring about beneficial behavioural and social change. There are also three specific concerns to consider:

1. **Unrealistic client expectations** – The proliferation of smart phones has resulted in a vast number of individuals having 24 hour-access to the internet and social media, and consequently they expect everything to be available at the touch of a button. Social marketers need to understand that using digital and social media requires continuous engagement and monitoring.

2. **Limited resources** – Although social media have many advantageous, social marketers should not be on all platforms just because they have to be seen to be doing so. For example, *safe*food has recently set up an instagram account but has to monitor what is posted on this channel. Due to the nature of Instagram, not all content being shared on other platforms will necessarily work.

3. **Unhealthy marketing** – As we noted, commerce is increasingly active in hyperspace and this activity is frequently antithetical to social marketing efforts. For example, in 2011 Facebook and Diageo announced a link-up. We will look at this in more detail in Chapter 8 (see Box 8.6), but at this point, it is sufficient to note the drinks company will benefit from Facebook's SWAT team of marketing (a term that originates from the Los Angeles police force and refers to the 'Special Weapons And Tactics' needed to control dangerous criminals); that this team will enable them not just to sell their drinks to young people but also recruit them as brand advocates; and that the particular interest is in developing countries. Have a try at Exercise 6.5.

EXERCISE 6.5   'HEINEKEN MAKES DEAL WITH GOOGLE IN SOCIAL-MEDIA PUSH'

Why would Heineken want to link up with Google in this way? Imagine you work for Balance North East (www.balancenortheast.co.uk), an NGO focused on reducing the harm caused by alcohol, especially to young people. What implications does this development have for your work? How would you respond? If you had two minutes with the Minister of Health for England what would you ask him to do about it, if anything?

(*Source:* http://online.wsj.com/article/SB10001424052702304584004576417301681632980.html.)

4. **Corporatisation** – The operating platforms for many digital media are becoming corporatised. In his book *The Master Switch* (2011), Timothy Wu shows how each new generation of communications technology – telephone, radio, television – began as a grassroots and free for all, but then rapidly was taken over and controlled by the corporate sector. The same, he argues, is now happening to digital media.

5. **The digital divide** – Getting and building a presence online costs money. Doing this in a sophisticated way is even more expensive. The result is that a digital divide has opened up between those with resources who can exploit the Internet, and those without who may even struggle to access it. Go back to Exercise 6.5 and imagine you are Head of Campaigns at Balance North East and one of your key tasks concerns "Educating and informing – giving you all the information and support you need to make you aware of and understand the issues related to alcohol so you can make informed choices." How might you use digital communications to achieve this? How would your efforts compare with those of Diageo and Heineken?

There is, then, as with other aspects of marketing, a need to adopt a critical perspective when assessing the contribution of digital media. We will return to this topic in the next two chapters.

Wrap-up

Communication, whether traditional or digital, is a complex process in which both communicator and audience are actively involved. This means that careful audience research is needed to decide whether, how and with what combination of other marketing activity it should be used. When designing a communication approach, social marketers have to decide whether the online and offline media can help resolve a particular social marketing problem, and if so what task it can perform, as well as guiding decision making about all aspects of content and message design. Relevant communication activities include problem definition; medium choice; content selection; images and links.

The communication job becomes more complex when the vagaries of human decision making are factored in – especially our tendency to decide things on emotional as well as rational bases.

It's disappointing that the principal acknowledgement of this emotional dimension of our lives in the health and safety sector comes in the form of fear-based communications, which raise many marketing questions. A more interesting line of thought is that other emotions, such as wellbeing, vitality, happiness, coolness and validation, could be engaged more effectively through branding and relational approaches with much greater strategic change potential.

The rise of mobile and social media has reinforced this need to embrace the role of individual agency and empowerment to bring about change. It is more true than ever that social marketers have to think in terms of doing things with, rather than to, their clients. This, however, reignites the questions about relative power that we discussed in Chapter 1, and the need not just for individual but also systemic change. To return to the Gettysburg Address, Lincoln warns us that the soldier's struggle, however brave, will amount to nothing without a proper democratic system – in his words, "government of the people, by the people, for the people." We will turn a critical eye onto these broader issues in the next four chapters.

Reflective questions

1. What is meant by the two-way communication process? Why is it important to the social marketer?
2. Define, in your own words in two or three sentences, each of the key words at the beginning of this chapter.
3. Explain the function of problem definition; medium; language; images and links in the communication process.
4. "The research into the effectiveness of fear appeal is inconclusive." Elaborate with illustrations.
5. Branding represents an alternative to fear campaigns. How? When? Where and Why?
6. What are social media? What should the social marketer consider when looking to use digital marketing?
7. Model and explain internal marketing as it applies to social marketing.

Reflective assignments

1. Conduct an Internet search and describe two common marketing communication models.
2. Locate and critique a social marketing communication example that includes a fear-based message.
3. Locate and review a social marketing example of good and poor branding.
4. Locate and document social marketing examples of Twitter, Facebook, Instagam, Snapchat and Linkedin.
5. Write a short paragraph on the how and why of each of the following: (a) communication; (b) branding; (c) fear appeals; and (d) digital marketing. *Cross reference* with (1) the four orientation principles of social marketing in Chapter 2; (2) research in Chapter 5; and (3) participation in Chapter 4.
6. Source and read any of the papers from Table 6.1 on digital social marketing.
7. Draw up your 'Rebels with a cause' communication, promotion and participation checklists.

Table 6.1 Examples of social marketing utilising social and digital marketing

Authors	Journal	Topic
Austin and Gaither (2016)	*Social Marketing Quarterly*	Examining Public Response to Corporate Social Initiative Types: A Quantitative Content Analysis of Coca-Cola's Social Media
Mowery (2016)	*Social Marketing Quarterly*	Using Online Message Testing to Evaluate TV Ads, Select Effective Messaging, and Improve Public Health Campaigns
Levit *et al.* (2016)	*Social Marketing Quarterly*	Application of the Transtheoretical Model and Social Marketing to Antidepression Campaign Websites
Antonishak *et al.* (2015)	*Social Marketing Quarterly*	Impact of an Online Birth Control Support Network on Unintended Pregnancy
Bowerman and DeLorme (2014)	*Social Marketing Quarterly*	Boaters' Perception of a Mobile App for a Marine Conservation Social Marketing Campaign
Ledford (2012)	*Social Marketing Quarterly*	Changing Channels: A Theory-Based Guide to Selecting Traditional, New, and Social Media in Strategic Social Marketing
Jones *et al.* (2017)	*Journal of Social Marketing*	Young Adults, Alcohol and Facebook: A Synergistic Relationship
Mulcahy (2015)	*Journal of Social Marketing*	Electronic Games: Can They Create Value for the Moderate Drinking Brand?
Guidry *et al.* (2014)	*Journal of Social Marketing*	Moving Social Marketing beyond Personal Change to Social Change: Strategically using Twitter to Mobilize Supporters into Vocal Advocates
Barn (2016)	*Journal of Marketing Management*	'Tweet Dreams are Made of This, Who are we to Disagree?' Adventures in a #Brave New World of #Tweets, #twitter, #Student Engagement and #Excitement with #Learning
Hodis *et al.* (2015)	*Journal of Marketing Management*	Interact with me on My Terms: A Four Segment Facebook Engagement Framework for Marketers
Moraes *et al.* (2014)	*Journal of Marketing Management*	The Use of Facebook to Promote Drinking Among Young Consumers

(*Source:* Flaherty 2017)

Notes

1 Lincoln, A. (1863) *The Gettysburg Address*, 19th November, Soldiers' National Cemetery, Gettysburg, PA.
2 http://en.wikipedia.org/wiki/Edward_Everett#cite_note-Simon41-7/.

3 Healthy Respect is a Scottish Government-funded national health demonstration project for young people and sexual health (2001–2008). For further information, contact Healthy Respect at NHS Lothian, Deaconess House, 148 Pleasance, Edinburgh. www.healthy respect.co.uk.

4 See for example, Olins, W. (2003) *Wally Olins On Brand*. London: Thames & Hudson.

5 The EVOKE game is available online at: www.urgentevoke.com.

6 Niamh Gately, Social Marketing Research Fellow with *safe*food, 2012.

References

2000AD (1998) Programme 1112, cover Judge Dredd by Kevin Walker, illustration of, 23–29 September.

Awagu, C. and Basil, D.Z. (2016) 'Fear appeals: the influence of threat orientations', *Journal of Social Marketing*, 6(4): 361–376. doi: 10.1108/JSOCM-12-2014-0089.

Bakewell, J. (2006) *The Guardian*, Review, 23 September.

Barry, T.E. and Howard, D.J. (1990) 'Review and critique of the hierarchy of effects in advertising', *International Journal of Advertising*, 9(2): 121–135.

Barton, J., Chassin, L., Presson, C.C. and Sherman, S.J. (1982) 'Social image factors as motivators of smoking initiation in early and middle adolescence', *Child Development*, 53: 1499–1511.

Bolling, K. and Owen, L. (1996) *Smoking and Pregnancy: A Survey of Knowledge, Attitudes and Behaviour*. London: Health Education Authority.

Burke, J. and Thompson, T. (2002) 'Rachel: Shock photo backed by boyfriend', *The Observer*, 3 March: 10.

Cacioppo, J.T. and Petty, R.E. (1989) 'The elaboration likelihood model: The role of effect and affect laden information processing in persuasion', in P. Cafferata and A. Tybout (eds) *Cognitive and Affective Responses to Advertising*. Lexington, MA: Lexington Books, pp.69–90.

Chaffey, D. and Ellis-Chadwick, F. (2016) *Digital Marketing: Strategy, Implementation and Practice*, 6th edn. London: Pearson.

Corcoran, A. (2017) Socio-Economic Groups in Ireland, [PowerPoint], Ipsos MRBI, Dublin, Ireland.

Dahl, S., Eagle, L. and Low, D. (2015) 'Integrated marketing communications and social marketing: Together for the common good?', *Journal of Social Marketing*, 5(3): 226–240. doi: 10.1108/JSOCM-07-2012-0031.

de Chernatony, L. (1993) 'Categorizing brands: Evolutionary processes underpinned by two key dimensions', *Journal of Marketing Management*, 9(2): 163–188.

Durgee, J.F. (1986) 'How consumer sub-cultures code reality: A look at some code types', *Advances in Consumer Research*, 13: 332–336.

Elliott, R. and Wattanasuwan, K. (1998) 'Brands as symbolic resources for the construction of identity', *International Journal of Advertising*, 16(2): 131–144.

Evans, D.W. and Hastings, G.B. (2008) *Public Health Branding: Applying Marketing for Social Change*. Oxford: Oxford University Press.

Flaherty, T. (2017) 'Digital Marketing and Social Marketing, the Case of Operation Transformation', poster presentation, 6 April, Whitaker Institute, NUI Galway, Ireland.

Foote, E. (1981) 'Advertising and tobacco', *Journal of the American Medical Association*, 245: 1667–1668.

Gossieaux, F. and Moran, E. (2010) *The Hyper-Social Organization: Eclipse Your Competition by Leveraging Social Media*. New York: McGraw-Hill.

Grindle, M. (2004) 'At what stage is our understanding of the interactive entertainment development industry in Scotland?', paper presented at *The Scottish Media and Communication Association Annual Conference*, 3 December. Dundee: University of Abertay.

Grindle, M. (2010) 'Can computer games save the planet? The role interactive entertainment might play in marketing sustainable consumption', paper presented at the *ISM-Open Conference Changing Times, New Challenges*, 3 November. Milton Keynes: The Open University.

Guardian (1938) From the Archives: Report of a Radio Broadcast of *The War of the Worlds* from *The Guardian*, November 1, 1938. Online: www.guardian.co.uk/fromthearchive/story/0,12269,1075 343,00.html. (Copyright Guardian News and Media Limited 2002.)

Hastings, G.B. and Leathar, D.S. (1986) 'Anti-smoking publicity in Scotland: A decade of progress', *New York State Journal of Medicine*, 86(9): 480–484.

Hawkins, D. and Mothersbaugh, D. (2010) *Consumer Behaviour: Building Marketing Strategy*, 11th edn. Maidenhead: McGraw-Hill International.

Hawkins, R. (2010) 'EVOKE – a crash course in changing the world', EduTech A World Bank Blog on ICT use in Education (Weblog). Online: http://blogs.worldbank.org/edutech/evoke-a-crash-course-in-changing-the-world (accessed May 2016).

Hedges, A. (1982) *Testing to Destruction: A Fresh and Critical Look at the Uses of Research in Advertising*. London: Institute of Practitioners in Advertising.

Henley, N. and Donovan, R. (1999) *'Unintended consequences of arousing fear in social marketing'*, Australian and New Zealand Marketing Academy Conference, Sydney, Australia. Online at: http://ro.ecu.edu.au/smatl_pubs/14/ (accessed May 2016).

Higbee, K.L. (1969) 'Fifteen years of fear arousal: Research on threat appeals', *Psychological Bulletin*, 62(6): 426–444.

Higgins, O., Sixsmith, J., Barry, M.M. and Domegan, C. (2011) 'A literature review on health information seeking behaviour on the web: A health consumer and health professional perspective'. Stockholm: ECDC.

Katz, E. and Lazarsfeld, P. (1955) *Personal Influence*. New York: The Free Press.

Kaufman, I.A. and Horton, C. (2015) *Digital Marketing: Integrating Strategy and Tactics with Values*. New York: Routledge.

Kubacki, K., Rundle-Thiele, S., Schuster, L., Wessels, C. and Gruneklee, N. (2015) 'Digital innovation in social marketing: A systematic literature of interventions using digital channels for engagement', in W. Wymer (ed.) *Innovations in Social Marketing and Public Health Communication: Improving the Quality of Life for Individuals and Communities*. Heidelberg: Springer.

Leathar, D.S. (1980) 'Images in health education advertising', *Health Education Journal*, 39(4): 123–128.

Lefebvre, R.C. (2009) 'The change we need: New ways of thinking about social issues', *On Social Marketing and Social Change*, 29 January. Online: http://socialmarketing.blogs.com/r_craig_lefebvres_social/2009/01/index. html/ (accessed May 2016).

Lefebvre, R.C., Doner, L., Johnston, C., Loughrey, K., Balch, G.I. and Sutton, S.M. (1995) 'Use of database marketing and consumer-based health communication in message design: An example from the office of cancer communications' "5 A Day for Better Health" program', in E. Maibach and R.L. Parrott (eds) *Designing Health Messages. Approaches From Communication Theory and Public Health Practice*. Thousand Oaks, CA: Sage Publications, pp.216–246.

Leventhal, H. (1960) 'Findings and theory in the study of fear communications', *Advances in Experimental Social Psychology*, 5: 119–186.

Lowry, R. (2000) 'Social Marketing and Communication: Persuading GPs to prescribe sugar-free medicines'. Open Wide Summer, Oral Health Promotion Research Group, London.

McDermott, L., Stead, M. and Hastings, G. (2005) 'What is and what is not social marketing: The challenge of reviewing the evidence', *Journal of Marketing Management*, 21(5–6): 545–553.

McQuail, D., Blumer, J.G. and Brown, J.R. (1962) 'The television audience, a revised perspective', in D. McQuail (ed.) *Sociology of Mass Communications*. Harmondsworth: Penguin.

Mays, D., Weaver, J.B. and Bernhardt, J.M. (2011) 'New media in social marketing', Ch. 12 in G. Hastings, K. Angus and C. Bryant (eds) *The SAGE Handbook of Social Marketing*. London: Sage Publications.

Monahan, J.L. (1995) 'Thinking positively: using positive affect when designing messages', in E. Maibach and R.L. Parrott (eds) *Designing Health Messages: Approaches From Communication Theory and Public Health Practice*. Newbury Park, CA: Sage Publications.

Murphy, J. (ed.) (1986) *Branding: A Key Marketing Tool*. New York: McGraw-Hill.

Noble, K.G., Farah, M.J. and McCandliss, B.M. (2006) 'Socioeconomic background modulates cognition–achievement relationships in reading', *Cognitive Development*, 21 (3): 349–368.

Packard, V. (2007) *The Hidden Persuaders*. Brooklyn, New York: IG Publishing.

Redmond, J. (2006) *How to Write a Poem*. Oxford: Blackwell Publishing, p.7.

Rogers, R.W. (1965) 'A protection motivation theory of fear appeals and attitude change', *Journal of Psychology*, 91: 93–114.

Rosengren, K.E. and Windahl, S. (1962) 'Mass media consumption as a functional alternative', in D. McQuail (ed.) *Sociology of Mass Communications*. Harmondsworth: Penguin, pp.166–194.

Rudolph, M.J. (1995) 'The food product development process', *British Food Journal*, 96(3): 3–11.

safefood (2015) 'Babies know the facts about Folic' – Internal Campaign Evaluation. Unpublished Report, safefood, Dublin.

Smith, A.M. (2011) 'Internal social marketing: Lessons for the field of services marketing', Ch. 20 in G. Hastings, K. Angus and C. Bryant (eds) *The SAGE Handbook of Social Marketing*. London: Sage Publications.

Tudor, A. (1996) 'On alcohol and the mystique of media effects', in T. O'Sullivan and Y. Jewkes (eds) *The Media Studies Reader*. London: Edward Arnold, pp.164–180.

Wu, T. (2011) *The Master Switch: The Rise and Fall of Information Empires*. New York: Vintage.

Chapter **7**

Competitive analysis

LOOK AND LEARN . . .

Uggina had woken up with a simple but brilliant idea in her head.

Her man Ugg was the strong silent type. He had once killed a grizzly bear with only his hands, but he did not have Uggina's skill for tracking animals. Nor had he mastered the spear, like Nugg who lived nearby. As a result they had not eaten meat for nearly three weeks. Uggina set about preparing another breakfast of unappetising wild millet porridge and, predictably enough, Ugg returned soon after empty-handed from yet another unsuccessful hunting trip.

She had noticed that the tribe at the other side of the valley did things differently; they hunted in groups. It was this that had given her the brilliant idea, which she now put to Ugg. She suggested that they combine their talents: she would track the animals and Ugg could use his strength to kill them. Now for the tricky bit, she thought, as she continued: "But if the animal we track is a deer or a wild ox it will run away before you can get your great hands and powerful arms on it." Ugg glowed with pride at this reference to his strength. "So why don't we approach Nugg and see if he would help us with his spear?" "Why should he?" asked Ugg, who didn't like Nugg much and envied his weapon-handling skills, "and anyway, who would get the meat?" "He might do it because he needs my tracking skills to find the deer, and your strength to protect him from any roving bears," she replied, "and we can all share the meat."

Ugg thought hard about Uggina's idea; thinking was not his forte but he could see the sense in it. No one was taking advantage of anyone else – this was a fair exchange from which all three of them would benefit. Furthermore, the alternative was another day of the awful millet porridge which Uggina managed to burn every time she made it. Maybe he should suggest to her another exchange: he would do the cooking if she would stick to thinking and see if she could come up with some more revolutionary ideas.

As we noted in Chapter 1, marketing is as old as human society. Uggina's story shows how its key principles of co-operation and mutually beneficial exchange were deployed by our earliest ancestors to overcome the disadvantages of being relatively weak and ill-protected from either the weather or our fellow creatures. Our key superiority as a species – our large brains – enabled us to work out, as Uggina did, that our chances of survival are greatly enhanced if we pool our resources and operate collectively; if we can find win–wins. So marketing is not something that emerged from the US business schools in the middle of the last century, but a timeless protocol for co-operation, mutual benefit and advancement. This book is all about reclaiming this wider purpose.

Uggina's story also tells us a great deal about the benefits of critically analysing the competition. We noted in Chapter 4 that the crucial function of strategic planning starts by looking internally, at our own personal or organisational strengths and weaknesses. Paradoxically, however, our appreciation of these is honed by looking around us at what our rivals are doing. Uggina's analysis of her local community helps her identify the importance of her own tracking ability and Ugg's strength. It also revealed a crucial gap in spear throwing ability – the benefits of which were apparent from Nugg's successes. In a sense the whole discipline of social marketing bears witness to the relevance of this lesson – as we noted in Chapter 1, it originated from attempts to imitate commercial marketing.

Assessing the competition can also sharpen our overall performance: it was Uggina's observation of the competing tribe that gave her her revolutionary idea for co-operation. We social marketers can also learn from the competing marketers around us – even when, as with the fast-food, alcohol and tobacco industries, their activities are inimical to ours. As we discuss below, branding is a particularly good example here.

Also, the story tells us something about relative power and its impact on our lives. The trio can track antelope, and defend themselves from bears, but supposing a woolly mammoth happens along? Or one of the large roaming wolf packs frighten off all the available game? Their only recourse is to make regular sacrifices to their deities to protect them from these calamities. We social marketers also face potent competition, but luckily don't have to rely on superstition to defend us: we can make intelligent, informed decisions about how to proceed.

Unfortunately, though, our competition is more intelligent than the average mammoth, and has learnt that size and wealth give it immense power. This power imbalance can make life difficult for social marketers, and hard decisions have to be made about how we respond to it. As we began to explore in Chapters 2 and 4, do we compete and challenge despite our relative weakness, or do we co-operate? In this chapter we take the discussion further and examine the concept of Corporate Social Responsibility (CSR), and the extent to which it represents a genuine solution or is just an evasive practice which reinforces the original problem. Does the much greater power of one party inevitably result in exploitation?

And where does regulation come into the picture? How and when should it be instigated?

Inevitably these questions of power pull us into broader issues of how corporate capitalism works, and the need to move beyond ad hoc competitive analysis and start making judgments at a systemic level. We will pick this up at the end of the chapter, showing how it underlines the value of independent critical thinking.

Learning outcomes

By the end of this chapter you should be familiar with the idea of competitive analysis and the benefits it can bring to social marketing. Specifically you should understand:

✓ That we in social marketing can learn from the strengths of others – even when those others are operating in direct competition to us

✓ The pros and cons of co-operation and competition

✓ The role of regulation and the need for evidence

✓ For social marketers the competition is both immensely powerful and systemic, and this raises much broader issues that are addressed by critical marketing.

Key words

Client power – competitive analysis – competitive strategy – co-operate or compete – CSR - direct and indirect competition – Porter's Four Forces – sustainable change.

It's a competitive business

As we noted in Chapter 2 competitive analysis underpins one of the four defining orientations of social marketing. This reflects its pivotal role in business. Burger King and McDonald's, Nike and Adidas, Coca-Cola and Pepsi are proverbial rivals; stock market ratings are the equivalent of sports leagues, takeovers and company failures the obvious results for the winners and losers in this jockeying for position. By contrast, among us gentle herbivores of the social marketing world, such rivalry seems counter intuitive. Surely social marketers are all on the same side, trying to do good – not put each other down? In reality however, competitive analysis can be a useful tool.

Marketing is concerned with profitably addressing needs, and we have already examined how this operates as far as the company and the customer are concerned, but there is a third 'C' in the equation: the competition. Like the natural world, business is also driven by the law governing the survival of the fittest. However, in this case the forces are not hidden Darwinian genes, but an overt managerial process guided by deliberate planning. Marketers seek to understand the behaviours of their competitors, just as they do those of their customers, so that they can control, influence or at least adapt to the resulting forces.

The ultimate aim is to establish sustainable competitive advantage, with the emphasis on sustainable. Above all else, studying your rivals informs your strategic planning; it helps define where you want to be not just in the next year, but the next decade. And this long-term vision is invaluable. Rumour has it that one Japanese car manufacturer is more than happy to show its competitors around its factories, and give them as much information as they want about its production methods. By the time they have copied them, its erstwhile host will have moved on, made improvements and left them far behind. The story is apocryphal, but its thrust is correct.

Good competitive analysis, as with so much else in marketing, starts by looking at the world through the eyes of the customer. What need are *they* trying to satisfy? What products do *they* use to satisfy the same need? What do *they* buy instead? Who do *they* see as the competition? Box 7.1 presents a simple competitive analysis for McDonald's.

BOX 7.1   WHAT CUSTOMER NEEDS DOES MCDONALD'S MEET?

Think for a few moments about what needs the fast food outlet are satisfying for a father and his two small children. As a good marketer you would seek to answer this question with a bit of market research asking the father and his children why they have come to the Golden Arches.

The obvious answer you are likely to get is food; McDonald's has to satisfy their hunger – but it is very likely that this is only part of the picture. Competitive analysis suggests questions specifically about what they consider to be the alternative – *the competing* - options can usefully extend your research. Questions like:

(i) Where might you have gone today if not to McDonald's?

(ii) What other places do you like going together?

(iii) How good are these alternative offerings?

The answers may produce predictable responses such as KFC or Burger King (because they have better free toys). A little more unsettlingly, but still reasonably predictable, the answer may be the new juice bar (because the food is healthier). However, the father and his children may also suggest less obvious alternatives, like a picnic in the park (because you can also feed the ducks and try out the swings) or a trip to the cinema to see the latest Disney (because it has been trailed on children's television and all their friends have seen it).

This simple exercise has two great benefits for McDonald's: it helps them think more incisively both about their rivals and (more importantly) their customers. As far as their rivals are concerned, the answers in Box 7.1 will enable McDonald's executives to see who they are up against – Burger King, the juice bar or the cinema. They can then think through how they should respond. Is it straight 'them or us' rivalry or are there also co-operative opportunities? For example, in the case of the juice bar direct competition is probably needed, perhaps by adding healthier options to the menu; the picnic option, on the other hand, may suggest that opening a franchise in the park has potential. Similarly, in the case of the cinema the best strategy may not be to compete head on, but to form an alliance and begin serving McDonald's meals to theatregoers.

As far as their customers are concerned, the answers in Box 7.1 start to give McDonald's a much better fix on the precise customer need they are seeking to meet. It becomes clear, for example, that this is about much more than food and hunger. Fun, entertainment and a child-friendly atmosphere are all also in there as exchange benefits. Indeed some people actually patronise McDonald's *despite* the food: a nutritionist friend living in Geneva takes her children there, although she has grave reservations about the menu, because it is one of the few child- friendly restaurants in town. Creating and delivering value, such as fun and a child friendly atmosphere, is – as we discuss in Chapter 10 – at the core of mutually beneficial marketing exchanges.

Solutions not problems

Thus our small competitive analysis has helped us uncover a valuable marketing insight: the distinction between the offering made (in this case, ostensibly at least, a meal) and the need satisfied (child-oriented entertainment). This is a vital distinction. Have a try at Exercise 7.1.

EXERCISE 7.1   CARLING STARLINGS

You work for Sensible Limits, an NGO concerned with youth alcohol problems. You are very much aware that the brewers of Carling lager are successfully reaching young people in your area and you want to learn more about how they are doing this. You have two opportunities to do so. First, you are familiar with a very successful cinema ad they produced featuring a flock of starlings that gradually came together to reveal the word 'BELONG' dressed up as the Carling logo go to YouTube and type in 'carlingstarlings'.

Second, a recently commissioned Memorandum for the UK Parliament Health Select Committee (www.publications.parliament.uk/pa/cm/cmhealth.htm) took an inside look at all the industry's marketing, and highlighted the starlings campaign (which had caused some disquiet among regulators when it appeared). Two quotes about this stand out:

1. "Carling celebrates, initiates and promotes the togetherness of the pack, their passions and their pint because Carling understands that things are better together," this is then split into "3 Aspects of Belonging: Initiation: Expressions of the moment when an individual joins a group and finds a happy home in the pack—the moment of belonging: Celebration: An expression of the sheer joy of belonging: Contagion: An expression of the magnetic power of the group—the power of belonging."
2. "Broadly speaking each piece of communication will either celebrate 'Join Us' by championing the benefit of togetherness or facilitate 'Join Us' by providing and enhancing experiences where togetherness is key."

List some of the lessons for Sensible Limits.

The interesting issue for Sensible Limits is how far the Carling marketing is from overtly selling beer – nothing is said about hops, brewing skills or even thirst. The pitch is to do with mates and social connectedness, not about beer as such. Given the skill and success of Carling, this provides a useful insight into the priorities of your target group. Unless you tread very carefully, messages about not drinking or drinking less risk being interpreted as a recipe for loneliness and social isolation. Perhaps Sensible Limits should be looking at healthier, non-alcohol related ways of belonging?

It's a timely reminder that marketers – whether commercial or social – don't sell products or services, they sell solutions. Consider for a minute this question inspired by Theodore Levitt (1960): 'What do Black and Decker make?' Jot down your answer(s).

The obvious response is perhaps drills, or more broadly, do-it-yourself equipment or tools. But a marketer would say no, the company doesn't sell drills, it sells holes. Drills just happen to be the best way of making them, but it may not always be so. New technology may, for instance, produce a laser-driven machine that can do the job better. Unless Black and Decker realise they are in the hole business rather than the drill business they will be as vulnerable to the competition as buggy-whip manufacturers were to the new technology of the internal combustion engine.

Browning's poem about three heroic horsemen bringing good news from Ghent to Aix helps reinforce this point. In the poem, three riders set out to deliver *"the news which alone could save Aix from her fate"* (Browning 1845); two of their horses die during the gallop and Roland – our hero's mount – expires on the streets of Aix as the tidings are delivered. Have a try at Exercise 7.2.

EXERCISE 7.2   HOW THEY BROUGHT THE GOOD NEWS FROM GHENT TO AIX

1	2
I SPRANG to the stirrup, and Joris, and he; I galloped, Dirck galloped, we galloped all three; 'God speed!' cried the watch, as the gate-bolts undrew; 'Speed!' echoed the wall to us galloping through; Behind shut the postern, the lights sank to rest, And into the midnight we galloped abreast.	. . . By Hasselt, Dirck groaned; and cried Joris, 'Stay spur! Your Roos galloped bravely, the fault's not in her, We'll remember at Aix'—for one heard the quick wheeze Of her chest, saw the stretched neck and staggering knees, And sunk tail, and horrible heave of the flank, As down on her haunches she shuddered and sank.
3	4
. . . 'How they'll greet us!'— and all in a moment his roan Rolled neck and croup over, lay dead as a stone;	. . . And all I remember is, friends flocking round As I sat with his head 'twixt my knees on the ground;

And there was my Roland to bear the whole weight Of the news which alone could save Aix from her fate, With his nostrils like pits full of blood to the brim, And with circles of red for his eye-sockets' rim.	And no voice but was praising this Roland of mine, As I poured down his throat our last measure of wine, Which (the burgesses voted by common consent) Was no more than his due who brought good news from Ghent.

In Browning's famous poem (abridged here) what did Joris, Dirck and our nameless hero really need?

What sales opportunity would you, an entrepreneurial marketer living in 19th-century Ghent, have been able to exploit? What would you have sold them?

The obvious answer is better horses. Or even a motorbike. But what they really needed – and any marketer worthy of the name would recognise this – was a telephone. Joris, Dirck and co. were not looking for a means of transport at all, but a means of communication. Competitive analysis aids this type of lateral thinking. McDonald's analysis of the competition stops them becoming obsessed with the product and keeps them focused on the need they are satisfying.

A broader Agenda

Competitive analysis also broadens beyond commercial rivals. McDonald's, for instance, will take careful readings of how its customers see the current obesity debate. Do they have any sympathy with the New York teenagers who tried to sue the company for making them fat, or support a ban on fast food advertising? This will help inform its consumer marketing – perhaps they should employ celebrity chefs or include healthier options on its menu. It also guides its stakeholder marketing. The rise in public concern about obesity has pushed the fast food industry to engage much more actively with policy makers.

This is even more apparent in the tobacco business. We noted in Chapter 4 when discussing strategic analysis that, as David Jobber, a leading business academic explains, "close relationships with politicians are often cultivated by organizations both to monitor political moods and also to influence them" (2004: 145). The importance of doing this is increased by the activities of tobacco control NGOs, as Jobber goes on to note: "the cigarette industry, for example, has a vested interest in maintaining close ties with government to counter proposals from pressure groups such as ASH". In this sense, competitive analysis is a natural progression from environmental scanning, as discussed in social marketing planning in Chapter 4.

Exercise 7.3 applies this thinking to a social marketing example.

EXERCISE 7.3 SCHOOL DINNERS – IDENTIFYING THE COMPETITION

Imagine that you are a social marketer and have been asked for help by Oldsville High School. Only about a third of their pupils eat school dinners; the others make alternative arrangements, either bringing their own or going out of school to local cafes. The school want you to make their new healthier lunches more popular.

Competitive analysis suggests that questions like these may be revealing:

(i) where do the two thirds of non-school diners eat at the moment?

(ii) what do they like about these alternatives?

(iii) why do the one third remain loyal?

As with our McDonald's and Carling examples – and Browning's poem – you may well find that the answers take you well beyond food and hunger. Local cafes, for instance, may offer a chance to rebel, to hang around with friends in an unstructured environment or simply to save money on the allowance disbursed by parents. On the other hand, the third who remain loyal are presumably rejecting the competitors' offerings, so asking them why they do so may uncover some hidden strengths in the school's dinners.

Porter's competitive forces

The nature of the competition is not just influenced by what other companies do, but by more fundamental forces in the marketplace. Michael Porter (2008) divides these into four categories (see Box 7.2).

BOX 7.2 PORTER'S COMPETITIVE FORCES

1. The power of the *buyer* or customer is of course crucial. Do they have access to alternative offerings that will satisfy their needs?

2. The *power of suppliers* and the extent to which they can control what the marketer does. The room for manoeuvre of BP, for example, may be significantly constrained by OPEC.

3. The degree to which offerings can be *substituted*. Generic, easily produced commodities, like potatoes or paper, are much more vulnerable to competition than are branded snacks or a unique piece of software.

4. Finally *new entrants* to the market can also increase competition, and the number of these will depend on how difficult it is to start up in a particular business. Setting up a new pharmaceutical company is, for example, much more challenging than a new beauty salon.

(*Source*: adapted from Jobber 2004: 678–680)

First, as you would expect, the buyer or customer has potential power. We have already explored this in some detail, but Porter reminds us that the amount of power the buyer has will vary according to market conditions. In a monopoly situation or a time of shortage, for instance, their power can shrink dramatically. The second force, the power of suppliers, is essentially the corollary of the first. The third force concerns the potential for substitution: are there alternative products or services available that can do the same job? In the commercial sector branding is used to capture this sort of power – a trainer is a trainer, but a Nike Air Max is unique.

Finally Porter considers the threat from new entrants to the market. The extent of this will be determined by how easy it is for others to move in and start satisfying the same consumer needs. In some sectors, such as pharmaceuticals and nuclear energy, the barriers are very high. In others, such as the small businesses service sector (e.g. hairdressers and cafes), entry is much easier and competition much more widespread – with a resulting tendency for businesses to appear and disappear on a regular basis.

As with other strategic decisions, a company's options for engaging with and tackling competition are going to be influenced by its internal capacity. What skills and resources can they call on? What strategic approaches can they realistically adopt? Can they compete on price, for example, or will differentiation (offering a valued alternative), focus (servicing a particular area or group), pre-emption (offering some innovation) or synergy (exploiting particular strengths) be feasible? This capacity will ultimately depend on the potential to develop a workable and effective marketing mix.

Porter's analysis is relevant to social marketing.

Buyer power in social marketing

The fact that social marketers deal with *voluntary* behaviour means their clients always have a choice – they have 'buyer power' (see Box 7.2) – and hence there is always *passive* or *indirect* competition (refer back to Chapter 2). Client power is a valuable concept in a discipline that also competes professionally with expert-driven approaches like public health and road safety, and reminds us of the need to satisfy our target's inherent self-interest by providing *real* benefits. In this context, *real* must incorporate both the objective (technical benefits such as symptom relief or greater safety) and the subjective (what the recipient feels about consuming the offering).

In competitive terms, there is, what seems to be, a natural tendency for social marketing offerings to be worthy, hard work, and as a consequence, inherently unattractive compared with our clients' alternative options. Thus a bad diet is fun and indulgent, a good one Spartan and dissatisfying; a sedentary life is restful and relaxing, exercise hard work and tiring. Furthermore we always seem to be asking people to give things up – chocolate, cigarettes, the rugged manliness that comes with driving an SUV. But as Richard Layard (2005) points out we put a greater premium on loss than gain: we get more upset from a £80 bill than we get happiness from £80 windfall. This suggests the Health Promotion Board of Singapore were right to turn the negative offering of anti-smoking into a positive in its Pro-Quitting campaign (Ogilvy & Mather 2012).

Similarly, social marketing seems doomed to offer long-term, probabilistic benefits (or often the absence of awful repercussions), whereas the competition brings short-term, definite

Figure 7.1 The delights of quitting

(*Sources:* MacAskill and Eadie 2002; MacAskill *et al.* 2002)

ones. The immediate pleasure of chocolate competes all too effectively with the deferred (and often elusive) advantage of weight loss; more dramatically, today's nicotine fix competes easily with the possibility of a heart attack in a couple of decades. 'Discounting' exacerbates this problem: rewards lose their value and costs are less onerous in the future.

This again compels us to think about what we are offering and the extent to which it meets people's real needs. If deferred gratification is such a weak product why do we focus on it? Especially when a little consideration shows that it is far from being the only benefit of a healthy lifestyle. Have a look at Figure 7.1, for example, which presents the results of research with prisoners and people on low income who have successfully given up smoking.

It shows the immense sense of achievement that successfully giving up smoking can bring to the most disadvantaged populations. Similarly back in Box 4.4 we saw that exercise is not by definition unpleasant – whole swathes of the population get a variety of (short-term) benefits as a result.

This takes us back to the discussion of fear messages and positive branding in the previous chapter. It also helps explain the World Health Organization's definition of health – "a state of complete physical, mental and social well-being and not merely the absence of disease or infirmity"[1] – which pushes us in a very positive direction.

Furthermore, if people want an enjoyable life today rather than the probability of more life tomorrow (and it is hardly surprising that they do), should we not be making sure that our products deliver this? Competitive analysis and customer power, just as with McDonald's, must lead us to think about our core business: is it just freedom from physical illness or a more fulfilled and rewarding life, as the WHO indicate? Is public health and safety about avoiding threats or realising opportunities; about drills or holes?

Competitive analysis reminds if we do not get this right, others surely will. Exercise 7.4 shows how the tobacco industry is working hard to provide attractive short-term offerings to potential new smokers. As we noted above, there is a Darwinian discipline at play here – we social marketers have to compete successfully or we will not survive.

EXERCISE 7.4   THE IMPORTANCE OF COMPETITIVE ANALYSIS IN SMOKING PREVENTION

Market research from the UK tobacco industry makes it clear the young are a key target and that image and emotion are vital appeals:

> "To smoke Marlboro Lights represents having passed a **rite of passage**."

> "Young adult smokers are **looking for reassurance** that they are doing the right thing, and cigarettes are no exception.
> Any break with a brand's heritage must be carefully considered in order not to throw doubt into the minds of young adult smokers."

> "Young adult smokers are also **searching for an identity**. Cigarettes have a key role to play as they are an ever-present statement of identity."
> "Smoking for these people (young smokers) is **still a badge**. A sign of maturity, discernment and independence."

> "Younger smokers give **more weight to imagery of cigarettes** and pay more attention and are open to fashionable brands and up-to-date designs."

Successful brands exploit these emotional needs and insecurities:

> "The success of Marlboro Lights derives from its being **the aspirational lifestyle brand . . . The Diet Coke of cigarettes**."

> "To be successful any Gallaher brand will have to tackle **Marlboro's coolness of image** – smokers do smoke the image as well as the taste."

> "We want to engage their aspirations and fantasies –
> 'I'd like to be there, do that, own that'."

How well will long-term, probabilistic health warnings compete here? Are there more attractive offers we could make?

(*Source:* House of Commons Health Select Committee 2000)

Case Study 8, demonstrates how careful and empathetic research can provide the sort of insights needed to devise offerings that meet psychosocial needs. "The Talk" campaign is innovative because it is aimed at the adult children of older males, rather than directly at the 'resistant' target. The focus on the community surrounding the target of the behaviour change is a significant shift away from individual behaviour change models. This novel approach could strengthen the campaign's impact, especially when combined with the humorous misunderstanding between father and son, which opened up the conversation. In this context simple fear inducement seems, at best, a limited response, as discussed in Chapter 6.

As we noted when discussing Exchange Theory in Chapter 3, insurance companies, like social marketers, have the problem of deferred gratification; they offer a benefit tomorrow that is both probabilistic and inherently unattractive. Very few of us actually want to claim on our household insurance because it assumes some misfortune has visited us first. The same is even more true of life insurance. The benefit that insurance companies push, then, is not so much financial paybacks later, but peace of mind now. They do not sell *in*surance; they sell *reas*surance.

Substitution, suppliers and new entrants

Porter's other three forces (Box 7.2) also have something of interest to offer, as Exercise 7.5 explores.

EXERCISE 7.5   APPLYING PORTER'S FORCES IN SOCIAL MARKETING

Have another look at Box 7.2. How well do Porter's other three forces – *substitution*, the *power of suppliers* and *new entrants* – help us think about social marketing problems? Jot down some ideas under each heading before continuing.

Substitution is an obvious development of client power. There are many easily substituted products for ours on offer. Celebrity diets present an attractive alternative to lifestyle change, and cleverly promoted four-wheel drives can deflect us from more ecologically sound modes of transport. Similarly, almost any other television channel is preferable to the one showing yet another tediously graphic speeding or drink driving ad.

More broadly, our issues compete for attention. Tobacco control, alcohol safety, and HIV/AIDS are all competing for the same health dollars. Furthermore, as lifestyle illnesses proliferate, resources become more stretched. For example, obesity has only emerged as a public health concern in the last twenty years, but it is estimated that by 2018 it will be absorbing 344 billion dollars a year – which is more than a fifth of the entire health budget (Lang and Rayner 2012).

In social marketing the **supplier** is, in many instances, very powerful – often more so than in the commercial sector. There are two reasons for this. First the supplier is frequently also the funder, with a resulting inclination to call the tune. Second, they do not have the laws of the market breathing down their neck as a commercial company does. They will not go bust if they get things wrong. As a result, in social marketing the demands of the supplier can sometimes supersede the needs of the client. For example, speed cameras might be imposed on a community despite the public's suspicions about the purity of the motives behind them or morning-after contraception discouraged because of the supplier's religious beliefs.

The absence of a profit motive means suppliers can't just buck the market, but create it. Thus governments will often decide what the priorities are for social marketers. This, of course, is no bad thing in a democracy, but serious problems can result. Recall how, in the UK, the May government's obesity strategy caused consternation in the public health community because a Brexit-driven need to focus on the economy had let food marketing off the hook.[2] Or on an international level how the focus on austerity has exacerbated inequalities.[3]

These pressures put an additional onus on social marketers. There is a need to question and, if necessary, challenge the social marketing agenda being set by suppliers. This can be difficult to do, but is essential for the discipline's long-term survival. It also reinforces the points made in Chapter 2 about the importance of building relationships with suppliers. We will return to this need for bigger thinking below.

Porter's fourth force – **new entrants** – brings us to a perhaps uncomfortably selfish notion of competition. Social marketers do compete with each other and other behaviour change specialists for funding and work. The recent upsurge of interest in the subject has brought a range of new providers into the market. This presents real threats, not just in terms of work, but to the discipline itself. If anyone can set up in business as a social marketer – if, in Porter's terms, the barriers are too low – there is a risk that prices, and then standards, will plummet. When medicine faced this threat a century or so ago it responded by setting up very considerable barriers to entry. We would not advocate such a strategy in social marketing, but we do need to set professional standards and agree reasonable criteria for qualifications.

More direct competition comes from a corporate sector which is coming under attack for the collateral harm it causes. A bit of do-gooding social marketing can help avert criticism and burnish the brand image – so tobacco companies run youth smoking prevention campaigns, the alcohol industry establishes health initiatives like the Drink Aware Trust in the UK (www.drinkaware.co.uk) and Bedrinkaware in Australia (www.bedrinkaware.com.au), and Coke – in the wake of concerns about its ecological performance in India – links up with the World Wide Fund for Nature (WWF).

This raises concerns about effectiveness. Are Philip Morris or Diageo really the best people to run public health initiatives? Is Coke actually more devoted to the planet or its profits? The evidence suggests that such concerns are well-founded; for example a review of tobacco industry youth prevention found that not only do they fail to prevent the onset of smoking, they also actually make things worse (Wakefield *et al.* 2006).

This shape-shifting also triggers questions about transparency. Have a go at Exercise 7.6.

> ## EXERCISE 7.6 COKE AND THE WWF
>
> "We have built our partnership on targets, very specific targets for achieving growth at Coke while maintaining no growth in the CO_2 emissions. Pursuing the best practices in sustainable agriculture, and the partnership brings together two of the biggest brands in the world. We have two great networks that are coming together in places around the world, and it's interesting, business leaders I've talked to, they've commented on the importance of businesses becoming leaders in addressing the world's problems because the best and the brightest don't just want to achieve more market share they also want to be leaders in solving the biggest problems that face the world."[4]
>
> Who said this?

You might guess that the speaker in Exercise 7.6 is Muhtar Kent, the $24m a year CEO of Coke, or possibly the company's marketing manager – but it is actually Carter Roberts who runs the WWF in the USA. How helpful do you think it is to have the leader of an NGO devoted to conservation and sustainability speaking up so enthusiastically about the Coca-Cola Corporation's potential for growth? Would he have done this if Coke had not given the WWF so much financial support?

From the perspective of the social marketing discipline though the greatest potential harm is more insidious. If these ineffective and ambiguous campaigns are presented to the world as examples of social marketing, the work of all social marketers will be diminished.

Levels of competition

Noble and Basil (2011) develop our thinking about competition, and show that it is useful to divide it into four levels:

- **Generic level competition** – this is the broadest level relating to the issue, rather than the service or product. For example, a computer recycling initiative is, in its most macro sense, about waste management and indirectly competes with energy, education, health and other social concerns for funding, support and space. At this level, our situational analysis from Chapter 4 – with its SWOT and environmental scanning as well as Harm Chain Analysis – is important. It assists in identifying these broad cultural, technological, legal, economic, social and political drives that, strategically, may act as barriers or benefits to our behaviour change programme.

- **Enterprise level competition** – still at the macro level, this is one stage less than generic. For computer recycling, there's also the options of reuse (give to children, donate to schools, ship to Africa) or reduce (keep computer for another year, use computer in work and don't purchase for home). This correlates to the traditional 'market' or 'business'. Substitutions and new entrants are significant threats here as they often create and script new markets, out-manoeuvring established organisations.

- **Product level competition** – refers to other known recycling facilities, such as the local dump, that are a viable and direct alternative, presenting real barriers to your recycling offering. In Porter's terminology, this is about present suppliers.

- **Brand level competition** – other recycling organisations, profit and non-profit, directly seeking your clients to engage in a computer recycling exchange with them as opposed to you, i.e. other firms, charities and entities in the same industry/business with the same offering as you, head-to-head competition). Piercy and Rich succinctly summarise the levels of competition when they say "the truth is customers just do not fit traditional industry definitions of markets: you think you make crisps, the retailer thinks that the category is salty snacks but the customer-defined market is lunch" (2009: 271). Thus, there's serious food for thought in a competition-level analysis for the social marketer because it explodes the mental market box that can limit our thinking. It also puts the spotlight on direct competitors.

EXERCISE 7.7   FOUR LEVELS OF COMPETITION

Think of a field of social marketing endeavour – tobacco control perhaps or energy conservation – and analyse it using Basil and Noble's framework.

Utilising Basil and Noble's framework in energy conservation has us identify, at the brand competition level, Carey Glass as an example of a leading **triple**-glazed **window** supplier and exporter in the UK and Ireland. They compete against 'window' products such as double glazing and UPVC. At the enterprise level, competition moves past windows into loft and cavity wall insulation, as well as solar panels, more efficient light bulbs and wood pellet burners. This brings us to our broadest type of competition – the generic level – where we have all products and suppliers concerned with all facets of energy conservation and energy-saving products and suppliers including novel, innovative wind, solar and water devices.

Active competition

There is of course, also a very direct way that we can think about competition in social marketing: in some instances other organisations – typically companies selling unhealthy products like tobacco, alcohol and energy-dense foods – push in completely the opposite direction. The WHO dubbed them the 'hazard merchants' a few years ago. Thus, one simple and compelling answer to the question why do so many people take up and continue smoking is because a raft of large and extremely powerful multinational tobacco corporations encourage them to do so. And they undoubtedly succeed, as study after study has demonstrated. Box 7.3 presents one fragment of this evidence base, the conclusion of a systematic literature review on the impact of tobacco advertising and promotion by the world renowned Cochrane Collaboration.

> ### BOX 7.3 TOBACCO ADVERTISING DOES HAVE AN EFFECT
>
> "Longitudinal studies consistently suggest that exposure to tobacco advertising and promotion is associated with the likelihood that adolescents will start to smoke. Based on the strength of this association, the consistency of findings across numerous observational studies, temporality of exposure and smoking behaviours observed, as well as the theoretical plausibility regarding the impact of advertising, we conclude that tobacco advertising and promotion increases the likelihood that adolescents will start to smoke."
>
> (*Source:* Lovato *et al.* 2003: 1)

Similar evidence bases are emerging for the promotion of energy dense food and alcohol. Reviews conducted by ISM (Institute for Social Marketing) for the Food Standards Agency (Hastings *et al.* 2003) and the World Health Organization (Hastings *et al.* 2005) have concluded that in each market commercial promotion is contributing to the public health burden.

Thinking beyond the WHO's hazard merchants, other industries may also present obstacles to social marketers. Car manufacturers can encourage speeding, as discussed above – and certainly have a vested interest in encouraging ecologically damaging forms of travel. The toy and entertainment markets may contribute to the sedentary lifestyles of young people. The armaments business has a role in human conflict. The evidence base in these fields may be less well formed than for tobacco, alcohol and food, but social marketers involved in ecological transportation, exercise promotion and conflict resolution would be unwise to ignore their potential influence.

So how should social marketers respond to this competitive activity?

First let us note that competitive analysis confirms that it is perfectly legitimate – indeed necessary – for us to respond. This reinforces our discussion in Chapter 2, that commercial marketing is part of the social context and that we not only *can* but *have* to make this context our business. Indeed our insights into marketing make our role in this arena particularly valuable. We understand the forces at work here; that there is, for example, so much more than advertising involved. It is the whole of the marketing mix – the products being developed, the pricing strategies used and the well-resourced distribution network – that makes commercial marketing so successful.

For example, while it is known that alcohol advertising contributes to youth drinking, product innovation is probably an equally important driver (Jackson *et al.* 2000). The advent of alcopops, heavily branded 'FAB's (flavoured alcoholic beverages like Bacardi Breezer) and shots has undoubtedly had an impact on drinking. A recent paper in the *American Journal of Public Health*, for instance, argued that it has transformed the youth alcohol market in the USA. The author provided a forensic case study of Smirnoff Ice, a leading brand of alcopops, and explained how "Diageo developed a sophisticated marketing strategy to reenergise its Smirnoff Vodka brand using 3 key components:

1. Develop a beverage that tasted like soft drinks.

2. Use the Smirnoff Vodka brand name but market the product as a malt beverage to compete effectively with beer in terms of price, availability, and advertising in electronic media.

3. Reorient Smirnoff Vodka itself as a young person's brand by adding new fruit flavors and using other marketing innovations" (Mosher 2012).

Similarly, tobacco, alcohol and energy dense foods are available at every turn. Box 7.4 gives one illustration of this; it shows posters offering special deals on snack food at an Australian cinema. It is worth bearing in mind that in its investigation into obesity, the UK government's Health Select Committee pointed out that a king-size Mars bar has as many calories as a three-course meal.

BOX 7.4   PROMOTING OBESITY?

Figure 7.2   Promoting obesity?

The ubiquity of obesity: calories galore being hawked to cinema goers.

And the film at the top of the bill? *Super Size Me*!

The most immediate response to this unhealthy marketing is to recognise, as we have already noted, that we social marketers have to match our competitors' game: we too need ubiquity, convenience and seductive branding.

Another response for the social marketer is to address the client and warn them about the activities of the hazard merchants. The Truth campaign in the US, as we noted in Chapter 2, did exactly this for tobacco companies, highlighting their unscrupulous business practices and deliberate attempts to attract youngsters to the habit. The ads were completely uncompromising – showing, for example, body bags being delivered to tobacco corporation headquarters to represent the numbers killed by smoking and ambushing executives with embarrassing questions. The result was a very high profile social marketing campaign which worked: it brought about a marked reduction in youth smoking rates (Farrelly *et al.* 2002). So we can compete and win.

To compete or co-operate?

When faced with a direct competitor like this, however, some form of co-operative response is also a possibility – as we noted in our McDonald's example. This is sometimes rather clumsily called 'co-opetition'. Some commentators suggest that this is the way forward for tobacco control: a tobacco-industry-funded academic, quoted in the journal *Science*, argued that "the real enemy" in tobacco control "is the death and disease smokers suffer", not the tobacco industry (Grimm 2005). Given the insights of competitive analysis, this is a simplistic argument – a bit akin to suggesting that the mosquito is a distraction in the fight against malaria. The problem is that for co-operation to work, as with relationship marketing, two conditions have to be present:

1. There must be some capacity to find mutual benefit.
2. The partners must have at least roughly equal power.

Neither is present with tobacco.

This is an instance where the competitive analysis throws up the conclusion that a head-to-head fight is the only solution: as long as we have tobacco corporations we will have smoking, along with its toll on life expectancy and inequalities – as illustrated in Case Studies 11 and 13, 'Civil society monitoring of tobacco industry point of sale marketing in Colombia'.

This sort of competitive analysis has led public health researchers to conclude that tobacco companies will have to be bought out and replaced by social enterprises who will continue to ensure a supply of tobacco to dependent smokers, but will do so with a clear public health agenda (Borland 2003; Callard *et al.* 2005). Instead of the current system, where tobacco companies are required by law to maximise returns to their shareholders – and hence to increase sales of tobacco – they would have the specific remit of reducing the public health burden from smoking. Thus they would procure only tobacco products that meet stringent public health goals (e.g. of reduced nitrosamines or with specified nicotine content) and produce generic cigarettes that meet only the nicotine needs of smokers. They will not be incentivised, as corporations are, to produce evocative brands or to try to meet any of the psycho-social needs of smokers discussed in Exercise 7.4.

Other competitors present a more complex picture however. There is a convincing evidence base to show that both food and alcohol marketing have a significant and unhealthy impact, especially on the young, as the Food Standards Agency and the World Health Organization reviews discussed above show.

At the same time however, the issues are less black and white than for tobacco. Taking alcohol as an example, most public health professionals would accept that this is not an irredeemably bad product. While it is becoming increasingly apparent that any level of consumption is risky, there are potential social and hedonistic benefits. And, if as we noted above, health is indeed more than the absence of illness, these broader benefits deserve to be considered. Similarly, while we should always remember that the majority of the world's population do not use alcohol, in many societies it is an acceptable and normal part of life. The problem is more one of abuse rather than use. This suggests that one of our two criteria for co-operation is being met: most alcohol manufacturers would argue that they share public health's interest in the safe use of their product.

There are complications however. The evidence base shows that the most effective public health response is to reduce per capita consumption, a measure that an alcohol corporation, driven as it is by a need to increase returns to shareholders, will find it very difficult to accept. So while public health and the alcohol producers might have some shared understanding of the problem, they differ on the solution.

The second criterion, of equal power, presents even greater problems. The alcohol industry is very big business, and the main producers such as Diageo are among the wealthiest of our global corporations. We need therefore to proceed with caution. Exercise 7.8 describes a collaborative project between a social marketer and Miller Brewing. How do you feel about this? What are the strengths and weaknesses of the collaboration?

EXERCISE 7.8   TO COMPETE OR CO-OPERATE?

In a rural, blue-collar community in the Northern US, drunk driving among young men is common practice. Forty per cent of 21–34-year-olds drive themselves home after an average of seven drinks at least twice a week. The competition has a monopoly; there is no other way of getting home, and its leading brand "I can drive myself home" has a huge market share. This is reinforced by the fact that brand consumption typically does not result in the negative consequences threatened by social marketers. Most of the men, on most occasions, do manage to drive home without mishap.

However, the brand also has at least one weakness. They know they are taking unreasonable risks, and feel guilty about it. An alternative offering might have potential, provided it did not come at too high a cost or interfere with their self-interest in having a good night at their local bar. The offering made was a free ride service, customised to each community and promising "no hassles, no worries,

(continued)

(continued)

more fun." It succeeded. Some 20,000 rides have now been given. Analysing the competition, and the target's perception of the competition, enabled the build-up of sustainable competitive advantage.

The case emphasises the need for social marketing to offer 'unique meaningful benefits', which both present better value than the competition and accommodate the customer's self-interest more effectively. Specifically, it underlines the value of emphasising the short-term benefits and reducing short-term costs in this process.

But did it also create problems?

(*Source:* Rothschild *et al.* 2006)

The example provides a good illustration of the dilemma. On the one hand it could be seen as a great example of the effective use of competitive analysis to deliver a simple and powerful intervention, and a major threat to public health – drunk driving – was reduced. On the other we might have concerns about the potential repercussions of a collaboration that effectively reinforced drunkenness – and actively delivered those drunks home to their families. From a competitive perspective it also enables the brewery to promote its products as actively as ever, with an undesirable implication that getting drunk is both acceptable and fun. This theme would ordinarily get them into trouble, but in this case they actually stand to get very positive public relations benefits from it.

Thinking more strategically, as we noted above, we have to ask questions about the impact these sorts of collaborations have on the standing of social marketing. Any company entering such an agreement would think very carefully about the impact it might have on its brand image – and so should social marketing. This is not necessarily an argument against the Miller collaboration, just a reminder that we need to think strategically about relationships with business on the one hand and civil society on the other. And in the case of alcohol this thinking has to be particularly careful, because the division made above, between use and abuse, is simplistic. The evidence shows that the two are in fact intimately related: the wider the availability and use of alcohol in a given jurisdiction, the greater the abuse that will result (Edwards et al. 2004, 2005).

The limits of corporate social responsibility

The idea for co-operation with industry has its most obvious manifestation in corporate social responsibility (CSR): the principle that companies should not just keep an eye on their financial bottom line, but also monitor and control their impact on health and social welfare. This is an attractive-sounding option; business is causing problems so it is right that it should be responsible for limiting these and cleaning up any mess that results. At first glance, it seems like a pleasing variant on 'the Polluter Pays' principle.

CSR is indeed a good thing. There is no doubting the genuine motives of many business leaders in this area. Furthermore, business is probably in the best position to self-regulate the minutiae of its activities. Advertising content, for example, or selling methods need technical and professional insight to guide control. However, CSR also has very real limitations. First of all it can only deal with the specific, not the general. Thus, while it can identify and remove an alcohol ad that transgresses a code of conduct, it can do nothing about the fact that there is simply too much alcohol advertising.

Second, and more fundamentally, corporations are required by law to put the interests of their shareholders – not society – first (see the 'fiduciary imperative'; see Box 1.1 in Chapter 1). The social bottom line will always be trumped by the fiscal one. As Niall Fitzgerald, former CEO of Unilever, succinctly put it, "Corporate social responsibility is a hard-edged business decision. [We do it] not because it is a nice thing to do or because people are forcing us to do it . . . [but] because it is good for our business" (Elliott 2003). As we discuss in Chapter 8, business textbooks are completely transparent about this ulterior motive.

So if you are a social marketer and a company offers to fund your campaigns as part of its CSR programme, you have to accept that you are signing up to work on their marketing team. If this makes you uncomfortable, perhaps you should think again. As we will discuss in the next chapter, it has certainly been the cause of concern in international development and ecological sectors. CSR also raises much bigger questions about the functioning of corporate capitalism to which we will also return.

Regulation

Thus co-operation may get us so far, but it has very real limitations. The alternative is to seek to contain – or at least constrain – the competition through regulation. This takes us back to the importance of stakeholder marketing; social marketers have to build relationships with policy makers and politicians that will encourage them to take action. The hazard merchants, as Jobber reminded us above, certainly put a great deal of effort and resource into such lobbying.

Regulation can take many forms, from self-regulatory codes of conduct to mandatory rules with clear and enforceable penalties for transgressions. The regulation of advertising in the UK comes into the first category; have a go at Exercise 7.9.

EXERCISE 7.9   CATCHING STARLINGS

Refer back to Exercise 7.1.

The self-regulatory codes on UK television advertising state that alcohol cannot be linked to the social acceptance or social success of individuals, events or occasions. More specifically, advertisements must not imply that drinking can enhance an individual's popularity, confidence, mood, physical performance, personal qualities, attractiveness or sexual success.

Does the Carling starling ad breach this code? Were the Advertising Standards Authority (ASA) right to reject complaints?

There is no clear-cut answer here. Advertising has become so subtle and creative that making judgements about the nature of particular messages is remarkably difficult. Furthermore, as we noted in Chapter 6, different audiences are likely to have different interpretations, so who decides when a breach has occurred – the middle-aged, middle-class adman on the ASA panel or the 15-year-old binger? The result is confusion and this confusion can and will be exploited. The real problem is not the complexity of the code, though this surely does not help, it is that these types of self-regulatory procedures are built on the assumption that public health and big business are both on the same side. As we have rehearsed several times already in this chapter, all too often they are not because they have different priorities – the first that of reducing unnecessary sickness and early death, the second that of boosting shareholder value.

Building the evidence base

In these circumstances, statutory regulation has to play a central role. A comparison with health and safety is useful here. When the industrial revolution first took hold and mass production began in earnest, factories were dangerous places where worker safety got little consideration. Children were employed as a matter of course and death and injury were commonplace. Box 7.5 gives an evocative illustration of working practices.

BOX 7.5   'COMING BACK BROCKENS'

In the early days of the Durham coalfields in the northeast of England, the pits comprised a central vertical shaft which, as it was sunk, passed through horizontal seams of coal. The miners worked out along these seams, leaving in place columns of coal to hold up the roof. Once they reached the limits of the seam they returned to the central shaft, removing the columns as they came, because the mine owners wanted every scrap of coal they could get. This was called 'coming back brockens'. The miners' great skill was to judge just how much pillar they could remove without the roof collapsing. The dangers involved are demonstrated by the fact that 'coming back brockens' was only practised in coalfields with no habitation up above (Holden 1994).

The official response to this hazardous state of affairs was not to encourage factory owners to produce comforting codes of conduct; it was to pass hard-nosed legislation like the Factories Acts which, for example, made it illegal to employ children. Now we know that marketing in the hands of a tobacco company is just as dangerous as a machine tool or overly-harsh shift regime, we also need to look to firm regulatory measures.

Statutory regulation needs a solid evidence base. Policy makers will not act unless they are confident that they can bring about genuine improvements; regulation necessarily means the infringement of liberty and there has to be credible justification for doing this. This high principle is reinforced by vested interest. We have already noted how companies actively cultivate policy makers, and their approaches become more energetic when regulation is on the cards. Indeed in the case of tobacco it has resulted in litigation: the tobacco industry recently took the UK Department of Health to court, arguing that its new regulation on point of sale (POS) advertising was disproportionate. They lost because there is a rigorous and convincing evidence base to show that POS advertising does influence young people to smoke.

Building this evidence base involves both primary and secondary research. The International Tobacco Control Policy Evaluation Project (http://itcproject.org), for example, is a longitudinal research programme designed to assess the impact of different tobacco control policy options such as advertising bans, on-pack warnings and price increases. It uses a multi-country design – originally four countries were involved (the UK, the US, Canada and Australia), but has now been extended to more than a dozen – and natural experiments to track policy impact. For example, it has been possible to show how the ban on tobacco advertising in the UK has resulted in significant public health improvements that are not evident in the US, where no such ban has been enacted (Harris *et al.* 2006).

An alternative approach to building the evidence base is to analyse secondary research, which because of the degree of contention involved, presents particular challenges. The medical community, which also has to make challenging, consensual decisions about a contested evidence base, has responded by developing the concept of 'evidence-based decision making' (Mulrow 1994: 309). This is built around the 'systematic review' (SR) which strengthens traditional literature reviewing by making it comprehensive, rigorous and transparent (refer back to Chapter 5). The process starts by laying down a clear protocol for searching all relevant data bases, the content and quality criteria that will be used to determine inclusion in the review, and the methods used to assess the relative quality of the included studies and their synthesis into conclusions. The contents of this protocol are included in the completed review and can therefore be subjected to detailed scrutiny and, if necessary, replicated by other researchers.

A technical paper prepared for the WHO by Hastings *et al.* (2006) describes how SR methods were, for the first time, applied to a marketing problem: the impact that food promotion may or may not be having on childhood obesity. Have a read of the report and consider how the SR procedures used made the work proof against criticism and helped it have a considerable influence on stakeholders.

Two factors were important in strengthening the review. SR procedures backed by consistent peer review made it largely unassailable to criticism. In particular, the transparency about the methods used meant that critics have to point out precise flaws or omissions; blanket disagreement or dismissal is untenable. Second, there was a clear acceptance that no final proof is possible. As with all social science research, we can only reduce uncertainty by testing hypothesis and judging the balance of probabilities. More recently, the same procedures have been used to assess the value of mandating the plain packaging of cigarettes. In this case the review became part of the UK government's official consultation on the subject.[5]

SR then provides a useful and robust way of building the regulatory evidence base. It is, however, very resource intensive. The plain packaging review, for instance, took two teams of researchers nearly 12 months to complete. In addition, it is inherently conservative. Only the most obvious and well-proven effects will be acknowledged. These are useful qualities in a public policy debate, where the stakes are high. As we noted in the introduction to the book, business is the engine of wealth creation, which means it effectively funds all our health and social services – and indeed social marketing. Checks and balances need to be applied with considerable caution.

However, as we discussed in Chapter 5, social marketers would argue that the value of SR in other areas, such as intervention design, is more limited. Furthermore, in the area of regulation it proceeds with grindingly slow caution. An alternative approach to the plain packaging of tobacco, for instance, is to adopt what is sometimes termed the 'precautionary principle': we know tobacco is really dangerous so why would we take the chance of letting tobacco companies do anything that *might* encourage consumption? Far better to play safe. This in essence is what the Australian government has done; it did not conduct an SR, it just acted to mandate plain packaging.

Wrap-up

In this chapter we have examined how competition, which is a defining characteristic of business, also has resonance for social marketers. Competitive analysis can help us think more effectively about our clients' needs, the vital strategic importance of relationships with our suppliers and the very nature of the discipline.

It has also brought us into the crucial area of direct competition: social marketers can and must address the activities of the hazard merchants if they are serious about facilitating beneficial social change. This does not preclude collaboration with commercial partners, but it does warn us to proceed with great caution.

We have also seen how competitive analysis links with a range of much bigger questions: if tobacco industry marketing is wrecking our lungs by encouraging us to consume tobacco, to what extent is all marketing damaging our planet by encouraging us to consume a massive array of carbon-rich products and services; if corporations are legally required to prioritise their shareholders interest, how can we ever expect them to prioritise the public interest; why do regulators mandate hard hats but go soft on television ads? This raises a much wider debate about how business and civil society interrelate, and pulls us inevitably into the field of critical marketing – which we will discuss further in the next chapter.

Reflective questions

1. What is meant by competitive analysis? Why is this important to the social marketer?
2. Model and discuss the role of competitive analysis in the social marketing planning process (from Chapter 4).
3. Explain how competitive analysis informs your social marketing positioning choices.
4. Discuss the two types of competition: direct and indirect and when they might emerge in social marketing.
5. Model and delineate Porter's four forces for social marketing.
6. The social marketer's competitive strategy, following competitive analysis, is either to co-operate or compete. Discuss with illustrations.

7. Provide examples of when and how the social marketer would adopt a 'co-operate' competition strategy in the food and drinks industry.

8. Provide examples of when and how the social marketer should adopt a direct competition strategy in the food and drinks industry.

9. What is CSR? What are its advantages? What are its disadvantages? What are the implications of CSR for the social marketer?

10. What is the role of regulation in social marketing?

Reflective assignments

1. Find three social marketing case studies or papers that demonstrate competition in action.

2. Locate and assess a social marketing competitive analysis example.

3. You are a team comprising (a) social marketing consultants, (b) a local City Council and (c) an advertising agency. You have been charged with developing and running an initiative to encourage waste avoidance. How will you use Competitive Analysis to help you to develop and evaluate your initiative? What strategy would you use?

4. You are a social marketer working with the National Roads Authority in your country. How might you use Competitive Analysis to assess your present behaviour change performance in relation to (a) policy makers and regulatory modifications to laws about drink driving, speeding and drug usage, (b) speeding drivers due to alcohol, drugs or tiredness, (c) non-use of seatbelts and child safety restraints, and (d) unsafe driving endangering vulnerable road users such as pedestrians, motorcyclists, cyclists and young children?

5. You have recently joined a multidisciplinary team considering human's impact upon the oceans. Specifically, you are examining different stakeholders concerned with food supply, human health, transport, energy and leisure, and tourism, and their demands upon our seas. How might a competitive analysis assist you?

6. Select one competitor of a social marketing organisation you are familiar with. Based upon your existing knowledge of this competitor, along with an analysis of readily available data, write down what type and level of competition they represent to your chosen organisation. How would you recommend your organisation proceed?

7. Complete your 'Rebels with a cause' checklist for competitive analysis.

Notes

1 WHO Preamble to the Constitution of the World Health Organization as adopted by the International Health Conference, New York, 19–22 June, 1946; signed on 22 July 1946 by the representatives of 61 States (Official Records of the World Health Organization, no. 2, p. 100) and entered into force on 7 April 1948.

2 www.theguardian.com/society/2016/aug/21/theresa-mays-first-test-was-obesity-strategy-and-she-has-failed-health-experts-say.

3 www.oxfam.org/sites/www.oxfam.org/files/bp174-cautionary-tale-austerity-inequality-europe-120913-en_1.pdf.

4   www.youtube.com/watch?v=lkR0WDvFK1Q.
5   http://phrc.lshtm.ac.uk/project_2011-2016_006.html.

References

Borland, R. (2003) 'A strategy for controlling the marketing of tobacco products: A regulated market model', *Tobacco Control*, 12(4): 374–382.

Browning, R. (1845) 'How they brought the good news from Ghent to Aix'. In his *Dramatic Romances and Lyrics*. London: author.

Callard, C., Thompson, D. and Collishaw, N. (2005) *Curing the Addiction to Profits: A Supply-side Approach to Phasing OUT Tobacco*. Ottawa, ON: Canadian Centre for Policy Alternatives and Physicians for a Smoke-Free Canada.

Edwards, G., West, R., Babor, T.F., Hall, W. and Marsden, J. (2004) 'An invitation to an alcohol industry lobby to help decide public funding of alcohol research and professional training: A decision that should be reversed', *Addiction*, 99(10): 1235–1236.

Edwards, G., West, R., Babor, T.F., Hall, W. and Marsden, J. (2005) 'The integrity of the science base: A test case', *Addiction*, 100(5): 581–584.

Elliott, L. (2003) 'Cleaning agent'. Interview with Niall FitzGerald, Co-Chairman and Chief Executive, Unilever, *The Guardian*, 5 July.

Farrelly, M.C., Healton, C.G., Davis, K.C., Messeri, P., Hersey, J.C. and Haviland, M.L. (2002) 'Getting to the truth: evaluating national tobacco countermarketing campaigns', *American Journal of Public Health*, 92(6): 901–907.

Grimm, D. (2005) 'Is tobacco research turning over a new leaf?', *Science*, 307: 36–37.

Harris, F., MacKintosh, A.M., Anderson, S., Hastings, G., Borland, R., Fong, G.T., Hammond, D. and Cummings, K.M., for the ITCPES Research Team (2006) 'Effects of the 2003 advertising/promotion ban in the United Kingdom on awareness of tobacco marketing: Findings from the International Tobacco Control Four Country Survey', *Tobacco Control*, 15(Suppl 3): iii26–iii33.

Hastings, G., Anderson, S., Cooke, E. and Gordon, R. (2005) 'Alcohol marketing and young people's drinking: A review of the research', *Journal of Public Health Policy*, 26(3): 296–311.

Hastings, G., McDermott, L., Angus, K., Stead, M. and Thomson, S. (2006) *The Extent, Nature and Effects of Food Promotion to Children: A Review of the Evidence*. Technical paper prepared for the World Health Organization, July. Geneva: WHO. Online: www.who.int/dietphysicalactivity/publications/Hastings_paper_marketing.pdf

Hastings, G., Stead, M., McDermott, L., Forsyth, A., MacKintosh, A., Rayner, M., Godfrey, C., Caraher, M. and Angus, K. (2003) *Review of Research on the Effects of Food Promotion to Children – Final Report and Appendices*. Prepared for the Food Standards Agency. Stirling: Institute for Social Marketing.

Holden, M. (1994) *Coming Back Brockens: A Year in a Mining Village*. London: Jonathan Cape, as quoted in the Marketing Matrix.

House of Commons Health Select Committee (2000) *Second Report – The Tobacco Industry and the Health Risks of Smoking*. Volume II, *Minutes of Evidence and Appendices* (October 2000). London: The Stationery Office.

Jackson, K.M., Sher, J.K. and Wood, P.K. (2000) 'Prospective analysis of comorbidity: tobacco and alcohol use disorders', *Journal of Abnormal Psychology*, 109(4): 679–694.

Jobber, D. (2004) *Principles and Practice of Marketing*, 4th edn. Maidenhead: McGraw-Hill International.

Lang, T. and Rayner, G. (2012) Ecological public health: the 21st century's big idea? *BMJ*, 345: e5466.

Layard, R. (2005) *Happiness: Lessons from a New Science*. London: Allen Lane.

Levitt, T. (1960) 'Marketing myopia', *Harvard Business Review*, 38(4): 45–56.

Lovato, C., Linn, G., Stead, L.F. and Best, A. (2003) 'Impact of tobacco advertising and promotion on increasing adolescent smoking behaviours', *Cochrane Database of Systematic Reviews*, (4): CD003439: p.1.

MacAskill, S. and Eadie, D. (2002) *Evaluation of a Pilot Project on Smoking Cessation in Prisons*. Glasgow: University of Strathclyde, Centre for Social Marketing.

MacAskill, S., Stead, M., MacKintosh, A.M. and Hastings, G.B. (2002) '"You cannae just take cigarettes away from somebody and no' gie them something back": Can social marketing help solve the problem of low income smoking?', *Social Marketing Quarterly*, VIII(1): 19–34.

Mosher, J.F. (2012) 'Joe Camel in a bottle: Diageo, the Smirnoff brand, and the transformation of the youth alcohol market', *American Journal of Public Health*, 82(1).

Mulrow, C.D. (1994) 'Rationale for systematic reviews', *BMJ*, 309.

Noble, G. and Basil, D. (2011)' Competition and positioning' in G. Hastings, K. Angus and C. Bryant (eds) *The Sage Handbook of Social Marketing*. London: Sage, ch. 9.

Ogilvy & Mather (2012) 'From anti-Smoking to pro-quitting', National Smoking Control Campaign, 2011, IPA Effectiveness Awards, Health Promotion Board of Singapore.

Piercy, N. and Rich, N. (2009) 'High quality and low cost: the lean service centre', *European Journal of Marketing*, 43(11/12): 1477–1497.

Porter, M.E. (2008) 'The five competitive forces that shape strategy', *Harvard Business Review*, January: 86–104.

Rothschild, M.L., Mastin, B. and Miler, T.W. (2006) 'Reducing alcohol-impaired driving crashes through the use of social markting', *Accident Analysis and Prevention*, 38(6): 1218–1230.

Wakefield, M., Terry-McElrath, Y., Emery, S., Saffer, H., Chaloupka, F.J., Szczypka, G., Flay, B., O'Malley, P.M. and Johnston, L.D. (2006) 'Effect of televised, tobacco company-funded smoking prevention advertising on youth smoking-related beliefs, intentions, and behavior', *American Journal of Public Health*, 96(12): 2154–2164.

8

Critical marketing[1]

STONE WALLS DO NOT A PRISON MAKE

Barney crept out of his hole and ventured once more into the wide world. In the seven weeks since his mother's sudden and unexplained disappearance the young white mouse had gradually learned to fend for himself. He now knew where to find food, the dead-ends to avoid and the misleading scents to ignore. His first efforts had been halting and inadequate and he hadn't eaten at all for the first two days. Now he not only dined whenever he wanted, he had also worked out how to quench his thirst. The water which he could so enticingly smell could be accessed if he climbed on top of the yellow pebble and stood on his hind legs against the wall. It had all been very scary at first, doing everything for himself, but now he had got to like it. It was an adventure and a challenge all in one; a test that he was passing more successfully every day. It might not be as comfortable and easy as when his mother had provided for him, but Barney had come to the conclusion that he preferred being his own mouse. Independence and self-empowerment, he thought to himself, you can't do better.

Then he heard the white-coats talking and scurried back to his hole. "Peter, that's me leaving now. Please can you make sure you fill the water bottle in the mouse cage before you go home?"

Barney is happy but utterly deluded. He thinks he is free, self-empowered and successfully making his way in the world, when in fact he is a laboratory mouse being manipulated and controlled at will by the white-coated scientists. It is tempting to sneer at his naivety, but we are all at risk of being just as gullible as Barney if we fail to question and challenge the world around us. If we simply accept things at face value, omit to scrutinise the rights and wrongs of the system we live in, or recognise that our seemingly independent decision making about how we live our lives is, on the one hand, actually greatly influenced by our social context and, on the other, having a profound impact beyond us as individuals.

Nowhere is this critical consciousness more important than in the world of marketing. As we explained in earlier chapters, social marketing came into being because it was recognised that marketing's well-established capacity to influence our behaviour might be useful outwith the marketplace. That which so successfully gets us to eat burgers and drink vodka might also be used to encourage healthy eating and moderate drinking – or even abstinence. This power-transfer makes sense, but it also begs enormous questions about the influence of commercial marketing, and the legitimacy this has. Who decides which behaviours commercial marketers are to change and how they go about it? When does justifiable encouragement become inappropriate manipulation? Is it ever acceptable to trick the unwary, hoodwink the naïve or exploit the vulnerable by simply invoking the fig leaf of *caveat emptor*?[2] Above all, who is checking whether the inevitably narrow focus of the business strategy is in conflict with the (hopefully) broad inclusivity of government strategy?

This chapter, then, will introduce and stress the importance of this principle of independent critical thought. It calls on us all to ask questions, challenge the status quo, look underneath the surface and expose assumptions to the harsh light of day.

It starts by reminding us that such thinking is not new to marketing; it dates back to the very origins of the discipline. It then points out that the need to be critical puts us all on the spot: we have to take responsibility for our behaviour and its impact on others. However, we are not alone; we revisit Foster Wallace (Chapter 2) and add a systemic view to our analysis. Specifically, the dominance of marketing and the resulting drive for ever greater consumption has to be addressed. Ideas of strategic planning, ubiquity – especially on the internet – and the deployment of multiple tools, that we have seen to be as valuable insights for social marketing in earlier chapters, become a threat when we think about materialism, inequalities and global warming. Next we move upstream, revisiting CSR and linking it to corporate influence on political power.

This brings us back to the need for regulation, but takes us beyond the control of ad hoc malpractice by the hazard merchants we discussed in Chapter 7. Rather, we explore the need for strategic regulation, guided by more enlightened aims than profits and shareholder returns – values such as physical, mental, social, and planetary wellbeing. Finally, though, we recognise that top-down solutions cannot work alone; they must be combined with the critical engagement of us all in the process of change.

This may seem like an ambitious agenda, but in reality it is just core business for a discipline which "critically examines commercial marketing so as to learn from its successes and curb its excesses" (see Chapter 1). It is also an essential first step if we want to move away from ad hoc amelioration to tackling the major challenges that face the world. Issues like inequalities, conflict and climate change. How can we start to put things right if we haven't taken the time and trouble to work out what is wrong; if we haven't undertaken some intelligent critical marketing?

Learning outcomes

By the end of this chapter you should be much more sceptical about the world of marketing. Specifically, you should be able to:

✓   Define and explain the fiduciary imperative and the dangers of corporate power

✓   See why a leading psychiatrist diagnosed the corporation with psychopathy

✓   Recognise the inequalities inherent in a system that perpetually chases money and self-interest to the exclusion of other values (think back to the discussion in Chapter 3)

✓   Understand some of the individual and collective harms that can be done by corporate marketing, and how these come about

✓   Think more critically about the commercialisation of hyperspace

✓   Appreciate that Corporate Social Responsibility is just as much marketing as are brand management and advertising

✓   Understand why these critical insights are so important to social marketing.

Key words

Critical thought – fiduciary imperative – inequalities – consumption – materialism – native Advertising – corporate social responsibility – individual and collective harm.

A century of critical marketing

The idea of addressing the social consequences of business is far from being a new issue for marketing. It takes us back to the origins, not just of social marketing thought, but also of marketing thought. An extensive review of the field published in the *Journal of Public Policy and Marketing*, points out that what the authors call 'marketing and society' has been a key part of marketing since it first became a distinct discipline at the turn of the twentieth century. They go on to note that well before the Second World War marketers were not limiting themselves to studying managerial issues, but addressing much wider social questions such as whether advertising is desirable or certain industries should exist at all (see Box 8.1). They were interested in how the relationship between consumers, marketers and Government could "facilitate the maximal operations of the system for the benefit of the host society" (Wilkie and Moore 2003: 118).

> ### BOX 8.1   MARKETING AND SOCIETY
>
> Wider social issues have always been a concern of marketing thought, as Wilkie and Moore's summary of the broader questions early marketers were addressing shows:
>
> • Are there too many middlemen? Does distribution cost too much?
> • Does advertising raise or lower prices?

- What control, if any, should be exerted over new combinations in distribution?
- Of the total costs paid by consumers, which elements are desirable? Indispensable?
- What about "non-essential" services such as credit availability; should these be eliminated?

(*Source:* Wilkie and Moore 2003: 116–146)

Their review goes on to conclude that this interest in the social impact of marketing needs to continue and indeed strengthen, a call reinforced by the discipline's premier *Journal of Marketing* in its millennium edition.

Social marketing has a crucial role to play in this renaissance. Just as our knowledge of marketing can help us deconstruct the practices of the hazard merchants, so we can contribute to the wider debate about the role and values of commercial marketing in a modern democracy. Thinking back to the Preface and forward to Chapter 9, we can start to become rebels with a cause. Naomi Klein and Joel Bakan have led an onslaught of commentators pointing out the deficiencies of corporate capitalism, from sweatshops to inflationary branding. Indeed Bakan concludes that the modern corporation is nothing more or less than a psychopath. Others have responded defensively, pointing out that corporations do a lot of good, not least by underpinning much of the wealth that funds modern medicine, social services and education. They also point out that while Bakan and Klein make a great job of flagging up deficiencies, they do not present much in the way of solutions; good box office, but light on direction.

Social marketing can help plug this gap with its combination of balance and practical solutions. In terms of balance, this whole book points out that the marketing used by corporations and so despised by its critics is not intrinsically harmful. On the contrary it can be used to great social benefit, as the case studies at the end of the book show. Protecting our marine environment (Case Study 2), helping children to build a smokefree future (Case Study 5) and encouraging sustainable tourism (Case Study 19) are all very desirable social outcomes. Social marketing demonstrates that marketing is an amoral technology that, provided it is controlled properly and deployed ethically, can bring about great good.

We all then have to think carefully about our use of and relationship with marketing. This raises the concept of individual responsibility, which we will discuss in detail in the next chapter, but needs some further mention here because it helps us get to the all-important idea of critical thinking (see Box 8.3).

Individual responsibility

When we discussed social cognitive theory in Chapter 3, we emphasised the dangers of victim blaming. None of us has complete control of our behaviour – environmental influences such as social norms or the absence of resources inevitably influence our options – so it is both wrong and ineffective to put the onus for change entirely on the individual.

The founding story of public health epitomises this view. In 1854 John Snow, a doctor working in London, found convincing evidence that a cholera epidemic in the district of Soho was being caused, not by bad air as the contemporary wisdom had it, but by polluted water. When the authorities refused to listen, he took matters into his own hands and had the handle removed from the public pump which was delivering up sewerage-contaminated drinking water. In this way he proved his point and resolved the problem all in one. He also hard-wired the public health discipline's focus on intervening upstream. The danger otherwise is that you end up blaming people for a predicament they find themselves in through no fault of their own. There was, for instance, little the individual Soho inhabitant could do about his or her poor-quality water, even had they known it was toxic.

Social marketing respects Dr Snow's insights, and shares the public health aversion to victim blaming. We too need to ask what we can do to make the system better so that healthy – and ecological, socially enhancing, politically intelligent, ethical – choices become the obvious and easy ones. But equally social marketers recognise systemic change is not enough; a degree of personal responsibility is essential. We are all perfectly capable of being miserable in paradise if we don't have internal balance. Kropotkin was right when he lauded the human capacity to co-operate and work together, but that collective instinct is also dependent on robust individuals. Barney the white mouse, hapless though his circumstances are, has his own strengths to bring to the party. And even in situations where the individual seems utterly parlous – the drug addict, the third or Majority World indigenous farmer facing starvation, the dying cancer patient – it is vital to recognise they still have immensely valuable resources to bring to the behaviour change table. Box 8.2 shows how a development agency made great progress because they benefited from the strengths of the local Quechua Indians. Their language will have brought all the learning from a thousand years of culture, their labour made projects possible, their intelligence and entrepreneurialism provided the essence of the Kamayoqs. The result is sustainable change based on a genuine partnership between actors who all have something of value to offer. Take a look at Case Study 14, which looks at the complexities of this type of working in the tanneries of Bangladesh.

BOX 8.2   KAMAYOQS

A development NGO called the Intermediate Technology Development Group (Practical Action) working in Peru has recognised the value that indigenous citizens provide and has moved away from the conventional practice of drafting in external experts with one of training up local people as Kamayoqs, which is the local Quechua tongue means knowledge bearers (Open University and BBC 2000).

The process "began by simply talking to the local people." These conversations were in Quechua, which is typically disparaged by officialdom, and the development workers put "great emphasis on local culture" because, they argue, change "has to be rooted in campesino institutions otherwise it won't be sustainable." Nonetheless "to begin with, people were mistrustful. They were used to a vertical relationship with state agencies, even with development agencies. For them, a vet was someone who turns up in a car wearing good boots and a new jacket and says 'This is what we're going to do'" (ibid.).

But cultural sensitivity combined with partnership working succeeded in removing these barriers. For example, the irrigation system, which dated back to the Incas, was renovated with due deference to its powerful religious significance and by teamwork: Practical Action provided the materials and "the campesinos did the work, they invested their labour" and so "now they're managing the irrigation system themselves. They've made it their own – that's what makes it sustainable" (ibid.).

Practical Action took the same approach to agriculture. Rather than parachuting in expensive external experts they helped local people access training in animal husbandry. The resulting system of Kamayoqs has three major advantages: it avoids expensive consultants' wages; it is sustainable because the Kamayoqs are and will remain locally based; and it sets in train a process of self-improvement. The last word should go to one of the Kamayoqs, a woman called Vicenta Cahuana: "I used to take orders from my husband and sometimes he was violent. In the past women didn't have rights. I began to think this has to change. I started to respect myself more. My husband got very uncomfortable. He said, 'Whatever you're learning, it's no good for this household because you're answering me back. You're not respectful any more since you've been running around.' In a friendly way, I told him I'm taking better care of the animals. I don't waste money getting them cured. Now he says carry on" (ibid.).

George Orwell squares the circle between John Snow and the Kamayoqs by pointing out that "two viewpoints are tenable" (social marketing would say essential): "the one, how can you improve human nature until you have changed the system? The other, what is the use of changing the system before you have improved human nature" (1970: 48). Any recipe for change, then, has to address the individual as well as the systemic.

Try doing Exercise 8.1.

EXERCISE 8.1   THE FREEDOM TO SMOKE?

The Surgeon General's report shows that 88% of US smokers take up the habit before the age of 18, and most of the other 12% have joined in before they are 21 (Surgeon General 2012). Adults, then, do not start smoking. It seems once we are mature enough to appreciate the downside of the cigarette – a lifetime's expensive addiction followed by a one in two chance of a painful premature death – we turn on our heels at the mere sight of a tobacco marketer. Furthermore, three quarters of

(continued)

(continued)

the adults who made a bad call in childhood and took up smoking, now regret it and would prefer to quit, but their dependence on nicotine ties them to tobacco. Unless they manage to break this dependence they have a 50% chance of becoming one of the estimated five million who are killed globally each year by tobacco.[3]

On the other hand, FOREST, the tobacco industry-funded lobby group, argues that tobacco use is about freedom of choice and free markets and rails against the interference of the nanny state and over-weaning 'health fascists' undermining legal and productive business. Tobacco marketing is a legitimate way for a long-established industry to go about its business.

Think through the arguments on both sides. Who do you agree with? Does the fact that the trade in tobacco is legal make it right? Is freedom a reasonable concept to use for a product that is only chosen by the immature and contains a highly addictive drug? Would you take a job in a tobacco company? Would you advocate banning tobacco?

There are no right or wrong answers to the exercise. It is there to stimulate questions; to remind us that we have a duty to challenge and be sceptical – to think critically (see Box 8.3). Only in this way will we identify problems, generate original solutions and change the world for the better. We will pick up this idea of personal responsibility in more detail in Chapter 9, and show how it connects directly to our rights and qualities as human beings.

BOX 8.3   CRITICAL THINKING

Critical thinking is the search for objective truth; it questions the assumptions underpinning what we think to be true, to uncover what we can objectively state to be true.

Defining qualities: analysis, questioning assumptions, search for objective truth.

Our corporate world

Turning now to Orwell's point about the system, think back to Chapter 2 and David Foster Wallace's (2008) story of the two young fishes who don't even realise that they are swimming in water, let alone that it is vital to their survival. He is reminding us that normalcy and familiarity can render the environmental influences on our lives almost invisible. Furthermore, the unobtrusiveness of these stimuli makes them all the more powerful; effects can simply slip under our radar.

Marketing is one of these very powerful influences. The increasing commercialisation of our lives – of the water we swim in – has profound effects on how we think, feel and behave. Thinking again about Exercise 8.1, the continued marketing of tobacco, even where this has been limited by legislation,[4] makes it more difficult to remember that nicotine is as addictive as heroin and tobacco killed more First World War soldiers than did the bullets. The importance of marketing to the tobacco industry is amply demonstrated in Case Study 13. In the same way, the massive budgets spent on promoting alcohol, especially in Europe and North America, encourage us to forget that worldwide most people are teetotal; in a statistical sense, at least, drinking alcohol is abnormal. Or consider obesity: given that in the US, Australia and the UK around two thirds of us are either obese or overweight, how much sense does it make to have such powerful marketing campaigns going on to convince us that every time we drink a sugary brown beverage or eat a fatty, salty, and sugary burger we are "unbottling happiness" and "lovin' it"? (Read Box 8.4.)

Furthermore, our analysis of the water we swim in has to move beyond individual products and examine the system more generally. Most of us now live in capitalist, free market economies which are increasingly dominated by multi-national corporations. Corporations depend on shareholders (also known as the stockholders in North America) to invest their money with them; in return shareholders get to share the profits of the business. Corporations, then, spend other people's money and, in order to guard against corruption, their obligation to look after the investors' interests above and beyond all others has been enshrined in law. As we noted in Chapter 1, this is known as the 'fiduciary imperative' and has become the driving force of the modern corporation.

BOX 8.4 "RESISTANCE IS FUTILE; YOU WILL BE ASSIMILATED"

For the *Star Trek* fans among us, the Borg are known as the ultimate invasion threat to humankind – a pseudo race with immense and awesome adaptability who savagely kidnap different species from all over the universe to serve as cybernetic implanted drones of the collective hive with its Borg Queen. The Borg relentlessly pursue one goal – total dominance – through central control and forced assimilation with no individuality, freedom or equality tolerated. One could argue the Borg Principle at its finest – "resistance is futile, you will be assimilated" – is operating in many of the corporations around the planet today.

There is business and there is corporate business

As our discussions in Chapter 1 suggested, the ability to do business is one of the things that separates us from the other animals. Barter, trade and the doing of deals are at the core of our capacity to operate collectively. This co-operation is also essential for our survival. We cannot possibly cater for all our worldly needs without the help of others, so we need a way of harnessing this help. Friends and family may well contribute voluntarily, but in a complex world their efforts will not suffice: strangers have to be brought into the equation. Business provides a mechanism for doing this.

Michael, the greengrocer in my Scottish hometown, epitomises the benefits of business. He provides a good range of the foods we need – from apples to courgettes – and if asked, will happily try and source items he doesn't normally stock. His prices are competitive, although most people would probably guess (often incorrectly) that he charges more than the local supermarket. Michael also provides a pleasant service, expertly modulated to his customers. The dowager ladies from up the hill get the personal touch and their bags packed, the children are handled with kindness and respect, and those customers who show a taste for it get a fine line in Scots wit and repartee. He even offers a home delivery service. Michael's business acumen is matched only by his unerring diplomacy: he never risks offending his customers. His adroit fencing of the inevitable anti-English jokes (many of his best customers come from south of the Tweed) is a joy to behold. When he retires from the shop, a job at the United Nations beckons.

What is more, Michael has succeeded in moving across the commercial border and becoming a real friend. He surely likes what we do for his bottom line, but he also genuinely likes us – and we him. Being his customer not only keeps our store cupboard well stocked, it also makes us feel good.

Contrast this small-town bliss with another Scottish business: the Royal Bank of Scotland (RBS). Superlatives and invective have been worn out describing the harm Fred Goodwin[5] and his colleagues caused: stupidity and insane greed brought the bank to the brink of ruin – and came close to taking the whole country with it during the 2008 financial crisis. It is tempting to see this as an anomaly, driven by particularly toxic business models in a temporarily out of control financial sector, but the misbehaviour continues – the bank is still making deeply disturbing headlines nearly a decade later.[6]

The problem is neither new nor a one-off. Steinbeck wrestled with exactly the same issues back in 1939 when writing about the predations of the banks on dustbowl farmers. He characterised the bank as a monster which "needs – wants – insists – must have"; "those creatures don't breathe air, don't eat side-meat. They breathe profits; they eat the interest on money" (1939: 39). Thirty years later, a Republican president, and former soldier, Dwight D. Eisenhower warned of the immense dangers of the "Military Industrial Complex" and its "unwarranted influence – economic, political, even spiritual" being "felt in every city, every Statehouse, every office of the Federal government", warning that "we must not fail to comprehend its grave implications. Our toil, resources, and livelihood are all involved. So is the very structure of our society." You can listen to his whole speech on YouTube.[7]

Move forward another thirty years and this time a Professor of Marketing, Michael Thomas, provides the admonishment: "We have unleashed a monster that no one can control, even that minority that profits from it. Unashamed self-interest is a vice, not a virtue. We must recognise that the usefulness of an activity is not necessarily measured by its profitability, and that what someone earns is not an indicator of their talents and abilities, still less of their moral stature" (Thomas 1999).

The essential difference between Michael the greengrocer and RBS is one of power: Michael is a vulnerable small business; RBS is a too-big-to-fail corporation. Many corporations are now much bigger than countries. Revisit the discussion of Lou Pingeot's research and the subsequent analysis by Oxfam in Chapter 1 to remind yourself just how big corporations have become. The power this gives them inevitably distorts their relationships with society. Try Exercise 8.2.

EXERCISE 8.2   WHAT ARE THE IMPLICATIONS OF CORPORATE POWER FOR SOCIAL WELLBEING?

Oxfam's report states: "Big businesses did well in 2015/16: profits are high and the world's 10 biggest corporations together have revenue greater than that of the government revenue of 180 countries combined. Businesses are the lifeblood of a market economy, and when they work to the benefit of everyone they are vital to building fair and prosperous societies. But when corporations increasingly work for the rich, the benefits of economic growth are denied to those who need them most. In pursuit of delivering high returns to those at the top, corporations are driven to squeeze their workers and producers ever harder – and to avoid paying taxes which would benefit everyone, and the poorest people in particular." It goes on to talk about corporate tax dodging, crony capitalism and the role of big business in exacerbating inequalities.

Do you agree with the report's conclusions?

(*Source:* www.oxfam.org/sites/www.oxfam.org/files/file_attachments/bp-economy-for-99-percent-160117-en.pdf)

Oxfam's report is shocking and the presentation dramatic, but much of the detail will be familiar to anyone who keeps up with the news. Tax minimisation by multinationals, the growth of the 'gig economy' and zero-hours contracts, and the emergence of a new class of worker christened 'the precariat', have all become matters of regular public debate. Similarly, there is no doubting the burgeoning gap between rich and poor: where once we talked of the 99% and the 1%,[8] now it is of the 1% of the 1%.

The impact of this power comes very close to home. This is Carole Cadwalladr, a reporter at the *Observer* newspaper, talking about her week as a member of the precariat working for Amazon (Amazon is the 73rd biggest economic entity in the world, making it bigger than Portugal, Poland and Colombia[9]): "At the Neath working men's club down the road, one of the staff tells me that Amazon is 'the employer of last resort'. It's where you get a job if you can't get a job anywhere else. And it's this that's so heart-breaking. What did you do before, I ask people? And they say they're builders, hospitality managers, *marketing graduates*, IT technicians, carpenters, electricians. They owned their own businesses, and they were made redundant. Or the business went bust. Or they had a stroke. Or their contract ended. They are people who had skilled jobs, or professional jobs, or just better-paying jobs. And now they work for Amazon, earning the minimum wage, and most of them are grateful to have that"[10] (emphasis added).

As social marketers we have to recognise that such power matters, and unless we are prepared to analyse its impacts and challenge its harmful effects our work is unlikely to be effective.

Adding charm

This begs the question as to why any of us would want to do business with an organisation ruthlessly focused on its own interests and making money out of others' needs. Why would anyone willingly engage with such a body? This is where marketing comes in, adding an all-important charm to the mix. As we have already noted, marketing long predates the corporation, but it has been adopted by the corporate marketer to help make the organisation's selfish intent less apparent.

Branding is a perfect illustration of this. Joel Bakan, in his (2004) book *The Corporation*, points out that one of the first brands was developed by the giant US corporation General Electric to try and give a human face to what was in reality a monolithic conglomerate focused on delivering maximum returns to its shareholders and management. Since these early days the brand has become a commonplace in the commercial sector, softening the image of corporate bodies, from Coca-Cola to Diageo.

Branding is of course just part of a much broader marketing effort which deploys new product development, packaging, distribution, pricing and multi-faceted communications to win our hearts and minds. Equally energetic efforts, in the form of corporate social responsibility, public relations and corporate affairs, are used to court stakeholders, policy makers and politicians. All to ensure that we love the corporation (or at least don't criticise it too much). We will return to these different marketing tools, and their potential problems, later in the chapter.

Such was Bakan's concern about the nature of the corporation that he consulted a leading psychiatrist, Dr Hare, to find out what he would make of a person with this combination of a single-minded focus on his or her own interests, along with the superficial charm provided by marketing. Dr Hare's diagnosis is presented in Exercise 8.3.

EXERCISE 8.3   THE CORPORATION AS PSYCHOPATH

"When we asked Dr Hare to apply his diagnostic checklist of psychopathic traits [italicised below] to the corporation's institutional character, he found there was a close match. 'The corporation is *irresponsible*, Dr Hare said, because 'in an attempt to satisfy the corporation's goal, everybody else is put at risk'. Corporations try to '*manipulate* everything, including public opinion', and they are *grandiose*, always insisting that we're the number one, we're the best'. A *lack of empathy* and *asocial tendencies* are also key characteristics of the corporation, says Hare – 'their behaviour indicates they don't really concern themselves with their victims; and corporations often *refuse to accept responsibility for their own actions and are unable to feel remorse*' . . . Finally . . . corporations relate to others *superficially*, 'their whole goal is to present themselves to the public in a way that is appealing to the public [but] in fact may not be representative of what the organisation is really like'" (Bakan 2004: 55–56).

Do you agree with Dr Hare's diagnosis? What, if anything, do you think could or should be done to make the corporation less selfish?

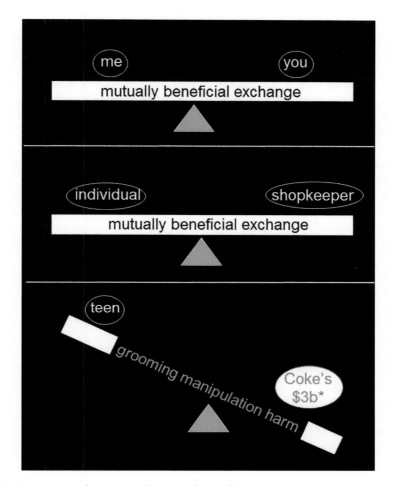

Figure 8.1 How power distorts marketing relationships

Note: * Coca-Cola annual marketing spend 2013

Whether you agree with his conclusion or not, it is clear there is an odd mismatch between the corporation, with its definitively selfish focus, and marketing which is supposed to be all about customer needs. Corporate marketing would seem to be a contradiction in terms, like 'military intelligence' or 'free trade' (see Figure 8.1).

The harm done by corporate marketing

Certainly a great deal of harm is done by corporate marketing. We discussed the ill health, premature deaths and personal damage inflicted by tobacco, alcohol and junk food marketing when we examined the competition in Chapter 7. More broadly we should also note the potential for psychological harm that comes with a system that promises to meet our every need. A core function of marketing is to scan and research our wants and preferences continuously so as to cater for them as effectively as possible. But doesn't this risk making us all overly materialistic? Isn't there a danger that we resort too much to retail therapy and get misled into thinking we can buy happiness? Might it not lead us to become spoilt and self-centred? Have a look at Case Study 18 on 'fast fashion'. Is there a danger that marketing by companies like Primark will pull consumers into excessive consumption and complicity in tragedies like the Rana Plaza garment factory collapse?

David Foster Wallace (2008), who we have already met, reminds us that we have a natural tendency to see the world in an egocentric way. What we see, hear, understand and experience is filtered through our own senses – through what he terms the 'lens of self'; everyone else's views and experiences come to us second hand; they have to be communicated to us. This creates a default position of perceiving everything as revolving around ourselves.

He goes on to highlight the dangers of this perspective. When things go wrong – the train doesn't arrive or the computer crashes – we take it as a personal affront, and give no allowance to the fact that other perfectly legitimate – indeed more important – priorities than our own might exist. We behave like over-indulged children.

Buddhists would agree with Wallace (2008) about the dangers of such an egocentric perspective, and the need to avoid it: "to conquer oneself is a greater victory than to conquer thousands in a battle".[11] The alternative, Wallace warns, is fruitless and self-destructive: "worship your own body and beauty and sexual allure and you will always feel ugly, and when time and age start showing, you will die a million deaths before they finally plant you."

Think for a minute how the cosmetics marketer overlooks these stark warnings. Take a look online at industry websites and think about the promises being made about beauty and eternal youth, be it Givenchy's perfume making "you look irresistible today,"[12] Max Factor's colour-correcting cream which ensures that you are "perfected" and can make your "glamour statement everyday"[13] or Oil of Olay's Total Effects Fragrance Free Anti-Aging Moisturiser, "Developed by Olay skin experts to give you younger-looking skin . . . delivers 7 anti-aging benefits in 1 formula" which "visibly smoothes fine lines and wrinkles, instantly evens skin tone appearance, smoothes and evens skin texture and instantly reduces the look of age spots."[14]

Foster Wallace (2008) takes his argument much further and states that "pretty much anything else you worship will eat you alive. If you worship money and things – if they are where you tap real meaning in life – then you will never have enough." He is alerting us to a fundamental contradiction at the heart of corporate marketing: **the offer of perpetual satisfaction to a species who can never be satisfied**. As Box 8.5 shows, like George Orwell, he is also echoing indigenous wisdom.

BOX 8.5 TWO WOLVES: A CHEROKEE PARABLE

An old Cherokee chief was teaching his grandson about life.

"A fight is going on inside me," he said to the boy. "It is a terrible fight and it is between two wolves. One is evil – he is anger, envy, sorrow, regret, greed, arrogance, self-pity, guilt, resentment, inferiority, lies, false pride, superiority, self-doubt and ego. The other is good – he is joy, peace, love, hope, serenity, humility, kindness, benevolence, empathy, generosity, truth, compassion and faith. This same fight is going on inside you – and inside every other person, too."

The grandson thought about it for a minute and then asked his grandfather, "Which wolf will win?"

The old chief simply replied: "The one you feed."[15]

In Cherokee terms, corporate marketing encourages us to feed the wrong wolf. The implications of this insight are profound. In Jeremy Seabrook's words, marketing is "the keeper of a dangerous but highly profitable secret – it knows how to promote a sense of universal neediness, to set up a wanting without end, a cult and culture of desire which must not be thwarted" (2015: 8) As he goes on to point out, however, this is a fragile power: all that is needed for it to fail is "that people should declare themselves content with what they have" (2008: 3). This throws into focus the role of individual responsibility in the social change process – something we will discuss in detail in the next chapter.

For now, let us just note that the problem is that we are seeking happiness not stuff; and stuff brings us about as close to happiness as Christmas tinsel does to redemption. To quote the Dalai Lama: "happiness is not something ready-made. It comes from your own actions." You cannot buy it any more than you can buy youth. Or, as the graffiti artist put it (Figure 8.2), what if the best things in life aren't things?

Figure 8.2 Graffiti

Inequalities again

Corporate marketing also raises concerns about inequalities. The perpetual quest to satisfy our every need comes at a price, both literally and figuratively. Do Exercise 8.4.

EXERCISE 8.4   THE PRICE OF ETERNAL YOUTH

Go online[16] or visit a shop and work out how much it would cost, over a one-year period, to use Oil of Olay's Total Effects Anti-Aging Moisturiser and access its "7 anti-aging benefits." (Notice in the how to use section it says "For best results, use daily.")

Work out how long it would take someone on your country's minimum wage to earn this amount. Don't forget to take deductions such as income tax into account.

The exercise demonstrates that we have a system that caters for our needs provided we have the resources to pay. As an MBA student recently remarked to a colleague, "why should marketers worry about the poor, they have no money?"[17] The result is a continuous accentuation of the gulf between the haves and the have-nots.

But the MBA student is missing a crucial point: we are all damaged by inequalities. As we noted in Chapter 1, it has now been well demonstrated that the best societies to live in are those with the smallest divisions between rich and poor; inequalities are bad for everyone including the privileged. This sounds counterintuitive, but Richard Wilkinson's and Kate Pickett (2010) book *The Spirit Level: Why Equality is Better for Everyone* provides the proof. It painstakingly demonstrates "that for each of eleven different health and social problems: physical health, mental health, drug abuse, education, imprisonment, obesity, social mobility, trust and community life, violence, teenage pregnancies, and child well-being, outcomes are significantly worse in more unequal rich countries."[18] Flick to the end of the book and think for a moment how many of our case studies this touches. Overall, their research shows the "pernicious effects that inequality has on societies: eroding trust, increasing anxiety and illness, (and) encouraging excessive consumption." (ibid.)

The blanket harm done by inequalities is explained by our interdependences; from its earliest origins humankind has flourished though co-operation and mutually beneficial exchange (refer back to our discussion of exchange theory in Chapter 3; remember also Uggina's lesson from Chapter 7). Many important benefits in life depend on us working together, rather than fragmenting into groups and individuals. Even the richest people depend on communally provided resources like roads, an educated workforce and an independent criminal justice system. Arguably the classic marketing tools of targeting and segmentation push in the opposite direction and so serve to accentuate differences. Try doing Exercise 8.5.

EXERCISE 8.5 THE DIVISIVE PERILS OF SEGMENTATION

". . . there is also a big social cost to segmentation and targeting: it divides us into exclusive groups. I find myself feeling superior because I drive a certain car, or sneering at someone for buying what I see as a second rate clothing brand. I hate this condescending tendency, but somehow it insinuates itself . . . The observation that we are all different is axiomatic, and indeed to be welcomed and celebrated. I just think that having a phenomenon as powerful and effective as corporate marketing focused on accentuating these differences is dangerous – especially when the only motive for doing so is to get us consuming more.

The second major problem with segmentation and targeting is that it institutionalises the notion that being able to afford something justifies its consumption. The ludicrous wealth of corporate CEOs leads seamlessly to Lear jets; bonus-happy city traders take us to jeroboams of vintage champagne; bejewelled despots provide the rationale for arms sales. Thus the pocket book pre-empts moral judgement or intelligent debate.

Third, and most fundamentally, segmentation and targeting hone and perfect the aim of the corporate marketer. It makes everything he or she does more powerful, just as a magnifying glass concentrates the power of sunlight. So everything we have been discussing in this book becomes turbo-charged; it accelerates and gains even more influence. And so we shop" (Hastings 2012).

Think about the points being made. Do you agree with them?

The selfish system

The discussion so far suggests that when seen from an individual's perspective, our system of corporate marketing can be selfish and flawed. From a global perspective the problems become even more worrying. Have a try at Exercise 8.6.

EXERCISE 8.6 THE LIFEBOAT

It was just over half an hour since the passenger ship had gone down and the eight strangers found themselves shocked but safe in a lifeboat. Their condition was better than might be expected, after all the boat was designed for fourteen, so they had plenty of blankets and supplies to go round. Then someone noticed that there were still people clinging to wreckage near where the ship had sunk and suggested they row over to pick them up. This caused a lively debate. It was pointed out that, while this would certainly be a nice thing to do, it would make things more difficult and

(continued)

(continued)

dangerous for them all. At the moment they were warm and well catered for, but if others got into the boat there would be less to go round. And if there were a lot of newcomers they might even swamp the boat. After some toing and froing it was decided to keep well away from the other survivors and concentrate on enjoying the energy dense biscuits and really rather good medicinal rum.[19]

Discuss the pros and cons of the passengers' decision.

Would you have done the same or behaved differently?

The behaviour of the passengers seems at best hard-hearted and at worst downright disgraceful. How could they so callously disregard the plight of their fellow human beings? However, before we get too indignant, we should note that the story is taken from a book of moral philosophy by Julian Baggini and the lifeboat is actually a metaphor for our planet. We in the rich north – the 'Minority World' – are behaving just as selfishly as the folk in the lifeboat. How did this come to be?

Textbooks date the modern business era back to the days of Henry Ford, when demand greatly outstripped supply, and all that mattered was mass production. As long as you could make it, people would buy it, and the maxim 'any colour you want as long as it's black' was not arrogant (though it sounds it now) it was just a simple statement of reality. Then, after the Second World War, the economic balance changed, supply increased and began to outstrip demand.

In the case of food, for example, historian Clive Ponting (2000: 790)) points out "After the mid twentieth century there was, for the first time in world history, enough food in the world to feed everybody adequately. The problem was that it was very unequally distributed." This might have been a good point at which to rethink the model. Instead, as Ponting continues, "By the late twentieth century the people of the industrialised countries of western Europe, Japan and north America ate half the world's food though they constituted only a quarter of the world's population. Much of the problem was caused by the fact that land in Asia, Africa and South America was devoted to growing crops for export to the major industrialised countries. A large proportion of this trade was simply to provide greater variety in the diet for people who were already well fed . . . in the second half of the twentieth century a domestic cat in the US ate more meat than people living in Africa and Latin America." The 1950s, when supply began to outstrip demand in our bit of the globe, marked the time when we in the rich minority countries rowed away from our planetary fellow passengers.

This might have been a good point at which to rethink the model; after all supply was only outstripping demand in the affluent north – much of the globe (the 'Majority World') was (and still is) living a life of great hardship. An enlightened stance might have been to look for ways of spreading the plenty in the Minority World more widely. Instead of wrestling with problems of redistribution and inequalities, the emphasis of business simply switched from production to selling. As one marketing textbook explains, "faced with stagnant markets and the spectre of price competition, producers sought to stimulate demand through increased selling efforts" (Baker 2003). A generation of sales reps stepped up to the plate and the growth of mass advertising gave them enormous reach. Vance Packard (2007) exposed the duplicity of this world in his book *The Hidden Persuaders*, uncovering a vast array of in-depth 'psychological' market research methods and correspondingly unscrupulous selling techniques. However, his book was rightly criticised for being piecemeal, descriptive and lacking insight into the fundamental economic and political forces underlying marketing: "His critique has no systematic basis. Packard sees the problem of covert 'persuasion' as a mere unsettling fad within the marketing establishment, and not as an inevitable outgrowth of the economic system" (Miller 2007: 19). Sixty years later, with the benefit of hindsight, these systemic problems are all too apparent.

Not so in the 1950s: the marketing text continues, the "spectre of price competition" remained: "if all the products are perceived as being the same then price becomes the distinguishing feature and the supplier becomes a price taker, thus having to relinquish the important managerial function of exercising control. Faced with such an impasse the real manager recognizes that salvation (and control) will be achieved through a policy of product differentiation" (Baker 2003: 5).

The marketer's version of history continues with the decline and fall of this flawed era of high-pressure selling, and the dawn of the enlightened age of marketing. Business came to see the benefits of replacing the old system of selling what could be produced with one of producing what could be sold. This has saved them from ruin and transformed what were dinosaur-like monoliths into consumer-focused modern companies. All because, the comforting narrative continues, marketing puts the consumer at the apex of the pyramid and focuses the whole business effort – from receptionist to CEO – on the Holy Grail of his or her complete satisfaction. We, the consumers, are now in charge. From this perspective, marketing begins to seem like an enlightened, almost democratic business model.

Except that, as we have already noted, the corporate structure gives this the lie – we are not in charge, the shareholder is. And seeking perpetual satisfaction is as futile as it is corrosive. And while we live in almost farcical plenty (a large UK supermarket, for example, has no fewer than 40,000 different product offerings) the Majority World continues to live in grinding need; the Hunger Project (2017), for instance, estimates that worldwide 896 million people are living on $1.90 a day or less, and 22,000 children die each day because of their poverty.[20] Referring back to Exercise 8.4, calculate how many days it would take someone living on this income to save enough to buy a bottle of Oil of Olay moisturiser.

This unfairness applies to much more important products than cosmetics. Joel Bakan describes its distorting impact in the pharmaceutical market: "of the 1,400 new drugs developed between 1975 and 1999, only 13 were designed to treat or prevent tropical diseases and three to treat tuberculosis. In the year 2000, no drugs were being developed to treat tuberculosis, compared to eight for impotence or erectile dysfunction and 7 for baldness" (2004: 49). All simply because we in the wealthy countries can afford to pay, so that is where the profit lies. The impact of these divisions is even more shockingly demonstrated by the appalling history of HIV medications. Between 1998 and 2003 the pharmaceutical industry systematically blocked the use of generic HIV medicines, costing $100 a year to administer, in order to defend its profits on the $15,000 a year branded versions. This resulted in an estimated ten million deaths in low income countries.[21] It is comforting to note, however, that, as the Fire in the Blood website and film explain, this story has a happy ending. A combination of individual agency, collective action and global pressure forced through systemic changes, and all those living with HIV now have access to the medicines they need. Chapter 9 (Spiritual Dimensions) and Chapter 11 (Systems Social Marketing) will look in more detail at these individual and systemic drivers.

For the most part, though, we end up as part of an extremely selfish system. We behave just like the people in the lifeboat. Do Exercise 8.7.

EXERCISE 8.7   WHAT MAKES US SELFISH?

We are all behaving like the people in the lifeboat. How has this come to be? Take a little time to think through how we have all been pulled into this morally questionable position.

Write down your thoughts.

The methods of corporate marketing

There are many answers to Exercise 8.7, but corporate marketing has to be a big part of them. It seduces and entices us into consuming more and more. This power comes from the three characteristics which we have explored in early chapters: strategic planning, ubiquitous deployment and a mix of powerful tools.

Strategic planning

Time is the key dimension of strategic thinking: doing something today in the knowledge that it will bear fruit tomorrow; analysing future possibilities and emerging trends; recognising that building trust and loyalty is a long-term endeavour. Nowhere is the corporate marketers' commitment to the long-term more apparent than in their attitude to children.

The textbook *Consumer Psychology for Marketing* tells us that "Children are important to marketers for three fundamental reasons:

1. They represent a large market in themselves because they have their own money to spend.

2. They influence their parents' selection of products and brands.

3. They will grow up to be consumers of everything; hence marketers need to start building up their brand consciousness and loyalty as early as possible" (Foxhall and Goldsmith 1994: 203).

Do Exercise 8.8.

EXERCISE 8.8   SUFFER THE LITTLE CHILDREN

Consider the quotation from *Consumer Psychology for Marketing* and think through what implications this has for society as a whole. You might like to consider:

a) child development and the stage at which youngsters can fully understand the persuasive intent of marketing;

b) family relationships and the concept of 'pester power';

c) how sensible it is, in a finite world, to encourage new generations to become 'consumers of everything'.

A decade ago the UK got a wake-up call when a UNICEF[22] report ('Report Card 7')[23] put it bottom among 21 developed countries for child wellbeing. It was a shocking judgement and the resulting furore encouraged UNICEF to commission a follow-up study[24] looking behind the statistics to understand why British kids are so badly off. This was an extremely thorough, in-depth exercise, which involved talking to and observing around 250 children and parents in the UK, as well as Sweden and Spain.

Now do Exercise 8.9.

EXERCISE 8.9   CHILDREN'S WELLBEING IN THE UK, SWEDEN AND SPAIN

Access the UNICEF Report 'Children's Wellbeing in the UK, Sweden and Spain: The Role of Inequality and Materialism'.[25]

Read the Executive Summary and consider its main conclusions.

To what extent do you think marketing is responsible for the UK's woeful showing in Report Card 7?

The UNICEF report reveals problems with all three of these levels of 'importance' that *Consumer Psychology for Marketing* ascribes to children. First, it shows children are wise enough to be deeply ambivalent about material possessions, pointing out that "the message from them all was simple, clear and unanimous: their well-being centres on time with a happy, stable family, having good friends and plenty of things to do, especially outdoors" (Nairn 2011: 1). They don't want to be seen merely as "a large market in themselves." Furthermore, they don't have any obvious sense of entitlement – they are disparaging about what they see as "spoiled kids," who don't have to wait, save up for and earn their rewards. A sensible reticence about the real potential benefits of consumption will, then, need to be overcome to access the child pound. Corporate marketers have to make children more materialistic to generate profits.

This brings us to the second level of marketing importance. Conduits work in two directions: if children give you access to parents, parents (especially insecure and vulnerable ones) give you access to children. This undermines family relationships. In particular, UK parents almost compulsively resorted to buying stuff in a failing attempt to compensate for the absence of quality time with their kids. The report speaks evocatively of "boxes and boxes of toys, broken presents and unused electronics" being "witness to this drive to acquire new possessions, which in reality were not really wanted or treasured" (Nairn 2011: 2). The irony that the need to earn the money to buy these products costs parents the very time that their children crave, seems to have been missed (or neutralised by relentless marketing).

On a more positive note, one might see the children's wisdom relative to their parents as boding well for the future – they are, after all, the next generation of parents and they will get the priorities right. Not if the marketers have their way. Remember, their third level of importance is that "they will grow up to be consumers of everything; hence marketers need to start building up their brand consciousness and loyalty as early as possible." That awful phrase "consumers of everything" is a chilling distillation of the impact of over-consumption on our planet. Nonetheless, the marketer eyes not threats to the planet, but opportunities for long-term sales. It is vital to get the next generation trooping into the malls.

Go back to Exercise 8.8 and re-examine your notes. Has the UNICEF research changed your mind in any way? Now consider what protections, if any, you think young people need from marketing. In particular, should we move to a much more controlled system as in Sweden, which does not allow any advertising to children up to the age of 12? (Note: Sweden came top for child welfare in the original UNICEF analysis.[26])

The UNICEF case underlines the strategic impact of corporate marketing. In his novel *Brave New World*, Aldous Huxley (1958) talks about propaganda acting "not so much like drops of water, though water, it is true, can wear holes in the hardest granite; rather drops of liquid sealing-wax, drops that adhere, incrust, incorporate themselves with what they fall on, till finally the rock is all one scarlet blob. Till at last the child's mind is these suggestions and the sum of these suggestions is the child's mind. And not the child's mind only. The adult's mind too – all his life long. The mind that judges and desires and decides – made up of these suggestions." Some might argue that corporate marketing is equally insidious; would you agree?

Ubiquitous deployment

Have you noticed how difficult it has become to buy a garment – even underwear – without a brand name? These logos are now integral to our clothes, so anonymising them is impossible; we are all becoming mobile billboards. As well as providing free advertising, corporate marketers also benefit in two additional ways from this: (a) they gain access to our credibility as a source of marketing messages – we are not only displaying but also actively endorsing their brand names; and (b) we are doing this voluntarily, with no gain, so there is no apparent sales pitch. Both these phenomena increase the power of their marketing.

The depth and breadth of corporate marketing's reach are powerfully illustrated by the Olympic Games. This is the ultimate global celebration of the power of amateurism, of humankind coming together to share our sporting accomplishments. As the International Olympic Committee's (IOC's) first Fundamental Principle puts it: "Olympism is a philosophy of life, exalting and combining in a balanced whole the qualities of body, will and mind. Blending sport with culture and education, Olympism seeks to create a way of life based on the joy of effort, the educational value of good example, social responsibility and respect for universal fundamental ethical principles."[27]

However, if you click on the IOC sponsorship site[28] you will also discover that "The Olympic Games are one of the most effective international marketing platforms in the world, reaching billions of people in over 200 countries and territories throughout the world." You will also learn that Coke has been a major sponsor since in 1928, though sugary beverages are hardly at the core of a successful athlete's diet. Do Exercise 8.10.

EXERCISE 8.10   OLYMPIC SPONSORSHIP

Do you think that Coke should be allowed to sponsor the Olympics? Consider issues of public health, inequalities and the marketing messages such link-ups promote. Visit the Coke and IOC websites to help you decide.

The IOC site explains that the TOP, or 'Olympic Partners' "worldwide sponsorship programme", was instigated in 1985 "to develop a diversified revenue base for the Olympic Games and to establish long-term corporate partnerships that would benefit the Olympic Movement as a whole." In cash terms it has at least paid off: the IOC's 2016 Olympic Marketing Fact File, available on the same site, boasts how combined revenues from TOP and other sponsorship activity have now exceeded $2 billion. In return, "the TOP programme provides each Worldwide Olympic Partner with exclusive global marketing rights and opportunities within a designated product or service category . . . The TOP Partners may exercise these rights worldwide and may activate marketing initiatives with all the members of the Olympic Movement that participate in the TOP programme."

It is clear then that sponsorship is about business, not philanthropy. Corporations become TOPs, for the same reason that they engage in all their other marketing activity, because it will enhance their bottom lines in a number of ways. One leading marketing text lists five of these: 'gaining publicity', 'creating entertainment opportunities', 'fostering favourable brand and company associations', 'improving community relations', and 'creating promotional opportunities'. Specifically, it notes, sports sponsorship provides the 'transferred values to the sponsor' of 'healthy', 'young', 'energetic', 'fast', 'vibrant' and 'masculine'. As the text observes: "the audience, finding the sponsor's name, logo and other symbols threaded through the event, learn to associate sponsor and activity with one another" (Jobber 2004: 506).

So the IOC takes money from Coke in return for the association with its core Olympic values and imbuing Coke with a healthy image. Do you think Coke deserves this healthy image?

If not, how does this fit with "the educational value of good example" in the IOC's first Fundamental Principle?

More widely, how does the strategy of selling the Olympic Games to corporate brand-building fit with its fifth Fundamental Principle that "the Olympic Movement shall have the rights and obligations of autonomy."[29] To what extent do you think freedom ceases to be freedom when it has a price tag?

So from our most personal garments to our treasured global icons, the brand is omnipresent. It colours the very water we swim in. Nowhere is this more apparent than in hyperspace.

Digital takeover

We noted earlier in the chapter how big corporations have now become, and that the tech giants – Google, Apple, Facebook and Amazon, or 'the Gafa' as they are sometimes collectively known – are some of biggest. All of these are intensely commercialised. Even Facebook, which we think of primarily as a social space to connect and reconnect with friends and family, gets 98% of its revenue from advertising.[30] The direction of travel was clear back in 2011 when Mark Zuckerberg's company announced that they had entered into a partnership with the drinks multinational Diageo; the social networking site said it was going to help the drinks firm strengthen its marketing by giving them access to a "'SWAT team' from its marketing, research and product engineering groups" (see Box 8.6, based on an announcement in the *Financial Times* [31]). The military language is interesting in an era which emphasises relationship marketing and customer service, and for a channel that is supposed to be principally about making friends and meeting people.

BOX 8.6   SOCIAL NETWORKING OR SELLING BOOZE?

Facebook strikes Diageo advertising deal

"Facebook has struck a multimillion-dollar advertising partnership with Diageo, owner of drinks brands including Smirnoff and Guinness, in the latest move by the social networking website to form closer ties with marketers . . . Diageo is one of a handful of large advertisers, including P&G, American Express and Wal-Mart, to which Facebook provides access to a 'SWAT team' from its marketing, research and product engineering groups."

Financial Times, 18 September 2011

Facebook are working with us to make sure that we are not only fan collecting but that *they are actively engaged and driving advocacy for our brands.* We are looking for increases in customer engagement and increases in sales and share ...

Kathy Parker,
Senior VP Global
MarketingDiageo

Now try Exercise 8.11.

EXERCISE 8.11   WHEN FRIENDS START TO SELL

Look at the image below. Consider how the Diageo/Facebook link-up blurs the edges between friendship and marketing. Is this desirable? Would you feel deceived? Is it reasonable for friends to market to friends?

Figure 8.3 Facebook and you

This cartoon presents one perspective; do you agree with it?

Since 2011 social media marketing has grown exponentially. We are all spending increasingly large parts of life online – through mobiles, tablets and PCs – seeking news and entertainment, connecting with friends and family and accessing the services we need. Nielsen's 2016 Total Audience Report,[32] for example, showed that US adults spend an average of 10 hours 39 minutes a day in front of a screen. But we hate the advertising that funds the great majority of this content. As a result, adblockers have become a standard tool, pop-ups enrage rather than enthral, and we are more likely to come out of plane crash alive than click on a banner ad. To square this circle, marketers have gone underground, using new tools like 'content marketing', 'sponsored content' and 'native advertising'. In each case the aim is to market to us without us realising it; to overcome our disinclination to pay attention by subterfuge. They are ways of sneaking advertising into supposedly objective editorial or 'content'. As John Oliver puts it, "ads are baked into content like chocolate chips into a cookie. Except it's more like raisins into a cookie, cos no one ******* wants them there."[33] As you can tell from the quote, John Oliver has a sense of humour and his video clip is as entertaining as it is disturbing.

In the clip, Ken Auletta, a long-standing contributor to the *New Yorker* magazine, explains the business model: "native advertising is basically saying to corporations who want to advertise 'We will camouflage your ads to make them look like news stories.' That's essentially it."[34]

So what do these forms of promotion look like? Editorial, of course: they are designed to imitate non-commercial content just as a chameleon blends into its background.

An early example of the genre was produced by the *New York Times* in June 2014 in its then "newly minted T Brand Studio, a nine-person team charged with creating content for brands" (Sebastian 2014) It took the form of a 1,500-word article on female imprisonment called 'Women Inmates: Why the Male Model Doesn't Work'. It is a sophisticated piece of journalism – Sebastian reminds us that a Native ad seeks "to mimic the editorial content surrounding it" and this is the celebrated *New York Times*. It contains statistics, charts, and video clips with real inmates, and as the subheading explains, addresses a vital social issue: "As the number of women inmates soars, so does the need for policies and programs that meet their needs" (*New York Times* 2014, quoted in Sebastian 2014). But actually it's an advertisement. It was paid for by Netflix to promote their new series of *Orange is the New Black*, which tells the story of one woman's experience in prison.

With the onset of native advertising a key principle of journalism has been jettisoned; that reporters should work independent from advertisers. Their one and only job, it was argued, should be to tell the news as objectively as possible – and this is difficult enough. They should not be distracted from it by a need to please the sponsor. You could argue this is not a new problem, that the conflict between money and truth is just as obvious with wealthy proprietors and greatly predates social networking. Few would doubt, for example, that Rupert Murdoch is able to exercise enormous power over journalism through his ownership of newspapers like the *Times* and the *Sun*. The difference is that media ownership is an extremely contentious issue and many complex regulatory procedures are in place to protect what is seen as a bastion of any democratic society: a free and unfettered press. By contrast, native advertising is the subject of minimal and largely voluntary controls.

Before its arrival, the need to build a wall between the journalism and the advertising was considered so vital it was informally referred to as "the separation of church and state," an allusion to one of the key drivers of the French Revolution. Now it is gone. As the newly developed native advertising department of *Time* magazine helpfully explains, the publication is now "helping marketers understand and develop the kinds of content programs that will help them connect organically with our audiences around every consumer passion point."[35] Try doing Exercise 8.12.

EXERCISE 8.12   REPURPOSED BOVINE WASTE?

Here are two senior figures in publishing talking about native advertising in the John Oliver clip[36]; the first is the CEO of Time Inc, the Executive Vice President of Advertising at the *New York Times Inc.*, the second is the Executive Vice President of Advertising of *The New York Times Co.*:

"Quite frankly I've changed church and state as you know. We took that away and we said the editors are now going to be working for the business side of the equation. But frankly I think they are happier, they're more excited about it, because no longer are we asking ourselves the question 'are we violating church and state?', whatever that was."

"Let me start by vigorously refuting the notion that native advertising has to erode consumer trust or compromise the wall that exists between editorial and advertising. Good native advertising is just not meant to be trickery, it is meant to be publishing sharing its story telling tools with the marketer."

Do you agree with their comments, or with John Oliver's irreverent reference to "repurposed bovine waste"?

(*Source: Native Advertising: Last Week Tonight with John Oliver* (HBO). 3 August 2014.)

A more considered response to the CEO and Executive Vice President comes from Ian Hamilton, an experienced and concerned journalist: "Native advertising breaks the contract between journalist and reader that lies at the heart of a free press. Unless paid-for content is clearly identified, both parties lose – the reader his or her faith in objective reporting, the journalist an often hard-won reputation for integrity. It is easy to see how we have got where we are. Traditional publishers face a life-or-death battle against falling advertising revenues but, by performing this sort of con trick on readers, they debase journalism and, ultimately, reduce the market for their own products."[37] (Incidentally, Ian Hamilton also notes, as does John Oliver, that the problem is partly of our own making; "we are all increasingly reluctant to pay for quality journalism"; this theme of personal responsibility is discussed further in Chapter 9.)

Perhaps we should not be surprised by the subterfuge of native advertising, given the well-established history of advergames, which perform an equivalent function for marketers targeting children. In this case they meld promotion with play in the form of a "video game which in some way contains an advertisement for a product, service, or company. Some advergames are created by a company with the sole purpose of promoting the company itself or one of its products, and the game may be distributed freely as a marketing tool. Other times, an advergame can be a regular popular video game, which may be sponsored by a company, and include advertisements within the game for the sponsoring company; for example you might see a character drink a particular brand of soft drink, or a race car might drive past a billboard advertising a certain snack food."[38] Crabs and Penguins, jointly designed by Coke and McDonald's, was an early example of the genre. (Refer back to the discussion of marketing to children above.)

Whatever our concerns for society about what Mara Einstein (2016) calls 'Black Ops advertising', the benefits for marketers are clear. Not only has camouflage enabled them to regain our (and our children's) attention, but it has made their message content more powerful. One of the basic parameters of advertising regulation is that ads have to be identifiable for what they are. The principal UK ad regulator, the Advertising Standards Authority, for example, is absolutely clear on this point; rule 2.1 of its code states "Marketing communications must be obviously identifiable as such." This is for the very good reason that we, the audience, can then be alerted to the partiality of the communication, and be prepared to respond critically to the sales pitch. Native advertising provides the marketer with a way under our radar. Thus Adage explains the subtlety of the persuasion 'baked into' the *New York Times*'s piece: "While the Times' paid post never explicitly tells readers to watch the show, it does delve deeply into the topic of women in prison. Piper Kerman, author of the book the show is based upon, is featured in the paid post."

The benefits for the digital platforms are also obvious. As we noted above, advertising revenue is their life's blood; Jonah Peretti founder and CEO of Buzzfeed, the leading news and entertainment site confirms this reality: "100% of our revenue comes from branded content. So we have a lot of partners who are marketers and major brands – 76 of the top one hundred brands."[39] And the business model has been remarkably successful; that is why the *Gafa* have become so dominant.

The implications of this power raise very broad concerns. Martin Moore,[40] Director of the Centre for the Study of Media, Communication and Power at King's College London, points out it will determine the sort of society we live in "because these tech superpowers are playing an increasing number of civic roles in our lives that affect our ability to participate in society and to communicate freely. With these civic roles they gain civic powers. This includes the power to communicate news, the power to enable collective action and the power to influence how we vote." And yet, he continues, "these are not public spaces, they are commercial private spaces, with their own rules and their own means of enforcing them." We will discuss the influence of business on our polity again below in the section 'Marketing to Power'.

A mix of tools

So far we have focused on the corporate marketers' attempts to influence us through different forms of communication. Three additional marketing tools also need to be considered: the price (the amount of money we can be persuaded to part with in return for a given product or service); the place (the distribution network and point of sale activity) and the product or service itself. The task of the marketer is to ensure that the 'right' decisions are made about each of these: the 'right' price is set, the 'right' outlet is located and/or designed, the 'right' product or service is made.

The definition of 'right' takes us back to the discussion we had earlier in the chapter and the core marketing idea of consumer orientation. On the face of it this means ensuring all three elements – price, place and product – are pitched so as to best satisfy us customers, which sounds most agreeable. However, a little thought throws up an inherent contradiction: as customers we would favour cheap prices, ready accessibility and high quality; but the marketer wants to make money. Specifically, as we have noted, the corporate marketer has an over-riding need to deliver increased shareholder value through higher profits, which in turn requires maximised margins and (especially) greater sales. Our consumption needs to be encouraged and accelerated. We have to be kept in the shops.

This reality can easily get lost in the rhetoric about customer satisfaction and consumer orientation, but is nonetheless clearly recognised in business textbooks: "the key principle of the optimum marketing mix is that which maximises shareholder value" (Doyle 2003: 291), thereby putting it in the frontline of the corporate mission. On this Doyle agrees with *Business Week* that "the fundamental task of today's CEO is simplicity itself: get the stock price up. Period." He goes on to quote, in turn, the mission statements of Coca-Cola, the Disney Corporation and Cadbury Schweppes – each emphasising the primacy of shareholder value.

Then to reassure us, lest we take fright at such transparency, he adds: "these shareholders are not the bloated capitalists of socialist propaganda, but rather the pension funds and insurance companies responsible for managing the savings of ordinary people." To be fair he was writing before the banks had imploded causing mass bankruptcy and home repossession. Before the scandal of profligate boardroom remuneration had been fully exposed. Before the socialists had been joined by the 99% in decrying the 1% of 'bloated capitalists'. And before Oxfam's 2017 analysis[41] showed us that the wealth of just eight men now exceeds that of the poorest half of humanity combined.

Interestingly, when it comes to the application of the marketing mix, the language becomes more direct. Thus rather than a route to our satisfaction, it now becomes the set of "controllable demand-impinging elements (instruments) that can be combined into a marketing programme used by a firm to achieve a certain level and type of response from its target market" (Baker and Saren 2010: 189). These instruments "influence demand to a greater or lesser extent." Or, as our blunt business academic puts it, "the marketing mix is the main way management seeks increases in sales"(Doyle 2003: 295).

Demand-impinging, achieving response, influence demand, increases in sales – there is no hiding the forceful purpose. The aim is to get us consuming, to boost sales and thereby corporate growth.

Each of the three marketing tools is, therefore, designed to stimulate our consumption: pricing is carefully calculated to maximise both the price we will pay and the number of us who will pay it; place, both in the sense of the distribution network and the configuration of each outlet, is designed to get us in with our wallets out; and the product itself is developed and tweaked to ensure it tempts us as seductively as possible. Have a go at Exercise 8.12.

EXERCISE 8.13   MARKETING AND CONSUMPTION

Consider how marketers use the marketing mix to get us to consume. Discuss how desirable this is, given the problems of global warming and a clear need for us to use less stuff. Is there a compromise to be had if marketers focus their efforts on reduced carbon options? If so, how would you ensure this happens?

Marketing to (get) power

Corporate marketers understand the lessons of David Foster Wallace about social context having a big influence on our individual behaviour. So, as we noted in Chapter 7, just as they put enormous effort into influencing us, so they also target those with the power to change the social context. Politicians, policy makers and other stakeholders can make life easier for the corporate marketer by introducing laws – for instance, by liberalising regulation, or by lobbying for such changes.

The more blatant attempts to get these groups onside – overt lobbying, donations to campaign funds, revolving door employment practices – already get considerable attention. For example, Box 8.7 shows that prior to the last general election, the financial services sector was revealed to be donating large sums to the ruling Conservative Party in the UK, just as the

government was debating the thorny issue of bank regulation. Do you think there is any connection between this funding and the gentle pace with which new controls were introduced,
or David Cameron's use of the UK's EU veto which some argue[42] has protected the City of
London from tighter European regulation?

BOX 8.7   BUYING POLITICAL INFLUENCE?[43]

Revealed: 50% of Tory funds come from City.

Donations from the financial sector have risen steeply since David Cameron became
leader of the Conservative Party.

When Cameron became Tory leader, the City gave the party £2.7m, or 25% of its
funds.

That figure rose to £11.4m in 2010.

Financiers in the City of London provided more than 50% of the funding for the
Tories last year, new research has revealed, prompting claims that the party is in
thrall to the banks. A study by the Bureau for Investigative Journalism has found
that the City accounted for £11.4m of Tory funding – 50.79% of its total haul – in
2010, a general election year. This compared with £2.7m, or 25% of its funding,
in 2005, when David Cameron became party leader. The research also shows that
nearly 60 donors gave more than £50,000 to the Tories last year, entitling each
of them to a face-to-face meeting with leading members of the party up to and
including Cameron.

However, the work of the corporate marketer in this arena is less widely discussed.
'Stakeholder marketing' uses the same techniques as consumer marketing, but now the
target is those who have power. The aim is to build and burnish corporate reputations;
in stakeholder marketing, corporate identity is as important as the brand is in consumer
marketing.

The two favoured and linked techniques are 'cause related marketing', where the corporation links up to a personable and self-evidently worthy issue such as child literacy and makes
sure this apparent good deed is well publicised; and 'corporate social responsibility' (CSR),
which, as we discussed in Chapter 7, links this specific act with longer-term commitments
to good practice. Corporate marketers are open about the self-serving nature of this activity
and clearly state that this is business not altruism. According to one text, for instance, it is
good at "enhancing reputation, building image and brands, creating relationships and loyalty
among customers and stakeholders, adding value, generating awareness and PR, driving trial
and traffic, providing product and service differentiation, developing emotional engagement
with the consumer and other stakeholders, and obviously increasing sales, income and volume" (Adkins 2003: 674). The same author underlines this quid pro quo agenda: "whatever
cause-related marketing is, it certainly is not philanthropy or altruism" (ibid.: 670).

The charity Christian Aid, however, is extremely critical of CSR and uses the notorious case of Shell in Nigeria to illustrate its concerns. Have a try at Exercise 8.14 before continuing.

EXERCISE 8.14   DOING WELL BY DOING GOOD

Read Christian Aid (2004) *Behind the Mask: The Real Face of Corporate Social Responsibility*, available at www.humanrights.ch/upload/pdf/050816_csr_behindthe-mask_2004.pdf. Discuss the pros and cons of CSR as used by Shell in the Niger Delta.

Then update yourself by consulting Amnesty International's more recent *The True Tragedy: Delays and Failures in Tackling Oil Spills in the Niger Delta* www.amnesty.org/en/documents/AFR44/018/2011/en/; and more recently still, www.amnesty.org/en/latest/news/2015/11/shell-false-claims-about-oil-pollution-exposed/.

Revisit your pros and cons.

In the early 1990s the oil giant shell wanted to quell discontent among the local Ogoni people, whose land in the Niger Delta it was despoiling, and called on Nigeria's military dictatorship for help. This resulted in savage repression, dozens of people being shot down and the subsequent execution of Ogoni leader Ken Saro-Wiwa. Shell's response to the resulting outcry was to invest heavily in CSR. It was the first major company to do so, and arguably is responsible for taking the strategy into the mainstream of business thinking.

However, the good deeds and fine promises have done little to improve the lot of the Ogoni people; over a decade later the Christian Aid report documented their continued suffering at the hands of Shell. And in 2011 a report by Amnesty International noted further extensive harm to the Ogoni. Two oil spills happened in the Niger Delta in 2008, which between them were as big as the Exxon Valdez disaster. In both cases no clean-up has happened and there were extensive delays before any remedial action was taken: "Eight months later, Shell finally appeared to recognize that people's food sources had been affected. On 2 May 2009, Shell staff brought food relief to the community. It included 50 bags of rice, 50 bags of beans, 50 bags of garri (a cassava product), 50 cartons of sugar, 50 cartons of milk powder, 50 cartons of tea, 50 cartons of tomatoes and 50 tins of groundnut oil" (Amnesty International and CEHRD 2011). And the problems continue; another report by Amnesty International, this time in partnership with the Centre for Environment, Human Rights and Development, published at the end of 2015, states trenchantly, "claims by oil giant Shell that it has cleaned up heavily polluted areas of the Niger Delta are blatantly false." Meanwhile, in 2016 Shell posted net profits of $4.58 billion.[44]

The marketing of infant formula provides another worrying example of the failure of CSR and voluntary corporate action. These are the words of Jasmine Whitbread, Chief Executive Officer, Save the Children UK: "I shouldn't be standing in front of you, on the 25 year anniversary of the Code, telling you so little has changed and that companies continue to encourage mothers to spend money they don't have on manufactured food most of them don't need. I shouldn't be standing in front of you because it shouldn't still be happening. But it is, because the voluntary code clearly isn't working, and children are dying as a result" (Save the Children & the Corporate Responsibility Coalition 2007: 3).

As with Shell in the Niger Delta, the tragedy continues today: "Tigers is a new film by Oscar-winning director Danis Tanovic based on the true story of a former Nestlé baby milk salesman in Pakistan called Syed Aamir Raza taking on the industry with the help of IBFAN (the International Baby Food Action Network) when he realises that babies are dying as a result of his work pressuring doctors to promote formula."[45]

It is perhaps little wonder, then, that Christian Aid concludes that what we need is not more voluntary responsibility from corporations, but accountability and statutory regulation. Unfortunately, as it also notes, a key function of CSR is to fend off regulation. John Hilary, Director of Campaigns and Policy at War on Want, confirms this view, pointing out that the Corporate Responsibility agenda as having been "created explicitly in order to get away from corporate accountability and regulation" (Worth 2007: 7). Revisit your answers to Exercise 8.14 and decide whether or not you agree. Then re-read Box 8.4; is CSR a classic example of the Borg Principle in action?

Finding solutions

Christian Aid and War on Want bring us back to the discussion in Chapter 7: the need for more robust and independent regulation, but this time not just for a minority of hazard merchants, but the whole corporate system. This certainly makes sense. If, as we noted in the last chapter, moves can be made to constrain tobacco marketing because it damages our lungs, it is simple logic to constrain marketing more generally because the excessive consumption it encourages is damaging our planet.

And the problems are fundamental so this regulatory process needs to be equally deep-seated. Arundhati Roy, for instance, calls for "another imagination – an imagination outside of capitalism as well as communism[46] . . . an imagination that has an altogether different understanding of what constitutes happiness and fulfilment."[47] Foster Wallace would surely agree; the materialism inherent in our current system often falls far short of offering anything that could genuinely be called happiness and fulfilment. This suggests a need for controls on business which have enlightened strategic intent; something more than the ad hoc control of bad practice we discussed in Chapter 7. Perhaps we should be thinking of a regulatory system that addresses priorities beyond those of the fiduciary imperative – instead of profits and shareholder returns, the focus could be on physical, mental, social, and planetary wellbeing.

India has taken an interesting and innovative step into this space. As Sanjeev Vyas explains in Case Study 22: "In August 2013, the Indian parliament passed the Indian Companies Act, 2013 made it mandatory for Indian companies and foreign companies operating in India of a minimum turnover and profitability to spend two percent of their average net profit for the past three years on CSR. There is a long list of permissible areas for CSR funding . . . ending hunger and poverty; promoting public health; supporting education; addressing gender inequality; protecting the environment; and funding cultural initiatives and the arts." The case study itself is a good example of the potential benefits of the law.

On the other hand, the NGO community has expressed reservations. This was one of the conclusions from a recent meeting of Global Reporting Initiatives: "A recent government bill stating that 2% of company's net profit must be devoted to corporate social responsibility may be welcome, but that still leaves 98%. Indeed, the rest of the business also needs to be sustainable. The 2% ruling could lead to forced philanthropy, 'tick box' behaviour, tokenism or even corruption, and masking of data to avoid having to comply. Time will show if this legislation will have a real impact on poor people's lives and prevent actual environmental degradation."[48] What are your views?

Clearly regulatory solutions are going to be complex and fraught. Furthermore, as Orwell and indigenous wisdom have reminded us, top-down system change has limited value if the individual is overlooked. Change has to come from the bottom up as well as the top down. In the next chapter we will explore this in more detail, and get into deep, even spiritual waters. This will be immensely challenging, but vital if we are to tackle complex and contested problems like climate change.

Wrap-up

This chapter has looked at the dark side of marketing, and you might have found this shocking. But the purpose is not to shock, it is to reinforce the importance of independent critical thought. Just as corporations sometimes have a vested interest in behaving badly, so they have a vested interest in covering this up. It is our responsibility as social marketers – and as citizens – to look beneath the surface and ask questions.

The Nazis were possibly the worst example of moral degeneracy in the 20th century. Yet *New York Times* journalist Charles Higham, in his forensically researched book *Trading with the Enemy*, shows that leading corporations like Ford, ITT and the Chase Manhattan bank worked with the regime throughout the war. ITT literally helped Hitler's regime to perfect the doodlebugs that so devastated London. This extreme example of keeping the focus on the bottom line was, he explains, hidden behind "an ice cream mountain of public relations." Our job is to look behind the ice cream.

This is an essential prerequisite for tackling the major, multifaceted and contested problems now facing humankind – the most profound of which is global warming. The solutions are surely elusive and challenging, but the first step is to take a thorough and critical look at our current ways of doing things. In Chapter 11 we will then go on to examine how systems thinking can help us build on these insights and so start to meet these massive challenges.

However, before this we need to do some introspection. A century before Orwell noted the link between the system and the individual, a Native American leader expressed the same thought more briefly: "there are no political solutions to spiritual problems."[49] Both men were recognising that any system is made up of individuals who have choices to make and values to maintain. Furthermore, as the next chapter will explore, failing to exercise these responsibilities is not just ethically unacceptable, it also damages us personally. We run the risk of leading our lives in the sort of fool's paradise inhabited by Barney the white laboratory mouse who we met at the start of the chapter. As Emmeline Pankhurst, leader of the movement for women's suffrage, trenchantly expressed it: *I would rather be a rebel than a slave.*

Reflective questions

1. What is 'fiduciary imperative'? Why is it important to marketing? What is its connection to social marketing?
2. Discuss what critical thought means to the social marketer.
3. The dark side of marketing results from an imbalance of power in the marketplace giving rise to individual and collective harm. Explain in detail.
4. Does marketing make us selfish? Answer with reference to the work of David Foster Wallace.
5. Social marketers should be *"concerned with analysis of the social consequence of marketing policies, decisions and activities"* (Lazer and Kelly 1997). Elaborate with examples.
6. Is marketing driving unsustainable consumption? If yes, what would you do about it?
7. Is CSR going to save the planet? If yes, how; if not why not?
8. How is CSR linked to cause related marketing?

Reflective assigments

1. Make sure you are comfortable with the concept of critical thought by writing a concise paragraph about it in your own words.
2. Locate three social marketing case studies or papers that demonstrate inequalities or the dark side of marketing.
3. You are social marketing manager with Jigsaw, a non-profit entity focused on mental health in young adults (18–35-year-olds) in inner cities around the country. You have been tasked with designing a mental health intervention specifically targeting suicide. How could you use critical thinking in your social marketing job?
4. How, where and why does critical thought integrate with our discussions of social marketing in Chapters 1 and 2?
5. Find a CSR or cause-related marketing example and using critical thinking assess the advantages and disadvantages of the example.
6. Revisit your debate with a friends or colleagues as to whether or not social marketers are really just out to satisfy their own ends like commercial marketers, or are they more altruistic as was argued in in Chapter 2. Applying critical throught, does your opinion alter? If so, how?
7. Consult the *Journal of Social Marketing* and/or *Social Marketing Quarterly* and read a classic or contemporary article(s) on the critical thinking in social marketing to advance your understanding of the theory and practice in this area.
8. Complete your 'Rebels with a cause' checklist for (a) critical thinking and (b) CSR.

Notes

1 This chapter builds on Hastings's *The Marketing Matrix: How the Corporation gets its Power and How We Can Reclaim It* (2012), which you may want to consult.
2 *Caveat emptor*: 'buyer beware'.
3 www.who.int/tobacco/mpower/mpower_report_tobacco_crisis_2008.pdf (accessed 5 April 2017).

4   Tobacco advertising has been banned in many countries. In the UK, for example, it disappeared in 2005 but marketing in a broader sense continues in the form of ubiquitous distribution, evocative packaging and carefully honed brands.

5   Fred Goodwin was CEO of RBS and his calamitous leadership epitomises the worst of the 2008 financial crisis: macho management, hubris and excessive greed. His crude attempts to destroy evidence about the mistakes made on his watch earned him the sobriquet 'Fred the Shred'.

6   www.ft.com/content/5ed96dfb-b141-3fde-b053-bdf143ae180d (accessed 5 April 2017).

7   Eisenhower, D.D. (1961) www.youtube.com/watch?v=8y06NSBBRtY (accessed 5 April 2017).

8   www.vanityfair.com/society/features/2011/05/top-one-percent-201105 (accessed 5 April 2017).

9   www.globaljustice.org.uk/sites/default/files/files/resources/corporations_vs_governments_final.pdf (accessed 5 April 2017).

10 www.theguardian.com/technology/2013/dec/01/week-amazon-insider-feature-treatment-employees-work (accessed 15 March 2017).

11 The Dalai Lama (and many other Buddhists).

12 www.givenchybeauty.com/en/fragrances/live-irresistible/range_1 (accessed 5 April 2017).

13 www.fashionmention.com/wp-content/uploads/2013/05/06/Candice_Swanepoel_MAX_FACTOR.jpg (accessed 5 April 2017).

14 www.olay.com/skin-care-products/total-effects/fragrance-free-daily-moisturizer?pid=075609001772 (accessed 5 April 2017).

15 www.sapphyr.net/smallgems/index.htm (accessed 5 April 2017).

16 www.olay.com/skin-care-products/total-effects/fragrance-free-daily-moisturizer?pid=075609001772 (accessed 5 April 2017).

17 With thanks to Professor Mike Saren.

18 www.equalitytrust.org.uk/spirit-level (accessed 5 April 2017).

19 This is adapted from Baggini: (2005 ch. 22).

20 www.thp.org/knowledge-center/know-your-world-facts-about-hunger-poverty/ (accessed 5 April 2017).

21 http://fireintheblood.com/ (accessed 5 April 2017).

22 The United Nations Children's Fund which was created by the United Nations General Assembly in 1946 to provide emergency food and healthcare to children in countries that had been devastated by the Second World War. It has continued ever since to provide long-term humanitarian and developmental assistance to children and mothers across the world.

23 UNICEF (2007) *Report Card 7*. www.unicef-irc.org/publications/pdf/rc7_eng.pdf (accessed 5 April 2017).

24 UNICEF (2010) Report 'Children's Wellbeing in the UK, Sweden and Spain: The Role of Inequality and Materialism', https://353ld710iigr2n4po7k4kgvv-wpengine.netdna-ssl.com/wpcontent/uploads/2011/09/IPSOS_UNICEF_ChildWellBeingreport.pdf (accessed 5 April 2017).

25 Ibid.

26 UNICEF (2007) *Report Card 7* (note 23 above).

27 https://stillmed.olympic.org/Documents/olympic_charter_en.pdf (accessed 5 April 2017).

28 www.olympic.org/sponsorship (accessed 5 April 2017).

29 https://stillmed.olympic.org/Documents/olympic_charter_en.pdf (accessed 5 April 2017).

30   https://s21.q4cdn.com/399680738/files/doc_presentations/FB-Q4'16-Earnings-Slides. pdf (see page 8).

31   Bradshaw, T. (2011) 'Facebook Strikes Diageo Advertising Deal' in *Financial Times*, 18 September 2011, www.ft.com/intl/cms/s/2/d044ea24-e203-11e0-9915-00144feabdc0. html#axzz1irtgC58l (accessed 5 April 2017).

32   www.nielsen.com/us/en/insights/reports/2016/the-total-audience-report-q1-2016. html (accessed 5 April 2017).

33   *Native Advertising: Last Week Tonight with John Oliver* (HBO). 3 August 2014. https://www. youtube.com/watch?v=E_F5GxCwizc (accessed 5 April 2017).

34   Ibid.

35   www.timeinc.com/advertise/content-solutions/native/ (accessed 5 April 2017).

36   *Native Advertising: Last Week Tonight with John Oliver* (HBO). 3 August 2014. https://www. youtube.com/watch?v=E_F5GxCwizc (accessed 5 April 2017).

37   Ian Hamilton (2017), personal communication, April 8.

38   www.businessdictionary.com/definition/advergame.html (accessed 5 April 2017).

39   https://dose.com/when-ads-look-like-news-can-we-believe-anything-e8c354987dde (accessed 5 April 2017).

40   Martin Moore (2017), *Observer*, 2 April, p.37.

41   www.oxfam.org/sites/www.oxfam.org/files/file_attachments/bp-economy-for-99-percent-160117-en.pdf (accessed 5 April 2017).

42   www.guardian.co.uk/politics/reality-check-with-polly-curtis/2011/dec/12/debt-crisis-conservatives (accessed 5 April 2017).

43   Nicholas Watt and Jill Treanor guardian.co.uk, 8 February 2011 www.theguardian.com/ politics/2011/feb/08/tory-funds-half-city-banks-financial-sector (accessed 30 August 2012). Link to full study: www.thebureauinvestigates.com/2011/02/08/city-financing-of-the-conservative-party-doubles-under-cameron/ (accessed 5 April 2017).

44   www.yahoo.com/news/shell-says-annual-profit-more-doubles-4-6bn-074840793.html (accessed 5 April 2017).

45   www.babymilkaction.org/tigers (accessed 5 April 2017).

46   Arundhati Roy (2011) *The Guardian*, www.theguardian.com/world/2011/nov/30/ arundhati-roy-interview (accessed 9 December 2011).

47   Arundhati Roy quoted in *New Internationalist*, October 2011 p. 30.

48   www.globalreporting.org/SiteCollectionDocuments/Mumbai-declaration-on-sustainability-reporting-for-sustainable-development.pdf (accessed 5 April 2017).

49   www.sapphyr.net/smallgems/index.htm (accessed 5 April 2017).

References

Adkins, S. (2003) 'Cause-related marketing: Who cares wins', in M.J. Baker (ed.) *The Marketing Book*, 5th edn. Oxford: Butterworth-Heinemann.

Amnesty International and CEHRD (2011) *The True 'Tragedy': Delays and Failures in Tackling Oil Spills in the Niger Delta*, 10 November. London: Amnesty International.

Boggini, J. (2005) The Pig that Wants to be Eaten. London: Granta.

Bakan, J. (2004) *The Corporation: The Pathological Pursuit of Profit and Power*. Toronto: The Penguin Group (Canada).

Baker, M.J. (2003) 'One more time – what is marketing?', in M.J. Baker (ed.) *The Marketing Book*, 5th edn. Oxford: Butterworth-Heinemann.

Baker, M. and Saren, M. (2010) *Marketing Theory: A Student Text*. London: Sage Publications.

Doyle, P. (2003) 'Managing the Marketing Mix', in M.J. Baker (ed.) *The Marketing Book*, 5th edn. Oxford: Butterworth-Heinemann.

Einstein, Mara, (2016) *Black Ops advertising: native ads, content marketing, and the covert world of the digital sell*. Berkeley, CA: Counterpoint Press.

Foxall, G. and Goldsmith, R.E. (1994) *Consumer Psychology for Marketers*. London: Routledge.

Klein, Naomi (2015) *This Changes Everything: Capitalism vs The Climate*. London: Simon & Schuster.

Hastings, G. (2012) *The Marketing Matrix: How the Corporation gets its Power and How We Can Reclaim It*. London: Routledge.

Higham, C. (1984) Trading with the Enemy. New York: Dell.

Huxley, A. (1958) *Brave New World Revisited*. New York: HarperCollins.

Jobber, D. (2004) *Principles and Practice of Marketing*, 4th edn. Maidenhead: McGraw-Hill International, p. 506.

Lazer, W. and Kelley, E. (1973) *Social Marketing: Perspectives and Viewpoints*. Homewood, IL: Richard D. Irwin, Inc.

Mara, (2016) *Black Ops advertising: native ads, content marketing, and the covert world of the digital sell*. Berkeley, CA: Counterpoint Press.

Miller, M.C. (2007) 'Introduction', in V. Packard, *The Hidden Persuaders*. Brooklyn, NY: IG Publishing.

Nairn, A. (2011) *Children's Wellbeing in the UK, Sweden and Spain: The Role of Inequality and Materialism*. London: Ipsos MORI.

Open University and BBC (2000) 'Looking for a Future: Sustainability and Change in the Andes', in *U213 International Development: Challenges for a World in Transition* (DVD recording). Milton Keynes: The Open University.

Orwell, G. (1970) *Collected Essays*, 2nd edn. London: Secker & Warburg.

Packard, V. (2007) *The Hidden Persuaders*. Brooklyn, New York: IG Publishing.

Ponting, C. (2000) *World History – A New Perspective*. London: Chatto and Windus.

Save the Children and the Corporate Responsibility Coalition (2007) *Why Corporate Social Responsibility is Failing Children*. London: Save the Children & CORE, p. 3. www.savethechildren.org.uk/sites/default/files/docs/Why_CSR_is_failing_children_1.pdf (accessed 5 April 2017).

Seabrook, J. (2015) *Pauperland: Poverty and the Poor in Britain*. London: Hurst and Company.

Sebastian, M. (2014). 'Native Ad Production Values Keep Growing with *Orange Is the New Black* Promo', *Advertising Age*, 13 June. Online: http://adage.com/article/media/york-times-runs-native-ad-orange-black/293713/ (accessed 5 April 2017).

Steinbeck, J. (1939) *The Grapes of Wrath*. London: Everyman's Library.

Surgeon General (2012) *Preventing Tobacco Use Among Youth and Young Adults*, Rockville MD.

Thomas, M.J. (1999) *Thoughts on Building a Just and Stakeholding Society*, 20th Anniversary Conference, Alliance of Universities for Democracy, Budapest (Hungary), 7 November.

Wallace, D.F. (2008) 'Plain Old Untrendy Troubles and Emotions', *The Guardian*, 20 September. Online: www.guardian.co.uk/books/2008/sep/20/fiction (accessed 5 April 2017).

Wilkie, W.L. and Moore, E.S. (2003) 'Scholarly research in marketing: Exploring the 'four eras' of thought development', *Journal of Public Policy & Marketing*, 22(2).

Wilkinson, R. and Pickett, K. (2010) *The Spirit Level: Why Equality is Better for Everyone*. London: Penguin.

Worth, J. (2007) 'Corporate responsibility: Companies who care?' *New Internationalist*, 1 December. Online: https://newint.org/features/2007/12/01/keynote (accessed 20 September 2017).

Chapter **9**

Spiritual dimensions

'THE CONFERENCE OF THE BIRDS'[1]

The birds of the air were anxious; they felt in urgent need of advice and leadership. So a great conference was organised where they came together to discuss what might be done. The Hoopoe spoke up and persuaded the gathering that they needed to go in search of the Simurgh or spiritual leader to provide them with the direction they lacked. After much debate and multiple attempts by different birds to avoid going on what would be an arduous journey, the quest got under way. It took many difficult years and involved crossing the seven valleys – of searching, love, understanding, friendship, unity, amazement, and death – each presenting its own challenges and lessons. As the pilgrimage proceeded, many birds abandoned the journey or were overcome by the ordeals they encountered. Eventually, now depleted to a band of just thirty, they arrived at a marvellous palace, which, the Hoopoe explained, was the home of the Simurgh. At first the palace guard would not let what had become a raggedy and disreputable looking gang enter the great mansion; but after a struggle they were admitted. Inside they searched everywhere for the Simurgh but the palace was empty. All they found was wall after wall lined with mirrors of every size and shape.

It was in these that they at last caught sight of their spiritual leaders.

'The Conference of the Birds', a 4,000-line epic poem, was written by the Sufi scholar Farid ud-Din Attar nearly a millennium ago. It tells of the hunt for a spiritual dimension to life, a sense of meaning beyond the everyday priorities that tend to dominate our existence. It may seem an odd tack to take in a social marketing textbook – more at home in a theology course or a treatise on moral philosophy perhaps. But consider for a minute. The greatest problems humankind faces, from non-communicable or lifestyle diseases (NCD) epidemics to global warming, problems we have rehearsed many times in earlier chapters, are, in essence, self-inflicted. Yes, there are systemic drivers – commercial marketing, inequalities, corporate power, addiction – but at base the uncomfortable truth is that we are voluntarily drinking the sugar-sweetened beverages and driving the SUVs which threaten our health and our planet. No one compels us to take intercontinental holidays or eat yet another plastic container of sugar, fat and salt. Similarly, the problems with native advertising and tech giants which were discussed in Chapter 8 are exacerbated by our complicity: we refuse to pay for good journalism; we are happy to swap our privacy for digital convenience.

It need not be so. Historical experience and two millennia of thinking show we are capable of better. We have moral agency and we can make the right choice even when it is the difficult one. Indeed, it is this capacity and desire "to follow after wisdom and virtue," to rebel against injustice and malignancy, that makes us human and cements our collective identity. In the last century this realisation was focused by the terrible events of the Second World War and resulted in the formation of the United Nations and the Universal Declaration of Human Rights. These rights had to be built on an understanding of what it is to be human, and this in turn necessarily incorporated the idea of responsibility. Rights without responsibility lead to tyranny; that is one reason why we do not let toddlers run the world.

Attar's allegory reminds us that this involves us all in an inward journey; a journey of self-discovery. It speaks of accountability, obligation and thinking through the full implications of our own decisions. Such introspection undoubtedly brings with it the need for effort: it is "up to us." Like the birds we have to stick at it. Human rights legislation recognises this essential dimension to our humanity and enshrines in international law not just the right to protection, but also the right to equal participation in the process of change, of creating a better world.

This chapter argues that these ideas of agency, morality and rights have fundamental implications for social marketing. We have to move beyond mere behaviour change and start thinking about people. Our job involves more than giving diets a healthy nudge or making the ecological option easy, fun and popular; we have to foster and encourage the innate human drive to think critically and act accordingly. We are not here to edit choice but to facilitate social progress. And at the core of social progress lies the well-rounded human being – in body, mind and spirit.

Learning outcomes

By the end of this chapter, you should be able to:

✓ Recognise the self-inflicted nature of many social problems

✓ Discuss the key lessons to emerge from the 19th-century fight against slavery

✓ Discuss the nature of humanity and lessons about this that emerged from the Holocaust

✓ Balance the ideas of rights and responsibilities

✓ Understand the basic precepts of Human Rights

✓ Explain the importance of moral agency and morality.

Key words

Rights – responsibilities – moral agency – slavery – morality.

Introduction: Self-harm on an industrial scale

In the WHO European region 88% of deaths are now caused by non-communicable diseases such as diabetes, cancer and heart disease.[2] In the public health literature, these illnesses have become known as 'industrial epidemics', because they are driven by commerce, and specifically the over-enthusiastic marketing of alcohol, tobacco and highly processed foods. Furthermore, there is compelling evidence that marketing does have exactly this kind of morbid power, especially over young people (Lovato et al. 2003; Anderson et al. 2009; Cairns et al. 2009) (see Chapter 7 for further discussion).

However, an alternative conception of what is happening is that this harm is self-inflicted; we are damaging and killing ourselves with our own consumption behaviour. Notwithstanding Coke's $3.3 billion annual adspend,[3] we are not forced to drink its sugary beverages; Diageo's multimillion pound link-up with Facebook (Bradshaw 2011) does not prevent us from saying no to drinking alcopops – or selling them to our chums. Yes, there is a power imbalance, and yes such unhealthy marketing needs to be contained, but nonetheless we do have a choice. We are capable of thinking for ourselves. And yet the WHO data suggest we are not doing so; that in fact we are happy to collaborate in our own destruction.

Our lemming-like tendencies extend beyond lifestyle diseases; we are co-operating in the impairment of our communities with equal enthusiasm. It is easy to blame big box retailers for stifling the social capital of small shops or the car industry for our choked and polluting roads, but their success is completely dependent on our patronage. This we enthusiastically provide; we don't just shop at Tesco and Walmart, we willingly indenture ourselves with their loyalty schemes. Tesco's Clubcard programme, for example, has over 16 million active members in the UK; its rival Sainsbury's has over 19 million.[4] The dictionary definition of loyalty is "a feeling of devotion, duty, or attachment to somebody"; it is unnerving that we use such a word to describe our relationship with a multinational corporation. Nor do SUVs drive themselves. We have freely bought into the conceit that we need a ton of metal with the technical capacity to cross the Sahara to get us a few hundred metres to the object of our retail devotion. Our behaviour doesn't even make economic sense: we willingly get ourselves into debt in our haste to kowtow to our materialist emperors. Statistics from the Money Charity show that average household debt had increased to £7,146 by December 2016, not including mortgages (see Box 9.1). The UK average salary was £28,000 in 2016 – slightly over £22,000 after tax – so on average every UK adult owed over two months of their disposable income.

BOX 9.1 UK CONSUMER DEBTS 2016 (NOT INCLUDING MORTGAGES)[5]

Outstanding consumer credit lending was **£192.95 billion** at the end of December 2016.

This is up from £178.8 billion at the end of December 2015, and is an increase of **£279.46** for every adult in the UK.

Per household, that's an average consumer credit debt of **£7,146** in December, up from a revised £7,047 in November – and **£522.70** extra per household over the year.

It also means the average consumer credit borrowing stood at **£3,821** per UK adult.

Our self-harming collaboration takes its most troubling form with anthropomorphic climate change (refer back to Chapter 1). This has been dubbed a 'wicked problem' because of its apparent complexity. But in at least one sense it is actually a very simple problem. Anthropomorphic, of course, means caused by humans – in other words, us. In particular, those of us who are in the wealthiest 20% of the world's population whose shopping behaviour is so utterly unsustainable. Planetary degradation is, in reality, just another lifestyle illness; one more symptom of our unthinking collaboration, our perpetual adoption of the line of least resistance. As the environmentalist George Monbiot[6] observes, "We'd never dream of killing gorillas or sharks, but let others do it: extinction is the bycatch of consumerism." We manage to live comfortably with these double standards and so "it's not ignorance that's wiping out so many species: it's our naked hypocrisy". We also manage to live comfortably with planetary degradation; a week after Monbiot filed his piece, the World Meteorological Organization's (WMO) annual greenhouse gas bulletin revealed that the "globally averaged concentration of carbon dioxide in the atmosphere" had "reached the symbolic and significant milestone of 400 parts per million for the first time." This, the UN body warned, marked "the start of a new era of climate reality."[7] A reality we blithely deny as we continue shopping.

Have a go at Exercise 9.1.

EXERCISE 9.1   SELF ANALYSIS

Think about your own consumption behaviour over the last month. Make a list of all the things you have bought.

Have any of your decisions or actions resulted in harm to yourself or to others?

To what extent are you able to answer the question?

To what extent had you considered these issues before doing this exercise?

It is often difficult to draw the link between our seemingly very small actions and momentous problems such as unfairness in the global trading system or climate change. This is particularly true of our consumption behaviour – shopping seems to be such an ordinary and unimportant activity. But the links are clear. Box 9.2, for example, is taken from Amnesty International's report on conflict minerals in the smartphone and battery markets; you can visit the NGO's website for more details.

> ### BOX 9.2   COLTAN – THE NEW BLACK GOLD[8]
>
> Coltan is a black-coloured mineral found in the Democratic Republic of Congo in West Africa. It is an essential component of all mobile phones. Decu is 8; everyday he and his twin brother walk to work at Ruashi mines; it takes two hours. There are no health and safety rules: they use their bare hands to separate the soil from mineral deposits. In the day they earn enough for a few pastries. The profits go to the mine owners and the phone companies. The state-of-the-art products and services go to us.

As we discussed in Chapter 8, one of the reasons we are discouraged from making these connections is because sophisticated marketing makes it counter-intuitive. It is extremely difficult to draw a direct line between the sleek, state of the art brand imagery of the latest iphone and Decu's miserable existence or the suicide of desperate Chinese workers in the Foxconn factory where the phones were assembled.[9] As Mark Dummett of Amnesty International points out, "The glamorous shop displays and marketing of state of the art technologies are a stark contrast to the children carrying bags of rocks, and miners in narrow manmade tunnels risking permanent lung damage."[10] However, although it is difficult and uncomfortable, we do have to make these connections; to accept our share of culpability. This was a key lesson to emerge from the fight against slavery which took place two centuries ago.

Learning from the abolitionists

William Wilberforce is often given the credit for the abolition of slavery, and there is no doubt that he and his colleagues do deserve a lot of thanks. However, the true heroes of the hour were people like us – ordinary citizens. Wilberforce himself recognised that nothing would be achieved without public support and in the dramatic speech to the House of Commons, with which he launched the campaign, he called on the British citizenry with the ringing phrase "we ought all to plead guilty" (Smith 2002), invoking both the moral and practical imperative of grassroots involvement.

The challenge was truly daunting. In 1787, when the anti-slavery movement began, there were actually more slaves than free people in the world. Furthermore, slavery represented massive economic interests: in the UK with its growing Empire, nearly 2% of gross domestic product was at stake. Wilberforce and his eight colleagues used many techniques that modern social marketers would recognise. They had a clear vision, "drawing connections between the near and the distant," for what they wanted to achieve. This was converted into achievable, pragmatic objectives – the cessation of trading rather than complete emancipation (the former would inevitably lead to the latter anyway). They engaged in classic strategic planning based on careful market research, a detailed situation analysis identifying key stakeholders and competitors, and shrewd tactical deliberation. They recognised that success would take time (eight of the nine originators were dead by the time their aim was accomplished) and hence progress needed continuous monitoring to inform adjustments to the strategy. Mass media communications were also deployed to great effect, and in the best social marketing traditions, they weren't afraid to use highly emotional appeals (Box 9.3).

BOX 9.3 ANTI-SLAVERY ADVOCACY

James Arnold, a doctor on a slave ship, gave this powerful evidence to the parliamentary hearing on the slave trade, which put it into the public domain where it was used in abolitionist leaflets:

A woman was one day brought to us to be sold; she came with a child in her arms. The captain refused to purchase her on that account, not wishing to be plagued with a child on board; in consequence of that she was taken back to the shore. On the following morning, however, she was again brought to us, but without the child, and she was apparently in great sorrow. The black trader who brought her on board said that the child had been killed in the night to accommodate us in the sale.

(Smith 2002: 3)

But the most important factor in their success was the role played by ordinary people. Abolition movements were established in towns across the country. These encouraged critical thinking, drawing "the dramatic, direct connection between British daily life and that of slaves." Tea, that quintessentially British symbol of civilised domesticity, became "the blood stained beverage." This critical thinking was converted into direct action – fundraising, letter writing to political representatives, petitions, protests, fliers, public meetings and boycotts of sugar and tea. Sugar sales, for example, slumped by a third as 300,000 people stopped using it in order to dissociate themselves from slavery.[11] The result was an unstoppable force and, despite the special pleading and massive commercial interests, the government simply had to move. A leading newspaper of the time expressed it trenchantly: "the sense of the people has pressed abolition on our rulers" (Smith 2002: 3).

Modern slavery

Notwithstanding the success of the Wilberforce initiative, slavery continues to be a major problem. As well as the iphone scandals noted above, for example, in 2016 "two of the world's biggest coffee companies, Nestlé and Jacobs Douwe Egberts, admitted that beans from Brazilian plantations using slave labour may have ended up in their coffee,"[12] and the year before it emerged that eggs supplied to most of the UK's leading supermarkets were collected using trafficked labour from Lithuania. In his video statement,[13] Laurynas Kelpsa explains "it's easy to control people who are scared, controlling your money, controlling your hours, controlling your sleep, controlling everything what you have . . . "

The journalist explained how the workers were victims of violence, subjected to the process of being debt-bonded on arrival, and put in accommodation riddled with bedbugs. They were also "denied sleep and toilet breaks, forcing them to urinate into bottles and defecate into carrier bags in their vehicle." The eggs produced in these conditions supplied "premium free range eggs for McDonald's, Tesco, Asda, M&S, and the Sainsbury's Woodland brand" as well as eggs marketed "under the Freedom Food brand, and for Noble Foods, owner of the Happy Egg Company."[14]

Have a go at Exercise 9.2.

EXERCISE 9.2 MODERN SLAVERY

In 2014 the UK government launched a major initiative to combat modern slavery. Its website states: "On 31 July 2014, the Home Office launched a modern slavery marketing campaign to raise awareness that slavery exists in the UK. This modern slavery campaign material has been developed in collaboration with partners (such as charities, the police and frontline staff) to support the nationwide campaign to end modern slavery".[15]

- What lessons from the original fight against slavery might be brought to bear on the modern problem?
- Do you think that, as a result of the UK government's campaign, journalists will conclude that "the sense of the people has pressed abolition on our rulers"?
- What are the lessons for social marketing?

It is uncomfortable, but the exercise makes us to think about our personal responsibility for the continued existence of slavery – and what we might do to stop it. On a positive note, it also suggests we have power; we can make a difference.

Moral agency

The fight against slavery reveals something fundamental about human beings: we have the ability to think through the implications of our actions, to distinguish between right and wrong and to act accordingly. We can plan for the future; forgo benefits today for rewards tomorrow. We can also think of others. We are capable of altruism, of putting ourselves in harm's way for the benefit of our fellow beings. Parents habitually make sacrifices for their children; soldiers are honoured for risking their own safety to protect their comrades. As a recent newspaper editorial argued, these are uniquely human qualities: "We are the only species capable of reflecting on our impact. We have moral agency. We can foresee the likely consequences of our actions, consider them, and then make choices."[16]

The editorial is pushing us to think through our personal responsibilities; to consider the consequences, both good and bad, of our actions; to recognise that "self-interest will only work to the common benefit if it is understood that we ourselves are mutually dependent creatures who harm ourselves when we harm one another", and above all that we all have "moral agency". We are, in the words of W. E. Henley's poem 'Invictus', "the masters of our fate and the captains of our soul".[17]

Sadly, good parents and heroic warriors notwithstanding, this moral agency seems to be in short supply. Lifestyle diseases, over-consumption and especially our disregard for the environment betray a disturbing lack of principled analysis, consideration for others or thought for the future. As the leader spells out, "In relation to the environment, these choices have frequently been wrong and show little sign of being right in time to save us from very large and damaging climate change."

This suggests that a crucial task for social marketing is to reawaken our moral agency, to reconnect us to the values we discussed in Chapter 3. In previous chapters we have noted the importance of addressing social structures and in Chapter 11 we discuss systems thinking and the need to address 'wicked problems' like obesity or global warming by recognising the complex set of external drivers – like inequalities and the economy – that have such a big influence on them and us. In this chapter this is balanced by looking inward at the human qualities that also influence how we behave. What it is about our make-up that enables us to feel as well as think, to consider morality in addition to convenience, and to do the right thing not because it is easy, fun and popular but because it is right. Why are we sometimes able to buck the unhelpful system, to succeed despite a harmful environment?

A decade ago the Institute for Social Marketing at Stirling University was commissioned to do a large qualitative and quantitative study into smoking in low-income communities. As we have noted several times already, smoking rates in the UK (and other rich countries) are much higher among the disadvantaged. In the Glasgow housing scheme which became the study location around two thirds of adults smoked – compared with less and one in five in wealthier neighbouring suburbs. The study adopted a novel approach: instead of interviewing smokers and asking them why they smoked, we talked to non-smokers to find why, despite their deeply unhelpful environment and social norms, they chose not to smoke. It was a challenging project if only because finding suitable non-smoking adults was quite hard, especially when we realised that many non-smokers had reasons for abstaining – such as lung disease or asthma – which had little to do with personal choice. Nonetheless the study did reveal a profoundly important finding: some people were clearly coping with life in the scheme far more effectively than others. They weren't resorting to props like tobacco or alcohol; they were fighting back against a deeply unsupportive system.

We should not have been surprised by these findings. Human beings are capable of amazing things, can adapt to difficult circumstances and overcome immense obstacles. An important task of social marketing is, perhaps, to help them to do so. Note this is not to ignore the dangers of victim blaming which were discussed in Chapters 3 and 8 and are very real, or underplay the importance of the system factors which we will address in detail in Chapter 11. It is simply a recognition that all systems are made up of individuals and social change will require activity at both levels.

Try Exercise 9.3.

EXERCISE 9.3 TWO WAYS OF TACKLING OBESITY

Zamzee	Fatworld
HopeLab set out to design technology that gets kids moving. Here's how we did it:	Fatworld constructs a small-scale society in which players decide what to eat, how much to exercise, what foods should be sold and what regulations

(continued)

(continued)

Connect the dots. In tackling the challenge, we wanted to both measure and motivate physical activity, enabling us to optimise the efficacy of our intervention. In a flash of insight, a HopeLab researcher had a great idea to combine an activity tracker with incentives and rewards for physical activity. If technology can reward kids by making sedentary behaviour enjoyable, then technology can be designed to make physical activity fun and rewarding.

Make a ruckus. We immersed ourselves in the lives of a diverse group of American kids in a project we called Ruckus Research. Our goal? To find out what makes young people sedentary or active and what motivates them . . . Based on what we learned, we created Zamzee, a programme that gives kids a wearable activity meter to measure their moderate-to-vigorous physical activity (MVPA) and access to a fun, motivational digital platform that encourages kids and their families to move more.[18]

should be imposed to determine their own health and that of their community. The game's goal is not to tell people what to eat or how to exercise, but to demonstrate the complex, interwoven relationships between nutrition, obesity and social factors like budgets, the physical environment, food subsidies and government policy.

In Fatworld, players also have an opportunity to influence public policy by visiting the Govern-O-Mat and to get a glimpse into their own character's health – if they can afford it – at the Health-O-Mat. Players can alter guidelines on merchandising for Fatworld, changing market dynamics to encourage certain products and discourage others. For example, the player could ban partially hydrogenated oils in Fatworld, effectively removing them from the store shelves. Or they could ban meat or fruit, for that matter.[19]

Which of these two approaches do you think is likely to be the most effective?

Zamzee is a good example of a pretested and customer-focused intervention. The website is able to cite randomised control trials to show that it has helped children to lose weight. But as Evgeny Morozov (2013) points out, it presents obesity as an individual problem: "being slim and being healthy are thus just the natural consequences of good individual behavior; they have little to do with structural factors like family income, access to healthy food or the risks of jogging around the neighborhood". Fatworld by contrast encourages players to think about the complex causes of obesity of which individual behaviour is only one. Its games developer Ian Bogost explains that "the game's goal is not to tell people what to eat or how to exercise, but to demonstrate the complex, interwoven relationships between nutrition and factors like budgets, the physical world, subsidies and regulations".

So Zamzee focuses on encouraging specific predetermined actions, whereas Fatworld wants us to analyse the obesity problem more broadly and decide what needs to be done at both a personal and systemic level. Zamzee tells us what to do; Fatworld asks us to think for ourselves. It raises a fundamental question for social marketing: is our job to get people to behave as we think they should – give up smoking, exercise more and so on; or is it to think of people in a more holistic way and enable them to fulfil their potential, to become not just targets of change, but agents of change? In short is social marketing about obedience or disobedience? Conformity or rebellion?

Voluntary servitude in the 21st century

The French philosopher Etienne de la Boétie (1548) argued strongly for rebellion. Five hundred years ago he set about explaining what is the great mystery of political science: why are we all so obedient? Throughout history he observed, regardless of polity, the vast majority of the population acquiesce to a tiny minority. This minority is not special in any way – in La Boétie's words they have "only two eyes, only two hands, only one body, no more than is possessed by the least man among the infinite numbers dwelling in your cities." And it matters not how they attain power; autocracies and democracies are alike in this respect: the power of the elite is utterly dependent on the co-operation of the populace; those at the top have "nothing more than the power that you [and I] confer upon" them.

The recent debates about the divisions in our society, which we discussed in Chapter 8, show that La Boétie's observations retain their resonance. When Oxfam's 2017 analysis[20] demonstrates that just eight men own as much as do half the world's population, the passivity of the population is perplexing. When the UK has become as economically divided as it was when Charles Dickens wrote *Hard Times* (Dorling 2012), the absence of protest is remarkable. When Thomas Piketty (2014) provides a blow by blow account of this unfairness and argues that it betrays a systemic problem – the "contradiction of capitalism" - our quiescence is startling.

La Boétie's answer to his own question also stands up to contemporary scrutiny. He argues that the elite use four basic techniques to ensure the 99% remain passive: the ready provision of both bread and circuses, a cloak of symbols and mysticism and the systematic reward of collusion. These still pertain today, with the only difference that they have been monetised and deployed on an industrial scale. Modern marketing has ensured that bread and circuses – ultra-processed food (as well as innumerable nicotine and alcohol products) and undemanding entertainment – have become ubiquitous (though we now pay for what was once freely bestowed by the Caesars); mystification is furnished by a multinational advertising industry, and the attractions of collusion now recruit not only millions of marketing professionals, but also – thanks firstly to stakeholder marketing and CSR in social marketing, and secondly to social media and 'relationship marketing' (Gummeson 1995; Hastings 2003) – consumers themselves.

The moral dubiety of much of this marketing becomes hidden in plain sight because it is so commonplace. Have a go at Exercise 9.4, which reproduces the parable of the Good Samaritan, and then retells it from a CSR perspective.

EXERCISE 9.4   CSR: AND THE GOOD SAMARITAN

The parable of the Good Samaritan

A man was going down from Jerusalem to Jericho, when he was attacked by robbers. They stripped him of his clothes, beat him and went away, leaving him half dead. A priest happened to be going down the same road, and when he saw the man, he passed by on the other side. So too, a Levite, when he came to the place and saw him, passed by on the other side. But a Samaritan, as he travelled, came where the man was; and when he saw him, he took pity on him. He went to him and bandaged his wounds, pouring on oil and wine. Then he put the man on his own donkey, brought him to an inn and took care of him. The next day he took out two denarii and gave them to the innkeeper. "Look after him," he said, "and when I return, I will reimburse you for any extra expense you may have."

The parable of the CSR manager

. . . But a CSR manager, as he travelled, came where the man was; and when he saw him, he beheld a good potential business opportunity. He went to him where he lay unconscious in the ditch and checked his identity papers to make sure he wasn't an African migrant – they are so unpopular with his company's customers. Then he texted a picture of the victim to the office to see if anyone in the marketing department could identify him. Joy of joys: the reply pinged back that the victim was actually a promising musician and something of a celebrity in the region, furthermore his fan base overlapped perfectly with the 12–16, C2DE demographic the company was trying to reach in its latest Facebook campaign. No question then, his boss added at the end of the text, it was well worth intervening – and if he managed to pull it off that promotion they had been discussing would be in the bag.

The CSR manager sprang into action: he rang the PR department for advice. They immediately saw the potential and told him to set his iPhone up to catch a swatch of selfies, and make sure he recorded everything the victim said as he came round. If he had anything with the company logo on with him, he should place it in camera shot – but be subtle about it, as this needed to look like a genuine helping-hand, not an advert.

The CSR manager ended the call and was about to follow the advice when he saw a Samaritan approaching. The newcomer was offering to help and said he had bandages, oil and wine. The CSR manager immediately recognised the threat: Samaritans were almost as unpopular as African migrants and one of them engaging in an act of benevolence would become the story, overshadowing his company's good work. He had to think fast. He reassured the Samaritan that all was under control, then gave him one of his business cards and asked him if he would help by taking it to the newspaper office in the next town with a message that the CSR manager would like to speak to the editor in an hour or so. The Good Samaritan did as he was asked.

The manager considered ringing back the PR department to advise them of this development, but decided it wasn't necessary. He was now ready to implement the CSR strategy. He put on his best Florence Nightingale manner and bent down to help the victim.

Sadly, however, by this time he had passed away.

What if anything do you think is lost in the retelling of the parable?

The potential losses are great. The Good Samaritan is a global morality tale. For two millennia it, and its equivalents in other cultures, have been used to guide and instruct each generation of children in the benefits of human decency, in the inalienable truth that helping one another when we are in need is not just right, but also the foundation of any civilised society. Thanks to CSR today's children get a toxic distortion of this moral lesson. They learn that people help each other only when it suits them to do so; when they can profit from it. They absorb this the hard way, because in their innocence they will start off thinking that Coke genuinely supports the ideals of the Olympic games (see Chapter 8). Some of them, as the CSR managers plan, will buy their products as a result. Much later, the fortunate ones will come to realise how badly they were deceived. To make matters worse, it is this twisting of decency, this pretence of altruism, which gives CSR its power. These are all deeply unhelpful lessons in an era when moral agency is so important.

La Boétie's solution to these challenges is as simple as it is difficult: we just need to end our collaboration; we should retract our permission. In 21st-century terms this means we should stop being consumers and start being citizens. The job of social marketing is to facilitate this change. To encourage the critical thinking, independence of spirit and self-actualisation it requires. To balance self-interest with mutuality and morality (recall Chapter 3).

In social marketing terms, La Boetie then argues for a whole-person approach. And if we consider for a moment the complexity of the relationship between behaviour and welfare, he seems to be onto something. Yes, we know of the link between tobacco and lung cancer, so encouraging people to avoid or quit smoking makes obvious sense. The same type of evidence and thinking applies for alcohol and ultra-processed foods. We can stretch this further to energy efficiency, recycling, public transport . . . but life is so much more than a collection of behaviours. The forces which make us happy, or feel fulfilled or give us purpose, cannot be identified and proven effective by an RCT or delivered by an intervention. Moral agency is not dispensed by a campaign poster or a clever slogan. To a large extent these qualities are not external at all, but lie inside each of us – however disadvantaged our community. It was these strengths that helped our Glasgow respondents to cope in such adverse circumstances; it is these strengths that social marketing needs to bolster and encourage.

In this sense moral agency becomes much more than a handy strategic tool. When Pandora let human vices escape her box, moral agency was the driving force of the hope that struggled out in their wake. It tells us something about the nature of our humanity. Nowhere is this more apparent than in the consideration of climate change, because it requires us to think about the future; about the world after our deaths; about a time and place where personal gain is no longer possible, and more profound issues assert themselves. The recent Papal Encyclical on sustainability spells out the implications: "When we ask ourselves what kind of world we want to leave behind, we think in the first place of its general direction, its meaning and its values . . . if those issues are courageously faced, we are led inexorably to ask other pointed questions. What is the purpose of our life in this world? Why are we here? What is the goal of our work and all our efforts? What need does the earth have of us? It is no longer enough, then, simply to state that we should be concerned for future generations. We need to see that what is at stake is our own *dignity*. Leaving an inhabitable planet to future generations is, first and foremost, *up to us*."[21] These questions are worth pondering. In particular, the last one: "What need does the earth have of us?" In a consumer capitalist world where our needs and satisfaction are perpetually prioritised, this focus on the inverse is salutary.

The use of the word 'dignity' is also crucial here. The dictionary links it to self-respect and a sense of personal pride. Thus it begins to explain why agency is so important; it suggests a fundamental human need to exercise judgement and make choices, even when these are difficult. The key benefit of doing this is self-enhancement: we learn how to make challenging decisions, with practice we get better at doing so and as a result we become more rounded human beings. In Charles Bukowski's words, "the more you learn to do it the more light there will be." The words come from his (1996) poem 'The Laughing Heart', which you can hear Bukowski reading online.[22] Listen to it three or four times and then do Exercise 9.5.

EXERCISE 9.5   A BUNCH OF DRUNKS

"I used to drink," Michael said. "A lot. It got to the point when I would have to stop at three different bars on my drive home from work. A half and half (a whisky and a half pint of beer) in each. Then when I got home I could break open a bottle of vodka. Did this for years before I woke up to the fact I was killing myself. So I got help. I went to Alcoholics Anonymous (AA) and it pulled me through.

"After my first AA meeting it took me three years to stop drinking. My life just got worse and worse. The redeeming feature was that I always went back to AA, probably 20 comebacks in three years. The same people were always there to help. They took me to meetings when I was unable to drive. I had constant panic attacks. I finally gave AA the chance to give me a chance. Some 40 to 50 people must have tried to help me in the three years before my last drink. I often wondered why they hadn't given up on me. People don't really give up on one another in AA. There's no formal arrangement. From their first meeting people are encouraged to obtain the phone numbers of AA members and to use them no matter the time of day (or night).

"There can be no progress without change; and change from a basis of honesty. The same person who came through the doors of AA is the person who will take you back out. The whole concept of change is central to your project and if a bunch of drunks can do it, then . . ."

What were the key factors that helped Michael break his addiction?

Michael's story gives a very clear sense that both environmental and personal qualities play a vital role in the process of change. On this latter, personal, level three of his comments are particularly resonant: "I finally gave AA the chance to give me a chance"; "the same person who came through the doors of AA is the person who will take you back out"; and "if a bunch of drunks can do it, then . . . Listening again to 'The Laughing Heart', which of Bukowski's words do you feel express similar sentiments – "your life is your life" perhaps, or "the Gods wait to delight in you"?

If this is a man

If our behaviour is not simply a function of external stimuli, let alone well-meaning interventions, but also a product of our internal qualities, we have to understand more about what these are, about what it is to be human. Primo Levi, the holocaust survivor, saw Auschwitz as an appalling but brutally effective experiment which was, inadvertently, capable of answering this question. In his book, *If This Is A Man*, he explains how the Nazis set about systematically dehumanising their victims so as to make it easier to mistreat and murder them. Life in the camps was deliberately designed to be as unbearable as possible so prisoners were pushed to behave selfishly, even brutally – to emulate their oppressors and abandon their humanity – in order simply to survive. And they were utterly defenceless: "we are slaves, deprived of every right, exposed to every insult, condemned to certain death . . . " Never had external stimuli been more destructive or debilitating, yet Levi maintains that the prisoners still possessed a vital level of agency: "but we still possess one power, and we must defend it with all our strength for it is the last – the power to refuse our consent" (1979: 47). However desperate our plight, we have an inner room which we can and must save from violation. This is our dignity. For Levi it is what makes us human.

Later in the book he takes this thinking a step further, using Dante's 'Divine Comedy'. In his poem, Dante invokes Vergil and the epic journey of Ulysses. Specifically, Levi quotes a speech the Greek hero made to embolden his men for the next stage of their voyage:

> *"Look inward, to your origins. For brutish ignorance*
> *Your mettle was not made; you were made human*
> *To follow after wisdom and virtue"* (Canto 26)

The words have a profound effect on his men and they become more than willing to continue their "foolhardy journey beyond the Pillars of Hercules" (symbolising the dangerous unknown) (Levi 1979: 119) because it offered the promise of wisdom. The power of the words was not a tribute to Ulysses' oratory, but confirmation that he was appealing to their irreducible humanity. Beings of their – our – mettle could do no other.

Try Exercise 9.6.

EXERCISE 9.6   *IF THIS IS A MAN* BY PRIMO LEVI

Read Chapter 11 on the Canto of Ulysses in Levi's book and think through what he is trying to tell us – especially what emerges from his conversation with Pikolo.

Two crucial messages emerge. First our internal drivers need to be focused on human betterment. In Dante's words we humans are made "to follow after wisdom and virtue." Second Levi warns that this quest will not be easy – it requires effort, hard work, the overcoming of adversity. Dante understood adversity as well as did Ulysses and his crew; he wrote his 'Divine Comedy' as an exile on the run from the powerful political factions of medieval Italy. Think back to the 'Conference of the Birds' that started this chapter. Attar's allegory reminds us that we are all involved in an inward journey; a journey of self-discovery. This introspection undoubtedly brings with it the need for effort: it is 'up to us'. It is also an endless task – "the search for meaning is itself the meaning" (Foley 2008: 74). But at the same time it is essential to our humanity – "the man who lives and does not strive is lost" (ibid.: 73). Once again, like the birds, we have to stick at it.

However living in a consumer society like ours obscures the benefits of striving. Obstacles become new product development opportunities and shopping the means of assuaging them. It is difficult to embrace toil and adversity when the dominant narrative is of customer service and perpetual satisfaction. Critical social marketing has a key role to play in deconstructing this damaging narrative.

Transcendence

Aldous Huxley extends this thinking when he talks of an innate human drive for "self-transcendence," adding a rather chilling reminder that this is an immensely powerful urge because humankind's self-knowledge – and particularly the realisation of our own mortality - underpin a compulsion "to escape from the tormenting consciousness of being merely ourselves" (1952: 36). We are continually seeking a sense of purpose to our lives. But again he warns that this is dependent on adversity: there are no simple solutions, self-transcendence takes hard work. Consequently, as Huxley goes on to discuss, this drive is extraordinarily susceptible to corruption. We are all reluctant "to take the hard, ascending way" and instead opt for "bogus liberation." Marketing, with its excellent 'because you're worth it' service with its siren call to consume ourselves to happiness, is bogus liberation writ large. Social marketing risks falling into the trap of copying this infantilising approach when it resorts to spoon-feeding and nudging.

More recent writers in the field of technology also express concerns about what they term 'solutionism' (Morozov 2013), i.e. IT being used to solve problems for us that we don't even know exist. This inures us from the consequences of our acts: my smart phone provides a service that my parents could barely have dreamt of and in the process suppresses my nagging concerns about the conflict minerals it contains. It also spoils us – we very rapidly demand more and more functionality. Comedian Louis C.K.[23] does a riff on how quickly we take remarkable innovations – from human flight to mobile phones – for granted. He concludes, with brutal honesty, "we live in an amazing, amazing world and it's wasted on the crappiest generation of, just, spoiled idiots that don't care." In a hi-tech world "digital keeps luring us on with the promise of perfection and infinite choice."[24] Morozov (2013) adds a third corrosive impact of solutionism: we learn to react rather than respond, "treating issues as puzzles to which there is a solution, rather than problems to which there may be a response."

And so the individual can be seen as the indivisible unit and motive force of social change. A key task of social marketing is to stimulate and empower this force. This takes us much deeper than mere behaviour change: it calls for humility to admit we do not have all the answers; a recognition that solutionism can do more harm than good; that we should not be seeking obedience but encouraging disobedience. The self-destructive collaboration that is driving both non-communicable disease and global warming is most vulnerable to critical awareness. For social marketers it once again raises the question of whether we should be concerned with behaviour or with people. The work of Levi, Dante, and Huxley suggests the latter.

Collective agency and human rights

Interestingly, a focus on the individual is not to deny the importance of the collective, but actually to reinforce it. Once we start to look critically at our society, to pick up the challenges of Fatworld, to address our own problems with alcohol as Michael did, it pushes us to consider others. If I am unhappy with the effects the system is having on me, at the same instant I come to recognise that others are also suffering. If my father dies of pneumoconiosis I begin to empathise with the fate of other coal miners or if a car knocks me off my bike the benefits of cycle paths for all become more apparent. French writer Albert Camus is precise about this, arguing that while our suffering in the face of a world that is difficult to understand and often unsympathetic (as he puts it "absurd") is individual, once we begin to criticise and act on these criticisms – that is to rebel – it immediately becomes collective. The stimulus to mitigate our individual hardship connects us with the humanity of others; the individual harm becomes a shared harm. Much as Descartes argued that our desire and ability to think demonstrates our individual existence, so Camus sees our desire and ability to rebel as proof of our collective existence. "I think therefore I am" is joined by "I rebel therefore we are" (2005: 8).

Camus and Levi were writing in the immediate aftermath of the Second World War, a time when it was recognised that there had been a profound failure of moral agency and there was a desperate hunger to prevent any repetition of the Holocaust and its related horrors. In this context, the idea that all human beings have the same fundamental qualities, share an "inherent dignity", and are equal "members of the human family" had powerful resonance (United Nations 1989). The view developed that the protection and nurturing of these qualities, and recognition of them as inalienable moral and legal rights, was the only progressive way forward. Under the auspices of the newly formed United Nations this resulted in the Universal Declaration of Human Rights.

As Szablewska and Kubacki (2017) argue, adopting a human-rights approach to social marketing brings a number of important benefit, especially regarding equality and empowerments. Case Study 6, 'Porto Tap Water' touches on the same points "drinking water is consecutively in the centre of a global crisis of scarce resources – exacerbated by social and environmental problems, accelerated urbanisation, climate change and increasing pollution levels – which affects millions of people and leads back to poverty and unequal power relations." Human rights can help address such unequal power relations.

Children are an obvious and vital case in point. The 1989 Convention on the Rights of the Child (CRC) (see Box 9.4) is the most widely-ratified international treaty in history. It enshrines in international law "the right of the child to the enjoyment of the highest attainable standard of health", that for any government "the best interests of the child shall be a primary consideration" and requiring administrations "to ensure the child such protection and care as is necessary for his or her well-being . . . and, to this end, shall take all appropriate legislative and administrative measures" (United Nations General Assembly 1989).

BOX 9.4   CONVENTION ON THE RIGHTS OF THE CHILD (EXTRACT)

Ratified by the UN General Assembly, 20 November 1989

Article 3

1. In all actions concerning children, whether undertaken by public or private social welfare institutions, courts of law, administrative authorities or legislative bodies, the best interests of the child shall be a primary consideration.

2. States Parties undertake to ensure the child such protection and care as is necessary for his or her well-being, taking into account the rights and duties of his or her parents, legal guardians, or other individuals legally responsible for him or her, and, to this end, shall take all appropriate legislative and administrative measures.

3. States Parties shall ensure that the institutions, services and facilities responsible for the care or protection of children shall conform with the standards established by competent authorities, particularly in the areas of safety, health, in the number and suitability of their staff, as well as competent supervision.

Article 24

1. States Parties recognize the right of the child to the enjoyment of the highest attainable standard of health and to facilities for the treatment of illness and rehabilitation of health. States Parties shall strive to ensure that no child is deprived of his or her right of access to such health care services.

2. States Parties shall pursue full implementation of this right and, in particular, shall take appropriate measures:

   a. To diminish infant and child mortality;

   b. To ensure the provision of necessary medical assistance and health care to all children with emphasis on the development of primary health care;

   c. To combat disease and malnutrition, including within the framework of primary health care, through, inter alia, the application of readily available technology and through the provision of adequate nutritious foods and clean drinking-water, taking into consideration the dangers and risks of environmental pollution;

   d. To ensure appropriate pre-natal and post-natal health care for mothers;

   e. To ensure that all segments of society, in particular parents and children, are informed, have access to education and are supported in the use of basic knowledge of child health and nutrition, the advantages of breastfeeding, hygiene and environmental sanitation and the prevention of accidents;

   f. To develop preventive health care, guidance for parents and family planning education and services.

Try Exercise 9.7.

EXERCISE 9.7   HUMAN RIGHTS AND SOCIAL MARKETING

Read Box 9.4.

What implications do you think the Convention on the Rights of the Child has for social marketing?

The CRC has fundamental implications for social marketing. First it means that measures social marketers would support, such as controls on harmful marketing or minimum unit pricing, are not just evidence-based actions which governments can be encouraged to take, they are legal obligations which they have to take.

It also challenges treasured assumptions. Take, for example, the Nuffield Ladder of Interventions (Box 9.5). The ladder's starting point is that any intervention is a threat to individual freedom and therefore should be (a) kept to minimum, and (b) justified by showing that whatever good it will produce will be sufficient to compensate for this inevitable harm. This builds on the idea of society being made up of autonomous individuals navigating their own way of life, a task which is constantly being threatened by those around them. It links to the dictum Henry David Thoreau (1849) made famous in his essay 'Civil Disobedience' – "that government is best which governs least".

An alternate view, as we showed in our discussion of exchange theory in Chapter 3, is that as individuals we are actually very vulnerable and frail; it is only by coming together with our fellow beings that we become strong and progressive. This means that the collective is not a threat to our liberty, but a facilitator of it. Note this doesn't diminish the role of the individual in ensuring collective progress, it emphasises it – as Thoreau went on to explain in his essay. This is why, as we discuss below, human rights law not only protects the individual, but also their right to participate in the process of progressive social change. Interventions, rather than being a threat to this, are a necessary part of it; individual freedom, for example, is reduced if governments do not take steps to curtail over-powerful vested interests.

BOX 9.5   THE NUFFIELD INTERVENTION LADDER[25]

Whether a public health measure is acceptable depends on whether or not it is 'proportionate'. For example, will the benefits of the measure be enough to justify the interference in people's lives and the financial cost? And how likely is it that the measure will achieve its aim?

We propose an 'intervention ladder' as a useful way of thinking about the different ways that public health policies can affect people's choices. Interventions that are higher up the ladder are more intrusive and therefore require a stronger justification:

| Eliminate choice |
| Restrict choice |
| Guide choice by disincentives |
| Guide choice by incentives |
| Guide choice by changing the default policy |
| Enable choice |
| Provide information |
| Do nothing |

Similarly, the supposedly oppressive influence of the 'nanny state' – being over-protective of its citizens – is also undermined when we consider that children have a *right* to protective legislation. Indeed, it completely inverts the argument, suggesting that the overbearing nanny is actually the unhealthy marketer, not the legislator, and she is a nanny from hell.

But the implications of human rights for social marketing take us beyond public policy. They reinforce the importance of moral agency ("the nature that underlies natural or human rights is the moral nature of a human being") and they emphasise the idea of human potential ("human rights are less about the way people are than about what they might become") (Donnelly 1985: 3 and 33). Human rights law can provide an environment in which this potential can be fulfilled, but in and of itself will not stimulate people to take up the resulting opportunities for personal growth. For this to happen people have to be recognised as active participants in the process of change.

The right to participation

For this reason, human rights legislation overtly enshrines it as a right that all of us should be able to participate in the process of change, from instigation right through to monitoring and evaluation. Here is the United Nations explaining these principles in its 'Right To Food Guidelines': "The process of designing and implementing [interventions] should also respect *participatory principles* and *empower* intended beneficiaries, who should be explicitly recognised as *stakeholders* . . . Fundamentally, a human rights based approach to poverty is about empowerment of the poor . . . This focus on the poor and the needy for their *empowerment* is amply reflected in calls . . . for those targeted to have a say in how services are provided, and for poor *communities to be empowered* to *control* the way money set aside for them is spent. In this context, it is clear that the design and operation of an effective RBM [rights based monitoring] system for the right to adequate food would be instrumental to the progressive realization of the right" (Food and Agriculture Organization of the United Nations 2006: 143, 47). Thus the idea of partnership working is not just encouraged, it is also laid down as a requirement in international law.

This fits perfectly with the core social marketing principles discussed in Chapter 2 such as client orientation and relationship building. Similarly, it strongly supports ideas about the co-creation, design and delivery of value, which we will discuss in Chapter 11 on Systems Social Marketing. Thus social marketing has a vital role to play in enabling participation, in providing society with Eisenhower's critical and aware citizenry (see Chapter 8) that will make the most of its hard-earned and mandated human rights. Young people can, for example, be encouraged to exert their rights to protection from tobacco industry predation, as they were with the American Legacy's Truth Campaign (Farrelly *et al.* 2002), and more recently in Cancer Research UK's 'Smoke This' and 'Make Them Pay' digital initiatives.[26]

The prize for doing this is indeed worth the winning: "human development is possible only through comprehensive human action coordinated by human rights." However, it carries with it risks as well benefits: "The 'human nature' that underlies human rights is quintessentially human, full of frailties but also fraught with the possibility of the greatest glory. Human rights are a practical political institution for widely realising these higher potentials . . . " (Donnelly 1985: 33). If social marketers are going to move from micromanaging specific behaviours to empowering people, they have to be prepared to let go control and take chances. This is not as radical as it might sound; it is just the natural endpoint for the social marketing commitment to client orientation. If we listen to and respect the people we work with to the extent that we claim, we should have the confidence to trust them with finding their own solutions.

Nga hapori hokohoko

The benefits of realising popular potential in this way are particularly apparent with indigenous groups. A few years ago one of us attended a social marketing conference in New Zealand. The organisers were very keen to involve Maori in the event, but knew they would have to do much more than issue an invitation to what was a *pakeha* (European) event.

Indeed, even the term 'social marketing' smacked of cultural imperialism. Discussion with the Maori community led to the idea of organising a *hui*, a traditional coming together of the community to discuss shared problems and opportunities. This *hui* would "provide a unique opportunity for discussion and debate on the role and relevance of social marketing to Maori." The key objectives (see Box 9.6) included its relevance to the 'Te Tiriti o Waitangi' (the crucial 1840 treaty between the Maori chiefs and the British Crown which became the "founding document of New Zealand as a nation"), the traditional role of marketing for Maori (reinforcing the point made in Chapter 1 that this is not a 20th-century business school invention), and what the future role of social marketing in Aotearoa (New Zealand) should look like.

BOX 9.6   THE OBJECTIVE OF A MAORI *HUI* ABOUT SOCIAL MARKETING

To answer the following:

- What is the social marketing paradigm?
- What is the role of the 'Te Tiriti o Waitangi'/Treaty of Waitangi in relation to social marketing?
- How effective are social marketing initiatives and activities in reaching Maori?
- What are the critical elements and processes involved in marketing with, or to, Maori?
- What expectations and issues should be considered when developing and designing effective marketing interventions with Maori?
- What is the traditional role of marketing to Maori? (Marketing and traditional Maori practices.)
- What should the future role of social marketing in Aotearoa (New Zealand) look like?

It was a powerful event. Maori do not pull their punches, as anyone who has experienced the *Hakka* can attest. There was concern that this was yet another attempt to manipulate; that this was just one more shot from an alien culture that had already caused many of the community's problems – not least in public health. But there was also a palpable respect for the process; for the effort at inclusion that was being made. The day culminated in a highly respected Maori elder and *tohunga* (cultural leader) presenting his view that social marketing does have something positive to contribute to Maori – and, crucially, offering a translation of the term into the Maori tongue: *Nga hapori hokohoko*. A literal translation is difficult so suffice it to say that this Maori phrase describes the notion of mutual or reciprocal exchange between people either as individuals or sections of a *whanau* (family), community, tribe or society.

It was a powerful reminder that in social marketing the concept of 'mutually beneficial exchange' is not a rhetorical sleight of hand, but a vital reality. I was at the *hui* as an 'expert' in social marketing, but I learnt just as much as I taught. I had been exposed to Arundhati Roy's alternative imagination "outside of capitalism as well as communism",[27] (see Chapter 8). "An imagination that has an altogether different understanding of what constitutes happiness and fulfilment."[28] She goes on to argue for greater recognition for indigenous peoples, "the people who still know the secrets of sustainable living" and "are not relics of the past, but the guides to our future."[29] Or as the liberation theologist argued, "it is not about giving them a fish; it is not even about teaching them to fish – it is about recognising their ownership of the river" (Codina 1985). We social marketers need to remember that, when it comes to their own lives, our clients always 'own the river'. Have a look at Case Study 19, which discusses the impact that tourism is having on the environment around the remote Ningaloo Reef off the Western Australian coast. Consider the conflicting values that need to be addressed.

Popular engagement in social change is also an important safety measure. Without it, human rights legislation risks becoming pious sentiment, or worse doing actual harm. Vanessa Pupavac, for example, explains how an over-zealous application by adults of the child's right to safety has dangerously constrained play, reducing school playtimes and even eliminating unsupervised play altogether: "Panics over strangers, concerns about environmental dangers, potential litigation over accidents (however remote) and fears over bullying are all leading to a constriction of children's play. The expanded meaning of protecting children from harm has required such all-encompassing dimensions that the eradication of risk effectively entails the elimination of unsupervised play" (2002: 72). The negative consequences included isolation, obesity and mental illness. The way to prevent this unintended harm is to encourage everyone to join the debate; a key function of social marketing is to help them do so.

A step towards systems

In this chapter we have looked in great detail at the individual and what it is to be human. This has taken us into very deep water, and led us, in the words of Pope Francis, to ask extremely challenging questions about "the purpose of our life in this world" and "Why are we here? What is the goal of our work and all our efforts? What need does the earth have of us?" Using Sufi wisdom, the terrible lessons of the Holocaust and abstract, almost theological philosophy, we have delved deep inside ourselves.

Interestingly this has also led us with equal force towards the collective, towards another innate human tendency – to live cooperatively and collectively. So we can revisit George Orwell's (1970: 48) observation which we first discussed in Chapter 8 ("two viewpoints are tenable: the one, how can you improve human nature until you have changed the system? The other, what is the use of changing the system before you have improved human nature") and conclude that he presents us with a false dichotomy: in reality the two – the individual and the collective – are indivisible.

In Chapter 11 we will bring this together with the idea of Systems Social Marketing. As a brief prelude to that we can conclude from this chapter that the job of social marketing can no longer be limited to micromanaging specific behaviours – to quit smoking, drink less, get moving – however beneficial these changes might be for the individual. Nor can it just be a matter of moving upstream and nudging people into these better behaviours by adjusting the 'choice architecture' or instigating policy measures, which are in any case increasingly hard-won or watered down thanks to the power and influence of corporate marketers. The problems we face defeat the capacity and compromise the ethics of such limited ambitions.

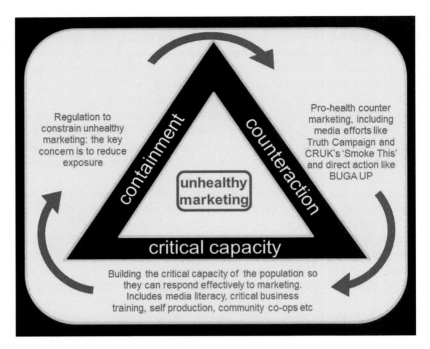

Figure 9.1 The 3Cs model

Rather, building on our discussion of the domain of social marketing in Chapter 1, social marketing can be seen to have three dimensions. First the effects of commercial marketing need to be **contained** by independent, comprehensive and robust regulation. The purpose should be radically to reduce everyone's exposure, and hence reduce the consumption both of health-harming products and 'stuff' generally. There is an obvious conflict of interest here for commercial marketers whose day job is to encourage consumption; they should not therefore be involved in developing or deploying these new rules, merely in obeying them. Second commercial marketing needs to be **countered** with robust social marketing and active deconstruction, as illustrated by the American Legacy's Truth Campaign and CRUK's 'Smoke This' and 'Make Them Pay' digital initiatives (see above). Third, and most importantly, **critical capacity** needs to be built in the population. Small steps in this direction have been taken with media literacy, but the idea has to be pushed much further, addressing not just advertising but also the whole neoliberal business system. The marketing mix, stakeholder marketing and the fiduciary imperative which requires corporations to prioritise profit each need to be unpacked and critiqued. Not so much media literacy as marketing and business literacy.

These three Cs of containment, counteraction and critical capacity the 3Cs model are mutually dependent: regulation without public support is severely weakened, while a politician's inclination to regulate is greatly increased by popular demand – and both are aided and abetted by effective counter marketing (see Figure 9.1). The move to smokefree public places in Scotland during 2006 perfectly illustrates this strategic potential: the near perfect alignment of public and parliament defeated a notoriously powerful multinational industry and delivered what many would consider to be the greatest single achievement of the McConnell government. Now visit Case Study 8 and see how you would use the 3Cs to answer their "Who holds industry to account when it comes to human safety?"

In conclusion, if the aim of corporate marketing is to encourage obedience, to get us to do as the marketer says, that of social marketing has to be more than simply saying "no, do as *we* say." It must be about enabling people to question current assumptions, understand the manipulative power structures these entail and withdraw their collaboration; about replacing obedience, not with another form of obedience, but with disobedience.

Wrap-up

We are the only species with moral agency: the ability to judge right from wrong and the capacity to act accordingly, regardless of adversity. This combination of morality and striving is not just a useful coping strategy, it is what defines us as human beings. It is what we mean when we talk of human dignity, of the human spirit or simply humanity. In the last century we so valued these qualities that we came together as a species to enshrine them as inalienable rights and commit their protection to international law.

And yet sixty years later we are self-harming on an industrial scale. The wealthiest 20% of us are consuming in a way that is destroying our bodies, our communities and our planet, and the global economic system is energetically encouraging the other 80% to follow suit. The cause of our predicament is that the most important, but least recognised, victim of our consumerism is the very humanity the UN set out to protect. We know what we are doing is wrong, but we continue doing it. Instead of rebelling against the marketing pressure to conform, we collaborate with it. As Swedish essayist Sven Lindqvist argues, "You already know enough. So do I. It is not knowledge we lack. What is missing is the courage to understand what we know and to draw conclusions" (Lindqvist 2002: 179). Social marketing has a vital role to play in helping us find this courage, draw our own conclusions and take appropriate action; to move from being passive consumers to active citizens – or, as Camus might express it, to become rebels with a cause.

Reflective questions

1. What is moral agency?
2. Critically discuss how human rights are reflected in the social marketing process.
3. Consider the pros and cons of an 'intervention ladder' as a means of thinking about how social marketing can and should influence people's choices.
4. Discuss how the concepts of participation and partnerships relate to each other.
5. Explain how the 3Cs, containment, counteraction and critical capacity, are mutually dependent.

Reflective assignments

1. Conduct an internet search on moral agency and morality.
2. Locate and review the UN's Human Rights Declaration.
3. Examine your experiences and document where you have seen morality and the lack of morality at work. What were your reactions, thoughts and feelings?
4. Apply the theory and thinking about morality to a behaviour change strategy of your choice.
5. Consult the *Journal of Social Marketing* and/or *Social Marketing Quarterly* and read a classic or contemporary article(s) on the moral agency of social marketing to advance your understanding of the theory and practice in this area.
6. Complete your 'Rebels with a cause' checklist for morality and spiritualty.

Notes

1   Based on Farid at din Attar (1974) 'The Conference of the Birds', translated by C.S. Nott. London: Routledge & Kegan Paul.
2   WHO (2016) http://apps.who.int/gho/data/view.main.CODREG6EURV?lang=en (accessed 5 April 2017).
3   WARC (2016) File: 20409_CocoCola_Euromonitor.pdf (downloaded from www.warc.com).
4   Express (2016) www.express.co.uk/finance/personalfinance/468092/Loyalty-cards-Tesco-Clubcard-V-Sainsbury-s-Nectar-card (accessed 5 April 2017).
5   http://themoneycharity.org.uk/money-statistics/january-2017-2 (accessed 5 April 2017).
6   www.theguardian.com/commentisfree/2016/sep/14/extinction-let-others-kill-albatross-gorilla-whale-shark-conumerism (accessed 5 April 2017).
7   http://public.wmo.int/en/media/press-release/globally-averaged-co2-levels-reach-400-parts-million-205 (accessed 5 April 2017).
8   www.amnesty.org/en/press-releases/2016/01/child-labour-behind-smart-phone-and-electric-car-batteries/ (accessed 5 April 2017).
9   www.telegraph.co.uk/news/worldnews/asia/china/9006988/Mass-suicide-protest-at-Apple-manufacturer-Foxconn-factory.html (accessed 5 April 2017).
10 www.amnesty.org/en/press-releases/2016/01/child-labour-behind-smart-phone-and-electric-car-batteries/ (accessed 5 April 2017).
11 www.monbiot.com/2016/10/19/the-flight-of-reason/ (accessed 5 April 2017).
12 www.theguardian.com/global-development/2016/mar/02/nestle-admits-slave-labour-risk-on-brazil-coffee-plantations (accessed 5 April 2017).
13 www.theguardian.com/world/2015/aug/10/lithuanian-migrants-chicken-catchers-trafficked-uk-egg-farms-sue-worst-gangmaster-ever (accessed 5 April 2017).
14 Ibid.
15 www.gov.uk/government/collections/modern-slavery#-promotional-materials (accessed 28 August 2017).
16 www.theguardian.com/commentisfree/2016/sep/01/the-guardian-view-on-pope-francis-an-unlikely-voice-for-the-environment (accessed 5 April 2017).
17 www.poets.org/poetsorg/poem/invictus (accessed 5 September 2017).
18 www.hopelab.org/portfolio/zamzee/ (accessed 5 April 2017).
19 https://itvs.org/about/pressroom/press-release/fatworld-online-game-explores-americaand (accessed 5 April 2017).
20 www.oxfam.org/sites/www.oxfam.org/files/file_attachments/bp-economy-for-99-percent-160117-en.pdf (accessed 5 April 2017).
21 Laudato Si (2015) http://w2.vatican.va/content/francesco/en/encyclicals/documents/papa-francesco_2050524_enciclica-laudato-si.html p9 (accessed 5 April 2017).
22 *Charles Bukowski – The Laughing Heart*. Uploaded 4 June 2011. www.youtube.com/watch?v=PepdFehviKo (accessed 5 April 2017).
23 Louis, C.K. (2016) www.thatvideosite.com/v/94.
24 Burkeman Oliver (2017) Get real: why analogue refuses to die. *Guardian* March 4 www.theguardian.com/lifeandstyle/2017/mar/03/analogue-refuses-to-die-oliver-burkeman.
25 http://nuffieldbioethics.org/report/public-health-2/policy-process-practice/.
26 CRUK (2016) www.youtube.com/watch?v=a9KSaUueok and www.youtube.com/watch?v=0vlKmlUOx-Y.
27 Arundhati Roy (2011) *The Guardian*, www.theguardian.com/world/2011/nov/30/arundhati-roy-interview (accessed 9 December 2011).

28   Arundhati Roy quoted in *New Internationalist,* October 2011, p.30.
29   Arundhati Roy (2011) *The Guardian,* op cit.

References

Anderson, P., de Bruijn, A., Angus, K., Gordon, R., and Hastings, G. (2009) 'Impact of alcohol advertising and media exposure on adolescent alcohol use: a systematic review of longitudinal studies', *Alcohol Alcoholism,* 44: 229–243.

Bradshaw, T. (2011) 'Facebook Strikes Diageo Advertising Deal', *Financial Times,* 8 September. Online: www.ft.com/intl/cms/s/2/d044ea24-e203-e0-995-0044feabdc0.html#axzzirtgC58l (accessed 5 April 2017).

Bukowski, C. (1996) 'The Laughing Heart', in *Betting on the Muse: Poems and Stories.* Santa Rosa, CA: Black Sparrow Press.

Cairns, G., Angus, K. and Hastings, G. (2009) 'The Extent, Nature and Effects of Food Promotion to Children: A Review of the Evidence to December 2008'. New York: WHO.

Camus, A. (2005) *L'Homme Révolté.*

Codina, V. (1985) 'Teología de la liberación y teología oriental: una aproximación', *Revista latinoamericana de teología (1985),* 2(5): 147–170.

De La Boétie, E. (1548) *The Politics of Obedience: The Discourse of Voluntary Servitude.*

Donnelly, J. (1985) *The Concept of Human Rights.* New York: Croom Helm.

Dorling, D. (2012) *Injustice.* New York: Policy Press.

Farrelly, M.C., Healton, C.G., Davis, K.C., Messeri, P., Hersey, J.C. and Haviland, M.L. (2002) 'Getting to the truth: Evaluating national tobacco countermarketing campaigns', *American Journal of Public Health,* 92(6): 901–907.

Foley, M. (2008) *The Age of Absurdity: Why Modern Life Makes It Hard to Be Happy.* New York: Simon & Schuster.

Food and Agriculture Organization of the United Nations (2006) *The Right To Food: Guidelines, Information Papers and Case Studies.* Rome: UN.

Gummesson, E. (1995) 'Relationship marketing: Its role in the service economy', in William J. Glynn and James G. Barnes (eds) *Understanding Services Management.* New York: Wiley, pp. 244–268.

Hastings, G. (2003) 'Relational paradigms in social marketing', *Journal of Macromarketing,* 23(1): 6–15.

Huxley, A. (1952) *The Devils of Loudon.* London: Chatto and Windus.

Levi, P. (1979) *If This Is A Man.* Harmondsworth: Penguin.

Lindqvist, S. (2002) *Exterminate All The Brutes.* New York: The New Press.

Lovato, C., Linn, G., Stead, L.F. and Best, A. (2003) 'Impact of tobacco advertising and promotion on increasing adolescent smoking behaviours', *Cochrane Database Syst Rev.,* 4: CD003439.

Morozov, E. (2013) *To Save Everything Click Here.* London: Allen Lane.

Orwell, G. (1970) *Collected Essays,* 2nd edn. London: Secker & Warburg.

Piketty, T. (2014) *Capital in the Twenty First Century.* Cambridge, MA: Harvard University Press.

Pupavac, V. (2002) 'The international children's rights regime', in D. Chandler (ed.) *Rethinking Human Rights.* London: Pluto.

Smith, R. (2002) 'Learning from the abolitionists: The first social movement', *BMJ,* 345: e830 doi.

Szablewska, N. and Kubacki, K.A. (2017) 'Human rights-based approach to the social good in social marketing', *Journal of Business Ethics,* pp. 1–18.

The Money Charity. (2017) *The Money Statistics February 2017.* Online: http://themoneycharity.org. uk/money-statistics/january-2017-2 (accessed 5 April 2017).

Thoreau, H.D. (1849) *Civil Disobedience.* www.gutenberg.org/files/71/71-h/71-h.htm.

United Nations General Assembly. (1989) 'Convention on the Rights of the Child', UN Treaty Series 1577 (November): 3.

Chapter **10**

Ethical issues

Laura has been going out with Daniel for three weeks now. He is a lovely boy – blonde hair, tall and quick-witted. He also captains the school football team and is the first boyfriend she has had who has made her feel really valued. They laugh a lot together. He doesn't criticise or try to change her; just accepts – likes her – for what she is rather than what she might be. She does not consider herself to be pretty or particularly accomplished, but she is 'comfortable in her own body' and Daniel has a gentle way of reinforcing this. The word love has begun to enter their conversations.

But Laura is anxious about sex. Fond though she is of Daniel, she does not feel ready to go this far. At 15 she isn't even sure it is legal, and she is anxious about possible repercussions – most especially pregnancy. Her friend Allison had to leave school early last year when she and Tommy Harlow had 'had an accident'; the school did an assembly about it. And the Social and Personal Development class on STDs had alarmed her.

But Daniel is clearly keen.

Now the local authority's new health promotion strategy has resulted in condom machines appearing in the school toilets. Daniel said this shows it is alright. Some of the other boys use the now readily available contraceptives to tease and embarrass the girls.

Her girlfriends are supportive but also uncertain. The teen magazines they all read seem to assume they will have sex – agony aunts, social workers, even doctors – offering advice on how best to do it. One magazine goes so far as to feature a 'position of the month', which had shocked Laura – though she pretended it didn't.

Against all this, Laura's parents are very religious and conservative. They barely mention sex, change the subject or the channel if the topic crops up, and believe fervently in the sanctity of marriage. But Laura's elder sister had rebelled and recently left home to live with her boyfriend in a nearby town. Her name had not been mentioned by her father since.

Laura reminds us that people's lives are complex, and the problems they face both agonising and multifaceted. She also shows how social marketing – however well-meaning – can have unforeseen repercussions, create discord with other influences and inadvertently undermine important support networks. Condoms may prevent unwanted pregnancy but they can also cause unwonted discomfort.

We social marketers are perennially interfering in people's lives, and this raises many moral dilemmas. We decide what behaviour is desirable, devise strategies to encourage it, choose who should get the benefits of our efforts (and who should not), criticise other people's campaigns and conduct endless research. All of these steps present ethical issues that have to be recognised, acknowledged and addressed.

This chapter starts by discussing why ethics are so important in social marketing and examines the principal dilemmas we face. Inevitably there are no simple solutions, as we saw in our discussion of theory (Chapter 3) and will note again when we discuss systems social marketing in the next chapter, but the chapter goes on to show how practical and theoretical approaches reinforce each other and help us to pick our way through the maze.

Learning outcomes

By the end of this chapter, you should be able to:

✓ Recognise that there are many important ethical dilemmas facing the social marketer

✓ Understand some basic points about ethical theory

✓ Explain the difference between *deontological theory* and *teleological theory*

✓ Understand the importance of human rights to ethical thinking

✓ Address practical ethical problems.

Key words

Deontological theory – ethical challenges – ethics – inequalities – morality – teleological theory – theories of rights.

Why we need ethics in social marketing

Ethical dilemmas arise because we deal with people and try to change what they do: our target customers, stakeholders, competitors and wider society are all impacted by our efforts.

Furthermore we focus on behaviours that are illegal, taboo or culturally sensitive – in recent years our work in the Institute for Social Marketing has covered illicit drug use, sex, addiction, speeding, domestic violence, prisoner health and childhood immunisation.

As a result, the social marketing solution often requires the difficult and stressful behaviour change options of people. For example, giving up addictive substances carries severe physiological and psychological repercussions, while encouraging increased fruit and vegetable consumption can have implications for the cost of a family's weekly shopping basket and for family relationships, particularly with fussy children.

As a result of concerns about inequalities, social marketers also tend to work with particularly vulnerable and hard-to-reach target groups. These groups include those in poverty, ethnic minorities, children and those with disabilities or pressing health needs. This poses challenges for research, segmentation and targeting.

However, the most fundamental reason that social marketers should be concerned with ethics is because ultimately their business is "messing with people's lives." It is imperative that we take time out and consider the morality and relevance of our values for others, and the effects (intended or otherwise) our campaigns have on those who engage with them.

One example of such a campaign that was compounded by difficult ethical dilemmas was a social marketing initiative to fluoridate the water supply of northeast England. Fluoridation is a remarkably simple and effective public health measure; it involves adding a small amount of fluoride to the water, the technology is foolproof and the benefits immense. Most strikingly, it ensures virtually perfect dental health for everyone, regardless of social background. But it also raises concerns about mass medication and 'nannying'. Box 10.1 gives a flavour of exactly how strongly some people feel about these issues.

BOX 10.1   SOCIAL MARKETING CAN RAISE VERY SERIOUS MORAL CONCERNS

During a campaign to fluoridate the public water supply a letter was received from an old soldier expressing very grave reservations:

we believe that neither you nor anyone else has the right to tell us what to consume – would you like us to tell you what to consume? Of course you wouldn't! Don't try to hijack the democratic system and individual rights in pursuit of ideological goals. Never try to deny consumers the right of choice in anything, choice also comes with democracy. Those rights were hard won on the battlefields of Europe, would you condemn those sacrifices to oblivion in your pursuit of self-gratification?

However, there are no easy answers; the option of not fluoridating also presents moral dilemmas. Is it right to deprive a community of a known public health benefit, especially one that has a proven effect on inequalities?

And all this assumes our social marketing efforts are successful. What happens when things don't work – do we just reinforce the negative behaviour, creating bad social marketing which makes the original problem worse? Do, for example, fearful messages about the side effects of smoking just provide teenage boys with a better prop for demonstrating how tough and rebellious they are? Is it unethical to make less than optimal use of limited government resources or charitable funds?

So yes, we need to address ethical considerations. In the commercial field, this forms an integral part of strategic thinking – good ethics are ultimately good business. The same thinking should apply in social marketing. But the first task is to pin down the ethical issues we face.

The key ethical challenges facing social marketers

EXERCISE 10.1   ETHICAL CHALLENGES IN SEXUAL HEALTH

You are a social marketing consultant who has been commissioned to undertake and evaluate an initiative on teenage sexual health in Dundee. You already know that there are above average levels of teenage pregnancy and sexually transmitted infections among 14–16-year-olds in the area.

What ethical dilemmas will you face with this project?

Looking back at the discussion of marketing planning in Chapter 4 will help.

In essence every stage of the marketing planning process discussed in Chapter 4 raises ethical as well as managerial challenges. As Figure 10.1 shows, we need to address six questions:

1. Which behaviours to address?

2. Are there potential competitors and how should we deal with them?

3. Which consumer groups to target?

4. What products/services to offer in their exchange?

5. How to use the marketing mix to make this offering?

6. How to conduct research to inform this process?

Each of these ethical questions is now addressed.

What behaviour?

Social marketers must make informed judgements about what problems to address or what behaviour to influence. These decisions have clear moral dimensions – should restricted budgets be spent on encouraging behaviours which are likely to improve the health and wellbeing of small numbers of people (e.g. intensive cessation counselling), or on large campaigns which reach large populations but with uncertain results (e.g. mass media anti-smoking campaigns).

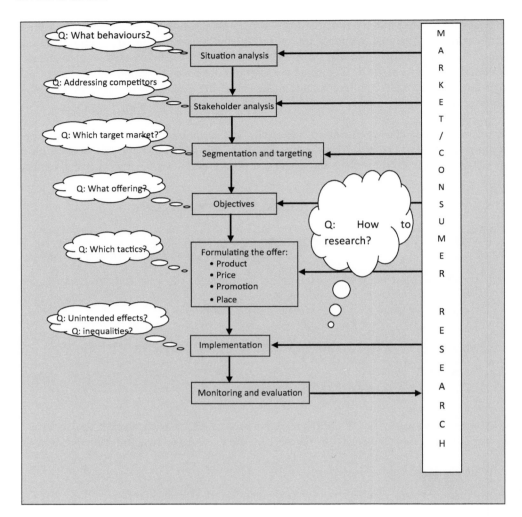

Figure 10.1 Ethical dilemmas in social marketing planning

(*Source:* adapted from MacFadyen and Hastings 2001)

More fundamentally, social marketers must make moral judgements about what behaviours are important to endorse or discourage, and for which groups of society particular behaviours are appropriate. Legislation provides obvious guidelines, but in other areas matters are less clear cut. For instance, in Exercise 10.1, addressing the sexual behaviour of teenagers below the age of consent, or to young people of certain religious backgrounds, presents particular problems.

It is important not to be arrogant and assume that we social marketers ('experts') know best. There may, for example, be situations where, on balance, certain 'dangerous' or undesirable behaviours may be permissible. Who determines that the best and only correct life choices should be that we all become: non-smoking, moderate drinking, blood donating, vegetarian, recyclers who live to become centenarians? Perhaps people do have the right to decide to take risks. It is important that, as social marketers, we avoid the easy trap of assuming that ours are the only legitimate priorities.

The letter in Box 10.1 actually gives us a glance into a small but typically well-organised anti-fluoridation movement. The reality is that any fluoridation programme, at least in the UK, is going to have to be progressed in the teeth of this opposition group. Difficult judgements have to be made about the legitimacy of their objections – are they based on sound science for example, or just prejudice and emotion? Then there are questions about how we deal with the competition – do we try to ally with them, as in the Miller Brewing-funded drunk driving initiative (see Exercise 7.8) or oppose and defeat them?

In Exercise 10.1 the Catholic Church may well represent serious opposition to, say, the promotion of condoms. As a social marketer you will need to think through how you respond to this.

Which target market?

Segmentation in the social marketing marketplace poses unique ethical problems. Despite the superiority of segmented versus undifferentiated campaigns, the decision to target (i.e. help) certain social groups to the exclusion of others can be extremely difficult. There may be an important trade-off between reaching less needy, but easy-to-reach groups (geographically or strategically), or very needy but hard-to-reach groups. For example, consumers in geographically isolated islands, very low income communities or convicted prisoners, may be difficult to 'reach' with mainstream initiatives, but can you really afford to ignore their needs?

Testing the efficacy of social marketing initiatives using an experimental research design shares this problem. The initiative is administered to one group but not another. Arguably, the control group participants sacrifice the opportunity for better health or safety to benefit others.

On the other hand, being targeted by a social marketing campaign may have deleterious consequences. Being publicly singled out for special support because of gender, poverty, disability, race etc. may leave consumers open to stigmatisation. For example, a government drugs prevention initiative in the northeast of England was unable to target young drug users for fear of stigmatisation. The programme had developed a range of intervention components for young people already using drugs. However, it would have been impossible to secure the necessary co-operation of schools, communities and parents who would not have wished their children labelled as drug users (Stead *et al.* 1997). A partial solution was found by combining blanket targeting with self-selection, where young people with similar interests (and presumably, similar attitudes/experiences of drugs) could opt-in to certain components (Home Office Drugs Prevention Initiative 1998).

In Exercise 10.1 there are similar dilemmas; will youngsters targeted with sexual health clinics suffer embarrassment or worse? Do girls come under pressure to have sex if boys are targeted with safer sex programmes?

What offering?

Ethical questions are also likely to occur when making decisions about the social marketing offering. As we have noted, social marketing is based on the principle of 'exchange'. A common point of understanding and fulfilment of needs must be reached for an exchange to take place. This ultimately results in some form of compromise between the principal actors. Because the behaviours involved are often deep rooted this may result in adopting more modest objectives or advocating behaviour which, while reducing risk, does still have negative repercussions. This level of compromise may seem defeatist and unethical.

For example, in our exercise Dundee is not exceptional; the UK as a whole has one of the highest rates of teenage pregnancy in Europe (United Nations Statistics Division 2011). Because so many young people are already sexually active, many would advocate that it is more important to prioritise safer sex than complete abstinence. This, and other harm minimisation campaigns, including the safer or more informed use of illegal drugs, raise key dilemmas in social marketing. Is it more important to have fewer people engaging in an undesirable behaviour, or to have more people doing it, but doing it more safely? Also, does it help to remember that in both cases we are running against the spirit, if not the letter, of the law?

Another ethical question which may arise when deciding on a suitable offering, is the level of involvement required on the part of the consumer. Some solutions, such as practising safer sex or going for cancer screening, require very active participation. Others do not require the consumer to do much, or indeed anything at all: a fluoridated water supply delivers better dental care without any action on the part of you or me. Indeed most people do not even know whether or not their water is fluoridated. This raises a crucial ethical issue: informed consent. Regardless of how much active participation a given programme demands, people have a right to know what is being done to them. This right applies however well intentioned and benevolent the programme.

Which marketing tactics?

In Chapter 4 we considered the value of the marketing mix as a management tool, helping us think through the effectiveness of different value co-creation tactics: of getting the right product, in the right place at the right time – and saying supportive things about it. We emphasised that 'right' in this context means in close alignment with consumer needs; but here we are concerned with it in an ethical sense – and there can be conflicts between these two perspectives. For example, in Exercise 10.1, a distribution strategy of putting condoms in school toilets may well encourage boys to think more seriously about using them, but at the cost of putting pressure on girls to have sex.

A closely related problem is that of ends and means. Because social marketers are typically involved in doing good, there is a temptation to assume that otherwise unacceptable tactics are justified. This type of thinking is most apparent in communications. Fear-based messages, whether they work or not, depend for their effectiveness in portraying alarming repercussions from a particular behaviour. Paradoxically, problems can then arise if these outcomes are not upsetting enough.

The anti-smoking campaign 'Every Cigarette is Doing You Harm' is a classic example. Developmental research showed that the target audience of young smokers did not find the prospect of disease and death in later life particularly disturbing; like many people under 40 they were inured by a combination of perceived immortality and short-termism. The campaign designers overcame this problem by emphasising the short-term health consequences of smoking using graphic images to illustrate the campaign's evocative strapline.

The problem is, it is not true. Doll and Peto's ground-breaking research on health consequences which followed British doctors up for fifty years, shows that people who quit by the age of 35 (as Doll himself actually did) show no long-term ill effects (Peto 1994).

This tendency for 'risk proliferation' may suggest a deeper ethical issue. Is the underlying assumption that our customers are ignorant, reckless and irrational children behaving in dangerous and unhealthy ways, and our job is to goad or trick them into behaving better? The additional danger here is that in our rush to put them right, we forget that behaviour is not just caused by the individual, but also – as we noted when we discussed social cognitive theory – by their social circumstances. In this way an over-reliance on threatening messages may simply be adding to consumers' feelings of stress and disempowerment. Whether it changes a particular behaviour or not, this is a serious moral concern.

Unintended effects

As we noted in Chapter 5 it can be difficult enough to establish whether your campaign has done what you wanted with the intended target group. From an ethical perspective though, it is equally important to think about people who may respond to your campaign because they misunderstand it, or are simply the wrong target. For example, in Scotland a smoking helpline established to assist adult smokers to quit was unexpectedly popular with underage smokers (Network Scotland 1997). This was not problematic in itself, but the system was not equipped to deal with the very particular needs of young smokers; as a consequence a demand had been created that could not be met.

Mission creep of this type can have very unfortunate results. The early attempts to warn people of the dangers of HIV resulted in a phenomenon dubbed 'the worried well', with people like children and the elderly, who could not possibly be at risk, becoming alarmed. Similarly, in Exercise 10.1, having wrestled with your conscience and decided that it is justified for 13-year-olds to receive a programme on safer sex, how comfortable would you be if 11- and 12-year-olds were also exposed to it?

There is a related issue here about keeping stakeholders informed and involved in your work. If you have indeed had to wrestle with your conscience to make decisions about the ethics of your campaign, are there other groups – such as parents or teachers – who have a right to be consulted or at least informed of developments?

Upstream interventions can also have unforeseen outcomes. Increasing the tax on – and thereby the price of – cigarettes has played an important role in reducing the UK's smoking prevalence (Townsend 1987). However, this proved a regressive policy, having most impact among the more privileged social groups, whose circumstances mean that they have found it easiest to quit. The least well off continue to smoke and the policy just makes them poorer (Marsh and McKay 1994).

Research issues

Conducting research into the sensitive, taboo and, at times illegal, behaviours of social marketing business requires careful consideration. The research process, particularly qualitative methods which depend on the intensive involvement of participants, may enhance fears, whether justified (e.g. discussion of cervical screening among those with experience of disease) or not (e.g. other respondents in a focus group hyping unreal risks), or cause embarrassment. It can also prompt risky behaviour, by, for instance, creating the impression that everyone is smoking tobacco or using drugs, encouraging impressionable participants to subscribe to a spurious norm. This is particularly problematic when the behaviour being researched is illegal, such as drug use, drunk driving or underage sex.

On the other hand research is certainly necessary, as we have discussed throughout this book, and it would present equal if not greater ethical dilemmas if we were to proceed without conducting it at all. By the same token, research has to be as reliable and rigorous as possible. This means researchers do have to probe, put respondents under pressure and check their answers for veracity.

In this sense, research ethics is a microcosm of all the ethical dilemmas social marketers face: a tension between individual vulnerability and overall effectiveness; a balance between means and ends.

How do we respond?

Let us leave aside complex issues of social marketing for a moment. How would you decide on a more everyday ethical problem? Try Exercise 10.2.

> ### EXERCISE 10.2   A SWEET DILEMMA
>
> You are in your local newsagent when you see a small child of 8 or 9 steal some sweets. Do you intervene? And if so, how – by telling the shop keeper or the parent, or confronting the child directly?

The chances are you will have used a combination of two ways of thinking about the dilemma: whether the action itself is right or wrong and whether the results of the action (intended or not) are desirable or not. You may also have considered the idea of human rights. Interestingly these echo the principal strands of ethical theory that we will discuss in a moment. We would say this with some confidence because that's typically what happens in the classroom.

In addition you probably looked for clues in the actions of others – what would your friends or peers do in the same situation? Or more generally, are there any codes of conduct or rules that give us some guidance about the correct course of action? Again you are not alone. Our responses to ethical dilemmas – just like our behaviour more generally – are influenced by our environment and social norms. This lies behind the increasing inclination in business, medicine and research to lay down formal rules and procedures to guide practice.

The theory

As with human behaviour (Chapter 3) there are many theories in the study of ethics. We will focus on the three that are of most immediate use: deontological theory, teleological theory and theories of rights.

Deontological theory

This view of ethical conduct is based on *the principle of duty* – the actual behaviour is emphasised, rather than its consequences. It institutes rules of good behaviour by focusing on motives rather than outcomes and assumes that a good intention is likely to produce good results. Kant expressed this in his 'categorical imperative': "I ought never to act except in such a way that I can also will that my maxim should become a universal law." Kant argues that we should act in ways that we hope all others would do.

Deontologists have been criticised for not focusing on the consequences of actions and ignoring the situational context of particular courses of action. For example, most would agree that it is in many instances wrong to lie, but can easily imagine circumstances when such a transgression would be justified – and many more where, while an outright lie is unacceptable, avoiding telling the whole truth would be.

It is important not to lie to consumers in social marketing, but there may be decisions to make regarding which truth to tell. For example, research to inform an initiative to encourage older men to climb stairs instead of taking the escalator found that the key message for this target was weight loss, rather than disease prevention. In cases such as this, social marketers have to choose between a traditional public health messages (to take exercise to avoid a heart attack), or a more superficial, but motivating message (take some exercise to be more slim and attractive).

Teleological theory

Teleological theory (or utilitarianism) describes the morality of a particular decision in terms of its consequences, rather than its motives (Mill 1978). An action or decision is argued to be ethically correct if it delivers the greatest good to the greatest number. This perspective rests on the assumption that morality is to promote human welfare by maximising benefits and minimising harm. To assess the consequences of actions, it is necessary to conduct a social cost-benefit analysis.

However, this perspective begs the question "who decides what is good?" For example, there are some who believe that only pleasure and happiness are intrinsically good, while others believe that there are other 'good' values, such as friendship, knowledge, health and beauty (Beauchamp and Bowie 1988). Furthermore, the drive to maximise total good may produce morally doubtful consequences. For example, in the UK, the greatest health benefits can be delivered most easily to those not in poverty. The health divide between rich and poor would likely be exacerbated if we relied only on teleological reasoning.

Theories of rights

Alternatively, decision-making can be framed in terms of its duty to ensure human rights (Waldron 1984). Theories of rights assume that there exist some universal human rights, to which we should all have equal access. These rights include: rights to life, safety, truthfulness, privacy, freedom of conscience, freedom of speech and private property. As we discussed in Chapter 9 there is a general consensus on these rights, and they have been laid down in both national and international law. Social marketers therefore have a duty to ensure they are not infringed.

This perspective may offer some clarity in the resolution of ethical questions. Take for instance, the case of access to a database of children's contact details which would be of great use for research on health behaviours, such as smoking or drug-use. Should this database be given to researchers to conduct research which will allow them to construct a random sample and produce new data that would contribute to evidence-based public policy? Or is this unethical use of confidential information? Deontological and teleological theories offer competing resolutions. Teleological theory would suggest that in the interests of the greater good – in this case the better public policy to protect children – access to the database should be agreed. Deontological reasoning, however, would focus on the wrong being done to those on the database, and therefore militate against access. Human rights thinking provides a way through this impasse. If we accept that everyone has equal rights to privacy, then a system of informed consent emerges as a solution.

Remember also our discussion in Chapter 9 about an additional human right: that to participation in the process of social change. This has ethical implications for the form our interventions take. In particular, we need to ensure that our activities are transparent and inclusive. Have a go at Exercise 10.3.

EXERCISE 10.3   NUDGING DILEMMAS

US academics Thaler and Sunstein (2008) have popularised the idea of 'nudging' people into correct behaviours. They discuss the possibility for altering the 'choice architecture' so we will choose the healthy option or take the sustainable alternative without even being aware of so doing. Desirable behaviours are designed into our lives, without troubling us to make decisions.

In your view, how does this fit into the human rights ideals of transparency and inclusivity?

Arguably nudging, while it may often be effective, falls short of the human rights ideal of participation. Furthermore, it raises the question of who decides which behaviours need nudging and the lack of transparency raises obvious dangers of manipulation. Finally, there is a potential opportunity cost: if people are not actively engaged in the change process they will miss an opportunity to learn – what is sometimes referred to as a 'teachable moment'.

Thus healthy or sustainable approaches to life will be less well understood. This becomes a matter of particular concern if, as we discussed in Chapter 9, a principal focus of social marketing is to help us, not just to do as others will (consciously or otherwise), but to develop into active and critical citizens.

The practice

This theory needs to be backed up by systems. As we noted in Exercise 10.2 we depend on social cues and guidance from those around us when making and carrying through ethical judgements as captured by the moral maxims for marketing in Exercise 10.4.

EXERCISE 10.4   MORAL MAXIMS FOR MARKETING

Listed below are a number of moral maxims for marketing that ask for some truthful soul searching. For each one, see if you can identify a work situation (even if it's not social marketing) where you have used the rule.

Contemplate the why, where, when and how. Are there any maxims you have not applied? Why?

The Golden Rule: Act in a way that you would hope others would act towards you.

The Professional Ethic: Take only actions which would be viewed as proper by an objective panel of your professional colleagues.

The TV/Newspaper Test: Always ask "would I feel comfortable explaining this action on TV or on the front page of the local newspaper to the general public"? (*The Wall Street Journal* or *Financial Times* Test).

When In Doubt, Don't: If you feel uneasy in your mind, heart or gut about a decision, there is probably a reason to question it. The individual should probably seek guidance from a trusted person before proceeding with the decision.

Slippery Slope: This maxim suggests that organisations must be careful not to engage in debatable practices that may serve as a precedent for undertaking other even more questionable strategies later (e.g. recent scandals that plagued several financial firms and the accounting profession are classic illustrations of the slippery slope).

Mother/Founder On Your Shoulder: Would your mother or the company founder be comfortable with the ethical decisions being made? Could you explain it to them in common sense terms they would understand?

Never Knowingly Do Harm: This asserts that a manager would not consciously make or sell a product not deemed to be safe. Called the "silver rule" because it does not hold marketers to as high a standard as the Golden Rule does.

Examine How Results Are Achieved: This statement focuses on the means rather than the ends in the selling of products. If attention is devoted to ethically accomplishing results, they are likely to be justly achieved.

Ethics Is Others: This comment implies that ethical individuals will always consider others in making decisions. It goes against the egoistic conception of individuals that always place themselves first.

(*Source:* adapted from Murphy *et al.* 2012)

These systems are being developed and increasingly it is difficult to get very far with a social marketing idea before you trip over, not just ethical issues, but also requirements to address these issues. Most typically this is driven by research ethics that has now become a mainstream aspect of any modern study. Prior to even starting, ethical approval by a formally constituted Ethics Committee is a pre-requisite for funding. As yet, interventions themselves do not have to be scrutinised in this way – ethical systems are not in place – and so require careful thought on behalf of the social marketer.

Without systems, it is easy to get lost. The case of Bill Mitchell illustrates how.

Bill Mitchell, a newly hired sales rep for Phalkirk Pharmaceuticals, was surprised to learn that there was a very extensive expense sheet to fill out after trips on the road. He spent almost an hour reading the instructions and filling out the first form after he finished training and made his first 'solo' trip through his territory. He realised that there were some expense categories that did not appear on the form. These included laundry. In his first draft of the expense account, he put laundry under miscellaneous.

His sales manager examined the report and suggested that, rather than a large miscellaneous total, it would be better to classify laundry under meal expenses, because individual receipts were not required and he was under the daily meal allowance. Bill was told that, while miscellaneous charges were usually examined very carefully, as long as meal totals were below the allowed limit, management never examined them.

Was Bill right? What would you have done?

A few months later, Bill was on the road dealing with the introduction of a new product when a good customer asked if he would like to attend a premiership football match. Bill offered, because of his relationship with the customer, to obtain tickets and host a total of three customers from the same firm to the game. Upon returning from the trip, he asked about how he should deal with the match tickets and was again told to find a category in which he had not exceeded the limit. By this time, he understood the process and felt comfortable about doing so.

Was Bill right? What would you have done?

Several months later, he called in from a long road trip and explained to his sales manager that, because of the difficulty in making appointments, he was going to miss his wife's birthday. The sales manager told him he should do something really special for his wife to make it up to her. After talking with his wife on the telephone, he felt worse than ever. He sent her €80 worth of flowers and claimed extra on his meals (which were still well under the limit) to cover the cost.

Was Bill right? What would you have done?

Several days after returning from the road trip, he was called into the marketing manager's office and asked about the flower expense. Bill explained that he felt justified to have the company pay for the flowers. The marketing manager listened carefully while Bill told the story of his wife's birthday. He went on to explain how it was commonly accepted practice among the sales force and sales managers.

Was Bill right? What would you have done?

Bill was fired for fraud on his expense account. Moral: ethical issues are very important and addressing them is most challenging when they are neglected by the systems in which we operate.

Wrap-up

Every step of the social marketing process raises ethical dilemmas, but marketing itself is amoral. As we have seen throughout this book it can be used as readily to encourage consumption of lethal and addictive drugs as it can to promote road safety. Social marketers therefore have to engage actively with ethics.

Theory and practice unite to help with this task. Thus we are naturally inclined to think about both the inherent rights and wrongs of a particular action and about the relative merits of its outcomes, thereby, even if unwittingly, picking up on the thinking of both Immanuel Kant and John Stuart Mill. An increasing sense that we all have certain basic human rights also helps us make progress. None of these philosophies provides the whole answer, but between them they can certainly help us analyse the challenges. The context in which we make our judgements, the views of our colleagues and peers, and formal systems such as Research Ethics Committees, help us carry this thinking into practice.

There are no easy or clear cut answers. We will make mistakes, people will get hurt – but as long as we try and apply ethical thinking to our work there is a better chance of doing good than harm. And, by way of consolation, if doing social marketing presents ethical dilemmas; not doing it presents more.

Reflective questions

1. What are ethics? Why are ethics important to the social marketer?
2. Model and explain how the social marketing planning process can guide one's thinking about ethics when designing a social marketing intervention.
3. "Social Marketing faces distinctive ethical challenges which are not faced by commercial marketing" (Brenkert 2002: 14). Elaborate.
4. Compare and contrast deontological and teleological theories of ethics.
5. Provide examples of deontological theory at work in social marketing practice.
6. Provide examples of teleological theory at work in social marketing practice.
7. How can deontological and teleological theories together with the theories of rights assist the social marketer?

Reflective assignments

1. Locate and examine three social marketing interventions from an ethical perspective.
2. Visit www.un.org/en/universal-declaration-human-rights/ and answer the questions to the case study.
3. How, where and why does ethics integrate with our discussions of research in social marketing in Chapter 5?

4. Apply deontological and teleological theory to a fear-based social marketing strategy of your choice.
5. Take the Theories of Human Rights and use it to evaluate a social marketing intervention of your choice.
6. You are marketing manager with the Chief Science Officer with responsibility for more young people choosing science as a career option. Specifically, you want to target young female teenagers, 16–18 years old and design an intervention whereby they select science degree offerings at university over and above art or business programmes. Address the following six ethical questions in designing your intervention: (1) Which behaviours to address? (2) Are there potential competitors and how should we deal with them? (3) Which 16–18-year-old girl groups to target? (4) What products/services to offer in their exchange? (5) How could you use the marketing mix to make this offering? and (6) How could you conduct research to inform this process?

References

Beauchamp, T.L. and Bowie, N.E. (1988) *Ethical Theory and Business,* 3rd edn. Englewood Cliffs, NJ: Prentice-Hall.

Brenkert, G. (2002) 'Ethical challenges of social marketing', *Journal of Public Policy and Marketing,* 21 (Spring): 14.

Home Office Drugs Prevention Initiative (1998) *Managing a Drugs Prevention Initiative: The Experience of NE Choices 1996–98.* Newcastle-upon-Tyne, Northumbria Drugs Prevention Team.

MacFadyen, L. and Hastings, G.B. (2001) 'First do no harm: The case for ethical considerations in social marketing'. Presented at Academy of Marketing Science 10th Biennial World Marketing Congress, *Global Marketing Issues at the Turn of the Millennium,* jointly organised with Cardiff University, 30 May–2 June.

Marsh, A. and McKay, S. (1994) *Poor Smokers.* London: Policy Studies Institute.

Mill, J.S. (1978) IEP http://www.iep.utm.edu/mill-eth/ (accessed 28 June 2017).

Murphy, P., Laczniak, G.R. and Prothero, A. (2012) *Ethics in Marketing: International Cases and Perspectives.* London: Routledge.

Network Scotland (1997) *Calls to Smokeline: Weekly Report 267.* Unpublished.

Peto, D. (1994) 'Smoking and death: the past 40 years and the next 40', *British Medical Journal,* 309(6959): 937–939.

Stead, M., Mackintosh, A.M., Hastings, G., Eadie, D.R., Young, F. and Regan, T. (1997) 'Preventing adolescent drug use: design, implementation and evaluation design of NE Choices'. Paper presented at Home Office, DPI Research Conference, Liverpool, December 3–5.

Thaler, R. and Sunstein, C. (2008) *Nudge: Improving Decisions About Health, Wealth, and Happiness.* New Haven, CT: Yale University Press.

Townsend, J.L. (1987) 'Cigarette tax, economic welfare and social class patterns of smoking', *Applied Economics,* 19(3): 355–365.

United Nations Statistics Division (2011) 'Table 10: Live births by age of mother and sex of child, general and age-specific fertility rates: latest available year, 2000-2009', in *Demographic Yearbook 2009 – 2010.* New York: United Nations, pp. 399–420. Online: http://unstats.un.org/unsd/demographic/products/dyb/dybsets/2009-2010.pdf (accessed May 2016).

Waldron, J. (1984) *Theories of Rights.* Oxford: Oxford University Press.

Chapter

11

Systems social marketing

ONE VOICE CAN CHANGE THE WORLD[1]

It is June 2007, and the senator and presidential hopeful Barack Obama is on his way to visit the small town of Greenwood, South Carolina (population 29,000) – about an "hour and a half from everywhere" – as part of his early campaign effort. After what seems like an endless drive, he finally pulls up to a small town's civic centre. It is late at night and the rain is pouring down relentlessly; nonetheless, he is surprised to find only a handful of equally wet and cold supporters in the room.

Edith S. Childs, a black woman wearing a church hat, is standing there smiling in the small gathering. She notices the look on Obama's face and suspects "maybe he thinks he is in the wrong place". She knew she must do something. Spontaneously she yells out to those assembled: "Fired up? Ready to go?" Slowly, a few join in and respond: "Fired up!" She asks again and again "Fired up? Ready to go?"

Each time, more shout back, louder "Fired up! Ready to go!" with growing enthusiasm and energy, until a shocked Obama looks to his aides, who shrug, not knowing what to make of the situation. "I'm standing there and I'm thinking, 'she's stealing my thunder'" he recalls. Childs continues, "Ready to go?" and the room responds loud and clear "Ready to go!" – and Obama, taken by the passion in the group, finds himself joining in and calling out "Ready to go". After five minutes or so, he begins to feel good. He asks his staff "You fired up? You ready to go?"

(continued)

(continued)

Soon after the campaign stop in Greenwood, the same chant was repeated at a larger Obama rally in Aiken, South Carolina. Before long, volunteers were carrying signs and wearing shirts printed with the slogan. The national press picked up on the craze; CNN interviewed Childs in Greenwood, and the *Los Angeles Times* and the *Washington Post* also interviewed her. She flew to New York to appear on CBS. When a Japanese reporter wrote a story on her, in Japanese, the president of Greenwood's Fujifilm plant translated it for her. In December 2009, almost a year after he assumed office, President Obama invited Edith Childs to the White House for the first holiday celebration hosted by the Obamas.

Obama recalled how that the chant helped motivate a movement: "It just goes to show you, how one voice can change a room. And if it can change a room, it can change a city. And if it can change a city, it can change a state. And if it can change a state, it can change a nation. And if it can change a nation, it can change the world."

This chapter, then, is about thinking big; about systemic change and the transformation of our communities, societies and the world we live in. It builds on the key ideas we have already discussed – how exchange between people is always about a blend of self-interest, mutuality and morality values; the individual and collective determinants of our health and wellbeing and the health of our planet; the need for coordinated approaches to change; and the benefits of long-term, strategic, critical thinking. It argues that, because we are social beings who live in mutually dependent communities, behaviour change is inextricably linked to social and systemic change in the same way one voice can connect to other voices in a room, a community, a city and a society.

This **interconnectedness** is present even for quite trivial and seemingly individual actions, as uncovered in a cautionary tale in Box 11.1.

BOX 11.1   A CAUTIONARY TALE FROM KIRIBATI

The island of Kiribati is in the middle of the Pacific. For many generations, the islanders lived by harvesting coconuts and fishing in the coastal waters. However, in 2004, officials began to realise that the tropical reefs off the island were become severely overfished. If fishing continued at the same rate, one of the island's main sources of food and livelihoods would be threatened, and the reefs be drained of their rich biodiversity.

In an effort to stop this overfishing, an agency teamed up with the local government and designed a creative programme to subsidise coconut farming. The idea was that local people would be incentivised to farm coconuts instead of catch fish and this would preserve the fish stocks and increase the incomes of the islanders giving them more stable and prosperous lives. It would be a classic win-win situation: more income for local people and less fishing.

Within a few years, more islanders had indeed taken up coconut farming and were enjoying higher wages. However, to everyone's horror, fishing increased by 33 per cent and the fish population had declined by a further 17 per cent. It turned out that when people could make more money from coconut farming, they also had more leisure time. And because they found fishing an enjoyable pastime, they spent more time casting their nets. They even bought more sophisticated fishing equipment with their newfound prosperity, increasing their daily catches and depleting the local ecosystem. Inadvertently, the individual behaviours affected the very survival of the community, simple rules gave rise to complex behaviours patterns and the crisis deepened instead of being resolved.

(*Source:* Omidyar Group 2017)

Now, travel back from the Pacific island of Kiribati to your world. What if you buy a piece of fruit or an item of clothing today? On the surface, these are a straight forward transaction, a simple quid pro quo marketing exchange between a customer and a retailer – some money in exchange for, say, a pineapple or a t-shirt. But closer analysis reveals complexities. The pineapple may have come from Costa Rica and the t-shirt from Bangladesh where press reports make clear workers in both countries are being very badly treated, in many cases underpaid and overworked, and your purchase may well have reinforced this inequality.

Unless you happen to live in Costa Rica or Bangladesh (in which case you most likely will not be able to afford the item in question), the pineapple or t-shirt will have been transported many, perhaps thousands of miles using fossil fuels, thereby contributing to the Larsen C ice-shelf break-up. The power of a voice, an individual shopper, is limited to refusing the pineapple or t-shirt, but taken to scale, this mindful decision could have considerable ramifications. If everyone turned their backs on unfair and unsustainable producing systems, our entire consumption structures – production, distribution, packaging and advertising activities – would have to alter. It is this leverage, this potential for full-scale systemic change, that makes thinking about how our societies operate and the geopolitical structures and social mechanisms that govern them so important for social marketers. This is what is meant by 'systems thinking'.

The need for systems thinking becomes even more apparent when we move from small decisions about shopping to large-scale problems with multiple stakeholders such as obesity, marine pollution and anti-microbial resistance. These sorts of problems are not only complex, but also typically conflicted because differing interests have to be accommodated. The oil industry will have one perspective, Friends of the Earth another and car-owners a third – with politicians caught in the middle trying to please multiple constituencies while also hoping to get re-elected. These types of problems become so intractable they are often termed **wicked problems**.

Churchman (1967: 141) explains that a 'wicked' problem is that "class of social system problems which are ill-formulated, where the information is confusing, where there are many clients and decision-makers with conflicting values, and where the ramifications in the whole system are thoroughly confusing." An easier way to think about wicked problems is to liken them to a bowl of spaghetti soup – in the way that it is messy and mixed up, with no beginning and no end, there is a high level of complexity associated with the behaviours and practices of wicked issues; there are multiple, interacting activities that can increase the wickedness the problem; there is separation in time and location between individual transactions and exchanges and their societal and environmental impact; and there is a strong interaction with the context or setting in which these activities are undertaken, spanning shopping, consumption and people's social life (Quested *et al.* 2013). The temptation is to ignore wicked problems. It is much easier and more pleasant to focus on simpler actions – a bit of recycling here and litter-picking there. But when, as with the Larsen C ice-shelf and planetary degradation, the problems are systemic, the solutions have to be equally wide ranging.

This chapter starts by exploring the idea of systems thinking and what a system is. At the heart of any social marketing system, lie the individual and the community they live in – thus community social marketing is our introduction to a localised system in action. Given the voluntary principles at the heart of social marketing, it will come as no surprise that the idea of value-based exchanges – working in partnership with community stakeholders to develop a consensus about what really matters – is a vital part of this process. This recognises the importance of people being mobilised to be directly and actively involved in the process of change (and links back to our discussion of client and collective orientations of social marketing in Chapter 2 and rights to participation in Chapter 9).

The chapter continues by examining how systems change hinges on social movements and community development in a value-exchange network. It then examines how social mechanisms can either facilitate or inhibit such a transformation. Finally, the theoretical and practical aspects of conducting social marketing strategies for societal change are drawn together in a concluding discussion about systems social marketing.

You fired up, ready to go? To be rebels with a cause? Read on.

Learning outcomes

By the end of this chapter, you should be able to:

✓ Define what a 'system' is with its underlying causal dynamics

✓ Discuss community social marketing (CSM)

✓ List the dominant CSM models

✓ Outline the central role of 'motivating a movement' in CSM

✓ Model the eystems eocial marketing planning

✓ Develop solutions that match the complexity of the challenge you are tackling

✓ Specify the indicator monitoring for longer-term systems social marketing impact.

Key words

Systems thinking – social marketing systems – causal dynamics – community social marketing – social movements – systems social marketing planning – systems analysis – value-based exchange mapping – indicator monitoring.

Joining up the dots – defining a system

Whether it is the island of Kiribati, your new t-shirt or the Larsen C ice-shelf, just as one water molecule cannot describe the viscosity or wetness of water, the social marketer cannot reduce or isolate the behaviour of a person to a discreet series of non-interacting events. Our social marketing principles clearly show change isn't just about individuals' behaviours, but the relationships and interactions between people. Social progress results from joining up the dots and addressing the multiple influences on an individual's behaviour (e.g. the effects of family, schools, community capacity and access, institutions roles, functions and broader cultural, political, technological and economic policies). To get a connected and unified perspective for deep and persuasive change in the face of wicked problems, the focus shifts to the linkages, relationships and interactions among individuals over time.

This brings us to systems. Briefly, a 'system' is made up of diverse entities which are connected to each other and so produce their own patterns of behaviour over time. Examples of familiar systems include transport, health and education where different individuals, people, organisations and institutions come together to do a particular job; in transport, the system gets us from A to B; in health, the system aims to cure and heal us from illness; and in the educational system, we gain new knowledge and skills. For the vast majority most of us, one of the biggest 'systems' we engage with, on a daily basis, is the commercial marketing system. Often described as a provisioning or consumption system, it can be the relatively simple Friday farmers' market made up of stalls, where local producers come as sellers to meet up with town residents and visitors as buyers. Alternatively, the marketing provisioning system can be a complex, dynamic melting pot of online and offline global producers, wholesalers, retailers, distributors, researchers, packers, advertisers and buyers separated by time, culture, geography, needs, wants, demand, supply and more. In either exchange system, the whole is much greater than the sum of its parts.

EXERCISE 11.1 SYSTEMS

Take a look around your world and jot down some animal, plant and social systems at work, based on our definition where a system is made up of diverse but connected entities producing their own behavioural patterns, i.e. the sum of the whole is greater than the sum of the parts.

Animal systems embrace ant colonies and flocks of sparrows, plant systems are seen in trees and flowers. The human brain represents another classic complex system as does the immune system and human genome. Social systems embrace the world wide web and social networks such as Facebook and Twitter (Mitchell 2017).

Social marketing systems

In a similar manner, a social marketing system is a network of linked exchanges between diverse individuals, community members and stakeholders, with the aim of achieving some form of social progress – as opposed to the profit motive or outcome of a commercial marketing system (look back to the Coke story from Chapter 1). For example, in the Rare Pride environmental campaigns, adaptive management is utilised to re-align upstream and downstream efforts regarding the fish conservation demand and supply factors operating for fishermen, their families, the local council, shops, markets and schools, and members of the community (Jenks *et al.* 2010). To see this in action, look at the stunning photo essay from Rare following Rodel, a lifelong fisherman in the Philippines, to explore the complex interplay of long-term conservation goals with the short-term economic and social forces he faces (http://us12.campaign-archive2.com/?u=6479fe156a130422afe4899a5&id=2f961fd7 de&e=3609ae0c7d).

As Rodel and Edith Childs show us, any social marketing system begins with the recognition that individuals in human communities are essentially different from each other in their mix of self-interest, mutuality, morality values (recall Chapter 3), beliefs, attitudes, behaviours, social skills, trust and understandings, communication and capabilities, to say nothing of access to resources. Think of this as 'multiple interpretations of value' going on in parallel in a social marketing system (Hillebrand *et al.* 2015). This heterogeneity is an essential element in the exchange processes at the heart of social marketing. As communities take shape, individuals creatively explore alternative beliefs and actions, widening the range and quality of the goods, services, experiences and ideas on offer, and in the process generate increasingly complex networks of exchange, both economic and social.

As these networks grow, system infrastructures begin to form, institutional practices and evolutionary processes lead to further change, innovation and invention – all contributing to the dynamics of the social domains found in a community and in particular to the many multi-level provisioning systems that exist within it. There is 'place and space' between people, their behaviours, value exchanges, their outcomes and impact.

For a more technical definition, Layton defines a social marketing system as "individuals or entities . . . and the value propositions they make in dealing with each other, the conceptual frames that limit the choices made, the interplay of power and influence in the networks they form, the ways in which these actors (which may themselves be marketing systems) interact through competition and/or cooperation, and the extent to which these interactions are complementary or supportive of a primary marketing system" (Layton 2014b: 5). This is exactly what is happening in community social marketing (CSM), which is in essence, a meso, focal system in action. 'Meso' refers to group behaviour such as a local sports or book club while 'focal' denotes a particular group of interest, e.g. Corrib Riding Club or the Galway Mindful Reading Circle.

Community social marketing

Community social marketing (CSM) requires the development of **localised meso systems**, that is to say, multiple and sometimes parallel value exchange clusters *between* different stakeholders, such as local residents, college students, hoteliers, businesses, local police, youth organisations and local authorities. Any CSM is a located system of interest that takes a values-based exchange barriers and benefits approach to behaviour changes for social progress, linking the immediate environment to the person in the way rebels with a cause combine their voices to bring about a movement. Anker and Kappel (2011) maintain CSM's framework allows members from the affected community or localised system to select the complex social problems they want to tackle, set programme goals and participate in the research, strategy development, and programme activities used to reach those goals. (Again, think back to our discussion of client and creative orientations of social marketing in Chapter 2.)

Read Case Study 3 to understand how CSM facilitates **behaviour changes for social progress** by emphasising connections between service users, service providers and service

Table 11.1 Dominant community social marketing models

Model	Description	Key features	Applications
Community preventative social marketing	Community directed framework where social marketers teach and work with community partners.	Community learning, participation, ownership and empowerment	Initiation of tobacco and alcohol use; promote physical activity; obesity prevention and prevention of eye-related injuries
Community-based social marketing	Focuses upon the barriers to behaviour change at the community level.	Barriers and benefits analysis	Environmental issues such as waste and pollution, water, energy, transportation, agriculture and conservation
Community readiness social marketing	Community change used for assessing the level of readiness of a community to develop and implement prevention.	Readiness assessment	Drug and alcohol use, domestic and sexual violence, HIV/AIDS and environmental issues
Community-led assets-based social marketing	Based on the concept that the client is the most important participant in the change process.	Audience insight, consumer solution generation	Used in health inequalities issues
Community social marketing	Partners with local organisations to inspire communities to take pride in their natural resources. Pride sparks and builds community support for the adoption of more sustainable behaviours.	Local partners identify target audiences, understand barriers to sustainable behaviour and tailor a plan that appeals to hearts and minds at every community site to help people and nature thrive.	Conservation, wildlife, fish, locally led, sustainable resource management solutions rooted in behaviour change

(*Source:* Fitzgerald 2015)

referral contacts. It also shows how, in contrast to a traditional mass media campaign, CSM involves active engagement on these multiple fronts. One of the case study's distinguishing characteristics is the partnerships created between social marketers and community members, remembering that communities are a system of networks based on locality, ethnicity, sexual orientation, occupation, and/or shared interests. Similar patterns are evident in Case Study 5.

When based on geographic bounded localities, community boards, coalitions or focal systems can be formed that typically include local public health professionals, lay leaders and activists, representatives of local businesses, churches, voluntary organisations, and residents. Pick any of the following case studies to see this in operation: Case Study 2, on 'Sea for Society' and the NUI Galway crew; or Case Study 17, which concerns colo rectal cancer; or Case Study 24, on making India open-defecation-free. Thus, in addition to enhancing the long-lasting success of social marketing interventions, CSM enhances community organising efforts by giving its members a more effective planning process (Bryant *et al.* 2000), as displayed in the dominant CSM models in Table 11.1.

What is common to each of the Community Social Marketing examples in Table 11.1 is an understanding of how community stakeholders' behaviours and values can act as benefits (value consensus) or barriers (value destruction) to systems change. Taking an exchange systems approach with community stakeholders will uncover information about local problems and the assets available to resolve them. This enhances the fit between problem diagnosis and solutions, between intervention strategies and local institutions and customs. With community stakeholders working together, network ties (recall social capital theory, Chapter 3) is strengthened with the new problem-solving and critical thinking skills acquired, thereby enhancing the community's capacity to tackle complex or wicked issues. Most importantly, communities are treated as change agents and active partners (refer back to Zamzee and Fatworld in Chapter 9) rather than passive target groups. Go to Case Study 5 to read about innovative youth engagement, empowerment, co-production and health optimisation

Echoing Obama's insight into how 'one voice' can change behaviours in a room, a town or a city, a distinguishing feature in all our CSM models in Table 11.1 is CSM's capacity to solve complex or wicked problems by '**motivating a movement**'.

EXERCISE 11.2   SOCIAL MOVEMENTS INSIGHTS INTO COMMUNITY SOCIAL MARKETING SYSTEMS

Motivating a social change movement to be precise, is about the mobilisation of different community stakeholders, via formal and/or informal means, around a social cause, such as fish conservation, meals on wheels or food waste management, homelessness or diabetes management. Such social movements are not as formal as, say, a political party, but at the same time are not unorganised members. They frequently begin with a small group or community of individuals, interested in a social issue, who band together and organise activities aimed at making a large-scale change. The group grows, often via personal networks, and becomes more formalised, engaging in collective action which tends to be sustained and intense.

Social movements draw attention to the language, communication and values used to diagnose the problem, how the community or group view it, and what solution is likely to be helpful (given the source of the problem). It is not just the ideas, but also the conversations and discussions of how beliefs and values align with behaviour, which allows social movements to be flexible and inclusive with a consequent potential to attract and mobilise large numbers.

Social movements have been associated with significant social changes, such as the women's suffrage movement and the American Civil Rights Movement and are associated with climate change, anti-gambling, feminism and the American Civil Rights Movement.

How do movements bind community stakeholders together? What mechanisms are operating? What missing elements do social movements bring to the table for social marketers who want social change as well as behavioural change?

(*Source:* Fry et al. 2017)

Social movements are important to community social marketing and systems thinking because they provide a **bottom-up** approach to improving things. Social movements recognise that transformation towards a better system is more complex than individual choice (Hoek 2016; Gray *et al.* 2016) in the same way CSM does. Social movements, often drawing on framing, social learning, social contagion theory and many of the social theories highlighted in Chapters 3 and 6, suggest change occurs via social connections, networks, webs and clusters to fuel the diffusion, adoption, copying and replication of new beliefs, attitudes, actions, practices and behaviours. For example, the highly successful activities of the US truth social marketing campaign, has evolved into a highly sophisticated brand that represents a savvy and active social movement (Hoek 2016). Truth denormalises smoking and exposes the tobacco industry's deceitful practices. Another brand that used social contagion theory to motivate CSM into movement is Stoptober, initiated by ASH UK, which aims to accelerate smoking cessation during a defined intense period by galvanising mass action (Hoek 2016). Have a look at Case Study 11, which describes the French version of Stoptober.

Edith Childs shows us that diagnosing Obama's discomfort and lack of enthusiasm (the problem), and articulating her 'fired up, ready to go' as a call to action (the flexible solution) with a motivational chant that resonated with fellow community members and their ideas, beliefs and preferences (memes) in the town hall, enabled and empowered each of them to participate and mobilise via a bottom-up approach. Obama, in turning to his staff and asking them if they were 'fired up and ready to go' equates to signalling or an information flow between one social network (community members in town hall) and another (Obama's staff). It had the effect of coordinating his team with the community groups and provided the much needed co-operative mechanism for shared learning and mutuality. Uncertainty and risk were reduced through the introduction of local alliances and through their joint mobilisation. And so the tiny seeds for a set of shared understandings towards a new tomorrow were sowed among the small gathering in Greenwood that wet and rainy night.

As so often happens with social movements and bottom-up change, the story could have ended there and the tiny seeds of shared beliefs, values and co-operation would not have taken root. In Obama's case, history tells us otherwise. The individual behaviours of those 20-odd community members responding to the call to action from Childs was picked up and tested in many different environments, such as the rally in South Carolina and the media channels provided by CNN, the *LA Times* and the *Washington Post*. Because it was found to be credible, flexible, inclusive and adaptive, the bottom up the movement continued to be diffused through social networks as far afield as Japan. This networking aspect – the ties, linkages and bonds – the self-organisation and emergence – highlights the importance of community **infrastructure** in social change. This can be tangible and symbolic; it frames or limits choice and values and is a critical part of the evolution of social practices in the co-evolutionary set of drivers. The network infrastructure, created on the way, provides the visible evidence of bottom-up/top-down change at work (Layton 2014a).

In the same way Obama tells how one voice can motivate a movement, Community Social Marketing gains much of its success from the synergy between community structures, social mobilisation (a bottom-up, top-down approach) and social marketing principles. By leveraging the wisdom of local groups and nurturing ownership of the problem-solving and solutions process, being inclusive of what is of value not just to the individual but also the community, CSM increases the likelihood of an intervention being successful and changes being sustained over time. Social agency and participatory problem solving come together for better segmentation, targeting, audience research, and intervention mix, design and delivery. Community participation also enhances the validity of formative research results, and strengthens participants' sense of social connectedness, control over their lives and ability to change. We see this repeatedly in our case studies, Case Study 20, such as where for some participants the project enabled a more positive attitude not just to safer driving, but also to adulthood, careers, and so on, thereby benefiting society as a whole; and Case Study 10, where the success to date has been built upon engagement with a variety of stakeholders across the community. Partnering with community leaders and local mental health services served to make interventions 'local'.

Through direct participation in all phases of the defining planning and implementation processes, some community stakeholders gain the social marketing skills needed to address other issues and work together to sustain and institutionalise solutions. That is to say, the community look to an adjacent or co-existing system – a system that interacts with the focal one, e.g. colon cancer treatment system interactions with the colon cancer screening system – and use their skills to alter its course. In the Florida case, individuals with health insurance can be treated through private hospitals (commercial marketing system), while those without insurance might be able to avail of assistance for screening through community churches (social marketing system).

For another example, the tobacco industry is a commercial marketing system which offers the consumer cigarettes to relax, be cool and part of the in-group, while a co-existing social marketing system, such as Truth or Moi(s) sans tabac, offers the client health and wellbeing, the chance to be the hero in their community and rebellion against exploitative tobacco firms. Often, social marketing and commercial marketing are adjacent or co-existing systems arising from the paradox of choice and values, reflecting our Competition Orientation from Chapter 2, and increase the community system's capacity to use marketing principles for policy advocacy, and service structure and delivery improvements.

In both our examples, social movements that grow out of micro needs – for colon cancer treatment or to quit smoking – have the potential to develop into much bigger concerns. Their CSM involvement might, for example, alert wealthy Floridians to the inequities of a privatised healthcare system that leaves the poor to depend on charity, and encourage them to join forces with their less privileged peers to advocate for a more profound system change. Or the smokers in Moi(s) sans tabac might become more concerned about the predations of young people by the tobacco industry. They might, for example, get 'fired up' about the need to protect the next generation from the trap of nicotine addiction into which they fell. In both cases we can see Albert Camus' ideas coming to life. Refer back to Chapter 9, where we discussed his insight that critical thinking and rebellion help us to realise that many of our problems are shared and so bring us together. He summed this up with the dictum: "I rebel therefore we are" (Camus 2005).

Like all systems approaches, CSM is challenging because the **social mechanisms** at work are complex, dynamic and, echoing David Foster Wallace (see Chapter 2), hidden in plain sight by familiarity. They include communication, language, signs, slogans and symbolic meaning as well as stories, empathy, creativity, learning and skills. As we see in Kiribati, CSM and social movements examples, **shared understandings** and **trust** or at least **mutual co-operation** and **exchange** among individuals are vital to social marketing. Importantly, developing these requires time (refer back to our discussion of relationship marketing in Chapter 2). Social mechanisms, triggered by co-evolution during the development of co-operation, are core to both the emergence of social system infrastructures and the operation of the stakeholders. They frame the processes of localised value-based exchanges and the emergence of self-organised structures at all levels of the focal system.

EXERCISE 11.3 SOCIAL MECHANISMS

Look at an average day in your life and see if you can identify social mechanisms at work? What social mechanisms are absent, broken or not working? Are some social mechanisms better with some groups, such as family and friends?

Your answer should include many of the ideas we have discussed in all the chapters so far, including communication, trust, commitment, exchange, risk, power, co-operation, competition, information, and many more (see Layton 2015 for a full listing of primary and secondary social mechanisms for marketing systems).

So if you want to change a room, a town or a local/regional community, community social marketing is an extremely efficient social marketing focal system approach, which takes the core notion of client and collective orientations but on a broader behavioural and social change agenda. But what if your mission is to change a state, a country or countries? What if you are the social marketing director with a WHO global movement and its 100 cities and towns from 30 countries from Moscow in Russia to Galway, the creative edge of Europe? Or you are working for Healthy Victoria to decrease Obesity in 12 Australian states? Or the UN to tackle climate change? Try Exercise 11.4.

EXERCISE 11.4   FROM SOCIAL MARKETING PLANNING TO *SYSTEMS* SOCIAL MARKETING PLANNING

Revisit the social marketing planning process in Chapter 4, p.86 and, bearing in mind our conversations about joined-up dots, connections, communities, structures and bottom-up mechanisms, put on your systems hat.

With your 'systems' perspective, list any two or three modifications you would make as a social marketing systems manager to get you from Social Marketing Planning (for behavioural change) to *Systems* Social Marketing Planning (for social change).

The full monty: systems social marketing

No doubt you'll have kept exchange and stakeholder analysis with its VETs and VATs from Chapter 4 as central pillars to best practice systems social marketing planning – as is segmentation and targeting and market and client research for a robust evidence base.

From our discussions on competition analysis, supported by strong critical thinking as seen in community social marketing, there's a sense that deep respect for **all the causal dynamics** in the system of interest is also central to the intervention(s) and social progress. So we can get from social marketing planning to *systems* social marketing planning:

1. Expand the traditional situational analysis to a more broadened systems analysis.

2. Incorporate the bottom-up mechanisms from CSM and social movements more explicitly into systems analysis to link the actions of individuals to behavioural patterns of group outcomes.

3. Clearly, when dealing with wicked problems, it is most likely *not* just a single intervention but multiple high-powered interventions or leverage points for deep transformation throughout the system.

4. Initiating, stimulating and implementing new value-based exchange clusters, based on mutuality, morality and self-interest, in any social marketing system takes time and space. But remember the 'timespace' during which you are seeking to alter and adjust the system is the same 'timespace' where change is happening of its very own accord as a result of the underlying dynamics. The only constant in life is change. So ongoing monitoring, listening, learning and adaptation in 'real' time are essential, as seen in Chapter 5.

To motivate a full systems movement for social impact, Layton (2015) eloquently summarises the practice shift that's required – the intervention(s) need to respond to the *heterogeneity*

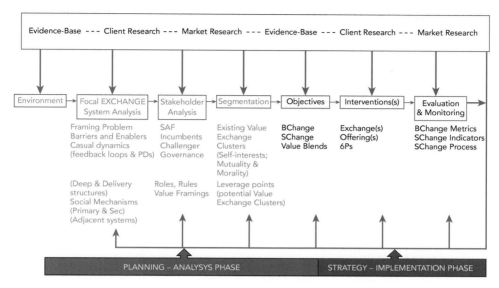

Figure 11.1 Systems social marketing – practice, planning and implementation

(*Source:* adapted from Domegan and Layton 2016)

found in system participants; the intervention(s) need to fit within and be part of the evolution of *behaviours, beliefs and the social practices* that grow out of the changes initiated by the intervention(s), that is, the intervention(s) need to draw on the causal drivers of change found in the *social mechanisms* that are at work; the intervention(s) need to ensure that the politics of the *stakeholders* created or resulting from the intervention are continually favourable; and they need to ensure, through a clear identification of the *localised value-based exchanges* it is hoped will result, that the tangible and intangible infrastructures which emerge from the self-organising networks initiated by the intervention(s) support or enhance their continued success.

We will now unpack the four systems social marketing planning constructs:

1. Situational analysis expands to become systems analysis:

   1.1 Frame the problem – define the focal system of interest, locate adjacent systems, if needed.

   1.2 Identify and analyse the causal dynamics and processes driving change:

   - co-evolution of beliefs, behaviours, practices
   - social mechanisms, linking individual to collective action
   - infrastructure – tangible and symbolic
   - feedback loops generating path dependences.

2. Segmentation: plan a strategic response on the basis of these understandings.

   2.1 Segment the flows of value-based exchanges (self-interest, mutuality and morality values) among system stakeholders and participants as they engage, or not, in exchanges.

   2.2 Segment the system based on leverage points, i.e. potential exchanges for changes that are feasible, impactful and timely to improve the system.

3. The offering/intervention expands to offering(s) or intervention(s)

   3.1 A deep systems intervention may generate enough ripple effects to improve the system.

   3.2 More likely, different but combined and connected initiatives will be required across the system, as one behavioural change initiative will not appeal to all groups and will not generate enough mobilisation or impact to resolve the wicked problem alone.

4. Evaluation and monitoring reflects the real timespace for processes to work across and within the systems. Nothing in life is static; systems are constantly evolving, altering, moving, adapting and rebelling. Sometimes the change is slow, incremental and unnoticed. Other times, the system can take a disruptive jump forward, as is often the case when a new technology emerges. The take-away message for the systems social marketer is simple: systems analysis is ongoing during the implementation phase – recall the conversations regarding formative, developmental and summative research in Chapter 5 – giving rise to indicator monitoring of the forces at work to empower constant adjustments throughout the implementation phase.

While all this sounds linear in the way these processes have been described, each step is interconnected, interdependent and likely to trigger modifications and responses in each other step, both in the focal system, to say nothing of adjacent complementary or competitive systems, all of which the social marketer needs to be alert and sensitive to.

Systems social marketing in practice

Moving on from the theory, we will now take a look at the practicalities of systems social marketing. There are a number of trailblazers in this field already mentioned above including the University of South Florida (USF) and their work on colorectal cancer (CRC) screening (Case Study 17). We will now look at this in more detail.

The five-year goal (2014–2019) of the CDC-funded, academic-community partnership is to identify, tailor, implement and evaluate a multi-level intervention to increase CRC screening. Work began with a systematic literature review, meta-analysis and key informant interviews which highlighted the key barriers/facilitators to CRC screening at the societal/policy, the community, the organisational, the interpersonal and the individual level.

A series of meetings were held with community representatives and stakeholders to understand better the situation. In the first instance, the problem was seen as a 'learning problem' with a need for researchers to work with academic-community partners to help them build a representative model of what was a complex and dynamic situation. The next step was to develop a shared vision and consensus on *what* the problem was and *how* to intervene. The challenges of learning had become those of coordination. The key concerns were about analysis; identifying leverage points, root causes, the best sequence and timing of interventions, and efficient practices (Hovmand 2014). As a result, the system modelling problem of interest was refined to "*How* to increase CRC screening rates to 80% by year 2018 among the priority populations".

The model was constructed at the 'strategic' level with an emphasis on involving community partners in the development, implementation, and scaling-up of a co-ordinated social marketing initiative for the rest of the state of Florida, emphasising the co-ordination and shared insights aspects of bottom-up and top-down change among Florida Prevention Research Center (FPRC) and community partners and American Cancer Society stakeholders. The USF team concluded it is possible that the only way to achieve this academic-community partnership's goal of increasing CRC screening rates to '80 percent by 2018' is to re-frame the situation as a 'transformation' problem, that is, the only solution might involve changing the **structure** of the system that is producing the undesirable dynamics or status quo.

Case Study 2 shows not only *what* the individual and collective barriers for a sustainable marine ecosystem are around Europe, but also *how* these barriers are connected to each other in the different EU contexts, whether one is looking at the problem from a country, regional or sector perspective. Here, Sea for Society translates into involving a vast array of diverse stakeholders from all over Europe from the very beginning, getting them involved in the planning stages, inviting them to help co-define the problem and generating solutions. As a result, 774 barriers and 653 options were generated with different mixtures of barriers and options emerging in the country-specific maps. The various maps identify how important barriers negatively influence each other and how these difficulties are interrelated and connected. The systems of interdependencies provide a contextualised dynamic complexity view of issues as they are perceived by participants and a composite management picture to initiate and manage change. The rich and informative 'Sea for Society' understanding of the causal dynamics at work, country by country, sector by sector, can be used as a strong basis for designing and legitimising synergistic behavioural and social change strategies.

Finally, go to Case Study 24, where programme managers focus on a total hygiene and sanitation approach in their social behavioural work and remove any gender stereotyping on the use of toilets. This is twinned with the financing of toilets with government administrative support to achieve their objectives. A policy of construction of latrines alone, accompanied without a change in the attitudes and social norms surrounding open defecation, would not guarantee latrine use. The guidelines recommend use of community-led and community-saturation approaches for motivating households to construct sanitary latrines, and community-based monitoring and vigilance activities to create peer pressure on the outliers to stop open defecation.

Systems social marketing indicators

Regardless of whether the focal system of interest is a health one such as USF's CRC study in Florida, or the BBC's Media Action role in Making India Open Defecation Free, or an environmental one such as NUI Galway's EU Sea Change project, time is a vital issue. Time enables short-term impacts which can give rise to long-term social change. In the way Childs, Obama, and Rebels with a cause pay attention to motivating a big bottom-up, top-down movement, the systems social marketer must ponder many issues. There's the co-evolution of beliefs, norms, and practices and the generation of new shared understandings. Values and co-operation, together with signalling and information flow, need attention. Finally, social and exchange networks with associated partnerships and alliances to reduce risk and improve choices can spring from the old, flawed system of interest.

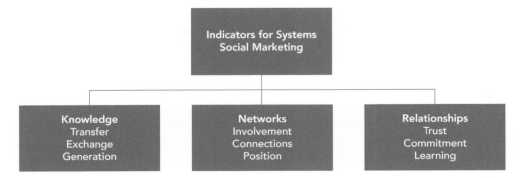

Figure 11.2 Indicators for systems social marketing

(Source: McHugh 2013)

To accentuate systems social marketing in action, Patricia McHugh (2013) explains **indicators** are useful in reducing broad concepts such as 'trust' and 'networks' to measurable forms, while maintaining the bonds between them. The advantage of indicators is that they integrate contributions from diverse parts of the system with dissimilar views, values, backgrounds, experiences, cultures, languages and expectations. There is strong evidence for three particular systems social marketing indicators: knowledge, relationships and networks, all displayed and categorised in Figure 11.2.

Knowledge or learning is a crucial first step in value co-creation and relationship marketing. It's about information acquisition, information dissemination and shared interpretation. The aim is co-learning which involves knowledge transfer as the flow of information from knowledge producers to knowledge users – for example, from researchers and scholars to policy makers and professionals, or from patients to doctors. (Knowledge exchange is shared learning and communication between problem solvers with a propensity to act as seen in Healthy Cities back in Chapter 3, where local police, hospitals, health agencies, retailers and resident communities work together to tackle college binge drinking.) Knowledge generation denotes the tacit and explicit knowledge shared continuously by all actors, that is, the experiential insights from the value-driven exchanges we discussed. Without learning, there can be no value co-creation with clients or stakeholders.

Relationship indicators, as we saw in Chapter 2 and again above, include trust and commitment. Finally, *network* involvement is about the identities, status, resources, access and other stakeholder characteristics.

To see systems indicators at work, go to Case Study 21. Sea for Society partners and associated partners, a total of 70 participants, completed an online survey of pre-validated scale items for demographics, relational processes, knowledge processes and networking processes. Partners and associated partners involved in Sea for Society showed high levels of agreement with the relationship outcomes of trust, commitment, learning and reciprocity. There was an overall positive attitude to sharing knowledge, generating knowledge and exchanging information and partners, and associated partners recognised the importance of networking and building networks. All three system indicator constructs – relationships, knowledge, and networking – were important to Sea for Society and its systems change. Network Involvement, one of the networking indicator dimensions, is the only indicator that does not exert any impact or predict any relationship in the empirical model.

As social marketers, what is important for us to remember is that our own and our clients' struggle to change is never isolated from society's efforts to transform. Indicators are our reminder and measurement of this big picture and how 'Rebels with a cause' can change the world.

Wrap-up

Listening to and learning from the people we want to work with, whether we term them consumers, clients, target groups or citizens, is the *sine qua non* of social marketing (Hastings, 2011). Nowhere is this better reflected than in *social marketing which sees both the individual and wider society as the client*. We call this 'systems social marketing', and the causal dynamics driving, or not, the value-based exchanges lie at the heart of the endeavour.

For any large-scale change to happen, there needs to be a co-operative system of values in place – people need to work together to agree on 'what really matters'. This is community social marketing at work, with its capacity to solve local problems by teaching community stakeholders social marketing principles and skills.

Systems social marketing expands this joint behavioural change agenda beyond the client and the community to larger networks of stakeholders. In this way, and propelled by networked partnerships of shared values, systems social marketing strategies can genuinely start to address the broad challenges of societal change presented by wicked problems. It deals with George Orwell's conundrum (see Chapter 8) and addresses both the individual and the systemic. Above all, it provides the necessary complexity and sophistication we need to tackle the great multifactorial problems – most notably global warming – that humankind now faces.

Reflective questions

1. Explain in one or two sentences, in your own words, each of the key words at the beginning of this chapter.
2. What has systems thinking to do with behaviour change?
3. Define what a 'system' is and list five systems you currently experience as part of your life.
4. Explain the key characteristics of community social marketing.
5. Describe the primary and secondary social mechanisms with examples from the real world around you.
6. What are the steps in social marketing planning? What are the steps in systems social marketing planning? Where are the steps similar and where are they different? Can you explain why these differences exist?
7. How can behavioural change be related to social change in social marketing?

8. Map two exchange clusters you are currently part of.
9. Map a value-based exchange network, web or cluster for a profit and a non-profit entity of your choice.
10. Define the term indicator. How might indicators be useful to the social marketer? List three systems social marketing indicators.

Reflective assignments

1. Make sure you are comfortable with the content of this chapter by writing a concise paragraph, in your own words, about community social marketing and systems social marketing.
2. Using the framework in Figure 11.1, identify the co-creation of value exchanges that an organisation of your choice successfully completes. Also outline the value-based exchange activities that the organisation does not perform well and consider why.
3. Locate and critique social marketing examples that include community social marketing.
4. You have been hired by the Alzheimer's Society to design a systems social marketing intervention aimed at farmers over the age of 65 with no family history of dementia. Specifically, the society wishes such individuals to undertake self-check for dementia and for farmers to be more proactive in seeking help/medical advice, if required. What might be the pitfalls facing you?
5. Go to www.euro.who.int/en/what-we-do/health-topics/environment-and-health/urban-health/activities/healthy-cities and investigate Healthy Cities. What hallmarks of systems social marketing does Healthy Cities display?
6. Go to the *Journal of Social Marketing* or *Social Marketing Quarterly*, and download and read an article on systems science to challenge your thinking on this topic.
7. Develop your own 'Rebels with a cause' checklist for systems social marketing.

Note

1   Sources: www.youtube.com/watch?v=QhWDFgRfi1Q and www.ibtimes.com/fired-ready-go-edith-childs-who-coined-slogan-obama-08-excited-clinton-2441838.

References

Anker, T. and Kappel, K. (2011) 'Ethical challenges in commercial social marketing', in G. Hastings, K. Angus and C.A. Bryant (eds) *The Sage Handbook of Social Marketing*, ch. 9. London: Sage.

Brennan, L., Binney, W., Parker, L., Aleti Watne, T. and Nguyen, D. (2014) *Behaviour Change Models: Theory and Application for Social Marketing*. Cheltenham: Edward Elgar. Brennan, L. and Parker, L. (2014) 'Beyond behaviour change: social marketing and social change', *Journal of Social Marketing*, 4(3).

Camus, A. (2005) *L'Homme Révolté, folio essais*. Espagne, p. 8. GH ref

Carvalho, H. and Mazzon, J. (2013) 'Homo economicus and social marketing: questioning traditional models of behavior', *Journal of Social Marketing*, 3(2): 162–175.

Cherrier, H. and Gurrieri, L. (2014) 'Framing social marketing as a system of interaction: a neo-institutional approach to alcohol abstinence', *Journal of Marketing Management*, 30(7–8): 607–633.

Churchman, C.W. (1967) Guest Editorial: 'Wicked Problems', *Management Science*, 14(4): Application Series, pp. B141–B142.

Corner, A. and Randell, A. (2011) 'Selling climate change? The limitations of social marketing as a strategy for climate change public engagement', *Global Environmental Change*, 21: 1005–1014.

Dibb, S. (2014) 'Up, up and away: social marketing breaks free', *Journal of Marketing Management*, 30(11–12): 1159–1185.

Domegan, C., Collins, K., Stead, M., McHugh, P. and Hughes, T. (2013) 'Value co-creation in social marketing: functional or fanciful?', *Journal of Social Marketing*, 3(3): 239–256.

Domegan, C. and Layton, R. (2016) 'Disruptive Social Marketing – Managing Complexity for Better Civil Engagement', ERSI 'Beyond Behaviour Change', Bristol, 1 December.

Fitzgerald, C. (2015) 'A Community Ready for the Future? A Social Marketing Study of Meals on Wheels Services in Ireland', PhD thesis, National University of Ireland, Galway, Ireland.

Fligstein, N. and McAdam, D. (2012) *A Theory of Fields*. Oxford: Oxford University Press.

Fry, M.L., Previte, J., and Brennan, L. (2017) 'Social change design: disrupting the benchmark template', Journal of Social Marketing, 7(2): 119–134.

Gray, R. J., Hoek, J. and Edwards, R. (2016) 'A qualitative analysis of "informed choice" among young adult smokers', *Tobacco Control*, 25(1): 46–51.

Hastings, G. and Domegan, C. (2014) *Social Marketing: From Tunes to Symphonies*, 2nd edn. London: Routledge.

Hedstrom, P. (2005) *Dissecting the Social: On the Principles of Analytical Sociology*. Cambridge: Cambridge University Press.

Hillebrand, B., Driessen, P.H. and Koll, O. (2015). 'Stakeholder marketing: theoretical foundations and required capabilities', *Journal of the Academy of Marketing Science*, 43: 411–428

Hoek, J. (2016) 'How Could Social Movements Promote Tobacco Endgames?', 41st Macromarketing conference paper presentation, Critical Social Marketing Track, Trinity College, Dublin, Ireland, 14 July.

Hovmand, P. S. (2014) *Community Based System Dynamics*. New York: Springer.

Jenks, B., Vaughan, P.W. and Butler, P.J. (2010) 'The evolution of Rare Pride: using evaluation to drive adaptive management in a biodiversity conservation organization', *Evaluation and Program Planning*, 33: 186–190.

Layton, R.A. (2014a) 'On the (Near) Impossibility of Managing a Macromarketing System', in *Macromarketing and the Crisis of the Social Imagination*, Proceedings of the 39th Annual Macromarketing Conference (edited by Alan Bradshaw, Mikko Laamanan and Alex Reppel), pp. 731–739.

Layton, R.A. (2014b) 'Formation, growth and adaptive change in marketing systems', *Journal of Macromarketing*, published online 22 September. DOI: 10.1177/0276146714550314.

Layton, R.A. (2015) 'Formation, growth, and adaptive change in marketing', *Journal of Macromarketing*, 35(3): 302–319.

Langford, R. and Panter-Brick, C. (2013) 'A health equity critique of social marketing: where interventions have impact but insufficient reach', *Journal of Social Science and Medicine*, 83(April): 133–141.

McHugh, P. (2013) 'The Use of Social Marketing and Innovation Theory for the Development of Process Indicators for Science Communication'. PhD thesis, National University of Ireland, Galway, Ireland.

Mitchell, M. (2017) 'What is Complexity?', Unit 1, *Introduction to Complexity*, Complexity Explorer, Santa Fe Institute, USA.

Rundle-Thiele, S.R. *et al.* (2013) 'Social Marketing: Current issues – future challenges', in K. Kubacki and S.R. Rundle-Thiele (eds) *Contemporary Issues in Social Marketing*. Newcastle upon Tyne: Cambridge Scholars Publishing.

Stead, M., Gordon, R., Angus, K. and McDermott, L. (2007) 'A systematic review of social marketing effectiveness', *Health Education*, 107(2): 126–191.

Quested, T.E., Marsh, E., Stunell, D. and Parry, A.D. (2013) 'Spaghetti soup: The complex world of food waste behaviours', *Resources, Conservation and Recycling*, 79: 43–51.

The Omidyar Group (2017) 'Why we need systems practice', Systems Practice: An approach to move from impossible to impact. https://model.report/s/ioneib/systems_practice_an_approach_to_move_from_impossible_to_impact (accessed February 14th, 2017).

Case study

1

A wicked problem and the SIMPle solution

Sinead Duane, Christine Domegan,
Aoife Callan, Sandra Galvin,
Martin Cormican, Kathleen Bennett,
Andrew W. Murphy and Akke Vellinga

Introduction

Antibiotics can be both a necessary and a lifesaving treatment option. However, after years of overuse and misuse of this once miracle drug, we are entering a new era where antibiotics will no longer work to cure infections. There are currently no new antibiotics under development. Antibiotic resistance (ABR), the term used to describe when an antibiotic has lost the ability to kill a bacteria effectively, is a major threat to public health. The consequences of ABR are far-reaching and include for example increased cost of illness through treatment failure and prolonged illnesses. Antibiotics make the treatment of infection possible and as ABR reaches critical levels action is urgently required to address this public health risk.

Situation analysis

ABR is a wicked problem and although it is having a major impact on our health, causes are far-reaching and span beyond our health system to sectors such as agriculture, veterinary, food production and public policy. There is little consensus between the major stakeholders from these sectors on how best to tackle the problem. For example ABR can spread through our consumption of antibiotics, be passed from person to person as we share bacteria, and can be directly and indirectly passed through our water system. As such ABR contributes to a collective action problem whereby the more we use antibiotics the greater the consequences (Anomaly 2013); an holistic collaborative approach is required to begin the change process (Duane et al. 2015; Edgar *et al.* 2009). Scientific discovery and changes in behaviour at an individual, community and population level must play a role in the solution (Amyes 2000).

This case study focuses on addressing ABR in our health system, and more specifically antibiotic prescribing by general practitioners (GPs) in the community.

Segmentation: ABR and general practice

GPs have been recognised as one contributor to the problem of ABR due to the over-prescription and inappropriate prescription of antibiotics (Cunney 2001; Lipsitch and Samore 2002; Vellinga *et al.* 2011; Wise *et al.* 1998). Examining the issue at a local level, Ireland is one of only three countries in Europe where outpatient antibiotic prescribing is increasing (Vellinga *et al.* 2010). Here, 80% of antibiotic prescribing takes place in the community by GPs (Murphy *et al.* 2011). Therefore improving the quality and quantity of antibiotic prescribing at this level will have a positive impact on the overall ABR issue. A major challenge however, is that many GPs and patients do not see ABR as a reason to stop using antibiotics (Costelloe *et al.* 2010). GPs can also feel pressurised by patients to prescribe an antibiotic (Public Health England 2010). We also know from previous research that although antibiotic prescribing guidelines are available in Ireland, in the case of urinary tract infections (UTI), less than 40% of antibiotic prescriptions for UTIs were according to those recommended (Vellinga *et al.* 2012). UTIs are the second most common infection presented in primary care and ABR is impacting on their treatment. UTIs are often treated empirically. This means that GPs make the decision to treat a UTI based on their clinical experience and the interaction with the patient, i.e. the symptoms the patient describes as opposed to waiting on the results of a microbiological analysis that confirms the infection which can take a few days to receive.

Although the researchers were aware that GPs were inappropriately prescribing antibiotics, we needed to understand why and in what circumstances they were deciding to do so.

Formative research

Rigorous formative research was instrumental in designing this social marketing complex intervention as well as its recruitment and retention strategies. The formative research explored the culture of antibiotic prescribing and consumption in the community for UTI from the perspective of both the GPs (*n* = 15) and community members (*n* = 6 community focus groups with 42 participants). It identified key barriers and facilitators to change. The topic guides were developed in consultation with a multidisciplinary team of experts and a review of the literature. Two decision-making theories also guided the development of the topic guide and the analysis process. The Trans Theoretical Model (TTM) (Prochaska and Velicer 1997) and the Buyer Behaviour and Decision Making Model (Howard and Sheth 1969) were adopted to understand the interrelating contextual factors and processes which contributed to the decision to prescribe or consume an antibiotic. Table CS1.1 summaries the key questions discussed.

Table CS1.1 Summary of key questions discussed within this research

GP Interview Questions	Focus Group Questions
Section 1: Usual practice for treating a UTI	**Section 1: General Health and GP Consultations**
Can you talk me through how you would normally diagnose someone with a UTI? What treatment do you recommend, how do you make this choice? Please describe the role of the patient in the diagnosis?	Activity to establish participants' health-seeking behaviours and current relationship with GPs
Section 2: Antibiotics	**Section 2: Awareness of Antibiotics**
Overall, what are your views on prescribing antibiotics? Positive/negative aspects? Do these views change for a UTI patient? Have you ever received any guidelines on prescribing antibiotics? Can you remember what the guidelines are? Do they include UTI? How did you feel about using these guidelines in practice?	Can you explain to me what an antibiotic is? Have you been prescribed any kind of antibiotic in the past year? Did you ask your GP/doctor any questions relating to the prescription? Can you describe the benefits and consequences of taking an antibiotic?
Section 3: Antimicrobial Resistance	**Section 3: Urinary Tract Infections Experiences and Associations**
Are there any adverse side effects to prescribing antibiotics? Do you know what the antimicrobial resistance patterns are in your area?	Scenario-based exercise describing symptoms experienced by a typical UTI patient. Discussions of personal experiences of having a UTI and the actions taken throughout the illness. Has anyone here ever experienced a Urinary Tract Infection (UTI) or known someone that has had one – what words or phrases would you associate with it? Please describe the steps you go through when deciding to go to see your GP and key priorities.

	Scenario-based exercise to discuss association between UTI illness and antibiotic.
Section 4: Intervention Design	**Section 4: Antibiotic Resistance**
Discussion of possible strategies to facilitate changing their attitudes and behaviours towards prescribing antibiotics for UTI.	Have you ever heard of the term 'antimicrobial resistance'? What does it mean to you? In what context did you hear it?
	Section 5: Intervention Design
	Discussion of possible strategies to facilitate changing their attitudes and behaviours towards consuming antibiotics for UTI.

(*Source:* Duane et al. 2016)

The results of the formative research and its influence on the design on the intervention are summarised in Table CS1.2. Although the UTI consultation itself was quite routine, the decision to prescribe or consume an antibiotic for a UTI is a set of complex interacting processes. The interaction between the GP and patient both at the time of consultation and from previous experiences was instrumental in determining its outcome – whether the patient received an antibiotic or not. Additionally, not every GP or patient were at the same stage of change. For example, some GPs were confident in prescribing an antibiotic for every suspected UTI they saw (habitual prescriber – pre-contemplator). Other GPs tried to avoid immediate antibiotic treatment by suggesting delayed treatment, whereby the patient waits to see if their symptoms improve for a few days before considering antibiotic treatment (questioning prescriber – contemplation/action).

Three profiles of patients emerged from the research; the young professional (quick fixers – pre-contemplation), the young mothers (advice seekers – contemplation/action) and the mature patient (experienced consulters – precontemplators). Each type of patient could be satisfied differently by the GP from a 'simple' UTI consultation. The 'quick fixers' adopt a low involvement approach and are satisfied to receive their antibiotic prescription. The 'advice seekers' adopt a higher involvement perspective, discussing treatment options for their illness; an antibiotic is not a satisfactory outcome in all instances. Finally, the experienced consulters have experienced a UTI and antibiotic treatment in the past, reinforcing the norm and expectations of treatment. In all cases, the GP's decision-making power hinges directly on the type of patient consulting for a UTI and vice versa. The findings indicated the interaction within the consultation and dialogue between the GP and patient which activate the outcome (Duane *et al.* 2016). As with other research, the GPs interviewed favoured an intervention that would support their skills (Velasco *et al.* 2012) and would not have a major impact on the duration of the consultation as time was also an important factor. GPs would not participate in an intervention if it unnecessarily elongated the consultation – which was usually short and straightforward. Focus group participants wanted a conversation with the GP about their illness and the treatment options available (Duane *et al.* 2013, 2016).

SIMPle intervention

Combining what we knew from the situational analysis with what we found in the formative research, the 'Supporting the improvement and management of prescribing for urinary tract infections' (SIMPle) study was designed by a team of multidisciplinary researchers. Our team combined knowledge and expertise from social marketing, health economics, microbiology, general practice and epidemiology to design this successful intervention. GPs were prioritised as the target of the SIMPle intervention as they were the gatekeepers who gave patients access to antibiotics through prescribing. SIMPle focused on the interaction between the GP and patient within the UTI consultation.

Objectives

SIMPle's overall aim was to design, implement and evaluate the effectiveness of a complex intervention on GP antibiotic prescribing and adult (18 years of age and over) patients' antibiotic consumption when presenting with a suspected UTI. More specifically we sought to increase the number of first-line antibiotic (nitrofurantoin) prescriptions, as recommended in the *Guidelines for Antimicrobial Prescribing in Primary Care in Ireland* (2011), for suspected UTIs in primary care by 10% in adult patients (Duane *et al.* 2013).

Intervention design

The SIMPle intervention was a three-arm cluster randomised control trial (RCT). Behavioural change was analysed at a general practice level and therefore involving all GPs within each of the 30 practices recruited was important. The 30 recruited general practices were randomised to one of the three intervention arms. Arm A (*n* = 10 practices) assessed improved antibiotic prescribing according to national guidelines; Arm B (*n* = 10 practices) improved antibiotic prescribing with the suggestion to delayed antibiotic treatment where appropriate; the control arm (*n* = 10) usual care. SIMPle incorporated four phases; Coding Workshop, Interactive Workshop, Patient Support and Follow-up. Figure CS1.1 illustrates a logic model of the SIMPle intervention.

Marketing mix

Product

In phase 1, the coding workshop, all GPs within participating practices were taught to code UTI patients (U71) within their patient management software. GPs would have been familiar with the concept of coding consultations for chronic illnesses, however not all GPs coded every consultation. They were less likely to code acute illnesses such as UTI. Demonstrating to the GP how to code UTI patients (U71) ensured they became familiar with the process and could ask the researcher any questions relating to coding. UTI consultation coding was important for a number of reasons. Firstly, it ensured accurate practice audit and feedback reports were generated, and secondly, it also helped to maintain accurate patient records. Consultation coding allowed the researchers to electronically extract consultation data to evaluate changes in antibiotic prescribing within participating practices.

Table CS1.2 Summary of results from formative research

Theme	Community member	GP	Influence on intervention design options
Knowledge of antibiotic resistance (ABR)	• Knew what ABR was but found it difficult to define or explain • Discussed becoming immune to antibiotics • Women were interpreted to be more knowledgeable than men • Believed antibiotics would always be available	• Knowledgeable about what it is and what contributes to it. • Focus on long term consequences • Overprescribing contributes to ABR • Other sectors had a role to play	• Simplify key messages and information • Reinforce short term consequences for patients
Treatment of UTI	• Severity of symptoms previous experiences and personal circums-tances • Antibiotic prescription was not a satisfactory outcome in all cases, patients also needed reassurance	• Common, easy to treat infection • Prescribed the same antibiotic routinely- could not recall why • Received no guidance on the impact it has on ABR • Dipstick impacted on the GPs decision to prescribe	• Different types of patient emerged, therefore it is not possible to satisfy everything each needing a different conversation • Keep the simplicity of the consultation • Review antibiotics prescribed • Provide evidence for change • Communication and interaction could impact on treatment

(continued)

Table CS1.2 (continued)

Theme	Community member	GP	Influence on intervention design options
The consultation	• Medical card status influenced when the patient decided to consult • Past experience developed expectations • Patients interpretation of a satisfactory outcome depended on past experience and knowledge • Satisfaction associated with consultation length, the duration, closeness of relationship and communication. • Wanted a conversation with their GP in relation to treatment	• Quick, easy uncomplicated consultation • Unpredictable nature • Wanted patients to be satisfied with outcome	• Integration into routine care • Focus on the interaction within the consultation • Facilitate a conversation
Time	• Different profiles of patient had different interpretations of time. Needed to get back to health quickly vs wanted. Reassurance on the duration of symptoms	• Many determinants of time impacted on consultation past experience with patient, busy waiting rooms, interpretation that UTI were easily treated	• Integration into routine care • Could not elongate the consultation
Intervention components	• Wanted material to be easy to understand • Mate sure it was relevant to them	• Wanted patients to be satisfied with outcome • Valued feedback on prescribe behaviours from experts	• Provide GP with evidence • Focus on interaction between GP and patient

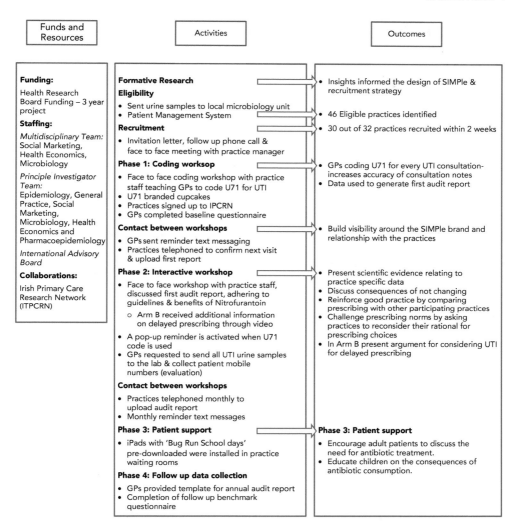

Figure CS1.1 SIMPle logic model

(*Source:* Duane et al. 2017)

Phase 2 began with an interactive workshop. Formative research uncovered issues which impacted on what antibiotic the GP chose to prescribe, the duration of the antibiotic and habit – they prescribed the same antibiotic each time. Practices in intervention arm A and B received information on the national antimicrobial prescribing guidelines and a factsheet outlining the importance of prescribing Nitrofurantoin (the only first line antibiotic the researchers were recommending). This factsheet emphasised the correct dosage and duration of the antibiotic prescription and current levels of community resistance. Practices were also given their first audit and feedback report. This report was very concise (two pages) but contained the evidence the GPs said they required to persuade them to change their antibiotic prescribing behaviours. The audit and feedback report illustrated what the practice

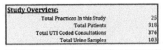
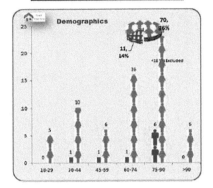
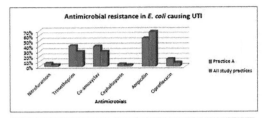
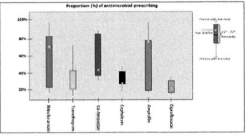

Product – Audit and feedback report

Supporting the Improvement & Management of Prescribing for UTI

Treatment of UTI in Primary Care

✓ **Nitrofurantoin** is recommended as a first line antibiotic for the treatment of UTI in adult patients (www.antibioticprescribing.ie)[1].

✓ Currently only 4% of *E. coli* causing UTI in the west of Ireland are resistant to **nitrofurantoin**. This is in contrast to 30.5% for co-amoxyclav, 30.5% for trimethoprim and 8.3% for ciprofloxacin[2].

✓ Resistance to **nitrofurantoin** is difficult for bacteria to maintain and does not spread within bacterial communities as readily as resistance to other antibiotics[2,3].

✓ Research has demonstrated that the uniform use of **nitrofurantoin** for treating UTI can be as effective as other antibiotics but dramatically reduces drug costs[2].

Product – Nitrofurantoin factsheet

Figure CS1.2 Examples of intervention material

was currently prescribing compared with other participating practices and the levels of ABR in their area. Presenting the GPs with an audit and feedback report at this stage allowed them the opportunity to examine what they were prescribing. Practices were encouraged to discuss the prescribing decisions they were making. They could also benchmark themselves against other practices in their area (Figure CS1.2). Therefore the GPs became aware of where changes could be made. By providing the practices with these reports we saved the GPs a lot of time as these could be used to fulfil their professional competency requirements. GPs also received CPD (continuing professional development) points for participating in the workshops.

The intervention practices received a monthly audit of their antibiotic prescribing for UTI by email. To standardise the intervention, control practices received a workshop which focused on their coding routine.

During the interactive workshop practices in intervention arm B also received additional evidence to support delayed prescription of antibiotics for suspected UTI. The GPs were also shown a video demonstrating how to have a conversation with patients about delayed pre-scribing (www.youtube.com/watch?v=4gFUNTP4DsM).

All GPs who coded UTI consultations U71 within their patient management software sys-tem received a reminder (electronic prompt) outlining the national antibiotic prescribing guidelines (including the web link www.antibioticprescribing.ie). For practices in arm B the reminder also urged the GP to consider delayed prescribing.

Phase 3 (Patient Support) introduced our award-winning multimedia application which included a game for children and an infomercial for adults addressing antibiotic awareness (Bug Run School Days; see www.youtube.com/watch?v=wecthQ7Md-Q). Bug Run School Days was designed to support prescribers and patients to begin the conversation in relation to the issue of ABR. It was was installed in the waiting room on an iPad which was supplied to participating general practices. Phase 3 was not introduced in the control practices.

After the six-month intervention period (phase 2 and 3), control practices were offered a workshop in which all the supporting materials to create an audit report were presented. At the end of the intervention, control practices received all the intervention material as well as their audit report.

Phase 4, the follow-up period, started at the end of the intervention and included a five-month period of passive data collection to evaluate sustainability (Vellinga *et al.* 2015).

Place

The SIMPle intervention was designed to be implemented within general practice in Ireland. SIMPle was conducted within 20 general practices, and an additional 10 general practices were recruited as control practices. Recruited general practices were required to use the same patient management software. This allowed the researchers to develop electronic prompts (reminders of recommended guidelines) within their patient management system which was activated when the GP coded the UTI patient U71. It also allowed for the electronic extrac-tion of patient information.

SIMPle was designed so that it could be implemented into routine care and sustainability was emphasised. All intervention components were implemented within each general practice at a time that was convenient. The researchers made appointments before each point of contact. Change was measured at practice level and therefore it was important that all GPs within participating general practices engaged with the researchers.

Figure CS1.3 UTI Diary app and patient text messages

Table CS1.3 Summary of the SIMPle marketing mix

	Marketing mix			
	Product	Place	Price	Promotion
Phase 1: Coding workshop	• Demonstration of how to code UTI patients (U71) within the GP patient management software	• In practice – appointments were scheduled at the convenience of practice staff	• Time – to participate in the workshop and to code thereafter • Rewarded at the end with accurate feedback reports • GP received CPD recognition	• Highlighting to the GPs that they needed to code to receive accurate audit and feedback reports • Factsheet on how to code within their patient management system • Cupcakes with U71 included on them • Access to coding demonstration video • Monthly text messages to the GPs to remind them to code U71 • Posters for waiting room informing the patients that an intervention was taking place
Phase 2: Interactive workshop	• An interactive workshop consisted of: • Presentation of what SIMPle was about • First audit and feedback report • GPs were encouraged to openly discuss their prescribing choices across phase 1 period – why they prescribed specific antibiotics	• In practice – appointments were scheduled at the convenience of practice staff	• Time – to participate in the workshop and prescribe antibiotic at every point • To reconsider their prescribing choices	• Monthly text messages to the GPs to remind them to code U71 • Pop-up enabled-reminding the GP of what to prescribe once they coded UTI patient U71 • Monthly audit and feedback report which included SIMPle branding • Sent a Christmas card from SIMPle team

(continued)

Table CS1.3 *(continued)*

Marketing mix			
Product	Place	Price	Promotion
• Nitrofurantoin mythbuster factsheet • In addition GPs in arm B received: • A video demonstrating how to begin a conversation with patients on delayed prescribing		• GP received CPD recognition	• Monthly telephone call from SIMPle team to receptionist to download study data • Patient information leaflet • CPD sign-up information
Phase 3: Patient Support • iPad with Bug Run School Days and infomercial uploaded was installed in waiting rooms	• Practice waiting rooms	• Free of charge	• Bug Run School Days and infomercial branded and continuously played • Practice visit to ensure no issues were arising • Monthly telephone call from SIMPle team to receptionist to download study data
Phase 4: Follow-up • Practices asked to continue coding U71		• Continue coding	• Practices received audit and feedback report made available • Monthly telephone call from SIMPle team to receptionist to download study data

Price

The formative research highlighted that time was a big pressure for the GPs, both in their general working environment and within individual consultations. Therefore we used this as leverage for exchange. By coding their UTI patients U71 we were able to remotely extract UTI patient data – this saved the GPs time spent in inputting data. It also allowed us to generate their practice-specific audit and feedback reports. The more the GPs coded the more comprehensive their reports were.

Promotion

The researchers developed the SIMPle logo which emphasised to the GPs that only a simple transition was needed to improve their treatment of UTIs. The researchers ensured that the branding for the study was consistent at any point of contact with the GPs, from the audit and feedback reports to sending the practices Christmas cards. We even brought cupcakes with us to the initial workshops to reinforce the study's message – to code UTI patients U71. GPs were also sent text messages on a monthly basis to remind them of the study and what they had been asked to do.

Evaluation

The medical research council in the United Kingdom describes complex interventions as "interventions that contain several interacting components" (Medical Research Council, 2006, p.7) that by their very nature are difficult to design and evaluate. Rigorous quantitative and qualitative research was central to the success of every aspect of the SIMPle study. In line with best practice, our research strategy was designed and published as a study protocol prior to the commencement of SIMPle (Duane et al. 2013). Our protocol outlined our intervention design, what change we were measuring (primary and secondary outcome measures), the methodology we were planning to use, and our analysis strategy.

Meticulously designing our study protocol at the beginning had its advantages. For example, it allowed us to design a remote electronic data collection system which helped reduce the data collection burden on participating practices. This system was based on consultation coding – a concept most GPs were familiar with even though they may not have been using it. By integrating our data collection system into the practices' existing patient management software we were able to reduce errors associated with manual data entry and preform additional analysis on our results (Galvin et al. 2015; Vellinga et al. 2015). We were also able to focus on very specific research questions, i.e. what type of antibiotic GPs were prescribing for UTI and the frequency of prescription? We also had an opportunity to adopt novel approaches to overcome hurdles that took place when trying to collect data from acute patients, i.e. UTI patients who may visit the GP once but should not have to reconsult. As part of SIMPle we developed both a two-way text message evaluation system and an award-winning smartphone application to collect data from patients in the days after their reconsulation (www.youtube.com/watch?v=nW-Od-yC30Y&feature=youtu.be). Both methods focused on patient symptoms (see Figure CS1.3) (Duane *et al.* 2007). It also allowed us to look at additional research questions such as reconsultation rates between male and female UTI patients (Tanden *et al.* 2016).

Outcome evaluation

SIMPle's primary objective was to improve the quality of antibiotic prescribing for UTI patients according to guidelines. The results are discussed extensively elsewhere (Vellinga *et al.* 2015). In summary, an absolute increase in the quality of prescribing of 20% was achieved for practices in the intervention arms, and patients attending an intervention practice were twice as likely to receive a prescription for a first-line antibiotic for their UTI as those attending a control practice. This change was 10% greater than anticipated. The changes made within general practices during the SIMPle intervention period were also sustained during the five-month follow-up period. This indicator of success highlights that it is possible to improve the quality of antibiotic prescribing in general practice by designing interventions which reflect real-life practices and the needs of the audience, in this case using interactive workshops and practice-specific audit and feedback reports.

Although this intervention successfully improved the quality of antibiotic prescribing, an unanticipated consequence of the intervention was that the amount of antibiotic prescriptions increased during the intervention period (Vellinga *et al.* 2015). This may be associated with message framing, however more research is needed to fully explain why.

Although RCTs are an excellent method of measuring the efficacy of new drugs, the complex nature of behavioural-related health research leads to methodological difficulties, as researchers underestimate the importance of the person and the process in the behavioural change activity. Their classic experimental design makes it difficult for their application to be transferred outside the trial setting, and this observation raises questions as to whether they are an appropriate method to evaluate complex interventions which involve multiple components interacting together within a specific environment (Stead and McDermott 2013). Taking SIMPle as an example, the researchers were able to identify a positive improvement in the quality of antibiotic prescribing. However, the increase in quantity is harder to explain. To help with understanding the impact of such changes a process and economic evaluation were also undertaken.

Process evaluation

Our process evaluation provided insights into the observed effects of introducing different intervention components which could help when rolling out SIMPle in the future (Duane et al. 2017). A process evaluation was conducted consisting of face-to-face interviews with GPs (n = 15), telephone interviews with patients (n = 12), and observation throughout the intervention period. The results of this evaluation are published elsewhere, however SIMPle was successful because it was built into routine care, we provided scientific evidence to support the changes we were implementing through practice-specific audit and feedback reports, and the intervention did not increase GP workload or overly burden the GP.

Economic evaluation

Funders may look beyond clinical effectiveness when deciding to fund the implementation of changes within clinical practice. Expected cost effectiveness may also be taken into consideration when deciding the sustainability of complex interventions. Therefore the cost effectiveness of SIMPle was also assessed as part of the suite of evaluation activities which were integrated (Gillespie *et al.* 2016).

Conclusion

To date the SIMPle study is the largest non-pharmaceutical trial to have taken place in Ireland. It was successful on a number of fronts. Firstly, due to the rigorous formative research and situation analysis the researchers recruited all 30 general practices within a two-week period. This is a very short recruitment period. All practices were retained for the duration of the intervention – we developed an intervention which rewarded the GPs with something they valued, i.e. an audit and feedback report. The change observed was double what we had estimated and changes in prescribing behaviours were sustained five months after the intervention period had finished. We even had general practices contacting us requesting further studies.

This was the first time that an electronic data extraction system had been implemented in a trial in Ireland – again this method was valuable as it was easy for GPs to use and reduced the data collection burden of participating in a study. Consultation coding (U71) resulted in over 3000 UTI patients' data being electronically extracted during the intervention period: data from these patients made it easier and more efficient to evaluate changes in the quality of antibiotic prescribing during the SIMPle intervention.

This case study has described the steps taken within the design, implementation and evaluation of the SIMPle study, and how the choices made throughout this process positively and negatively impacted on the emerging results. The testing of such interventions has been identified as a weakness of social marketing in the past, which often rely on interviews and focus groups to evaluate change activities (Rundle-Thiele *et al.* 2013). The SIMPle complex intervention was an RCT. This is a gold standard evaluation method which is frequently used in the health domain to measure the effectiveness of clinical outcomes, e.g. the type of antibiotic prescribing undertaken by GPs (Oakley *et al.* 2006). It is important that social marketers apply such rigorous evaluation methods to ensure the sustainability of our change activities in the future (Gordon *et al.* 2006; Rundle-Thiele *et al.* 2013).

For a summary of the SIMPle intervention visit www.youtube.com/watch?v=buyeYTt1uQs.

Acknowledgements

The authors would like to acknowledge the participation and support of the staff of the 30 general practices who took part in the SIMPle study and all patients who participated in the provision of data and in the formative research. The authors also acknowledge the staff of the Galway University Hospital laboratory. Practice data collection was facilitated through the Irish Primary Care Research Network (IPCRN). We would also like to thank the Health Research Board for funding the SIMPle project.

Case study questions

1. SIMPle successfully improved the quality of antibiotic prescribing within participating practices, however it also resulted in an increase in prescribing. What changes in the strategy design would you implement to prevent this from happening?

2. Like the SIMPle research team, you have been tasked with evaluating a similar social marketing intervention. Design and describe how you would undertake a process evaluation to analyse the interaction between intervention components.

3. SIMPle's intervention components were constrained as it was an RCT. Now that we have shown favourable results describe how you would scale your social marketing activities up and out.

References

Amyes, S. (2000) 'The rise in bacterial resistance: Is partly because there have been no new classes of antibiotics since the 1960s', *British Medical Journal*, 320(7229): 199.

Anomaly, J. (2013) 'Collective action and individual choice: rethinking how we regulate narcotics and antibiotics', *Journal of Medical Ethics*, 39(12): 752–756.

Costelloe, C., Metcalfe, C., Lovering, A., Mant, D. and Hay, A.D. (2010) 'Effect of antibiotic prescribing in primary care on antimicrobial resistance in individual patients: systematic review and meta-analysis', *British Medical Journal*, 340(c2096).

Cunney, R. (2001) *Strategy for the Control of Antimicrobial Resistance in Ireland (SARI)*. Dublin: National Disease Surveillance Centre.

Duane, S., Callan, A., Galvin, S., Murphy, A.W., Domegan, C., O'Shea, E., Cormican, M., Bennett, K., O'Donnell, M. and Vellinga, A. (2013) 'Supporting the improvement and management of prescribing for urinary tract infections (SIMPle): protocol for a cluster randomized trial', *Trials*, 14(1): 441.

Duane, S., Domegan, C., Callan, A., Galvin, S., Cormican, M., Bennett, K., Murphy, A. W. and Vellinga, A. (2016) 'Using qualitative insights to change practice: exploring the culture of antibiotic prescribing for urinary tract infections: The SIMPle Study', *British Medical Journal Open*, 6(1).

Duane, S., Domegan, C., Callan, A., Galvin, S., Cormican, M., Murphy, A.W. and Vellinga, A. (2017) 'Changing antibiotic prescribing in general practice: the results of the SIMPle process evaluation', *International Journal of Healthcare*, 3(1): 68.

Duane, S., Domegan, C., McHugh, P., Devaney, M. and Callan, A. (2015) 'Tomorrow's world: collaborations, consultations and conversations for change', Ch. 15 in W. Wymer (ed.) *Innovations in Social Marketing and Public Health Communication*. Heidelberg: Springer.

Duane, S., Tandan, M., Murphy, A.W., Vellinga, A. (2017) 'Using mobile phones to collect patient data: lessons learned from the SIMPle study', *JMIR Research Protocols*, 6(4): 61.

Edgar, T., Boyd, S.D. and Palamé, M.J. (2009) 'Sustainability for behaviour change in the fight against antibiotic resistance: a social marketing framework', *Journal of Antimicrobial Chemotherapy*, 63(2): 230–237.

Galvin, S., Callan, A., Cormican, M., Duane, S., Bennett, K., Murphy, A.W. and Vellinga, A. (2015) 'Improving antimicrobial prescribing in Irish primary care through electronic data collection and surveillance: a feasibility study', *BMC Family Practice*, 16(1): 77.

Gillespie, P., Callan, A., O' Shea, E., Duane, S., Murphy, A.W., Domegan, C., Galvin, S. and Vellinga, A. (2016) 'The cost effectiveness of the SIMPle intervention to improve antimicrobial prescribing for urinary tract infection in primary care', *Journal of Public Health*, 1–8.

Gordon, R., McDermott, L., Stead, M. and Angus, K. (2006) 'The effectiveness of social marketing interventions for health improvement: what's the evidence?', *Public Health* 120(12): 1133–1139.

Howard, J. A. and Sheth, J.N. (1969) *The Theory of Buyer Behavior*. New York: Wiley.

Lipsitch, M. and Samore, M.H. (2002) 'Antimicrobial use and antimicrobial resistance: a population perspective', *Emerging Infectious Disease*, 8(4): 347.

Medical Research Council (2006) 'Developing and evaluating complex interventions: new guidance'. Online at: www.mrc.ac.uk/documents/pdf/complex-interventions-guidance/ (accessed 18 March 2017).

Murphy, M., Byrne, S. and Bradley,C.P. (2011) 'Influence of patient payment on antibiotic prescribing in Irish general practice: a cohort study', *British Journal of General Practice*, 61.

Oakley, A., Strange, V., Bonell, C., Allen, E., Stephenson, J. and Team, R.S. (2006) 'Health services research: process evaluation in randomised controlled trials of complex interventions', *British Medical Journal*, 332(7538): 413.

Prochaska, J.O. and Velicer, W.F. (1997) 'The transtheoretical model of health behavior change', *American Journal of Health Promotion*, 12(1): 38–48.

Public Health England (2010) 'Health matters: antimicrobial resistance'. Online at: www.gov.uk/government/publications/health-matters-antimicrobial-resistance/health-matters-antimicrobial-resistance (accessed May 2017).

Rundle-Thiele, S., Kubacki, K., Leo, C., Arli, D., Cairns, J., Dietrich, T., Palmer, J. and Szablewska, N. (2013) 'Social marketing: current issues and future challenges', in S. Rundle-Thiele and K. Kubacki (eds) *Contemporary Issues in Social Marketing*. Newcastle upon Tyne: Cambridge Scholars Publishing.

Stead, M. and McDermott, R. (2013) 'Evaluation in social marketing', in G. Hastings, K. Angus and C. Byrant (eds) *The SAGE Handbook of Social Marketing*. London: Sage.

Tanden, M., Duane, S., Cormican, M., Murphy, A.W. and Vellinga, A. (2016) 'Reconsultation and antimicrobial treatment of urinary tract infection in male and female patients in general practice', *Antibiotics*, 5(3): 31.

Velasco, E., Ziegelmann, A., Eckmanns, T. and Krause, G. (2012) 'Eliciting views on antibiotic prescribing and resistance among hospital and outpatient care physicians in Berlin, Germany: results of a qualitative study', *British Medical Journal Open*, 2(1).

Vellinga, A., Cormican, M., Hanahoe, B. and Bennet, K. (2011) 'Antimicrobial management and appropriateness of treatment of urinary tract infection in general practice in Ireland', *BMC Family Practice*, 12.

Vellinga, A., Galvin, S., Duane, S., Callan, A., Bennett, K., Cormican, M., Domegan, C. and Murphy, A.W. (2015) 'Intervention to improve the quality of antimicrobial prescribing for urinary tract infection: a cluster randomized trial', *Canadian Medical Association Journal*, 188(2): 108–115.

Vellinga, A., Murphy, A.W., Hanahoe, B., Bennett, K. and Cormican, M. (2010) 'A multilevel analysis of trimethoprim and ciprofloxacin prescribing and resistance of uropathogenic Escherichia coli in general practice', *Journal of Antimicrobial Chemotherapy*, 65(7): 1514–1520.

Vellinga, A., Tansey, S., Hanahoe, B., Bennett, T., Murphy, A.W. and Cormican, M. (2012) 'Trimethoprim and ciprofloxacin resistance and prescribing in urinary tract infection associated with Escherichia coli: a multilevel model', *Journal of Antimicrobial Chemotherapy*, 67(10): 2523–2530.

Wise, R., Hart, T., Cars, O., Streulens, M., Helmuth, R., Huovinen, P. and Sprenger, M. (1998) 'Antimicrobial resistance: is a major threat to public health', *British Medical Journal*, 317(7159): 609.

2

Seas of energy

Using a systems research approach for a wicked problem

Patricia McHugh, Christine Domegan,
Marzia Mazzonetto, Sinead Duane,
John Joyce, Michelle Devaney,
Michael Hogan, Benjamin J. Broome
and Joanna Piwowarczyk

Introduction

Planet Earth and all mankind depend on the ocean and its marine resources for their survival. The health of the human race and the sea are inextricably intertwined: around half of the oxygen we breathe is produced by marine plants and phytoplankton; the seas account for 71% of our planet's surface and contain 97% of our planet's water. According to the European Commission's EU Blue Growth programme (2012), the 'blue' economy represents 5.4 million jobs and generates a gross added value of almost €500 billion a year, with further growth possible. In Europe, the fishing industry employed 141,110 full-time equivalent jobs in 2011, had a fishing fleet of 84,909 vessels with a total gross tonnage of 1.8 million tonnes, and had an overall production value of around €23 billion (Joyce 2012). Furthermore, the ocean provides a whole range of services that are important for human safety and health.

In the words of the European Marine Board (2013: 4), "the marine environment contributes significantly to human health through the provision and quality of the air that we breathe, the food we eat, the water we drink and in offering health-enhancing economic and recreational opportunities". These are critical components contributing to and accelerating Europe's wicked marine problem. This case study – Sea for Society – uses Interactive Management (IM), a group methodology, to uncover the barriers contributing to a wicked problem, and it also identifies and prioritises solutions that can assist in the design of future social marketing interventions.

Problem definition

The seas are immense, but their resilience, and that of marine ecosystems, are not unlimited (Joyce 2012). Society either ignores or is ignorant of the fact that our behaviours are threatening the health of our seas, leading to their gradual deterioration by pollution, coastal development, logging, dredging, ocean acidification, waste dumping and overfishing. Despite the importance of Europe's sea area, it is under increasing threat from environmental pressures, including wind and ocean energy, aquaculture and the exploitation of mineral resources, all of which exert environmental pressure leading to the continued deterioration of our seas.

So what does this mean for social marketing? And what makes this a wicked problem? One of the factors that makes this a wicked problem is the fact that European citizens are not fully aware of the true extent of the medical, economic, social, political and environmental importance of the sea to Europe and indeed to the rest of the world. Furthermore, stakeholders have conflicting understandings of what constitutes a sustainable marine resource. Together, society's conflicting misunderstandings and awareness issues perpetuate the complexity of Europe's wicked marine problem, as no single person, entity or country has the resources or the expertise to bring about lasting social change. This case study showcases a methodology, using a systems approach for Sea for Society, to reach effective systemic resolutions using collaboration and dialogic efforts on the part of each stakeholder group, by providing insights into their current values, attitudes, behaviours and actions to co-design, co-create and co-deliver solutions for social and collective action (Duane *et al.* 2016; Gordon and Gurrieri 2014; Hastings and Domegan 2014; Kania and Kramer 2011).

Competitive analysis

Man and nature compete as "no area of the oceans remains unaffected by human activities" (McKenzie-Mohr *et al.* 2012: 109). Following a comprehensive literature review, this study identifies six behavioural factors that emphasise Europe's wicked marine problem. These include the sea as (1) a place to live, (2) a source of food, (3) a means of transport, (4) a source of energy, (5) a support for human health, and (6) a place for leisure and tourism (see Figure CS2.1). All six behavioural factors are interconnected, and only by understanding the barriers to, and opportunities for, each behavioural factor, can an effective mobilisation strategy be put in place to move towards a 'Blue Society' in which humankind lives in sustainable harmony with the sea.

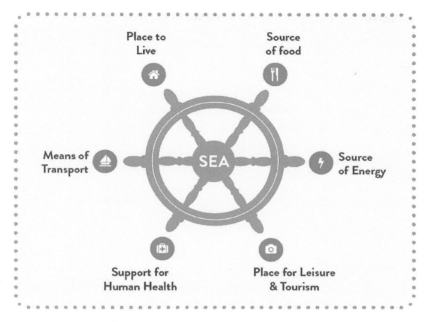

Figure CS2.1 Competing factors

Stakeholder analysis

Stakeholders in this study are classified as primary (p), secondary(s) or influencers (i). Primary stakeholders are defined as those groups whose economic and societal welfare was dependent on the oceans, e.g. fishers, aquariums, naval service and city councils. Secondary stakeholders are those whose economic and societal welfare was dependent on the economy of the primary stakeholders, e.g. hotels, beach artists and environmental agencies. Influencers are those who influenced activities in the ocean but are not dependent on the sea for their economic and societal welfare, e.g. researchers, the media and the government. Judgemental sampling frames were compiled and agreed by multi-disciplinary expert panels in each of the European countries drawing upon secondary sources, e.g. national databases, commercial listings and trade publications. In total, 249 stakeholders across eight countries were recruited to participant in the study.

In addition, as it was not possible to examine all six of the competing factors from Figure CS2.1 in each of the European countries involved, this study identified three Geographical Forums (GF): the Atlantic Region comprising of France/Belgium, Ireland and Portugal; the Baltic Region with Sweden and Poland;and the Mediterranean region including Greece, Italy and Spain. Each country within each of the Geographical Forums was assigned two factors to examine. In order to capture the geographical differences, each factor was applied to three different regions of Europe, based on geographic spread/shared waters, so that all six behavioural factors were covered per Geographical Forum (see Table CS2.1 below) without duplication. In total, 16 workshops would be held across Europe to examine the behavioural factors across the three Geographical Forums.

Table CS2.1 Geographic distribution of theme subjects for consultation

GF 1 – Atlantic Region	GF 2 – Baltic Region	GF 3 – Mediterranean Region
France/Belgium	*Sweden*	*Greece*
Human Health/Energy	Human Health/Energy	Transport/Leisure and Tourism
Ireland	*Poland*	*Italy*
Food Supply/A Place to Live	A Place to Live/Leisure and Tourism/Food Supply	Food Supply/Energy
Portugal		*Spain*
Transport/Leisure and Tourism		Human Health/A Place to Live

Aims and objectives

The overall aim of this study is to bring together researchers, marine and land-based organisations, government and non-governmental bodies, individuals and youth, in a mutual learning, consultation and joint action programme aimed at laying the foundation for a 'Blue Society'. A Blue Society recognises that "humankind can coexist with, and benefit from the oceans and its resources without harming it" (Domegan *et al.* 2016b).

Specific aims of the study are:

- to outline the steps involved in conducting an Interactive Management stakeholder consultation;
- to identify the barriers to a sustainable marine ecosystem in relation to the behavioural factor energy;
- to generate solutions for a sustainable marine ecosystem in relation to the behavioural factor energy.

Research method

Warfield's Interactive Management (IM) was the chosen research methodology because of its theoretical basis in systems science and sophisticated problem-solving techniques for wicked problems (Warfield and Cárdenas 2002). IM is a methodology which specialises in facilitating group discussion and consensus building. It facilitates the brainstorming of multiple ideas while providing a "roadmap" for strategy development, and has the ability to "collectively visualise the structure of a shared problem" (Domegan *et al.* 2015: 1). Unlike other methodologies such as focus groups, IM focuses on one trigger question, with the stakeholder participants leading the discussion. It allows multiple stakeholders from multiple sectors and settings to work together to solve problems – in this case examining the barriers and benefits to maintaining sustainable marine ecosystems and how they can be overcome from a multilevel perspective.

Data collection

The stakeholder consultations consisted of four steps, assisted by interpretative structural modelling (ISM) software.

Step 1: Idea generation

At the beginning of each consultation, facilitators provided the context of Sea for Society and defined what they meant by sustainable marine ecosystems. Stakeholders across France/ Belgium, Sweden and Italy were asked the same trigger question: "What are the barriers to a sustainable marine ecosystem in relation to energy?" The purpose of the trigger question was to stimulate conversation. Stakeholders were supported in generating their barriers with starting statements, such as 'lack of', 'absence of' or 'failure to', and given the opportunity to reflect on the question and think of as many barriers as possible in private. Each stakeholder was then asked to share and clarify each of their barriers before it was placed on a board for discussion. Idea generation continued until no new barriers were identified by the stakeholders.

Step 2: Idea categorisation

Each stakeholder was asked to vote for the top barriers for a sustainable marine ecosystem that emerged in Step 1; this established the top weighted barriers for categorisation. Once the voting process was complete, paired comparison took place, meaning all the remaining barriers were compared with the top weighted barriers. This process continued until categories were formed, usually consisting of at least five barriers. After similar barriers were grouped together, the participants named the category. Once all the barriers were categorised and named, a second round of voting established the primary, most voted for barriers in each category.

Step 3: Structuring barriers

The 12 barriers that received the highest votes were entered into the ISM computer software, where a series of relational questions, "Does Barrier A significantly aggravate Barrier B?", were asked of the stakeholders. A yes/no vote was taken and entered in the software. Structuring continued until all relational barriers were voted upon and structural barrier maps were generated (Figures CS2.2, CS2.3 and CS2.4.).

Step 4: Generating solutions

To conclude the IM consultation, stakeholders were divided into sub-groups to work with two categories from Stage 2. They were provided with the facilitation question "What are the options for overcoming the barriers to energy?", and asked to explain their solutions with the entire group. All stakeholders then discussed the proposed solutions they perceived to be the most feasible, impactful and timely.

Findings

Structural barrier maps and pathways of aggravation

Across the three Energy stakeholder consultations 136 barriers were generated. Table CS2.2 presents a breakdown of the number of barriers generated in each country.

Table CS2.2 Breakdown of barriers generated for the behavioural factor energy

Energy – 136 barriers
Sweden – 60 barriers
Italy – 35 barriers
France/Belgium – 41 barriers

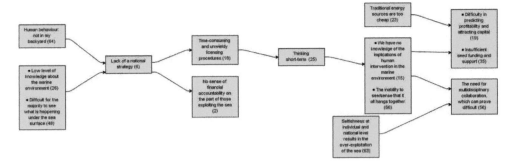

Figure CS2.2 Swedish structural barrier map generated during energy consultation

Figures CS2.2, CS2.3 and CS2.4 provide evidence of the structural barrier maps that were generated from the energy stakeholder consultations in Sweden, Italy and France/Belgium. The structural barrier maps should be read from left to right. Barriers to the left of the map significantly aggregate (make worse) barriers on the right.

For example, in the Swedish map in Figure CS2.2 to address 'Thinking short term' change agents must address the barriers to its left, beginning with the barriers on the far left which cause the most aggravation – "Human behaviour, not in my backyard," "Low level of knowledge about the marine environment" and "Difficulty for the majority to see what is happening under the sea surface."

Five different barrier aggravation pathways are evident in Figure CS2.2 with directional arrows indicating aggravating barriers. Five aggravation pathways exist as not all barriers aggravate each other. For example, "Traditional energy sources are too cheap" does not aggravate "Lack of a national strategy." Barriers grouped together in the same box, such as "We have no knowledge of the implications of human intervention in the marine environment" and "The inability to see/sense it all hangs together" are reciprocally inter-related and significantly aggravate one another.

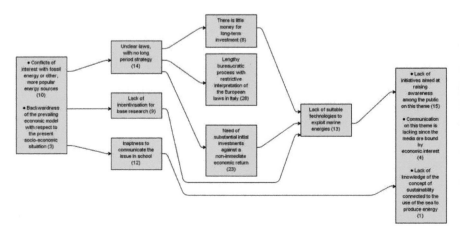

Figure CS2.3 Italian structural barrier map generated during energy consultation

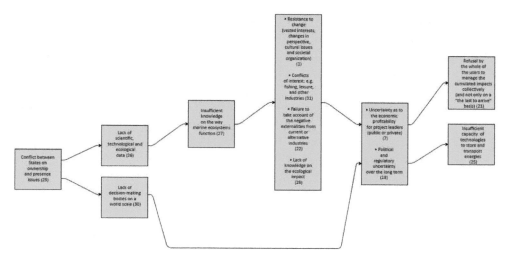

Figure CS2.4 France/Belgium structural barrier map generated during energy consultation

In Figure CS2.3, Italy illustrates another five different barrier aggravation pathways for energy. In this case, "Conflicts of interest with fossil energy or other more popular energy sources" and "Backwardness of the prevailing economic model with respect to the present socio-economic situation" cause the most aggravation for the energy behavioural factor in Italy. In the case of France/Belgium (see Figure CS2.4) one barrier exerts the highest level of aggravation, i.e. "Conflicts between states on ownership and presence issues". Also, France/Belgium exhibits two different aggravation pathways in the same figure.

Value can also be derived from the idea categorisation stage (stage 2) of the IM process where top-voted categories perpetuating energy problems across Sweden, Italy and France/Belgium were identified through voting. Table CS2.3 below illustrates the top three voted categories for energy. Taking these three categories alongside the structural barrier maps provides an understanding of the individual barriers and themed categories accelerating energy problems for a sustainable marine ecosystem.

Options

In the Swedish, Italian and French/Belgian stakeholder consultations, 130 options were generated with Table CS2.3 displaying the top three barrier categories for possible energy interventions - conflict, research and innovation and knowledge deficit. Table CS2.4 presents a breakdown of the number of options generated in each country.

While these 130 options are not to be interpreted as fully designed interventions, taken in conjunction with the structural barrier maps above in Figures CS2.2, CS2.3 and CS2.4, these

Table CS2.3 Top three voted barrier categories for energy

Energy
Conflict (70 votes)
Research and innovation (66 votes)
Knowledge deficit (51 votes)

Table CS2.4 Breakdown of the options generated for the behavioural factor energy

Energy – 130 options
Sweden – 54 options
Italy – 25 options
France/Belgium – 51 options

stakeholder options can be very informative and useful for the design of an intervention strategy. A Sea for Society intervention strategy that aligns with these stakeholders' options is also more likely to receive support across Europe. Table CS2.5 illustrates the top voted options for the conflict, research and innovation and knowledge deficit categories.

Table CS2.5 Top voted for options for energy

Energy	
Top voted barrier categories	Top voted for options
Conflict	• Favour private investment by simplifying the authorisation process, by reducing times and by creating guarantee funds; these should be created by public entities, in order to allow privates to access bank lending (10 votes)
	• Insert in the organisation charts of the decision-making organs some professionals with a good knowledge on the use of the sea as energy source (9 votes)
	• Spreading the concept of a new economy that includes the 'natural capital' in addition to human capital (8 votes)
	• Promote the emergence and development of solutions by the players concerned (8 votes)
	• Accredit conscientious and independent journalists/media (credibility) (8 votes)
Research and innovation	• Identify and promote the services provided by ecosystems (10 votes)
	• Create a national strategy (10 votes)
	• Share the scientific knowledge between economic players and end-users locally (9 votes)
Knowledge deficit	• By developing the concept of environmental accounting, so that both individuals and the community can understand that investing in marine energy will generate savings and will improve life quality (15 votes)
	• Assess the impact on ecosystems including global warming, biodiversity, carbon footprint (13 votes)
	• Promote the ocean through art, increase the number of artistic exhibitions/shows on the various treasures of the seas and the oceans (e.g. the Plankton shows), create 'the *chevaliers de la mer*/knights of the sea' = citizens (model) (9 votes)

These findings acknowledge the multi-faceted nature to energy problems across Sweden, Italy and France/Belgium, and rather than illustrate exact solutions for energy in each country, the options taken in context with the structural barrier maps outline leverage points for energy interventions. Context becomes critical as the barriers driving energy issues vary from country to country, and by consequence a one-size-fits-all solution for each country is impractical and redundant. In Sweden social marketing efforts that connect people with the seas and what's happening under the surface are appropriate to their context, as an intervention of this type can connect society with blue spaces and subsequently tackle conflict and knowledge barriers. Alternatively, in Italy dialogue processes to bring awareness to energy sources can reduce the conflict that co-exists between fossil energy and other more popular sources of energy. In France the level of conflict related to energy is at a macro, policy level, and so any intervention strategy designed to tackle energy issues should acknowledge the role of upstream policy actors, decision makers, regulators and municipalities.

Discussion

Interactive Management is but one systems methodology a social marketer could utilise in problem diagnosis. It is a particularly valuable systems research approach in understanding wicked problems, as the group methodology involves stakeholders from the very beginning – getting them involved in the planning stages, inviting them to help co-define the problem and generating solutions. It gets at multiple interpretations of the same issue for different audiences, how these mental interpretations are connected and interlocked, and how they differ from location to location, sector to sector. Interactive Management offers the potential to move beyond a power-over client orientation to a power-with stakeholder orientation (Domegan *et al.* 2013).

Unlike other qualitative research methodologies that bring together like-minded participants, Interactive Management offers social marketers the advantage to bring together participants from diverse, and even conflicting, backgrounds using nominal group technique. While a diverse group of stakeholders will not agree on all barriers and solutions, Interactive Management "helps focus the group towards a common set of goals, while preserving the individual differences" (Broome 2004: 194).

Interactive Management also encourages dialogical interaction (Ballantyne and Varey 2006), collaborative learning and extended active participation. It helped Sea for Society stakeholders within and across marine ecosystems to "explore critical issues in depth and learn to work together productively" (Broome 2004: 193–194). As a systems research approach it is suitable for social marketing as the theoretical constructs that inform it draw from both behavioural and cognitive sciences, with a strong basis in general systems thinking that is suitable for complex social, ecological and managerial contexts (Domegan *et al.* 2016a).

Case study questions

1. Briefly describe the steps involved in an Interactive Management consultation.

2. Why do you think it is important to classify different stakeholder groups for an Interactive Management consultation?

3. What does Interactive Management as a research methodology offer social marketers that other linear methodologies do not?

References

Ballantyne, D. and Varey, R. (2006) 'Introducing a dialogical orientation to the service-dominant logic of marketing', in R.F. Lusch and S.L. Vargo (eds) *The Service Dominant Logic of Marketing: Dialog, Debate and Directions* (pp.224-235). New York: M.E. Sharpe, Inc.

Broome, B.J. (2004) 'Reaching across the dividing line: building a collective vision for peace in Cyprus', *Journal of Peace Research*, 41(2): 191–209.

Domegan, C., Collins, K., Stead, M., McHugh, P. and Hughes, T. (2013) 'Value co-creation in social marketing: functional or fanciful?', *Journal of Social Marketing*, 3(3): 239–256.

Domegan, C., McHugh, P., Devaney, M., Hogan, M., Broome, B., Duane, S., Joyce, J., Murphy, D., Mazzonetto, M. and Piwowarczyk, J. (2015) 'Advancing Theory and Research in Social Marketing: Interactive Management for Complex Problem Thinking'. Paper presented at the World Social Marketing Conference, Sydney.

Domegan, C., McHugh, P., Devaney, M., Duane, S., Hogan, M., Broome, B.J., Layton, R.A., Joyce, J., Mazzonetto, M. and Piwowarczyk, J. (2016a) 'Systems-thinking social marketing: conceptual extensions and empirical investigations', *Journal of Marketing Management*, 32(11–12): 1123–1144.

Domegan, C., McHugh, P. and Joyce, J. (2016b) *Sea for Society: At a Glance – Conversations, Consultations and Calls for Action*, EU Sea for Society Project, Whitaker Institute, NUI Galway, Ireland.

Duane, S., Domegan, C., McHugh, P. and Devaney, M. (2016) 'Beyond restricted to complex exchanges: the social marketing change agenda', *Journal of Marketing Management*, 32(9–10): 856–876.

European Commission (2012) *Blue Growth – Opportunities for Marine and Maritime Sustainable Growth*. Communication from the Commission to the European Parliament, the Council, the European Economic and Social Committee, Brussels, Belgium.

European Marine Board (2013) *Linking Oceans and Human Health: A Strategic Research Priority for Europe*. Position Paper 19 of the European Marine Board, Ostend, Belgium.

Gordon, R. and Gurrieri, L. (2014) 'Towards a reflexive turn: social marketing assemblages', *Journal of Social Marketing*, 4(3): 261–278.

Hastings, G. and Domegan, C. (2014) *Social Marketing: From Tune to Symphonies*, 2nd edition. London: Routledge.

Joyce, J. (2012) *Toward a Blue Society Summary Report*, EU Sea for Society Project, AquaTT, Dublin, Ireland.

Kania, J. and Kramer, M. (2011) 'Collective impact', *Stanford Social Innovation Review*, 9(1): 36–41.

McKenzie-Mohr, D., Lee, N.R., Schultz, P.W. and Kotler, P. (2012) *Social Marketing to Protect the Environment: What Works*. Thousand Oaks, CA: Sage.

Warfield, J. and Cárdenas, R.A. (2002) *A Handbook of Interactive Management*. Iowa City: Iowa State University Press.

Case study **3**

Meals on Wheels

A community-led approach and stakeholder analysis

Christine Fitzgerald, Christine Domegan and Tom Scharf

Introduction

Meals on Wheels (MOW) services provide nutritional support for older people by delivering either a hot or chilled meal to their home. Currently, MOW services are going through a transitional period, moving away from historical charity origins towards approaches characterised by public–private partnerships of varying kinds in different communities. The service is also tasked with meeting the needs of a growing and diverse client base; the older population aged 60 and over is projected to grow significantly, with the number of older people living in their own homes predicted to double by 2021 (CSO 2013). Such demographic change is likely to increase demand for MOW services. It is in light of these transient complex social issues and community setting that the role of key stakeholders in MOW services to respond to the needs of a growing and increasingly diverse older population is examined and understood.

Problem definition

This research addresses the challenges associated with MOW key stakeholders' behaviours through the application of a community social marketing model: the Community

Readiness Model (CRM). Building on increasing recognition of the value of community-led approaches, this research examines behaviour change from the perspective of a community, rather than the traditional focus on the individual, encompassing the environment in which behaviours occur.

In the domain of social marketing, recognition is growing of the value of community-led approaches in overcoming the challenges associated with traditional social marketing programmes (Bryant *et al.* 2007). Such community-led approaches see community social marketing programmes dominating the literature (Bryant *et al.* 2007; McKenzie Mohr 2000; Plested *et al.* 2006; Stead *et al.* 2013). Community social marketing facilitates an understanding of how the behaviours of community stakeholders can act as benefits or barriers to change. Such a collaborative and community-centred approach enhances the synergy between programmes and communities, where community resources and relationships are strengthened and sustained. Bringing about effective community behaviour change requires the development and management of transformational partnerships with local stakeholders to ensure that communities are actively involved in addressing local issues and in ensuring community needs, barriers and motivators are accurately understood (Jones and Wells 2007; Sprague Martinez *et al.* 2012).

Due to the state of transition in MOW services, these services are currently moving to different variations of a MOW community model, ranging from public–private partnerships to commercially-based MOW services. In light of changes at policy level, coupled with a challenging economic climate which has seen funding cutbacks in the provision of community-based supports, the application of the CRM to the MOW acts as a measure to assess community readiness in the environment where behaviour change occurs. Such community consultation is essential to ensure that MOW are shaped by both users and stakeholders. The application of the CRM to this area provides a systematic approach to measure attitudes, efforts, knowledge and resources within the MOW community, which are key to assessing the community's readiness to change to a more personalised approach. Informed by current thinking in social marketing research, the inclusion of a multi-level perspective in this study extends current approaches; bridging a gap in MOW research by incorporating the perspectives of current, former and potential MOW users as well as those of relevant community stakeholders. The application of the CRM to the MOW community ensures that community-based programmes are successfully implemented and community needs are met; an essential component in the social marketing planning process (Selem 2011).

Incorporating the community mobilisation tool CRM supplemented with a community-led process of mapping, identifying and selecting key stakeholders ensures multi-level perspectives of community, leading to a transferable and systematic process to obtain a representative selection of key stakeholders.

Stakeholder analysis

To overcome a lack of clarity and guidance in the CRM process of identifying key informants, stakeholder theory literature was critically reviewed to assist in establishing a more comprehensive and transparent approach to identifying key informants (Marr 2008; Schwalbe, 2010). The terms 'key informant' and 'key stakeholders' possess similar traits, with the majority of relevant literature existing most commonly using the term 'key stakeholder'. While the literature may have used the term 'key stakeholder', for the purpose of application of the CRM this was adapted to include reference to 'key informants'. Table CS3.1 combines two key stakeholder approaches as outlined by Schwalbe (2010) and Marr (2008), resulting in a more robust process than the original CRM process. This approach was adhered to in this study, making the identification process more systematic, resulting in a more robust list of key informants.

Defining key informants

Based on the CRM literature, a variety of terms exist surrounding the definition of key informant criteria, with definitions varying to include leaders (Plested *et al.* 1998) with others stating that a key informant is not necessarily a leader (Oetting 2001). This lack of clarity and consistency surrounding the definitions of key informants associated with the CRM signified a need for a consistent and more rigorous approach in ensuring accuracy in identifying key informants. This gap in the literature was addressed through the development of a structured and defined step in the CRM process for identifying key informants. When considering who would be a suitable key informant, Oetting *et al.* (2001) suggest keeping the following question in mind: *who would know what is going on in this area?* Key informants should be people who represent different segments of the community. They should be selected from members of the community who know about the problem being examined, existing prevention programmes aimed at the problem, and various segments of community leadership (Plested *et al.* 1998). They should be leaders or working in the community on a day-to-day basis (Plested *et al.* 1998). A key informant is a person who is likely to know about the problem or issue of concern, not necessarily a leader or decision maker. Depending on the problem, different key informants can be used, but they are all going to be people who are involved in community affairs and know what is going on (Edwards *et al.* 2000). Key informants should be selected from community members who know about the issue being examined (Jumper-Thurman *et al.* 2001). Jumper-Thurman *et al.* (2001) discuss how key informants should be in touch with various segments of the community leadership, and would be leaders or professionals working in the community on a daily basis (Jumper-Thurman *et al.* 2001). From this context, a key informant is seen as simply a person who knows the community, knows about the problem or issue and can provide specific data about what is happening in that community (Oetting 2001). The following definition of a key informant was developed and used in this study to best respond to its central research question, i.e. someone who is involved with the MOW community and can provide information about what is happening in that community.

In order to develop a sampling approach for the key informant interviews, the CRM literature was reviewed for guidance and insight from previous applications of this process. However, it was identified that a gap in the literature existed in relation to this crucial part of the CRM process. In light of this, a systematic process for the identification of key informants was developed, which is outlined in Table CS3.1.

The combined approach outlined in Table CS3.1, used to identify key stakeholders in the MOW community, was developed for this study. Through following a series of actions, this approach ensures the systematic identification, mapping and selection of key stakeholders to be involved in conducting key informant interviews in the application of the CRM.

Table CS3.1 Identification process for CRM key stakeholders

Step	Task	Action
1	Identify all stakeholders	Brainstorming session with the community in question
2	Create a stakeholder register	Create a document that contains details of stakeholders identified
3	Identify key stakeholders	Identify key stakeholders based on KII criteria
4	Identify process stakeholders	Stakeholders contributions (Inputs and outputs) are examined
5	Identify a narrow list of key stakeholders	Identify a narrow list of key stakeholders, based on the KII criteria
6	Key stakeholders mapping	Mapping of key stakeholders geographically

(*Source:* Adapted from Marr 2008; Schwalbe 2010)

Mapping key informants

In response to a paucity of a systematic and representative selection process for key inform-ants in the social marketing domain, literature on stakeholder and key stakeholder theory

Table CS3.2 Primary stakeholders and key elements

Stakeholder	Key elements
Customers	Customer relationships essential Need for long-term commitments to nurture relationships Customers must be understood in order to provide a sustainable and relevant service Customer focus
Suppliers	Strong relationships Collaborative culture Good communication
Employees	Central to building customer commitment Customer needs knowledge
Shareholders	Customer satisfaction Loyalty Strong relationships Sustainability
Regulators	Close coordination Responsive
Local Community	Support Trust

(*Source:* Adapted from Hult *et al.* 2011)

was reviewed to assist in the systematic identification of potential stakeholders. Schwalbe (2010) defines stakeholders as people involved in and affected by project activities, including the project sponsor, project teams, support staff, clients, users, suppliers and competition. Marr (2008: 31) defines a stakeholder as 'a person, group of people, or institution that has an investment, share or interest in an organisation and who may significantly influence the success of this organisation'. A systematic approach for identifying key stakeholders was developed based on information drawn from Schawalbe (2010) and Marr (2008). In reviewing literature relating to stakeholder groups, a particularly useful article by Hult *et al.* (2011) was identified whereby an extensive review of 58 marketing articles was conducted, resulting in the identification of the six primary stakeholder groups, customers, suppliers, employees, shareholders, regulators and the local community. Based on the stakeholder literature (Hult *et al.* 2011), Table CS3.2 was developed to ensure that the process of identifying and selecting key informants was done in a systematic and rigorous manner. The process of identifying and selecting key informants as outlined in Table CS3.2 focused on assisting the selection of potential participants to take part in the key informant interviews. Due to the composition of the MOW service, it was not possible for the key informant participants from each of the stakeholder groups identified by Hult *et al.* (2011) to take part in the key informant interviews. This was largely due to the content of the key informant interview, with the focus of the questions not relevant to some of the stakeholder groups, such as suppliers, service users and regulators.

Aims and objectives

- This research addresses the challenges associated with MOW stakeholders' behaviours through the application of a community social marketing model: the CRM.

- Building on increasing recognition of the value of community-led approaches, this research examines behaviour change from the perspective of a community, rather than the traditional focus on the individual, encompassing the environment in which behaviours occur.

- Drawing on research gaps, this research bridges this gap by developing and testing a systematic process to identify stakeholders/key informants for community-based social marketing efforts, based on a review of the CRM literature which is transferable to broader social marketing stakeholder efforts.

Research

The CRM was applied to the MOW community, utilising a three-phased research approach:

Phase One focused on understanding service users' experiences with MOW, allowing for a deeper understanding of the current MOW target audience. Semi-structured interviews were used in this phase in order to gain insight into the MOW service from the perspective of both current and former MOW users, living in both urban and rural geographic areas. Including the perspectives of MOW users in both urban and rural areas allowed for greater insight into the barriers and benefits of MOW use.

Phase Two explored perceptions of MOW from older people who had not previously used MOW services. This second phase consisted of focus groups conducted with people aged 65 and over from the community, who had not used MOW and were therefore seen as potential MOW users. The aim of the focus groups was to gain insight into how MOW are perceived by potential users, and to identify the perceived benefits and barriers to future use of MOW.

Phase Three focused on the key stakeholders involved in the provision of MOW. Through application of the CRM, key informant interviews were conducted using nine-point anchored rating scales to score and ascertain the MOW community's stage of readiness on each dimension. Dimension scores are averaged to provide an overall community readiness score ranging from 1 to 9 (1 indicated no awareness and 9 indicated high levels of community ownership).

Central to the CRM process for this study were consultative processes with the community, with additional semi-structured interviews and focus groups constructed with service users at different stages of service use, to shape and inform the CRM application and the key informant selection process.

Discussion

The resultant systematic process offers a transferable approach to identifying relevant and representative stakeholders across multi-levels, as well as the opportunity to build community capacity while building sustainable efforts for community-based social marketing efforts.

By adhering to a systematic and collaborative process of working with stakeholders, this approach lends itself to a co-creative means of engagement, while providing a transferable means of understanding the different complexities at play in community systems. The community-led process of stakeholder analysis outlined in this case study can be used on its own, or to complement broader social marketing efforts, including use with the CRM, to which it adds an additional step in the CRM process, making the CRM a more systematic tool for wider applications.

Case study questions

1. Outline the rationale for community-led approaches in stakeholder analysis and what benefits these approaches can bring.

2. What gaps were identified in stakeholder theory and what was done to address this challenge?

3. Briefly describe the steps involved in mapping key informants.

References

Bryant, C.A., McCormack Brown, K.R., McDermott, R.J., Forthofer, E.C. and Bumpus, S.A. (2007) 'Community-based prevention marketing: organising a community for health behaviour intervention', *Health Promotion Practice*, 8: 154–163.

CSO (2013) 'Total population by census district in County Galway.' Available at: www.cso.ie/census/table8.htm (accessed 30 June 2017).

Edwards, R.W., Jumper-Thurman, P., Plested, B.A., Oetting, E.R. and Swanson, L. (2000) 'Community readiness: research to practice', *Journal Community Psychology*, 28 (3): 291–307.

Hult, T., Mena, J., Ferrell, O.C. and Ferrell, L. (2011) 'Stakeholder marketing: a definition and conceptual framework', *Academy of Marketing Science*, 1: 44–65.

Jones, L. & Wells, K. (2007) 'Strategies for academic clinician engagement in community-participatory partnered research', *Journal of the American Medical Association*, 297 (4): 5407–5410.

Jumper-Thurman, P., Plested, B.A., Edwards, R.W., Helm, H. and Oetting, E.R. (2001) 'Using the Community Readiness Model in native communities', *Cultural Competence Series Monograph 9*, CSAP and SAMHSA, pp. 129–158.

McKenzie Mohr, D. (2000) 'New ways to promote pro environmental behaviour: promoting sustainable behaviour: an introduction to community-based social marketing', *Journal of Social Issues*, 56(3): 543–554.

Marr, B. (2008) *Managing and Delivering Performance*. Oxford: Elsevier.

Oetting, E.R., Jumper-Thurman, P., Plested, B. and Edwards, R.W. (2001) 'Community readiness and health services', *Substance Use and Misuse*, 36: 825–843.

Plested, B.A., Edwards, R.W. and Jumper-Thurman, P. (2006) *Community Readiness: A Handbook for Successful Change*. Colorado: Tri-Ethnic Center for Prevention Research.

Plested, B.A., Jumper-Thurman, P., Edwards, R. W. and Oetting, E. R. (1998) 'Community readiness: a tool for effective community-based prevention', *Prevention Researcher*, 5(2): 5–7.

Schwalbe, K. (2010) *Information Technology Project Management, Course Technology*. Boston, MA: Cengage.

Selem, M. (2011) 'Examining a Business Community's Readiness to take on Sustainability'. Dissertation, Illinois, University of Illinois.

Sprague Martinez, L.S., Freeman, E. and Perea, F.C. (2012) 'From engagement to action: assessing community readiness for disparities mobilization', *Journal of Health Disparities Research and Practice*, 5(2): 101–112.

Stead, M., Arnott, L. and Dempsey, E. (2013) 'Healthy heroes, magic meals, and a visiting alien community-led assets-based social marketing', *Social Marketing Quarterly*, 19(1): 26–39.

Case study **4**

Reduce Your Juice

A digital social marketing programme for reducing residential electricity use

Rebekah Russell-Bennett,
Rory Mulcahy, Ryan McAndrew,
Tim Swinton, Jo-Anne Little and
Neil Horrocks

Introduction

Reduce Your Juice (RYJ) has transformed traditional energy efficiency programmes into a model that effectively connects with today's digitally connected consumer.

This innovative programme reimagines traditional energy efficiency approaches in a digital world. It incorporates an evolutionary recipe that embraces design thinking, integrated digital channels and a participant-focused experience which has shown impressive results for a part of the market that is growing rapidly – mobile connected consumers. In response to the Australian Federal government's call for programmes that trialled different approaches for assisting low-income earners to reduce their electricity, the Reduce Your Juice project sought to demonstrate the use of a digital approach to energy efficiency engagement. The programme was designed to help 1,000 low-income young adult renters (aged 18–35) across

Greater Brisbane to make better decisions about their energy use in order to become more independent and secure lasting energy savings.

The programme ran for three years from July 2013 through to May 2016 and was valued at $6,448,065, including $5,540,281 from the Australian Government and $1,212,711 from industry. Two waves of consumer engagement occurred between May 2015 and December 2015 which involved participation in a six-week intervention.

This has been a collaborative project that brought together sustainability agency CitySmart, research partner QUT and marketing communication agency BCM Partnership to deliver a successful intervention, showing the importance of building strategic partnerships between industry and the research sector to create innovative, evidence-based outcomes.

Problem definition

Energy bills are one of the largest household expenses for the target group, second only to rent and groceries (ABS 2011). Despite this, energy consumption doesn't rate highly on the agenda of the target group because they have more important, pressing concerns in their life and are therefore not highly involved with their energy consumption. This low involvement means lack of motivation and inertia for altering energy use behaviours even when knowledge of the benefits of changing behaviour is high. The nature of energy consumption itself is problematic in that the target group can't visually see energy being consumed or don't interact with it until they receive their quarterly bill, thus going into crisis mode which typically achieves very little change. The lack of understanding and information means that the target group vastly underestimate the impact of high consumption appliances such as air conditioners, electric hot water and laundry appliances on their energy bills. Indeed, households that participated in the Reduce Your Juice programme reported 40% higher energy bills than the average South East Queensland households.

Energy efficiency is a significant issue for rental households on low, fixed and unreliable incomes. These households are particularly impacted by increases in retail energy prices as a result of poor quality housing, limited ability to reduce energy use through upgrading to more energy efficient appliances and fixtures, and the higher proportion of income they spend on this essential service (ABS 2013).

Young adults comprise over 30% of low-income earners[1] nationally (ABS, 2015) and are not especially targeted by energy efficiency programmes. The opportunity existed to target this emerging group of adults to help establish their behaviour for the future. Evidence suggests that young adults have less energy efficiency knowledge and are less likely to take action, making the challenge more significant. In Brisbane, around 47% of young low-income adults rent their home and budgetary constraints often mean that homes is not energy efficient (ABS 2012).

The background and formative research thus revealed that young low income earners have high electricity bills with a low care factor and short attention span but are hyperconnected.

Table CS4.1 Competitive analysis

Competitive source	Formative research
Competing behaviours	• Electricity use habits that are ingrained and hard to change
Competing benefits and motivations	• Lack of belief that solutions will change anything
	• Lack of care until the bill arrives
	• Electricity bills are controlled by the companies not the consumer
	• Desire for temperature comfort
	• Belief that nothing more can be done
Personal influencers	• Children don't care about the bill and therefore saving electricity
	• The household is rarely united in a quest to lower the use of electricity
Societal influence	• Multiple appliances in the house are the norm even for low-income households
	• Desire by low-income households to have the possessions of middle-class homes (aspirational)
	• Air-conditioning in Queensland is perceived as essential and not a luxury

Competitive analysis

Formative research revealed the following as competitive influences:

Competing behaviours by the individuals themselves. This includes decreasing the temperature of the air-conditioning to keep cool or increasing temperature to keep warm, leaving power switches on, use of high energy appliances such as a dryer or spare fridge.

Competing benefits and motivations for the behaviour. This includes the need for comfort, convenience, minimising effort, status, myths and perceptions, as well as scepticism towards possible solutions.

Personal influencers who provide mis-information or seek to maintain the status quo. In this household this can be children or household members who prefer the competing behaviour. Outside the household this can be friends, family or other reference groups.

Societal influence that maintains the current behaviour. This refers to the standards, culture or social norms that govern electricity use behaviours. This can include the types and number of appliances that are deemed necessary to maintain quality of life and the vigilance with which a household should monitor its usage, as well as general pro-environmental concerns.

Stakeholder analysis

Internal stakeholders included the employees and researchers involved in the three main organisations developing the programme; CitySmart, Queensland University of Technology and BCM Partnership.

External stakeholders included consumers, the federal government department funding the programme and Centrelink, electricity distributors and retailers, electricity consumer groups such as Energy Consumers Australia, media and social welfare groups concerned with the protection of vulnerable energy consumers represented by Queensland Council of Social Service.

Aims and objectives

The programme set out to test and demonstrate:

- the effectiveness of interactive digital learning
- the effectiveness of energy efficiency rewards
- the effectiveness of digital and social communication media
- the cost effectiveness of programme components.

Research questions were developed as the initial step in designing the research approach. The research questions were designed to guide the research design and achieve the project objectives.

Research questions:

1. Can a digital engagement learning programme change energy consumption behaviours?
2. What is the impact of communication and rewards on the energy consumption behaviours of the programme participants?
3. Does a split incentive for participants (a) generate contact with landlords to install energy efficient appliances and (b) result in landlords implementing an energy efficient intervention to gain a rebate?

Research design

The programme employed a combination of approaches including games, communications and rewards to achieve behaviour change. A variety of data were collected from different sources at different points in time to be able to analyse the effectiveness of the trial. CitySmart worked with research partner QUT to develop a rigorous research and evaluation approach for the trial that reflected research best practice. CitySmart then worked with QUT to develop the social marketing strategy to underpin the design of the programme and BCM for the design and implementation of the user engagement strategy through game and integrated digital communications development.

To enable the first stage of the testing of research question 1, mandatory pre- and post-programme surveys were completed by both a control group and intervention group six weeks apart. The pre-programme data provided a baseline to evaluate any changes in energy attitudes, perceptions and behaviours over the programme period. The intervention and control group surveys were completed at two different seasonal points (winter and summer) to account for any temperature effects. The data were analysed using Paired T-tests and repeated measures ANOVA to determine if the changes between time periods were significantly different. Where dichotomous/binary data measured at two time points occurred, such as True or False for questions about Knowledge and Yes or No for Habits, McNemar's test statistic was used to determine if there were statistically significant changes.

Optional online surveys were conducted to provide explanatory data for the research analysis from a sample of participants and were also completed by the control group. These surveys went beyond the three research questions.

As any changes over the six-week intervention period could be attributed to factors other than participation in the RYJ programme, a control group ($n = 734$) with a similar demographic profile was used. This enabled the second and final stage of testing research question 1. The control group completed two surveys six weeks apart however they had no involvement in the programme. The control group was a separate recruitment process to the intervention group and was not a random allocation.

Four distinct treatment groups were used to test research question 2 through difference testing based on the level of communication and type of rewards received by participants. Treatment groupings enable a sound methodological evaluation to compare different aspects of the intervention at multiple data collection points across time and draw on a quasi-field experiment approach.

Research question 3 was tested using data collected by Energex which matched Reduce Your Juice participants with households that participated in Energex's Positive Payback programme.

Digital analytics were also used to monitor participant engagement with the landlord engagement offer during the programme.

Intervention

The programme used a digital engagement approach with a combination of multiple interventions. The learning components were designed to address the barrier of information failure to help participants change their energy consumption behaviour and were delivered using a range of digital channels, including an app with mini-games and a supporting suite of integrated digital communications (email, social media and SMS).

The programme design takes into account the involvement level and nature of energy efficiency for the target group in conjunction with their digital behaviour. Acknowledging the low involvement nature of energy consumption, the programme seeks to stimulate learning and behaviour change via a fun, intrinsically motivating experience which uses a unique blend of games and gamified digital interactions. RYJ uses a mobile-led, integrated digital media approach to deliver bite-sized interactions designed to help participants learn in order to improve their energy usage behaviours.

RYJ trialled the use of energy efficiency product rewards in comparison to other non-energy related 'lifestyle' reward products to address capital constraint barriers. Products are used as rewards for participants who complete designated actions at different points in the programme.

To address split incentive barriers, a landlord engagement component assisted participants to engage their landlords to upgrade their home's energy efficiency, incentivising both parties through rebates.

Theoretical base for intervention

The research insights indicated that a 'behavioural' approach to facilitate learning and change would be more appropriate than a high involvement cognitive approach which relies on thinking and processing information (Skinner 1938). Therefore, a behavioural learning theoretical framework of instrumental (operant) conditioning was selected. This theory posits that individuals are motivated by rewards following a behaviour rather than an information or attitude change. With the target group not being sufficiently motivated to invest time in acquiring knowledge, knowledge and attitude change was unlikely to precede behaviour – instead the behaviour precedes the formation of knowledge and attitudes towards energy. The second theoretical framework used reflected the nature of digital engagement; the experiential learning hierarchy whereby people learn by doing rather than from thinking (Ray 1973).

These two behavioural theories were combined to form a fit-for-purpose programme model to fulfil the project requirements and appeal to the needs of the target group – instrumental learning (where behaviour is shaped through positive reinforcement and reward) (Skinner 1938) complemented by an experiential learning approach (learning by doing) (Ray 1973).

Target behaviours

Methodology adapted from Community Based Social Marketing (CBSM) was used to ensure the intervention would be targeted towards the best areas for change for the target group. A large number of potential behaviours were analysed and scored based on their impact (cost saving), ease of change (including barriers and benefits), and penetration within the target group. The complexity and nature of performing each behaviour were also considered as part of the analysis (e.g. simple, short term, complex, repetitive, long term, or habitual).

Behaviours were shortlisted based on their scores with priority given to the cost benefit and ease/likelihood of performing the behaviour. Following the scoping session, behaviours were logically grouped into three clusters which formed the primary focus for the programme:

Cool

- Use a fan rather than the air-conditioner
- Set your air-conditioner to 24 degrees in summer

Switch

- Switch off lights
- Switch off appliances to avoid standby

Wash

- Use a clothesline or drying rack, rather than the dryer
- Wash full loads of washing
- Wash in cold water

Programme design principles

Based on the research and insights, guiding programme design principles were developed to underpin the development of all aspects of the programme.

RYJ set out to be:

- innovative
- fun and entertaining
- relevant
- easy and informative
- responsive
- positive and helpful.

Games and gamification

The RYJ mini-games form a core component of a broader gamified programme (see Figure CS4.1). RYJ used 'serious games' to virtually engage players to learn about the energy efficiency behaviours targeted. Serious games involve simulations of real world situations to help solve a problem, rather than being a game designed for entertainment purposes. Serious games are particularly relevant given the invisible, intangible nature of energy consumption in the real world. RYJ employed three mini-games to 'virtually' engage participants in the three key areas for behaviour change, using simulation to demonstrate and reinforce energy related concepts such as cause and effect of behaviours on energy consumption.

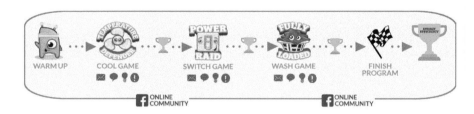

Figure CS4.1 The gamified programme

Note: images of Reduce Your Juice characters are the property of Green Heart CitySmart Pty Ltd and cannot be reproduced without permission

The RYJ programme used a mix of behaviour change tools and techniques including games, gamification, communication and rewards to encourage engagement and progression through the programme.

The game required participants to select a character from the 'Watt Family' as their character (see Figure CS4.2). This created emotional connection with the game.

Figure CS4.2 Reduce Your Juice characters

Note: images of Reduce Your Juice characters are the property of Green Heart CitySmart Pty Ltd and cannot be reproduced without permission

Outcomes

Selecting an appropriate and rigorous evaluation approach is critical for determining the effectiveness of a programme. Many social marketing programmes do not adequately plan or resource the evaluation component which leads to a lack of scientifically rigorous evidence or the measurement of the wrong outputs. The ultimate result of this flaw is an inability to determine if public funding has been well-spent and if the programme has indeed achieved the desired objectives in a credible manner. Thus a significant amount of time and resources was invested in determining the evaluation approach for RYJ.

The approach selected was the logic model (see Figure CS4.3), an approach used by funders of complex social programmes both in Australia and internationally to evaluate the effectiveness of the programme. The model consists of four stages that are causally related; inputs, outputs, outcomes and impact. The first stage is the most controllable and

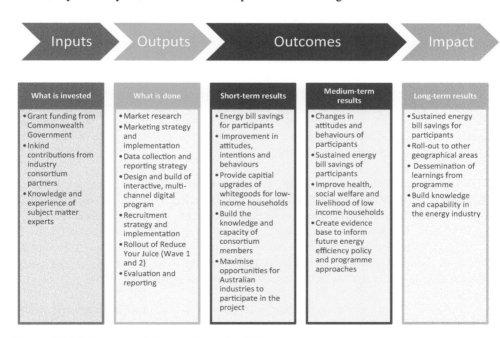

Figure CS4.3 Logic model to evaluate the RYJ programme

is short term while the final stage is the least controllable and is long term. The level of difficulty of measurement increases at each stage of the model. The first two stages inputs and outputs are process measures and should be measured progressively to enable non-linear development. The use of two waves of implementation with the first wave being a smaller pilot enabled process evaluation to be undertaken with adaptive changes made prior to full implementation in wave 2. The second two stages are outcome measures and are the core of overall evaluation.

The key results of the programme were:

- 12.3% improvement in energy consumption on previous year compared to a control group
- $54.82 average saving on quarterly electricity bills ($219.28 annual saving)
- 22.5% improvement in energy habits
- 78% of starters completed the programme
- 97.2% recommended RYJ to friends and family
- significant improvement in attitudes, bill control, self-efficacy.

On a relatively small- scale basis of delivery to 1,000 participants, each dollar invested by the Commonwealth yielded a dollar of benefit due largely to the high set-up cost. The economic viability of a digital approach significantly improves at scale, for example delivery to 10,000 and 100,000 participants would deliver $2.02 and $2.70 in benefits for each dollar invested, thus providing a strong economic case for future investment.

Discussion

The development of a new and innovative programme was full of complexity and risk, however the appropriate resourcing and collaborative, positive approach of the multi-disciplinary team was crucial in delivering a successful final product. The innovative approach of the RYJ programme provided many benefits and expanded the capacity and experience of the participating consortium and partnering organisations. This includes the broadening of knowledge surrounding energy efficiency for young low-income renters, as well as in the delivery of a complex, sophisticated digital solution integrating multiple digital channels to benefit both user experience and research and evaluation.

In developing an innovative programme, the use of agile development techniques and the infiltration of this mindset among the team proved an effective way of managing multiple risks and uncertainty while working towards achieving the programme goals. The use of agile marketing was also effective in testing and refining content and messages with the target group to create a more relevant experience to resonate with participants. Holding the customer at the heart of all approaches proved beneficial for the outcomes of the programme, with strong customer results achieved and positive feedback received.

The programme results reinforce the relevance and usefulness of digital channels applied appropriately to create a meaningful experience for participants, especially surrounding the use of serious games and gamification to change energy related behaviour. The use of fun and entertainment has been shown to be an effective way to help participants learn and change, especially with the mundane, low involvement nature of energy efficiency behaviours. Gamification techniques were especially helpful in bringing together the multiple elements of the intervention into a fun experience for participants designed to elicit action.

Recommendations to take into consideration in the development of future energy efficiency policy and programme approaches include the following:

1. Make digital engagement a part of the Low Income Household approach.

2. Incorporate emerging digital engagement techniques and tools into future programmes.

3. Recognise that trust is a key component to engagement and with new digital engagement tools; trust doesn't need a physical presence.

4. Investigate the economies of scale that can be achieved from widespread implementation of effective digital delivery approaches.

5. Ensure that future energy efficiency programmes incorporate effective collaboration to ensure success.

6. Ensure that energy efficiency programmes include a calculation of the full value chain of energy productivity improvements.

7. Incorporate benchmarking into behaviour change programmes.

8. Recognise the growth in the digitally connected consumer segment.

Case study questions

1. What do you think are the advantages of using a digital approach in a social marketing programme rather than face-to-face?

2. What do you think are effective ways of recruiting people to participate in a digital programme?

3. How can smaller organisations with limited funding offer innovative digital solutions as part of a social marketing programme?

Note

1 A low-income household for this study was defined as a household with income in the bottom two quintiles – below \$50,700 (ABS 2015). The equivalent personal income equated to a maximum of less than \$41,548.

References

ABS (2011) *Household Expenditure Survey, Australia: Summary of Results, 2009–10*. Retrieved from: www.abs.gov.au/AUSSTATS/abs@.nsf/DetailsPage/6530.02009-10?OpenDocument#Data (accessed May 2016).

ABS (2012) *Australian Social Trends, March, Australia*. Retrieved from: www.abs.gov.au/AUSSTATS/abs@. nsf/Previousproducts/4102.0Main%20Features2Marc:h%20Quarter%202012?opendocument&tabname=Summary&prodno=4102.0&issue=March%20Quarter%202012&num=&view (accessed May 2016).

ABS (2013) *Household Energy Consumption Survey, Australia: Summary of Results, 2012*. Retrieved from: www.abs.gov.au/ausstats/abs@.nsf/Lookup/4670.0main+features100032012 (accessed May 2016).

ABS (2015) *Household Income and Wealth, Australia, 2013–14*. Retrieved from: www.abs.gov.au/AUSSTATS/abs@.nsf/DetailsPage/6523.02013-14?OpenDocument (accessed 31 January 2016).

Ray, M. L. (1973) 'Marketing communications and the hierarchy of effects', in P. Clarke (ed.) *New Models for Mass Communications Research*. Beverly Hills, CA: Sage.

Skinner, B.F. (1938) *The Behavior of Organisms: An Experimental Analysis*. New York: Appleton-Century-Crofts

Case study **5**

Innovative youth engagement

Empowerment, co-production and health optimisation (tobacco-free generation 2034: the Fife Project)

Marisa de Andrade, Karen Cooper and Kay Samson

Introduction

The Fife Project seeks to contribute to the creation of an environment that supports young people to choose not to smoke by enhancing their knowledge of the health harms of smoking and reducing the attractiveness of tobacco use. In doing so, the work aims to develop a tobacco-education initiative that is tied to national health policy objectives and outcomes and that can be delivered effectively at a local level.

The project builds upon an innovative research intervention carried out in Fife secondary schools in 2014. Informed by an asset-based approach, co-production and co-design, the

'Pop-Up Radio Project' sought to creatively engage with pupils in Fife's secondary schools in order to explore the impact of two tobacco-education school interventions – Smoke Factor (SF) and Smoke-Free Class (SFC) (see de Andrade 2014; de Andrade, Angus and Hastings 2015). During this project pupils responded positively to informal delivery of the tasks they were set and enjoyed engaging in fun activities. The young people also supported 'getting involved' in sharing ideas for education initiatives and welcomed the idea of making informed choices rather than being told what to do.

In response to these findings, three distinct phases of work were proposed and carried out between July 2015 and March 2016:

Phase (i): An evidence-scan or review of the literature on ways of engaging young people to enhance their choices around tobacco-education initiatives. This was to include asset-based approaches and co-production, alongside a variety of innovative methodologies aimed at empowering young people to make informed choices and decisions about risk and health promoting behaviours.

Phase (ii): Pilot preparation to include a review and discussion of the most appropriate methods of engaging young people on the subject of tobacco-education.

Phase (iii): Design of a framework/toolkit to be used with young people in school classrooms. Building upon the findings and of the previous two phases, this phase of the project aimed to draw together the information in order to develop practical activities and learning outcomes linked to health policy objectives and outcomes.

This case study will both summarise the findings of these activities and provide a detailed overview of how a toolkit for young people might be taken forward and evaluated.

Problem definition

To ensure that the project reflects existing policy aims and objectives it was imperative that the work would be directly linked to local and national priorities. This section outlines some of the key messages to emerge from recent policy documentation.

The programme of sessions outlined in the Fife Project meets the aim of "Getting it right for every child" (GIRFEC), which is to put children and their families at the heart of decision making. GIRFEC supports *asset-based* approaches which encourage young people and communities to come together to achieve positive change by using their own skills, capabilities, resources and experiences of the issues relevant to their lives (Foot and Hopkins 2010; Ripon and Tait 2015). Drawing upon personal and community knowledge, asset-based approaches aim to enhance opportunities for personal health options and choices and create local conditions for health improvement (Morgan and Ziglio 2007).

A Tobacco Control Strategy for Scotland 2013 set in out the actions which it hopes will lead to a tobacco-free generation by the year 2034. The focus of the strategy is to encourage children and young people to choose not to smoke. This includes reducing the attractiveness of tobacco and providing services and support for those who wish to stop smoking. In order to create a tobacco-free generation, a five-year strategy was set out to cover a range of actions across the following themes:

Prevention – creating an environment where young people choose not to smoke.

Protection – protecting people from second-hand smoke.

Cessation – helping people to quit smoking.

This multi-faceted approach seeks to balance a range of national and local actions that complement and reinforce each other. The need to work in partnership and with individuals and communities to achieve health targets is also advocated by the Scottish Government/COSLA.

The strategy draws upon evidence which suggests there are three levels of influence associated with a young person starting to smoke – **individual, personal environment and social and cultural environment**. Effective smoking prevention approaches must therefore address each of these levels. As health behaviours do not exist in isolation, any tobacco-control strategies aimed at young people must also encourage them to negotiate decisions about tobacco, and ensure that these decisions take into account the potential interactions between smoking and other health-damaging behaviours.

Initiatives must also seek to make young people aware of the health harms of tobacco use and must aim to build awareness and support among young people of the health, social, financial and environmental advantages of choosing not to smoke. This includes ensuring that there are continued efforts to reduce the availability, attractiveness and affordability of tobacco to young people. The strategy also highlights that national and international research findings should provide an evidence base aimed at informing the development and delivery of tobacco control policy.

Aims and objectives

The Fife Project:

- is a co-produced schools-based education programme contributing to the creation of an environment that supports young people to choose not to smoke
- enhances young people's knowledge of the health harms of smoking and reducing the attractiveness of tobacco use
- facilities critical thinking
- focuses on solutions (assets) rather than problems (deficits) and is health promoting;
- is comprised of six classroom sessions to be delivered to school-children in S1 (aged 11 to 12 years); these six sessions directly precede a 'competition' activity (for further details see below and Group Activity 9 of the delivery strategy)
- aids young people in developing their understanding of key issues through a series of innovative, co-produced group and individual activities
- inspires creativity, fosters co-working and develops confidence and independence of thought.

Research

Recent policy and research debates around the health and wellbeing of young people have identified the need to examine effective youth strategies and explore the role of adolescents in designing and delivering services. The ways in which young people might be empowered to collaborate with and co-produce health education and smoking education programmes is of particular significance. The international literature will guide the development of the Fife Project by ensuring that evidence-based decisions are made regarding the use of effective engagement activities.

A bibliographic search was carried out in December 2015 across eight academic databases. Due to the extensive literature base and fast-paced nature of policy-focused research, the search was restricted to international peer-reviewed literature, written in English and published between January 2005 and December 2014. Key search terms were selected in relation to a range of youth health and smoking-related criteria and also to reflect the involvement of adolescents and community members in the design and delivery of initiatives. In total, 127 records met the criteria set by the reviewer and were included.

The review sought to explore the range of existing opportunities for youth smoking prevention and the predominant strategies used by practitioners. Four 'types' of initiative were identified: school-based programmes; community-based programmes, media-based programmes and programmes targeting specific youth groups and/or vulnerable young people.

Factors influencing the development, design and success of projects were explored and the existing research on theoretically-designed programmes was outlined, including young people's decisions to engage in programmes and their perceptions and management of their health and risk-taking. Central to this was the idea that people's health is interdependent and can transcend the individual. Attention was primarily drawn towards the influence of peers on smoking, risk and health. The findings lend support for family peer and community involvement to ensure there is exposure to a variety of people, activities, and social groups in order to guide and encourage behavioural change.

To develop an evidence base of effective programmes, attempts were made to explore 'what works' in youth initiatives. A key focus was the role of young people in designing and implementing initiatives and peer-led and youth involvement in programme delivery, including working as peer educators, mentors, role models, buddies, advisors or collaborating in youth partnerships.

Adolescent participation also included 'youth voice' via participation in the development and design phases of intervention. This could include focus or advisory groups, role playing or problem solving. Such activities provide a means of ensuring that an intervention is culturally and social relevant. They also help foster respectful relationships and provide young people with the development of individual skills, including competence, social and cognitive development and feelings of usefulness. Involving young people in participatory research was also highlighted as a viable means of encouraging co-design and co-evaluation.

Technology-driven interventions have gained recent popularity and provide new and innovative ways of working with young people. These include social media campaigns and digital and visual media. The need for messages and programmes to be relevant, believable and enjoyable was highlighted as a means of fostering co-design and co-evaluation, and a positive way of enhancing participation and retention on programs.

The findings suggest a need for locally/culturally tailored and targeted interventions that offer a comprehensive, multifaceted, multichannel approach (Small *et al.* 2013) and are open to incorporating young people's perspectives, needs and preferences. Evaluations support the use of a collaborative, youth-centred approach which draws upon well thought-out methods of delivery and theoretically informed aspects of design (Robinson and Vale 2012; Baker *et al.* 2012).

In light of information gathered across the review, the following recommendations are offered:

i) *There is a need to address the social and relational contexts of health behaviours.*

The research suggests it is important to explore young people's own frames of reference around health issues in order to better understand how social relationships might help empower and motivate positive changes. Central to their needs is having supportive people and communities around them, most notably their peers. This is in line with previous reviews and studies which suggested a young person's peers, and their corresponding social identity, are by far the most significant factor linked to teenage smoking practices (Heikkinen *et al.* 2009; Lee *et al.* 2014). Drawing upon an integrated and interrelated social approach to understanding health behaviours will ultimately enable programmes to be socially marketed to appeal to and effectively communicate with youth sub-groups and ensure that young people's needs are more adequately addressed via focused resources and crafted, authentic messages (Lee *et al.* 2014).

ii) *There is a need to listen to community and youth-identified needs: co-production and empowerment.*

Listening to and collaborating with community members and young people provides opportunities to better understand the foundations from which young people's health behaviours are established and carried out. There is a need to learn from individual experiences, access local resources, appreciate personal perspectives on health and create spaces for young people to voice their concerns (Baker *et al.* 2012; Erbstein 2013; Fields *et al.* 2014: 313).

Interventions based on diffusing behavioural changes and group practices may also work best in well-defined close communities, where peer supporters are in regular contact with members of a stable community (Starkey *et al.* 2009). Developing programmes by and within social identity groups not only provides a recognition of existing social networks, community and cultural knowledge (Erbstein 2013), but crucially also creates opportunities to share reciprocal knowledge and information at all levels and stages of the project, from initial focus groups to gather information on ideas and concepts, to testing and development, implementation and delivery. Engaging in the co-production of activities with young people means that by listening to their ideas and setting programme agendas youths can be reframed as active designers in creating programmes and as genuine collaborators in the production of effective interventions, rather than passively serve as the recipients of educational programmes. Such approaches ultimately provide ways of reaching out to vulnerable, diverse and multi-ethnic youths whose own needs, choices and support structures may vary widely. Listening to ideas about relevant cultural and community needs will only enhance the potential for capturing young people's interests and tapping into their behavioural norms.

iii) *It is important to customise and tailor interventions to meet the contemporary needs and preferences of young people.*

Across a variety of health domains, adolescents have highlighted their preferences for message content and presentation. Indeed, as Remafedi and Carol note, 'the vehicle of prevention is as important as the message' (2005: 254). There is strong evidence to suggest that multi-media campaigns may be effective in reaching young people and in making programme content accessible and relevant. This might mean either designing a stand-alone intervention resource or embedding a programme within existing social networking platforms. Social media for health promotion can provide a cost-effective, convenient and easy means of generating, sharing and receiving digital content and health information across a diverse group of individuals. In particular, messages involving digital media that interface with social media like Facebook, Twitter and YouTube offer the potential to vary and personalise programme content and select relevant components in order to create individually tailored programme appeal (Whittaker *et al.* 2008).

iv) *Programmes should seek to engage with young people in programme evaluation.*

Prior systematic reviews have reported recurring methodological limitations of programme evaluations, including high rates of attrition and small sample sizes (Bryant et al. 2011). However, in order to understand the potential effectiveness of interventions, evaluations should aim to explore the mechanisms of change as well as potential outcomes. To understand how and why studies 'work' there is a need to incorporate formative process evaluations to ensure that feedback can be immediately referred to policy makers, practitioners and programme developers in order to enhance the likelihood of effective content, implementation and delivery. Central to this approach is the need to incorporate on-going evaluative work with young people. This ensures that researchers can be aware of local impact effects and culturally specific understandings of programme implementation. Furthermore, listening to and acting upon young people's feedback will not only help ensure that future programmes are suitable and relevant but also will ultimately provide more favourable opportunities for youths to translate and feedback the findings within their community. This can only serve to increase the likelihood that young people will be pro-active in making well-informed positive decisions about their health.

The Fife Project

Drawing upon the policy literature helps to guide the development of the Fife Project by ensuring that appropriate information is included in the design and effective communication activities are devised. This includes communicating any knowledge in a style and format that reflect the needs of the target audience and make the learning opportunities enjoyable. Engaging young people in this process will ensure their views are listened to and taken on board throughout the design, development and implementation stages.

At a local level, the aim of Fife's health and wellbeing strategy is to support organisations and partnerships to promote ways of working to support good health. In particular, it highlights that good social and community networks and participation in developing initiatives can help to build better health and stronger communities. It further supports the need for activities that will build skills, resources and knowledge to enable individuals to take control of their own health. Incorporating individual, group and community tasks within the Fife Project will help increase the young people's knowledge about the inter-related nature of health.

In light of local strategic priorities which aim to support individuals to make healthy decisions and improve opportunities for wellbeing, the activities within the Fife Project will encourage adolescents to interpret and analyse information, to be creative, and to work with each other and their teachers to co-ordinate and develop ideas and to promote better choices for themselves and their peers. The work will reflect the curriculum for excellence in that it will help them to be a successful learner, a confident individual, a responsible citizen and an effective contributor. The information provided during the sessions will therefore put young people at the centre of the initiative and build upon their strengths to promote resilience and support informed choice.

Furthermore, in line with the approaches advocated in this strategy, the Fife Project will implicitly promote positive health choices, enabling young people to make clear informed decisions about tobacco use via active participation in individual and group activities utilising a range of contemporary communication strategies.

Intervention and outcomes

The Fife Project

THE COMPETITION PROCESS

The proposed competition is an opportunity for the young people to develop a creative and innovative promotional campaign aimed at engaging and inspiring other youths in their community to make positive choices about their health.

The competition can be introduced to run not only across individual classes and year groups but also within and across Fife schools. The young people will be encouraged to use the skills and information derived from their classroom sessions to work together in small groups with the aim of creating a resource that will promote individual and community-level change.

Set over an agreed period of time, the young people will work together to design and make their resource. The grand final of the competition will bring together all participants to showcase their efforts and talents. The young people will be an integral part of the event final, contributing their ideas and presenting their final piece of work. The work will then be judged and a winning team appointed. This might involve a panel comprising young people and staff, alongside local community members, education and health experts, and/or a live voting system for audience members.

(continued)

(continued)

The competition will enable the young people to gain considerable recognition for their efforts in front of a wide range of friends, family, teachers, head teacher(s) and local members of the community – along with relevant Fife-wide figures from the media (including local radio presenters and journalists), public figures and celebrities (including footballers, TV presenters), and prominent councillors and members of the education services and the NHS.

All participants will be awarded certificates and the winners will receive publicity for their work to be used/viewed within the local community and made available more widely through appropriate channels (for example, on social and/or visual media and across other public domains).

To complement and assist with the classroom activities, details about available resources/factsheets are provided where necessary. These resources aim to give further information on each of the topics discussed. Teachers are however encouraged to add any additional relevant materials and to update and/or replace resources according to new available information, timescales and age-appropriate learning. A summary outlining the key skills and learning outcomes is presented after the sessions.

While the aim of the initiative is to ensure that teachers are provided with enough flexibility to tailor the project to the needs of the children in their classes, it is also important that they receive guidance in how to deliver the activities. As such, regular 'Teacher Tips' will be included to support classroom delivery. These tips have been designed to allow for a degree of consistency across classes/schools and to ensure that work can be effectively completed within the timescales, without being overly-prescriptive or restricting teacher creativity. The programme is also based upon the idea of co-production and design, with classroom activities being led, to a large extent, by the young people themselves. As such, it is suggested that rather than regularly provide a list of key information, or learning points, the young people will be encouraged to discuss and identify the relevant facts and points of interest at the end of each session.

At this stage it is anticipated that the Fife Project will be a pilot intervention. In the long-term however, it is the intention that this proposed toolkit could be rolled out and delivered to schoolchildren in different years, as well as across schools in Fife and beyond.

Sessions 1 and 2: Marketing

Aims
The aim of the first two sessions is to lay the foundations for the programme and associated competition: this will provide the young people with information about the initiative, the planned activities, and the learning objectives.

Session 1 will begin by introducing young people to the tobacco industry. They will be encouraged to think about what tobacco companies do and their aims and objectives.

They will also consider how and why cigarettes are targeted at the public, the strategies the companies use to promote their products, and their effectiveness.

Following an introduction to marketing, in Session 2 the young people will explore what makes a successful business by examining some of the key roles and thinking about how a company might develop and deliver products. They will be encouraged to identify their own key strengths, abilities and weaknesses and learn how these can be used to work in collaboration with others to develop a successful team/company.

Session 1: What is marketing?

Introduction to the competition: To include an outline by the teacher about what the programme will involve, how many sessions there will be, and how the young people will be encouraged to actively participate in each session in order to broaden their knowledge and skills.

GROUP ACTIVITY 1: WHAT IS MARKETING?

The aim of this activity session is to think about why you buy items and how this links to what you want and what you actually need.

Consider something you have bought recently – an item of clothing perhaps or a computer game, or new mobile etc. Think through why and how you bought it. What made you think of it in the first place? What encouraged or discouraged you? Would you buy it again? How did you buy it, e.g. shop, online? What did you like/dislike about it and the process of buying it? How did you feel once you had your product and how does it make you feel now? (Hastings and Domegan 2014)

TIPS FOR TEACHERS

Divide the class into an equal number of small groups. Try to mix participants rather than keep friendship groups. Give the children about 10 minutes to think about an item they have recently bought and to answer the specific questions. They can either be given the time to work individually and to feed back to their group, or to think of a few examples within their group and provide feedback to the class. The young people can be encouraged to write down their answers and to discuss within their groups.

Following a class discussion of the answers, ask the children to consider the question: **What is marketing?** Provide the young people with a hand out or diagram. It would

(continued)

(continued)

be helpful to work through this with them. (Further information about the activity and suggested resources can be found in the list at the end of this session and in Hastings and Domegan 2014.)

In order to link the marketing strategies to tobacco use, consider discussing the following points with the class: Tobacco marketing is designed to appeal to certain markets by using certain imagery, e.g. for males, females or adolescents. Think about or show examples of product design, packaging, distribution and pricing 'the marketing mix'. Ask them to think about how this imagery can result in misconceptions about the harmfulness of the products and lead to the development of particular attitudes about smoking.

INDIVIDUAL RESEARCH ACTIVITY: CRITIQUE ADVERTISING CAMPAIGNS

The aim of this activity is to help you recognise the persuasive strategies marketing companies use. Using the skills that you have learned during this session, select two advertising campaigns, one you view as positive and cleverly designed and another you feel is not very effective. Think about why is this is the case. What do you like/ dislike about each example? Why? Also consider the following questions:

Who is the campaign/product aimed at? What facts are made available to the consumer? What are the key messages that the company want the consumer to think about and remember? What does the brand do for someone? What are the benefits and what are the main physical features of the product? What lifestyle are you being sold? Examine the emotional side of the campaign as well. How does using the brand make the customer feel? How would others view the users of the brand? How does the brand benefit the customer? How do the company make sure that the consumer will remember these messages? Is there anything that could be improved in the advert? Is there anything else that you, as a young person, would look for in a campaign?

Can you think of an alternative lifestyle or story that would also work? Devise a way of recording your search, e.g. journal, blog, Pinterest-style collection of images, illustrating where you searched for resources, how you focused your ideas, what aspects of the campaign you considered etc. Be prepared to present your findings and critical evaluations at the next session. Your findings can be presented in any format.

TIPS FOR TEACHERS

Hand out a sheet with information about the aims/objectives of the task, the questions the young people must answer and any restrictions. These might include, for example, restricting the analysis to a particular time period, or for a particular age range etc. Encourage the young people to think about how they will present their findings in an interesting, creative and informative way.

Key learning points and issues of interest (repeat at the end of each session)

Thinking about the activities, resources and classroom discussions you have had today, then please consider the following questions. These questions can be completed individually, in pairs or groups:

1. What were the key facts that you learned about today?

2. What information will you take away with you/remember?

With the competition in mind, please keep a record of your answers and think about how this information might be used to help develop your ideas at the end of the six sessions.

Before you go . . . opportunities for evaluation (repeat at the end of each session)

Please ensure that the young people are provided with approximately 5-10 minutes to complete and hand in their answers to the following questions at the end of each of the sessions:

3. What did you enjoy most about this session?

4. What was your least favourite part of the session? Why?

5. How would you make today's session more interesting and/or relevant?

6. What (if anything) are you going to do differently now?

Session 2: Creating a business

> Complete Individual Research Activity from Session 1.
>
> Session 2 begins with the young people presenting their individual research tasks. What do the findings tell us? Why did the young people look at specific websites/go to places for information? How much did they find? How is it presented to the class, e.g. a few notes/pictures/lots of facts and figures? Discuss the range of information and sources used and the variety of presentation skills.

GROUP ACTIVITY 2: FORMING A COMPANY

> Now using your experiences of working in your groups and individually to complete the previous activities, we will start to think about how it is possible to use individual skills and personality traits to work in the tobacco business. You will now begin working in small groups to form an advertising/marketing company. This group will also form your team for the forthcoming competition . . .
>
> *(continued)*

(continued)

Each company contains a number of key roles. You must make sure you have the right people for the right tasks. This is not about 'who is better?' . . . it is about knowing that we all bring different strengths to a team and being able to recognise our own strengths. Who is the leader? Who is the researcher? Who will manage the creative team? Who will pitch once the team has a product? Use your own experiences/knowledge/personality to decide how you will get the best business team.

TIPS FOR TEACHERS

Divide the class into an equal number of groups. Try to mix participants rather than keep friendship groups.

Write down a company role for each young person, e.g. Creative Team Leader, CEO, etc. and put them into a 'hat'. Each young person must then pick a piece of paper out of the hat to discover their role.

In turn, the young person must then either agree to take on the role and provide the rest of the group with a reason why they would like to take on the position.

If the young person does not want to accept the role they have chosen they must argue a case for why they would work more effectively in another role. Encourage the young person to reflect on their key strengths, abilities and personality characteristics. The young people can then vote on whether they agree with the change of job or whether they think the team member would work effectively in a given position. Then give the class groups 15 minutes to decide and agree upon their roles.

GROUP ACTIVITY 3: DESIGNING A COMPANY NAME

Any successful company must have a recognisable brand name. This has to reflect the image that the team want to portray. It must also reflect the people involved in the team and be something that will appeal to young people. Think about the key marketing strategies that have been learned. What do you want the name to represent? What is it saying about the company?

Be prepared to explain to the class what your company name is and to justify your choices and final design.

INDIVIDUAL RESEARCH ACTIVITY: ADVERTISING YOUR COMPANY

Design a logo for your company. What will you include in your design? What information do you want to provide? How will it catch the eye of the public? Think about the reasons for each of your decisions and be prepared to explain these to your classmates.

To be completed during the next session.

TIPS FOR TEACHERS

This can be a creative task, ranging from painting, collage, computer design etc. Provide as many opportunities for creativity. This might be undertaken in an art classroom or under the supervision of an art teacher.

The task will be started in class and time will be given to complete the activity at home and in Session 3. The group then get to vote on and choose the best logo for their business in the following session.

Outcomes and Key Skills learned in Sessions 1 and 2

- Following Sessions 1 and 2 the young people will have learned about basic marketing strategies and principles. In line with the policy and literature evidence sweeps, the activities will encourage them to develop the skills to interpret and think critically think about products and images. This will aid their creative decision making later in the competition round.

- Effective youth programmes should also pay attention to the diversity of youths and recognise their individual strengths. The activities in Session 2 directly address this issue and ask the young people to explore and consider how their strengths can be used in collaboration with others.

Sessions 3 and 4: Image and smoking

Aims

Sessions 3 and 4 will focus on tobacco use. The young people will think about what information the media present to the public about smoking, and then compare this to the actual lived experiences of people in their community who smoke.

In Session 3 the young people will utilise the critical thinking skills they have developed in earlier sessions to explore how images in the media create certain ideas about smoking and people who smoke. Session 4 will then explore some basic facts about cigarette ingredients and the potential implications of using tobacco, including effects on appearance and overall health. This will lead to discussions about the realities of smoking, the health choices that people make, and the consequences of their tobacco use. At this stage, the young people should begin considering ideas and relevant topics of interest for their competition resource. They will work in groups and in pairs to develop their thoughts and to carry out activities.

Session 3: Smoking and health

Complete the Individual Research Activity from Session 2. All students should complete their individual logo design. Then ask each company to vote on their favourite logo. Allow approximately 10 minutes for the groups to decide and vote. They should then explain the reason for their choice.

GROUP ACTIVITY 4: MEDIA IMAGES AND SMOKING

You will be presented with a series of images or screen shots from the movies/ TV programmes. Looking at these images, think about and answer the following questions:

What do you think their role or profession is in the film/programme? e.g. hero/ villain/etc.

How is the character/person portrayed? Are they a rebel? Cool? Dangerous? Depressed?

What is their age/appearance like? Do they look good? Aged and tired etc.?

When do they smoke? To impress? When stressed? Late at night? With friends? Alone?

Explore these questions and create a group poster to detail your findings. The aim is to build up a picture about what you see and how you interpret these images. It might help to divide your paper into sections, starting with '**Description**': What do you see, or what image do you think you are being 'sold'? Then consider a second section, '**What you like**' about the images portrayed, and a final section on '**What you dislike**'. What do the findings tell you? Be sure to include why you feel like this way. If members of the group have different opinions then make sure that your poster summarises these different views.

TIPS FOR TEACHERS

This session will require a set of images or screen shots from films, or magazines and TV programmes. Each image should include a character or person who is smoking or who is a smoker. It may help to include individuals and characters from films that may not be well known to the young people. This will encourage them to try and interpret what they are seeing and to explore how they view the images.

To enable each group to work on a poster, large sheets of paper might be provided to facilitate opportunities to brainstorm ideas and answer the key questions.

Following completion of the activity, encourage each group to feed back their findings and discuss their poster. Once each group has presented their answers to the questions, the correct information can be provided about the images/characters etc. Explore how accurate the young people's interpretations are and what they did/did not correctly interpret. Also ask them how they feel about their responses in light of the information provided.

Session 4: Images vs Reality of Smoking

A series of short individual and group activities will take place during the session. This will allow the young people to build up a picture of the different and inter-related aspects of smoking and image.

GROUP ACTIVITY 5: WHAT IS IN A CIGARETTE?

Cigarettes are made from the dried leaves of tobacco plants – after the leaves are dried they are treated with chemicals and turned into cigarettes. Over 4000 chemicals are included in cigarette smoke, many of these are highly poisonous and more than 60 can cause cancer. Do you know what chemicals are included? See game: www.w-west.org.uk/scooby-do-or-scooby-dont.html

TIPS FOR TEACHERS

It might be useful to expand this game to add more information and additional ingredients, e.g. tar/CO etc. (as included in the smoke-free class competition info sheet).

(continued)

(continued)

Or make something very similar for them to work with, e.g. boardgame/white board/ mobile game, e.g. adding different chemicals and what they are used for (e.g., hydrogen cyanide is a poison used in gas chambers). Another possibility is to add in additional ingredients and ask the young people to decide which chemicals they believe are/are not included in the cigarettes.

See the website game, below. Upload a photo and see how smoking changes your appearance: www.w-west.org.uk/wrinkled-or-smooth.html

GROUP ACTIVITY 6: SMOKING AND IMAGE

Discussion: how does this make you feel? Is it what you expected? How does this reflect what you learned about the media images in the previous session?

INDIVIDUAL RESEARCH ACTIVITY: REAL LIVES AND THE CONSEQUENCES OF HEALTH CHOICES

Work in pairs for this activity.

You are a researcher and you want to find out some real-life stories about health choices and smoking. Identify a local person and – with permission – interview them about their experiences. The individual might be someone you know well, e.g. a family member or neighbour, or it could be someone you regularly associate with and who you know is/was a smoker.

In order to find out about their experiences and knowledge of smoking you will need to obtain key information from them. Be sure to include information on the following.

Why did the smoker take up the habit? When did they start smoking? Discuss their habit and how it affects their daily life. You can also talk about cost. Keep in mind that you are not asking them to justify to you why they still smoke but you want to find out why they started and what led them to their current situation. What the effects are on them and if they have any regrets.

Think about what you have learned in previous sessions. Ask them about the role of advertising and the media on their decision making.

Were they drawn into an advertising campaign? Was it peer pressure? Do they know the facts that you have learned about smoking today, i.e. in terms of how the habit affects their health and what goes in the cigarettes? What are their future plans? How do they feel about it now? Ensure that your plans for interviewing and your questions are checked and agreed with your teacher prior to carrying out the activity.

Create a way (any medium) for your company to illustrate the health experiences and choices of real people via a *storyboard* detailing their experiences in a sequential series of images. This can be, for example, an advert/poster, film, series of photos, or piece of music or theatre. It could include a series of digital photographs or hand-drawn images or any other visual means of presenting a story. Again, be as creative as you can. Try and make the information as interesting as you can and report in a way that reflects what your interviewee has told you. How would they like to see their information used, what are the key messages they wanted you to remember?

Whatever the creative format chosen it must not last any longer than five minutes so think about how you will ensure that the relevant information and facts are made clear to the audience.

It must include *real facts* and *experiences* and detail the health choices people have made and the outcomes of these choices.

TIPS FOR TEACHERS

The young people will need to receive clear instructions about what the aims are for the activity and how they should go about collecting information. Encourage them to think about who they want to approach to participate and why. The interviewee should be carefully selected and amicable – this is not about confrontation. Ensure that the young people discuss this issue in pairs.

Include a handout detailing a series of potential questions the young people can ask. Give them time to add any additional questions and think about how they might approach someone and the practical considerations of conducting an interview. Provide each pair of young people with enough time and then check each plan and series of questions.

Also include an information sheet and a consent form on school headed paper that the young person must present to any participant. This includes providing potential participants with details about the nature of the work and gaining their signed consent to take part. Please note that it should be made clear to participants that the presentations designed by the young people will not be kept by the school and the information provided will be for the sole use of the classroom session and for children to learn about adult health choices.

Outcomes and key skills learned in sessions 3 and 4

- At the end of Sessions 3 and 4 the young people will have developed the skills to critique existing mediated messages about tobacco use and also assess, analyse and evaluate media in order to learn to create their own media messages.

- The interview session will mobilise the young people's creativity and help foster connections between them and their communities. This will enable them to redefine the personal and social issues of smoking. The activity will also help them to document local health issues and enhance critical reflections about health behaviours and experiences at an individual and social level.

- The activities draw on the tradition of storytelling, enabling the young people to make an impact by developing a narrative and a way of illustrating lessons learned and knowledge. They will also learn to see smoking from a 'human perspective' which contrasts with the previous media and marketing strategies they have learned about. The activity also aims to mobilise their creativity and community engagement.

- The work will reflect the curriculum for excellence in the young people who will work together to contribute effectively and gain confidence in their creative skills.

Sessions 5 and 6: Making choices and tackling addiction

Aims

In Sessions 5 and 6 the young people will explore the choices that individuals have to make about their health. This includes considering what is 'good' and 'bad' health. By building on the information learned in the previous sessions, they will be encouraged to begin thinking about how to take charge of their health and make positive decisions. This should help provide information and inspiration for competition design ideas.

Session 5 will explore health and addiction, including examining what addiction is and what impact can it have on individuals. The activities will help the young people to link individual and social decisions about health options. They will start working creatively to think about how to influence other young people and make a difference to their health decisions.

Session 5: What is good health?

Complete and present the individual Research Activity from Session 4.

Discussion: How does the information you have gathered differ from the media images we explored in the previous sessions? How would this make a consumer feel? What can you learn? Discuss the storyboards and interviews and explore what has been learned.

GROUP ACTIVITY 7: GOOD AND BAD HEALTH

This activity involves thinking about health more broadly. In your groups you will begin to discuss 'good' and 'bad' health. This brainstorming activity will involve you setting out your thoughts on paper. Divide the sheet into two sections and write down any words or thoughts you would associate with each term.

Also think about some of the reasons for good and bad health. What leads people to experience bad health – is it simply luck, or are there things people can do to improve their health? Try and think about individual decisions as well as other factors. Who influences your health – family? Peers? How?

The role of addiction should also be discussed. What skills would you need to quit an addiction? Willpower? Family support? Peer support? Knowledge about risks? What else do you need (social, cultural, economic factors)? How do young people learn to use these skills and strategies to cope with addiction? Particularly when faced with companies' marketing strategies? With the information your group has gained, create an infographic that is eye-catching and informative. It can include any information and/or statistics that you think are relevant and that you believe reflect the range of influences on people's health and behaviours.

TIPS FOR TEACHERS

During the brainstorming activity provide some basic information about health and addiction, along with any other related topics. This might include some of the suggested resources.

To enable each group to work on a poster, large sheets of paper might be provided to facilitate opportunities to brainstorm ideas and to answer the key questions. Also provide various materials to create an infographic, arts, crafts, magazine cuttings etc. Some examples can be shown in order to aid creative designs. Encourage the young people to look up any relevant facts or figures to enhance their work.

Following completion of the activity, each group should feed back their findings and discuss their infographic. In particular, note any differences between the groups and ask the young people to explain how they came to their decisions about good/bad health. What influenced them? Past experiences? People in their community? The media? Ensure they are aware of the range of influences and the interconnected nature of health.

GROUP ACTIVITY 8: ADDITION – A SOCIAL ACTION PROJECT

Your company has been tasked with designing a social action project, promoting ways to help young people give up an addiction. This could be smoking, alcohol or something else. Think about how you will tackle this issue. Do you want to create

(continued)

(continued)

a local, one-off event for the young people to attend, or a product to help provide information, such as an app? Would you like to set up an online support group? Try and be as creative as you can.

Incorporate the marketing strategies you learned about in Sessions 1 and 2. Also make sure that you include any health information facts that you feel are relevant. Consider what information you think the young people would need in order to make informed decisions and access the support they need. Also signpost to any resources that might be of use. What is the best way to tell them? What format will it take, e.g. a leaflet, poster, an infographic or a short movie etc.? Additional time will be provided in Session 6. You will then present your company activity to the class.

Session 6: The competition

Complete the Individual Research Activity from Session 5.

In this final session, the young people will complete the 'Tackling Addiction' task and present it to the class.

Discussion: What have you learned? How does this illustrate what knowledge you have gained over these last sessions? What have the sessions taught you? Is there anything else that could or should be included in this programme? How and why would this be useful? Try and note down some of these thoughts and pass them on to your teacher.

Provide any opportunities for questions and discussion about the tasks that have been completed over the course of the previous five sessions.

TIPS FOR TEACHERS

Encourage the young people to reflect upon what they have learned over the course of the last five sessions and ask them to talk about what they have enjoyed and what they have gained from the different activities. This might be something like working effectively with other class members, or learning new creative skills.

It might also be useful, in their groups or 'companies', to note down some of the main points that have interested them and the skills they have gained. Is there anything that they did not feel was useful or that could have been better delivered or explained? How could it be improved next time? What else would you have liked to learn about? Revisit the key learning points and information the young people have identified at the end of each session.

This will provide valuable feedback for future projects and ensure that valuable lessons are learned for any further project development.

Thinking about the previous sessions will also allow the young people to begin considering how they can use the skills and knowledge that they have acquired in the next phase of the programme, the Competition.

Clarify that the young people will continue to work in their group 'companies' and that they will be expected to use their new skills to best effect during the next phase of the programme.

GROUP ACTIVITY 9: THE COMPETITION

In your 'company' groups you will work collectively on an issue that you identify and agree upon is a topic for *individual and community-level change*. You must try and use as many of the creative and analytical skills as you can in order to be innovative and original. The work can be fun, humorous or serious and it can be designed in any way that you feel would be useful and effective for your peers in school and/or your community. *The focus is on the positive choices that young people should make about their health.*

> *The idea is to design a creative and innovative promotional campaign to inspire other young people to make better health choices and develop their unique potential.*

Any of the information and strategies that have been presented in the previous sessions can be used.

There are no boundaries, however:

> *Each project must be no longer than 10 minutes in length. The group must allocate tasks to each member and each person must ensure they agree to this task and work with their team to make certain it is completed.*

> *The work can be delivered in any format – a film, an infographic, a poster, a storyboard etc. Draw upon what you have seen and heard in the previous sessions and present it as your company project.*

Be prepared to present this work to your class and potentially to a wider audience – your school, or within your local area.

There will be a vote to select the winning team and they will then progress to compete against other class projects and other schools.

The overall winners will be decided at a grand event later in the academic year.

> **TIPS FOR TEACHERS**
>
> The guidance notes and any further details about the project should be pre-sented to the young people. It would be helpful to clarify any project deadlines and to specify the number of sessions they will have to work on their project. If possible, ensure the young people are encouraged to continue their work outside the school environment.
>
> Help each group to discuss their ideas and provide them with any relevant resources and websites, including those previously mentioned in the sessions.

Outcomes and key skills learned in sessions 5 and 6

- Following these sessions the young people will be able to better reflect upon the inter-connected nature of health behaviours. They will be aware of the broad spectrum of influences, including peers, family and community.

- Through group critical dialogues the young people have explored addiction as a youth-centred issue and examined how and why individual experiences link to peer decision making and local community issues. They collaboratively worked to develop narratives around a research theme and help to plan ways to address the health needs of others.

- The sessions build upon the research skills and critical thinking the young people have learned previously. They will now begin to think about how their knowledge and skills can be utilised to focus on the end-users – young people in their school/local community. The competition will not only capture young people's voices and views it will also provide tangible evidence of the learning and skills they have developed.

Discussion

In addition to developing knowledge about smoking and health choices, the series of struc-tured activities aim to challenge the young people in group and individual tasks, enabling them to utilise their creativity and enhance their communication skills. The activities also seek to develop critical thinking and analytical abilities. Each session builds upon the previ-ous lessons learned in order to provide the students with a clear overview of the different aspects of tobacco use and health more broadly (i.e. biological, social, political). These core areas play an important and interrelated role in influencing their knowledge enhancement and personal decision making about their health.

The project ensures that rather than seeking to intervene in existing health-related behav-iours, the young people are invited to take the lead in developing creative outputs and estab-lishing core messages to promote knowledge and understanding. Engaging adolescents in collaborative and social sessions promotes ways of developing personal and co-responsibility as well as creative ownership. In line with the findings of the wider literature evidence base, this aims to increase young people's self-awareness and self-efficacy and empower them to make informed and healthy lifestyle choices.

Going forward, any programme of activities requires careful monitoring to ensure effective implementation and use and to ascertain whether the programme can be improved or better delivered. Careful monitoring and consultation with participants will help ensure the young people continue to be consulted on the initiative and provide opportunities for them to be involved in co-evaluation. A formative process evaluation would further ensure that feedback can be immediately referred to policy makers and programme developers in order to enhance the likelihood of effective content, implementation and delivery.

Case study questions

1. Why were the self-evaluation questions included after each session in this case?

2. What important communication skills might the young people gain from this case?

3. What key skills will the young people learn to help them take control of their health?

References

Baker, L., McClain, M-C., Hurst, V., Grossman, S., Dehili, V., Flagg, S., Marshall, D. and Prevatt, F. (2012) 'A review of motivational smoking cessation programs for adolescents in the schools', *Education Research and Perspectives*, 39: 104–135.

Bryant, J., Bonevski, B., Paul, C., McElduff, P. and Attia, J. (2011) 'A systematic review and meta-analysis of the effectiveness of behavioural smoking cessation interventions in selected disadvantaged groups', *Addiction*, 106: 1568–1585. doi: 10.1111/j.1360-0443.2011.03467.x

de Andrade, M. (2014) *The Impact of Tobacco-Education Interventions in Fife Schools: Asset-Based Approaches, Co-Production and Innovative Engagement*. NHS Fife Report.

de Andrade, M., Angus, K. and Hastings, G. (2015, Nov.) 'Teenage perceptions of electronic cigarettes in Scottish tobacco-education school interventions: co-production and innovative engagement through a pop-up radio project', *Perspectives in Public Health*. doi: 10.1177/1757913915612109.

Erbstein, N. (2013) 'Engaging underrepresented youth populations in community youth development: tapping social capital as a critical resource', *New Directions for Youth Development*, 138: 109–124.

Fields, A., Snapp, Sh., Russell, S.T., LLicona, A.C., Tilley, E.H. and The Crossroads Collaborative. (2014) 'Youth voices and knowledges: slam poetry speaks to social policies', *Sexuality Research and Social Policy*, 11(4): 310–321.

Foot, J. and Hopkins, T. (2010) 'A glass half-full: how an asset approach can improve community health and well-being'. Local Government Improvement and Development, 32. Retrieved from www.local.gov.uk/web/guest/health/-/journal_content/56/10171/3511449/ARTICLE-TEMPLATE (accessed 12 April 2016).

Hastings, G. and Domegan, C. (2014) *Social Marketing*, 2nd edition. New York: Routledge.

Heikkinen, A.M., Broms, U., Pitkaniemi, J., Koskenvuo, M. and Meurman, J. (2009) 'Key factors in smoking cessation intervention among 15-16-year-olds', *Behavioral Medicine*, 35(3): 93–99.

Lee, Y.O., Jordan, J.W., Djakaria, M. and Ling, P.M. (2014) 'Using peer crowds to segment black youth for smoking intervention', *Health Promotion Practice*, 15(4): 530–537. doi: 10.1177/1524839913484470.

Morgan, A. and Ziglio, E. (2007) 'Revitalising the evidence-base for public health: an assets model', *Global Health Promotion*, 14(2): Suppl: 17–22. doi: 10.1177/10253823070140020701x.

Remafedi, G. and Carol, H. (2005) 'Preventing tobacco use among lesbian, gay, bisexual and transgender youths', *Nicotine and Tobacco Research*, 7(2): 249–256.

Rippon, S. & Hopkins, T. (2015) *Head, hands and heart: asset-based approaches in health care*. Available at: http://www.health.org.uk/sites/health/files/HeadHandsAndHeartAssetBasedApproaches InHealthCare.pdf (accessed 18 September 2017).

Robinson, L.M and Vail, S.R. (2012) 'n integrative review of adolescent smoking cessation using the Transtheoretical Model of Change', *Paediatric Health Care*, Sept-Oct: 26(5): 336–345. doi:10.1016/j.peadjc.2010.12.001

Scottish Government (2013) *Tobacco Control Strategy: Creating a Tobacco-Free Generation*. Edinburgh: Scottish Government. Available at: www.gov.scot/Resource/0041/00417331.pdf

Small, S.P., Kushrer, K.E. and Newfeld, A. (2013) 'Smoking prevention among youth: a multi-pronged approach involving parents, schools, and society', *Canadian Journal of Nursing Research*, 45(3): 116–135.

Starkey, F., Audrey, S., Holliday, J., Moore, L. and Campbell, R. (2009) 'Identifying influential young people to undertake effective peer-led health promotion: the example of A Stop Smoking in Schools Trial (ASSIST)', *Health Education Research*, 24(6): 977–988.

Whittaker, R., Maddison, R., McRobbie, H., Bullen, C., Denny, S., Dorey, E., Ellis-Pegler, M., Van Rooyen, J. and Rodgers, A. (2008) 'A multimedia mobile phone-based youth smoking cessation intervention: findings from content development and piloting studies', *Journal of Medical Internet Research*, 10(5).

Case study **6**

The Porto Tap Water programme

Ana Sofia Dias and Sara Balonas

Introduction

Water as a resource remains one of the top concerns on the international agenda. Despite all the efforts, drinking water is consecutively in the centre of a global crisis of scarce resources – exacerbated by social and environmental problems, accelerated urbanisation, climate change and increasing pollution levels – which affects millions of people and leads to poverty and unequal power relations. However, in developed countries, the perception is totally different: water, seen as a commodity, is available in quantity and quality to be consumed directly from the tap, but bottled water consumption is very high. Undoubtedly, commercial marketing gets people to pay for products they don't need.

Problem definition

Portugal has one of the best public waters of Europe. In 2015, the water safety indicator (for controlled and good quality water) reached 99 per cent, meaning that Portugal's population can drink tap water with confidence (Martins *et al.* 2016). Tap water is regularly analysed and supervised by governmental authorities and health institutes that validate its excellent quality. In fact, as shown in the ERSAR (the water and waste services regulation authority) annual report, data confirm the excellent tap water quality in Portugal (Martins *et al.* 2016). Why, then, is bottled water chosen instead of tap water?

Several studies and investigations, as well as a survey on tap water consumption in Porto, point to a gap between the perceived and the real quality of tap water. In Porto 63 per cent of city residents drink, on average, between 0.5 and 1.5 litres of water per day (Maia *et al.* 2015). Of these 37 per cent don't have preference regarding the type of water to consume; 33 per cent elect tap water; and 30 per cent choose bottled water (Maia *et al.* 2015). Moreover, only 18.5 per cent of the population under 40 years elects tap water (Maia *et al.* 2015) which foreshadows the future persistence of bottled water consumption behaviour. Indeed, most of the residents of Porto are unaware of the treatment and strict quality control to which tap water is submitted. And yet, in Porto, the analysis of water supply proves its excellent quality – continuously reaching results above 99 per cent[1]. In 2014, the public company that manages the Porto Water won the seal "Quality of Service of Public Water Supply"[2].

Competitive analysis

High consumption of bottled water can be associated with an essentially cultural phenomenon (Wilk 2006): the manufactured demand leading to the generalisation of purchase and consumption. Between the 1970s and 1980s, bottled waters became a trend driven by the yuppies – young urban professionals who in a period of economic growth followed a frenetic lifestyle that encouraged consumption of convenience products and services. The context made bottled water (a consumer product) a symbol of a status that communicates lifestyle and sense of belonging to a real or desired group (Silva, cited in Queiroz *et al.* 2012).

Part of water's symbolic power is precisely rooted in geographical and class/status associations (Wilk 2006). Consumerism and advertising are pointed out as reasons for the purchase of branded water (Olins 2003; Queiroz 2012), even if this is not always synonymous with superior quality. Framed by the brand, the waters have increased their perceived value (Barden 2014). Boosted by advertising messages, they explore meanings and influences far beyond their basic function (Wilk 2006).

Stakeholder analysis

A cross-section of stakeholders was identified as relevant, including the following:

- The internal public – staff of the municipal institutions and companies as disseminators of tap water quality
- Influencers – trendsetters, prosumers, millennials
- Prescribers – opinion leaders, health professionals, media in general
- Intermediate public – condominium owners and managers, HORECA channel, public institutions.
- Young people – public in school age, future influencers of behaviour
- Porto citizens in general – trendsetters and followers.

Research

Contrary to the twentieth century, a time in which branding stood out mainly in the supply of consumer goods and services, today everything can be a brand. For the private sector, public sector, public utility or non-governmental organisations, branding is an undeniable marketing tool. Therefore if social marketing learns from conventional marketing the best strategies aiming at campaign or programme success, the potential of brands applied to behavioural change and social good can't be ignored.

What is required is to know the challenges that arise for branding in the social marketing plan: the desired behaviours are the product. Therefore the cost of the behaviour, as well as the access and the promotion of its benefits, must be explored in accordance with it. Brands are essential in the positioning of products, services, behaviours and organisations in consumers' life through the creation of associations (Evans and Hastings 2008). It is about facilitating behavioural change by creating and communicating a persuasive value. As French said "branding within social marketing is a key consideration as it is a subset of creating social value. Developing trusted social brands leads to greater influence on behaviour that promotes social and personal good and wellbeing" (French, cited by Dias 2015). One of the reasons for this is that we need to "develop emotional connections to influence attitudes beliefs and behaviour" (French, cited by Dias 2015). Brands are more than a simple matter of communication and persuasion: they're about relationship, value and exchange (Evans and Hastings 2008).

In sum, brands as holders of great power and influence in society can also fulfil "a great social purpose" (Olins 2003). One of the dimensions through which they can bring benefit to society is precisely their role in presenting a campaign programme and raising trust and credibility regarding a social issue (Hilton 2005).

Aims and objectives

The Porto Tap Water case study aims to stress that the success of a social marketing plan is strictly related to attitudes and beliefs change but the final goal is fulfilled only with a concrete action – behaviour change (Lee & Kotler 2011; Weinreich 2011). In this process, institutions best positioned to help people change their attitude and behaviour are the brands (Hilton 2005), specifically aiming to:

- increase trust in tap water quality
- increase consumption of tap water, considering the benefits of public water over the competition (bottled waters)
- increase Águas do Porto brand value
- involvement in the promotion strategy of the city (Porto).

Intervention

Águas do Porto, the public company for water management and distribution in the city of Porto, launched a two-year programme for behavioural change aiming to encourage the consumption of tap water. Designed by a consultant company, the programme was developed in accordance to social marketing practices and principles. The first concern was to find the insight which would guide the intervention plan. With the support of the empirical results from the survey made by CEGEA of the University of Porto, it was possible to understand the cause that influences the preferences of water consumption in Porto providing clues to unlock the desired behaviour. For Porto consumers what influences their behaviour can be

Table CS6.1 Traditional marketing mix applied to the Porto Tap Water programme

Product	Increase its value through communication. From the product to packaging: accessibility/portability. The creation of packages/bottles overcome one of the weaknesses pointed to tap water: the fact that it is not portable, an increasingly important requirement in the current lifestyle.
Price	Competitive advantage: tap water is cheaper than bottled water.
Placement	Availability outside home: dissemination of existing water supply points in the city of Porto and creation of new access points to public water.
Promotion	An integrated communication plan: offline campaign, online communication, social networks, events, public relations, activation, environment media.

summarised as "I choose the water, depending on the quality and reliability that it transmits me" and "I choose the water for convenience/portability."

From this point, the approach to the problem of tap water consumption summoned all relevant marketing variables to the process such as product portability (packaging), distribution (greater promotion and dissemination of contact points) and perceived value (what the product worth's to those who consume it). Making the offer appealing, affordable, available and appreciated (Hastings 2011) has always been taken into account in the plan.

Concerning 'product', the first listed variable, the strategy was to transform a simple commodity into a product with its own personality and attributes. Porto Tap Water has a set of distinctive characteristics that represent competitive advantages. From these advantages, which add value to the product and are associated benefits to consumers, key messages were set.

Thus it was defined that Porto Tap Water and its consumption would be positioned as of quality, reliable, convenient, cheap, good health, portable, cool and trendy. The positioning of the product in the market led, in a strategic and logic perspective, to the creation of a brand

Table CS6.2 Attributes and key messages for Porto Tap Water

Control	Quality that you can drink.
Health	Drinking water is good.
Safety	Water with safe quality.
Price	A good for all.
Taste	A sign of rigorous control.

Figure CS6.1 Icons to communicate the five attributes of Porto Tap Water

as the "creative link between trust in brands" and a "social issue in which a change of attitude can make all the difference" (Hilton 2005: 60). The strategy included necessarily a symbolic perspective of the brand: the creation of a connotation between an essential good, the water, and the "quality" and "vitality" perceived about the city of Porto. In fact, Porto is recognised as a city of strong emotions, the centre of a "northerner" pride which is seen in its culture, history, heritage and products. In addition, the brand explores the potential of the sense of belonging, of "a common thing", i.e. water as a unifying element of Porto citizens.

Moreover if it is easier to create a personality which is associated with a functional benefit rather than simple saying it (Aaker 2012), the creative line led to the signature *É boa todos os dias!* (As good as it gets) – a typical expression of the oral speech of Porto people. In a very familiar and customised way, this signature summarises the key argument that crosses the whole programme: trust and quality. The brand has a confident and assertive tone, but is also trendy and positive, which refers to the perception and attitude change and adoption of an underrated social behaviour.

In sum, the brand created the conditions to consistently over time make the benefits of tap water consumption more immediate and tangible for the consumers (Keller 1998).

The variable "placement" is particularly critical because there is a need to solve one of the identified weaknesses of the tap water, i.e. the fact that it is not portable, an increasingly important requirement nowadays. Thus points of access to tap water were created throughout the city, making it available outside home and a public design contest led to the production of the official Porto Tap Water bottle (one in glass and another in an eco-friendly material).

The stakeholders involved in the programme were hierarchically divided into four groups (final, internal, intermediate and prescribers/influencers) that were successively segmented as recommended in social marketing best practices. The design of a specific marketing programme for each 'client'/segment, sustained in a profound understanding of the public and their vision of the problem, the insight (French *et al.* 2011), was a precondition for the success of the behavioural

Figure CS6.2 Porto Tap Water logo

Table CS6.3 Targeted key arguments/message content

	TARGET		KEY ARGUMENT
FINAL PUBLICS	Population in general – consumers	Trendsetters	Control, safety and quality of the water, convenience and portability, taste, sustainability
		Followers	Control, safety and quality of the water, convenience and portability, price, taste
	School publics	Elementary school	Health, taste, quality, environment, portability
		High School	Sociocultural (sense of belonging), taste, portability
		Schools – Universities	Taste, health, trust and quality, portability
	Tourists		Water safety, promotion of the city, portability
INTERNAL PUBLICS	Employees of the Águas do Porto company	Monitors of Pavilhão da Água	Control, quality, convenience and portability
		Pickets and managers	Control, quality, convenience and portability
	Employees of the municipal institutions and companies		Control, quality, convenience and portability
PRESCRIBERS/ INTERMEDIATE PUBLICS	Owners and condominium managers		Control, responsibility in the process, legislation
	HORECA channel		Promotion of the city, safety, quality, sustainability
	Public Institutions		Promotion of the city, safety, quality, sustainability
INFLUENCER PUBLICS	Opinion leaders: "Water Ambassadors"		Control, safety, quality, convenience, price, taste
	Health professionals		Health and quality
	Social Communication		Control, safety, quality, convenience, price

change campaign, as well as identification of the groups of influencers (Lee and Kotler 2011). Finally, to ensure this client orientation, key arguments were strategically adapted for each target segment.

This means that the communication plan was designed to impact different publics with a range of target actions and in this manner disseminated the key messages to contribute to an effective change of behaviour. The integrated communication plan included an offline campaign, online communication, social media, street activation, environment media, public relations/press and events.

The definition of the social marketing mix included the traditional 4Ps plus two others: public and partnerships (Weinreich 2011). People are central in any social marketing programme

Figure CS6.3 Flyer part of school kit

and, particularly in this case, internal and external audiences have been impacted by specific messages and actions, supported by a strategic partnership plan. This is because the establishment of partnerships supported the credibility and notoriety of the programme, allowing synergies (co-branding actions), conquering new communication and distribution channels and broadening the reach of the messages.

Programme phases

The programme started on March 2015 and continued until March 2017. Throughout this period, it had been developed based on a change process divided into four big moments, to be implemented over two years: (1) inform, (2) educate, (3) change attitudes and perceptions, and (4) induce new behaviours.

Outcomes

Some data can be already signed out and analysed later in depth:

- around 400 employees of the municipal company Águas do Porto were impacted through several editions of the awareness and involvement actions of the programme
- official bottles for Porto Tap Water was distributed in March 2017 to solve the portability problem and ensure a future preference for tap water
- the programme was presented in four scientific events which led to a Master's thesis case study and reached international visibility
- the Facebook page created for the programme (www.facebook.com/bebaaguadoporto) has around 600 fans (only organic results)
- the campaign was present in approximately 50 public events in Porto.

Discussion

In marketing and communication, convergence of all strategies and tools around the emotion factor is evident. As Elliott and Wattanasuwan (1998: 134) stated, "any voluntary consumption involves, in a conscious or unconscious way, symbolic meanings." Branding, per excellence the emotional tool of marketing, focuses more and more on the symbolic dimension and emotions. With emotions as an influential factor in the perspective of social psychology, in what concerns attitudes and behaviours change, and in the psychology of consumption, in what relates to the engagement with the brand, the symbolic dimension of brands can not be ignored in the strategic definition of a social marketing programme.

Focusing on the Porto Tap Water case, its consumption represents, first and foremost, an attitude and behaviour consistent with the personality of the city and its population, without neglecting the quality perceptions associated with Porto products. As it is a brand with a socio-symbolic positioning strategy, it validates its meanings through a discursive construction in a social context (Elliott and Wattanasuwan 1998). Indeed, in this social marketing programme, branding plays a key role in defining and communicating with target audiences. When consuming Porto Tap Water, people are presenting themselves to society as part of a trending 'attitude' of the city, which brings them more immediate benefits and positive reinforcement (Keller 1998), for example, by being 'accredited' or recognised for avoiding the consumption of bottled water, which has negative consequences.

In sum the strategy consists of 'controlling the power of language and images to bring about broader social change' (Anholt 2005: 251), combining, as the target becomes engaged with the brand (the greater the engagement, the greater the likelihood of consume behavioural change; Strategic Social Marketing, s/d) the central importance of the symbolic dimension.

This case raises some relevant aspects for discussion, namely:

- the importance of monitoring and evaluate social marketing programmes. Quite often, the promoters of social marketing programmes don't have the needed time and knowledge to neutrally evaluate and adjust the strategies;

- communication that promotes a social change "must follow a long and deep process to modify beliefs, ideologies and change long-term attitudes" (Ruiz 2003). Despite the branding is part of the strategy, advertising, sponsorships, events, and other communication and marketing actions also contribute to achieve the objectives of the behavioural change programme under review. In the present case, the integrated intervention mix is strong in events but it must be more effective in terms of communication mix: online/social media, PR/press;

- analyse the efficiency of branding is required - using indicators such as reputation, brand loyalty, perceived quality and brand associations in behavioural change programmes through the results achieved with the Porto Tap Water case.

Case study questions

1. How can branding be evaluated in social marketing programmes concerning its efficiency?

2. Taking the competitive analysis in consideration, specifically, the manufactured demand, what are the potential risks in the implementation of this programme?

Notes

1   www.aguasdoporto.pt/noticias-aguas-do-porto/ersar-confirma-agua-da-torneira-em-portugal-e-de-excelente-qualidade www.aguasdoporto.pt/rede-publica/1o-trimestre-2016#22

2   www.aguasdoporto.pt/noticias-aguas-do-porto/aguas-do-porto-nomeada-para-premio-qualidade-do-servico-de-abastecimento-publico-de-aguado-ersar

References

Aaker, D. (2012) *Building Strong Brands*. New York: Simon and Schuster.

Anholt, S. (2005) 'Branding de locais e de países', in R. Clifton and J. Simmons (eds), *O Mundo das Marcas* (pp. 241–254). Lisboa: Actual Editora.

Barden, P. (2014) 'Brands as frames', in A. Samson (ed.) *The Behavioral Economics Guide 2014* (pp. 78–84). S/l: *Behavioral Economics*. [eBook]. Online at: www.behavioraleconomics.com/.

Dias, A. (2015) 'O simbólico como estratégia para a alteração comportamental: o caso Águas do Porto', Master's thesis, University of Minho.

Elliott, R. and Wattanasuwan, K. (1998) 'Brands as symbolic resources for the construction of identity', *International Journal of Advertising*, 17: 131–144. Online at: http://sspa.boisestate.edu/communication/files/2010/05/Elliot-Brands-as-Symbolic-Resources.pdf

Evans, W. and Hastings, G. (2008) *Public health branding: applying marketing for social change*. New York: Oxford University Press.

French, J., Merritt, R. and Reynolds, L. (2011) *Social Marketing Casebook*. London: Sage Publications.

Hastings, G. (2011) *Social Marketing: Why Should the Devil have All the Best Tunes?* Amsterdam: Elsevier.

Hilton, S. (2005) 'O valor social das marcas', in R. Clifton and J. Simmons (eds), *O Mundo das Marcas* (pp. 47-66). Lisboa: Actual Editora.

Keller, K. (1998) 'Branding perspectives on social marketing', in J. Alba and J. Hutchinson, *NA – Advances in Consumer Research*, 25 (pp. 299–302). Utah: Association for Consumer Research. Online at: http://acrwebsite.org/volumes/7887/volumes/v25/NA-25.

Lee, N. and Kotler, P. (2011) *Social Marketing: Influencing Behaviors for Good*, 4th edition. Los Angeles, CA: Sage Publications.

Martins, A., Machado, I. & Guerreiro, S. (2016) 'Volume 2 – Controlo da qualidade da água para consumo humano', in Entidade Reguladora dos Serviços de Águas e Resíduos (eds), *Relatório Anual dos Serviços de Águas e Resíduos em Portugal (2016)*. S/l: ERSAR.

Maia, M., Alves, H. & Martins, C. (2015). *Inquérito ao consumo da água da torneira – Beba a nossa água: Relatório Final*. Porto: Centro de Estudos de Gestão e Economia Aplicada da Universidade Católica do Porto.

Olins, W. (2003) *A Marca*. Lisboa: Editorial Verbo.

Queiroz, J., Rosenberg, M., Heller, L., Zhouri, A. and Silva, S. (2012) News about tap and bottled water: can this influence people's choices?, *Journal of Environmental Protection*, 3: 324–333. doi: 10.4236/jep.2012.34041.

Ruiz, A. A. (2003) 'Publicidad social: enfoques y métodos de análisis.', in Benet, V.J. and Aldás, E.N. (Eds.), La publicidad en el Tercer Sector. Tendencias y perspectivas de la Comunicación Solidaria, Vol., Cap. IV. Barcelona: Icaria editorial, 4: 129–141.

Strategic Social Marketing (s/d) One Page Key behaviour change influences summary. Online at: http://strategic-social-marketing.vpweb.co.uk/Free-Tool-Box.html.

Weinreich, N. (2011) *Hands-on Social Marketing: A Step-by-step Guide to Designing Change for Good*, 2nd edition. Los Angeles, CA: Sage Publications.

Wilk, R. (2006) 'Bottled water: The pure commodity in the age of branding', *Journal of Consumer Culture*, 6(3): 303–325. doi: 10.1177/1469540506068681.

7

Development of strategies to promote solid waste management in Bourj Hammoud, Lebanon

Amena El Harakeh, Farah Madi and Marco Bardus

Introduction

Background to the project

The case study reported here presents the preliminary steps of a social marketing plan addressing solid waste management by focusing on waste minimisation in Bourj Hammoud, a suburb of Beirut, the capital city of Lebanon. This marketing plan was developed by a group of graduate environmental health students enrolled in the Master of Public Health at the American University of Beirut during a 14-week Social Marketing course (taught in Spring). The plan was developed in collaboration with the Ministry of Social Affairs (MOSA), based in Bourj Hammoud. The Social Marketing course is based on service learning. The implementation of service learning activities, including meetings with the community partner organisations, was entirely supported by the Center for Public Health Practice, hosted at the Faculty of Health Sciences. We report here the findings of formative research which informed the strategy and the development of the plan. The implementation of the campaign depends on resources that the Ministry is currently trying to identify and allocate from its own budget. As a research unit in AUB, we are trying to apply for grants to support the process and outcome evaluation of the campaign.

Contextualising the issue of solid waste management in Lebanon

Since July 2015, Lebanon has been suffering from a national waste crisis after the closure of the Naameh landfill, the main landfill in the country, which has been receiving waste since 1994 and should have been shut down twelve years ago (AUB 2015). The Lebanese government did not have a contingency plan to properly manage solid waste and this has led to growing piles of garbage in streets and leachates into nearby rivers in Greater Beirut and Mount Lebanon. Among the contributing factors to the solid waste management crisis was the settlement of thousands of asylum-seeking Syrian refugees in different regions in the country (MOE/EU/UNDP 2014). In 2013, the latter phenomenon led to the production of around 2.0 million tons of municipal solid waste. The increased production of solid waste augmented the pressure on existing sorting and composting facilities and landfills (MOE/EU/ UNDP 2014). Additionally, the emergence of open dumps and open burning practices due to the growing population along with the absence of a sustainable waste management solution further intensified the magnitude of the situation.

In addition to the factors mentioned above, a major contributor to the inadequate management of waste in Lebanon is the absence of legislation and policies that tackle the issue of solid waste management; there are only fragmented legal guidelines, unclear responsibilities and minor duties for authorities management. Political interferences, the lack of expertise in the field is the main reason behind the absence of proper implementation and enforcement of a comprehensive solid waste management plan (MOE/LEDO/ ECODIT 2001). The previous national strategy relied on outsourcing waste management to the private company 'Sukleen' which was responsible for waste collection, transportation, minimal processing to sort out recyclable material, and placement in the landfill. A draft law regarding integrated solid waste management was prepared by the Ministry of Environment (MOE) in 2005, approved by the council of ministers in 2012, and then sent to the Lebanese parliament for ratification (MOE/LEDO/ECODIT 2001). However, no action was taken regarding this matter.

Improper waste management is associated with critical health and environmental consequences. Open dumps and leachate runoff lead to the deterioration and contamination of soil and eventually impact land use (MOE/EU/UNDP 2014). This is mostly witnessed in regions where informal tented settlements are located because people there burn part of their waste and dispose of the rest in rivers and open channels. This severely impacts the quality of air and surface and groundwater resources. (MOE/EU/UNDP 2014).

Some health hazards resulting from improper solid waste management were revealed by a recent study conducted by a research team at the American University of Beirut. Air samples were measured on a rooftop of a residential building located near an open dump and indicated alarming levels of air dioxins and emergence of another carcinogen, namely dibenzanthracene (Saliba *et al.* 2015). The exposure of children and adults to these toxins is associated with an increased likelihood of developing cancer (Saliba *et al.* 2015), specifically colorectal, larynx and stomach cancer (Elliott *et al.* 1996; Federico et al., 2010; Ranzi *et al.* 2011). Other serious health consequences include the possible development of congenital abnormalities (Cordier *et al.* 2004, 2010) and increased mortality from respiratory diseases, along with a higher risk of respiratory wheezing in children (Hsiue *et al.* 1991; Ranzi *et al.* 2011; Shy *et al.* 1995).

In such a critical situation, promoting a proper and integrated solid waste management plan for the residents of Bourj Hammoud, in one of the most densely-populated cities of the Middle East, constitutes a fundamental goal to the Ministry of Social Affairs (MOSA) in Bourj Hammoud. This goal, which has been a priority since the rise of the waste crisis, was highly influenced by the opening of the dump in Bourj Hammoud. Given the fact that a large proportion of Beirut's current waste is being placed in Bourj Hammoud's Dump, influencing the residents' knowledge and behaviour concerning proper waste management is of high priority.

This case study presents a plan for a community-based initiative designed using social marketing principles to address the solid waste management situation in Bourj Hammoud by focusing on reduce and reuse as strategies to decrease the generation of waste by its residents. Moreover, following a meeting with the municipality of Bourj Hammoud on 15 April, 2016, we were informed of four pilot studies that were conducted on sorting and recycling. This information confirmed the convenience and appropriateness of the campaign's focus. Through this campaign, we tried to influence residents' knowledge and behaviour for a sustainable management of solid waste starting with waste prevention. The decreased amounts of waste generated will on the long run contribute to less pressure on municipal solid waste management scheme in Bourj Hammoud and reduce health disparities that result from improper solid waste management (Hilal *et al.* 2015). Since this campaign is based on the involvement of residents in the waste management plan, it will improve their civic engagement through promoting an environmental friendly lifestyle (Hilal *et al.* 2015). Moreover, if the plan succeeds, it will present Bourj Hammoud citizens as innovators in waste reduction, a strategy and concept that are absent in Lebanon, thus influencing other neighbouring cities to adopt reduce and reuse as strategies to manage waste. The main focus of this campaign is to enhance knowledge and to engage citizens in Bourj Hammoud in waste reduction and reuse through sending messages tailored to each target audience.

Situation analysis

Literature review: prior campaigns

A first recycling campaign implemented by MOSA in Bourj Hammoud during 2015 was relatively successful. Most of the residents were responsive and started sorting in their houses; however, several obstacles prevented the progress of the campaign and those relate to the absence of recycling bins, inability of collecting trucks to move in the narrow streets of Bourj Hammoud, and the refusal of residents to place recycling bins next to their buildings. Hence the willingness of Bourj Hammoud's residents to recycle and the growing waste crisis in

Lebanon triggered us to plan a social marketing campaign to reduce unneeded amounts of food and utensils in order to minimise waste generation in Bourj Hammoud. Taking into consideration that no reduction campaign was previously implemented in Lebanon, it is difficult to find benchmarks to validate our plan; however, AUB has recently initiated a campaign to enhance waste reduction among university students, which was similar to a campaign that took place in the Prince George campus of the University of Northern British Columbia (UNBC) (Smyth *et al.* 2010). In the campaign implemented in UNBC, various educational and policy techniques were proposed to encourage waste reduction. Some of these techniques influenced our campaign and include the educational material prepared for waste reduction and the packaging reduction strategy.

SWOT analysis

Below are the results of our SWOT analysis, conducted for the Ministry of Social Affairs (MOSA).

Strengths

- **Education and preparation.** The staff at MOSA have an educational background and a general insight about the environmental problems that occur in Lebanon. In their capacity-building programme, they discuss current health topics with residents; in one of the previous sessions, waste sorting was spontaneously raised by many members of the community.

- **Responsiveness.** The staff respond to people's needs and concerns in a timely manner.

- **Partnerships and networks.** MOSA has strong connections with non-governmental organisations (NGOs), centres and other governmental agencies. For example, MOSA coordinates with the Ministry of Education in the implementation of a health promotion programme at public and semi-private schools. Moreover, in their recycling campaign, MOSA collaborated with TERRE Liban, an NGO devoted to the creation and implementation of environmental education within Lebanon.

- **History of programmes offered.** MOSA offers a great variety of health and environmental programmes that target different age groups. The latest was the recycling campaign that was partially successful and had to stop because of infrastructural weaknesses (i.e. a lack of integrated waste management facilities in the area). The success of such programmes enhances MOSA's reliability and increases the residents' trust in the quality of its work.

- **Good reputation.** MOSA is a governmental centre and this increases its influence in Bourj Hammoud. Accordingly, residents follow the recommendations and apply the safety measures developed by MOSA, particularly in crises and emergency situations.

Weaknesses

- **Limited workforce.** The number of staff may not always be sufficient to conduct needed projects or to reach out to as many residents as possible.

- **Contingency programmes.** In some cases, MOSA has to prioritise projects over others because of emerging needs. Although the implementation of earlier projects does not stop, the effectiveness of their work might be affected.

Opportunities

- **New partnerships.** MOSA receives continuous support and services from NGOs. Since MOSA is a governmental centre that has been successfully responding to people's needs, it is possible that other governmental agencies would like to collaborate with MOSA. The MOE could be interested in supporting the waste management initiatives developed by MOSA, including this waste reduction campaign.

- **The environmental threat demands action.** The unpleasant smell of the accumulated waste and the health threats (not only diseases) that might emerge because of the waste crisis drove residents towards revolution.

Threats

- **Competition with the municipality.** The municipality is planning recycling projects with several NGOs and this might be more encouraging for residents than waste reduction because they had previously engaged in recycling.

- **Social background.** Most of the residents are of low socioeconomic status and do not purchase excess amounts of food. This might reduce the efficiency of the waste-reduction method.

- **Landfill reopening.** The reopening of Naameh landfill and Bourj Hammoud open dump might affect people's interest in waste reduction and their willingness to engage in waste reduction activities.

- **Limited governmental funding.** The governmental funds allocated to MOSA are limited which requires them to find alternative financial resources.

- **Political instability.** The unstable political situation in Lebanon affects the sustainability of any ongoing or potential community project.

Segmenting the population in Bourj Hammoud

The priority target audience is divided into two segments: (1) households and (2) students attending schools in Bourj Hammoud. We used a differentiated marketing approach, based on income for households, and age/class for students in schools. The demographic information related to target audience was retrieved from a meeting with the deputy mayor. According to the deputy mayor, there are 20,000 households and 28 schools in the area. The population size in Bourj Hammoud during the day is around 220,000 people, proportionally distributed according to their income levels: 80% is considered of low socioeconomic status and 20% of middle/high socioeconomic status. The population includes people who work in the area but do not necessarily reside there. The whole population is affected by the waste crisis and the national waste management strategy that does not include any of the 3Rs (reduce, reuse and recycle).

The first target audience, households, was selected due to their major contribution to waste production in Bourj Hammoud, according to the deputy mayor. By choosing households to be a target audience, the aim is to influence the knowledge, attitudes, and behaviours of both men and women living in the household. In fact, men and women are the purchasers of food and other goods. Influencing their behaviour will lead to reducing the amount of waste produced starting from the quantity and type of products bought. According to a focus group conducted at MOSA with eight housewives from the area of Bourj Hammoud (see details below), knowledge regarding the waste problem and positive attitude towards recycling and reducing were present. However, the participants expressed their intention to recycle if the infrastructures allowed, and were more likely to reduce waste (e.g. paper) than other goods. This was further confirmed by our observations and knowledge in regard to the waste management in Lebanon following the waste crisis.

The second segment of our target, students in schools aged 6 to 14 years old, were selected based on MOSA's experience with the previous recycling campaign that addressed students in schools. Further segmentation of students is done according to their age/class. The first segment includes students from grade 1 until 5 (aged 6 to 10), and the second segment includes students from grade 6 until grade 9 (aged 11 to 14). We are aware that there might be students who are older in a class. We consider these cases to be a minority and that the general messages that tackle both segments of students may result in a better response. Those who are above grade 9, almost older than 14 years, were excluded from the plan due to the absence of high schools in Bourj Hammoud. As MOSA was previously able to successfully promote recycling among this target group, we believe that promoting waste reduction would be equally accepted.

The choice of our target groups was also based on theoretical considerations. According to the Social Cognitive Theory, adults, and parents in particular, are considered to be role models in the eyes of their children (Bussey and Bandura 1999). On the other hand, children have a remarkable effect on their parents and can impact their behaviours and attitudes (Mandel 2013). This is another factor for choosing students which is to reinforce the behaviour at the household level. Taking into consideration this dual influence between children and parents, changing the behaviour of children will be complementary to that of their parents, which will eventually lead to a maximum impact.

We also considered other important stakeholders as potential target groups of our initiative. These include the schools' administrators, food and beverage shops, and the municipality. In addition to the 28 schools, there are more than 700 supermarkets, mini-markets, snack and juice shops, and bakeries in Bourj Hammoud, so the opportunities to engage with the target group are many. However, we considered them as potential partners and stakeholders, as we believe their role will be to endorse and support the campaign efforts, hence indirectly affecting the knowledge, attitudes and behaviours of our target audiences.

Formative research

On 8 March, 2016, a focus group discussion was organised and delivered by MOSA with a convenience sample of eight female residents from Bourj Hammoud representing the household segment. During the focus group discussion, key influential groups and competing forces were identified, as well as the benefits and barriers to reducing and reusing waste. Below we summarise the results of the focus group discussion, coupled with an insight from the literature and formative research done with MOSA.

Key influential groups

At the household level, local authorities represented by the municipality and MOSA are major influential groups that can motivate residents to support their own waste reduction behaviour. The municipality expressed its willingness to collaborate with the campaign organisers and to assist in encouraging residents to reduce waste through recognition and other incentives. Moreover, MOSA was interested in involving several stakeholders from Bourj Hammoud to increase the effectiveness of the campaign (see Figure CS7.1). For instance, restaurants, and through partnerships, can assist in directing the behaviour of residents towards waste minimization particularly food waste. Restaurants will be interested in joining the campaign because this will improve their image as environmental friendly places. On the other side, supermarkets, who are considered major market players, might oppose the implementation of this campaign because it will reduce their profit. This is why we chose to partner with both, restaurants and supermarkets, and focus on their important civic role and how this campaign will not harm their businesses. It will only orient customers to choosing certain products over others.

On the level of schools, participants suggested that teachers and administrators impact the involvement of students in waste reduction. Teachers and administrative directors can contribute to the campaign by supporting and endorsing the activities delivered and by providing guidance to students.

Competing behaviours, forces and choices

The national crisis led to the evolution of competing priorities within the waste management scheme. Residents might have perceived waste minimisation as an unnecessary step while waste was disposed of without proper segregation in open dumps. Additionally, the municipality was working on four recycling pilot projects, hence creating some internal competition with a related behaviour. Furthermore, residents are not used to engaging in waste reduction activities. According to the focus group discussion and MOSA workers,

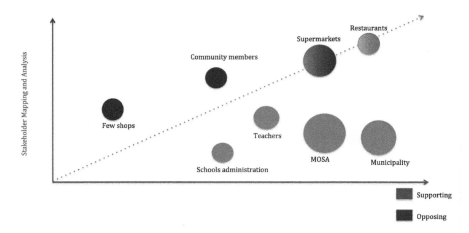

Figure CS7.1 Stakeholder mapping

most residents did not purchase only what they need but were also influenced by market trends. Additionally, they did not take into account the importance of reducing waste generation while purchasing goods.

Perceived barriers

According to the focus group discussion, perceived barriers and costs included the following themes:

- *Unclear concept*: Lack of understanding about waste reduction and how the concept is different from recycling. Residents felt that waste reduction is not clear even though some were engaging in waste reduction activities without knowing it. They believed that if their understanding of the concept improves, they would be able to better participate in reducing or reusing activities. Moreover, this knowledge gap was consistently reported in the literature (e.g. Cox *et al.* 2010; Sharp *et al.* 2010).

- *Effort needed*: Need for time and effort to engage in reducing and reusing because this is a new concept that requires rethinking while shopping. Both households and students will be exerting extra effort to change from producing excess waste to preventing the generation of unneeded waste.

- *Inability to see benefits*: Inability to identify the benefits from reducing waste especially with the opening of the dump in Bourj Hammoud.

- *High perceived cost*: Higher cost associated with waste reduction when compared to producing excess waste, because they will have to purchase reusable bags instead of free plastic ones and glass containers instead of cheaper alternative products, etc.

- *No social support*: Lack of social support because reducing activities might be socially associated with being 'stingy', as the Lebanese and Arab culture is based on sharing abundant food and goods within the family and with guests.

Perceived benefits

Likewise, the benefits emerging in the focus group discussion included the following themes:

- *Space saving solution*: The focus on reducing waste generation in a crowded area such as Bourj Hammoud will allow citizens to save spaces in their houses and neighbourhood and to reclaim them from waste.

- *Responsible citizens*: Residents will recognise the importance of their participation in waste reduction practices and activities in such a national crisis and will be delighted by the 'responsible citizens' identity that they will hold.

- *Social cohesion*: Since almost all households are targeted in this campaign, social cohesion can result from participating in this campaign because all residents will follow the same plan, gather in events and share their experiences.

According to the literature, common benefits of waste reduction include the following themes:

- *Health benefits*: Waste reduction and reuse are preventive approaches which result in numerous health benefits and protection from risks associated with waste generation (Zorpas *et al.* 2015).

- *Reduced environmental impact*: Waste reduction, unlike recycling, helps in preventing the environmental impact of both waste production and waste treatment (Yano and Sakai 2016). Reusing material also reduces the amount of carbon dioxide emissions associated with the production of new items (Cox *et al.* 2010).

- *Saving natural resources*: This method also helps in preserving the finite natural resources by reducing both waste generation and energy consumption (United States Environmental Protection Agency 2016).

- *Cost-effectiveness*: Although some residents might link waste reduction to higher cost, this strategy is cost effective and provides residents with opportunities to save money (reduce food waste, use refillable containers etc.) (UK Department for Environment, Food and Rural Affairs UK 2013).

Aims and objectives

The goal of our campaign is to reduce waste production in Bourj Hammoud. The campaign raises awareness about the importance of reducing waste production and provides the target population with several potential methods that can be used to 'reduce', tailored specifically for each segment of our campaign. In other words, the campaign educates the target population to integrate 'reducing' in their daily practices, aiming to indirectly protect participants' health and the environment. In brief, we want our target population to know the benefits of reducing, believe that reducing protects their health and saves the environment, and replace their wasteful practices with more environmentally friendly activities. Specifically, our campaign will aim to increase the number of Bourj Hammoud households and students that recognise the significant health benefits of reducing waste and believe that protecting the environment will be good for the entire society. Additionally, we aim to increase the number of households who believe that by reducing waste they can reduce the impact of the waste crisis on the long term. Ultimately, we want our target audience to start reducing waste and to adopt innovative techniques suggested by our campaign.

Formulation of strategy

Product

The core product includes the valuable knowledge and benefits that result from the information and activities delivered through this campaign. For households, these include information on methods to: plan the purchase of goods from shops; reduce food waste production at home; reuse products. For both households and students, the strategy includes the delivery of messages on the importance of such behaviours from an environmental and health perspective. The actual product includes PowerPoint or other presentations, videos, posters, and a guide/manual that will be distributed to households and be used to support the campaign goals. Additionally, we will provide an educational kit for students (including posters to be hung in classrooms and on bulletin boards, game materials, as well as magnets with 'reduce messages' that will be provided as take-home material) and guidelines for teachers. The team agreed on the choice of deliverables with MOSA team and these will be written in Arabic to reach the largest number of households and students.

Place

The behaviour of waste reduction (and waste production) takes place at home, especially when preparing food and cleaning afterwards. Students in schools are also responsible for waste production as they are spending most of their day in school. However, the exact moment when waste is generated is highly unpredictable. Considering these factors, households and schools will be considered the place where the behaviour takes place. The physical spaces of the household and of schools will contain posters and visual cues that will prompt the behaviour as described below in the promotion section. All households will be invited to attend regular awareness and educational sessions at MOSA on ways to reduce waste. Those training sessions will be supported with presentations and posters. Additionally, banners and posters will be hung in MOSA and in partner supermarkets and restaurants to enhance their behaviour.

Schools will be recruited through invitations to join the campaign addressing the respective principals. The MOSA team having previously delivered activities in some of the schools in Bourj Hammoud, provided us with feedback regarding the most appropriate and visible areas in which the posters could be hung in the schools other than classrooms, including bulletin boards and playgrounds near cafeterias and waste containers. Presentations, training sessions, and games will take place in classrooms or theatres.

Promotion

Since our target audience is composed of low and high socioeconomic status, some messages will target both segments and some will be specific to each segment. Different messages will be delivered to households through presentations, posters, brochures, and interactive activities; these include:

- highlighting the destructive impact of waste on the environment, complemented with the need to reduce the use of plastic bag consumption;

- encouraging people to buy in bulk such as buying a gallon of water rather than six small bottles which will reduce the cost and amount of waste, saving up space at home. Food items with price tags on them are going to be brought to the training sessions to explain further how to buy our items for a healthier lifestyle and at less cost in the long term;

- encouraging people to buy their food in glass jars instead of cans to preserve their health and reuse glass jars;

- encouraging people to use reusable bags instead of plastic bags;

- restraining the purchase of items that are not needed and may end up in the garbage;

- encouraging people to cook/order smaller amounts of food to reduce food waste. And in case they are eating outside, to take away the amount left and give it away;

Messages for households included in the campaign

"Reduce waste. Reduce disease."

"Don't throw away food! Someone else needs it."

"Save your money, you need it for other things."

"Be a vector for change, reduce garbage!"

"Leave space in your house for your children to play."

"Empty the drawer and get it all in one."

"Buy to reuse!"

For the schools, since our target population is students aged 6 to 14 years old, the media channels that will be used in the promotion of reduce and reuse behaviours will be attractive, easy to read, and easy to understand. The promotion material includes presentations, an educational kit and a set of posters, which deliver the following ideas:

- Encourage reducing and reusing will help decrease the amount of accumulated waste which negatively affects the environment and human health. This will be displayed with cartoon images of waste and sick children and parents (fever, coughing, etc.). The negative messages in the framing of this behavior are expected to be effective since the negative consequences of the waste crisis are already present and felt by all of the Bourj Hammoud population, starting with the odour and respiratory complaints.

- Encourage students to find ways to reduce paper waste by writing on both sides of the paper and encouraging students to give previously used books to school library since there is a system already in some schools that collects used books and redistributes them to new students.

- Encourage students to use refillable water/juice bottles and lunchboxes with different colours and provide pictures of children using them. The age of children in the posters is the same as that of the two segments, thus two sets of posters will be produced.

Furthermore, a competition will be held to see which grade level can generate the lowest amount of waste by monitoring wastebins in classrooms on a selected day in the month. The results will be publicised on bulletin boards and shared with other classes, teachers, and parents. The announcement of results will be followed by a 'Best Waste Reduction Class Ambassador Award' presented to the winning class in each school. Furthermore, and in order to maintain the participation of all schools in Bourj Hammoud in this campaign, schools joining the campaign will be issued a Certificate of Appreciation and given the chance to share their success with other schools, the district, and the larger community.

To ensure a committed participation in the programme, students will be encouraged to sign a pledge to bring a waste-free lunch to school. An example of a pledge could be "In order to use fewer natural resources and send less waste to the landfill, I agree to bring a waste-free lunch every Tuesday" and then expand it to other week days. The pledge is used for this age group, which is in the teenage phase, due to the increased sense of responsibility that they develop. A certificate, 'Environmentally Committed Leader', is given at the end of the year to those students who would show the highest commitment.

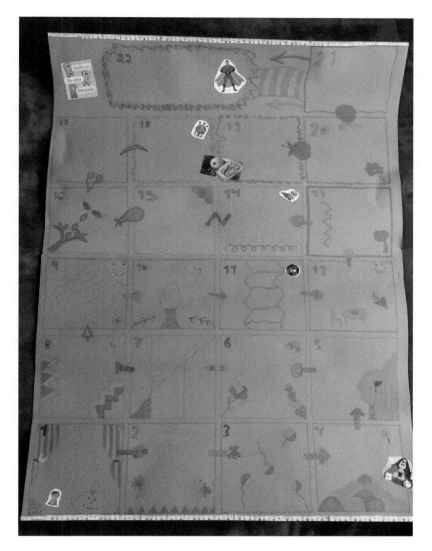

Figure CS7.2 Sample of classroom activity for students aged 6 to 10 years

Messages for school students included in the campaign

"Reduce waste. Reduce disease."

"Plastic is out. Recycling is in. Be cool!"

"Do not abuse paper. Reduce and reuse!"

"Don't Waste the Taste."

"Don't throw food! Someone else needs it."

"Books to library not to garbage."

Price

The main focus is to decrease the monetary and nonmonetary cost for households who will effectively engage in reducing waste generation. For the households, costs that should be taken into account will include the following:

- The perceived cost of buying in bulk for people with low socioeconomic status. The message to be delivered here is that although the short-term cost is higher, in the long term it is more cost effective.

- The extra time spent in planning what items to buy in order to reduce waste is a perceived nonmonetary cost.

- The cost of reusable/cloth bags compared to the free nylon bags. The counterargument is that the reusable bags have a longer lifetime and could use less space when compared to nylon bags which accumulate in drawers at home. Moreover, the cost of reusable bags is minimal when compared to nylon bags which have very high environmental cost (Wagner n.d.).

- The cost of buying food in glass containers is higher than that of buying them in cans or plastic bags. However, glass containers can be reused for other purposes and present a lower health hazard when compared to cans (Korfali and Hamdan 2013).

- Culture plays an important role in framing the lifestyle of the Lebanese people, for example takeaways are not a natural part of Lebanese culture and so they are hesitant in requesting them.

- Cooking a smaller quantity is not very common because a large quantity is better within the Lebanese mindset.

- The cost of commuting to MOSA was calculated to be less than $1 which is not a major monetary cost that residents participating in the campaign have to bear.

For the students, the costs include:

- The cost of extra time invested in the daily preparation of the lunchbox and water bottle.

- Students do not have to pay for transportation since the campaign will be being delivered in their classrooms once per month.

- The cost associated with planning the delivery time of the campaign will depend on each school's strategy (either delivered within the curriculum or during extracurricular activities on weekends). The latter will most probably have a higher monetary and nonmonetary costs on both schools and students. These include the cost of opening the school for an extra day and the need for additional energy and human and thus it would be advisable to disregard this option.

- Another cost for students is the time taken from the recess to ensure that they are consuming their lunch as a way to reduce food waste in schools. Students usually invest a lot of time playing during the recess and forget to eat their food, which might end up in the garbage.

- Moreover, the short-term monetary cost of buying a lunchbox and refillable bottles may be perceived to be higher than buying plastic bottles and double packaging the lunch using papers and plastic bags; however, comparing the lifetime of both indicates the cost-effectiveness of the former choice.

Partnerships

A partnership with food and beverage shops can have an influential role in enhancing reduction behaviours among residents. These shops will be encouraged to partner with us under the title of Corporate Social Responsibility which implies giving back to their community and the environment. We will invite the shop owners to attend a meeting at the municipality because of the influential and regulatory role that the municipality has over these partners. In this meeting, we will inform them about our campaign, focusing on the environmental and health impacts of waste in Bourj Hammoud. We will communicate with them our plan and messages. We will then ask who would be willing to hang up posters and banners in their shops, including messages and slogans stressing the environmental and health impacts of waste along with messages on reducing food waste and packaging.

Supermarkets will be encouraged to promote recycled and reusable items such as napkins and glass-filled items and reusable bags. Posters will also be placed at each store's entrance/exit and on the displays where reusable bags are sold. Food shops will be encouraged to reduce double packaging and wrapping items excessively as this would reduce costs too. Also, they would be encouraged to buy recycled items such as napkins which cost less. Restaurants will be asked to encourage the 'takeaway' strategy in which any food remaining on plates will be placed in a box (with minimal packaging) to take home and eat or even give away. Supermarkets will be encouraged to promote recycled and reusable items such as napkins, and glass-filled items, and reusable bags.

The municipality will have an encouraging and follow-up role to ensure that those partners are collaborating in spreading the word and reducing waste production. From MOSA's side, certificates of recognition will be distributed to all partners as an incentive to encourage sustainable behaviours among them.

As mentioned before, schools and more specifically the administration and teachers are very important partners in this campaign since we are addressing students and part of the campaign will take place there. Thus, trainers delivering the sessions will have to work with teachers to incorporate the campaign's messages into classroom studies and to ensure the monitoring of students' behaviours (reduce and reuse). The schools will also also involved in the campaign by competing with other schools, providing their students with certificates, and maintaining the games and activities inside the classrooms.

Acknowledgements

The authors wish to thank focus group discussion participants and the personnel at the Ministry of Social Affairs, in particular Ms. Bernadette Kreidi, who closely worked with our team. We also wish to thank the Center for Public Health Practice for supporting the collaboration with MOSA by initially coordinating the meetings and then organising transportation to MOSA facilities.

Case study questions

1. What are the major challenges to the implementation of the social marketing plan for solid waste management in Bourj Hammoud?

2. What are alternative 'price tactics' that might be applied in this case?

3. What is the role of 'promotion' in achieving the goals of the plan?

4. What role can public health professionals and social marketers play in influencing the national government to solve the problem in Bourj Hammoud?

References

AUB (2015) AUB Task Force on Solid Waste Management: Addressing the Lebanon Trash Crisis. Online at: www.aub.edu.lb/communications/media/Documents/sep-15/task-force-waste-EN. pdfhttps://www.aub.edu.lb/communications/media/Documents/sep-15/task-force-waste-EN.pdf (accessed 23 October 2015).

Bussey, K. and Bandura, A. (1999) 'Social cognitive theory of gender development and differentiation', *Psychological Review*, 106(4): 676. Online at: www.ncbi.nlm.nih.gov/pubmed/10560326 (accessed 1 May 2016).

Cordier, S., Chevrier, C., Robert-Gnansia, E., Lorente, C., Brula, P. and Hours, M. (2004) 'Risk of congenital anomalies in the vicinity of Municipal Solid Waste Incinerators', *Occupational and Environmental Medicine*, 61(1): 8–15.

Cordier, S., Lehébel, A., Amar, E., Anzivino-Viricel, L., Hours, M., Monfort, C. and Robert-Gnansia, E. (2010) 'Maternal residence near municipal waste incinerators and the risk of urinary tract birth defects', *Occupational and Environmental Medicine*, 67(7): 493–499.

Cox, J., Giorgi, S., Sharp, V., Strange, K., Wilson, D. C. nd Blakey, N. (2010) 'Household waste prevention—a review of evidence', *Waste Management & Research*, 28(3): 193–219.

Elliott, P., Shaddick, G., Kleinschmidt, I., Jolley, D., Walls, P., Beresford, J. and Grundy, C. (1996) 'Cancer incidence near municipal solid waste incinerators in Great Britain', *British Journal of Cancer*, 73(5): 702–710.

Federico, M., Pirani, M., Rashid, I., Caranci, N. and Cirilli, C. (2010) 'Cancer incidence in people with residential exposure to a municipal waste incinerator: An ecological study in Modena (Italy), 1991–2005', *Waste Management*, 30(7): 1362–1370.

Hilal, N., Fadlallah, R., Jamal, D., El-Jardali, F., K2P Evidence Summary: Approaching the Waste Crisis in Lebanon: Consequences and Insights into Solutions. Knowledge to Policy (K2P) Center. Beirut, Lebanon; December 2015

Hsiue, T.R., Lee, S.S. and Chen, H.I. (1991) 'Effects of air pollution resulting from wire reclamation incineration on pulmonary function in children', *Chest*, 100(3): 698.

Korfali, S.I. and Hamdan, W.A. (2013) 'Essential and toxic metals in Lebanese marketed canned food: Impact of metal cans', *Journal of Food Research*, 2(1): 19–30.

Mandel, P. (2013) *Children as Change Agents: The Influence of Integrating Environmental Education into Home Learning Projects on Families and Community Members*. Online at: http://digitalcommons. fiu.edu/cgi/viewcontent.cgi?article=1098&context=sferc (accessed 1 May 2016).

MOE/EU/UNDP (2014) *Lebanon Environmental Assessment of the Syrian Conflict & Priority Interventions*. Online at: www.undp.org/content/dam/lebanon/docs/Energy%20and%20Environment/Publications/ EASC-WEB.pdfhttp://www.undp.org/content/dam/lebanon/docs/Energy and Environment/ Publications/EASC-WEB.pdf (accessed 1 May 2016).

MOE/LEDO/ECODIT (2001) *State of the Environment Report 2001*. Online at: www.moe.gov. lb/getattachment/The-Ministry/Reports/State-Of-the-Environment-Report-2001/Chap-8-Water.pdf.aspxhttp://www.moe.gov.lb/getattachment/The-Ministry/Reports/State-Of-the-Environment-Report-2001/Chap-8-Water.pdf.aspx (accessed 23 October 2015).

National Public Health Partnership (NPHP) (2001) Promoting active transport: a portfolio of interventions. Melbourne: NPHP.

Ranzi, A., Fano, V., Erspamer, L., Lauriola, P., Perucci, C. A. and Forastiere, F. (2011) 'Mortality and morbidity among people living close to incinerators: A cohort study based on dispersion modeling for exposure assessment', *Environmental Health: A Global Access Science Source*, 10(1): 22–28.

Saliba N. *et al.* (2015) AUB press release December 1, 2015. Online at: www.aub.edu.lb/news/2015/Pages/carcinogen-waste-fires.aspx (accessed 1 May 2016).

Sharp, V., Giorgi, S. and Wilson, D.C. (2010) 'Delivery and impact of household waste prevention intervention campaigns (at the local level)', *Waste Management & Research*, 28(3): 256–268.

Shy, C.M., Degnan, D., Fox, D.L., Mukerjee, S., Hazucha, M.J., Boehlecke, B.A., Bromberg, P.A. (1995) 'Do waste incinerators induce adverse respiratory effects? An air quality and epidemiological study of six communities', *Environmental Health Perspectives*, 103(7/8): 714–724.

Smyth, D.P., Fredeen, A.L., Booth, A.L. (2010) 'Reducing solid waste in higher education: The first step towards 'greening'a university campus.' Resources, Conservation and Recycling, 54(11): 1007–16.

UK Department for Environment, Food and Rural Affairs (2013) *Waste Prevention Programme for England. Call for evidence.* Online at: www.gov.uk/government/consultations/waste-prevention-programme-for-england (accessed 1 May 2016).

United States Environmental Protection Agency (2016) Reducing and Reusing Basics. Online at: www.epa.gov/recycle/reducing-and-reusing-basics#benefits (accessed 1 May 2016).

Wagner, J. (n.d.) *The Effects of Plastic Bags on Environment: Health Guidance.* Online at: www.healthguidance.org/entry/14901/1/The-Effects-of-Plastic-Bags-on-Environment.html (accessed 1 May 2016).

Yano, J., Sakai, SI. (2016) 'Waste prevention indicators and their implications from a life cycle perspective: a review', *Journal of Material Cycles and Waste Management*, 18(1): 38–56.

Zorpas, A. A., Lasaridi, K., Voukkali, I., Loizia, P. and Chroni, C. (2015) 'Promoting sustainable waste prevention strategy activities and planning in relation to the Waste Framework Directive in insular communities', *Environmental Processes*, 2(1): 159–173.

"I know what I'm doing"

Communicating a safety message to change the attitudes and behaviours of older men

Linda Brennan, Glen Donnar, Lukas Parker and Natalia Alessi

Introduction

Drowning is an all too frequent occurrence in Australia where the climate is conducive to outdoor activities, and lifestyle and leisure choices often revolve around water. Males represent more than 80 per cent of all drowning deaths, and a third of all such incidents (34%) concern people aged 55 and over (Royal Life Saving Society – Australia 2016). Alcohol and illicit drugs are a contributing factor in many drownings, but the relaxation of inhibitions, lowered perception of risk and masculine dynamics of competence and autonomy also increase the risk. Even more tellingly, experience on the water does not lower the risk, with aquatic leisure activities not considered a risk by either experienced or inexperienced water users because potential negative consequences are not conceived as tangible, present or realistic. This is a key reason why social marketing campaigns targeting middle-aged or older men commonly fail to change behaviours or attitudes about water safety. This case study of the Royal Life Saving Society – Australia's 2014 campaign, *'The Talk' – Reducing Drowning in People over 55*, provides recommendations on how to design social marketing strategies that are applied across the social system, rather than just targeting the individual.

Problem definition

Australians identify an outdoor, active lifestyle, including water-related leisure activities, as an integral aspect of the national character, even into older age. However, 2016 research shows that a third of all drowning deaths (34%) are people aged 55 and over (Royal Life Saving Society – Australia 2016).[1] Males are four times more likely to drown than women, despite both being relatively equally represented in aquatic leisure consumption (Australian Bureau of Statistics 2012). Tellingly, the 45–54 age group registered a 26% increase over the 10-year average to 2015 (Royal Life Saving Society – Australia 2015). In addition, in their 2016 report on drowning, the Royal Life Saving Society – Australia (RLSSA) warns of the increase in drowning risk when combining aquatic activities with the use of alcohol or illicit drugs. Where alcohol was known to have been consumed prior to drowning, 40% of those victims recorded a blood alcohol content (BAC) reading at least four times over the legal limit to drive (i.e. 0.2mg/L) (Royal Life Saving Society – Australia 2016; see also Driscoll *et al.* 2003).

This combination of factors represents a unique social marketing challenge. How does social marketing address a difficult-to-reach market, i.e. male, mature, and highly resistant to messaging about safety? It therefore also represents an opportunity to address men's well-documented resistance to safety messaging (Keller and Honea 2016; Noble *et al.* 2014). This case study of the RLSSA's 2014 campaign, 'The Talk' – Reducing Drowning in People over 55,[2] showcases a social-system approach to social messaging that challenges the prevailing presumption in advertising that awareness alone will lead to a spontaneous, self-directed behaviour change by individuals. Our case study seeks to deepen our understanding of how social marketing campaigns could effectively address older males and meaningfully change their behaviour. In this context, initiatives need to look beyond safety messaging to tackle the systemic issues that lead to unsafe behaviour during aquatic activities.

Competitive analysis

This study identifies six competitors[3] based on extant research into drowning (see for example, Croft and Button 2015; Peden *et al.* 2016; Schmidt *et al.* 2016; Turgut and Turgut 2012; Zhu *et al.* 2015). These include (1) Inherent Competitors; (2) Human Competitors, including (2a) Internal factors and (2b) External factors; (3) Cultural Competitors; (4) Site Competitors; (5) Environmental Competitors and (6) Recreation-related Competitors. All are considered to be threats, behavioural influences or alternatives for people engaged in activities that include water proximity. The summary, presented in Figure CS8.1, excludes drowning deaths as a result of suicide or homicide, deaths from natural causes, shark or crocodile attacks, or hypothermia.

In addition to these competitors, three high-risk factors have been identified. These include (1) the role of alcohol and illicit drugs; (2) the non-use of lifejackets; and (3) the role of pre-existing medical conditions. While there are other causally associated factors, these are the

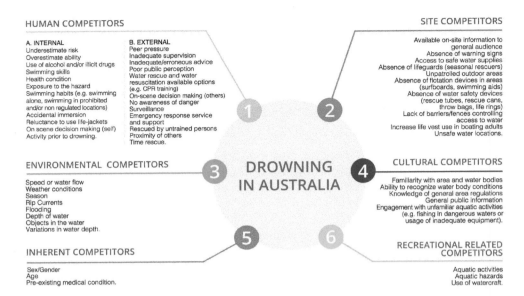

Figure CS8.1 Competitor analysis

(*Source:* developed for this study based on RLSSA and AWSC documents)

most salient among the target population of mid-life and older males. Factors 1 and 2 fall into the category of preventable causes and can be addressed with social marketing. While Factor 3 may be preventable, with aging it is somewhat inevitable; thus, a broader set of stakeholders is required to address the health concerns of middle-aged and older men.

Stakeholder analysis

Stakeholders are identified as individuals; business, non-profit organisations and governmental institutions that engage with the population in varied forms (Buyucek *et al.* 2016; Hastings and Domegan 2013). Stakeholders can be direct or indirect and their contribution to the development of strategies depends on their connection to each other and to the issue of drowning. As such, the range of activities undertaken by stakeholders is varied, and includes the provision of support, information, training, education, awareness, guidance, participation, research, as well as encouraging the growth of sport and recreational activities. This study identifies five different groups of participants that have a stake in reducing drownings, including (1) Community; (2) Regional; (3) State/Territory; (4) National; and (5) the Australian Water Safety Council. Table CS8.1 illustrates the stakeholders and the roles they play in reducing the risk of recreational and sport activities.

Aims and objectives

The overall aim of the Australian Water Safety Strategy 2016–2020 is to reduce the number of deaths by 50% by 2020 (Australian Water Safety Council 2016). The Australian Water Safety Strategy 2016–2020 further aims to increase awareness and initiate behavioural change among the population that engages with recreational activities involving bodies of water.

Table CS8.1 Stakeholder map

	Description	Example	Contribution
INDIVIDUALS	Individuals around water	Friends and peers	Supervision of water activities by responsible and sober adults
	People who swim	Personal responsibility	Individual responsible engagement with water activities (e.g. do not swim alone, do not swim drunk, do not swim in prohibited or non-regulated locations)
COMMUNITY	Community groups	Swimming and Lifesaving Clubs	Rescue volunteers in strategic points supervising leisure water activities
	Local Council	Aquatic Centres, Beach Lifeguard Services, Parks and Aquatic Reserves	Provide safe and adequate water leisure services
	Business Sector	Boat, Kayak and SUP Hire	Provide equipment and services that allow for safe water leisure consumption
		Caravan Parks	
		Hotel, Motel and Holiday Rentals	
	Schools	Primary, Secondary, Tertiary (e.g. TAFE)	Provide education and training about water safety, assist with access to target audience
	Business sector	Health Clubs, Sportswear, Safety Gear	Provide support, training, information and networking opportunities for all members who are involved in sport and leisure services throughout Australia
REGIONAL	Regional government agencies	Regional Infrastructure and Services Goulburn Valley Water	To increase the participation and profile of active recreation at state level, supporting the growth and development of community recreation at a state level
	Regional water safety agencies	FarmSafe (and others)	Help with the improving of health and safety in rural communities

(continued)

Table CS8.1 *(continued)*

Description	Example	Contribution
State/territory water safety agencies	State and Territory Branches of Royal Life Saving and Surf Life Saving, offices of AUSTSWIM	Provide lifesaving and drowning prevention programmes; Provide swimming education across all states in Australia; Provide beach safety services
Related organisations	State/Territory-based associations of aquatic facility managers, i.e. Aquatic Recreation Institute (NSW); Leisure Institute of WA (LIWA)	Provide support for managers and staff of professional facilities
State/territory government agencies	State/territory Water Safety Councils, i.e. NT Water Safety TaskForce, Play it Safe by the Water (VIC)	Water Safety Policy; Water Safety promotions via water safety weeks; Coordination of water safety plans
Business sector	Water parks, private service providers, retailers of equipment, manufacturers of safety equipment	Provide safe and fit for purpose services, materials and equipment
The Australian government	Department of Health, Office of Sport	Provision of water safety policy; Provide of funding to peak water safety bodies
National Coordination Mechanism	Australian Water Safety Council	Develops the national water safety strategy (AWSS); Conducts conferences, workshops to support focus on the AWSS
National peak water safety agencies	Royal Life Saving Society Australia; Surf Life Saving Australia; AUSTSWIM	RLSSA to lead efforts to reduce drowning and promote swimming, lifesaving and water safety; SLSA to reduce drowning in the coastal environment; AUSTSWIM – to support the teaching of teachers of swimming and water safety

STATE/ TERRITORY

Other members of the Australian Water Safety Council	Australia New Zealand Safe Boating Education Group (ANZBEG), and related NGOs	The identification and discussion of boating issues
Other members of the Australian Water Safety Council	Australia Leisure Facilities Association (ALFA), and related NGOs	Progression and development of leisure facilities in Australia
Other members of the Australian Water Safety Council	Surfing Australia, related NGOs	To establish, guide and promote the development of safe surfing across states in Australia
Other members of the Australian Water Safety Council, and related NGOs	Divers Alert Network	To promote safety in the diving industry
	Swimming Australia	To promote the sport of swimming
	Australian Swimming Coaches & Teachers Association (ASCTA)	Development practices in the education, accreditation, professional development and on-going support for swimming coaches, and swimming and water safety teachers
	Swimming Pool and Spa Association (SPASA)	Work with member association of business in the area of swimming pools and spas to promote a safe swimming culture
	Australian Local Government Association (ALGA)	Representation of government raising concern to national level

(Source: Developed for this study, based on Australian Water Safety Council 2016)

Of particular concern is the cohort of males aged 45 to 64 where drownings have increased over the last ten years despite efforts that have successfully decreased deaths overall (RLSSA 2016). In line with lowering the numbers of fatalities, it is also an objective to lower the number of non-fatal drowning incidents and morbidities associated with near drownings, including the long-term impacts of extended periods without oxygen to the brain. Given the nature of this problem, a new approach is required: one that does not rely on the mature male to change his behaviour spontaneously and self-directedly after being the subject of special advertising. This new approach uses a holistic social marketing approach that incorporates a consideration of the behavioural eco-system (Brennan et al. 2016), rather than a narrow focus on individual and peer group behaviour change.

Table CS8.2 outlines the activities undertaken by the RLSSA at each level of the market system (i.e. with the stakeholders identified in Table CS8.1). Each level operates within a set of intervolved activities that takes place before and after the micro-social system is engaged. This means that all stakeholders play their part in ensuring that the problem is being addressed from multiple perspectives.

Table CS8.2 Social marketing activities by level – overall RLSS strategy

Level	Typical focus of social marketing activities	RLSS Strategies
Macro (Government and peak bodies)	1. Advocacy	1. Yes
	2. Public policy negotiations	2. Yes
	3. Public relations	3. Yes
	4. Technical assistance	4. Yes
	5. Financial assistance	5. No
Macro/Meso (National)	6. Public communications	6. Yes
	7. Publicity	7. Yes
	8. Strategic partnerships and alliances	8. Yes
	9. Seminars, consultations and meetings	9. Yes
	10. Conferences and exhibitions	10. Yes
Meso/Micro (Regional and State)	11. Sponsorships	11. Yes
	12. Community participatory action	12. Yes
	13. Training and education resource development	13. Yes
	14. 'Sales' promotions	14. Yes
	15. Online social marketing (information)	15. Yes
	16. Freemiums and giveaways	16. Yes
Micro (Community)	17. Advertising	17. Yes
	18. Social media	18. Yes
	19. Mobile applications	19. Yes
	20. Interpersonal interactions	20. Yes
	21. Direct media such as noticeboards, flyers, brochures, wearable marketing	21. Yes

Research

In addition to the scope of the problem, research shows that the more experienced people become, the more they rely on heuristic existing behavioural repertoires (Kahneman 2011; Tversky and Kahneman 1974; Wright 2016). Unfortunately, when behaviours become either automatic, or unconscious habits become the principal basis for performance of behaviour, new repertoires are difficult to establish. This is especially so if the new repertoire requires a change to lifestyle. The more expert and experienced people are, the more likely they are to reject messaging that challenges their autonomy or competence (Mackie and Asuncion 1990; Quistberg et al. 2014). Learning new repertoires requires breaking old habits, which is increasingly difficult in an environment where people do not perceive any danger or any need for change (Brennan et al. 2014).

Additionally, people engaged in pleasurable behaviours in a leisure situation do not think rationally about their safety (Moran 2011), instead they concentrate on the experience of leisure. They do not want to be inconvenienced or uncomfortable on the way to having fun (Quistberg et al. 2014). As a result, it becomes extremely difficult to connect previous pleasurable experiences to a potential, future risk or threat such as drowning. Phrases such as "I can take care of myself" and "I know what I'm doing" confirm that people do not actively think, for example, about using lifejackets except when out of sight of 'safe' land (Wright 2016) or in difficult weather conditions (Chung et al. 2014). Particularly, given that land is readily visible in inland waterways, which lowers the perceived risk of drowning as a consequence. Further, familiarity decreases the perception of threat (De Pelsmacker et al. 2011; Mangione et al. 2012). That is, men who have pursued a particular aquatic leisure activity for many years will not consider the activity to be potentially unsafe – after all, they have "survived" a long time without incident (Steensberg 1998).

Factors that contribute to men's drowning statistics include over-trusting in skills and behaviour repertoires developed earlier in life and an *actual* level of capability that does not match their *perceived* level of capability. That is, they are not as fit or healthy as they believe. In addition, older people often have more available leisure time, leading to increased opportunity risk. In this context, older people are more likely to be on their own when exposed to a drowning risk (Franklin et al. 2010) and men represent 70% of those that have an incident (Steensberg 1998). Finally, older people may have medical conditions that affect their ability to respond to risk quickly and effectively if an incident occurs. All of these risks are enhanced when alcohol is involved (Franklin et al. 2010). Thus, an individual behaviour change strategy using social advertising as the principal tool will not shift long-standing behavioural repertoires. Any intervention needs to provide a support infrastructure for skills development, skills renewal and maintenance, as well as normalising the use of safety devices such as lifejackets, and support people in learning life-saving skills and avoiding alcohol around water. Therefore, many participants need to be mobilised to provide the required supporting infrastructure.

Intervention

As a consequence of message resistance and a reliance on behavioural repertoires that are or may now be unsafe, the RLSSA initiated a campaign aimed at older males that uses their adult children as the key communicator of the safety message. The ad was designed to encourage families to talk about water safety with a view to shifting cultural norms through reverse socialisation (Watne *et al.* 2011), that is, where children socialise parents into new ways of thinking and acting. To be successful, this strategy needs to provide the child with the ammunition needed to persuade the parent. In the case of drowning, this would include wider, integrated social-system support from the stakeholders and the social marketing activities described earlier (see Table CS8.1 and Table CS8.2).

Launched in November, in time for the Australian summer holiday season, the 15-second and 30-second spot ads that were part of the 2014 campaign depict an adult son trying to talk to his aged father about water safety. The ad shows an awkward start to a conversation as the son attempts to engage his father while they fish on a pier, declaring, "Dad, we need to have the talk." The father humorously misconstrues the intent, responding with "What, you're going to talk to me about the birds and the bees?" This permits a light-hearted segue into broaching the main issue, i.e. that over-55 year olds are more vulnerable in and around water than they think.

Figure CS8.2 Promoting YouTube video with social media

(*Source:* RLSSA Twitter account)

The campaign was promoted via stakeholders and social media (YouTube, Facebook and Twitter). The ads appeared nationally as a community service announcement and were supported by a national media campaign and release. The 15-second and 30-second ads were featured on the RLSSA's YouTube channel, and promoted on their Facebook and Twitter feeds (see Figure CS8.2), collectively gaining over 27,000 video views. The 30-second ad on YouTube was promoted on the RLSSA's Facebook page, having a reach of 41,700, receiving 535 clicks and 481 reactions. A PR campaign accompanied this media campaign, including over 100 radio interviews and 16 TV interviews.

Impact

The RLSSA report which was released at the launch of the "The Talk" campaign made recommendations designed to reduce drowning deaths in people aged 50 years and over, including to:

- Create, implement and evaluate a national public awareness campaign targeting known drowning hazards and risks for older people. The awareness campaign could target the role of underlying medical conditions in drowning, high-risk activities for older people and strategies to reduce these risks or the role of alcohol and drugs in drowning.

- Encourage participation in aquatic activity as a way of providing older people with water safety skills while at the same time improving their health and well-being in a low impact setting.

- Explore the presence and impact of underlying medical conditions on drowning in older people.

- Create and implement interventions targeting older people and specially males and the use of watercraft.

While it is part of greater research, "The Talk" campaign is innovative because it is aimed at the adult children of older males, rather than directly at the 'resistant' target. The focus on the community surrounding the target of the behaviour change is a significant shift away from individual behaviour change models. This novel approach could strengthen the campaign's impact, especially when combined with the humorous misunderstanding between father and son, which opened up the conversation.

Evaluation of the campaign

Advertising is not enough in a social system, which is why aiming the campaign at adult children is likely to be more effective. And while younger people are more likely to be safer as a result of previous campaigns, greater attention and increased initiatives are required to aid older people, especially males (Steensberg 1998; Franklin et al. 2010). Reaching out to adult children potentially amplifies the safety message because family members can be a trusted source of information. A personal source of information is also more likely to be persuasive, rather than a direct appeal from an advertisement.

In terms of communication, the campaign ads direct adult children to a mobile phone application. The app distils the campaign messages into a list of five 'dos':

1. Know your limitations.

2. Be aware of medical conditions.

3. No alcohol around water.

4. Wear a lifejacket.

5. Learn lifesaving skills.

Authentic to the idea that the adult child is socialising the parent, the ad does not directly acknowledge older people's experience or ask them to utilise this to develop new repertoires. Yet, there is potential to break old habits if the child can persuade the parent to think or behave differently, which is feasible if the leisure experience is a shared one. Hence, the supporting evidence provided for the child to use while 'talking' to their parent is valuable for the persuasion task.[4] If the message is effectively communicated throughout the social system, the child's task is easier because there are multiple credible sources of information available.

There is, however, limited elaboration on associated solutions to recalibrate the behavioural repertoires evident in the campaign. While noting that people do not engage in rational decisions when engaged in leisure activities, especially those activities involving prospective danger and threats (emotional processing dominates), it is important to create repertoires that are inherently safe *before* participating in water activities. While the ad shows the five key safety recommendations, it does not define them as new repertoires and attitudes. This could be problematic if the older male believes he already possesses the necessary skills and knowledge to navigate aquatic activities without incident. The five listed 'dos' in the campaign are, also, neither clearly connected to each other, nor linked to a definite problem (i.e. one recognised by the older male). Additionally, there is an overall focus on stopping or prohibiting behaviour, rather than supporting behaviour change (other than having adult children speak to parents), with limitations. Existing medical conditions and alcohol are listed before lifejackets and *learning* lifesaving (rather than renewing, updating or teaching it). The situation portrayed in the ad is not in the key location or scenarios for older male drowning, e.g. the father is neither alone nor on a boat. Further, the ad recommends the wearing of lifejackets, yet the father and son shown in the advertisement are land bound in a safe locale and not wearing jackets.

Most interestingly, "The Talk" is not really shown; a voice-over talks over it. The 30-second ad declares "Don't be shy about talking to your parents about the facts of life", but itself exhibits this shyness. This potentially positions reverse socialisation as slightly embarrassing and possibly stigmatises the act of talking about water safety. The expression of the father, initially dismissive, does change as he nods gravely, but this lasts for only three seconds of the ad. Moreover, because the exchange is presented entirely from the son's point-of-view, it may not engage the ultimate target of the safety message. As males are accustomed to deflecting negative messages as not personally relevant, especially if they challenge their autonomy or competence, this could result in 'switching off' rather than 'switching on' to the safety message.

The campaign is designed to encourage talking about safety in safe circumstances in order to ensure that risks are managed before safety becomes an issue. In this context, the 'how to have "The Talk"' website recommends choosing the right moment and provides suggestions for how to get started. The 15-second ad, however, does show the son using one of the suggestions provided on the supporting website.[5] Media coverage at the time of launch showed young people giving their parents 'The Talk'[6] and older Australians being informed of the statistics relating to older people drowning.

Conclusion

The use of communication tools alone in social marketing communications campaigns is insufficient to encourage target audiences, particularly when they are difficult to reach and to persuade, to change their attitude and behaviour. Rather than an approach to social messaging that presumes that awareness will lead to spontaneous, self-directed behaviour change, multi-layered engagement activities and a broader social-systems approach are required to facilitate and support behaviour change. Campaigns need to address Human, Site and Cultural Competitors in an integrated manner to support change, and avoid reactance or resistance. The RLSSA campaign cleverly talks to and co-opts family members, typically more likely to be trusted and accepted, to transmit the safety message to the target. Such a social-systems approach could be ideal for other situations where individuals are less receptive to direct messages. That said, campaigns are less likely to be successful if the message given is unclear or ambiguous. It is critical for campaigns to provide clear direction on how to change behaviour repertoires and to ensure they respect the target's autonomy and competence, especially in the case of experienced older males. In so doing, we may be able to use the dictum, "I know what I'm doing", to encourage rather than resist attitude and behaviour change.

Case study questions

1. Given that there are many stakeholders involved in water safety in Australia, and limited resources (financial, social) how can deaths from drowning be reduced? What is the role of industry in this situation? Explain whether or not you think corporate social marketing could be useful in this case study.

2. Is there too much going on? Would you advise the RLSS to work on one level of the market instead of across all four layers? Explain your reasoning and offer some alternative recommendations.

3. Is a market system approach that excludes industry representative of the market? Why or why not? Who holds industry to account when it comes to human safety? How might industry be engaged in reducing drownings of older males?

Notes

1 More than one quarter of drowning deaths (75) occur in inland waterways, including rivers, creeks, lakes and dams. In 2015–16, 21% of all drownings happened in a river, creek or stream, although with coastline activities being perceived as 'Australian', a significant number of deaths occurred on beaches (63) and ocean or harbour locations (53) (Royal Life Saving Society – Australia, 2016).

2 www.lifesavingwa.com.au/programs/seniors-water-safety.
3 Competitors are conceived as factors that intervene, moderate or vary an individual's behaviours in the environment.
4 www.royallifesaving.com.au/programs/thetalk/how-to-have-the-talk.
5 www.youtube.com/watch?v=J0CALtF46jY.
6 www.sunshinecoastdaily.com.au/news/folks-we-have-to-talk/2465374/.

References

Australian Bureau of Statistics (2012) *1301.0 - Year Book Australia, 2012*. Online at: www.abs.gov.au/ausstats/abs@.nsf/Lookup/by Subject/1301.0~2012~Main Features~Sports and physical recreation~116 (accessed 1 May 2016).

Australian Water Safety Council (2016) *Australian Water Safety Strategy 2016–2020*. Online at: www.watersafety.com.au/AustralianWaterSafetyStrategy/2016-2020Strategy.aspx (accessed 1 May 2016).

Brennan, L., Binney, W., Parker, L., Aleti, T. and Nguyen, D. (2014) *Social Marketing and Behaviour Change: Models, Theory and Applications*. Cheltenham UK: Edward Elgar.

Brennan, L., Previte, J. and Fry, M.-L. (2016) 'Social marketing's consumer myopia: Applying a behavioural ecological model to address wicked problems', *Journal of Social Marketing*, 6(3).

Buyucek, N., Kubacki, K., Rundle-Thiele, S. and Pang, B. (2016) 'A systematic review of stakeholder involvement in social marketing interventions', *Australasian Marketing Journal (AMJ)*, 24(1): 8–19.

Chung, C., Quan, L., Bennett, E., Kernic, M. A. and Ebel, B.E. (2014) 'Informing policy on open water drowning prevention: An observational survey of life jacket use in Washington State', *Inj Prev*, 20(4): 238–243. doi:10.1136/injuryprev-2013-041005.

Croft, J. L. and Button, C. (2015) 'Interacting factors associated with adult male drowning in New Zealand', *PLoS one*, 10(6): e0130545.

De Pelsmacker, P., Cauberghe, V. and Dens, N. (2011) 'Fear appeal effectiveness for familiar and unfamiliar issues', *Journal of Social Marketing*, 1(3): 171–191.

Driscoll, T., Harrison, J.E. and Steenkamp, M. (2003) *'Alcohol* and drowning in *Australia'*, *International Journal of Injury Control and Safety* Promotion, 10(4).

Franklin, R.C., Scarr, J.P. and Pearn, J.H. (2010) 'Reducing drowning deaths: The continued challenge of immersion fatalities in Australia@, *Med J Aust*, 192(3): 123–126.

Hastings, G. and Domegan, C. (2013) *Social Marketing: From Tunes to Symphonies*: Routledge.

Kahneman, D. (2011) *Thinking, Fast and Slow*. New York: Farrar, Straus and Giroux.

Keller, S.N. and Honea, J.C. (2016) 'Navigating the gender minefield: An IPV prevention campaign sheds light on the gender gap', *Global Public Health*, 11(1-2): 184–197.

Mackie, D.M. and Asuncion, A.G. (1990) 'On-line and memory-based modification of attitudes: Determinants of message recall-attitude change correspondence', *Journal of Personality and Social Psychology*, 59(1): 5.

Mangione, T.W., Chow, W. and Nguyen, J. (2012) 'Trends in life jacket wear among recreational boaters: A dozen years (1999–2010) of US observational data', *Journal of Public Health Policy*, 33(1): 59–74.

Moran, K. (2011) '(Young) men behaving badly: Dangerous masculinities and risk of drowning in aquatic leisure activities', *Annals of Leisure Research*, 14(2–3), 260–272. doi:10.1080/11745398.2011.615719.

Noble, G., Pomering, A. and Johnson, L. (2014) 'Gender and message appeal: Their influence in a pro-environmental social advertising context', *Journal of Social Marketing*, 4(1): 4–21.

Peden, A.E., Franklin, R.C. and Leggat, P.A. (2016) 'Fatal river drowning: The identification of research gaps through a systematic literature review', *Injury Prevention*, injuryprev-2015-041750.

Quistberg, D.A., Bennett, E., Quan, L. and Ebel, B.E. (2014) 'Low life jacket use among adult recreational boaters: A qualitative study of risk perception and behavior factors', *Accident Analysis & Prevention*, 62: 276–284.

Royal Life Saving Society (2015) *National Drowning Report 2015*. Online at: www.royallifesaving.com. au/__data/assets/pdf_file/0006/14559/RLS_NDR2015_Report_LR.pdf (accessed 1 May 2016).

Royal Life Saving Society (2016) *National Drowning Report 2016*. Online at: www.royallifesaving.com. au/__data/assets/pdf_file/0004/18085/RLS_NDR2016_ReportLR.pdf (accessed 1 May 2016).

Schmidt, A.C., Sempsrott, J.R., Hawkins, S.C., Arastu, A.S., Cushing, T.A. and Auerbach, P.S. (2016) 'Wilderness Medical Society practice guidelines for the prevention and treatment of drowning', *Wilderness & Environmental Medicine*, 27(2):236–251.

Steensberg, J. (1998) 'Epidemiology of accidental drowning in Denmark 1989–1993', *Accident Analysis & Prevention*, 30(6): 755–762.

Turgut, A. and Turgut, T. (2012) 'A study on rescuer drowning and multiple drowning incidents', *Journal of Safety Research*, 43(2): 129–132.

Tversky, A. and Kahneman, D. (1974) 'Judgment under uncertainty: Heuristics and biases', *Science*, 185: 1124–1131.

Watne, T., Lobo, A. and Brennan, L. (2011) 'Children as secondary socialisation agents for their parents', *Young Consumers*, 12(4): 285–294.

Wright, M. (2016) 'Beach safety education: A behavioural change approach', in M. Tipton and A. Wooler (eds), *The Science of Beach Lifeguarding* (pp. 235–239). Australia: CRC Press, Taylor & Francis Group.

Zhu, Y., Jiang, X., Li, H., Li, F. and Chen, J. (2015) 'Mortality among drowning rescuers in China, 2013: A review of 225 rescue incidents from the press', *BMC Public Health*, 15(1): 1–8.

Case study 9

Walk to School 2014

Krzysztof Kubacki, Kellye Hartman, Annemarie Wright, Haruka Fujihira and Sharyn Rundle-Thiele

Introduction

Regular physical activity remains the backbone of a healthy lifestyle and provides children with a wide range of physical and cognitive benefits, including the development of healthy musculo-skeletal and cardiovascular systems, the strengthening of mental health, greater confidence and social skills (WHO 2015). One of the main consequences of insufficient physical activity is obesity, and obese and overweight children face an increased risk of poor health outcomes later in life even if they achieve a healthy weight by adulthood (Deckelbaum and Williams 2011).

The World Health Organization (WHO) directs that children and teenagers aged 5–17 years gain significant health benefits by accumulating a minimum of 60 minutes of physical activity every day. This should include vigorous-intensity muscle- and bone-strengthening activities at least three times per week. The WHO (2015) suggests that the daily goal of 60 minutes can be achieved in multiple short bouts throughout the day.

Notwithstanding the importance of physical activity for developing children, there is evidence that physical activity rates decline and sedentary forms of activity increase (e.g. watching TV and spending time on the Internet) as children become older. For example, in the United States only 8% of adolescents engage in the recommended level of physical activity (Troiani *et al.* 2008). The situation in Australia is not much better. Findings from the Australian Health Survey 2011–2012 indicate that only a third of Australian children meet the daily 60 minutes of physical activity recommended by the World Health Organization (2015). Similarly alarming is that around 75% of children spend more than two hours per day on screen-based entertainment (Department of Health 2014).

According to the American Academy of Pediatrics the multiple causes of obesity, including low levels of physical activity, need to be tackled early during childhood (Shonkoff *et al.* 2009), and behaviour change programmes should facilitate the establishment of active living habits early in life. One way to achieve this is by engaging in 'active transport' which refers to travel to a destination by foot or bicycle (NPHP 2001). Active transport has been positively associated with higher daily levels of physical activity and lower levels of obesity (Ainsworth *et al.* 2012; Mendoza *et al.* 2011).

Walking to and from school has been identified as a prime opportunity to increase physical activity levels among children (McMinn *et al.* 2011). Walking is low cost (Rosenberg *et al.* 2006), no equipment is required, and it can be easily integrated into the daily routine (Brophy *et al.* 2011; Pucher and Buehler 2008). However, the rates of active school travel have been declining among Australian children (Crawford and Garrard 2013). In the state of Victoria, less than one in five children walk to school (Australian Bureau of Statistics (ABS) 2011), and car travel is the dominant mode of travel to and from school (64.1%) (Department of Transport 2009).

Social marketing is a key behaviour change approach which has been effective in supporting healthy living habits (Barlovic 2006). A recent systematic review of 23 social marketing interventions targeting children found that social marketing has been successful in improving physical activity behaviours among children (Kubacki *et al.* 2015).

The case study that follows describes the process and outcome evaluation of the Victorian Health Promotion Foundation's (VicHealth) Walk to School 2014 campaign, and illustrates how social marketing can support the achievement of positive outcomes.

Intervention

About VicHealth

The Victorian Health Promotion Foundation (VicHealth) is a pioneer in health promotion – i.e. the process of enabling people to increase control over and improve their health. VicHealth's primary focus is promoting good health and preventing chronic disease.

About Walk to School

VicHealth's Walk to School is a high profile annual community event that encourages primary school students (aged 5–12 years old) and their families across Victoria to walk to and from school as often as possible during the month of October. VicHealth has funded Walk to School since 2006.

Walk to School focuses on positive health outcomes, particularly increased levels of physical activity, and raises awareness of the environmental and social benefits of active travel (walking to and from school), such as reduced traffic and parking congestion, children connecting with their family, friends and neighbourhoods in their journeys, and opportunities for children to develop road safety skills and independence. The following evidence and research informed the design and delivery of Walk to School:

- National guidelines recommend that children aged 5–12 engage in at least 60 minutes of moderate to vigorous physical activity every day (Department of Health and Ageing 2004);
- High levels of persistent physical activity participation in childhood are correlated with adult levels of activity (Telama *et al.* 2005);
- Only one in five children aged 5–17 get the recommended amount of physical activity every day (ABS 2013a);
- Active transport choices – walking and cycling instead of driving – contribute to individual achievement of recommended physical activity levels (Australian Institute of Health and Welfare (AIHW) 2012);
- Less than 20% of Victorian children walk to school (Australian Bureau of Statistics 2013b).

By engaging primary school-aged students and their families, as well as schools and local councils, VicHealth aims to promote behaviour and attitudinal change, as well as policy and environmental change, to support sustainable increases in active travel for the long term.

Aims and objectives

Walk to School 2014 aimed to:

- actively promote the benefits of walking to and from school to children, their families, and the general community;
- build active transport habits among Victorian primary school children, by encouraging them to walk to and from school during October 2014.

The Walk to School *2014* campaign objectives were to:

- engage 56 local councils through the Walk to School grants programme (a 10% increase on 2013 levels);
- secure the active participation of 348 Victorian primary schools in Walk to School activities (a 15% increase on 2013 levels);
- secure the participation of 36,800 primary school students in Walk to School activities (a 15% increase on 2013 levels);
- record walks totalling 472,650 km by participating students (a 15% increase on 2013 levels).

Social marketing activity

Walk to School 2014 took place between 6 and 31 October and was supported by an integrated programme of activity throughout the year. The key elements of the Walk to School 2014 campaign are described below.

Local government grants

VicHealth delivered a grants' programme, offering funding for Victorian local governments to support Walk to School activities through promotions and school engagement in their local communities. Councils were also required to deliver initiatives that promoted ongoing active travel among local primary school students, to ensure walking behaviour was supported and encouraged in the community beyond the end of the Walk to School 2014 campaign. Fifty-two of Victoria's 79 councils received a Walk to School grant in 2014.

Digital platform

VicHealth updated the existing Walk to School website (www.walktoschool.vic.gov.au) and Android and iPhone apps (see Figure CS9.1) to ensure they supported the 2014 campaign effectively. The website allowed parents, schools and councils to create accounts and keep track of their Walk to School activity. The app allowed parents to register their children and track their walks to and from school during the campaign, and included a simple game and digital rewards to incentivise walking.

Updates to the Walk to School website aimed to increase efficiencies and improve user experiences. These included a new collateral order function for schools and councils, customised reports available to councils, the introduction of mobile-friendly web pages, and the inclusion of social media feeds on the home page to provide current, dynamic content.

Community partnership

To reach a broader Victorian audience and support the growth of the Walk to School campaign, VicHealth brokered an in-kind community partnership with an elite sporting organisation. The partner organisation promoted the campaign through its local member networks including social media and email newsletters, provided ambassadors for media engagement activities, and helped secure prizes for schools (such as free sports clinics and equipment) and incentives for participating students (such as co-branded bag tags). With a focus on family engagement and school programmes, the community partner was able to add value to the campaign, and in return was recognised as the Official Community Partner on all key campaign materials.

Figure CS9.1 Walk to School 2014 app

Collateral

A range of branded collateral was produced to support council, school and student participation. Free promotional posters, classroom calendars for tracking walks (see Figure CS9.2), information sheets for schools and parents (see Figure CS9.3), stickers and signs (see Figure CS9.4) were distributed via participating schools and councils.

To make Walk to School information accessible to parents from non-English speaking backgrounds, VicHealth trialled selected translations of the Walk to School information sheet for parents, which were particularly welcomed by participating primary schools in culturally diverse communities.

Paid, earned and owned media

A programme of paid digital advertising was delivered to raise awareness of Walk to School *2014* among parents of primary school-aged children, and encourage sign-ups. Digital advertising was chosen to ensure accurate targeting could be achieved, with relatively low costs for state-wide coverage. Key advertising channels included social media, online and mobile platforms, and Google Adwords.

By engaging a public relations (PR) agency, VicHealth was able to deliver a strong programme of PR and media activity to increase the reach of campaign messages to parents and the broader Victorian community. PR and media activity included local and mainstream media activity, and new ambassador engagement and workplace engagement programmes. The workplace programme promoted Walk to School as a health and wellbeing opportunity

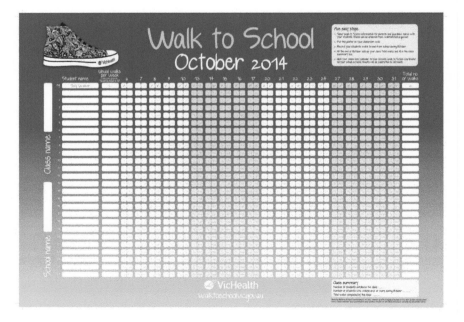

Figure CS9.2 Walk to School 2014 classroom calendar

Information for parents and guardians

Walk to School encourages primary school children to walk to and from school every day in October, to highlight the ways walking improves children's health and wellbeing.

Walking to and from school can help children get the daily physical activity they need – and there are plenty of other benefits too. Walking to school can help to reduce traffic congestion, parking difficulties and the associated environmental impacts.

How your child can get involved

Your child can take part simply by walking to and from school! There are lots of ways for children and families to get involved, and we encourage you to find an option that suits your family.

You might like to:

- walk with your child to and from school and enjoy the chance to talk, help your child learn road safety skills, and get to know the local neighbourhood together
- arrange for your child to walk with other families or friends, giving them time to socialise and share their journey
- drive part of the way to school and walk the rest, particularly if you live a long way from school, or have limited time
- mix it up – if your child enjoys riding their bike or scooter, that's fine too!

Taking part through your child's school

If your child's school is taking part in Walk to School, your child's teacher will record how many times students walk to and from school during October, using a classroom calendar. Schools with the highest participation levels in each region will be eligible for some great prizes – so each time your child walks, they'll also be increasing their school's chances!

Taking part as an individual

If your child's school is not taking part in Walk to School, your child can still participate by signing up, with your permission, using the Walk to School app or at www.walktoschool.vic.gov.au. Your child can then record their walks during October.

The free app includes a game that allows children to create their own imaginary Walk to School journey, and collect bonus creatures and objects for their world with each walk they record. The app is available for free from the iTunes store and Google play.

Competitions and prizes

Regardless of how many times they walk, children can enter fun walking-themed competitions each week, and have a chance of winning some fantastic prizes. Competitions will be promoted on the Walk to School website and Facebook page throughout October.

For more information about Walk to School visit www.walktoschool.vic.gov.au, and follow Walk to School on Facebook and Twitter for the latest news and updates. If you have any questions you can contact walktoschool@vichealth.vic.gov.au.

For more information about VicHealth, visit www.vichealth.vic.gov.au.

Figure CS9.3 Walk to School 2014 information sheet for parents

Figure CS9.4 Walk to School 2014 school sign

through more than 50 large Victorian employers with high proportions of parents with primary school-aged children in order to extend the reach of campaign messages to a broader audience. Earned media delivered strong results, with significant reach and on-message coverage throughout the state.

Social media engagement through the Walk to School Facebook (www.facebook.com/WalkToSchool) and Twitter (https://twitter.com/WalkToSchoolVic) accounts was used to increase awareness of the campaign among parents of primary school-aged children and to engage stakeholders. Key campaign information, news items, competitions, shareable content and participating school and student experiences were shared through these channels in the lead-up to and throughout the campaign period.

Competitive analysis

There is a range of campaigns and programs that target primary schools or primary-aged children and/or encourage walking or other active transport. These include the following:

- The *Walking School Bus* programme, previously funded by VicHealth and still active in some local government areas.

- The Bicycle Network's national *Ride2School*, which runs throughout the year with a week of focused activity in March.

- The Pedestrian Council of Australia's *Walk Safely to School Day* which takes place in May and focuses on road safety.

- Murdoch Children's Research Institute's *Stepathon* which encourages children to count their steps for one week in September to raise money for child health research.

- Physical Activity Australia's *Walktober* encourages all Australians to walk in October for active travel, exercise, leisure or pleasure.

- Diabetes Australia's *Walk to Work* is a single day event which aims to help employers and employees build walking into their daily routine.

Walk to School is set apart from these campaigns by the length of the programme – most of the other campaigns in this space focus on a day or week of activity – and by the community-level engagement through councils and schools. These unique aspects provide opportunities for local collaboration, tailored approaches and local action to promote and enable longer-term active transport behaviours.

Stakeholder analysis

Councils were identified as key stakeholders, as they have existing health and wellbeing priorities that align to the Walk to School campaign, links to the local community, and influence over local infrastructure, networks, and social norms. Councils were heavily engaged through the design and delivery of Walk to School *2014*, in particular via the grants programme described above.

Engagement with primary schools was also critical to the delivery of the campaign. VicHealth offered free resources to participating schools, and incentivised participation through competitions and prizes. Where councils were funded to deliver local Walk to School activities, they were the key conduit to schools. Otherwise, VicHealth liaised directly with primary schools via letter, email, phone and social media to support their participation.

VicHealth mapped and engaged other key stakeholders to ensure relevant organisations were consulted and kept informed throughout the campaign development and delivery. This allowed VicHealth and stakeholder organisations to share insights, avoid duplication or conflicting messages, and cross-promote key messages through their owned channels.

Research

An integrated evaluation programme was developed by VicHealth, VicHealth's Social Marketing Research Practice Fellow, Social Marketing @ Griffith, and a market research company. The programme design and delivery was measured through:

- a weekly campaign metrics and outputs report which allowed real-time analysis of activities and outcomes, and optimisation of activities throughout the campaign;
- participation data collected from schools and individuals via the Walk to School website, app and classroom calendars, with an additional data field to capture baseline walking rates;
- walking data from a sample of classroom calendars and online participation data;
- an independent evaluation of the grant programme;
- observations at three participating primary schools;
- online surveys for councils and primary schools;
- surveys of parents of primary school-aged children in Victoria.

Social Marketing @ Griffith was specifically responsible for the last two data collections and for the outcome and process evaluation of the Walk to School 2014 campaign and its influence on key audiences of carers, schools and councils. Online survey data were collected before and after the campaign between September 2014 and December 2014. The project was approved by the Griffith University Human Research Ethics Committee.

Outcome evaluation

The aim of the outcome evaluation was to measure the change in self-reported walking behaviours.

In order to evaluate whether the Walk to School 2014 campaign changed behaviour (getting primary school-age children to walk to school more often), a repeated measure design was used.[1]

Two groups of respondents were recruited to participate in the carers' online survey:

- an intervention group (respondents with children participating in Walk to School 2014); and
- a control group (respondents with children not participating in Walk to School 2014).

There were 966 respondents at Baseline, including 372 respondents in the Intervention group and 594 respondents in the Control group. During Walk to School 2014 the survey was completed by 802 respondents, including 294 respondents in the Intervention group and 508 respondents in the Control group. At the Follow-up stage the survey was completed by 793 respondents, including 338 respondents in the Intervention group and 455 respondents in the Control group.

Process evaluation

The aim of the process evaluation was to gain an understanding of the experience of the programme among participating schools, councils, and carers with primary school-age children.

Respondents with children participating in the Walk to School 2014 campaign also took part in the process evaluation.

Email invitations were sent to 1,829 schools (536 registered to participate in Walk to School 2014 and 1,293 non-participating schools) by VicHealth with a response rate of 6% (105 completed responses). Email invitations were sent to 63 Victorian councils by VicHealth resulting in a response rate of 73% (46 completed responses). The link to the survey was emailed to schools in mid-November 2014, following the completion of the Walk to School 2014 campaign.

Outcomes

Campaign results

The Walk to School 2014 campaign achieved most of its objectives.

Outcome evaluation

The analysis of the data showed that overall walking rates were higher after the Walk to School 2014 delivery (M = 3.0, SD = 3.8) when compared to before the Walk to School 2014 (M = 2.6, SD = 3.7).[2] Further analysis indicated that children participating in Walk to School 2014 (Intervention group) walked more often than children who did not participate (Control group).

Further examination revealed a positive change over time for the Intervention group that was higher than that for the Control group. The results indicate that walking to and from school rates increased for children who participated in the Walk to School 2014 campaign between Baseline (M = 3.8, SD = 3.9) and during the campaign (M = 4.7, SD = 3.7), and that walking to and from school rates were sustained at follow-up (M = 4.6, SD = 4.0).

Process evaluation

Carers, school representatives and local councils were asked to evaluate their experience with the Walk to School 2014 campaign. Satisfaction and enjoyment with Walk to School 2014 was measured for carers, schools and councils. Schools and councils were also asked how easy it was for them to administer the Walk to School 2014 campaign.

The results indicated that the majority of carers, schools and council representatives were satisfied with Walk to School 2014 and that the majority enjoyed Walk to School 2014. The results indicated that the majority of schools and councils found Walk to School 2014 easy to administer.

Discussion

The easiest way of increasing the levels of regular physical activity among children is walking to and from school due to its low cost and universal accessibility (Rosenberg *et al.* 2006). Walking can be integrated into daily routines by most families with school-age children (Brophy *et al.* 2011). However, there has been a significant decline in the use of active forms of transport to and from school (Salmon *et al.* 2005). VicHealth's Walk to School 2014 aimed to counteract this decline by building active transport habits among Victorian primary schoolchildren. This initiative actively promoted the benefits of walking to and from school to children, their families and the general community, and established October 2014 as a month 'to walk to and from school'.

The Walk to School 2014 campaign achieved its aims with the results demonstrating that it had a positive impact on increasing walking behaviour among the participants. The number of children who walked to and from school increased significantly more among children participating in the Walk to School 2014 campaign relative to those who did not participate.

The results of the process evaluation indicated that the overall experience with the Walk to School 2014 campaign was very positive for carers, with high satisfaction levels and enjoyment reported among respondents. The result from schools showed the majority of school representatives were pleased with their experience with the Walk to School 2014 campaign and enjoyed participation. The feedback from Victorian councils was also very positive in regard to their experience with the Walk to School 2014 campaign. The majority of councils reported they were satisfied and enjoyed their experience in the Walk to School 2014 campaign. A very positive aspect of the campaign for both schools and councils was the fact that it was easy to administer.

Acknowledgements

The authors wish to acknowledge research assistance provided during the data collection stages of this project by Dr Joy Parkinson, Anna Katariina Kitunen, James Durl, Cuong Pham and Patricia David.

Case study questions

1. Social marketers use a marketing mix to bring about behaviour change. What are the key components of the Walk to School 2014 campaign's marketing mix?

2. Social marketing segmentation tailors campaigns to segments with common characteristics. Taking one of the segments identified in Schuster *et al.* (2015), propose changes to the Walk to School 2014 campaign's marketing mix to adapt it to that particular segment.

3. You have been invited by VicHealth to submit a proposal for a Walk to School campaign next year. Use the campaign description and evaluation provided to create a social marketing campaign idea to pitch to VicHealth.

Notes

1 In a repeated measure design each individual is asked the same question at different time points and the degree of change (or not) is measured. Data were collected at Baseline (one month before Walk to School 2014), During Walk to School 2014, and at Follow-up (one month after Walk to School 2014).
2 A 3 (time) × 2 (intervention and control groups) repeated measure ANOVA was undertaken to determine whether sustained behaviour change was evident following participation in the Walk to School 2014 campaign. Post hoc analyses further examined whether significant differences between the Intervention and Control group existed at each time point and whether change rates differed between groups.

References

Australian Institute of Health and Welfare (AIHW) (2012) Risk factors contributing to chronic disease. Cat. no. PHE 157. Canberra: AIHW. www.aihw.gov.au/publication-detail/?id=1073 7421466.

Ainsworth, B. and Macera, C. (2012) *Physical Activity and Public Health Practice*. Broken Sound: CRC Press.

Australian Bureau of Statistics (ABS) (2011) 2011 Census Quick Stats: Victoria. Online at: www. censusdata.abs.gov.au/census_services/getproduct/census/2011/quickstat/2?opendocument &navpos=95 (accessed 1 May 2016).

Australian Bureau of Statistics (ABS) (2013a) *Australian Health Survey: Physical Activity, 2011-12*, 4364.0.55.004. Canberra: Australian Bureau of Statistics.

Australian Bureau of Statistics (ABS) (2013b) *CensusAtSchool Australia, 2013 National Summary Tables*. Canberra: Australian Bureau of Statistics.

Barlovic, I. (2006) 'Obesity, advertising to kids, and social marketing', *Young Consumers*, 7(4): 26–34.

Brophy, S., Cooksey, R., Lyons, R., Thomas, N., Rodgers, S. and Gravenor, M. (2011) 'Parental factors associated with walking to school and participation in organised activities at age 5: Analysis of the Millennium Cohort Study', *BMC Public Health*, 11: 14–14.

Crawford, S. and Garrard, J. (2013) 'A combined impact-process evaluation of a program promoting active transport to school: Understanding the factors that shaped program effectiveness', *Journal of Environmental and Public Health*, 816961–14.

Deckelbaum, R.J. and Williams, C.L. (2001) 'Childhood obesity: The health issue', *Obesity Research*, 9(Suppl. 4): 239–243.

Department of Health (2014) Australia's physical activity and sedentary behaviour guidelines. Online at: www.health.gov.au/internet/main/publishing.nsf/Content/health-pubhlth-strateg-active-evidence.htm (accessed 1 May 2016).

Department of Health and Ageing (2004) *Australia's Physical Activity Recommendations for 5-12 year olds*. Canberra: Department of Health and Ageing.

Department of Transport (2009) *Victorian Integrated Survey of Travel and Activity 2007 (VISTA 07)*. Melbourne: Department of Transport, pp. 5–6.

Kubacki, K., Rundle-Thiele, S., Lahtinen, V. and Parkinson, J. (2015) 'A systematic review assessing the extent of social marketing principle use in interventions targeting children (2000-2014)', *Young Consumers*, 16(2): 141–158.

McMinn, D., Rowe, D., Murtagh, S. and Nelson, N. (2011) 'The Strathclyde evaluation of children's active travel (SE-CAT): Study rationale and methods', *BMC Public Health*, 11: 958–978.

Mendoza, J.A., Watson, K., Baranowski, T., Nicklas, T.A., Uscanga, D.K. and Hanfling, M.J. (2011). 'The walking school bus and children's physical activity: A pilot cluster randomized controlled trial', *Pediatrics*, 128: e537–e544.

National Public Health Partnership (NPHP) (2001) Promoting active transport: a portfolio of interventions. Melbourne: NPHP.

Pucher, J. and Buehler, R. (2008) 'Making cycling irresistible: Lessons from the Netherlands, Denmark and Germany', *Transport Reviews*, 28: 495–528.

Rosenberg, D., Sallis, J., Conway, T., Cain, K. and McKenzie, T. (2006) 'Active transportation to school over 2 years in relation to weight status and physical activity', *Obesity*, 14: 1771–1776.

Schuster, L., Kubacki, K. and Rundle-Thiele, S. (2015) 'A theoretical approach to segmenting children's walking behaviours', *Young Consumers*, 16(2): 159-171.

Shonkoff, J.P., Boyce, W.T. and McEwen, B.S. (2009) 'Neuroscience, molecular biology, and the childhood roots of health disparities: Building a new framework for health promotion and disease prevention', *Jama*, 301(21): 2252–2259.

Telama, R., Yang, X., Viikari, J., Välimäki, I., Wanne, O. and Raitakari, O. (2005) 'Physical activity from childhood to adulthood: A 21-year tracking study', *American Journal of Preventive Medicine*, 3: 267–273.

Troiani, V., Peelle, J.E., Clark, R. and Grossman, M. (2009) 'Is it logical to count on quantifiers? Dissociable neural networks underlying numerical and logical quantifiers', *Neuropsychologia*, 47(1): 104–111.

WHO (2015) Physical activity and young people. Available at: www.who.int/dietphysicalactivity/factsheet_young_people/en/ (accessed 1 May 2016).

Case study **10**

Cycle Against Suicide

The creation of a community-based social marketing programme to promote mental health in Ireland

Amy Cannon, Olivia Freeman and Patrick Kenny

Introduction

Many social marketing programmes aiming to promote sustainable behaviour change are based around information-intensive campaigns and rely heavily or exclusively on media advertising (McKenzie-Mohr 2013). However, a community-based social marketing (CBSM) approach (McKenzie-Mohr 2000) is not only an attractive alternative to 'expert-driven' solutions but can also be used in conjunction with other behaviour change tools and involve local communities in the co-delivery of programmes. Community-based interventions involve multiple, often simultaneously implemented, levels of interventions or 'programmes' (as opposed to a single intervention such as individual psychotherapy). The main advantages of a CBSM approach are its cultivation of the community's local knowledge, its efficient and effective use of a community's resources and its empowerment of the community in the process of social change.

In Ireland, a country experiencing a high rate of youth suicide relative to other European countries, the voluntary charitable organisation Cycle Against Suicide is in the business of fostering positive social change on a national scale. Cycle Against Suicide understands the synergistic power of mobilising communities, local organisations and local media channels to deliver change-programmes in resource-constrained contexts.

Problem definition

While suicide has been a feature of Irish life for generations, the country has recently experienced an alarming growth in suicide among young people. In 2013, the country had the fourth-highest suicide rate among 15–19-year-olds in the EU (Eurostat 2016). Death by suicide is the 'tip of the iceberg' – for example, a population-based study by McMahon *et al.* (2014) revealed that for every recorded suicide, more than 3,000 young girls reported self-harm.

The reluctance of young people to seek help for mental health problems is increasingly acknowledged as a challenge to effective early intervention approaches and engaging with appropriate help services is recognised as an important protective factor (National Office for Suicide Prevention 2015). Dozens of voluntary and mixed-funding mental health organisations have been established to provide help at multiple levels including online services, wellbeing skills training and one-to-one therapeutic services. These organisations make the public aware of their services through both traditional and digital media channels. According to a national study of youth mental health in Ireland (Dooley and Fitzgerald 2013), despite effective treatments being widely available, less than one-fifth of young people experiencing serious personal, emotional, behavioural or mental health problems avail themselves of professional help. Historically, suicide was an illegal act in Ireland until 1993 and there remains a certain stigma associated with the experience of suicide and mental health. Gulliver *et al.* (2010) identify a number of barriers and facilitators to help-seeking behaviour (see Table CS10.1). These barriers and facilitators are key to informing Cycle Against Suicide's strategic priorities, aims and objectives.

Table CS10.1 Uncovering barriers to help-seeking behaviour

Barriers	• Perceived stigma and embarrassment
	• Problems recognising symptoms (poor mental health literacy)
	• Preference for self-reliance
Facilitators	• Social support and encouragement from others
	• Emotional confidence
	• Good mental health literacy

(*Source:* Gulliver *et al.* 2010)

Cycle Against Suicide: background

Cycle Against Suicide is an all-Ireland voluntary charitable organisation founded in 2012 by Irish entrepreneur Jim Breen. It is based on a model of working with communities to collectively address social stigma in a positive and collaborative manner. Cycle Against Suicide comprises a board of directors, and a team of national and local project managers, consultants and mental health organisation officers. Cycle Against Suicide collaborates with target audiences, mental health organisations and communities in the co-delivery of its programmes. In particular it liaises with these associations in order to:

- encourage positive conversations about mental wellness;
- offer encouragement to seek out support;
- create an accessible platform for mental health organisations to communicate their services directly with target audiences.

Cycle Against Suicide's messaging platform stems from its tagline: "It's OK not to feel OK; and it's absolutely OK to ask for help." It employs an evidence-based approach constructed on research from the European Alliance Against Depression (EAAD) and OPSI (Optimising Suicide Prevention Programmes and their Implementation in Europe) outlining levels of interventions to target suicide prevention. Interventions include school-based programmes and awareness-raising events, including an annual community cycle (see Table CS10.2).

Competitive analysis

Social marketing theory emphasises that effective programme design begins with an understanding of the barriers to engaging in an activity (Andreasen 1995). Numerous barriers may exist for any behaviour at many levels (McKenzie-Mohr and Smith 1999). In order to understand ways in which Cycle Against Suicide could successfully encourage activation of its audiences, it was important to understand the barriers that might

Table CS10.2 Summary of Cycle Against Suicide programmes

Programme	Approach
1. *Schools Programme*	Whole-school approach
• Ambassador School Programme	
• Student Leaders' Congress	
• Student Leader Ambassador Programme	
• Anchor Schools	
2. *Awareness-Raising Events*	Community-wide approach
• Annual Cycle	
• Community Spin-Offs	
• Fun Runs	
• School Spins	
• Events Against Suicide	

Table CS10.3 Audience, desired behaviour, bundle of benefits and barriers

Audience	Desired Behaviour (Product)	Benefits (Exchange)	Barriers (Price)
Consumers/ Service user groups *(Primary Audience)*	Voluntary help-seeking	Satisfaction knowing that I have found the assistance I need through this tough time through (or a result of) my attendance of a Cycle Against Suicide programme. I will do what I can to support my peers in the understanding that there are many options for specialised mental health support.	I choose not to seek help due to fear of stigma/poor mental health literacy/negative perception of specialised support services.
Community	Voluntary participation	Satisfaction knowing that I have used my personal and/or professional skills to assist in my local community. I will do what I can to support my local event and influence my peers to do the same.	I choose not to participate or volunteer time to community-based mental health charities due to poor mental health literacy/dedicating time to different social or commercial endeavours/lack of interest.
Mental Health Organisations	Voluntary alignment with community-based programmes	Positioning my service in Cycle Against Suicide's CBSM programme will mean more people in crisis will understand our service. Our organisation will be more successful and I will apply for more funding. To help me adopt the desired behaviour, I will get advance notice of events close to my target markets and leverage these avenues to market my services.	I choose to stay with current model of promotion because of a perceived lack of evidence achieved by community-based programmes/ seeing Cycle Against Suicide as a force of competition for funding, media coverage or volunteer engagement.
Media	Voluntary alignment with community-based programmes	Reporting on mental illness without bias and prejudice or sensationalism makes the media outlet a more accurate and responsible publisher. To help me adopt the desired behaviour, I will use programmes such as Cycle Against Suicide that help me avoid biased, stigmatising language and labels, and as a potential source for positive success stories.	Preference to report about other charities competing for the same attention; choosing sensational headlines to sell papers, drive online traffic and increase viewership.

impinge on that activation process as well as the benefits that might flow from it (see Table CS10.3). For example, a resident or local association may have chosen not to participate with a programme due to commitments with other charitable organisations; media channels may have preferred to report about other charities competing for the same audience; mental health organisations might have shown a preference towards their own channels of self-promotion, or even classified Cycle Against Suicide as a competitive threat for funding, media coverage or volunteer engagement. Acknowledging these legitimate sources of competition was key to enhancing commitment, forming alliances with a number of stakeholders and acting speedily on competitive threats.

Stakeholder analysis

The success of a CBSM programme is dependent on the goodwill and involvement of a range of stakeholders beyond the target audience. Cycle Against Suicide treats all stakeholders as partners in the shared goal of suicide prevention as opposed to treating stakeholders as passive consumers of messages and programmes (Lefebvre 2012). Stakeholder involvement engages with corporate brands as sponsoring partners; Irish celebrities as brand advocates; community organisations as local promoters; and a network of volunteers to help set up and deliver programmes. Cycle Against Suicide has continued to grow partnerships year on year. Table CS10.4 provides a sample of Cycle Against Suicide's partner entities.

Aims and objectives

The main aim of Cycle Against Suicide is to positively change the Irish public's mindset and behaviour around mental health. It seeks to do this by creating public awareness

Table CS10.4 Cycle Against Suicide stakeholders

NGO Partners	Cycling Ireland, Gaisce (personal development programme for young people), Athletics Ireland, Gartan Outdoor Centre
Corporate Partners	MSL, Chain Reaction Cycles, Sam McCauley, Ernst and Young, TLI Group, Fyffes, Aspen Grove, GPS, Musgraves Group, TNS Distribution, Zest, Tetra Ireland, City Cycles, Kerry Coaches, Dalata Hotel Group, Gomac Signs, Coca Cola, Elverys, Permanent TSB
School Partners	Institute of Guidance Counsellors, The Le Chéile Trust, The Loreto Trust, CEIST Trust, Edmund Rice Schools' Trust, Education and Training Board Ireland Joint Managerial Body, National Association of Principals and Deputy Principals, Transition Year Support Service (PDST)
Third Level Partners	Ulster University, University of Limerick
State Sector Partners	Departments and Ministries of Health, Education, Justice and Equality, Children and Youth Affairs, *An Garda Síochana*, Ombudsman for Children, The Civil Defence
Media Partners	2FM, *The Ray D'Arcy Show*, *Fit Magazine*

of organisations working to prevent suicide and by fostering cohesion and cooperation between these organisations. Cycle Against Suicide designs programmes aimed at creating attitudinal and behavioural change in relation to help-seeking and disclosure.

The organisation's core aims are to:

- prompt positive, non-stigmatising conversations about mental health in Ireland;
- offer reassurance and encouragement to young people to seek out available local supports;
- direct people to where this critical help can be found.

Table CS10.5 Cycle Against Suicide strategic plan

Initial Priorities, 2012-2015	Strategic Objectives, 2016- 2018 (long-term)
Schools Programme To expand the reach of Cycle Against Suicide throughout the educational system	*Measurable increase in numbers seeking help* • 80% positive affirmation regarding the mind-set that "It's OK not to feel OK" • 80% positive affirmation regarding the intention of talking about emotional wellbeing in times of need • 70% positive affirmation regarding actual help-seeking behaviour among those who were experiencing an emotional crisis
Awareness-raising Events To actively engage in the expansion and development of awareness-raising events	*Establish brand and message* • Firmly establish Cycle Against Suicide as an instantly recognisable national brand at 65% recognition level of total population on the island of Ireland • Firmly establish its message, "It's OK not to feel OK; and it's absolutely OK to ask for help", as an instantly recognisable phrase from Cycle Against Suicide at 65% recognition level of total population on the island of Ireland
Communities Against Suicide To actively engage in the research and development of the 'Communities Against Suicide Programme' in order to achieve a sustained level of engagement and ongoing awareness building	*Measurable increase in Cycle Against Suicide engagement* • By December 2018, to have engaged with 65% of the population through a Cycle Against Suicide awareness raising event or social marketing campaign.
Collaborative Network To establish partnerships with a number of mental health/suicide prevention organisations and high-risk advocacy groups	*Grow collaborative network* • By December 2018, to have established partnerships with five Northern Ireland-based and ten Republic of Ireland-based mental health/ suicide prevention organisations and high risk advocacy groups

With the consideration of established barriers towards help-seeking and disclosure (stigma, preference to self-reliance and poor mental health literacy), Cycle Against Suicide piloted a number of programmes designed to facilitate behaviour change towards mental health help-seeking. School-based programmes focused on the construction of emotional confidence, wellness skills and good mental health literacy; awareness-raising events were designed to encourage social support and the community-wide reduction of stigma.

Having been founded in 2012, the strategic priorities for the first three years included successfully piloting and launching programmes and building a network of stakeholders and collaborators. Long-term objectives include attitudinal change and help-seeking disclosure, (evaluated according to the Depression Stigma Scale (see Griffiths *et al.* 2004), and the promotion of professional help-seeking, evaluated using metrics from the World Mental Health Surveys International College Student Project (WMH-ICS). Table CS10.5 outlines the initial and long-term strategic priorities for Cycle Against Suicide.

Research

Organisations are required to demonstrate that their interventions or campaigns 'work'. Corporate sponsors want to ensure that their funds are being spent wisely, persons involved in the design and delivery need to know whether or not they are succeeding so that they can modify or fine-tune their approach accordingly, and compliance with programmes set out by governing bodies (such as the Charities Regulatory Authority in Ireland) must be met. The final two sections of the case study describe Cycle Against Suicide's main interventions and offer an evaluation of the success of each of these.

Intervention

Working in the community: school-based programmes
The Ambassador School programme
The Ambassador School programme encourages schools to become actively involved in mental health promotion and facilitates the sharing and showcasing of good practice in the area of mental health education. The programme is aimed at second level students. In 2014, 30 schools achieved the award, and in 2015 this increased to 45 schools. In 2016, 83 schools achieved Ambassador School status. The programme provides a five-level framework (see Table CS10.6) for schools to integrate mental health activities into the school plan and includes project work on an annual wellness theme chosen by student leader ambassadors, a 'mental health week' organised by students and supported by a range of stakeholders, and a programme to integrate mental health in the schools' curricula. The Ambassador School Programme incentivises participating schools with a school-wide invite to the annual Student's Leaders' Congress. In 2015 Jim Breen, founder of Cycle Against Suicide, visited 19 schools, and 41 schools in 2016.

Student Leader Ambassador programme
Each year, Cycle Against Suicide creates and empowers a network of young leaders throughout Ireland through the Student Leader Ambassador programme. Leaders are peer-nominated and selected by the school due to their leadership in the school-wide promotion of positive mental health. All students nominated receive a Certificate of Achievement, while a small group of exceptional nominees receive the Student Leader Ambassador award

Table CS10.6 Five-level framework

Level 1: Mental health education

Schools are asked to demonstrate how they integrated mental health education into their curriculum throughout the year. This is facilitated through existing curricula and enhanced through guest speakers and programmes. Alternatively schools create a school-based curriculum tailored to their own context and student needs.

Level 2: Project work

To consolidate learning, schools are asked to engage their students in project work based on the annual wellness theme chosen by Student Leader Ambassadors. Schools registered for the annual Student Leaders' Congress are invited to showcase their projects.

Level 3: Simple things

Schools aiming for Ambassador School status require the identification of 'simple things' that they think will support student wellbeing in their school context and plan how this can be implemented.

Level 4: Mental health week

With the help of the school, students organise a 'Mental Health Week' in their school. This promotes positive mental health strategies and includes the involvement of local mental health services in line with the Cycle Against Suicide core aim of encouraging help-seeking behaviour.

Level 5: Get active

To promote the link between physical and mental health, Ambassador Schools organise a physical activity of their choice to generate local and community awareness and promote the message: "It's OK not to feel OK, and it's absolutely OK to ask for help."

and are invited to participate in a residential retreat where they take part in an intensive leadership programme organised by Cycle Against Suicide. By building a number of local reference groups with well-connected youth opinion leaders, Cycle Against Suicide builds local insight into target audience problems. The School Leader Ambassador programme accommodates 15 students per year.

Student Leaders' Congress

The Congress brings together senior cycle students (aged 15 to 18) and teachers from all over Ireland in a forum comprising of student leaders, celebrity spokespeople and live entertainment. Co-delivered with student leaders, a portion of the event involves students discussing mental wellness projects they have engaged with, conducting peer interviews and interacting with a range of mental health organisations exhibiting on the day. The congress is broadcast through 2FM, a leading youth-oriented station run by the Republic of Ireland's national broadcaster, RTÉ. In 2015, 3,800 attended the Congress at the RDS. In January 2017, Cycle Against Suicide will hold two consecutive congresses at the University of Limerick allowing the participation of 6,000 students and teachers. The Congress is open to schools in both Northern Ireland and schools in the Republic of Ireland, however the uptake in NI is poor due to a lack of brand recognition. In 2015 there were just two schools from Northern Ireland out of 103 schools and in 2016 there was no school from the entire province of Ulster (Northern Ireland plus the northern counties of Donegal, Cavan, Monaghan in the Republic) registered for the Congress.

Table CS10.7 Student leaders' aims/activities

Student Leaders' Congress Aims	Student Leaders' Congress Activities
• To promote help-seeking behaviour and Cycle Against Suicide's core message: "It's OK not to feel OK; and it's absolutely OK to ask for help." • To facilitate safe engagement with mental health issues with a view to giving students useful life skills and evidence-based strategies. • To showcase school-based initiatives promoting positive mental health highlighting student leadership in action. • To create a dynamic and memorable experience for student leaders.	• An exhibition of mental health and youth services. • A showcase of student project work and school-led initiatives; demonstrating student leadership in action. • Interactive collaborative sessions where students contribute their ideas and local initiatives to the larger audience. • Streaming of videos from the event on Twitter and Facebook. • A broadcast of the Congress by Ireland's national radio station RTÉ 2FM. • High-profile speakers in panel discussions. • Music and entertainment to make the event engaging and memorable.

Awareness-raising events

The Cycle Against Suicide annual cycle attracts more than 3,000 adult and student cyclists to participate in a 14-day, 1,400-km cycle around the island of Ireland, passing through 85 communities, visiting 28 schools and engaging with 20,000 students. Each day, two positive mental health events, co-delivered by local students, local mental health and suicide prevention organisations and local celebrity spokespeople, are held in 'anchor' locations including schools, colleges, universities and community centres. Refreshments for the cyclists are provided by the community, local organisations and local businesses. The Homestay programme, organised by local coordinators throughout Ireland, welcomes participants of the event into local families' homes and 'host' cyclists with a meal and a bed for the night. This allows the community to lend support in a very tangible way without taking part in the cycle itself. As well as the main event, locally organised student 'School Spins' and monthly community 'SpinOffs' take place after the main cycle ends. These events are locally organised events owned by the community and championed by Cycle Against Suicide 'community leaders'. Entertainment, refreshments and a mental wellbeing event are incorporated into larger events.

Outcomes

Participation and engagement: figures and feedback

Cycle Against Suicide has achieved positive outcomes across its busy schedule of events. Success is attributed in part to the mobilisation of local community channels including local media and local social networks. Participatory media such as Twitter, Snapchat and Instagram have offered alternative forums for community members to become fellow storytellers, network builders and co-creators of value.

One of the main national events – the annual cycle – has grown significantly from 7,500 cyclists in 2014 to 9,000 cyclists in 2015 and 10,000 cyclists in 2016. In addition to the participation of cyclists 8,400 people volunteered across a range of ancillary activities connected to the 2016 cycle.

Attendance at the annual Student Leader's Congress has also grown from 30 students at a pilot congress held in 2013 to 3,200 participants in 2014, 3,600 participants in 2015 and 4,000 participants in 2016. This upward trajectory is due to continue with 6,000 students expected to attend the congress when it is held in the University of Limerick in 2017.

Student and local leaders are hugely valuable for the promotion and co-design of programmes. After training, a number of students and local leaders evaluated their experiences to help refine the various programmes. Comments from a group of student leaders included:

> *The most beneficial aspect of the programme was learning the concise reasoning behind Cycle Against Suicide – to promote help-seeking behaviour and to promote community-based supports. I now feel that I have a better understanding of what we are doing to erase the stigma around mental health.*
> *Caroline, St. Louis Community School, Kiltimagh, Ireland*

> *I think the most beneficial aspect was being able to work on our own skills relevant to student leadership that we can take back into our own communities and many related areas, not just directly associated with Cycle Against Suicide.*
> *Eamon, Jesus and Mary Secondary School, Enniscrone, Ireland*

> *I believe the most beneficial aspect was definitely seeing so many motivated student leaders coming together, tossing up ideas and brainstorming new plans for the student domain. Like-minded people coming together in unity was very special.*
> *Roisin, Regina Mundi College, Cork, Ireland*

Media reach 2016

Cycle Against Suicide social media platforms were launched on January 2013 and in 2016 there were 60,000+ followers across their various social media platforms. Social media managers encourage volunteers to spread the word by sharing their personal experiences with Cycle Against Suicide. The annual event also receives extensive coverage in traditional media channels.

Table CS10.8 Cycle Against Suicide social media platforms

News articles	474
Appearances on live TV programmes	9
Regional radio interviews	110
Twitter followers	9,500 followers in 2015; a 12,200 increase was reported throughout the annual cycle period 2016
Facebook followers	39,000 followers in 2015; an increase to 42,000 was reported throughout the annual cycle period 2016

Discussion

Cycle Against Suicide's community-based model works on the premise that help-seeking behaviour is shaped and influenced at the interpersonal, organisational and community level. The approach employed by the organisation involves a careful selection of the behavior to be promoted (help-seeking); identification of the barriers and benefits associated with the selected behaviour (stigma, low mental health literacy); design of a strategy that utilises behaviour-change tools to address these barriers (social support, emotional confidence); piloting of the intervention on a small segment of the community; evaluating the impact once it has been broadly implemented and refining the programme to maximise strategic impacts. From internal reviews and questionnaires, the Cycle Against Suicide programmes have brought about positive changes in the standards of socially acceptable help-seeking behaviour at the individual and community level, although more work remains to be done to achieve the long-term behavioural change objectives.

The success to date has been built upon engagement with a variety of stakeholders across the community. Partnering with community leaders and local mental health services served to make interventions 'local'. The generation of media coverage and advocacy for the various interventions also facilitated the overall progress of the campaign. Finally, creating networks of trained mental health leaders, such as student ambassadors, local event leaders and celebrity spokespeople, created a network of representatives that positively endorsed the brand and provided credible and trustworthy promotion of programmes.

Case study questions

1. There is much to be commended from a CBSM intervention. What are the potential benefits of actively involving the community in social marketing activities?

2. Engaging with the community is not without its drawbacks. What are the challenges in actively involving the community in social marketing activities?

References

Andreasen, A. (1995) *Marketing Social Change: Changing Behavior to Promote Health, Social Development, and the Environment*. San Francisco, CA: Jossey-Bass. http://doi.org/0787901377.

Dooley, B. A. and Fitzgerald, A. (2013) *My World Survey: National Study of Youth Mental Health in Ireland*. Online at: http://researchrepository.ucd.ie/handle/10197/4286 (accessed 1 May 2016).

EAAD (2016) Multi-level intervention. Online at: www.eaad.net/mainmenu/research/ospi-europe/results/ (accessed 1 May 2016).

Eurostat (2016) *Suicide death rate, by age group*. Online at: http://ec.europa.eu/eurostat/web/products-datasets/-/tsdph240 (accessed 1 May 2016).

Griffiths, K., Christensen, H., Jorm, A., Evans, K. and Groves, C. (2004) 'Effect of web-based depression literacy and cognitive behavioural therapy interventions on stigmatising attitudes to depression', *British Journal of Psychiatry*, *185*(August), 342–349. http://doi.org/10.1192/bjp.185.4.342.

Gulliver, A., Griffiths, K. M. and Christensen, H. (2010) 'Perceived barriers and facilitators to mental health help-seeking in young people: A systematic review', *10*(113): 1–9.

Joint National Listenership Research (2016) My MRBI | JNLR. Online at: http://info.ipsosmrbi.com/jnlr (accessed 8 September 2016).

Lefebvre, C. (2010) 'Social models for social marketing: Social diffusion, social networks, social capital, social determinants and social franchising', in G. Hastings, C. Bryant, and K. Angus (eds), *The SAGE Handbook of Social Marketing* (pp. 32–43). London, UK: Sage Publications. http://doi.org/10.4135/9781446201008.n3.

Lefebvre, C. (2012) 'Transformative social marketing: Co-creating the social marketing discipline and brand', *Journal of Social Marketing*, 2(2): 118–129. http://doi.org/10.1108/20426761211243955.

McKenzie-Mohr, D. (2000) 'Promoting sustainable behavior: An introduction to community-based social marketing', *Journal of Social Issues*, 56(3): 543–554. http://doi.org/10.1111/0022-4537.00183.

McKenzie-Mohr, D. (2013) *Fostering Sustainable Behavior: An Introduction to Community-Based Social Marketing*. BOOK, New Society Publishers. Retrieved from https://books.google.ie/books?id=g6D3POVUkfMC.

McKenzie-Mohr, D. and Smith, W.A. (1999) *Fostering Sustainable Behavior: An Introduction to Community-based Social Marketing*. BOOK, New Society Publishers. Retrieved from https://books.google.ie/books?id=2ZnKy6BMpTQC.

McMahon, E. M. *et al.* (2014) 'The iceberg of suicide and self-harm in Irish adolescents: A population-based study', *Social Psychiatry and Psychiatric Epidemiology*, 49(12): 1929–1935. http://doi.org/10.1007/s00127-014-0907-z.

National Office for Suicide Prevention (2015) *Connecting for Life: Ireland's National Strategy to Reduce Suicide 2015–2020*.

Case study **11**

Moi(s) sans tabac

The first collective challenge for smoking cessation launched by Santé Publique France

Karine Gallopel-Morvan,
Olivier Smadja, Anna Mercier,
Elodie Safta, Jennifer Davies,
Romain Guignard, Pierre Arwidson
and Viêt Nguyen Thanh

Introduction

The campaign 'Moi(s) sans tabac' was launched in France during 2016 by Santé Publique France.

SANTÉ PUBLIQUE FRANCE[1]

Santé Publique France is a national public health agency answering to the Minister of Health. Its mission is to protect public health under the rubric 'foresee, understand, act'. As the leading primary agency for scientific expertise in public health, it is charged with population health surveillance and epidemiology, health promotion and education, responding to public health threats and emergencies. In fulfilling these obligations, the agency works with many partners in the public and academic sectors.

It is the French version of 'Stoptober',[2] the English annual campaign established in 2012 by the National Health Service and adopted by *Public Health England* when it was founded in 2013. It challenges smokers to give up tobacco for a month, offering supportive communication advice and services along the way. Why 28 days? Because if a smoker gives up for a month, she increases her chance of quitting completely fivefold (West and Stapleton 2008). France decided to launch its own version of the campaign because Stoptober had increased the quit attempt rate by 50% compared with other months (Brown *et al.* 2014). 'Moi(s) sans tabac' began in November 2016, targeting 20- to 49-year-old smokers. It is France's biggest ever anti-smoking campaign. It needed the managerial, communication, partnership and press relations skills of six fulltime staff members at Santé Publique France over a 12-month period, the partnership of 14 regional health authorities and regional ambassadors to implement the campaign at a local level and the collaboration of more than 90 public and private organisations.

Problem definition

There is a high level of smoking in France: 34.6% of those aged 15 to 75 years were either regular or occasional smokers in 2015 (Andler *et al.* 2016). Prevalence went up between 2005 and 2010 but has stabilised since then. In comparison, adult smoking rates in the UK are 15.8%[3] and 19.4% in Québec. The consequences of this smoking culture are severe: tobacco is the greatest cause of premature death in France, killing 73,000 people each year (Bonaldi *et al.* 2016), and costs the country an estimated €120m (Kopp 2015). Reports from the Cour des Comptes[4] (2012, 2016) highlight a number of loopholes which explain this failure to reduce smoking levels: the inadequate implementation of tobacco control legislation (e.g. ad bans and underage sales controls); inadequate health promotion budgets; a lack of engagement at a local level; a lack of precision in the national strategy; and a French culture which resents interference in what is still often seen as a freedom of choice (Gallopel-Morvan 2009; McNeill *et al.* 2015). To rectify these problems, the French government instigated a National Programme to Reduce Tobacco use (PNRT) in 2014. Among its provisions are the introduction of plain packaging (2017), a fund dedicated to the fight against tobacco, a reinforced programme of support for smokers who want to quit and a range of local initiatives. 'Moi(s) sans tabac' is part of the PNRT.

Competitive analysis

'Moi(s) sans tabac' faces two forms of competition. First there is the tobacco industry which uses its prodigious stakeholder and consumer marketing skills to push back against any tobacco control measures. Secondly smokers themselves can respond defensively to avoid or deny the implications of anti-smoking efforts. To reduce such reactions, 'Moi(s) sans tabac' is a deliberately upbeat campaign, using a collective and engaging appeal to support smokers to quit. The intention is to renew it each November.

Stakeholder analysis

The target for the campaign is 20 to 49-year-old smokers, especially those in low-income groups where smoking is particularly marked. Data show that more than 8 million smokers want to quit (Baromètre Santé 2014), but encounter difficulties due to their nicotine addiction. 'Moi(s) sans tabac' is designed to give them the support they need. It aims to get into local communities and connect with people's lives. In the UK, the campaign is built around local government funded smoking cessation services, but as these don't exist in France, different partners have had to be found. The fact that the campaign was part of PNRT, based on sound science and respect and equality, helped this process.

L'Assurance maladie is a public body charged with reimbursing health and maternity care costs following illness, accident or childbearing and also with running health education campaigns. It is a major partner in the campaign, along with Santé Publique France and the Minister of Health. It provides: (i) access to both health professionals and insured smokers; (ii) (with Santé Publique France) a mobile application providing e-coaching to quit; (iii) financing targeted at low-income groups; and (iv) a home for 'Moi(s) sans tabac' on its website.

Regional health authorities (RHAs) are public bodies that manage health provision at a regional level in France. The arguments used to persuade them to join the campaign were that, as well as being part of the PNRT, current anti-smoking efforts were too weak and all media materials (posters, press releases, branding) would be provided ready to use. In the end 14 of the 17 RHAs joined. Their job was to roll out both the campaign and the media in their region. An early obstacle was the lack of human and financial resources; this was successfully resolved with a dedicated funding bid which enabled the participating RHAs to recruit 14 local Ambassadors who promoted the campaign among key local figures, oversaw quality control and reported back on progress.

Health professionals of all kinds – doctors (both general practitioners and specialists), nurses, pharmacists, dentists, midwives – were involved in the campaign because of their close links to the population. Their job was to raise the possibility of quitting with their smoking patients and tell them about the campaign and the support it offered. Professional organisations in the health sector were also invited to join the campaign.

For the first time, Santé Publique France built a network of public and private partners to boost the profile and impact of the campaign: Arcelor Mittal, Google, Twitter, the PSA Group, health bodies and employment bodies and the Ministry of Defence were all, for example, recruited to the cause. The aim was to expose as many smokers as possible to the message and access them in the workplace. The attractions of the campaign for the partners included the opportunity to impact the health of their employees by helping them to quit smoking in a way that was purely voluntary, along with the chance to gain name recognition (partners' logos were included in publicity). There were also several different ways of participating: via digital communications, conventional channels and by staging special events. The only limitations on partners were that their actions should not undermine those of Santé Publique France and that 'Moi(s) sans tabac' should not be exploited commercially. To ensure respect for these principles a charter was created.

Many other public, third sector and private organisations became associated with the campaign, including schools, ministries, media (France Télévisions, Radio France), local government, sporting organisations, hospitals and health facilities. In many cases the initiative came from these organisations, as word about 'Moi(s) sans tabac' spread. In the end, more than 90 partners signed up and a special website was created to keep them informed about the campaign.

Aims and objectives

Table CS11.1 Campaign aims and objective

Smokers	Partners
To encourage them to quit smoking in November 2016 (or thereafter)	To get across the campaign's quit message and create a buzz
To encourage non-smokers to support them	To provide information about the details of the campaign and its services
To tell/remind them that support services are available (the app, the quitline, the website)	To help health professionals talk to their patients about quitting and inform them about the services and kit available via 'Moi(s) sans tabac'
To encourage smokers to use these services during their quit attempt and get the quit kit	To run accessible events and services to support smokers (for example, in the workplace)
To encourage smokers to sign up for advice sessions and services	To run collective actions such as group challenges
To consult their doctor about quitting	To encourage local media coverage
In the medium and long term, to reduce the number of smokers and resulting harm	In the medium and long term, to create a desire to join the fight against tobacco

Research

Desk research and existing knowledge, combined with meetings with prospective partners, showed that there was an appetite for 'Moi(s) sans tabac', provided resources were made available. In view of this, and time constraints, no concept testing was felt to be necessary.

Intervention and outcomes

To meet the objectives a social marketing strategy was devised. Communication tools were developed to adapt the campaign to the French context.

1. The brand

A logo was created by Santé Publique France which communicated the key message: the challenge of quitting for a month and the vision of a better life without tobacco. It encapsulated the brand's key values: (i) the rational promise that after 30 days without tobacco, the smoker was five times as likely to quit forever; (ii) the emotional promise that this will be easier and even enjoyable together; (iii) a positive and encouraging tone built around the symbol V for victory and a warm yellow and red design (see Figure CS11.1).

Figure CS11.1 The brand, logo and slogan for 'Moi(s) sans tabac'

2. Product: support materials and services

A range of support materials and services was developed and brought together with existing provisions, including a website (www.tabac-info-service.fr) detailing the benefits of quitting and related advice, a redesigned mobile application providing ecoaching, support videos and general encouragement, and a telephone helpline providing personalised help from an expert. In addition a quit kit, adapted from the English Stoptober original by the Ligue Nationale Contre le Cancer and Santé Publique France, was developed for DIY quitters (see Figure CS11.2).

3. Price: keeping it low

A key point of the campaign was to make the cost of quitting as low as possible. Therefore no or minimum charges were made of smokers – the quit kit was free, the telephone advice available for the cost of the call, etc.

4. Place: making it accessible to the smoker

The aim was to make 'Moi(s) sans tabac' as accessible as possible by locating it in close proximity to smokers' lives. For example, the quit kit was made available through high street pharmacies, in the workplace and online. Similarly, partners were encouraged, to organise events in the workplace and alongside recreational activities.

- a preparation guide
- a 30-day calender giving encouragement for each succcesful day
- leaflet on how to beat stress and the desire to smoke
- an amusing sticker saying "I Will Succeed"
- a calculator to show how much money is being saved
- a campaign badge

In addition, partners were encouraged to organise their own events and support services.

Figure CS11.2 The quit kit

Figure CS11.3 Campaign visuals and events

5. *Promotion: supportive communications to inform and motivate*

A national communication campaign (led by Santé Publique France, the Ministry of Health and l'Assurance Maladie) and related local communication campaigns (led by regional health bodies) were launched in three waves:

- *Wave 1, September 2016*: campaign launch among health professionals using a combination of massive mailing, advertising in professional press, digital communications (including a dedicated site (http://pro.tabac-info-service.fr/) and professional networks. Alerting and gaining the support of this group was vital to the success of the campaign.

- *Wave 2, October 2016*: a multiple media campaign (including TV, OOH, POS, digital, PR, product placement in soaps etc.) targeting the public with the message **Prepare To Quit Smoking** with the aim of recruiting both smokers and non-smokers to the cause. This was supported at a local level with events, a promotional lorry, regional press coverage and social media activity (see Figure CS11.3).

- *Wave 3, November 2016*: the launch of the collective challenge, "We will quit smoking together." This message went out at both a national and local level using every available media, both conventional and digital; the call was for smokers to give up and non-smokers to support them. Local activity benefited from the free use of nationally produced communication materials (see Figure CS11.4).

Figure CS11.4 Campaign materials produced for partners and supporters

Early lessons

This French adaptation of Stoptober is a unique experiment, and it is early days – the campaign has yet to be formally written up and published. A full evaluation is underway, and this will show whether the campaign met its cessation objectives. Even at this stage, however, there are indicators of success. It is the first time that so many partners have come together across France in the name of tobacco control, and they have done so with energy and enthusiasm. It is also the first time the idea of 'social contagion' has been used, and this too has been welcomed. This positive response on its own suggests that 'Moi(s) sans tabac' will become a regular fixture in France's public health calendar. In future years though thought should be given to the size of the project team – the current staff of six could barely keep tabs on the vast array of events that took place across France.

Case study questions

1. Which criteria and methods could be used to evaluate the effectiveness of the 'Moi(s) sans tabac' campaign?

2. Imagine you decide to implement a campaign such as 'Stoptober' and 'Moi(s) sans tabac' in your country or in a regional area. How could you adapt it to the context, the culture, etc. of your country/your regional area?

3. What are the theoretical models used in the 'Stoptober' and 'Moi(s) sans tabac' campaigns?

Notes

1 www.santepubliquefrance.fr.
2 www.nhs.uk/oneyou/stoptober.
3 www.ons.gov.uk/peoplepopulationandcommunity/healthandsocialcare/healthand lifeexpectancies/bulletins/adultsmokinghabitsingreatbritain/2016.
4 The independent body charged with monitoring public life.

References

Andler, R., Richard, J.B., Guignard, R., Nguyen-Thanh, V., Pasquereau, A., Beck, F., Deutsch, A., et al. (2016) 'Consommation de tabac et utilisation d'e-cigarette en France en 2015 : premiers résultats du Baromètre cancer 2015', *Bulletin épidémiologique hebdomadaire*, 30–31: 502–7.

Bandura, A. (1977) 'Self-efficacy: Toward a unifying theory of behavioral change', *Psychological Review*, 84(2): 191–215.

Bonaldi, C., Andriantafika, F., Chyderiotis, S., Boussac-Zarebska, M., Cao, B., Benmarhnia, T., Gremy, I. (2016) 'Les décès attribuables au tabagisme en France. Dernières estimations et tendance, années 2000 à 2013', *Bulletin épidémiologique hebdomadaire*, 528–540.

Brown, J., Kotz, D., Michie, S., Stapleton, J., Walmsley, M. and West, R. (2014) 'How effective and cost-effective was the national mass media smoking cessation campaign 'Stoptober'?', *Drug and Alcohol Dependence*, 135: 52–58.

Christakis, N.A. and Fowler, J.H. (2008) 'The collective dynamics of smoking in a large social network', *New England Journal of Medicine*, 21: 2249–2258.

Cour des comptes (2012) Rapport d'évaluation pour le Comité d'évaluation et de contrôle des politiques publiques de l'Assemblée nationale, Les politiques de lutte contre le tabagisme, décembre, 332 p., available at "http://www.ccomptes.fr" www.ccomptes.fr.

Cour des comptes (2016) La lutte contre le tabagisme : une politique à consolider, février, 33 p., available at "http://www.ccomptes.fr" www.ccomptes.fr.

Doran, G.T. (1981) 'There's a SMART way to write management's goals and objectives', *Management Review*, 70: 35–36.

Einstein, S. and Epstein, A. (1980) 'Cigarette smoking contagion', *International Journal of the Addictions*, 15(1): 107–114.

Fishbein, M. and Ajzen, I. (1975) *Belief, Attitude, Intention and Behaviour: An Introduction to Theory and Research*. Reading, MA: Addison-Wesley.

Gallopel-Morvan K. (2009) Comment changer l'image du tabac en France?, in Rapport sur le tabagisme, rapport coordonné par Maurice Tubiana, Académie Nationale de Médecine, p.5 et 17–20

Kerckhoff, A.C. and Back, K.W. (1968) *The June Bug: A Study of Hysterical Contagion*. New York: Appleton-Century-Crofts.

Kopp, P. (2015) Le coût social des drogues en France, Note de synthèse, OFDT, 10 p., available at www.ofdt.fr/BDD/publications/docs/eisxpkv9.pdf

McNeill, A., Guignard, R., Beck, F., Marteau, R., & Marteau, T. M. (2015) 'Understanding increases in smoking prevalence: case study from France in comparison with England 2000–10', *Addiction*, 110(3): 392–400.

Rosenstock, I.M. (1974) 'Historical origins of the health belief model', *Health Education Monographs*, 2: 328–335.

Taylor, D., Bury, M., Campling, N., Carter, S., Garfield, S., Newbould, J. and Rennie, T. (2006) *A review of the use of the Health Belief Model (HBM), the Theory of Reasoned Action (TRA), the Theory of Planned Behaviour (TPB) and the Trans-Theoretical Model (TTM) to study and predict health related behaviour change*, National Institute for Clinical Excellence, December, London.

West, R. and Brown, J. (2013) *Theory of Addiction*, 2nd edition. Oxford: Wiley Blackwell.

West, R. and Stapleton, J. (2008) 'Clinical and public health significance of treatments to aid smoking cessation', *European Respiratory Review*, 17(110): 199–204.

12

Food waste in higher education institutions

'Smaller Eyes than Belly Movement'

Sara Balonas and Susana Marques

Introduction

As in other countries, food waste is a current problem in Portugal. According to a study on food waste carried out in Portugal in 2012, it is estimated that more than one million tons of food per year will be wasted from primary production (332,000 tons), food processing/industry (77,000 tons), distribution (298 thousand tons) and home food management (324 thousand tons) (PERDA, 2012, cited by Governo de Portugal 2014). Although lower than the European average, it is timely to think about the implementation of measures that would reverse the current situation. Currently there are increasing awareness campaigns to reduce food waste. In Portugal, 2016 has been declared *The Year Against Food Waste*.

European Union is also seriously committed to reduce food waste as this will have a great effect on reducing the resources used in food production. This will bring more efficiency and less environmental impact. In 2014, The European Parliament has recommended that member states cut food waste by half by the end of 2016 .

Universities can play a crucial role concerning food waste and sustainability – they provide the appropriate environment to stimulate reflection and action. This present case is focused in the specific context of universities, in particular the University of Minho, a public Higher Education Institution pioneering the launch of a programme to reduce waste food in Portuguese canteens. This intervention is named *Movimento Menos Olhos do Que Barriga* (Smaller Eyes than Belly Movement) and focuses on reducing consumer plate waste in the university canteens. It was designed in line with social marketing branding, integrated communications and social activism concepts.

Problem definition

The Food Service of the Social Action Services of University of Minho, situated in north Portugal, conducted a study in 2013 on waste management, concluding that daily levels of food waste were considerably high: the University of Minho generated around four tons of food waste per month in their canteens.

Competitive analysis

As competitive attitudes and behaviours, we point out routines in the use of canteens. Dishes are served by university staff and according to nutritionists, users accept the quantities without intervening in the process. Therefore it is a passive behaviour to be combated. Moreover there is the idea that one pays the same for a full or less full plate, associated with an idea of 'being entitled' to the full portion, without questioning if it will actually be consumed.

In sum, there is an habit associated with a tacit acceptance and an idea of acquired right that the behavioural change strategy will have to consider when designing an intervention.

Stakeholder analysis

Four broad categories of stakeholders were identified, consisting of:

- University of Minho academic community: staff, students, teachers and non-teachers in schools;
- indirectly, family and friends of the members of the academic community (via word-mouth effect);
- local non-profit institutions that potentially benefit from the intervention (social canteen);
- regional and national media as partners.

Aims and objectives

The aims were to:

- inform and engage the approximately 18,000 students, workers and teachers at the university against the food waste resulting from meals in the canteens and consequently reduce that waste;
- develop a meaningful and clear social proposition – reduce food waste by 50% from four to two tons through behaviour change/reducing plate waste;

- inform students, workers and teachers about the social value of not wasting – food is used for needy families;

- promote an attitude and positive behaviours at social and environmental level.

Research

Research on food waste is increasing. Concerning consumer-related food waste in food service environments, as reviewed by Aschemann-Witzel *et al.* (2015), it is being argued that nudging strategies (e.g. switching to a tray-less system, reducing plate size and welcoming repeated helpings) can reduce waste. According to the EU project FUSIONS (2014) the causes of wastage need to be clearly identified within each single activity and the supply chain process. It then becomes necessary to set very specific proceedings for monitoring food waste generation in the different chain segments and in each type of activity, and find out appropriate methods for any single situation.

In a (2013) WRAP Report on *Out of Home Consumer Food Waste*, it was concluded that food is mainly left because portions are too big. Over half of meal leavers linked leaving food to various aspects of portion sizes. Two-fifths of meal leavers stated that one of the reasons why they had left food was because the portion was too big and one in ten stated they ordered/ served themselves too much. Meal leavers do not feel a sense of ownership or responsibility over the food left, do not believe the amount of food they get is within their control and many will not ask for information on portion sizes. Overall, close to three-fifths of respondents are not concerned by leaving food at the end of their meal.

Use of theory

Rangun *et al.* (cited by MacFadyen *et al.* 1999) suggest a typology of the benefits associated with a behaviour change. The benefits may be tangible, intangible, relevant to the individual or relevant to society. Where the product benefits are intangible and relevant to society (difficult to personalise and quantify), it is harder for social marketers to justify the need for behaviour change. This complex process of achieving effective behavioural change can benefit from participatory approaches (French 2011: 22). We are witnessing a mutation in society in which a citizen ceases to be seen as a passive individual and becomes part of the solution to social problems. For social marketing there seems to be an increasing attention to so-called community activism: "Listening and learning from the people with whom we want to work . . . is the sine qua non of social marketing" (Hastings 2011: 6), underlining the "power of ordinary people" in two respects:

- in a conventional sense, people can and will resist change if they feel that it does not take their needs into account;

- more subtly, they are not interested in social marketing programmes focused on the process but rather on the results; focused on the individual and not on the current lifestyles.

More individual and collective empowerment, in addition to a balance between experts and citizens, says Hastings.

This can be achieved through an intervention framework that integrates elements of the community affected by a given social problem with social marketing specialists, through their participation in problem selection, goal setting, participation in research, strategic development, and activities definition (Hastings 2011: 6). As Marques and Domegan (2011) point out, this aspect stresses the importance of relational marketing by providing "a new logic that sees consumers as the engines of the value creation process." That is "as value co-creators" (2011: 44). The intervention builds on these contributions.

Simultaneously, the intervention was also designed based on branding and integrated social marketing communications literature. As argued by Alden *et al.* (2011), social marketing communications work better when the brand promise is promoted with consistency and synergy across the different elements of the communications mix (e.g. advertising, public relations, sales promotion and social media). They also emphasise that communications are more effective when the focus is not on providing information but on pro-social behaviour change and actions such as trial and maintenance.

"Branding plays a very important role in social marketing by helping individuals to communicate and signal to themselves as well as others that they are engaging in desirable behaviours so they are better able to realise more immediate benefits and receive positive reinforcement" (Keller 1998: 300). In fact brands are more than a simple matter of communication and persuasion: they are about relationships, value and exchanges (Evans and Hastings 2008). Moreover, brands as holders of great power and influence in society can also fulfil "a great social purpose" (Olins 2003: 262).

For Hilton (2005) the institutions best positioned to help people change their attitude and behaviour are branded institutions, and that's why their cultural and economic power is an important component of their social value (2005: 60). In sum, "we need to understand and develop emotional connections to influence attitudes beliefs and behaviour" (French cited by Dias 2015).

The intervention

Based on the WRAP study on waste and waste management, the Food Department of the Social Action Services of the University of Minho decided to develop a communication campaign challenging the University's Communication Sciences Course in 2013. Instead of a traditional campaign, a behavioural change strategy was developed by a group of students with the teacher's support. The *Movimento Menos Olhos do Que Barriga* campaign strategy was launched on 16 October 2013 (World Food Day) by the students themselves who invited other students as volunteers to implement the intervention strategy in canteens as a guerilla action.

Branding was embedded throughout the intervention. The Movement was communicated through a visual logo and a statement referring to a popular expression easily recognised and altered in order to generate humour and surprise. The benefits of changing attitudes were clearly communicated: leftover meals will be sent to needy families.

Groups of young volunteers carried out 'patrol' actions using T-shirts alluding to the Movement, entering into canteens/bars in bulk, as inspectors who examine the dishes of

Figure CS12.1 Visual logo

Figure CS12.2 Poster

Figure CS12.3 Disposable cutlery

each consumer, in order to evaluate food waste. Groups visited the tables with an information flyer and a brief explanation of the patrol's purpose. Those who demonstrated having more than a portion size, were asked not to take the food they knew they would not consume. Via the Facebook page, the whole community could participate in challenges and follow the initiatives that took place throughout the school year.

The strategy was followed by three-year continuous interventions with 23 patrols in action, as well as disseminated actions during the academic year such as activities integrated in the reception and integration of the university's new students, vox pops throughout the city and university campuses, and a massive distribution of flyers and stickers. Having been considered a pioneering initiative in Portugal, the Movement received considerable media coverage: publication of articles in five national newspapers as well as reports on the various national television channels and on several national radio stations.

Outcomes

Quantitative results were obtained in terms of food waste reduction – approximately a 50% decrease. The rise in the number of meals served in canteens stresses a significant environmental and social impact, demonstrating a change in habits and attitudes towards a problem of sustainability, according to the University Food Department. They also concluded that in a year, the leftovers sent to nonprofit organisations resulted in an increase; from 12,650 soups to 13,448, and from 3,784 meals to 6,088 meals.

Focusing on a global improvement in waste reduction, the creation and practice of a positive influence on values, attitudes and behaviours regarding the same waste means environmental sustainability is a strong outcome of this project. Those responsible for the Food Department of the university say there is a sustainable daily behaviour change: the majority of the canteen users ask only for the amount of food in the dish that they know they will consume.

The Movement has already been awarded with three distinctions: PRA-TØ – Recognition of Practices and Acts for Zero Food Waste, in the 'Initiative and Mobilisation' category; and 'Excellence in Work', both in 2013 and in 2015.

The scope of the project also involves the implementation of the Movement in other Higher Education Institutions and the dynamisation of the following practices:

- development of mechanisms for measuring the results of the Movement, whenever these are applied in school or business institutions with a canteen;

- development of partnerships with composting companies for the recovery of food waste;

- support for institutions that assign leftovers to social canteens.

Thus the Smaller Eyes than Belly movement guarantees a continuum of actions for an effective behaviour change.

Discussion

The outcomes presented above suggest different angles for discussion:

1. In the University of Minho, before the behavioural social change programme, the school community didn't feel that they were part of the process of deciding the amount of food they could put on the plate. The movement provided a change in the way consumers behave, allowing them a sense of ownership or responsibility over the food left.

2. The benefits associated with a behaviour change were not known, namely, the existence of the social canteens. The social programme connected the behaviour of canteen customers to the users of the social canteens, the needy families. Moreover, canteen users are symbolically rewarded for their responsible behaviour with a pin. In the present case, defining the goal of reducing from 4 to 2 tons per month made the tangible benefit relevant.

3. The students' engagement is one of the key points of the intervention. Consumers need to feel involved and committed. Being developed and delivered by students this case stresses the social activism process. In this sense, as pointed by Hastings (2011: 7), communities are treated as agents and partners and not as passive message consumers.

4. The movement follows good practices regarding branding and integrated social marketing communications. The adoption of a visual logo and an easily recognisable statement (a popular expression with cultural roots) in all communication supports the behavioural change through the creation and communication of an influential value. Immediate benefits and positive reinforcement (Keller 1998) were main concerns in the branding strategy. Simultaneously marketing communications promoted the brand promise with consistency and synergy across the different elements of the communications mix, emphasising a pro-social behaviour change and action (Alden et al. 2011).

5. The imperative of a long-lasting programme. Several social marketing specialists (French *et al.* 2011) believe in the need for social change programmes to be citizen-oriented, as they must create value for citizens and develop a continuous relationship with them, ensuring that they become part of the solution to the social challenges society are facing (2011: 3). To make that happen, more than a traditional awareness campaign is necessary. A continuum of actions of interaction with the school community must be guaranteed, taking into account the events of a year, as has been happening since 2013.

6. Accountability: communicating results and social care leads to trust in the movement and awards actions. It is important to know people's expectations in exchange for their support for the cause. Companies that clearly communicate the conditions in which they act in favour of the cause, in interaction with the nonprofit organisation, will be in tune with the consumer–citizen of our times. Long-term commitment, and explicit involvement with a third-party organisation, are factors that can help build trust and reduce scepticism (Balonas 2013: 100).

7. Reducing food waste in university canteens is a demanding, complex and multifaceted challenge. Naturally, it requires different levels of interventions and change. The focus of this case was engaging with students, teachers and staff, making them part of the solution.

Case study questions

1. Communication that promotes a social change "must follow a long and deep process to modify beliefs, ideologies and change long-term attitudes" (Ruiz 2003). How does the social marketer keep the movement active in the long term, if it is strongly dependent on students' involvement and taking into account that they are a fluctuating population?

2. How could you improve the branding and integrated communication strategy?

References

Alden, D., Basiland, M. Desphande, S. (2011) 'Communications in social marketing', in G. Hastings, K. Angus and C. Bryant (eds) *The SAGE Handbook of Social Marketing* (pp: 167–177. London: Sage Publications.

Aschemann-Witzel, J., Hooge, I., Amani, P., Bech-Larsen, T. and Oostindjer, M. (2015) 'Consumer-Related Food Waste: Causes and Potential for Action Sustainability', 7: 6457–6477, open access.

Balonas, S. (2013) 'Social Causes Advertising: phenomenon characterization in Portugal, through television'. PhD thesis, University of Minho.

Dias, A. (2015) 'Symbolic as a strategy for behavioral change: The Águas do Porto case study'. Master's thesis, University of Minho.

French, J. (2011) 'Why nudging is not enough', *Journal of Social Marketing*, 1(2): 154–162. doi: 10.1108/20426761111141896.

French, J., Merritt, R. and Reynolds, L. (2011) *Social Marketing Casebook*. London: Sage Publications. ISBN: 978 0 85702 543 2.

FUSIONS (2014) 'Drivers of current food waste generation, threats of future increase and opportunities for reduction', Bologna. ISBN: 978-94-6257-354-3.

Governo de Portugal (2014) 'Prevenir desperdício alimentar: Um compromisso de todos'. Online at: www.portugal.gov.pt/pt/o-governo/arquivo-historico/governos-constitucionais/gc19/os-ministerios/mam/documentos-oficiais/20141017-mam-desperdicio-alimentar.aspx (accessed 4 July 2017).

Hastings, G. (2011) *Social Marketing: Why Should the Devil have all the Best Tunes?*. Amsterdam: Elsevier.

Hastings, G., Angus, K. and Bryant, C. (eds) (2011) *The Sage Handbook of Social Marketing*. London: Sage Publications.

Keller, K. (1998) 'Branding perspectives on social marketing', in J. Alba and J. Hutchinson (eds), *NA: Advances in Consumer Research*, 25 (pp. 299–302). Utah: Association for Consumer Research. Online at:http://acrwebsite.org/volumes/7887/volumes/v25/NA-25 (accessed 1 May 2016).

MacFadyen L., Stead, M. and Hastings, G. (1999) 'A Synopsis of Social Marketing', Stirling, Institute for Social Marketing. Online at: www.stir.ac.uk/media/schools/management/documents/social_marketing.pdf (accessed 1 May 2016).

Marques, S. and Domegan, C. (2011) 'Relationship Marketing and Social Marketing', in G. Hastings, K. Angus and C. Bryant (eds), *The Sage Handbook of Social Marketing*, Ch. 1. London: Sage Publications.

Olins, W. (2003) *A Marca*. Lisboa: Editorial Verbo.

Ruiz, A. (2003) 'Publicidad social: enfoques y métodos de análisis', in V.J. Benet and E.N. Aldás (eds), *La publicidad en el Tercer Sector: Tendencias y perspectivas de la Comunicación Solidaria* (pp. 129–141). Barcelona: Icaria editorial.

WRAP (2013) 'Waste and Resources Action Programme: Understanding out of home consumer food waste'. Final summary report, UK. Online at: www.wrap.org.uk/sites/files/wrap/OOH%20Report.pdf (accessed 1 May 2016).

Case study **13**

Civil society monitoring of tobacco industry point-of-sale marketing in Colombia

Juan Miguel Rey-Pino, Liliana Andrea Ávila-García, Jaime Arcila Sierra and Marian Lorena Ibarra Ávila

Introduction

In Colombia 17.3% of men and 5.6% of women are smokers. Among children, boys (11.9%) are less likely to smoke than men, but girls (7.9%) are more likely to do so than women. This tobacco use results in over 26,000 deaths per year – or 15.9% of all deaths in the country (IECS and IETS 2013). Because tobacco marketing is so clearly implicated in the onset of teen smoking, Colombia's relatively high levels of underage smoking have focused attention on the need for its regulation.

Latin America as a whole, and Colombia in particular, has made good progress on implementing laws and policies to control tobacco marketing (Shammah et al. 2015). Colombia ratified the Framework Convention on Tobacco Control (FCTC) in 2006 (an international treaty sponsored by the World Health Organization to combat tobacco which makes detailed provisions for the control of marketing) and then passed Law 1335 in 2009 which was designed to protect children with a range of tobacco control measures. In particular, it prohibited all forms of advertising and commercial communications for tobacco products, including the sponsorship of cultural and sporting events. Unfortunately, however, a confusion arose because the Ministry of Industry and Commerce (SIC), which has responsibility free competition and consumer protection, subsequently issued two Circulars (005 and 011) in 2012 regulating the display of cigarette packs at point of sale (POS) – despite the fact that Law 1335 had already banned all such promotion. This inadvertently created a loophole, which the Tobacco Industry (TI) has energetically exploited: it has been able to obey the circulars and in the process defy Law 1335. Careful monitoring carried out by the Veeduría Ciudadana para el Control del Tabaco (VCCT), a coalition of civil society organisations, has revealed the extensive use of POS marketing by the TI.

Problem definition

Law 1335 comprised a series of measures to achieve a range of objectives in line with the FCTC regulations, including: the prohibition of the sale of tobacco to minors (Article 2); the design of a public policy of tobacco control (Article 5); the creation of educational programmes to prevent tobacco consumption (Article 8); the regulation of health warnings on the labelling and packaging (Article 13); recognition of the rights of non-smokers (Article 17 et seq), and importantly for this case study, the total ban on all forms of advertising and promotion of tobacco products (Article 15 and 16), including sponsorship (Article 17). These latter controls are comprehensive, prohibiting "Any form of promotion of tobacco or its derivatives" and "any natural or legal entity from posting billboards, banners, murals, posters or similar mobile or fixed publicity promoting tobacco products."

The constitutionality of this legal provision was studied by the Constitutional Court of Colombia (Case C-830, 2010), which examined the impact of the measures on freedom of trade and normal commercial practice. Importantly, the Court accepted the global consensus on the harmfulness of tobacco for consumers, passive smokers and the environment. Consequently, it agreed that the measures were both proportionate and constitutional, concluding that the law "should be understood as a total ban on advertising of tobacco products along the terms formulated by the FCTC." The FCTC defines "advertising and promotion of tobacco" as "any form of communication, recommendation or action with the aim, effect or likely effect of promoting directly or indirectly a product of tobacco or the use of tobacco."

Circulars 005 and 011 of the Ministry of Industry and Commerce were issued with the goal of regulating the display of cigarettes at points of sale. The circulars were addressed to owners and managers of commercial establishments selling tobacco and its derivatives such as cigarettes in shops, mini-markets, liquor stores and department stores. Unfortunately, however, they were developed in ignorance of the previous prohibition of all types of tobacco promotion and effectively permit various forms of display of tobacco products in showcases, counters or "racks intended for this purpose." The TI has exploited the resulting confusion to install captivating POS advertisements which directly and indirectly promote tobacco products. In this way it has successfully undermined the FCTC, Law 1335 and the clear intent of the Colombian government to protect young people from tobacco marketing.

Aims and objectives

This case study describes the critical marketing approach adopted by the Colombian Civil Society organisation *VCCT* to analyse and expose the nature and extent of TI POS marketing.

Strategy formulation

The strategy began with a theoretical analysis of the role of POS promotion in marketing, and then proceeded to a detailed monitoring exercise of the actual POS activity taking place in Colombia.

The role of POS promotion in marketing

Display of a product at the point of sale is an advertising and promotional strategy aimed at influencing the patterns of purchase and consumption (Hastings *et al.* 2008). There is in fact a great quantity of scientific literature that stresses the value of the display at the point of sale as a factor of communication and promotion. This type of advertising is known generically as communication management at POS or, more simply, as Below the Line (BTL) merchandising (Kotler and Armstrong 2013; Vázquez Casielles and Trespalacios Gutiérrez 2012). Within the marketing process, defined as all strategies and tools that facilitate relationships between buyers and sellers, are the strategies of product, price, distribution and promotion-communication (De Juan Vigaray 2005; Martínez Martínez 2005).

Thus, POS is the meeting point between buyer, seller and manufacturer and a place where various techniques of persuasion and communication are carried out to persuade consumers to acquire a brand or product. This form of publicity is sometimes referred to as Point of Purchase Advertising (POPA). It is the most direct form of communication between the customer (Liljenwall 2003).

A series of actions at the POS fall under the name of merchandising and serve to optimise the presentation and persuade the consumer. These actions include:

- the choice of brands and variations of the product;
- the internal arrangement (spread of the products at the retailer);
- the presentation of the brands on the display racks;
- the design of the window display (shop window design);
- the ambiance of the interior.

The functions of merchandising can be summarised as a means to reinforce the positioning of the brand in the competitive environment, coordinate and communicate the strategy of choice to the target customer, properly manage the sales area, trigger interest and attention, and to encourage comparison and direct the customer towards the purchase. Displays at the point of sale therefore represent a communication tool and strategic promotion especially for:

- products that are largely undifferentiated from others where communication and the packaging itself can determine the sale;

- products where the only form of communication for a number of reasons (expense, legality, etc.) is the point of sale (Ailawadi *et al.* 2009).

The most common Point of Purchase Advertising communication strategies used by the TI are:

- the use of *branding* that evokes psychological and functional benefits such as status, health and glamour;

- the use of *packaging* to communicate and evoke product qualities (Orth and Malkewitz 2012; Rundh 2005);

- the way to compensate for the loss of other channels due to legal impediments (Porcu et al. 2012).

There are two types of tools used at the point of sale as a means of communication: those that constitute a form of advertising (Point of Purchase Advertising) and those that promote a product. A number of elements that stand out among the Point of Purchase Advertising are the following:

- *Signage* on hanging features or on masts.

- *Displays*. This is very characteristic element of Point of Purchase Advertising. It carries out the function of product differentiation. The effect of the display is to arouse the curiosity of the consumer. Depending on its complexity, it can offer a wide range of additional information that can be extremely creative and attractive to the consumer. Among the various forms are case-stacker displays, a combination of counter and floor displays, counter displays, coupon dispensers, dealer-loader displays, dump-bins, easel cards, one way sell displays, pack-out displays, pallet displays, pole-topper displays, premium displays, pre-pack displays and revolving-floor displays.

- *Point of Purchase Advertising* is bolstered by commercial jingles played through the public address system, by commercial spots and by commercial information via video screens, by adhesives attached to any medium and by other electronic media, lettering on the floor, brochures and neon signs and pennants.

Among the more common forms of promotion at the point of sale are price, incentive and events. In-kind offers such as samples, clearance items, gifts (known in commercial communication and advertising as advertisement objects) or contests with prizes are especially effective. All have demonstrated effectiveness in encouraging the purchase.

Monitoring of communications at the point of sale in Colombia

Given the different advertising and promotion strategies applied by the TI in the framework of the provisions of Law 1335 and the recommendations of the FCTC, *VCCT* launched an initiative to monitor the display of tobacco products throughout points of sale in Colombia's cities. The monitoring was intended to verify the implementation of these provisions and identify the violations. The monitoring includes the systematic collection of data obtained by observing the formal trade in traditional retailers (local convenience stores, supermarkets and mini markets) as well as informal trade such as street vending. The project was accompanied by a photographic record of the displays and a campaign to identify the promotional and advertising strategies.

This monitoring identified the following marketing TI strategies:

- The use of the PoS and the packaging of tobacco products as the main vehicles for promoting tobacco in Colombia.

- The widespread and systematic use of glossy, sophisticated and often illuminated stands to exhibit their products and ensure that these are highlighted.

- The placing of cigarette products and their displays in strategic locations near sweets and other products within reach and sight of children and young people, normalising their presence and consumption.

- The exhibition of cigarettes as a promotional platform to feature existing brands and launch new ones and as a vehicle to promote innovations such as changes in image, price or flavour.

Discussion

Both the theoretical analysis and the monitor suggest that the TI is using POS to promote its products, maintain the loyalty of its current customers, and seek new clients, in particular young people. This is taking place in defiance of Law 1335 which was supposed to have instituted a complete ban on all tobacco marketing. *VCCT* is now in a position to use this evidence to advocate for government action. In this way, a critical marketing perspective provided the means for real public health progress, and might ultimately ensure that young Colombians benefit from the full protections intended by their government.

Case study questions

1. How did a critical marketing perspective help *VCCT*?

2. What is the role of civil society and its organisations in the development of public health?

3. How in this case do the activities by the TI at the point of sale affect the consumer?

4. What does the case tell us about how regulations work?

References

Ailawadi, K.L., Beauchamp, J.P., Donthu, N., Gauri, D.K. and Shankar, V. (2009) 'Communication and promotion decisions in retailing: a review and directions for future research', *Journal of Retailing*, 85(1): 42–55.

De Juan Vigaray, M. (2005) *Comercialización y Retailing*. Madrid: Pearson.

Hastings, G., MacKintosh, A. M., Holme, I., Davies, K., Angus, K. and Moodie, C. (2008) 'Point of sale display of tobacco products', Cancer Research UK. Stirling: University of Stirling.

IECS and IETS (2013) *Carga de enfermedad atribuible al tabaquismo en Colombia*. Documento Técnico N°09, Noviembre.

Kotler, P. and Armstrong, G. (2013) *Fundamentos de Marketing* (11th edition). Boston, MA: Addison-Wesley.

Liljenwall, R. (2003) *The Power of Marketing at Retail*. Washington, DC: POPAI International Martínez Martínez, I.J. (2005) *La Comunicación en El Punto de Venta*. Madrid: ESIC.

Martínez Martínez, I.J. (2005) *La Comunicación en El Punto de Venta*. Madrid: ESIC.

Orth, U. R. and Malkewitz, K. (2012) 'The accuracy of design-based judgments: a constructivist approach', *Journal of Retailing*, 88(3): 421–436.

Porcu, L., Del Barrio-García, S. and Kitchen, P. (2012) 'How Integrated Marketing Communications (IMC) works? A theoretical review and an analysis of its main drivers and effects', *Communication & Society*, 25(1): 313–348.

Rundh, B. (2005) 'The multi-faceted dimension of packaging: marketing logistic or marketing tool?', *British Food Journal*, 107(9): 670–684.

Shammah, C., Gutkowski, P. and Andreis, M. (eds) (2015) La salud no se negocia (3rd edition). *Niños en la Mira de la Industria Tabacalera*. Fundación Interamericana del Corazón Argentina.

Vázquez Casielles, R. and Trespalacios Gutiérrez, J.A. (2012) *Estrategias de Distribución Comercial*. Madrid: Paraninfo.

Case study **14**

Reducing the negative environmental impact of SMEs in Pakistan's leather and tanning industry

Anne M. Smith and Aqueel Imtiaz Wahga

Introduction

In the year 2000 the Norwegian Agency for Cooperation and Development (NORAD) and the Pakistan Government began to work together to reduce the environmental impact of small and medium-sized enterprizes (SMEs) in Pakistan's private sector.[1] Initial work began with the leather and tanning industry; one that was particularly known to be responsible for water pollution impacting on the availability of clean water to local communities. A social marketing programme was launched to change SME owners'/managers' behaviour so as to reduce waste and negative environmental impact. At the same time SMEs would benefit from developing new capabilities, improving working conditions, increasing efficiency and cost savings, enhancing product quality, reputation and profitability. The programme was judged to be successful and was subsequently extended to other industrial sectors. However, while many SME owners adopted the new behaviours, others did not. This case study particularly focuses on the differences between adopters and non-adopters of pro-environmental behaviours to suggest how those implementing social change programmes can best target their interventions and accelerate the adoption process.

Problem definition

Studies have highlighted how organisations, and not individuals, are the main cause of many environmental problems (Smith and O'Sullivan 2012). Pakistan's leather and tanning industry has, in the past, been particularly problematic from an environmental perspective. This sector is of substantial economic and social importance, directly employing 500,000 people (Vogt and Hassan 2011: 47) and indirectly many others, for example from the agricultural sector and chemical industry. Leather is Pakistan's third largest export earning industry with almost 60% of exports destined for European markets. However, traditional production methods involve unhealthy working conditions and the discharge of waste into water supplies, thereby endangering human wellbeing as well as the natural environment. The industry is dominated by SMEs which, unlike larger businesses, often lack the resources (technology, knowledge, human and finance) to implement environmental measures such as newer, cleaner production technologies and methods.

Competitive analysis

Three main categories of competition can be identified from the case. First, at the individual SME owner/manager level, negative beliefs, attitudes and behaviours will prevent the achievement of desired behavioural change and therefore programme aims and objectives. These include:

- Inertia, i.e. acceptance of existing behaviours based on traditional practices or habit.
- Perceived costs of change, i.e. both financial costs and the time to learn about the new methods.
- Lack of knowledge (or belief) in the business benefits of change.
- Lack of environmental awareness/concern.

Second, SMEs may wish to adopt new technologies and methods but lack the finance, knowledge, skills and other resources necessary for change. Third, the existing infrastructure may not support adoption (for example availability of technologies, training and finance and government action to support behavioural change or deter existing behaviours, e.g. incentives and fines).

Stakeholder analysis

NORAD: The overall objective of Norway's development policy is to fight poverty and bring about social justice. The Norwegian government, through the Norwegian Agency for Cooperation and Development (NORAD), is involved in a range of projects aimed at addressing social problems in developing countries and provides substantial funding.

Pakistan Government: The Pakistan Environmental Protection Agency was established to enforce the Pakistan Environmental Protection Act, 1997. The agency works to "promote research and the development of science and technology which may contribute to the prevention of pollution, protection of the environment, and sustainable development; identify the needs for, and initiate legislation in various sectors of the environment; provide information and guidance to the public on environmental matters; specify safeguards for the prevention of accidents and disasters which may cause pollution; and encourage the formation and working

Figure CS14.1 The Leather Products Development Institute at Sialkot

of nongovernmental organizations, community organizations, and village organizations to prevent and control pollution and promote sustainable development" (http://environment. gov.pk/about-us/). In addition, the agency can fine and even close down businesses which do not comply with environmental legislation.

The Pakistan Gloves Manufacturers and Exporters Association (PGMEA): The PGMEA is a regional association of Pakistan's leather industry (the national association is the Pakistan Tanners Association (PTA)). It was the industry-level institution which managed the programme, acting as liaison between NORAD, the Cleaner Production Centre (see below) and the industry. The PGMEA continues to manage the current programme including the ongoing work of the Leather Products Development Institute (LPDI) (see Figure CS14.1) which focuses on developing design skills among workers including sketching, cutting and stitching, thereby minimising leather waste during production. The PGMEA's main interest is in increasing the export volume of leather and leather products through meeting the environmental demands of international buyers.

The Cleaner Production Centre: The CPC is an outcome of the collaborative arrangements between NORAD, PGMEA and the Pakistan Government. Its focus is the environmental capacity-building of SMEs in Pakistan's leather industry. The initial project was signed in 1998 and implementation began in 2000. The main objective of the CPC was to study the engineering techniques of leatherworking in SMEs and identify how they could reduce their environmental footprint while also becoming eco-efficient. This environmental support institute raises the level of eco-literacy among owner-managers and workers by organising workshops and seminars. The CPC also arranges on-the-job training showing how SMEs can conserve resources and reduce the pollution load by adopting cleaner production techniques (CPTs). Currently, the CPC does not receive any financial support from NORAD or the Pakistan Government. It is managed and funded by the PGMEA. While the CPC continues to guide leatherworking firms in Sialkot about adopting cleaner production, there is also a laboratory, Tti laboratories, on site which offers product-testing services to a wider range of industries.

Buyers of leather goods: Major international buyers of Pakistan's leather goods can, through their pro-environmental purchasing policies, have a major influence on their suppliers.

SME owner/managers in the leather and tanning industry: As the target audience these were a major stakeholder group with a considerable interest in the change programme and the perceived benefits (or drawbacks) which it would achieve. They have the power to accept or reject change.

Local communities: Local communities have a significant interest in the programme from at least three major perspectives. First, as employees of SMEs (and also owner/managers as above) in this sector they are dependent on business success. Second, the programme involves improved working conditions in terms of health and safety, for example wearing protective gloves and shoes. Third, reduced pollution will improve the quality of drinking water for them and their families, reducing health risks.

Other stakeholders: These may include SME owner/managers in other industries who benefit from the extension of the programme; those in other industries reliant on the leather and tanning industry etc.

Aims and objectives

The main aim was to minimise negative environmental impact by making changes to the product (leather goods) or by improving production methods. The programme aimed to achieve the following changes in the industry:

- Control discharge of pollutants such as harmful solid waste and heavily polluted water.
- Reduce treatment/production costs with the introduction and implementation of 'cleaner production techniques' (CPT) in the industry.
- Encourage green businesses in Pakistan.

Achieving these aims required SME owner/managers to adopt the following behaviours:

- Engage in process improvement with the help of technical assistance from the 'cleaner production centre'.
- Install water meters to aid in water conservation.
- Control air pollution by the installation of dust collectors.
- Reduce water pollution by the construction of grit chambers trapping the sludge from the effluent.
- Use desalting tables to curtail the element of salt in effluents.

The intervention

The initial phase of this intervention took place between 2000 and 2003 and was later extended to 2006. It is currently in its fourth phase. The initial intervention was mainly funded by NORAD and designed collaboratively with industry association, industry consultants and the export promotion bureau of Pakistan. The target audience comprised SME owners/managers in the leather and tanning industry in Pakistan who were using environmentally degrading technologies and production methods.

The various components of the intervention can be classified according to the elements of the marketing mix as follows.

Product

The 'product' offered to SME owner/managers comprises benefits, tangibles and intangibles (service).

- **Benefits** included cost savings through reduced resource consumption and waste generation; improved production efficiency and reduced compliance costs (fines). Increased financial gain would be achieved through enhanced product quality and improved reputation with buyers and other stakeholders. Improving working conditions would benefit SMEs through their reputation as a good employer, improved employee morale and well-being. Other benefits included the development of a continuous improvement capability contributing to competitive advantage and long-term growth.

- **Tangibles** relate to the new clean production technologies (CPT) offered for adoption for example, water meters, dust collectors, grit chambers, chrome recovery plant and protective clothing for employees.

- **Services** aimed to provide the facilities required by SMEs to enable them to adopt cleaner technologies. For example, the CPC provided testing laboratories and information centres offering the expertise and knowledge which were lacking. Other vital services included training programmes and on-site visits (see Place and Promotion below).

Price

Much of the financial cost was borne by the CPC, for example they provided financial support for installing new machines and developing infrastructures including the provision of water meters and dust collectors free of charge. They also developed grit chambers specifically for SMEs and purchased a dumper to collect solid waste. From the SMEs' point of view this significantly reduced the financial cost of adopting new technologies although, as highlighted later, other costs such as time spent away from the business, time for staff to retrain and production downtime were also incurred.

Place

The CPC is located in Sialkot, a city which houses a large number of export-oriented leather-working firms. However, to reduce the need for travel and increase convenience, training and consultancy are also conducted in-house at SME premises. Leather technologists from the CPC visit SMEs, observe their production processes and advise on how to adjust chemical combinations to reduce chrome (which could be a carcinogen), implement water and energy conservation measures through reconfiguration of the production process, install water flow meters, and take health and safety measures for example by equipping employees with masks, rubber gloves and shoes.

Promotion

Information about the programme was disseminated by the CPC through their news bulletins, industry reports and training programmes, including lectures and seminars. The CPC also established an information centre to provide technical information about the latest technologies and knowledge about how pollution can be reduced with the help of solid waste management systems. As illustrated consultants from the CPC also visited SMEs to promote the benefits of the new technologies. As the programme developed, case studies were developed of SMEs who had adopted the new technologies and methods. Peer groups were formed to work on, for example, water and energy conservation and later to cascade the practices in other SMEs.

Research and evaluation

Although no formal research was conducted prior to the intervention, the programme designers included industry experts (consultants and agencies) who were familiar with the attitudes and behaviours of the target audience. During and post-intervention, consultants involved in the programme collected data from SME owners/managers as to their opinions with respect to adopting the new technologies and production methods. They concluded that adopters and non-adopters differed according to the following characteristics:

- adopters were better educated and widely travelled entrepreneurs who had greater exposure to environmentally relevant market opportunities;

- non-adopters were less educated entrepreneurs and lacked awareness and knowledge of environmental issues.

The findings (summarised below) show notable differences between those who adopted the new behaviours and those who did not across three criteria: perceived business benefits and costs; environmental concern/awareness; and perceptions of government/infrastructure factors (A = adopter; NA = non-adopter).

Business benefits and costs

- Customer pressure is the main reason for adopting new methods, primarily coming from the European markets (A).

- Some SMEs want to increase their goodwill (A).

- Environmental engagement does not make economic sense (NA).

- Training and knowledge transfer focused on environmental awareness are considered a waste of time; some small firm owners prefer to stay with their unit to avoid revenue losses (NA).

- Entrepreneurs are not willing to invest in environmental initiatives at the cost of the usual financial needs of their businesses (NA).

Environmental concern/awareness

- A few others voluntarily want to address the environmental problems because they are damaging natural resources (for example, marine life is endangered) and also causing health problems for individuals and communities (A).

- Despite having environmentally concerned staff, some entrepreneurs are not willing to invest in environmental initiatives (NA).

- Lack of awareness of environmental impact (NA).

Government/infrastructure factors

- Pressure from government to become environmentally responsible (but not a significant reason) (A).

- Ineffective implementation of environmental rules and regulations (NA).

- Inspection of firms by environmentally incompetent staff from the government resulting in weak legislative implementation (NA).

- Even if the community raises concerns about environmental impacts, the factory owner is very influential so pressure from local authorities does not matter (NA).

- Unplanned expansion of firms does not allow for the provision of effective common facility/service support (NA).

Finally, SME owner/managers commented on features of the intervention/programme which had, or could, influence them positively or negatively:

- Perceived ownership of the programme by the industry-related consortium of firms, the Pakistan Gloves Manufacturers and Exporters Association (PGMEA), was a positive factor.

- If SMEs perceive a direct benefit, for example by getting a solution to their problem, only then will they adopt environmental measures (seminars do not provide the solution so small firm owners, generally, do not even attend these). However, medium-size firms do attend such events relatively frequently.

- The people involved are important. They should be informally dressed and use the local language so as not to be considered a tax-officer or a person who will just waste their time.

Outcomes

The success of CPT in this industry has been apparent. After the first two phases of implementation changes include:

- 25% reduction in water usage.
- 30 to 40% reduction in effluent.
- 20% reduction in waste production.

- 20 to 30% reduction in treatment costs.

- 10% reduction in the use of chemicals.

(*Source*: Pakistan Gloves Manufacturers and Exporters Association, 2009)

Consequently CPT initiatives have been extended to other industries and further extensions are planned, including cutlery, metal finishing, sports goods, textiles, sugar, surgical instruments and paper.

Discussion

The case study illustrates a number of factors relating to the adoption of new behaviours and technologies first described by E. M. Rogers in 1962[2] and often used in marketing studies. First there is the difference in adopter/non-adopter characteristics. In particular customers who are 'early adopters' often exhibit the characteristics found in this study (although there can be differences depending on the nature of the product). Adopters of CPT were better educated and widely travelled entrepreneurs who have had greater exposure to environmentally relevant market opportunities. Non-adopters were less educated entrepreneurs and lacked awareness and knowledge of environmental issues. Those who are most likely to adopt new behaviours are often referred to as 'the low-hanging fruit' in that they are more accessible and easier to reach.

Rogers also describes five product (or innovation) characteristics that can affect the speed of adoption. These are:

- Relative advantage – What are the benefits, advantages or efficiencies that the new product has over alternatives?

- Compatibility – How well does this new product fit with the potential adopter's needs, value system, existing products and technologies etc.?

- Complexity – How difficult it is to understand, learn about or use the new product?

- Trialability – Can the new product be tested on a limited basis?

- Observability – To what extent are the benefits visible?

Social marketing interventions need to address the above characteristics to encourage the target audience to adopt new behaviours. Question 1 below asks you to develop a detailed target audience profile (the 'low-hanging fruit') for early adopters of CPT, while question 2 asks you to recommend how a social marketing intervention should be designed to optimise the potential for success in changing the behaviour of SME owner/managers. The five characteristics outlined above will be useful here.

Finally, although this case study emphasises the successes of social change programmes on a local level, further consideration needs to be given to the need for systemic change. As highlighted above, some SME owner/managers resist change, as for them the costs outweigh the benefits. In addition there is evidence that the Pakistan government could do more to enforce changes thereby increasing the perceived costs of non-adoption. The negative impact of this industry on the health of workers in other developing countries has also been highlighted. For example, the World Health Organization has identified the significant negative impact of the leather tanning industry on the health of the local population and particularly children in Bangladesh. A recent report states:

> *Children as young as eight working in the tanneries of Bangladesh producing leather that is in demand in the west are exposed to toxic chemical cocktails that are likely to shorten their lives*

and in addition:

> *About 90% of those who live and work in the overcrowded urban slums of Hazaribagh and Kamrangirchar, where hazardous chemicals are discharged into the air, streets and river, die before they reach 50.*
> *(ZoomBookmarkSharePrintListenTranslate)*

Case study questions

1. Based on the case study, and particularly the research findings, develop a detailed target audience profile for an intervention to reduce the environmental impact of working practices of SMEs. This should focus the intervention on potential early adopters (the 'low-hanging fruit').

2. Many developing countries are dependent on a large number of SMEs for employment, production and exports. Yet many SMEs provide poor working conditions and are responsible for substantial environmental damage. By analysing the case study above recommend how a social marketing intervention should be designed to optimise the potential for success in changing the behaviour of SME owners/managers.

3. Outline the main features of the social marketing system as described in the case study. In your view where are the potential areas for collaboration/fit or conflict between the social marketing system and the marketing system for leather goods. How can a Community Social Marketing approach influence the quality of life of workers and local communities?

Notes

1 SMEs, in Pakistan, are defined differently by various institutions. According to the SME policy of Pakistan (2007), an SME is considered to employ up to 250 people with paid-up-capital up to Rs. 25 Million and annual sales up to Rs. 25 Million. For details see this link: www.smeda.org/index.php?option=com_fsf&view=faq&catid=3&faqid=48.
2 For a later edition see E.M. Rogers, (2003) *Diffusion of Innovations*, 5th edition. New York: Free Press.

References

Smith, A.M. and O'Sullivan, T. (2012) 'Environmentally responsible behaviour in the workplace: An internal social marketing approach', *Journal of Marketing Management*, 28(3–4): 469–494.

Pakistan Glove Manufacturers and Exporters Association (2009) Annual Report 2008–2009. Sialkot, Pakistan: author.

Vogt, P. and Hassan, Z.A. (2011) 'Value Chain Analysis of the Gems, Jewellery and Leather Sector in Pakistan', European Comission, Framework Contract EuropeAid: 127054/C/SER/multi - Lot 10 Trade, Standards and Private Sector.

Websites

www.unep.org/dtie

www.sci-pak.org/LinkClick.aspx?fileticket=wGo5jzzTfU4=

http://tribune.com.pk/story/33904/sialkot-industries-re-open-with-a-clean-slate/

http://tribune.com.pk/story/16489/new-technique-leads-to-35-fall-in-tannery-pollution/

Case study **15**

Changing population salt intake behaviour

Lessons from the UK salt reduction strategy

Michael Barry and Maurice Murphy

Problem identification

High blood pressure is very prominent worldwide, and the associated dangers and consequences of high blood pressure can be detrimental to one's health. Cardiovascular disease, including heart disease, stroke and related diseases, is the major cause of death in Ireland, accounting for almost 40% of all deaths (Irish Heart Foundation 2010). A diet high in salt has been linked to an increased incidence of high blood pressure. Populations around the world are consuming too much salt, largely as a result of the high salt content of processed foods. A relatively modest reduction in salt intake has the potential to prevent a significant number of heart attacks and strokes annually (Bibbins-Domingo et al. 2010).

It is estimated that about 15% of total dietary salt intake is from discretionary sources (salt added in cooking and at the table), 5% is from naturally occurring sodium in unprocessed foods, and about 80% comes from manufactured or processed foods (Food Safety Authority of Ireland 2005). The FSAI report in 2005 called for greater engagement with the food industry to reduce the salt content of foods on the market.

In 2003, the Scientific Advisory Committee on Nutrition in the United Kingdom, considering the extensive evidence for a direct link between salt intake and high blood pressure, recommended that the average consumption of 9 grams of salt per day in adults in the UK should be decreased to 6 grams per day to reduce high blood pressure and lower the burden of cardiovascular disease (Scientific Advisory Committee on Nutrition 2003).

The UK is leading the world in salt reduction through the implementation of progressively lower voluntary salt targets for more than 80 categories of foods. New revised UK-wide salt reduction targets for 2017 set even more challenging and wide-ranging targets than the previous targets for 2012. The revised targets have been developed and agreed by the UK's Department of Health working closely with industry, NGOs and stakeholders. The 2017 targets recognise the progress that has already been made by the food industry and aim to encourage further reduction. Salt levels in many foods covered by previous targets have reduced significantly, some by 40–50% or more, and more than 11 million kilograms of salt have been removed from foods. However, average UK salt consumption remains high at approximately 8.1–8.8g per day so there is still a considerable reduction required to meet the desired maximum daily intake of 6g per day for adults.

The UK salt reduction strategy: upstream social marketing intervention

1. Ascertain the present level of salt in food, then set a new lower salt target and ensure a system is in place to audit the changes.

In the UK, the creation of specific salt reduction targets for various food categories along with monitoring the progress of food companies in meeting these targets has seen significant positive results. Developing a list of priority food products for salt reduction by national health bodies has proven effective, due to the high nature of salt in foods such as bread, meat, fish and processed meats which contribute to the majority of the salt content in the population's diet.

2. Collaborate with the food industry in reformulation of food products to achieve the new lower salt targets as well as adherence to food labelling requirements.

Reformulation is seen as hugely important in terms of salt reduction and improving public health. An unobtrusive salt reduction (stealth) strategy appears to be the most attractive and effective method for reformulation and is government-led. This strategy reduces the salt content of a food product gradually and without highlighting the fact that reductions are taking place. The reductions in salt largely go unnoticed and taste is also unaffected as these reductions are carried out slowly over time. People's tastebuds change to the new salt level, and because the reduction is done gradually over time, it does not come as a shock to the palate.

3. Ensure government support with the associated threat of mandatory salt reduction legislation in the event of non-compliance.

The move to a low salt target must not be rushed by government or national health authorities in order to achieve the desired outcome. The reductions should be gradual and must be achieved slowly over time. The process may be slow, and this is certainly a limitation, but for the strategy to be truly successful, this needs to remain the case. In order for population salt intake to be significantly reduced the programme needs to be incremental, gradual and invisible. Drawing attention to salt reduction in products can have negative implications on consumer perceptions of taste and this silent unobtrusive salt reduction strategy avoids this. Government and public health bodies need to be aware of this.

4. Ensure that all non-governmental organisations dedicated to the salt reduction agenda are well-resourced and funded to continuously lobby all interested parties for lower salt targets.

Those non-governmental organisations dedicated to the salt reduction debate should be responsible for tailoring specific programmes for salt reduction to meet the requirements of different countries. Active campaigning by these organisations can have a huge influence on the decisions and actions made by the food industry. It is essential to have these advocacy organisations apply pressure to force change and hold both government and food industry organisations to account. It is essential for all social marketers attempting to reduce salt consumption to work with CASH (Consensus Action on Salt and Health), WASH (World Action on Salt and Health) and the WHO and utilise their resources.

The influence chefs and in particular celebrity TV chefs may have on salt reduction cannot be underestimated, and they should be lobbied to promote healthier eating through a campaign against salt.

5. Food labelling to change consumer behaviour: A classic pull strategy.

It is important to understand how food manufacturing labelling requirements can be improved to better inform consumers of salt content. It is generally understood that food labelling should be a simple process; however this has not always been the case. The number of varying food labelling systems in Ireland, the UK and worldwide has caused mass confusion among the public. There is overwhelming enthusiasm among social marketers towards the Traffic Light System (TLS) due to its simplicity. The TLS informs the consumer, in a clear and concise fashion, on the level of salt in a product with the use of a colour-coded system: red for a high level of salt, amber for an intermediate level, and green for a low level.

The simplistic nature of this labelling system has increased people's awareness of how much salt is contained in the foods they buy. The TLS is also displayed on the front of the packaging.

Case study questions

1. Why is the Traffic Light System (TLS) favoured over other labelling systems?

2. Why are consumers not told of the specific reductions in salt content?

3. Could this approach be applied to the area of sugar reduction rather than any proposed sugar tax?

References

Bibbins-Domingo, K., Chertow, G., Coxson, P., Moran, A., Lightwood, J., Pletcher, M. and Goldman, L. (2010) 'Reductions in cardiovascular disease projected from modest reductions in dietary salt', *New England Journal of Medicine*, 362: 590–599.

Irish Heart Foundation (2010) 'Cardiovascular Disease'. https://irishheart.ie/ (accessed 3 March 2015).

Food Safety Authority of Ireland (2005) *Salt and Health: Review of the Scientific Evidence and Recommendations for Public Policy in Ireland*. Online at: www.fsai.ie/uploadedFiles/Science_and_Health/salt_report-1.pdf (accessed 1 May 2016).

Scientific Advisory Committee on Nutrition (2003) *Salt and Health*. Online at: www.sacn.gov.uk/pdfs/sacn_salt_final.pdf (accessed 1 May 2016).

Case study **16**

The Act-Belong-Commit mental health promotion campaign

Rob J. Donovan and Julia Anwar McHenry

Introduction

Mental *health promotion* seeks to improve the wellbeing of all people regardless of whether or not they have or are at risk of a mental illness, whereas mental *illness prevention* targets known risk factors, including early interventions for the signs and symptoms of mental disorders. To be optimally and sustainably effective, mental health promotion and illness prevention initiatives need to bring about systemic change at the policy and structural levels (Anwar McHenry and Donovan 2013; Herrman *et al.* 2005).

Act-Belong-Commit is the world's first population-wide mental health promotion campaign, designed to build population mental health and to prevent mental illness. Using a community-based social marketing approach, this evidence-based campaign targets individuals to engage in behaviours that build mental health and wellbeing, and attempts to create supportive environments for positive mental health and wellbeing by involving community organisations and policy makers. Under a mass media advertising umbrella, the campaign relies heavily on social franchising to reach both the general community and specific target groups through a formal partnership programme (Donovan and Anwar McHenry 2015).

The Act-Belong-Commit message provides a colloquial 'ABC for mental health' and represents the three major behavioural domains that the scientific literature and members of the general population both consider contribute to good mental health (Donovan *et al*. 2003; Donovan *et al*. 2006; Donovan *et al*. 2007; (Donovan and Anwar McHenry 2016; Kirkwood *et al*. 2008). The campaign is explicitly behaviour-based, providing a framework for individuals, health professionals and policy makers with respect to what people can and should do to keep mentally healthy. More specifically, they are articulated as follows:

Act: Keep alert and engaged by keeping mentally, socially, spiritually, and physically active.

Belong: Develop a strong sense of belonging by keeping up friendships, joining groups, and participating in community activities.

Commit: Do things that provide meaning and purpose in life like taking up challenges, supporting causes, and helping others.

That is, the campaign encourages individuals to be physically, spiritually, socially, and mentally **act**ive, in ways that increase their sense of **belong**ing to the communities in which they live, work, play and recover, and that involve **commit**ments to causes or challenges that provide meaning and purpose in their lives. There is substantial scientific evidence that these three behavioural domains contribute to increasing levels of positive mental health (and, in fact, to physical health) (Donovan *et al*. 2006). Furthermore, although different groups may articulate the domains differently and place different emphases on each, these three domains appear universal across different cultures.

This chapter draws on a number of previous publications to describe the implementation, evaluation, evolution, and diffusion of the campaign (i.e. Donovan and Anwar McHenry 2015, 2016; Koushede *et al*. 2015). We will also comment on some of the broader societal implications of the campaign beyond mental health promotion.

Problem definition

As Koushede et al. (2015) note, an individual's mental health, like physical health, is fundamental to their short- and long-term thriving, their ability to work and their ability to contribute positively to society. However, it is estimated that over the life course, approximately 50% of the population will experience mental health problems (OECD 2013a), and, in the upcoming decade, mental health problems are estimated to constitute one of the major global burdens of disease (Whiteford *et al*. 2013), with wide-ranging social and financial implications for society as a whole. For example, according to Koushede *et al*. (2015), in the Member States of the European Union the cost of mental health problems is estimated to be between 3% and 4% of GNP due to a loss of productivity and increased expenses for social services and the healthcare system (OECD 2013b).

Within Australia, more than 3.6 million or approximately one fifth of Australian adults (aged 16 to 85 years) are estimated to experience mental ill-health, and almost 600,000 children and youth between the ages of 4 and 17 experience mental health problems each year (NMHC 2014). Mental illness is the leading cause of non-fatal disease burden in Australia, with an estimated cost of more than 2% of GDP (NMHC 2014).

Given this increasing burden of disease and consequent monetary costs, in recent years there has been an increased focus on population mental health and recognition that treatment alone is unlikely to make a significant difference to the escalating rates of mental illness being experienced worldwide (Anwar McHenry and Donovan 2013; WHO 2005). It has been recognised that interventions focusing on prevention and promotion are critical in enabling individuals to protect their mental health (Anwar McHenry and Donovan 2013; Department of Health 2012), with recent economic evaluations suggesting that investing in mental health promotion is cost-effective in the short term as well as in the long term (Knapp *et al.* 2011; McDaid and Park 2011).

Competitive analysis

Those wishing to implement mental health promotion face a number of systemic and other competing interests. First, in government health budgets, mental health and mental illness fall far below physical health services, facilities, and high-technology equipment in terms of governments' (and medical professionals') priorities. Numerous photo opportunities abound for politicians in opening gleaming new hospitals and operating theatres with the latest in high technology facilities. On the other hand, there is very little interest (and not much to film) in announcing more funding for medication or counselling services, or upgrading wards for mental illness patients.

Second, within mental health per se, despite the recommendation to invest more in upstream prevention and promotion interventions to reduce the burden of disease from mental ill-health predictions, downstream services tend to receive a greater proportional allocation of funds when compared to upstream initiatives (NMHC 2014). That is, most attention by governments and policy makers has been on mental illness treatment and service delivery both in Australia and globally (Reavley and Jorm 2014). Reluctance to invest in mental health promotion has been attributed to a perception of limited evidence supporting cost-effectiveness relative to treatment (Rush *et al.* 2004). It may also be due to stigma around mental illness in the community extending to systemic stigma among health professionals and governments.

What community-wide programmes do exist tend to focus on raising awareness of specific mental illnesses, promoting coping strategies and stress reduction tips, help-seeking for the early detection and treatment of mental health problems, and de-stigmatising mental illness, with interventions to build positive mental health limited to a number of school and worksite interventions (Barry *et al.* 2005; Jané-Llopis *et al.* 2005; Patterson 2009; Saxena and Garrison 2004). Hence, while mental health promotion is talked about a lot more right around the globe than a few decades ago, the reality is that apart from Act-Belong-Commit, there appear to be no government-funded, comprehensive, population-wide mental health promotion programmes in the English-speaking world.

Apart from the above, another reason why mental health promotion has not been implemented is because mental health/illness professionals have not had an easily understood and practical framework to work with as exists for physical health. It was deemed far easier for health professionals to identify and focus on the specific causes of a physical illness, for example, smoking and lung cancer or saturated fat intake and heart disease, and then mount campaigns to change smoking and diet habits than it is to promote mental health.

The Act-Belong-Commit campaign was designed to fill this vacuum by providing both individuals and health professionals with a practical framework for promoting mental health. Furthermore, to give meaning to the mantra that 'mental health is everybody's business', the framework was designed for use not just by health professionals but also by any organisations offering or wishing to offer mentally healthy activities.

Stakeholder analysis

The Act-Belong-Commit framework was designed for implementation at the population level in community, organisational and clinical settings, as well as specific target groups. The campaign's stakeholders therefore include individuals and communities targeted by the campaign, organisations who use the campaign to provide targeted support and interventions to their immediate clients, members, communities and staff (including mental illness service providers, and schools), state government departments such as health (in particular), education, sport and recreation and Aboriginal affairs, and local municipal governments. The ministers responsible for these government departments, as well as individual members of parliament, are also considered key stakeholders, along with our funding organisations.

Stakeholders are managed via representation on our Steering Committee, as well as via invitations to attend or launch functions and e-newsletter updates. Regular face-to-face and electronic contacts are maintained with key funders and major supporters.

The participatory research and consultation into a feasibility study for the 2005–2008 pilot of the campaign in six regional areas in Western Australia involved extensive involvement of stakeholders in the state physical and mental health areas, along with forums of local community organisations in the pilot towns. This consultation resulted in WA Country Health Services (responsible for delivery of health services in non-metropolitan areas of the state) becoming an early partner by providing staff time and physical location resources to the campaign.

Aims and objectives

The campaign's overall vision is articulated as: *a society that values mental health and where everyone has the opportunity to be mentally healthy*. The campaign's supporting mission statement is: *to enhance population mental health by creating supportive environments that strengthen individual and community resilience.*

The specific communication and behavioural objectives include the following:

1. To increase individuals' mental health literacy in terms of what they can and should do to keep mentally healthy.

2. T encourage individuals to maintain 'healthy' levels of activity within the act, belong, and commit domains (according to their capacity and opportunity).

3. To encourage organisations that offer mentally healthy activities, to partner with the campaign to increase participation in their activities.

4. To increase the awareness of organisations of all types, that there are policies and practices they could introduce to provide a mentally healthy environment for their constituents.

5. To enhance the capacity of the mental health sector to deliver effective mental health promotion by fostering mutually beneficial relationships.

Research

In 2002 the Health Promotion Foundation of Western Australia ('Healthway') commissioned research to inform the development of a mental health promotion campaign in Western Australia (WA). Adopting a grounded theory approach, Donovan *et al.* (2003) used qualitative research methods to first examine lay people's perceptions of mental health and the behaviours thought to protect and promote good mental health. The subsequently developed grounded theory was followed by an extensive review of the scientific literature on factors influencing mental health and wellbeing. This showed that while terminology and depth of understanding differed, there was much commonality between lay people's and behavioural scientists' views on what factors build resilience and good mental health and wellbeing. Various implementation strategies were developed on the basis of the research findings. Healthway then appointed the researchers to conduct a two-year pilot of the campaign in six regional towns throughout the state in 2005–2007. On the basis of the positive pilot study results, the campaign was launched state-wide in 2008 with further funding from the Mental Health Commission of Western Australia (WA). The origins of, evidence for, and rationale of the campaign are described elsewhere (Donovan et al. 2003, 2006).

Process and impact evaluations of the campaign are conducted annually among the general population (e.g. Anwar McHenry *et al.* 2012) and organisations that partner with the campaign (e.g. Jalleh *et al.* 2013). The general population questionnaire measures the reach of the campaign and campaign impact in terms of individual behaviour change, changes in beliefs about mental health and mental illness, and perceived societal impacts such as the effectiveness (or otherwise) of the campaign in increasing openness towards mental health issues and reducing the stigma surrounding mental illness. The partner questionnaire measures the extent to which organisations have benefited from the partnership in terms of staff capacity, organisation awareness, promotion of events, and obtaining funds for specific activities (Donovan and Anwar McHenry 2015).

Intervention

The campaign makes extensive use of social franchising to facilitate individuals' participation in mentally healthy activities and for the delivery and implementation of the campaign at a local community level (Donovan and Anwar McHenry 2015).

Act-Belong-Commit (the 'franchisor') partners with a diverse range of community groups (e.g. theatre groups; women's health groups; sporting groups; recreational and hobby groups; see under 'Partners' at actbelongcommit.org.au), local governments, and state-wide organisations. Franchisees are provided with initial and ongoing training, overall strategic direction, scientific resources, merchandising, mass media advertising, publicity, and event sponsorship (Donovan and Anwar McHenry 2015). The social franchise model differs from the commercial model in that an assurance of moral consensus or enthusiastic embrace of the social cause needs to be presen, with similar understandings about how objectives should be attained to enable franchisees to actively contribute and take ownership over the initiative (Volvery and Hackl 2010). Hence our franchisees sign a Memorandum of Understanding (MOU) to maintain the integrity of the campaign messages. Importantly in an area where funding is limited, the social franchise model enables the Act-Belong-Commit campaign to expand its impact and geographical reach without necessarily increasing the size and hence the ongoing costs of the franchiser 'hub' (Beckmann and Zeyen 2013).

As noted above, franchisees sign an MOU with Mentally Healthy WA to ensure brand consistency and message integrity, the continual learning and sharing of activities and strategies between partners, and the provision of regular process evaluation data to support overall evaluation of campaign impact (Donovan and Anwar McHenry 2015). Partnerships with sectors other than health (i.e. sport, recreation, the arts, education, charities, etc.) allow the involvement of local people in implementation, which is considered essential for health promotion campaign success in addressing the social determinants of mental health and wellbeing more effectively (Annor and Allen 2008; Barnett and Kendall 2011; Quinn and Biggs 2010).

The campaign has a number of online downloadable resources, including a self-help guide (*A Great Way to Live Life: The Act-Belong-Commit Guide to Keeping Mentally Healthy*), which not only provides individuals with a tool for enhancing their mental health, but also provides the clinician with a helpful tool in the clinical setting. The Guide contains self-assessment questionnaires on the Act-Belong-Commit domains and can be completed online. Other resources include a mobile phone app, a website search tool to find clubs and organisations in one's areas of interest in geographic areas, various fact sheets, curriculum materials for schools, and print and video advertisements (actbelongcommit.org.au).

Outcomes

The 2015 annual population survey of 600 respondents across the state shows high campaign reach (75%), with 10% of those reached by the campaign reporting trying to do something to improve their mental health as a result of their exposure to the campaign (Jalleh *et al.* 2014).

Although conceived as a primary prevention intervention, many individuals with a mental illness experience have contacted the campaign and reported being influenced by it to take up activities that have assisted their recovery or enhanced their quality of life. To quantify this impact, in the 2013 and 2014 general population surveys we included questions on whether the respondent had sought professional help for a mental health problem in the past 12 months and whether they had ever been diagnosed with a mental illness. Campaign impact was generally higher on most measures among those with a mental illness or had sought help, but particularly on changing the way respondents thought about mental health (41% vs 24%), and doing something for their mental health as a result of their exposure to the campaign (21% vs 9%) (Donovan *et al.* 2016). Feedback from individuals with a mental illness in informal group discussions with campaign personnel indicated that one of the major factors facilitating their involvement is that they see the campaign as "for everyone", and hence can get involved without their involvement being defined by their mental illness.

At a societal level, the campaign is perceived to be making people more open about mental health problems and reducing the stigma around mental illness. The campaign is also having further effects at a systemic level, with the training in the previous 12 months of around 250 mental health professionals in the campaign principles and how they can apply these to patients in recovery. Reaction by the health professionals to the workshops has been very positive, and this has been validated in follow-up surveys showing that the attendees are applying the principles in practice, both with their colleagues and consumers and carers (Robinson *et al.* 2016).

Discussion

In the eight years that the campaign has been conducted state-wide, there have been major changes in people's perceptions of mental health and an acceptance that individuals can do things to protect and improve their mental health in the same way that there are things they can and should do to keep physically healthy. Perhaps one of the most significant outcomes of the campaign is the sheer number and variety of community organisations (e.g. from knitting groups to dragon boat clubs, stamp collectors, and surf lifesavers) that saw that the campaign messages were relevant to them and their organisation's activities. In that sense, this campaign actually walks the talk that "mental health is everybody's business".

The finding that individuals with a diagnosed mental illness or experiencing a mental health problem are being encouraged by the campaign to do something of their own volition to alleviate symptoms or implement solutions is particularly encouraging. These data suggest that population-wide mental health promotion campaigns can not only impact the mental health and wellbeing of the general population, but also can impact the mental health and wellbeing of those with a diagnosed mental illness or experiencing a mental health problem. At the clinical level, this suggests that clinicians, especially those following a person-centred approach (Thorne 2007), could find this framework helpful in their work. At a broader level, given that depression is a major risk factor for suicidal behaviour and that the stigma around mental illness inhibits early help-seeking behaviour (Corrigan 2004; Stuart *et al.* 2012), by encouraging those with early signs of depression to do something for their mental health, and by reducing perceived stigma, the campaign has the potential to increase early help-seeking and deal with problems before they become more serious and require more treatment than otherwise, including deterioration to the point of suicide (Donovan *et al.* 2016). Hence such campaigns have the potential to achieve direct economic savings via secondary prevention, and perhaps reduced risk or reduced severity of relapse among those in recovery.

By building individual and community resilience, Act-Belong-Commit has a primary prevention role for mental illness. However, Joiner's theory of why people suicide suggests that Act-Belong-Commit also serves as a powerful primary prevention intervention for suicide (if not secondary and tertiary prevention also). Joiner's Interpersonal – Psychological Model of Suicidal Behaviour (Ribeiro and Joiner 2011) proposes that people suicide when they have both the desire and the ability to die by their own hand. According to Joiner, the desire or motivation to suicide is driven by two factors: low or 'thwarted' belongingness and perceived burdensomeness. Joiner's motivational factors have clear overlaps with 'Belong' (particularly) and 'Commit'. 'Belong' is about building and maintaining connections with others, including community and civic organisations and institutions. 'Commit' involves doing things that provide meaning and purpose in life, including taking up causes and volunteering that helps society and other individuals. In Joiner's theory, both of these are clearly protective factors against suicide and hence form the building blocks for suicide prevention interventions.

At a broader societal or civic engagement level, the 'Belong' concept attempts to bring people from various walks of life together in public spaces to participate in community events and celebrate community achievements. Such public participation, including where volunteerism brings people together who would not otherwise interact, reinforces social inclusion, neutralises and reduces prejudices, and promotes solidarity. These characteristics promote strong supportive societies that enhance what Aristotle might have called civic virtue, and what others would call harmony. In short, 'Belong' and 'Commit' promote good citizenship (Donovan 2013). It is noteworthy that with respect to young Muslim men from Western countries going to Syria and Iraq to fight with the Islamic State, comments by journalists, political commentators, politicians, and behavioural scientists have centred around these young men lacking a sense of belonging to their (or their parents') adopted countries, and a lack of meaning and purpose in their lives. Notwithstanding individual psychological and other elements (e.g. criminal backgrounds), as for suicide, the Belong and Commit domains are clearly protective factors against 'Jihadist radicalisation'.

Finally, the campaign messages have shown applicability across cultures through the involvement of various ethnic groups in Australia and via the campaign's diffusion across Australia and overseas (Koushede *et al*. 2015; Nielsen *et al*. 2016). Organisations in the UK, Japan, Fiji, USA and Mongolia have shown interest in the campaign, with Denmark becoming the first national hub outside Australia, followed by Norway signing up to the campaign in 2016.

Case study questions

You have been asked to assess the feasibility of implementing the Act-Belong-Commit campaign in your country. Given this scenario, you are required to answer the following questions.

1. What research would you undertake and with whom? Delineate your research objectives and methods.

2. What stakeholders would you consult and for what purposes?

3. If the research showed the campaign was feasible, but you were given limited funds, what communication strategies and channels would you use in the first year of the campaign?

References

Annor, S. and Allen, P. (2008) 'Why is it difficult to promote public mental health? A study of policy implementation at local level', *Journal of Public Mental Health*, 7(4): 17–29.

Anwar McHenry, J. and Donovan, R.J. (2013) 'The development of the Perth Charter for the Promotion of Mental Health and Wellbeing', *International Journal of Mental Health Promotion*, 15(1): 58–64.

Anwar McHenry, J., Donovan, R.J., Jalleh, G., and Laws, A. (2012) 'Impact evaluation of the Act-Belong-Commit mental health promotion campaign', *Journal of Public Mental Health*, 11(4): 186–195.

Barnett, L. and Kendall, E. (2011) 'Culturally appropriate methods for enhancing the participation of Aboriginal Australians in health-promoting programs', *Health Promotion Journal of Australia*, 22: 27–32.

Barry, M.M., Domitrovich, C. and Lara, M.A. (2005) 'The implementation of mental health promotion programmes', *IUHPE - Promotion and Education* (Supplement 2): 30–35.

Beckmann, M. and Zeyen, A. (2013) 'Franchising as a strategy for combining small and large group advantages (logics) in social entrepreneurship: A Hayekian perspective', *Nonprofit and Voluntary Sector Quarterly* (online).

Corrigan, P. (2004) 'How stigma interferes with mental health care', *American Psychologist*, 59: 614–625.

Department of Health (2012) 'No health without mental health: Mental health strategy implementation framework', London, Centre for Mental Health, Department of Health, Mind, NHS Confederation Mental Health Network, Rethink Mental Illness, Turning Point.

Donovan, R.J. (2013) 'When it comes to mental health promotion, there's a lot more said than done. A lot more'. *Obsessive Hope Disorder: Reflections on 30 years of Mental Health Reform and Visions of the Future* (J. Mendoza, S. Rosenberg, A. Bresnan, A. Elson, Y. Gilbert, P. Long, K. Wilson, J. Hopkins and G.Y. Caloundra). Moffat Beach, ConNetica Consulting.

Donovan, R.J. and Anwar McHenry, J. (2015) 'Promoting mental health and wellbeing in individuals and communities: The 'Act-Belong-Commit' campaign', in W. Wymer (ed.), *Innovations in Social Marketing and Public Health Communication: Improving the Quality of Life for Individuals and Communities* (pp. 215–226). Cham, Switzerland: Springer International Publishing.

Donovan, R.J. and Anwar McHenry, J. (2016) 'Act-Belong-Commit: Lifestyle medicine for keeping mentally healthy', *American Journal of Lifestyle Medicine*, 10(3): 193–199.

Donovan, R.J., Henley, N., Jalleh, G., Silburn, S.R., Zubrick, S.R. and Williams, A. (2007) 'People's beliefs about factors contributing to mental health: Implications for mental health promotion', *Health Promotion Journal of Australia*, 18(1): 50–56.

Donovan, R.J., Jalleh, G., Robinson, K. and Lin, C. (2016) 'Impact of a population-wide mental health promotion campaign on people with a diagnosed mental illness or recent mental health problem', *Australian New Zealand Journal of Public Health*.

Donovan, R.J., James, R., Jalleh, G., and Sidebottom, C. (2006) 'Implementing mental health promotion: The Act-Belong-Commit Mentally Healthy WA campaign in Western Australia', *International Journal of Mental Health Promotion*, 8(1): 33–42.

Donovan, R.J., Watson, N., Henley, N., Williams, A., Silburn, S., Zubrick, S., James, R., Cross, D., Hamilton, G. and Roberts, C. (2003) Mental Health Promotion Scoping Project. Perth, Report to Healthway. Centre for Behavioural Research in Cancer Control, Curtin University.

Herrman, H., Saxena, S. and Moodie, R. (eds) (2005) *Promoting Mental Health: Concepts, Emerging Evidence, Practice*. Geneva: World Health Organization.

Jalleh, G., Anwar McHenry, J., Donovan, R. and Laws, A. (2013) 'Impact on community organisations that partnered with the Act-Belong-Commit mental health promotion campaign', *Health Promotion Journal of Australia*, 24(1): 44–48.

Jalleh, G., Donovan, R.J., and Lin, C. 2014. Evaluation of the Act-Belong-Commit Mentally Healthy WA Campaign: 2014 Survey Data. Perth, School of Public Health, Curtin University.

Jané-Llopis, E., Barry, M., Hosman, C. and Patel, V. (2005) 'Mental health promotion works: A review', *Promotion and Education*, 12(Supplement 2): 9–25.

Kirkwood, T.B., May, C., McKeith, I. and Teh, M. (2008) 'Mental capital through life: Future challenges', Foresight Mental Capital and Wellbeing project, London, The Government Office for Science.

Knapp, M., McDaid, D. and Parsonage, M. (eds) (2011) *Mental Health Promotion and Mental Illness Prevention: The Economic Case*. London: London School of Economics and Political Science.

Koushede, V., Nielsen, L., Meilstrup, C. and Donovan, R.J. (2015) 'From rhetoric to action: Adapting the Act-Belong-Commit Mental Health Promotion Programme to a Danish context', *International Journal of Mental Health Promotion*, 17(1): 22–33.

McDaid, D. and Park, A. (2011) 'Investing in mental health and well-being: Findings from the DataPrev project', *Health Promotion International*, 26(S1): i108–i139.

Nielsen, L., Sørensen, B.B., Donovan, R.J., Tjønhøj-Thomsen, T. and Koushede, V. (2016) '"Mental health is what makes life worth living": An exploration of Danish lay people's understanding of mental health and mental health promoting factors', *International Journal of Mental Health Promotion*.

NMHC (2014) *The National Review of Mental Health Programmes and Services*. Sydney: National Mental Health Commission.

OECD (2013a) *Health at a Glance 2013: OECD Indicators*. Paris: OECD.

OECD (2013b) *Mental Health and Work: Denmark*. Paris: OECD.

Patterson, A. (2009) Building the Foundations for Mental Health and Wellbeing: Review of Australian and International Mental Health Promotion, Prevention and Early Intervention Policy. Hobart, Australia: Department of Health and Human Services.

Quinn, N. and Biggs, H. (2010) 'Creating partnerships to improve community mental health and well-being in an area of high deprivation: Lessons from a study with high-rise flat residents in east Glasgow', *Journal of Public Mental Health*, 9(4): 16–21.

Reavley, N. and Jorm, A.F. (2014) 'Mental health reform: increasing resources but limited gains', *Medical Journal of Australia*, 201: 375–376.

Ribeiro, J.D. and Joiner, T.E. (2011) 'Present status and future prospects take up the interpersonal–psychological theory of suicidal behaviour', in R.C. O'Connor, S. Platt and J. Gordon (eds) *International Handbook of Suicide Prevention: Research, Policy and Practice* (pp. 169–179). New York: Wiley.

Robinson, K., Donovan, R.J., Jalleh, G. and Lin, C. (2016) *Act-Belong-Commit in Recovery: Train the Trainer Pilot and Intensive Pilot Study*. Final Report. Perth, Mentally Healthy WA, Curtin University and the Mental Health Commission, Government of Western Australia.

Rush, B., Shiell, A. and Hawe, P. (2004) 'A census of economic evaluations in health promotion', *Health Education Research*, 19(6): 707–719.

Saxena, S. and Garrison, P.J. (2004) *Mental Health Promotion: Case Studies from Countries*. Geneva: World Health Organization and World Federation for Mental Health.

Stuart, H., Arboleda-Florez, J. and Sartorius, N. (2012) *Paradigms Lost: Fighting Stigma and the Lessons Learned*. Oxford: Oxford University Press.

Thorne, B. (2007) *Person-Centred Therapy: Dryden's Handbook of Individual Therapy*. London: Sage. pp. 144–170.

Volvery, T. and Hackl, V. (2010) 'The promise of social franchising as a model to achieve social goals', in A. Fayolle and H. Matley (eds) *Handbook of Research on Social Entrepreneurship*. Cheltenham: Edward Elgar.

Whiteford, H.A., Degenhardt, L., Rehm, J., Baxter, A.J., Ferrari, A.J., Erskine, H.E., Charlson, F.J., Norman, R.E., Flaxman, A.D., Burstein, N.J.R., Murray, C.J.L. and Vos, T. (2013) 'Global burden of disease attributable to mental and substance use disorders: Findings from the Global Burden of Disease Study 2010', *The Lancet*, 382(9904): 1575–1586.

WHO (2005) 'Mental health action plan for Europe: Facing the challenges, building solutions'. First WHO European Ministerial Conference on Mental Health, Helsinki, Finland. Copenhagen: WHO Regional Office for Europe.

Case study **17**

From concept to action

Integration of systems thinking and social marketing for health disparities elimination

Brian J. Biroscak, Carol A. Bryant, Claudia X. Aguado Loi, Dinorah Martinez Tyson, Tali Schneider, Laura Baum, Aldenise Ewing and Peter S. Hovmand

Introduction

The Florida Prevention Research Center (FPRC) at the University of South Florida (Tampa, Florida, USA) is partnering with a community coalition[1] known as the CCC, which stands for Colorectal Cancer Prevention Community Committee. The CCC initiative involves developing, implementing, and evaluating a community-centred social marketing strategy designed to address colorectal cancer (CRC) screening disparities in the Tampa Bay region. Our case study demonstrates how, through the co-creation of social marketing activities in conjunction with an academic-community partnership, innovative solutions may be generated for eliminating health disparities.

Problem definition

Figure CS17.1 indicates Florida counties with high incidence rates of late-stage CRC. The area encircled encompasses some of the counties with increased late-stage CRC, and this is where we are focusing our efforts.

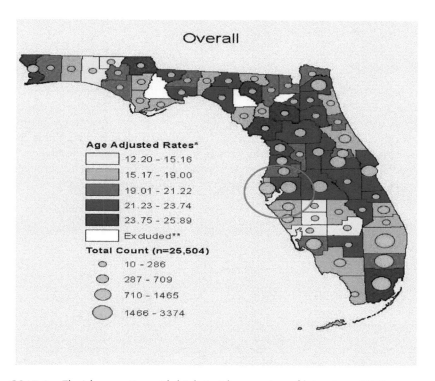

Figure CS17.1   Florida counties with high incidence rates of late-stage CRC

The FPRC and the CCC are co-creating the next iteration of the former's social marketing planning framework, known as Community Based Prevention Marketing (CBPM). The first CBPM framework was designed to teach community coalitions how to use social marketing for programme development (Bryant *et al.* 2009), and the second CBPM framework was planned to teach coalitions how to use social marketing for policy development (Bryant *et al.* 2014). The next iteration, called CBPM for Systems Change, is an eight-step framework (Figure CS17.2) designed to lead community coalitions through the process of using 'systems thinking' to formulate and implement social marketing strategy. Although the term 'systems thinking' has been applied quite liberally by many authors, we use it in reference to the 'system dynamics modelling' tradition that came out of the Massachusetts Institute of Technology (MIT) (Forrester 1958).

Aims and objectives

The five-year goal (2014–2019) of this CDC-funded academic-community partnership is to identify, tailor, implement, and evaluate a multi-level intervention to increase CRC screening. The specific aims of the case study reported here included:

- to examine disparities in late stage CRC incidence and screening rates to identify priority populations;
- to identify appropriate and feasible evidence-based interventions (EBIs) for priority populations; and
- to conduct formative research with priority populations and key stakeholders to assess the EBIs' acceptability and to tailor EBIs to better meet priority population(s') preferences and needs.

Situation analysis

In CBPM Step #1 (Figure CS17.2), this academic-community partnership created a foundation for success (e.g. readiness assessment). As outlined by Green and Kreuter (2005), a situational analysis is essential to assess the capacity of the community planning team and uncover potential barriers/facilitators. CCC members completed a readiness checklist to assess their group's capacity to identify gaps in building a successful foundation. Situation analysis findings were summarised, e.g. as a 'word cloud' (Figure CS17.3) and PowerPoint presentation, and presented back to the CCC for reflection. The readiness assessment addressed the following types of questions:

- Does the group have the resources and member interest needed to implement the *CBPM for Systems Change* framework?
- What are the group's strengths/weaknesses?
- Are there external partners needed?

Audience segmentation

In CBPM Step #2 (Figure CS17.2), the CCC selected two priority populations as the focus of the to-be-developed social marketing strategy: (a) Florida residents aged 50–64 years

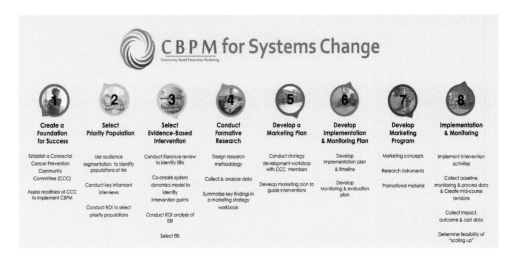

Figure CS17.2   The CBPM steps for Systems Change

Figure CS17.3   CBPM word cloud

without health insurance but with a healthcare provider, and (b) Florida residents aged 50–64 years with health insurance. To arrive at these choices, FPRC faculty and staff conducted classification tree analysis, i.e. a nonparametric, multivariate approach similar to multivariate regression analysis called chi-square automatic interaction detection (CHAID). It has been used in commercial marketing to identify segments of the population and their responsiveness to certain strategies. CHAID examines correlates of several health-related risk factors or behaviours, and it assumes there is statistical interaction among the factors (van Diepen and Franses 2006). One of its major advantages is the use of a tree-like display to summarise results that makes it easy for a community group to identify and compare audience segments.

Figure CS17.4 shows the first three levels of the classification tree from our CHAID analyses. In our study, 'up-to-date screening status' was the dependent variable and served as the seed structure for segmentation. Through an iterative, chi-square test of independence, mutually exclusive and exhaustive segments were identified based on independent variables considered (e.g. race/ethnicity, age, insurance coverage, access to a regular health provider, BMI, education, health status, gender). CCC members were provided with CHAID results and then participated in a return-on-investment (ROI) exercise to select the two priority populations as the focus of their social marketing efforts.

The CCC members, even those who did not have statistical training, were able to recognise differences in screening rates between subgroups and the unique combination of characteristics that defined each segment, in large part because of the tree format CHAID uses to display results. They also were able to understand the importance of selecting a small number of segments that are likely to provide a good return on investment for their programme-planning efforts. As a result, CCC members were then able to focus efforts in the next CBPM steps on these defined audience segments.

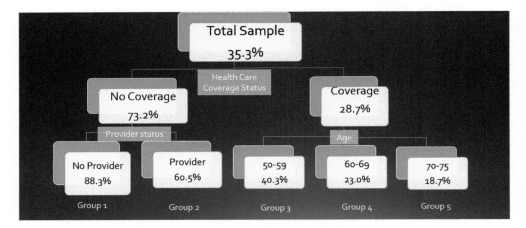

Figure CS17.4   CHAID results

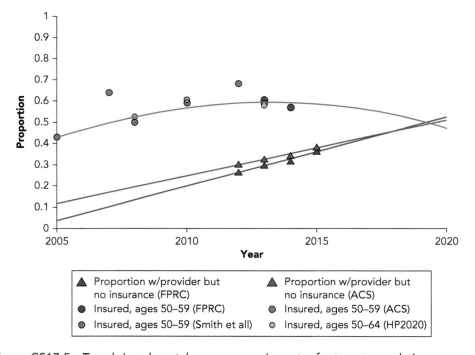

Figure CS17.5   Trends in colorectal cancer screening rates for target populations

Competitive analysis

In CBPM Step #3 (Figure CS17.2), FPRC faculty and staff conducted a systematic review and meta-analysis to identify evidence-based interventions (EBIs) that might be effective for increasing CRC screening rates among the priority populations of interest. This activity is considered to form part of a 'competitive analysis' because those who will be needed for implementation of the eventual interventions (e.g. health insurance administrators, primary care physicians, individual patients) have multiple options that compete for their time and resources, with respect to CRC screening. The goals of this review were to (1) identify the evidence-based CRC screening interventions published from August 2009 to December 2014, (2) describe the types of intervention strategies used in each study, and (3) document the effectiveness of each intervention in promoting CRC screening rates. A total of 101 studies met a set of eligibility criteria gleaned from previously published, peer-reviewed CRC systematic reviews.

The following summary includes only the randomised controlled trials ($n = 51$), further classified into the following categories: 36 'Client-Centred' studies, 2 'Provider-Centred' studies, 1 'System-Centered' study, and 12 RCTs classified as 'Combination'. The main findings suggested that our to-be-developed social marketing strategy for promoting CRC screening should consider the following:

- address multiple system levels (e.g. patient, provider, and health system);

- integrate, at minimum, patient and provider reminders;

- add an educational component (patient and provider);

- remove barriers to CRC screening (e.g. in-person delivery of screening test);

- give patients a choice of screening tests (where feasible).

Additionally, as part of CBPM Step #2 (Figure CS17.2), FPRC faculty and staff conducted key informant interviews, having been advised by CCC members of potential interviewees, to begin developing an understanding of consumer needs and wants as well as competitor actions. The following summary presents the key barriers/facilitators to CRC screening, identified from the 18 key informant interviews. Themes were organised using a socio-ecological perspective (McLeroy et al. 1988; Stokols et al. 1996).

- Societal/policy level:

  ○ Statewide policy decision to not expand a social health care program for families and individuals with limited resources, termed 'Medicaid' (barrier).

  ○ Federal policy decision under the 'Affordable Care Act' or ACA[2] that insurance plans will provide free preventive screenings (facilitator).

- Community level:

  ○ Lack of gastrointestinal (GI) clinics in certain ZIP codes (barrier).

  ○ Outreach and awareness campaigns (facilitator).

- Organisational level:

  ○ Providers' lack of knowledge about evidence-based interventions to increase CRC screening (barrier).

  ○ Screening reminders produced from up-to-date medical records (facilitator).

- Interpersonal level:

  o Lack of referral or ineffective communication from primary care provider (barrier).

  o Primary care provider recommendations (facilitator).

- Individual level:

  o Lack of knowledge and awareness related to risk and need for screening (barrier).

  o Patient knowing a family or friend who was diagnosed with CRC (facilitator).

Research

In addition to secondary research (see 'Competitive Analysis' above), CBPM Step #3 involves primary research in the form of *system dynamics modelling*. System dynamics modelling is the use of informal causal maps and formal computer models with simulation to uncover and understand endogenous (or 'feedback') sources of system behaviour (Richardson 2011). Specifically, we have applied an approach called *Community Based System Dynamics*, which is a highly participatory method for involving communities in the process of understanding and changing systems from the perspective of system dynamics (Hovmand 2014). This approach included the use of group model building, which is a method of involving participants and other stakeholders in the modelling process, from system conceptualisation to model formulation to intervention analysis and implementation.

There were many advantages of working with community groups to set goals, analyse the problem, and develop solutions. For example, we learned that CRC screening is impacted by multiple factors, requiring a multi-faceted intervention to increase screening rates. By working together, community members gained a sense of ownership that will sustain their interest and commitment to the project. Their participation also makes it more likely that the intervention will be integrated into existing community structures (Bryant 2009).

The first group model-building (GMB) session was held in Tampa, Florida. The output of one of the group activities, where CCC members were split into two groups (based on priority patient population) was a constructed 'connection circle' to identify key variables related to CRC screening and how those variables were interrelated. At that time, the core modelling team envisioned a computer model with a heavy emphasis on epidemiologic aspects of CRC (e.g. incidence, prevalence, etc.). However, by the second GMB session, it became apparent that this academic-community partnership required a model with a greater emphasis on social determinants of CRC dynamics (e.g. social norms regarding screening).

Subsequently, the modeling problem of interest was refined to 'How to increase CRC screening rates to 80% by year 2018 among the priority populations'. Screening data from a variety of sources (e.g. Behavioral Risk Factor Surveillance System [BRFSS]) suggested that this problem was dynamic (i.e. changing over time) among the two priority populations. The modelling problem type was primarily a 'learning problem', i.e. modellers working with academic-community partners to help them build their own model of this dynamic situation. By the time of the fourth GMB session, the situation had transitioned to more of a 'coordination problem', i.e. developing a shared vision and consensus on *what* the problem was and *how* to intervene. By the time of the fifth GMB session, the problem type had transitioned to what amounted to an 'analysis problem', i.e. identifying leverage points, root causes, best sequence and timing of interventions, and efficient practices (Hovmand 2014).

The primary purpose of the system dynamics model was to help this academic-community partnership design a social marketing strategy for implementing evidence-based interventions that will increase CRC screening rates among the priority populations. Such a model should help these partners (and stakeholders elsewhere) to visualise the major system components and how they were interrelated. The model was constructed at the 'strategic' level with an emphasis on involving community partners in the development, implementation, and scaling-up of a coordinated social marketing initiative for the rest of the state of Florida. To achieve this, a qualitative system dynamics diagram was created using participatory modelling activities with FPRC and CCC partners (GMB session #'s 1–2) and American Cancer Society stakeholders (GMB session #3).

Formulation of strategy

The FPRC and its CCC partners have progressed to CBPM Step #4 (Figure CS17.2) to conduct formative research regarding, for example, health communication materials created for other CRC screening campaigns (e.g. pre-testing campaign brochures). The next step for FPRC faculty and staff, along with our community partners, is to complete activities corresponding to CBPM Steps #5 ('Develop a Marketing Plan'), #6 ('Develop Implementation & Monitoring Plan'), #7 ('Develop Marketing Programme'), and #8 ('Implementation & Monitoring').

Outcomes

Although our application of 'systems thinking' represents but one specific school of thought (i.e. 'system dynamics modeling'), we see similarities between Hastings and Domegan's (2015) phases of value co-creation and the steps of our emergent CBPM framework. Our project's initial outcomes pertain more to the early, co-discovery phase of value co-creation. For instance, we asked our community partners (CCC members) to complete evaluation forms at the conclusion of our committee meetings. To date, attendees have rated the CBPM framework activities and materials as overwhelmingly positive. Additionally, at the conclusion of each GMB workshop, our core modelling team conducted a debriefing session using a freely available 'script' (Lavallee *et al.* 2010). We have learned that social marketers are capable of facilitating many of the activities included in GMB scripts; however, without a system dynamics modeller on the team, CBPM framework users may be limited in the extent to which they can proceed from creating connections between system variables to creating formal simulation models that can inform social marketing strategy development.

Discussion

Although we are still in the process of social marketing strategy-development and implementation, our case study demonstrates how an academic-community partnership might co-create social marketing activities to generate innovative solutions for addressing health disparities. From a systems perspective, our case demonstrates how a dynamic problem (e.g. CRC screening disparities) can be reframed throughout the course of a project: from a 'learning' problem to a 'coordination' problem to an 'analysis' problem (Hovmand 2014).

It is possible that we may soon discover, through the use of computer simulation modelling, that the only way to achieve this academic-community partnership's goal of increasing CRC screening rates to '80 percent by 2018' is to reframe the situation as a 'transformation' problem, i.e. the only solution might involve changing the *structure* of the system that is producing the undesirable dynamics or status quo. However, there are many different classes of options for changing the structure of a system to produce more of what one wants and less of that which is undesirable. Hastings and Domegan (2015: 269) have stated: "In essence, no significant social change is possible without a change in values." Although *changing the mindset out of which a system arises* is believed to be among the highest 'leverage points' to intervene in a system (Meadows 2008), the decision of where, how, and when to intervene will be made primarily by our community partners.

Conclusion

Multiple authors have written about the potential for combining 'systems thinking' with the strategies and tools of social marketing. For example, French and Gordon (2015: 183) sought to help social marketers "identify and understand the relevance of systems thinking in social marketing and how it can help deliver value and engender social good". Hastings and Domegan (2015: 270) aimed to help social marketers see 'the big picture' by bringing together "the practical and theoretical aspects of conducting social marketing strategies for societal change". However, we are unaware of empirical examples that combine social marketing with the systems thinking tradition that is 'system dynamics modelling' (Sterman 2000). Our case study illustrates how, through the co-creation of social marketing and systems thinking activities, academic-community partnerships may generate innovative solutions for addressing health disparities.

Acknowledgements

This publication was supported by Cooperative Agreement Number, 1U48DP005024-01, funded by the Centers for Disease Control and Prevention – Prevention Research Centers Program. Its contents are solely the responsibility of the authors and do not necessarily represent the official views of the Centers for Disease Control and Prevention or the Department of Health and Human Services.

Case study questions

1. Discuss the value of 'audience segmentation' as illustrated in this case study.

2. Discuss the advantages of using a participatory approach to 'systems modelling' as illustrated in this case study.

Notes

1 A community coalition is a group of community members, organisational representatives, and other stakeholders who work together on problems of shared to interest to achieve common goals.
2 The Affordable Care Act (or ACA) is a federal statute passed in 2010 as a regulatory overhaul of the US health care system designed to increase health insurance quality and affordability.

References

Bryant, C.A. (2009) 'Community-based health promotion', in J. Coreil (ed.), *Social and Behavioral Foundations of Public Health,* 2nd edition (pp. 273–290). Thousand Oaks, CA: Sage Publications.

Bryant, C.A., Courtney, A. H., McDermott, R.J., Lindenberger, J.H., Swanson, M.A., Mayer, A.B., . . . Biroscak, B.J. (2014) 'Community-based prevention marketing for policy development: A new planning framework for coalitions', *Social Marketing Quarterly,* 20(4): 219–246. doi:10.1177/1524500414555948.

Bryant, C. A., McCormack Brown, K., McDermott, R.J., Debate, R.D., Alfonso, M.A., Baldwin, J.L., . . . Phillips, L.M. (2009) 'Community-based prevention marketing: A new planning framework for designing and tailoring health promotion interventions', in R. DiClemente, R.A. Crosby and M.C. Kegler (eds), *Emerging Theories in Health Promotion Practice and Research: Strategies for Improving Public Health,* 2nd edition. San Francisco, CA: Jossey-Bass.

Forrester, J. W. (1958) 'Industrial Dynamics', *Harvard Business Review,* 36(4): 37–66.

French, J. and Gordon, R. (2015) *Strategic Social Marketing.* London: Sage Publications.

Green, L.W. and Kreuter, M.W. (2005) *Health Program Planning: An Educational and Ecological Approach,* 4th edition. New York: McGraw-Hill Higher Education.

Hastings, G. and Domegan, C. (2015) *Social Marketing: From Tunes to Symphonies,* 2nd edition. New York: Routledge.

Hovmand, P.S. (2014) *Community Based System Dynamics.* New York: Springer.

Lavallee, A., Hower, T. and Hovmand, P. (2010) Scriptapedia/Debriefing. Online at: https:// en.wikibooks.org/wiki/Scriptapedia/Debriefing (accessed 1 May 2016).

McLeroy, K.R., Bibeau, D., Steckler, A. and Glanz, K. (1988) 'An ecological perspective on health promotion programs', *Health Educ Q,* 15(4): 351–377.

Meadows, D.H. (2008) *Thinking in Systems: A Primer.* White River Junction, CT: Chelsea Green Publishing.

Richardson, G.P. (2011) 'Reflections on the foundations of system dynamics', *System Dynamics Review,* 27(3): 219–243. doi:10.1002/sdr.462.

Sterman, J.D. (2000) *Business Dynamics: Systems Thinking and Modeling for a Complex World.* Boston, MA: McGraw-Hill.

Stokols, D., Allen, J. and Bellingham, R.L. (1996) 'The social ecology of health promotion: implications for research and practice', *Am J Health Promot,* 10(4): 247–251.

van Diepen, M. and Franses, P.H. (2006) 'Evaluating chi-squared automatic interaction detection', *Information Systems,* 31(8): 814–831. doi:http://dx.doi.org/10.1016/j.is.2005.03.002.

Case study **18**

Fast fashion

A wicked problem for macro-social marketing

Ann-Marie Kennedy, Sommer Kapitan,
Neha Bajaj, Angelina Bakonyi and
Sean Sands

Introduction

Fast fashion is deemed a wicked problem in that it is multifaceted, interconnected and self-perpetuating. Fast fashion is a reasonably new retail strategy whereby the fashion cycle has become 'fast', however clothing quality and price have decreased. The production of fashion until recently was based on seasons, however today's technologies allow manufacturers, distributors, and retailers to supply fashion to the marketplace in much faster timeframes in a matter of weeks. The negative effects of this strategy include environmental degradation, human and labour rights violations, and excessive consumption due to low pricing and faster fashion cycles. The seemingly positive outcomes include increased profits for retailers, employment for people in developing countries, access to clothing for lower socioeconomic groups within developed countries, and constantly updated fashions. These positive and negative effects permeate through the micro (individual consumer), meso (supplier and retailer), and macro (government and global economy) levels of society, creating a situation in which no one group can be blamed and no one group takes overall responsibility. The market system is, thus, flawed. For the problem of fast fashion to be mitigated, system wide, macro-social marketing needs to be undertaken (Kennedy 2015).

Problem definition

Many argue whether fast fashion is actually a problem at all. Superficially, there are positive effects that seem to assist businesses and help emerging economies to grow, however, in terms of sustainability and beneficial labour/economic growth in the developing countries, is this the case?

Slave labour, child labour, abuse and unsafe working conditions for those making the textiles and clothing, as evident in tragedies such as Rana Plaza in Bangladesh, make fast fashion a problem that needs to be addressed. Fires at the Ali Enterprises garment factory in Karachi, Pakistan, and at Tazreen Fashions in Dhaka, Bangladesh, killed 401 workers in 2012. When the Rana Plaza building containing a garment factory collapsed in 2013 in Bangladesh, 1,129 were killed and 2,515 were injured (Bain and Avins 2015; Sobhan 2012). As exploitative and dangerous as the race to the bottom may be for workers in the developing world, ending fast fashion sourcing from developing markets would still be detrimental to those countries' economies and wellbeing.

In Bangladesh alone, the garment industry is responsible for more than 3 million jobs, and is considered a chief part of the exports and manufacturing industry that has lowered the poverty rate from 80% in the 1970s to less than 30% today, and grown GDP by an average 5% since 1995 (Bain and Avins 2015). It is argued by developing nations that even though clothing and textile factories break basic human and labour rights, positions in the garment industry are superior to other employment options in the areas.

Equally, consumers enjoy a feeling of relative affluence with their ability to purchase plentiful, inexpensive clothing items and experience a positive mood boost from the novelty of owning new fashions. Consumers today are able to purchase clothing cheaply and often, leading to a trend in over-consumption and consumerism. However, the effects on the environment due to dumping of products and waste, as well as excessive use of natural resources in production, present only part of the problem with this strategy. American, UK, and Australian consumers throw away some 12.7 million tonnes of textiles per year (roughly 68 pounds or 31 kg per person per year), of which 1.6 million could be recycled or reused (Hawley 2008). In production of textiles and clothing, 2 trillion gallons of water and 145 million tonnes of coal are used each year (Cline 2013; Siegle 2011).

Competitive and stakeholder analysis

To understand this wicked problem, one must first understand what is happening at each stakeholder level. This section addresses the macro, meso and micro viewpoints of the fast fashion issue.

Micro-level viewpoints

Deal-conscious consumers who pride themselves on coupon clipping or simply on getting items on sale are not likely to value a higher-dollar garment more than lower-priced knockoff designs, despite the lower quality of material, design and stitching. Inexpensive clothing has in this way become "a symbol of consumer democracy" (Cline 2013: 33), with retailers such as H&M touting that their fast-fashion clothing is "for everyone, not just the elite" (Strauss 2004). In a value-conscious environment of ubiquitous and cheaply priced clothing, sales prices that show a marked difference over a consumer's reference price increase perceptions of additional value, yielding psychological satisfaction from the transaction itself that fuels purchase behaviour (Grewal *et al.* 1998; Thaler 2008). Encountering a sale on clothing or an extraordinarily low price thus feels good, further driving effects from identity-seeking and a desire "to cultivate a distinctive personality" (Tian *et al.* 2001), factors which might further encourage consumers to buy fashion at low prices.

Product replacement intervals are shorter when something becomes unfashionable, which happens the more rapidly items are introduced (from seasonally thirty years ago to twice weekly new stock arrivals at some fashion outlets today; Cline 2013). Even when quality changes or differences in durable goods are not apparent, the more rapidly new offerings hit the marketplace, the more it motivates replacement behaviour from consumers (Grewal *et al.* 2004). The more frequent the introduction of an offering, the more cues in the marketplace that improvements have been made, even if — as in the case of new clothing appearing every week at a retailer — it is hard to tell what is improved or better in a new colour, cut or hemline (Grewal *et al.* 2004).

The impact of psychological obsolescence and voluntary replacement of garments from rapid introductions of new offerings translates to the American marketplace as a whole purchasing 20 billion new garments a year (Cline 2013).

Meso-level viewpoints

Retailers and suppliers are uniquely positioned in the fashion industry to seek out and source capabilities to exploit a competitive advantage (Layton 2014). For multinational businesses, this often involves searching for the least expensive production services and can come at the expense of fair labour standards. The shift to global sourcing in the clothing industry is largely due to the cost of the production in the apparel industry; clothing and textile industries are labour intensive. Companies have shifted sourcing to countries such as Morocco, Turkey and India that can quickly respond to the standard required and also have lower labour rates (Perry *et al.* 2014).

Practices that allow a front-line retailer to remain competitive and attract more consumers with lower prices for fashion have larger downstream consequences for the supply chain. To reduce costs further, buyers have established overseas sourcing offices in their main producing countries and shifted more responsibilities to these overseas sourcing offices, driven by cost and the skills of the staff based there. This has saved between 4% and 8% of the wholesale price they paid as commissions to sourcing agents and manufacturers (Gereffi and Frederick 2010).

Working conditions in the clothing industry can be particularly challenging for female workers (International Labour Organization 2014). Informal and home-based work is more common among women than men. Long and unpredictable working hours and safety concerns can make it difficult for women to combine family responsibilities with work. Low wages, weak collective bargaining opportunities and lack of equal pay for work of equal value can make women vulnerable to exploitation inside and outside the workplace. Poor or non-existent maternity protection and various forms of violence, abuse and harassment are also still present in the textile and apparel industries (International Labour Organization 2014).

Unethical practices within the clothing industry have been a key issue and practices including child labour, forced labour, and excessive overtime hours without rest are still prevalent across many countries in all stages of garment production (International Labour Organization 2014; Nimbalke *et al.* 2015). The Australia fashion report 2015 (Nimbalke *et al.* 2015) highlights that 17 countries are known to use child and/or forced labour in cotton production, and countries such as Uzbekistan have been known for unethical practices in cotton production. The report also highlights the action that companies have taken against such unethical practices: 29 companies have taken significant steps to avoid using Uzbekistani cotton in their products (Nimbalke *et al.* 2015).

A 2014 report from the U.S. Fashion Industry Association, a major lobbyist behind the elimination of the global apparel quota system, reveals that 81% of members from fashion brands to retailers, importers and wholesalers consider rising production costs among the greatest business challenges they face. While 77% already source from Bangladesh, 65% of its members plan to increase sourcing from Bangladesh (Lu 2014). "Despite last year's tragedies in several of its garment factories, Bangladesh is still regarded as a popular sourcing destination with growth potential," the report concludes (Lu 2014).

Macro-level viewpoints

Macro-level, government viewpoints surround not only economic growth through trade, but also human and labour rights. Free trade agreements are purported to decrease barriers for developing nations and enable them to develop their economy and its infrastructure. However, while trade has expanded globally, clothing prices have actually decreased; the average price of garments imported by the United States from China in 2013 was lower than in 2008.

Garment prices in Bangladesh decreased by 40% in the mid-2000s. Similar price reductions have also been reported in other countries (Gereffi and Frederick 2010; International Labour Organization 2014). However, significant government action is still required to improve working conditions in the industries, as only regulatory bodies have the legitimacy to enforce labour legislation and protect workers' rights (Gereffi and Frederick 2010).

Aims and objectives

The aims and objectives for solving the multitude of 'wicked' problems created by fast fashion are currently unclear and agreement on specifics is very difficult. Such specifics include definitions of the problem, the perpetuating factors for the problem, and responsibilities regarding the problem, let alone solutions to it. Thus, taking the viewpoint of each of the groups above allows for examination of how each stakeholder might have a differing and conflicting understanding of the situation and whether or not a solution is needed. Some potential objectives and aims could surround:

- micro-level aims and objectives, which might include thought and behavior change to encourage demand for fair trade and ethical clothing at a price that supports a living wage;
- meso-level aims and objectives, which include thought and behaviour change to encourage the use of suppliers who practise fair and ethical treatment of their employees and the environment, and who pay a living wage;
- macro-level aims and objectives, such as thought and behaviour change on employment and trade laws to favour supply from ethical and fair trade partners and to favour minimum price floors, along with the introduction of a living wage.

Formulation of strategy

There are a plethora of strategies that are currently being undertaken at multiple levels of society to combat these issues. Many of these are not undertaken by NGOs, but instead community groups and organisations. There is no coherent strategy in evidence today.

One suggested strategy is the slow fashion movement (Ertekin and Atik 2015). The slow fashion movement is based on the slow food movement and advocates long fashion cycles and sustainable practices. By slowing down the number of collections each year, the movement posits that higher quality garments can be manufactured. Higher quality garments mean more durable garments and less consumer waste. The reduced number of releases also slows the consumption cycle of fashion for consumers and helps curb their levels of consumerism. Beyond this, sustainable practices including environmental and employment practices are put forward. Other aspects to the movement include a push to use local resources and support local brands, renewed support for artisan design and secondhand purchases, and other related practices to increase the life-span of garments (Cataldi et al. 2010).

Retailers do at times implement steps to mitigate some of their impact on the world. Some retailers have sustainable fashion lines (e.g. H&M), while others also have clothing recycling stations in their stores (e.g. Uniqlo). Unfortunately, many consumers see these tactics as just lip-service, since the same organisations tend to be some of the worst offenders for fast fashion. Further, many fashion retailers have codes of ethics which their suppliers must meet, but these can be circumvented through suppliers faking reports or subcontracting parts of their contracts.

The interconnected nature of fast fashion provides another calling card of a wicked problem: it is almost impossible to see the ripple effect of strategies that are implemented. Thus, negative effects of social marketing interventions are difficult to plan for and could be disastrous. For instance, encouraging consumers to purchase only ethical and fair trade clothing could potentially encourage the collapse of developing economies that rely on the garment industry, such as Bangladesh.

Conclusion

Wicked problems such as fast fashion present social marketers with a major challenge. They are challenged not only by the interconnected nature of each perpetuating factor, but also by their level of control or influence in such global situations. The multi-agency, multi-country interventions needed are complex and require careful and continual management and monitoring. These changes may take generations.

Case study questions

1. Only a few aims and objectives have been identified in this case. Think of some more aims and objectives for social marketers.

   a. Are any of the aims and objectives contradictory?

2. Take a look at the following organisations' websites and identify what strategies they are following to address fast fashion:

   a. The Ethical Fashion Forum www.ethicalfashionforum.com.

   b. The Centre for Sustainable Fashion www.sustainable-fashion.com.

   c. Fairtrade International www.fairtrade.net.

   d. Slow Fashioned www.slowfashioned.com.

3. Come up with one strategy to address downstream (consumer level), midstream (retail and supply level) and upstream (government level) social marketing.

   a. What are the narratives or messages that each stakeholder group might rely on? What narratives or messages will be most persuasive for each stakeholder group?

   b. Consider how these might work together as a broader macro-social marketing strategy. Can they work together? Is there overlap in messaging?

   c. What are the intended and unintended consequences of your strategies?

4. Consider your strategies in question 3. Who do you imagine will implement the strategies you have identified?

   a. Will it be one group or multiple groups?

   b. Who would fund the groups?

   c. What opposition would they face?

References

Bain, M. and Avins, J. (2015) 'The thing that makes Bangladesh's garment industry such a huge success also makes it deadly', *Quartz*, April 24. Online at: http://qz.com/389741/the-thing-that-makes-bangladeshs-garment-industry-such-a-huge-success-also-makes-it-deadly/ (accessed 1 May 2016).

Cataldi, C., Dickson, M. and Grover, C. (2010) 'Slow Fashion: Tailoring a Strategic Approach towards Sustainability'. Doctoral dissertation, Master's thesis.

Cline, E. L. (2013) *Overdressed: The Shockingly High Cost of Cheap Fashion*. New York: Penguin.

Ertekin, Z.O. and Atik, D. (2015) 'Sustainable markets motivating factors, barriers, and remedies for mobilisation of Slow Fashion', *Journal of Macromarketing*, 35(1): 53–69.

Gereffi, G. and Frederick, S. (2010) 'The global apparel value chain, trade and the crisis: Challenges and opportunities for developing countries', *World Bank Policy Research Working Paper Series, No. 5281*.

Grewal, D., Monro, K.B. and Krishnan, R. (1998) 'The effects of price-comparison advertising on buyers' perceptions of acquisition value, transaction value, and behavioral intentions', *Journal of Marketing*, 62(2): 46–59.

Grewal, R., Mehta, R. and Kardes, F.R. (2004) 'The timing of repeat purchases of consumer durable goods: The role of functional bases of consumer attitudes', *Journal of Marketing Research*, 41: 101–115.

Hawley, J. (2008) 'Sustainable Fashion: Why now? A conversation exploring issues, practices, possibilities', in *Economic Impact of Textile and Clothing Recycling*. New York: Fairchild Books, pp. 207–232.

ILO (2014) 'Wages and working hours in the textiles, clothing, leather and footwear industries'. Issues Paper for discussion at the *Global Dialogue Forum on Wages and Working Hours in the Textiles, Clothing, Leather and Footwear Industries* (Geneva, 23–25 September), GDFTCLI/2014. Online at: www.ilo.org/wcmsp5/groups/public/---ed_dialogue/---sector/documents/publication/wcms_300463.pdf (accessed 1 May 2016).

Kennedy, A. (2015) 'Macro-social marketing', *Journal of Macromarketing*. Published online 23 November, available at DOI: 10.1177/0276146715617509.

Layton, R. (2014) 'Formation, growth, and adaptive change in marketing systems', *Journal of Macromarketing*, 35(3): 302–319.

Lu, S. (2014) *2014 U.S. Fashion Industry Benchmarking Study*. A monograph of the United States Fashion Industry Association. Online at: www.usfashionindustry.com (accessed 1 May 2016).

Nimbalke, G. *et al.* (2015) 'The Truth Behind the Barcode'. Australian Fashion Report 2015.

Perry, P., Fernie, J. and Wood, S. (2014) 'The international fashion supply chain and corporate social responsibility', in *Logistics and Retail Management*, 4th edition (pp. 77–99). London: Kogan Page.

Siegle, L. (2011) *To Die For: Is Fashion Wearing Out the World?* London: Fourth Estate.

Sobhan, Z. (2012) 'Progress and Globalization in Bangladesh: The Tazreen Fashions Garment Factory Fire'. Vice Media, December 2. Online at: www.vice.com/read/progress-and-globalization-in-bangladesh-the-tazreen-fashions-garment-factory-fire (accessed 1 May 2016).

Strauss, M. (2004) 'H&M seeks high profits from low prices', *The Globe and Mail*, 29 September.

Thaler, R.H. (2008) 'Mental accounting and consumer choice', *Marketing Science*, 27(1): 15–25.

Tian, K.T., Bearden, W.O. and Hunter, G.L. (2001) 'Consumers' need for uniqueness: Scale development and validation', *Journal of Consumer Research*, 28(1): 50–66.

19

Whale sharks, Ningaloo Reef, Western Australia

Sarah Duffy and Roger A. Layton

Introduction

Wicked problems, such as the damage industry inflicts on our environment, expose our society to vulnerabilities, and in some situations may prevent future generations from using those resources. How to manage natural resources in a way that balances current and future use and prevents or minimises damage is an issue grappled with around the globe. Recently, Kennedy (2016: 354) pointed out that wicked problems persist due to "institutionalised behavioural norms, which reflect society's value and belief systems." For example, this might take the form of opportunistic behaviours enacting the idea that one can take or use the environment as much as one wishes without thought for the balance of the ecosystem or the needs of others in the present or future.

To resolve complex wicked problems such as this, a 'macro-social marketing' perspective is suggested (Kennedy 2016; Kennedy and Parsons 2011). 'Macro' means to take an over-all perspective, in this context one that involves analysing a social marketing issue from a societal level. In order to do this macro-social marketing argues for systems thinking. Systems-thinking is complex and some of the issues it requires one to think of are: the numerous individuals and entities involved in the situation; their resources; their interactions with the environment and one another; the particularities of the issue studied; the history and the environmental context. This may seem like an overwhelming task, however the best way to avoid feeling like this is to take the first step and clearly define your unit of analysis, i.e. the issue.

We will apply a systems perspective to think through a complex wicked problem surrounding the management of a tourism industry that is reliant on whale sharks in Western Australia. Whale sharks are what is known as a common pool resource (CPR) and confront unique challenges which we will discuss in what follows. The whale shark tourism industry faces a complex wicked problem, i.e. how can they conduct their industry in a way that preserves the fragile natural environment it is reliant upon without damaging this and preventing their own future prosperity?

Problem definition

This case study focuses on whale shark tourism in the World Heritage Area, Ningaloo Reef, Western Australia. Ningaloo is Australia's largest fringing coral reef, skirting the west coast for 300 kilometres. The region is a striking colour palate of turquoise Indian Ocean hemmed by white sand and edged by the vast red desert. The reef may be visited from two towns, Exmouth and Coral Bay, which are located over 1,200 km north of the state's capital city Perth. The reef's key defence from being 'loved to death' is its low profile and isolation. This is changing as the region has received global recognition and accessibility has improved. Ningaloo Reef has a colourful history and at times has experienced a fierce tug of war between development and conservation.

Whale shark tourism is a key source of local pride and point of difference for the region. Whale sharks are a protected species and a popular drawcard for tourists. Whale sharks, similar to coral reefs, fisheries and forests, are what is known as a common pool resource, i.e. they may be depleted and they are owned 'in common'. A sustainable tourism industry has developed in Exmouth and Coral Bay offering the opportunity to swim with whale sharks, however there are challenges faced in order to strike a balance between protection and growth.

This case study provides a brief history of tourism at Ningaloo Reef. We then define what is meant by the term 'common pool resource' and identify some of the unique challenges to be faced. This will be followed by an examination of the whale shark tourism industry at Ningaloo Reef. Finally, there will be a discussion of some of the interventions that are striving to resolve or ameliorate this wicked problem.

Tourism at Ningaloo Reef

Tourism is the largest component of Exmouth's economy; it is linked to the three other local industries, i.e. the military, pastoralism and mining. As mentioned at the outset, it is critical to consider all of the individuals and entities involved in a social marketing system. Before delving into the tourism industry, a brief overview of the other industries will be given so you will be able to see how these impact the whale shark tourism industry.

The military have had a profound impact on Exmouth. The town was gazetted in 1963 to serve a US Military base that was established during the Cold War to enable communication with their submarines in the Indian Ocean. When the Cold War ended, the base remained with a skeleton staff, reducing the town's population by 30%. Funds were left by the US military to help the town fill the vacuum they left; this money was put towards key infrastructure projects. The first was a civilian airport terminal, the second project improved the road accessibility, and the third was a marina. The military base is now operated by contractors, run by a skeleton staff of approximately 100 employees. Raytheon, the military contractor, is the town's largest single employer. This is a substantial reduction from the 3,000 staff employed during the Cold War.

The first pastoral station was established in the region in 1876. Over time revenue from the industry declined, largely due to falling wool prices. However, many of the pastoral stations included kilometres of coastline with unrivalled access to surf breaks, fishing, diving and snorkelling spots along the Ningaloo Reef. The stations have now diversified their operations and embraced tourism to supplement their income. In 2008 Rip Curl teamed up with a local station owner and launched a bid to host an international surfing event at Gnarloo, the site of popular surfing documentaries. In response to this, the North West Surfers' Alliance mounted a protest citing the negative impact of large-scale surfing competitions. The concerns centred on crowding and detrimental environmental impacts. Preventing publicity of a surf break is a well-documented social norm within the surfing community (Nazer 2004). The movement attracted over 3,000 signatures to its petition and Rip Curl took the world championship event to Bali instead. Potentially, a million dollar injection to the local economy was lost (Murphy 2009).

Unlikely bedfellows, the tourism industry as it currently exists in Exmouth, is both threatened by and would suffer without the oil, gas and mining industries (Duffy 2016). Significant oil and gas production occurs offshore in the Carnarvon basin and in the Exmouth Gulf. The oil and gas industry provides consistent employment opportunities and has funded small-scale community infrastructure projects. However, a spill similar to that in the Gulf of Mexico would spell disaster for the tourism industry. The oil, gas and mining industry have measures in place to mitigate this risk; they frequently consult with the local community and run training drills to hone the response effort. However, so long as they continue their operations, spillages are a possibility. On the positive side, due to the oil/gas/mining industry Exmouth may be reached daily by two Qantas flights, whereas Monkey Mia, also a world heritage area on the West Australian coast, and also reliant on tourism, may only be reached a few times a week by a regional airline. The reason for the discrepancy in frequency and price is that Exmouth's airport (Learmonth) is regularly accessed by the oil, gas and mining industry. The town remains divided on the presence of oil and gas exploration in the region and has actively rejected some projects from going ahead. There is tension between development and growth for the town and preservation of the established way of life (Duffy 2016).

Whale shark tourism

Ningaloo is one of the best places in the world to encounter the remarkable Whale Shark, the world's largest fish, which gather in greater numbers at Ningaloo than have been recorded anywhere else. From 1828 to 1987 there were just 320 sightings of the whale shark recorded in the scientific literature. Whale sharks were seen by fisherman and others frequently out on the reef, but it was not until local doctor Geoff Taylor began to film whale shark sightings in the early 1980s that word spread that they visited regularly (Taylor 1994). In 1992 a documentary film was made using footage Taylor had captured, sparking worldwide interest in whale sharks and Ningaloo Reef. This same year the American Military vacated Exmouth, leaving a gap in the local economy and an urgency to find an alternative industry.

Both Exmouth and Coral Bay are destinations that revolve around natural, water-based attractions. There are a variety of ways visitors can enjoy the reef, including fishing, snorkelling, sailing, glass bottom boat tours and so forth. Recent research from Tourism Australia estimates that the area hosts over 200,000 visitor nights a year (TRA 2014). This is particularly significant since the permanent population of Exmouth is 2,393 residents (ABS, 2011 Census) and Coral Bay has a population of 221 people (ABS, 2011 Census). Research from Tourism Australia tells us that most of the visitors to Exmouth are from Western Australia and nearly double the visitors come from overseas than from other states in Australia. International visitors stay the longest, interstate visitors the shortest. Domestic visitors predominantly travel as a family unit (35%), whereas International visitors mostly travel alone (48%). There was a higher proportion of 'grey nomads' in the domestic traveller category with 17% of visitors aged over 65. The backpacker age bracket was represented more highly by international visitors with 21% aged 15 to 24. Caravan/camping parks are the most popular accommodation choice for visitors. Exmouth's economy relies on the pristine beauty of their natural resources. Without careful management in place, the region could suffer negative consequences that would have a significant impact on the environment, economy and local community. The next section will discuss this in more detail.

What is a common pool resource?

A common pool resource (CPR) is identified by two defining characteristics. The first is that the exclusion of users through physical barriers or legal means is difficult or prohibitively costly. This is problematic because the second characteristic of a CPR is that consumption can deplete the resource or is rivalrous (Dietz et al. 2003). The depletability resulting from use means that open-access arrangements can lead to a situation where no individual bears the full cost of resource degradation, but are benefitting in the short term from their use (Hardin 1968). Rivalrous means that the resource is not endless and that one person's use diminishes or prevents another person's use. An influential researcher in this area, Hardin (1968) suggested that without coercion or privatisation the ruin of our CPRs is inevitable, essentially arguing that if there is no one to stop us we will 'use up' the resource. Hardin (1978) claimed there are only two solutions to the commons dilemma, i.e. privatisation or government intervention.

We now know that the future is not so bleak. Due to the efforts of commons scholars, we have insight into how the structure of situations in which resources are used affects management decisions and use patterns (Acheson 2003; Carlsson and Sandström 2007; Dietz et al. 2003; Healy 2006; Ostrom 1990). One of the most important implications of this work is that people have the capacity to plan, cooperate and communicate with one another in order to maximise a resources capacity and can do this successfully without government intervention (Burger and Gochfeld 1998).

All commons are not created equal. They are unique and vary depending on the social context. Control of the commons and the mechanisms that do this (e.g. property rights, informal rules) can be democratic or otherwise, access can be equal or unfair (Burger and Gochfeld 1998). These mechanisms influence how the CPR is managed, how the rules are constructed and applied, the alignment between activities, incentives and sustainable outcomes, the level of investment in infrastructure, and ultimately if the resource is maximised or depleted or somewhere in between.

CPR issues cannot be examined at an individual level alone, one must consider the activities and consequences for a CPR at a macro level. They will have serious consequences for those associated with them and involve issues such as fairness and equity. Saunders *et al.* (2015: 165) recently categorised social marketing as the "application of marketing principles to enable individual and collective ideas and actions in the pursuit of effective, efficient, equitable, fair and sustained social transformation." Thus any industry or social marketing system that is operating in a way that is depleting a common pool resource is contrary to this definition.

Challenges of CPR management

The challenge of CPR management in a social marketing sense is how to reduce or prevent externalities (Agrawal 2001). In the case of a tourism destination, these are often resource degradation, rivalry and over-crowding. Externalities can be a positive or negative consequence of a transaction experienced by third parties. From a social marketing perspective, we are interested in reducing negative externalities. Free riders are regularly at the heart of these types of issues as they are benefitting from using the resource without investing in the infrastructure to maintain or enhance the resource. If users free ride the collective benefit will suffer (Ostrom 1990). Further to this, those who do invest in a CPR might not achieve as high a return due to free riders or if the actions of others diminish or destroy the resource. For example, if visitors to Ningaloo Reef overfish their quota, or stand on the coral when snorkelling, these activities will be diminished for others in the future.

Table CS19.1 first shows the nature of the CPR and lists the type of externality that threatens the resource. It is essential to identify the threat in order to assess the risk and consequences. If the resource can be enhanced this is indicated next and has implications for investment. The use is classified which has consequences for the health of the resource and the likelihood of government intervention. The type of intervention is specified, followed by the possibility of exclusion. Type of use and the level of demand are listed as this influences planning. The existence of a shared future among users is shown. Finally, in recognition that humans will behave in ways that are rewarded, the alignment of rewards and conservation of the resource is considered. This case study will focus on whale shark tourism in detail, however this table is presented in order to show the different types of CPRs that exist, management regimes and the challenges faced.

From the study of CPRs a list of design principles has been developed and are shown in Table CS19.2. These principles have been found to be pivotal in the successful management of a CPR. There are very few situations where all principles will be operating in a positive way. However, one may apply these to a CPR in order to identify which constructive structural elements are present and which are lacking (Ostrom 1990). In the next section, we will provide an overview of the whale shark tourism industry before applying the design principles.

Overview of the whale shark tourism industry

Swimming with a whale shark is a 'bucket-list' experience: it is risky, lasts a full day and is an intimate event. The experience takes place in the open ocean, which is under minimal control of the provider and involves a wild animal that is also out of the control of the provider. Varying between 4 and 12 metres in length, the whale shark is the world's largest fish.

Table CS19.1 CPR classification

Example	Externality	Access rights of users	Rule-making power	Resource can be enhanced	Specified use	Intervention	Exclusion	Transferability	Type of use and level of demand	Shared future among users	Incentives aligned with sustainable outcomes
Whale shark tourism industry	Congestion, rivalry and resource degradation	Access and withdrawal	Some input – Limited	Yes	Non-extractive	State government – limited entry	Impossible – migratory	Not without sanction from management regime	Commercial Increasing	No	Incentives to invest in value-added facilities are weakened by open access (free riding tourists and adjacent industries). However, operators have personal incentive to conserve the resource.
Fish Stocks, Ningaloo Marine Park	Resource degradation	Access and withdrawal	Limited to non-existent	Yes	Extractive	State government – license required	Unfeasible	No	Recreational Increasing	Locals – yes Tourists – no	Incentives to invest in value-added facilities are weakened by open access (free riding tourists and adjacent industries). Individuals have strong incentives to stretch or break the rules for personal benefit.

Urban spaces (parks, streets, vacant land) (Foster, 2011)	Congestion, rivalry and resource degradation	Access	Limited to non-existent	Yes	Non-extractive	government	Impossible	No	Recreational	Yes	None
Lobster Fisherman Maine {Wilson, 2007 #1088;Acheson, 2003 #410}	Resource degradation, Rivalry	Access, withdrawal, informal management, exclusion	Informal – mutually agreed upon & enforced	Yes	Extractive	Self-governance	Possible through territorialism	Yes	Commercial and recreational, increasing	Yes	Yes, individuals have strong incentive to preserve the resource to ensure future benefit
Surfing Breaks (Nazer, 2004)	Congestion and rivalry	Access, withdrawal, informal management, exclusion	Informal	No	Non-extractive	Self-governance – no formal intervention – the resource is managed through informal norms	Possible through territorialism	Impossible	Recreational – Yes increasing		The resource itself cannot be depleted, however use is sullied without adherence to informal norms governing behaviour providing incentives for individuals to follow the norms

(continued)

Table CS19.1 (continued)

Example	Externality	Access rights of users	Rule-making power	Resource can be enhanced	Specified use	Intervention	Exclusion	Transferability	Type of use and level of demand	Shared future among users	Incentives aligned with sustainable outcomes
Common Land in England (Pieraccini, 2010)	Resource degradation	Access, withdrawal, informal management	Limited	Yes	Extractive	Formal governance and limited self-governance	Possible	Yes	Commercial – increasing	Yes	Changes have been made to minimise gaps between legal measures and customary practices in an attempt to align management practices with more sustainable outcomes
Sustainable tourism (Healy, 2006)	Resource degradation, congestion	Locals – Access Tourists – Access	Locals – limited opportunity via the commission that manages the falls Tourists – None	Yes	Non-extractive	State government	Impossible	No	Recreational – increasing		The efforts of management are ultimately to increase visitation to Niagara Falls, however they do focus on mitigating impacts

Table CS19.2 Design principles

1A. User Boundaries	Clear and locally understood boundaries between legitimate users and nonusers are present
1B. Resource Boundaries	Clear boundaries that separate a specific common pool resource from a larger social-ecological system are present
2A. Congruence with Local Conditions	Appropriation and provision rules are congruent with local social and environmental conditions
2B. Appropriation and Provision	Appropriation rules are congruent with provision rules; the distribution of costs is proportional to the distribution of benefits
3. Collective-Choice Arrangements	Most individuals affected by a resource regime are authorised to participate in making and modifying its rules
4A. Monitoring Users	Individuals who are accountable to or are the users monitor the appropriation and provision levels of the users
4B. Monitoring the Resource	Individuals who are accountable to or are the users monitor the condition of the resource
5. Graduated Sanctions	Sanctions for rule violations start very low but become stronger if a user repeatedly violates a rule
6. Conflict-Resolution Mechanisms	Rapid, low-cost, local arenas exist for resolving conflicts among users or with officials
7. Minimal Recognition of Rights	The rights of local users to make their own rules are recognised by the government
8. Nested Enterprises	When a common pool resource is closely connected to a larger social-ecological system, governance activities are organised in multiple nested layers.

(*Source:* Cox et al. 2010)

A filter feeder with no teeth, the whale shark is docile allowing divers and snorkelers to interact at close quarters, swimming beside them. Based on this novel marine-based human-animal interaction opportunity, a tourism industry has developed (Duffy 2016).

Whale Shark tours first began operating in NMP in 1989. The governing body the Department of Parks and Wildlife (DPaW) established the first licensing agreement in 1993 (Coleman 1997). The state intervened in this industry in an effort to minimise the negative externalities of its operation and as part of a broader initiative state wide to ensure that natural assets were effectively managed. Negative impacts have the potential to impact on different levels of the system:

- the micro level (whale shark and swimmer)

- the meso level (the Exmouth economy)

- the macro level (tourism in Western Australia).

At the micro level, if swimmers are too close to the whale shark, they may be injured if hit by its powerful tail. Without regulation, the tourist experience could be negatively affected by congestion. The whale shark may also suffer. There are numerous videos and images online of tourists in other parts of the world interacting with whale sharks in ways believed by marine scientists to have an adverse impact on their health. Two studies (Norman 2002; Quiros 2007) investigated the behaviour manifested by whale sharks during interactions with tourists. Both studies found that whale sharks react to vessels and swimmers alike by diving down, porpoising (i.e. diving up and down like a porpoise), shuddering, eye rolling and banking (i.e. exposing their thick dorsal flank in a shield-like fashion). Across both studies close proximity to the whale shark, touching the animal, and obstruction of their path by a swimmer were among the reasons found to trigger these reactions. Overcrowding may disturb the whale shark and could impact their likelihood to return, causing changes to migratory pathways (Norman 2002). Whale sharks swim very close to the surface and are vulnerable to boat strikes, and increased boat traffic escalates the potential for collisions to occur. Additionally, as migratory animals whale sharks are more complex from a governance perspective since their protected status varies across their migratory pathway. For example, within Australia the whale shark is listed as 'vulnerable' under the Environment Protection and Biodiversity Conservation Act 1999. Globally, the whale shark is listed by the World Conservation Union on the Red List of Threatened Species as 'vulnerable' and the population is believed to be dwindling. The Taiwanese hunt and consume whale sharks, presenting a threat to the species.

If the whale sharks were to depart the region or the industry was no longer functioning at its present levels there would be a significant impact at the meso level on the local community. Swimming with whale sharks is a key drawcard for the region and forms the basis of the area's unique selling proposition (Duffy 2016). In 2005 the industry's contribution to the local economy was AU$12 million annually, and since then the number of tours and passenger numbers has more than doubled, suggesting the financial loss for the town would be substantial (Catlin et al., 2012). There are numerous murals, statues and representations suggesting that the whale shark forms an integral part of the town's identity and are a source of local pride. Additionally their presence was a formative part of the justification for the region's listing as a World Heritage Area.

At the macro level, whale sharks have become increasingly significant for the state of Western Australia (Duffy 2016). They feature on the state's emblem and are a unique drawcard for visitors to the state. Exmouth is the fourth most popular destination according to the most recent visitor survey (TWA 2013). The whale shark industry contributes to the state economy directly through attracting visitors, taxes collected and providing employment for the bureaucracy that manages the industry. Without management of these risks, substantial consequences may arise.

The intervention: managing WS tourism

We have applied the design principles to assess the whale shark tourism industry. They are shown in Table CS19.3.

Management goals for tourism in Ningaloo Marine Park are to offer low impact commercial tourism activities which add to the recreational and educational experience of Marine Park users and to ensure that tourist operations do not negatively impact on the ecological or cultural heritage values (Infrastructure 2004). The boundaries of NMP have facilitated the

Table CS19.3 Design principles applied to the whale shark tourism industry

1A. User Boundaries	Clear and locally understood boundaries between legitimate users and nonusers are present.
Supply	MET The industry is managed by a state government body, the Department of Parks and Wildlife (DPaW). There are 15 licenses conditionally dispensed by the DPaW for a duration of five years (Mau 2008).
Demand	MET A tourist may participate without a tour however, barriers are high to circumvent this system.
1B. Resource Boundaries	Clear boundaries that separate a specific common- pool resource from a larger social-ecological system are present.
Supply and Demand	MET Resource boundaries apply equally to the demand and supply side of the industry. The tours are conducted within the confines of Ningaloo Marine Park as specified by state government legislation.
2A. Congruence with Local Conditions	Appropriation and provision rules are congruent with local social and environmental conditions.
Supply	UNMET There is conflict between the regulator (DPaW) and the whale shark operators suggesting that there is some degree of incongruence with the local social conditions.
Demand	MET Based on interviews conducted with both domestic and international tourists the rules were well received and no causes of contention were expressed.
2B. Appropriation and Provision	Appropriation rules are congruent with provision rules; the distribution of costs is proportional to the distribution of benefits.
Supply and Demand	MET 100% of the cost of the management programme is recovered from the whale shark operators. This cost is passed on to tourists. Based on the interviews conducted, tourists felt the cost was high, but many expressed a sense of satisfaction from supporting research and a sustainable industry.
3. Collective-Choice Arrangements	Most individuals affected by a resource regime are authorised to participate in making and modifying its rules.
Supply	UNMET There is a strong feeling among the whale shark operators that although they can make suggestions their suggestions are easily disregarded by DPaW if they disagree.
Demand	UNMET Tourists are not involved in making or modifying rules. However, they are able to vote with their feet so to speak.
4A. Monitoring Users	Individuals who are accountable to or are the users monitor the appropriation and provision levels of the users.
Demand	MET WSOs are formally monitored by DPaW, this cost is borne by the tourists consistent with the licensing conditions. Informal monitoring also takes place, that is, the whale shark operators monitor one another on the water and will informally deal with contraventions, similar to the lobster fishermen in Maine (Acheson 2003).

(continued)

Table CS19.3 *(continued)*

Supply	MET WSOs are required to communicate to tourists the rules relevant to them and monitor their compliance.
4B. Monitoring the Resource	*Individuals who are accountable to or are the users monitor the condition of the resource.*
Demand	MET There are two resources, Ningaloo Reef and the whale sharks. Due to the high mobility of the whale sharks and their vulnerability it is difficult to monitor them and isolate the impacts of tourism. However, all whale sharks swum with are photographed and this information is supplied to DPaW. The condition of Ningaloo Reef is monitored, due to the nature of this resource it is a more complex undertaking. The monitoring is conducted by a variety of research bodies rather than users. It is difficult to distinctly separate the effects of adjacent industries such as recreational fishing and oil and gas exploration for example.
5. Graduated Sanctions	*Sanctions for rule violations start very low but become stronger if a user repeatedly violates a rule.*
Supply and Demand	MET Both formal and informal sanctions graduate in severity depending on the violation and if it has been repeated.
6. Conflict-Resolution Mechanisms	*Rapid, low-cost, local arenas exist for resolving conflicts among users or with officials.*
Supply and Demand	UNMET There is no independent, swift conflict resolution mechanism. The options are formal legal procedures or lobbying the Minister.
7. Minimal Recognition of Rights	*The rights of local users to make their own rules are recognized by the government.*
Supply	UNMET Interviews suggested that the locals ability to make their own rules were often not recognised and a significant cause of resentment and contention.
8. Nested Enterprises	*When a common pool resource is closely connected to a larger social-ecological system, governance activities are organised in multiple nested layers.*
Supply	MET It was found that local, regional and state level staff were associated with the administration of the region, it was noted the Federal Government had no direct involvement, although they issued a mandate to the state government.

(*Source:* Duffy and Layton 2016)

development of a set of social arrangements for regulating the preservation, maintenance and consumption of its resources (Duffy 2016). In general, the intervention in the form of a management system to govern human-whale shark interaction has focused on licensing, education, research and monitoring, executed by DPaW in consultation with commercial operators (Coleman 1997; Mau 2008).

In a tourism context, the users with the greater level of market demand for the resource are usually external to the region, which influences how the rules of use are developed, institutionalised and enforced. A large proportion of external users with high levels of demand is a challenge, since studies have found that a shared future among resource users is a key determinant of sustainable resource management (Dietz *et al.* 2003). However, with a comprehensive management programme in place it seems that the industry may avoid this complication. Some studies have suggested that successful resource management is more likely if 'outsiders' can be excluded from use (Ostrom 1990). A shared future may not always be the pivotal factor: it is notable that fishing, an activity that is most important to Western Australian tourists, has been identified locally as the most significant environmental threat (Jones *et al.* 2009).

Tour operators, whose concern for preservation may exist, facilitate interactions with the resource, however they are also concerned with economic gain. Additionally, there are many opportunities for unsupervised interactions to take place in such an expansive location or for the pressures of market demand to take priority. As the demands on whale shark tour operators have increased there has been shift away from largely local operators towards more experienced tour operators from the capital, Perth, which may have the unintended effect of eroding the local connection (Dietz *et al.* 2003). The strict regulation of the industry strives to prevent such occurrences. Only those holding a license may conduct whale shark tours and there are strict specifications. A photographer who is also collecting data on the whale shark is present as an observer. This is an example where the design principles hold, underscoring the importance of rules and the monitoring of rules in use.

The design principles provide a yardstick to appraise the management against as shown in Table CS19.3. However, they are static and capture only a snapshot in time. This can be problematic and unless regularly updated also misleading. In addition, it fails to explain why some conditions exist and why others do not. The design principles are an important tool for understanding, however it is critical that these are updated regularly and thoroughly investigated.

Issues of fairness and equity

In many cases, a social marketing intervention will take the form of public policy. The reasons for public policies are often complex; one of their chief functions is to police markets, i.e. to create, modify, and control behavior and outcomes in market exchange or to substitute acts of authority for acts of exchange (Hurst 1982). Efforts to control behaviour are evident in the whale shark industry as public policy intervention attempts to resolve the allocation of a scarce resource (Duffy 2016). Returning to our definition of social marketing, fairness is an outcome that social marketing efforts strive for. Fairness relates not only to the distribution of costs, but also to ensuring the benefits of a scarce resource are distributed equally.

The cost of the regulation needs to be considered in the light of fairness. The government will incur costs implementing public policy, and often so too will those who must comply with the regulation (the whale shark tour operator). The high cost of swimming with a whale shark (approximately \$320–\$420) can be prohibitive to some tourists. The allocation

Table CS19.4 Property rights held by key actors

	Commercial whale shark tour operator	Recreational whale shark swimmer	DPaW
Access	X	X	X
Withdrawal	X	X	X
Management			X
Exclusion			X
Alienation			X

(*Source:* Duffy and Layton 2016)

Table CS19.5 Comparison of CPR management, NMP

	Whale sharks	Fish stocks
State government managed	Y	Y
License required for use	Y	Y
100% cost recovery	Y	N
Powerful lobby	N	Y
Information provided to users about resource health	Y	N
Extractive experience	N	Y

(*Source:* Duffy and Layton 2016)

of both the costs and perceived benefits of regulation may contribute to the polarisation of those involved. It is useful to compare the management of whale sharks with local fish stocks (also a CPR) to compare this issue to a similar context.

In comparison to the whale shark industry, the license fees for recreational fishing recover just 35% of the management programme (Duffy 2016). The state government absorbs the surplus management cost. In contrast to the whale shark tour operators, recreational fisherman are represented by a powerful lobby group. The disparity in the cost of the management programme is interesting considering swimming with a whale sharks is a non-extractive experience, whereas recreational fishing is extractive.

Conclusion

In a world experiencing a diminishing supply of pristine environments, as a social marketer it is critical to understand the unique nature of a CPR, how this impacts growth, and the intervention strategies for coping with adverse effects arising from their use and issues of fairness and equal access (Duffy 2016). The work of commons scholars is extensive and rigorous, encompassing a range of commons problems and contexts over more than forty years (Acheson 2003; Agrawal 2001; Dietz *et al.* 2003; Gibson *et al.* 2005; Ostrom *et al.* 1999). Governance of common pool resources is a tricky balancing act, as not only is there potential to deplete the resource but also excessive regulation can severely stunt economic growth

(Techera and Klein 2011). The design principles suggest that in order for a resource to be sustainably managed certain conditions must exist. These are clear boundaries, fair rules, a balance in private and public funding, thorough monitoring programmes, graduated sanctions, accessible and low-cost conflict resolution, the right to self-organise and collectively devise rules, and finally consideration of related systems. Not all of the ideal conditions are present in the whale shark tourism industry; conspicuously absent are low-cost conflict resolution and contribution to rule making. Tension can be attributed to these missing conditions. However, overall the industry appears to be ably negotiating a precarious balance between development and growth, issues of fairness and equal access and protecting the local environment and way of life (Duffy 2016).

Case study questions

1. Think of a common pool resource you are familiar with:

    a. Identify the key stakeholders involved.

    b. Discuss some of the potential challenges this common pool resource faces.

2. Apply your knowledge of social marketing and common pool resources to recommend a solution to one of the challenges you have identified. Ensure you justify your solution.

    a. In your answer, think of a potential obstacle your intervention may face and how you would overcome it.

References

ABS, A. B. o. S. (2011) Census. *Exmouth, Coral Bay, Cape Range National Park (C) Population Data.* Online at: www.abs.gov.au (accessed 1 May 2016).

Acheson, J.M. (2003) *Capturing the Commons: Devising Institutions to Manage the Maine Lobster Industry.* Upne.

Agrawal, A. (2001) Common property institutions and sustainable governance of resources', *World Development*, 29(10): 1649–1672.

Burger, J. and Gochfeld, M. (1998) 'The tragedy of the commons 30 years later', *Environment: Science and Policy for Sustainable Development*, 40(10): 4–13.

Carlsson, L.G. and Sandström, A.C. (2007) 'Network governance of the commons', *International Journal of the Commons*, 2(1): 33–54.

Catlin, J., Jones, T. and Jones, R. (2012) 'Balancing commercial and environmental needs: Licensing as a means of managing whale shark tourism on Ningaloo reef', *Journal of Sustainable Tourism*, 20(2): 163–178.

Coleman, J. (1997) 'Western Australian Wildlife Management Program No. 27: Whale shark interaction management, with particular reference to Ningaloo Marine Park' (pp. 1–39). Fremantle, WA: Western Australian Department of Conservation and Land Management.

Cox, Michael., Arnold, Gwen, and Toma, Sergio (2010) 'A Review of Design Principles for Community-Based Natural Resource Management', Ecology and Society, 15(4): 38.

Dietz, T., Ostrom, E. and Stern, P.C. (2003) 'The struggle to govern the Commons', *Science*, 302(5652): 1907–1912.

Duffy, S. (2016) 'New Perspectives on Marketing Systems: An Investigation of Growth, Power, Social Mechanisms, Structure and History'. PhD dissertation, University of New South Wales.

Duffy, S., Layton, R. and Dwyer, L. (2016) 'When the Commons call "Enough", does marketing have an answer?, *Journal of Macromarketing*, under review.

Duffy, S., Layton, R. and Dwyer, L. (2017) 'When the Commons call "Enough" Does Marketing Have an Answer?', *Journal of Macromarketing*, 37(3): 268–285.

Gibson, C. ., Williams, J.T. and Ostrom, E. (2005) 'Local enforcement and better forests', *World Development*, 33(2): 12.

Hardin, G. (1968) 'The tragedy of the commons', *Science*, 162(3859): 1243–1248.

Hardin, G. (1978) 'Political requirements for preserving our common heritage', *Wildlife and America*, 31: 1017.

Healy, R.G. (2006) 'The commons problem and Canada's Niagara falls', *Annals of Tourism Research*, 33(2): 525–544.

Hurst, J.W. (1982) *Dealing with Statutes*. New York: Columbia University Press.

Jones, T., Hughes, M., Wood, D., Lewis, A. and Chandler, P. (2009) 'Ningaloo coast region visitor statistics: collected for the Ningaloo destination modelling project' (pp. 1–61). Queensland, Australia: Sustainable Tourism Cooperative Research Centre.

Kennedy, Ann-Marie (2016) 'Macro-social marketing', *Journal of Macromarketing*, 36(3): 354–365.

Kennedy, Ann-Marie and Adrian Parsons (2012) 'Macro-social marketing and social engineering: a systems approach', *Journal of Social Marketing*, 2(1): 37–51.

Mau, R. (2008) 'Managing For Conservation and Recreation: The Ningaloo Whale Shark Experience', *Journal of Ecotourism*, 7(2–3): 213–225.

Murphy, S. (2009) 'Quarrel Coast', *ABC Landline*. Australia: Australian Broadcasting Commission.

Nazer, D.K. (2004) 'The tragicomedy of the surfers' commons', *Deakin Law Review*, 9(2): 655–713.

Norman, B. (2002) 'Review of current and historical research on the ecology of whale sharks (*Rhincodon typus*), and applications to conservation through management of the species'. Fremantle: Western Australian Department of Conservation and Land Management.

Ostrom, E. (1990) *Governing the Commons: The Evolution of Institutions for Collective Action*. Cambridge: Cambridge University Press.

Ostrom, E., Burger, J., Field, C.B., Norgaard, R.B. & Policansky, D. (1999) 'Revisiting the commons: Local lessons, global challenges', *Science*, 284(5412): 278–282.

Quiros, Angela L. (2007) 'Tourist Compliance to a Code of Conduct and the Resulting Effects on Whale Shark (Rhincodon typus) Behavior in Donsol', Philippines. Fisheries Research, 84(1): 102–108.

Taylor, G. (1994) *Whale Sharks: The Giants of Ningaloo Reef*. Melbourne: Angus & Robertson.

Techera, E.J. and Klein, N. (2011) 'Fragmented governance: Reconciling legal strategies for shark conservation and management', *Marine Policy*, 35(1): 73–78.

TRA (2014) Exmouth overnight visitor fact sheet. Perth: Tourism Western Australia.

TWA (2013) Western Australia overnight visitor fact sheet, YE Dec 10/11/12 (pp. 1–13). Perth: Tourism Western Australia.

Case study 20

Wheels, Skills and Thrills

Alan Tapp

The problem: too many car crashes caused by poor driving from young disadvantaged men

Tackling risky driving by young men from deprived areas has proven extremely difficult. A call for innovative ideas led to the funding by the Department for Transport in 2009 of a project called Wheels, Skills and Thrills 1 (WST1). Led by Alan Tapp, this project worked alongside a community developer and with a group of young men from one of the most deprived areas in Bristol and ran from 2010–11. The intervention combined social marketing, advanced driver training, and early versions of in-vehicle data recorders known as 'black boxes'. Outcome measures found significant and sustained improvements in driving skills linked to safer driving (Tapp *et al.* 2013) and in this case study we explain how this happened and the role of social marketing.

Disadvantaged young men's driving is high risk

Young male drivers from economically and socially deprived locations are significantly more likely to be involved in road collisions than other road users (Abdalla *et al.* 1997; Constantinou *et al.* 2011; Durkin and Tolmie 2010; Fleury *et al.* 2010; Hasselberg *et al.* 2005; Moller 2004; Sharpe 2006). Despite a significant decline in overall road user casualties in recent years, a disproportionate number of young drivers continue to be involved in car crashes. In the UK only one in eight drivers is aged under 25, yet one in three drivers who die are in this age group. Causes of collisions among young people are multifactorial, including tendencies towards recklessness and thrill seeking, feelings of invincibility and over-confidence (Clarke and Robertson 2005; Falk and Montgomery 2009) and a lack of observation and anticipation (Cavallo and Triggs 1996), all of which combine to create 'skill-risk optimism' (White *et al.* 2011) in that young drivers believe that they possess high-level skills and also that they are very unlikely to have an accident, when the statistics demonstrate the opposite on both counts. Deprivation typically has a multiplying effect on youth and gender (Hasselberg *et al.* 2005; Lumsden 2009)with the influence on driving of disruptive behaviours, emotional disturbance, poor anger management, increased short-termism and living for the moment, and increased recklessness and thrill seeking.

Attempts to solve the problem using traditional methods haven't worked

A recent review of road safety interventions aimed at young drivers by the Transport Research Laboratory (DfT forthcoming) confirms that meeting these behavioural challenges has proven extremely difficult for the road safety sector across the world. Apart from Graduated Driver Licensing (this involves delaying the awarding of driving licenses to teenagers until they are older; it has worked well in other countries but is currently ruled out of consideration by British policy makers) very little progress has been made. Attempts to change high-risk driving behaviours by traditional driver training and education approaches have met with little success (Helman et al. 2010), and while initiatives such as schools-based education projects involving firefighters have proven very *popular* with the public, parents and indeed many within the road safety sector itself, there is little evidence of their *effectiveness* in improving safety outcomes (McKenna 2010). Popular interventions include ideas such as firefighters visiting schools and graphically describing the trauma of having to visit the scene of a car crash involving teenagers. Often accompanied by graphic images, the immediate effect is extremely powerful with a very quiet set of young people filing out of the room. But as Frank McKenna, a leading road safety authority, explained: "These educational interventions are incredibly popular. Parents, teachers, firefighters, the media, everyone loves them. They tick every box except one: there's not a scrap of evidence that they work." There is little doubt that, taken as a whole, evidence for the influence of such interventions on subsequent crash involvement is weak (McKenna 2010).

Another major approach for road safety is the use of so-called fear appeals such as the Think! campaign (see http://think.direct.gov.uk/). However, fear appeals have little effect on those most likely to be involved in crashes, such as young male drivers. Young men, particularly those suffering the greatest social disadvantage, are better able to deflect such appeals. Either they feel that fear appeals don't apply to them as they consider themselves to be more skilful drivers (this phenomenon known as self-enhancement bias is the tendency for drivers to over-estimate their own driving ability and under-estimate that of others) or these approaches merely emphasise the element of risk that motivates their behaviour in the first place.

We faced many other problems unique to driving. Driving is an extremely interesting and difficult-to-change behaviour. In addition to self-enhancement bias, drivers typically publicly contest the link between speed and danger. This link, and the quantification of it, have been the subject of considerable academic study (Elvik 2005). It is common (even among some driver trainers) to find the argument that speeding is not risky provided the skill levels of drivers are high enough to handle the speed. Assessing risk requires accurately assessing probabilities – a calculation most people are poorly equipped to make accurately (Roberts 2013). Crashes are complicated and have multiple causes, and the role of speed in crashes is complicated to unravel and difficult to prove. These complexities have to be simplified by drivers making everyday decisions, hence their use of 'availability heuristics' (the tendency to use easily available information to make decisions) in deciding that "speeding today is safe" because "each time I've done this before I have been fine." Levels of support or opposition to speed limits are also affected by drivers' attitudes to breaking or complying with laws in general, and speeding laws in particular, e.g. drivers whose high confidence in their own skills, and high need for personal autonomy and control in deciding their own driving decisions, lead them to conclude that speed limit laws should not apply to them (Corbett and Simon 1992). Other drivers privately clearly consider speeding to have various benefits. Deliberate (instrumental) motives include exceeding the posted limit because the driver is in a hurry or wants to save time, and speeding as a thrillseeking experience (McKenna 2010). Some young drivers may also feel pressure from others. In their exploration of social contagion Corbett and Simon (1992) found the need to conform and to avoid the social pressures of not conforming were important motives, with some drivers feeling that that driving *more slowly* than a speed limit (in which the mean speed was higher than that limit) may be regarded as *more unsafe* than exceeding the limit themselves, hence providing a moral rationale for exceeding limits. The concern for advocates of 20mph limits may be that group pressures such as these may be in play and may even be exacerbated in the 20mph limits imposed on roads whose design may encourage faster speeds. Finally, Corbett and Simon (1992) found 'inadvertent speeders', who either did not know there was a speed limit in force, or had not realised how fast they were going. Their studies found many who drive on 'auto-pilot' claim to speed 'without realising it'. Such habitual or 'automatic' (inattentive/inadvertent) driving has once again been observed in many countries.

The solution: Wheels, Skills and Thrills – a new approach to safer driving for young men

To summarise the argument so far, there had been numerous calls for standard approaches to improving safety through education and training (which have not worked well) to be replaced by evidence-based and innovative approaches (McKenna 2010; WHO 2013). This need for innovation provided the impetus for the original WST1 programme. The start point was this: young men (aged 17–23), particularly those from deprived backgrounds typically have a difficult relationship with education and authority. It may therefore be unsurprising that 'being told what to do' by authority figures does not sit well. Perhaps social marketing may have more promise in changing driver behaviours (Smith 2006). Behaviour change programmes in road safety had traditionally relied on the 3Es of education, enforcement and engineering with the mistaken assumption either that all people lack are the skills to drive properly, or that people need to be forced to behave properly – either through road design or by the force of law. These approaches left out a 'third way': the use of marketing techniques that concentrate on driver motives, and examining how these motives may be changed so that drivers *want* to drive more safely.

The team felt that advanced driver training held promise, but that a new approach was needed. Hitherto the evidence base was somewhat mixed: it was noted that while some training courses had found improvements in situational awareness (Walker *et al.* 2011) and attitudes, skills and knowledge (Stanton et al. 2007), others were unsuccessful, with this lack of success attributed by Helman (2012) to a focus on skills (aspects of vehicle handling for example) that were not related to crash reduction. In other words, if road traffic collision reduction was the aim, the wrong training was being given. Helman suggested more attention should be paid, for example, to practising hazard perception skills. He also found insufficient attention had been given to factors such as the difficulty of transferring the training context into subsequent driving.

The Institute of Advanced Motoring (IAM) were experts in advanced driver training and had a course that they offered. However, this tended to attract the attention of older men who liked formal, traditional ways of doing things. Thus, marketing principles were used to work with the IAM to re-design the IAM's advanced driver training programme to optimise its appeal to young lads by ensuring it was enjoyable, presented attractively, appealed to the self-image of the audience and had value as 'cultural capital' (participants can 'show off' their skills to each other, and validate these skills with 'advanced status'). This re-design focused on skills that were of interest to the cohort (e.g. cornering, smooth driving) while also addressing deficiencies that contributed to their risky behaviour (e.g. observation and anticipation). Care was also taken with the 'branding' of the new course. While the primary aim remained safe driving, driver *skills* were emphasised. In fact the word 'safety' was banned from the project, even among the team. Another major concern was a clash of styles between mainstream and anti-authority that could have led to project failure. An example might be that an emphasis on, say, how to hold the steering wheel properly (this was an important feature of the traditional IAM course) would have been off-putting to the cohort: such things would have created 'social risk' for individuals in their own peer group. Hence, a coaching policy of 'letting the little things go' (ignoring some driver mistakes on 'the proper way' of driving) was introduced, something that did not immediately come naturally to some of the driver trainers, but which was successfully implemented. On the other hand, the observers' advanced driving skills were seen as a marketing plus, and a 'demonstration drive' by the IAM advanced trainers in which they undertook a rapid progress commentary drive proved a great success in establishing respect for the coaching programme. A final relationship-building component was that the cohort themselves named the project – 'Wheels, Skills and Thrills'.

The final major element of WST1 was an early prototype black box that was fitted into participants' cars and deployed as an accelerometer to measure aggressive driver manoeuvre 'events'. An 'event' might consist of heavy braking or cornering at aggressive speeds. It was found that not surprisingly our drivers typically would trigger many aggressive events in a single journey.

An interesting reality check for us was the lack of success of recruiting participants based on the attractiveness of a 'free advanced driving course'. The difficulties of gaining the trust of a 'hard to reach' audience from a traditional 'working-class' area were highlighted. We had to rely on a local community worker who lived locally and was known and trusted by potential participants, and we needed to bolster the attractiveness of the intervention by offering free monthly karting sessions at a local indoor facility.

Figure CS20.1 summarises the WST intervention.

What did we do?

The following bullet points illustrate elements of the programme that we explored.

Figure CS20.1 The components of WST

Initial recruitment and engagement

- We researched the levels of incentives required to recruit and retain participants. This was hard to do. The role for our community worker who lived locally was crucial in creating the initial degree of trust required to allow initial engagement. A significant incentive to participate was the offer of free karting sessions at a local indoor track. This was seen as initially attractive, but once interest in the advanced driving skills became more established, different motives for participating took over.

- We tested neighbourhood leaflet drops, and publicity in local area facilities such as clubs etc. These were of limited success. Once more the community development officer was instrumental in attracting interest.

- Once recruited, the advanced drivers established credibility with a 'demonstration drive' in which the participant accompanied the advanced driver on a commentary drive that showcased advanced skills including vehicle handling, road positioning, observation and anticipation. The highly skilled driving and commentaries were very impressive.

- A careful approach to socialising was adopted that started with individualised approaches in which driver trainers got to know participants individually.

- Tone of voice throughout is important but particularly at the beginning of the project. Research the importance of 'self-image reinforcement' and not, initially, challenging cohort assumptions that they are 'good drivers'. In other words, driver trainers avoided 'telling off' participants for poor driving, instead inviting self-reflection about how they could have driven a section road better, and so on.

Training and development

- The programme began with a 'baseline drive' to initiate the pre-post-control measures.

- Trainers initiated training with vehicle-handling skills development as this was the most attractive (and easiest) material to begin.

- Trainers then moved to implicit (cognitive/judgement) observation/anticipation skills. They sought to build cognitive over-rides to overcome copycat driving and automaticity and looked for ways to help in breaking bad habits.

- We briefly introduced higher levels of the Goals for Driver Education model[1] such as moving from mechanical driving skills to attitudinal development (for example, exploring the downside of peer approval/pressure, use of humour to get points across, etc.).

- We considered the use of driver performance feedback available from black boxes as part of training and development. For example we considered the use of behaviour-change incentives based on telematics measures. One possibility was a competitive element, either individualised or between participants. For operational reasons this was ruled out.

- We considered retention options including the use of team building and socialising between participants, versus individualised/personal models. Team building was a strong component of our final delivery, with karting sessions and post-training award ceremony as examples.

- We aimed to finish the programme on a high note with driver trainers and the community officer helping to build maturity, personal/social and self-esteem. We provided a new narrative about what good driving consists of and sought to build resistance to peer pressure and resistance to the use of reckless driving as cultural capital. We also aimed to reduce self-enhancement bias ('I am a better than average driver') but implicitly, i.e. by allowing participants to reach their own conclusions about their actual rather than perceived level of skill.

What happened? What were the results?

The outcomes of the project were very encouraging. Driving events, graded as red or amber, were sharply reduced and remained steady after the trial (Figure CS20.2) and trainer assessments of driving ability were also significantly improved (Table CS20.1) (Tapp *et al.* 2013). An assessment of each participant's driving was made before the programme and then repeated after completion.

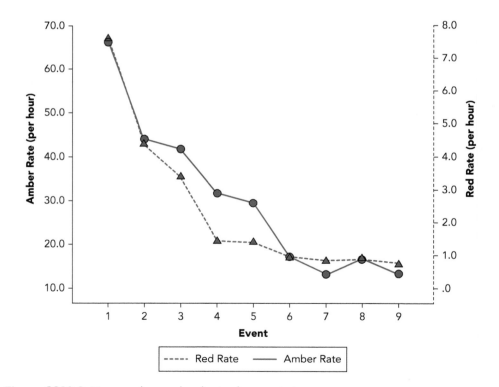

Figure CS20.2 Mean amber and red rates by event stage

Table CS20.1 Pre-post intervention drive-check results (lower scores reflect higher skill levels)

	Pre	Post
Driver 1	33	15
Driver 2	25	17
Driver 3	33	36
Driver 4	40	18
Driver 5	36	17
Driver 6	30	31
Driver 7	33	14
Driver 8	41	17
Driver 9	35	17
Driver 10	32	25
Driver 11	33	27
Driver 12	39	14
Driver 13	37	23
Driver 14	42	28
Driver 15	31	15
Driver 16	28	25
Driver 17	36	17
Driver 18	30	19
Driver 19	32	26
Driver 20	25	21
Driver 21	35	16
Driver 22	40	18
Average Score	**34**	**21**

A final point to note on WST was its unexpected benefits with respect to participant and community outcomes outside of driver behaviour. Qualitative community reports were received of participants' increased sense of worth and personal confidence, leading to reported reductions in anti-social behaviour and increased commitment to work and family. This seemed significant because for young people debut crimes related to cars are predictors of chronic criminal careers (Broughton 2006; Owen and Cooper 2013). The exposure to role models and advanced driving skills offered improved confidence in life skills, and there was evidence that for some participants the project enabled a more positive attitude not just to safer driving but also to adulthood, careers and so on, thereby benefiting society as a whole.

Looking to the future: from WST to WST2

The funding available for WST was relatively modest and the team are in the process of creating a second project that will lead to a 'market ready' solution. The future of road safety programmes such as WST might lie in the private sector, perhaps run by insurance companies as part of a 'profit model'. The premise would be that WST2 reduces the chances of collisions for high-risk insurance customers, and hence it will be of sufficient commercial value to car insurers that they will be motivated to run it themselves. Insurers have already significantly developed telematics (black boxes) into their offer, and so the 'customer management' aspects of WST2 (penalising high-risk driving and rewarding low-risk driving for each individual driver) would be quite straightforward for the sector. While high-risk drivers (young men from deprived areas) are currently typically regarded as 'off-limits' to most mainstream insurers, a proven risk-reducing agent such as WST2 would enable these 'off-limits' drivers to be brought into the mainstream of insured customers, expanding the total market base.

This profit model would make the role of social marketing even more crucial in an attractive programme design, and in recruiting and retaining participants. The Institute of Advanced Motorists (now called IAM RoadSmart) remains committed to helping with the programme delivery. A programme such as WST must always be ready for rapid change and be prepared to adapt to new circumstances. One of the key changes is that since the original programme black-box telematics have rapidly developed. As noted above telematics-based feedback and incentives to reduce driving risk, as used by the insurance sector, are in a phase of rapid growth, although sector claims of behaviour change have to date been unverified by scientific study (Tong *et al*. 2016). Future research versions of WST will provide insights by using up-to-date black boxes and new in-car camera technology in terms of not only measurement and performance feedback but also their use to incentivise change. In other notable developments, driver training has continued to develop as a science, with increasing recognition (e.g. the Goals for Driver Education) that higher order skills such as hazard perception and driving skills associated with lifestyle and risk are particularly important for road safety outcomes.

Case study questions

Note

1   http://ec.europa.eu/transport/road_safety/consultations/doc/2009_06_22_training_education_consultation_paper_annex.pdf.

References

Abdalla, I.M., Raeside, R., Barker, D. and McGuigan, D.R.D. (1997) 'An investigation into the relationships between area social characteristics and road accident casualties', *Accident Analysis and Prevention*, 29(5): 583–593.

Broughton, J. (2006) *The Correlation Between Motoring and Other Types of Offence*. London: Department for Transport.

Cavallo, A. and Triggs, T.J. (1996) 'Directions for improving young driver safety within Victoria: A discussion paper', Monash University Accident Research Centre, Melbourne, Vic.

Clarke, S. and Robertson, I.T. (2005) 'A meta-analytic review of the Big Five personality factors and accident involvement in occupational and nonoccupational settings', *Journal of Occupational and Organizational Psychology*, 78: 355–376.

Constantinou, E., Panayiotoua, G., Konstantinoua, N., Loutsiou-Ladda, A. and Kapardis, A. (2011) 'Risky and aggressive driving in young adults: Personality matters', *Accident Analysis and Prevention*, 43(4): 1323–1331.

Corbett, C. and Simon, F. (1992) 'Decisions to break or adhere to the rules of the road, viewed from the rational choice perspective', *British Journal of Criminology*, 32(4): 537–549.

Department for Transport (forthcoming) TRL review of young driver interventions for DfT.

Durkin, K. and Tolmie, A. (2010) *The Development of Children's and Young People's Attitudes to Driving: A Critical Review of the Literature.* Institute of Education, University of London, September. London: Department for Transport.

Elvik, R. (2005) 'Speed and road safety: Synthesis of evidence from evaluation studies' in *Transportation Research Record: Journal of the Transportation Research Board* no. 1908. Washington, DC: Transportation Research Board of the National Academies. pp. 59–69.

Falk, B. and Montgomery, H. (2009) 'Promoting traffic safety among young male driver by means of elaboration-based interventions', *Transportation Research Part F: Traffic Psychology and Behaviour*, 12(1): 1–11.

Fleury, D., Peytavin, J.F., Alam, T. and Brenac, T. (2010) 'Excess accident risk among residents of deprived areas', *Accident Analysis and Prevention*, 42(6): 1653–1660.

Hasselberg, M., Vaez, M. and Laflamme, L. (2005) 'Socioeconomic aspects of the circumstances and consequences of car crashes among young adults', *Social Science and Medicine*, 60(2): 287–295.

Helman, S. (2012) 'Driver training testing and licensing, and the safety of new drivers', Transport Research Laboratory. Online at: www.roadsafe.com/pool/files/events/youngdriversexpert-meeting/Roadsafe%20expert%20meeting%202012%20Shaun%20Helman.pdf (accessed 1 May 2016).Lumsden, K. (2009) *Do We Look Like Boy Racers? The Role of the Folk Devil in Contemporary Moral Panics.* Online at: www.socresonline.org.uk (accessed 1 May 2016).

Helman, S., Grayson, G. and Parkes, A.M. (2010) 'How can we produce safer new drivers? A review of the effects of experience, training, and limiting exposure on the collision risk of new drivers', *TRL Insight Report (INS005)*. Crowthorne: Transport Research Laboratory.

McKenna, F. (2010) 'Education in road safety-are we getting it right?', *RAC Foundation Research Report 10/113*.

Møller, M. (2004) 'An explorative study of the relationship between lifestyle and driving behaviour among young drivers', *Accident Analysis and Prevention*, 36: 1081–1088.

Owen, N. and Cooper, C. (2013) 'The start of a criminal career: Does the type of debut offence predict future offending?', *Research Report 77*. London: Home Office.

Roberts, I. (2013) 'Why improving public health may lead to more injury not less'. In D. Mohan (ed.) *Safety, Sustainability and Future Urban Transport.* New Delhi: Eicher.

Shope, J. T. (2006) 'Influences on youthful driving behavior and their potential for guiding interventions to reduce crashes', *Injury Prevention*, 12(1): 9–14.

Smith, W.A. (2006) 'Social marketing: an overview of approach and effects', *Injury Prevention*, 12(1): 38–43.

Stanton, N.A., Walker, G.H., Young, M.S., Kazi, T. and Salmon, P.M. (2007) 'Changing drivers' minds: The evaluation of an advanced driver coaching system', *Ergonomics*, 50(8): 1209–1234.

Tapp, A., Pressley, A., Baugh, M. and White, P. (2013) 'Wheels, Skills and Thrills: A social marketing trial to reduce aggressive driving from young men in deprived areas', *Accident Analysis & Prevention*,58: 148–157.

Tong, S., Lloyd, L., Durrell, L., McRae-McKee, K., Husband, P., Delmonte, E., Parry I. and Buttress, S. (2016) 'Provision of telematics research', Transport Research Laboratory, PPR755.

Walker, G.H., Stanton, N.A. and Salmon, P.M. (2011) 'Cognitive compatibility of motorcyclists and car drivers', *Accident Analysis and Prevention*, 43: 878–888.

White M.J., Cunningham L.C. and Titchener K. (2011) 'Young drivers' optimism bias for accident risk and driving skill: Accountability and insight experience manipulations', *Accident Analysis and Prevention*, July, 43(4): 1309–1315.

WHO (2013) *WHO Global Status Report on Road Safety 2013: Supporting a Decade of Action.* Geneva: WHO.

Case study **21**

An evaluation of Sea for Society using system indicators

Patricia McHugh and Christine Domegan

Introduction

A 'Blue Society' is a marine vision in which citizens are ocean literate and have an understanding of the ocean's influence on them and their influence on the ocean (Ocean Literacy Network 2015). The current level of ocean literacy within society presents serious social and environmental challenges, both in complexity and scale. Globally, when individuals or organisations attempt to tackle environmental issues such as the damage and degradation to marine ecosystems, long-term success stories, with lasting effects, have been all too rare. Countless collaborative initiatives have been tried but very few have sustained their pro-environmental actions to deliver wider impacts on society.

Traditional social marketing campaigns or interventions tackling environmental change measure behaviour change using outcome indicators. Outcome indicators detail the *what* of a social marketing campaign or intervention, measuring participant numbers, demographic information and reported changes in behaviour, knowledge, beliefs or values (Florida Prevention Research Centre 2003). Outcome indicators look at finding and funding a single solution at an individual level, such as one single community group or priority group in a specific location, with the hope that the most successful intervention will scale-up or replicate to extend its impact more widely (Kania and Kramer 2011). An example of outcome indicators at work is 'Give Swordfish a Break', a campaign that targeted North Atlantic restaurants, hotel and other food establishments between 1998 and 2002 by asking them not to include swordfish on their menus until such a time when stock levels replenished. Once swordfish stock numbers reached an acceptable numbers, food businesses could revert to their original behaviours. This is an example of where numeric data determine success – they deal with the visible symptoms of a problem at an individual level and respond by providing an immediate fix.

Problem definition

Problems relating to the environment are spiralling from simple, localised area issues to complex, wicked challenges. A pressing environmental problem today is marine habitat destruction. Pollution, coastal development, inland dams, logging, destructive fishing, dredging, draining of wetlands, tourism, climate change, and dynamiting coral reefs, in addition to individual human behaviour across different cities, regions, countries and continents, all contribute to marine habitat destruction. With this in mind, no single individual or organisation can possibly be charged with the responsibility of decreasing marine habitat destruction. Outcome indicators, on their own, will not suffice in creating systemic change as large-scale solutions are not known or obvious. At the individual-level, no single person or entity has the resources or the expertise to bring about lasting social change. For marine habitat destruction reaching effective systemic resolutions requires being client focused, and it also brings in a stakeholder orientation to widen the sets of priority groups who "are and could be involved in" the design and delivery of solutions for social and collective action (Brennan *et al.* 2016: 222). As social marketers, the following questions prevail, namely how can social marketing progress beyond outcome indicators, and what other stakeholders can and should participate to bring about real positive change in protecting the environment?

Evaluation efforts require new thinking and a shift towards dynamic evaluation work, where system indicators become the norm in assessing how things are changing or not, in addition to outcome indicators. System indicators detail *what* is happening in an intervention but most importantly they further understand *how* change is happening, and if change is not occurring system indicators question the shortcomings of an intervention (McHugh and Domegan 2017). System indicators in social marketing consider who-to-engage-with, what-to-work-on-together and how-change-happens on small and large scales (McHugh and Domegan 2017). They explain, rather than question, the marketing system that surrounds social behaviours, power bases and actions (Arndt 1985; Gordon and Gurrieri 2014). System indicators build critical capacity for skills, knowledge, attitudes and values which in turn improve future decisions, actions and behaviours (Mackay and Horton 2003).

Formative evaluation indicators are used in the early stages of an intervention to determine priority group selection and segmentation criteria and to establish intervention aims, objectives and baseline behaviours. Summative evaluation indicators measure the effects and changes that occur after a social marketing intervention. Outcome indicators are an example of summative evaluations indicators. They can occur directly after an intervention or long after the campaign to look for evidence of "decay and recidivism" (Florida Prevention Research Centre 2003: 6). Both types; formative and summative evaluation indicators are extensively applied in social marketing programmes detailing metrics, such as participant numbers, budgets, return on investment, promotional materials disseminated, and percentage changes in behavioural intentions, knowledge, beliefs, awareness, attitudes and the behaviours themselves (McHugh and Domegan 2017; French 2012; Stead and McDermott 2011).

Aims and objectives

The overall aim of this study is to analyse Sea for Society mobilisation activities using a system indicator evaluation framework. Mobilisation in Sea for Society is more than a simple strategy; it is a complex process that involves new interactions, capacity building, collaborative projects, multidisciplinary teams and collective action.

Specific aims of the study are:

• to offer a conceptual framework for system indicator evaluations;
• to define three systems indicator constructs – relationships, knowledge and networks;
• to outline the reflections and key takeaways on manifesting a Blue Society.

Context

Sea for Society (SFS) was a European Project that brought together a multidisciplinary partnership from 13 countries. SFS represented a European-wide mobilisation initiative that connected stakeholders and citizens to better understand the effects of their everyday choices, decisions and behaviours on the ocean in order to develop and enrich the concept of a 'Blue Society'.

In SFS, the majority of the evaluation work centred on the individual citizen, feeding their choices, knowledge, attitudes and behaviours up to the governance level to guide national and European decisions, policies and regulations (see Domegan *et al.* 2016). Significant summative evaluations were conducted at the client level, or what Gordon and Gurrieri (2014) term 'participants', using outcome indicators such as number of mobilisation initiatives held, materials distributed, audience reach, knowledge and attitude levels, and pledges made for pro-environmental behaviours.

To build on the outcome indicator evaluations, a conceptual framework for system indicator evaluations (see Figure CS21.1) was designed for Sea for Society to measure the knowledge flows, network interactions and relational processes underpinning the movement towards a Blue Society.

System indicators

Three system indicators – relationships, knowledge, and networking – have been adapted for Sea for Society to reflect on what is being co-ordinated, how that coordination is occurring, and the mechanisms that forge interrelationships and interconnections between Sea for Society partners and associated partners (Hastings and Domegan 2014; Roberts 2011).

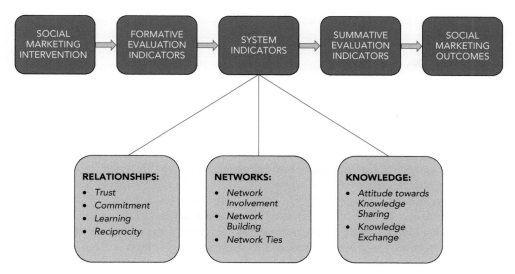

Figure CS21.1 Conceptual framework for system indicators

(*Source:* adapted from McHugh and Domegan 2017)

Relationships

Social marketing relationships empower change agents and their behavioural groups or communities in becoming strategically connected, active and informed, promoting inclusive approaches to effective social change (APSC 2007; Prahalad and Venkat 2004). Inclusivity in relationships allows social marketers to better understand the mechanisms underlying exchanges, feedback loops and balanced partnerships between actors in a behavioural system. Genuine, inclusive relationships can lead to successful partnerships with enhanced expertise and personal growth (McHugh and Domegan 2017). Four relational indicators were investigated in Sea for Society: trust, commitment, learning and reciprocity.

Knowledge

Knowledge processes identify flows of communication and explore the shared learning and communication patterns which stem from webs of interactions (McHugh and Domegan 2013). The investigation of knowledge processes in social marketing is important because knowledge is subjective and constructed as a result of people's values, attitudes, behaviours, actions and experiences. Understanding how knowledge is created and shared in communities, societies and between individuals allows social marketers to appreciate the complexity and scale of the social problem under investigation (McHugh and Domegan 2017). It also assists in co-designing more appropriate and acceptable solutions if wider social impact is to be achieved. The knowledge indicators investigated in Sea for Society were attitude to knowledge sharing and knowledge exchange.

Networking

In behavioural systems, individuals from different levels and backgrounds integrate and share their individual skill sets, insights and intellectual capabilities to facilitate the empowerment of mutual interests and knowledge (McHugh and Domegan 2017). Network processes in social marketing foster collaboration and participation. Networks acknowledge the need for bottom-up and top-down interactions; total market approaches which challenge social marketers to "think more about the marketplace, rather than individuals, as they analyse problems, propose solutions and implement and evaluate actions" (Lefebvre 2011: 67). Network involvement, network ties and network building were the networking indicators studied in Sea for Society.

Stakeholder analysis

This study assessed what Gordon and Gurrieri (2014: 261) call "other stakeholders – the non-governmental organisations and government departments involved in delivering the project." These other stakeholders were labelled partners and associated partners in Sea for Society. Partners were defined as those that were involved for the full 42-month term of the project and their involvement spanned both the consultation and mobilisation phases. Associated partners were those who became involved in the mobilisation phase of the project. Both stakeholder groups were seen as 'connectors', enabling and fostering dialogic exchanges and collaboration between the vision for the SFS initiative and the public (McHugh and Domegan 2017).

Research method

This study was conducted online through a web survey with the SFS partners and associated partners. In total, the project's partnership consisted of 70 individuals and all 70 were invited to complete the online survey. The online survey contained pre-validated scale items for demographics, relational processes, knowledge processes and networking processes, and the survey took approximately 15–25 minutes to complete.

Dillman's Tailored Design Method was employed to administer the online survey in order to increase the amount of responses collected (Dillman 2007). Three emails were sent out to all of Sea for Society partners and associated partners over the course of four weeks. The first email outlined the objective of the survey, its link and a contact email should any questions or queries arise. Two weeks later, partners and associated partners received their first reminder email. Three weeks after the original email, another reminder email was sent where individuals who had completed the survey were thanked. The survey was then officially closed and the data were prepared for analysis.

A total of 60 Sea for Society partners and associated partners participated in the online survey, producing an open rate of 85.7%. Of the 60 respondents, 52 surveys were deemed useable for further analysis producing a response rate of 74%. Forty-two partners responded and ten associated partners responded. Each SFS country was represented in the online survey with responses from Belgium, France, Greece, Ireland, Israel, Italy, Norway, Poland, Portugal, Spain, Sweden, the United Kingdom and Switzerland.

Outcomes

Sea for Society examined and showed support for all three system indicators – relationships, knowledge and networking. In particular, trust, commitment and learning were found to be important relational indicators in Sea for Society. However, partners did not see the value or importance of reciprocity or feel any obligation to return favours to others even though they may have exchanged their knowledge and skill sets with that particular partner.

Attitudes towards knowledge sharing and knowledge exchange in addition to network building and network ties were also found to be strong indicators among Sea for Society partners and associated partners. Network Involvement, however, did not exhibit any impact in the Sea for Society study as partners and associated partners felt it was more important to extend their own personal and organisational networks with specific individuals, who could enhance their knowledge and learning capabilities, as opposed to becoming involved in and remaining in a dedicated Sea for Society network (McHugh and Domegan 2017).

This study shows that system indicators are an integral component of any social marketing programme or intervention. System indicators have the potential to measure progress from social marketing ideations to social marketing outcomes. Building capacity for more effective and meaningful interventions through relationship, knowledge and networking is fundamental in achieving a wider social impact. System indicators allow social marketers time for paucity, in the wake of complex and wicked social problems, to truly learn and reflect on the successes and challenges of achieving change (McHugh and Domegan 2017). In Sea for Society, the combined assessment of system indicators with summative evaluations provides a roadmap of how change can be scaled-out and scaled-up in future marine and human-ocean related projects.

Reflections and key takeaways for manifesting a blue society

Sea for Society was a collective movement towards improving human-ocean dynamics. This collective movement in perceptions, attitudes, awareness, knowledge and values represents a complex behavioural and social change process. In Sea for Society, system indicators provided a good indication that Sea for Society was at a critical turning point in entrenching, recognising and accepting the values of the ocean and seas to daily life. From this study, key takeaway messages have been generated to assist social marketers and change agents in manifesting a Blue Society going forward.

Key takeaways from relationship indicators

Partners and associated partners involved in Sea for Society showed high levels of agreement with the relationship indicators of trust, commitment and learning. Going forward, there is a need for stakeholders to continue to learn together. Learning is inextricably linked with knowledge. As reflection takes place, learning can occur as a result of the feedback loops that identify what worked well and the learnings that can take place to improve challenging experiences, mistakes or failures in the future.

Key takeaways from knowledge indicators

Sea for Society showed high levels of support for, and agreement with, the knowledge indicators in terms of having an overall positive attitude to sharing knowledge and exchanging information. Going forward, reflection is critical to the success of knowledge exchange. Reflection allows partners and management to pause, reflect and take stock of the collective knowledge generated in a project.

Key takeaways from networking indicators

In Sea for Society, partners and associated partners recognised the importance of networking and building networks. Going forward, cross-sectoral partnerships need to be maintained between partners and associated partners regardless of the completion of the project. Manifesting a Blue Society requires a networked approach and partners need to build and capitalise upon the opportunity to create 'networks of networks' in the future.

The consideration of these key takeaway messages and the application and further enhancement of system indicators in social marketing paves the way for social marketers to stand on the shoulders of giants and learn from one another in co-designing and co-delivering marine interventions that improve human-health and human-ocean dynamics and assist in the manifestation of a 'Blue Society' in the future.

Case study questions

1. Why do you think it is important to include system indicators in social marketing?

2. Briefly describe the different types of evaluation indicators that social marketers can use.

3. What do you think were the core learnings from using system indicators in Sea for Society?

References

APSC (2007) *Tackling Wicked Problems: A Public Policy Perspective*. Contemporary Government Challenges Series, Barton, ACT, Commonwealth of Australia.

Arndt, J. (1985) 'On making marketing more scientific: The role of observations, paradigms, metaphors and puzzle solving', *Journal of Marketing*, 49(3): 11–23.

Brennan, L., Previte, J. and Fry, M.L. (2016) 'Social marketing's consumer myopia', *Journal of Social Marketing*, 6(3): 219–239.

Dillman, D. (2007) *Mail and Internet Surveys: The Tailored Design Methods*, 2nd edition. New Jersey: Wiley.

Domegan, C., McHugh, P., Devaney, M., Duane, S., Hogan, M., Broome, B., Joyce, J., Daly, O. and Murphy, D. (2016) 'Systems-thinking social marketing; conceptual extensions and empirical investigations', *Journal of Marketing Management*, 32(11–12): 1123–1144.

Florida Prevention Research Centre (2003) *'Evaluating your Social Marketing Programme"* Social Marketing and Public Health Preconference, June 18–19 2003.

French, J. (2012) 'Guidance on Evaluation of Small Scale Social Marketing Projects', Strategic Social Marketing Ltd.

Gordon, R. and Gurrieri, L. (2014) 'Towards a reflexive turn: social marketing assemblages', *Journal of Social Marketing*, 4(3): 261–278.

Hastings, G. and Domegan, C. (2014) *Social Marketing: From Tune to Symphonies*, 2nd edition. Abingdon: Routledge.

Kania, J. and Kramer, M. (2011) 'Collective impact', *Stanford Social Innovation Review*, 9(1): 36–41.

Lefebvre, R. (2011) 'An integrative model for social marketing', *Journal of Social Marketing*, 1(1): 54–72.

Mackay, R. and Horton, D. (2003) 'Expanding the use of impact assessment and evaluation in agricultural research and development', *Agricultural Systems*, 78(2): 143–165.

McHugh, P. and Domegan, C. (2013) 'From reductionism to holism: how social marketing captures the bigger picture through system indicators', in K. Kubacki and S. Rundle-Thiele (eds) *Contemporary Issues in Social Marketing* (pp. 78–94). Newcastle upon Tyne: Cambridge Scholars Publishing.

McHugh, P. and Domegan, C. (2017) 'Evaluate development! Develop evaluation! Answering the call for a reflexive turn in social marketing', *Journal of Social Marketing*, 7(2). doi: 10.1108/JSOCM-10-2016-0063.

Ocean Literacy Network (2015) Understanding the ocean's influence on you and your influence on the ocean. Online at http://oceanliteracy.wp2.coexploration.org/ (accessed 1 May 2016).

Prahalad, C. and Venkat, R. (2004) 'Co-creating unique value with customers', *Strategy and Leadership*, 32(3): 4–9.

Roberts, N. (2011) 'Beyond smokestacks and silos: Open-source, web-enabled coordination in organisations and networks', *Public Administration Review*, 71(5): 677–693.

Stead, M. and McDermott, R. (2011) 'Evaluation in social marketing', in G. Hastings, K. Angus and C. Bryant (eds) *The SAGE Handbook of Social Marketing* (pp. 193–207). London: Sage Publications.

The Taj Must Smile

Sanjeev Vyas

The Taj Must Smile is a public–private partnership in health communication outreach with key messages promoting healthy behaviours for reproductive, maternal, and child health in the country. The social and behaviour change communication (SBCC) campaign aimed to be a multi-stakeholder campaign involving the private sector, civil society, celebrities and key opinion leaders, and media coming together to make every Indian aware of healthy behaviours.

Introduction

The overall goal and approach of the US Agency for International Development (USAID/India)-funded Improving Healthy Behaviors Programme (IHBP), managed by FHI 360 from June 2011 to March 2014, was to improve the adoption of positive healthy behaviours through the institutional and human resource-capacity building of national and state institutions and the development of strong, evidence-based SBCC programmes for government counterparts. The project focused on four programme areas: family planning (FP)/reproductive health; maternal and child health (MCH); tuberculosis; and HIV/AIDS. Technical advice from IHBP focused on strengthening institutions and human resource capacity for SBCC in the Ministry of Health and Family Welfare (MOHFW), including the National AIDS Control Organisation (NACO), the Central TB Division (CTD), and the National Institute of Health and Family Welfare (NIHFW), a MOHFW-affiliated training institution.

At the request of the National Health Mission, a government-led country-wide programme had been initiated to improve health outcomes in India through a continuum of care or life-cycle approach called RMNCH+A (Reproductive, Maternal, Neonatal, Child, and Adolescent

Health). IHBP created a series of 360-degree communication materials, initially on reproductive health and maternal health followed by campaigns on HIV/AIDS, tuberculosis and adolescent health. These campaign materials were developed and produced after extensive testing with target groups with the help of leading research and communications agencies.

As part of its scope of work, IHBP had the mandate to extend the impact and scope of its work through generating interest and leverage in project-supported areas by the Government of India (GOI) and the private sector. The project aimed to achieve a 1:1 leveraging ratio to USAID funds expended.

Problem definition

As a cornerstone of its leveraging strategy, IHBP decided to take the spread of these government-approved health campaigns and messages to a wider audience, preferably through the private sector organisations, by building a public–private partnership on health communication.

PPPs were seen to be a viable strategy for health communications as this mechanism will generally match financial resources, provide in-kind contributions, and share knowledge. Assets leveraged are deeply linked to harnessing the complementary resources of expertise, networks, and innovation toward a strategic end. Furthermore, partners leverage assets to produce an outcome that is equal to or greater than the sum of its parts.

Competitive analysis

However, given the scant success of PPPs in health in India and no notable initiative in health communication, it was a challenge to develop a strategy that would bring in private sector organisations to help spread the campaign messages among vulnerable and marginalised communities and groups. The aim was to devise a strategy that could create a movement which the entire nation could rally around. It was important that private-sector partners should participate alongside and thereby complement government efforts in raising awareness for the key campaign messages, thereby saving the lives of thousands of women and children.

The three models of PPP shown in Figure CS22.1 (market-based, balanced, and socially based) hinge on whether the primary intended outcome of the intervention is commercial (profit making) or social (improving public health). While every PPP has a double bottom line (in terms of having to produce both a commercial return on investment and a social return on investment), the three models can be differentiated in terms of their varying degrees of commercial and social investment.

Given that the classic example of the socially-based PPP model is CSR programmes, in which commercial enterprises help to expand social activities that are typically led by governmental or non-profit organisations, there was a case for a socially-based PPP in health communication, where IHBP could contribute limited seed capital and invite in-kind investments from potential CSR and NGO partners.

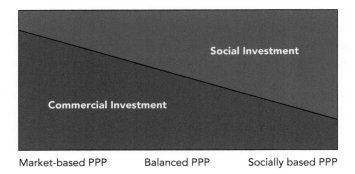

Figure CS22.1 Graphic depicting commercial-social mix defining the type of PPP

(*Source:* Jeff Barnes; Designing Public–Private Partnerships in Health, July 2011)

Stakeholder analysis

In August 2013, the Indian parliament passed the Indian Companies Act, 2013 (the 'New Act'), which replaced the Companies Act of 1956, thereby making India the first country to legally enshrine a corporate social responsibility (CSR) law.

The law came into effect from April 1, 2014, and the rules as outlined in Section 135 of the Companies Act made it mandatory for Indian companies and foreign companies operating in India of a minimum turnover and profitability to spend 2% of their average net profit for the previous three years on corporate social responsibility (CSR). Annual CSR reports are a requirement of the law and must cover information about the CSR policy, the CSR commit-tee, the amount of CSR expenditure and details of where the money has been spent. While companies are not penalised for failing to spend their required amount, they must publicly disclose why they were not able to.

There is a long list of permissible areas for CSR funding. These include such purposes as: ending hunger and poverty; promoting public health; supporting education; addressing gen-der inequality; protecting the environment; and funding cultural initiatives and the arts. The New Act encourages companies to spend their CSR funds in India and in areas where they operate, but money cannot be spent on activities undertaken that are part of the normal course of the company's business or on projects for the exclusive benefit of employees or their family members.

With CSR gaining prominence in corporate India, IHBP identified CSR Foundations as its primary potential partners. In order to understand their needs and gaps, an exten-sive stakeholder mapping exercise was undertaken. A secondary analysis of the top 100 CSR spenders from industry data was undertaken. Additonally, 15 CSR managers were interviewed with the objective of identifying how and why the communication campaign materials offered by IHBP could be of value to them. Some viable paths that emerged were: community health interventions; workplace health; employee volunteering programmes; and cause-related marketing.

Clearly, there was an opportunity for IHBP and USAID along with the Ministry of Health and Family Welfare to play the role of *aggregators and/or incubators* – to identify organiszations that had a useful mix of corporate members and have these groups co-convene as a strategic group of potential partners to promote the cause of maternal health through communication. This strategy was seen to be in sync with the Mission's India Partnership Strategy that aims at investing in partnership platforms and alliances that address industry-wide challenges, bringing together resources and expertise from a range of sectors and organisations, linking US expertise with the Indian private sector, and tapping into broad knowledge networks.

As such, a creative ignition platform was required to build a multi-stakeholder movement that could continue to have resonance and could be easily adopted even after the end of the project. This platform could then be converted into a national movement that would draw the attention of corporate CSR, NGOs, media and other institutions, and be a ready platform that influencers, celebrities and key opinion leaders could easily associate with. An umbrella pitch was required for the multiple stakeholders with whom IHBP wanted to engage that could eventually provide outreach via important preventive health messages to the public at large.

For IHBP to have the largest possible impact on the target group, enlisting influencer support was crucial to share the message effectively. Celebrities, health influencers, NGOs and corporate organisations who actively engaged their target audience and were also involved in similar social impact activities were identified. However, to ensure the message ddidn't become fragmented given that they were reaching out to people across India on an array of topics, it was decided that an umbrella campaign 'theme' should be devised. 'The Taj Must Smile' campaign was born of this need.

About 'The Taj Must Smile': aims and objectives

In spite of being a booming economy, India has remained woefully behind in terms of medical literacy. Many deaths happen purely because people don't know about simple healthy behaviours which can help prevent disease and subsequent death. Health indices paint a very grim picture of India. Maternal mortality in India in 2012 stood at 178 per 100,000 live births, putting the nation behind 128 countries. Tuberculosis (TB), claimed 500,500 deaths on average per year. Taboos regarding menstruation result in many adolescent girls suffering from infections. The rural and urban base of the pyramid groups were not aware of behaviours which could be adopted to prevent these diseases. While investments in health infrastructure are essential, any additional behaviour change communication efforts would supplement the government's ongoing efforts.

'The Taj Must Smile' leverages the fact that India's monument of pride, the Taj Mahal, was built in circa 1632 by the Mughal emperor Shah Jahan as a symbol of eternal love for his wife, Mumtaz Mahal, who died giving birth to their 14th child. Mumtaz Mahal died during childbirth probably because of a lack of awareness of health-related issues, poor health-seeking behaviour, and access to quality healthcare which was not as developed in seventeenth-century India as it is today. However, some four hundred years later, although India has made much progress in reducing the number of maternal deaths, the country still has the dubious distinction of having one of the world's highest maternal mortality rates (MMR). The Taj will 'smile' when more Indians embrace the measures they can take to have a healthy life for themselves and their children.

The campaign sought to reinforce the national symbolism, while highlighting the underlying problem relating to women's health awareness, by drawing comparisons to the childbirthing tragedy of Mumtaz. Further, 'The Taj Must Smile' ignition platform was a theme wide enough to include closely related issues of family planning and adolescent health along with a core of maternal and child health.

Research

A market landscape ananlysis of PPPs related to healthcare in India was conducted in 2012. This analysis was aimed at gaining market insights related to private sector organisations in partnerships with central or state government and the key areas in which these interventions were operating. This 'outside-in' analysis helped in mapping the market and identifying potential partnership opportunities.

At this point it was important to understand what would be the value proposition for stakeholder groups identified. What would encourage and motivate them to partner USAID, the Health Ministry and IHBP, and join 'The Taj Must Smile' campaign? Stakeholder consultancies were organised to understand these important issues and some of the things that resonated positively with potential partners emerged:

a. It was prestigious for private sector to be seen partnering with the Government of India and USAID in priority health areas as their efforts received additional credibility.

b. They were keen to gain access to evidence-based 360-degree communication campaigns (including TV & Public Service Radio Ads, posters, handbills, banners and billboards, wall paintings, interactive educative games, street-theatre scripts) developed by IHBP and endorsed by the government.

c. Access to the communication campaigns freed their own resources and saved time developing SBCC materials.

d. The private sector was happy to receive technical assistance from IHBP to build capacity in frontline health workers conducting IPC and outreach,and help with impact measurement tools.

A request to USAID and the government to allow partners adopting the SBCC materials (and using their own resources to print and broadcast these campaigns) to add their corporate branding received a favourable response. This made the PPP 'visible' and was an added attraction to the private sector.

The value proposition (or the promise of value we can deliver to our stakeholders in terms of relevancy, value and unique differentiation) to go with was defined as an opportunity to partner with the Government of India and USAID with free access to evidence-based, 360-degree health communication campaigns to build a healthy India.

A desk review and information from industry sources were compiled to develop a 'hot list' of about 100 potential corporate foundations, businesses, bilateral programmes, NGOs, and academic institutions that could be approached for partnerships. Initial meetings organised to test the value proposition showed that the campaign track of Maternal and Child Health for community health programmes found favour with corporate foundations, bilateral programmes, and NGOs. However, there was relatively lesser traction for partnerships in the area of family planning/reproductive health (given the controversies surrounding previous government efforts in this area) and other health tracks.

Intervention

IHBP partnered with two key organisations to deliver 'The Taj Must Smile' campaign. While Weber Shandwick PR was roped in for leading media advocacy and enlisting celebrities to lend support to the campaign, Idobro (a social enterprise idobro.com that facilitates an active and deeper model of engagement to map and implement market-based solutions) was signed up as the knowledge partner. IHBP collaborated with leading umbrella trade and industry bodies such as ASSOCHAM (Associated Chambers of Commerce of India), PHDCCI (PHD Chambers of Commerce and Industry), FICCI (Federation of Indian Chambers of Commerce and Industry) and CII (Confederation of Indian Industries) to reach out to their members active in CSR initiatives in health.

The project participated in a variety of private sector events, such as industry conferences, exhibitions and seminars, to showcase its communication campaigns and explore potential partnerships. Some of these events also provided speaker opportunities with the inclusion of panellists or presenters.

Along with the support of Weber Shandwick and Idobro, IHBP organised a series of communication workshops aimed at senior executives from the CSR functions of private businesses and NGOs. The idea here was to showcase the 360-degree communication campaigns while sharing the consumer insights and creative ideas behind those campaigns. INHP invited the private sector representatives to a partnership whereby partners would have free access to all communication templates which they could then print or broadcast after adding their corporate branding.

A total of 14 private sector organisations signed MOUs with IHBP and a bilateral programme utilised the communication campaign materials in a variety of ways within their programme catchment areas (see Appendix 1).

While some reprinted the leaflets and posters and used these for their community outreach events such as health camps or put them up at schools and community halls, others played the public service ads on TV screens at health facilities.

Some partners extended the reach of these messages through their mobile phone or interactive radio services (mHealth programmes) and even by buying time on national and local radio and television networks.

'The Taj Must Smile' campaign also undertook a massive outreach effort and a Facebook page which along with a Twitter handle and YouTube were the main social media tools together with conventional media outreach through newspapers, radio and television channels. Enlisting influencer support to help to share the message effectively was identified as a key media advocacy strategy. The team identified celebrities who actively engaged the majority of our audience and were also involved in similar social impact activities. Additionally, renowned doctors were requested to endorse newspaper articles supporting key campaign messages.

Celebrities and influencers played a pivotal role and provided *pro bono* support. Video messages from Olympic gold medallist Mary Kom, as well as renowned celebrities including Gauhar Khan, Ronit Roy and Mouni Roy and singer Shaan, supporting women and child health issues, were recorded and uploaded on YouTube and Facebook. Articles from several celebrities were published in national and regional newspapers under 'The Taj Must Smile' umbrella. DD National (a government TV channel), NDTV (a leading news channel) and All India Radio, (he widest radio network) aired programmes and public service announcements disseminating key messages.

Alongside these news articles and videos IHBP's communication materials were posted on Facebook and Twitter, reaching many more people with messages on positive healthy behaviours.

Outputs

'The Taj Must Smile' campaign was hugely successful and over 800,000 impressions of the campaign messages were disseminated across Facebook. Over 58 million viewers were reached through programmes and *pro-bono* public service announcements on India's leading news channel, NDTV and the government-owned DD National television channels. The STAR Plus TV channel also weaved the key message around care for a pregnant woman in their popular TV serial *Saraswati-Chandra* where a doting husband explains to his newly-pregnant wife the importance of taking adequate rest, eating nutritious food, and including green, leafy vegetables in her diet, as well as iron and calcium supplements, for a safe pregnancy. Some other events hosted by IHBP received coverage in the national news on television, thereby reaching millions of viewers across the country.

Radio announcements across the country's largest radio channel, the government-owned All India Radio, expanded the campaign's reach phenomenally. Multiple stories about the campaign were launched across 41 media titles.

Discussion

'The Taj Must Smile' campaign was a unique, highly visible and successful PPP initiative in health communication and helped in increasing the outreach of important maternal and child health, reproductive health, adolescent health, and tuberculosis messages to the poor and vulnerable communities, both directly through government media spends and those of the partner organisations. It also helped IHBP surpass the 1:1 leveraging target. It successfully leveraged US$23,426,088.56 over its lifetime, and the central and state health ministries as well as private sector players continue to use the communication materials even in the year 2016–17 and beyond, thus demonstrating the sustainable impact of 'The Taj Must Smile' campaign.

The campaign partnerships helped partners realise the need and scope of SBCC in their community interventions. Furthermore, partners are collaborating among themselves and with other organisations to take some of the learnings forward and thus adding impact to their CSR initiatives. A good example here is the TTMS campaign partner IL&FS that went on to adopt the Prevention of Parent-to-Child Transmission (PPTCT) of HIV/AIDS and the Stigma and Discrimation by healthcare providers campaign, developed by IHBP for the National Aids Control Organisation, MOHFW. This was in partnership with 'Arogya' – the CSR programme of Oil India Limited, a Fortune 500 company, in the states of Assam, Andhra Pradesh and Rajasthan under a Global Fund grant.

'The Taj Must Smile Campaign' has won global recognition for its creativity, innovation, and impact. Some of the global communication awards won in 2015 were as follows:

1. The IPRA Golden World Awards in the NGO Campaign and Public Sector Campaign categories.

2. The Stevie Bronze award – Communication Campaign of the Year in Public Service Category at the 12th Annual International Business Award for Corporate Communications, Investor Relations & Public Relations.

3. The Spikes Asia Award for the best Public Relations Campaign.

4. The South Asia SABRE Award in Public Affairs/Government Relations category.

Private sector partners found great value in associating with 'The Taj Must Smile' campaign which is evident from their contribution of resources in furthering the key messages through their programmes or channels.

Partner speak

Since IL&FS is working with various state governments, particularly with Department of Health, we intend to scale up such initiatives and use these materials for any further engagement with them on menstrual hygiene, family planning, and maternal health.

Dr Arun Varma, Vice President and Group Head, Health
Initiatives, IL&FS ETS, Ltd., National Capital Region, Noida

We thank IHBP for providing us with material that is very user friendly and relevant for use in our comprehensive health interventions. It has added immense value to our effort in reaching out to communities with health messages in a most effective manner.

Ms Anagha Mahajani, General Manager – Programme
Research and Monitoring, Ambuja Cement Foundation, Mumbai

With the help of IHBP partnership, we were able to produce a digital toolkit by converting the menstrual hygiene content provided to us as a Java toolkit, which is currently being used in the MIRA channel.

Mr Hilmi Quraishi, Director – Social Initiatives,
ZMQ Development, Gurgaon

We are extremely thankful to IHBP for showing such positive intent toward the introduction of the menstrual hygiene program in Satya Bharti Schools. The support provided has been extremely good and has helped us in planning out a smooth implementation strategy. Such partnerships help in channelising common resources for good of the society.

Mr Antony Joseph Nellissery, General Manager –
Programmes, Bharti Foundation, Gurgaon

A partnership of this kind with IHBP surely helps Jubilant Bhartia Foundation to extend its capacity as a foundation to collaborate with esteemed international organisations like USAID and the Government of India to bring health care consciousness among the vulnerable population of the country.

Mr Vivek Prakash, General Manager CSR, Jubilant
Bhartia Foundation, National Capital Region, Noida

We have invested in the maternal health campaign and are using it in health camps in the interiors of Bihar, Odisha, Jharkhand, and Uttar Pradesh. Doctors are very happy and show appreciations to Bafna and team for the posters and leaflets with very important messages which should be adapted by every women during pregnancy and after.

Mr Surendar, Product Manager, Bafna
Pharmaceuticals Ltd., Chennai

Case study questions

1. How do you create a communication campaign that stands out in a cluttered social impact category such as maternal health is in India? Think of yourself as the CSR Manager of a medium-sized enterprise and come up with a a similar health issue in your country and identify key aspects of a social marketing campaign in that area.

2. As a communications person, would you recommend the strategy of creating a buzz around a campaign among stakeholder groups who are technically not its end beneficiaries? For e.g., with TTMS, our end beneficiaries were the base of the pyramid populations in urban and poor geographies, but we reached out to a very urban population to help spread the message? Why or why not?

3. What possible advantages and disadvantages do you perceive in creating a platform or an umbrella campaign?

4. Do PPPs always result in win-win partnerships? Why do many PPPs fail? What are the specific opportunities and challenges according to you in developing PPPs in health? Divide your groups into two and conduct a short debate in support of and against PPPs.

5. Given the limited and ever shrinking donor resources available for social and development issues, what alternate strategies can you think of for leveraging resources from corporate businesses, civil society, academia, media, celebrities and local governments? How would your strategy look at tapping some of these potential alternate funding sources? What are the challenges you perceive and how will you overcome those to build a win-win strategy?

Resources

1. Commission on the Private Sector & Development – Report to the Secretary General of the United Nations 2004 – Unleashing entrepreneurship: Making business work for the poor: Chapter 4: Engaging the private sector www.scribd.com/document/24309231/Unleashing-Entrepreneurship (accessed 17 September 2017).

2. Engaging with the Private Sector in the Post-2015 Agenda: Consolidated Report on 2014 Consultations – United Nations Development Group www.unglobalcompact.org/library/2781 (accessed 17 September 2017).

3. Handbook on Corporate Social responsibility in India – Confederation of Indian Industries & PwC India 2013 www.pwc.in/assets/pdfs/publications/2013/handbook-on-corporate-social-responsibility-in-india.pdf (accessed 17 September 2017).

4. Funds for NGOs – Grants and Resources for Sustainability www.fundsforngos.org/free-resources-for-ngos/counts-leverage-usaids-global-development-alliance-concept-paper/ https://www.facebook.com/TheTajMustSmile/ (accessed 17 September 2017).

5. Understanding Private Sector Values: An Assessment of How USAID Measures the Value of Its Partnerships August 2011 www.usaid.gov/sites/default/files/documents/1880/Understanding%20Private%20Sector%20Value_Assessment%20Report_Final.pdf (accessed 17 September 2017).

6. The Taj Must Smile – Facebook Page www.facebook.com/TheTajMustSmile (accessed 17 September 2017).

7. The Improving Health Behaviors Project www.fhi360.org/projects/improving-healthy-behavior-project-ihbp (accessed 17 September 2017).

8. Exploring FHI360 – Publication: The Taj Must Smile Nov 2014 www.fhi360.org/resource/taj-must-smile (accessed 17 September 2017).

9. The Taj Must Smile Webpage www.empowershe.org/TajHome.html (accessed 17 September 2017).

10. Rahul Roy and other celebrities support The Taj Must Smile www.mp3fordfiesta.com/mp3/rohit-roy-supports-the-taj-must-smile-campaign-part-2.html (accessed 17 September 2017).

11. Gauhar Khan supports The Taj Must Smile Campaign http://mp3ecoboost.com/mp3/5kKAwld9EvU2/gauhar-khan-supports-the-taj-must-smile-campaign.html (accessed 17 September 2017).

12. The Communication Initiative Network – Convening the communication and media development social and behavior change community www.comminit.com/global/content/taj-must-smile-campaign (accessed 17 September 2017).

13. YouTube www.youtube.com/watch?v=drjwnfJoPDo (accessed 17 September 2017).

14. International Public Relations Association: IPRA Golden World Awards 2017 www.ipra.org/golden-world-awards/winners/ (accessed 17 September 2017).

15. IPRA Golden World Awards – Winners 2015 http://content.presspage.com/uploads/542/ipragoldenworldawards-winners2015.pdf (accessed 17 September 2017).

16. The International Business Awards – PR Award Winners Communications or PR Campaign of the Year – Public Service (Bronze Stevie Winner – The Taj Must Smile).

17. India PR and Corporate Communication Awards 2015 www.exchange4media.com/iprcca2015/top5.aspx (accessed 17 September 2017).

Appendix I IHBP signed MOUs with 14 private sector organisations and collaborated with one bilateral programme

S.No.	Partner	Geography	Activities/interventions
1.	Ambuja Cement Foundation (Ambuja Cement, Ltd.)	Himachal Pradesh (Darlaghat), Gujarat (Ambujanagar)	mHealth maternal and child health programme using FP and MH campaign videos embedded in CommCare for ANC and PNC visits through *sakhis*
2.	Bafna Pharmaceuticals, Limited	Bihar, Uttar Pradesh, Odisha	Manufacturer of the Raricap range of IFA tablets and syrups. Organises health camps in small towns and villages to check haemoglobin (Hb) levels and raise awareness about anemia; detailing to doctors through salesforce.
3.	Bharti Foundation (Bharti Airtel, Limited)	Haryana, Punjab, Rajasthan, West Bengal, Uttar Pradesh, Tamil Nadu	The Foundation runs schools across India; proposes to use menstrual hygiene campaign to increase awareness on menstrual hygiene among schoolgirls and mothers in 254 schools.
4.	Centre for Market Research and Social Development	Delhi	Community outreach activities to generate awareness on FP, MH, and AH under its Health and Family Welfare project in the urban slums of Delhi, covering 100,000 people in 34 villages with a focus to supplement/strengthen the government health programmes.
5.	Dimagi Software Innovations Private, Limited	Jharkhand, Himachal Pradesh	Developing a standardised MCH application, CommCare, for the Jharkhand government, which will function as a mobile-based job aid support for *sahiyas* to deliver better; collaborating in a mHealth programme with the an Ambuja Cement Foundation in Himachal Pradesh.
6.	Fem Sustainable Social Solutions (femS3)	Cities of Agra, Mumbai	Community outreach on water and sanitation through NGO partners. femS3 used FP and MH campaign in their community outreach programme.

No.	Organisation	State(s)	Description
7.	Gram Vaani Community Media Private Limited	Jharkhand	Community radio services and a mobile phone-based voice interaction platform (*Mobile Vaani*) in rural India.
8.	IL&FS Education & Technology Services Limited (IETS)	Assam, Uttar Pradesh, Himachal Pradesh, Delhi	ITES is implementing the CSR programme for Oil India Ltd. (OIL) in two districts of Upper Assam (Dibrughar and Tinsukia) to reduce the infant mortality rate (IMR) and maternal mortality rate (MMR). The FP, MH, and adolescent health (AH) campaigns have been translated and dubbed by ITES into Assamese; IL&FS is using FP and MH campaigns under its community health interventions around its highway project sites in Jharkhand, Delhi, Punjab, and HP. IL&FS adopted the Prevention of Parent to Child Transmission (PPTCT) of HIV/AIDS and Stigma & Discrimination campaigns in partnership with Oil India Limited under a Global Fund grant for Assam, Andhra Pradesh and Rajasthan.
9.	Janani (a part of DKT)	Bihar, Uttar Pradesh	Utilising FP, MH, and AH campaigns as a part of demand creation for services through 150+ Surya and franchise clinics.
10.	JSPL Foundation (Jindal Steel & Power, Limited)	Jharkhand, Chattisgarh, Odisha	JSPL is integrating the FP, MH, AH, and HIV/AIDS campaigns for its community healthcare initiatives: 'Kishori Express' – health of adolescent girls; 'Sshodasi' – a low-cost sanitary napkin initiative; and 'Vatsalya' – a community initiative for safe motherhood through strengthening of existing health services, in the intervention areas of Jharkhand, Chattisgarh, Odisha, Haryana and Arunachal Pradesh, with a focus to supplement/strengthen the government MCH programme in the project areas.
11.	Jubilant Foundation (Jubilant Life Sciences, Limited)	Uttar Pradesh (Gajraula district), Haryana (Jhajjar district)	Community interventions in FP, MH, AH across 34 villages around Jubilant Life Sciences plant in Gajraula (Amroha) district of UP; outreach on health issues through doctor posted in medical van in Jhajjar district of Haryana (in partnership with CSR of Panasonic Limited).

(continued)

Appendix I (continued)

S.No.	Partner	Geography	Activities/interventions
12.	RPG Enterprises (RP Goenka Group)	Maharashtra, Madhya Pradesh, Rajasthan, Gujarat	Employee volunteer programme in villages surrounding its facilities in Jaipur (Rajasthan), Jabalpur (MP), Halol and Baroda (Gujarat), Vasai, Mumbai, and Nagpur (Maharashtra), and Mysore (Karnataka).
13.	World CSR Alliance (a division of Grow Brands Worldwide Private, Limited)	Web presence	Existing online platforms like social media assets, websites and syndications to create a multiplier effect for the campaign. It will also sponsor a TV series (infomercials/ documentary/ talk show) to promote 'The Taj Must Smile' campaign.
14.	ZMQ Development	Haryana, Uttar Pradesh	Digitisation of IHBP campaigns for mobile delivery; integration of FP/MH content in their mobile application 'MIRA Channel – Mobile Lifeline Channel for Women', which targets GOI's RMNCH+A strategy. ZMQ is also using the materials to disseminate health messages and reach the base of the pyramid communities through organised human networks such as SHGs (self-help groups), micro-finance institutions (MFIs), health workers such as Mahua Mahila Vikas Sanasthan (MMVS), the Mewat Development Agency (MDA), SHG federations, polio programme partners.
15.	JHUCCP and DFID for Project Ujjwal	Bihar, Odisha	JHUCCP repurposed the FP campaign developed by IHBP and is making extensive use of the same as part of the Demand Generation Strategy under Project Ujjwal – Reproductive Health and Family Planning Project for Bihar and Odisha, funded by DFID. The Enter-Educate shows use the branding line *Khushi Ka Manatar Show* to pull in crowds and inform them about modern contraceptive methods.

Case study **23**

Identification of behavioural change strategies to prevent cervical cancer among Malay women in Malaysia

Julinawati Suanda, Desmond Cawley,
Maria Brenner, Christine Domegan
and Neil Rowan

Introduction

Although preventable, cervical cancer has become a major health problem in developing countries (Tavafian 2012). In Malaysia, cervical cancer is in the top five of cancers and the third most common cancer among women (NCR/2011). Furthermore, compliance with cervical cancer screening in Malaysia is currently still voluntary. In 2010, the Director General of Health Malaysia distributed a circular directing the implementation of the Human Papillomavirus (HPV) Vaccine Programme among female teenagers, aged 13, in Malaysia (Wong *et al.* 2008). Pap smear screening was first introduced in Malaysia in the late 1960s (Oon *et al.* 2011). Malaysian women have been offered free Pap smear screening since the launch of 'Healthy Life Style Campaign against Cancer' in 1995 (Othman and Rebolj 2009). Nevertheless, despite these programmes and campaigns, there was no significant reduction in cervical cancer prevalence until the year 2000 (Wong *et al.* 2008); only 47.3% of women in Malaysia underwent screening between January 2000 and September 2008 (Othman and Rebolj 2009).

In terms of effectiveness, Pap smear screening along with HPV vaccination will save thousands of lives as well as increase life expectancy if adopted by Malaysian women (Ezat and Aljunid 2010). Therefore, expenditure on Pap smear testing and HPV vaccinations, combined with preventative efforts, are paramount in the treatment for cervical cancer disease. Pap smear testing is offered free-of-charge in public health centres while HPV vaccination is given free to school children aged 13. Statistically, according to the National Cancer Registry (NCR) published by the Ministry of Health Malaysia (MOHM), cases are higher among Indian women for cervical cancer in Malaysia (NCR 2011). Consequently, it is timely to investigate ways to address this problem. The approachable suggestion in this present study was the continuity and appropriate strategies to promote awareness of the disease and to increase participation in Pap screening. In doing so, it is important to re-evaluate the efficiency of existing strategies used by the Ministry of Health Malaysia and to identify the most appropriate approach to addressing this problem that would embrace stakeholders.

Problem definition

Cervical cancer has been reported as the third most common cancer in Malaysia. The NCR (2011) reported that a total of 18,219 new cancer cases were diagnosed and registered in the NCR 2007. It comprised of 8,123 males and 10,096 females. The actual number is potentially much larger as the NCR 2007 estimates that almost 10,000 cancer cases are unregistered every year. The ten leading cancers among the population of Malaysia in 2007 were breast, colorectal, lung, nasopharynx, cervical, lymphoma, leukaemia, ovarian, stomach and liver. The five most frequent cancers among Malaysian males in 2007 were lung, colorectal, nasopharynx, prostate and lymphoma, while the five most common cancers in females were breast, colorectal, cervical, ovarian and lung. Pap smear testing was offered free of charge since 1996, however a reduction in cervical cancer cases was not observed until the early 2000s. Since 2012, teenagers (aged 13 and over) are administered free-of-charge the HPV vaccination in the schools with parental consent. Despite these interventions, only 30 to 40% of all deaths from cancer are registered in Malaysia where ca. 18,000 new cancer cases occur per year with a further estimated 10,000 cases going unregistered (Malaysia's National Cancer Report of 2011). The order of decreasing reported incidence of ethnic groups to cervical cancer was Indian, Chinese and Malay, with the latter representing the largest ethnic group in Malaysia.

There is a pressing need to investigate and deploy effective behavioural change strategies to prevent cervical cancer in Malaysia. The MOHM started a Healthy Lifestyle Campaign in 1991 carrying the theme 'Be Healthy for Life', emphasising community roles, regardless of age and sex, to lead a healthy and wholesome lifestyle. This campaign emphasises five main concepts including: healthy eating, managing stress, adequate exercise, physical activity and not smoking. Annual media campaigns have been conducted since 2006 to assess the achievements of the Healthy Lifestyle Campaign. It is therefore timely to understand the health prevention practices and behaviours by Malay women towards cervical cancer. It is also important to understand the factors which influence cervical screening and clinical attendance. It is envisaged that the knowledge generated in this study will be translated to inform cancer prevention in other ethnic groups. Specifically, this research is focused on studying the Malay women to explore the relationship between socioeconomic status, perceived health beliefs and social marketing strategies. Although Malay women as an ethnic group have the lowest number of cervical cancer cases reported annually in Malaysia, possible reasons for decreasing trends in cervical cancer diagnosis are explored. This provides the basis for further research in other ethnic groups, such as Indian women who have a growing incidence of cervical cancer and can inform future social marketing strategies with other groups.

Stakeholder analysis

Malay women from both rural and urban settings, Ministry for Health of Malaysia (MOHM), husbands, children, General Practitioners, nurses, health care workers, employers and laboratories offering cervical cancer methods are relevant pap smear stakeholders.

Aims and objectives

The overall aim of this study is to explore Malay women's insight towards cervical cancer and their experiences through perceived beliefs of awareness and behavioural change strategies used by the Ministry of Health Malaysia (MOHM).

Specific objectives of the study are:

- to determine the health prevention behaviours practised by the Malay women in preventing cervical cancer;

- to explore the Malay women's knowledge of cervical cancer and their experiences of accessing the cervical cancer screening service;

- to examine the reactions of Malay women towards the strategies by the MOHM.

Research methods

The objectives of this study were met by combining social marketing with health promotion in order to influence and communicate behavioural change and to solve health problems through application of the Health Belief Model (HBM). The Health Belief Model was utilised to help the exploration of participants' health behaviour to address the strategic social marketing efforts. Instruments tested for HBM were the perceived beliefs (perceived barriers, benefits, severity and susceptibility) and cues to action, while knowledge and suggestions in the campaign and awareness gained by the participants in this study were also tested (Figure CS23.1). Analysis included whether or not HBM and behavioural change marketing were influenced by participants' socio-demographic factors. The theoretical framework underpinning this research is HBM that was developed by a group of social psychologists among the U.S. Public Health Service in the 1950s. HBM is referred to as a psychological health behaviour change model and was originally used to understand non-compliance with the recommended health action towards the tuberculosis screening programme by the US Public Health Service (Strecher and Rosenstock 1997). HBM addresses five major

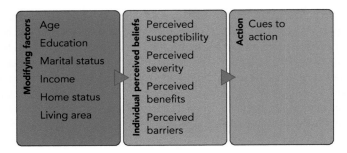

Figure CS23.1 Health belief model framework and health belief model constructs with modifying factors

(*Source:* adopted from Rosenstock *et al.* 1988)

constructs for compliance with recommended health action, namely: (i) perceived barriers of recommended health action; (ii) perceived benefits of recommended health action; (iii) perceived susceptibility of the disease; (iv) perceived seriousness of the disease; and (v) cues to action (Rosenstock *et al.* 1988). The uniqueness of this current study is that it combines the deployment of HBM with social marketing elements to perceive the effectiveness of available strategies by MOHM. Through the HBM framework, participants can share their experiences, knowledge and awareness of cervical cancer and cervical cancer prevention. This current study also reveals the preferred campaigns by the participants through suggestions made. In a study of scales measurement using HBM constructs the purposes were divided into two sections: (1) to assess the predictors for cancer examination; and (2) to examine the ability of the scales to predict self-reported physical activities.

In order to meet the philosophical underpinning and overarching aim of this research, this current study decided to utilise Husserl's descriptive phenomenology to guide the qualitative methods. By exploring Husserl's phenomenology, this current study employs the approach especially in accessing participants' intention, perceived thinking and imagination or reaction towards cervical cancer. All of the aforementioned behaviours happened consciously and the participants were aware of that (Dowling 2007). Subsequently, experiences were captured without any prejudice and participants have been provided ample space and time to share theirs. Since this study has chosen to stay in line with Husserl's methods, the study has been developed in such a way from the aim and objectives, through the research methods.

Phase I was carried out through face-to-face interviews with 18 Malay women (eight from urban [Kuala Lumpur] and ten from rural areas [Kelantan] in Malaysia) using open-ended questions framed upon HBM. Phase I also involved English-Malay translation, back-translation and analysis of findings using Giorgi's data analysis framework and NVivo version 10. A total of 18 women (Table CS23.1) were interviewed in Kuala Lumpur and Kelantan, Malaysia. Participants in this study were among Malay women. They were those who had attended cervical screening clinics on at least one occasion, in any of the government clinics or hospitals that offered cervical screening. The clinics or hospitals were in the areas of Kuala Lumpur (for urban) and Kelantan (for rural) only. According to the statistic by NCR (2011), women in Malaysia could be suffering from cervical cancer between the ages of 20 and 75 years. Thus participants of the cervical screening were between the ages of 20 and 75 years only. This study excluded the women who refused to participate and those who were not approached by the 'gatekeepers' (gatekeepers in this current study were among the health personnel and were responsible for carrying out this study at their sites; see Mander, 1992). Chinese and Indian women were not included in this study, as this study only focused on investigating Malay women in Malaysia. Since this study is only focused on the clinics under the monitoring of Ministry of Health Malaysia, only government clinics and health centres were involved in the research areas in Kuala Lumpur and Kelantan.

Purposive sampling was used in this study to select the participants. This approach also allowed for probing of respondents' backgrounds, in respect of age, marital status, socioeconomic background and number of uptakes (McCaffery et al. 2006). Samples were not chosen randomly as not every member of the particular community is eligible to partake in this study. Purposive sampling was appropriate to further the knowledge of Malay women about cervical screening and their experiences towards the service. This technique was adopted as the participants' backgrounds were identified accordingly with the criteria listed. The target group for this study were Malay ethnic, aged from 20–75 years who attended the government clinics between 9am and 5pm from Sunday to Thursday in Kelantan and from Monday to Friday in Kuala Lumpur.

Malay, as the largest ethnic population in Malaysia, was chosen as the target group due to its record of the least diagnosed cervical cancer cases, according to the National Cancer Registry from 2002 until 2007, followed by the Chinese and Indian women (NCR 2003–2005; NCR 2011). Saturation is reached at a point where similar themes were provided as answers to the questions posed (Mason 2010). However, in this particular study, not all the questions that had reached saturation were void, as some were retained in order to expand themes and to help with the discovery of new information. Saturation points were discovered as the transcription process occurred simultaneously during the interview process.

Data collection and analysis

Semi-structured interviews were carried out with women who attended the selected centres in urban (Kuala Lumpur) and rural (Kelantan) settings, for cervical screening, as can be seen in Figure CS23.2. The qualitative phase was a crucial level in which the researcher gained a better understanding of the cervical cancer prevention behaviours among the targeted population (Creswell 2006). Data collection was conducted in 'Malay' as their first language. A small number of participants were chosen as it is valuable to understand Malay women's experiences of using the cervical screening service. It took at least one to two days to explore and to draw a conclusion after each conversation before starting a new interview. Also, the time scheduled for interviews depended on what free time the participant had and not all who were invited could or were willing to participate in the interview. As the two locations were separated geographically, the researcher's time to interview more participants was limited. The number of interviewed participants met the research objectives and fulfilled the research purpose.

Data collected and analysed at this stage were aimed at developing an instrument to follow on quantitative phase II. The data collection was performed by face-to-face narrative interviews, using open-ended questions, to gain information from the participants on life experience and knowledge of cervical cancer (Watson et al. 2008). Each interview was

Table CS23.1 Summary of sociodemographic profile of participants

Participants' Profile	Urban	Rural	n = 18	(%)
Average age of respondents	41 years old	35 years old	-	-
Age range	24–62 years old	26–54 years old	-	-
Number of years married				
0–10	2	5	7	(38.9)
11–15	3	3	6	(33.3)
21 and above	3	2	5	(27.8)
Occupation				
Own business	3	1	4	(22.2)
Unskilled worker	2	1	3	(16.7)
Housewife	3	8	11	(61.1)
Husband's occupation				
Own business/	2	4	6	(33.3)
Self-employed	2	0	2	(11.1)
Administrative	1	0	1	(5.6)
Skilled worker	1	1	2	(11.1)
Unskilled worker	0	2	2	(11.1)
Defence	0	1	1	(5.6)
Manufacturing	2	0	2	(11.1)
Retired	0	2	2	(11.1)
No information				
Number of children				
1–2	2	7	9	(50.0)
3–4	3	2	5	(27.8)
5–6	0	1	1	(5.6)
7–8	1	0	1	(5.6)
No information	2	0	2	(11.1)
Number of pap smear screens	2	6	8	(44.4)
1–2	3	2	5	(27.8)
3–4	2	1	3	(16.7)
5–6	1	1	2	(11.1)
11 and above				

audio-taped, guided by an interview protocol and guide, and also by the recommendations of the regional ethics committee. The structure and nature of the interview were guided by questions based upon the Health Belief Model's framework of behavioural change approach to health. A gatekeeper was used to help facilitate the study. On the day of meeting the gatekeeper, the researcher also checked the environment's condition was suitable for inter-views. During the interview sessions, notes were taken with an electronic recorder as well as field notes. Field notes were written inclusive of the facial expressions or body language of the participants and were also assisted by using drawings to illustrate more detail about the situation (Flick 2009).

In phenomenology, bracketing is essential for underpinning the Husserlian method. In Giorgi's phenomenological research method, the application of bracketing is a process to prove validity and demonstrate the phenomenological approach throughout the research process, not only during the data collection but also during data analysis (Gearing 2004). In order to learn about the participants' lived experiences, the researcher had to set aside her own knowledge on cervical cancer to allow the story to be told naturally.

Data were analysed using Giorgi's data analysis framework (De Castro 2011; Giorgi 2005; Whiting 2002). In addition to Giorgi's framework, NVivo software was also used assist in the analysis of data and this involved the following steps:

1. Interviews were conducted by the researcher who 'bracketed' during that particular time.

2. The raw data were then transcribed, translated and back-translated. Subsequently, the researcher decided to use a computer-aided qualitative data analysis to help with cod-ing. Through coding, themes emerged accordingly and supported the aims of the study. Emerging themes were either similar to or different from one participant to another.

3. Transcripts were uploaded into NVivo to allow the process. NVivo also helped the researcher to see the statements made by participants being placed under certain themes. Coding data using NVivo saves the researcher's time and also helps to organise complex data.

4. From there, themes were extracted, sub-themes were recognised and data were organised (Table CS23.2).

5. Finally, these themes were organised again and this stage eliminated redundancy of themes and also all codes evolved were clustered in a bigger theme.

6. Transferability of data was ascertained through comparison with previous studies.

The aforementioned steps have considered the application of NVivo computer-aided data analysis software to assist with the analysis process, especially in theming the transcribed data. After the interviews were transcribed, audio data were transferred into written form, entered in the computer, backed-up, and printed. The transcription process was carried out immediately after the researcher completed each interview. It took about two months to complete all 18 interviews. The challenge that the researcher had to face during the transcrip-tion process was when it came to the dialect used by the Kelantanese women (in rural areas).

Translation and back-translation were completed according to Brislin's Seven Step Translation Model, adapted by Lopez et al. (2008). The researcher applied NVivo to ease the organisa-tion of data management. NVivo made a tremendous contribution in organising the theming process and producing the themes by coding (cluster) the related statements made by the participants into nodes (themes).

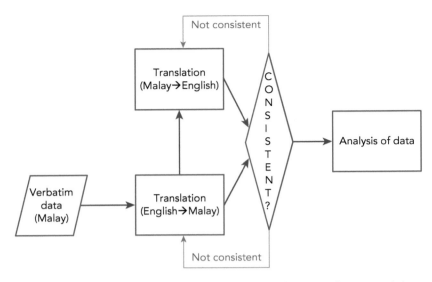

Figure CS23.2 Translation procedures adapted from Brislin's Translation Model

Findings and discussion

Five main themes emerged in Phase I of this study that informed objectives 1 to 3, namely individual beliefs, action, knowledge and experiences, improvements, and existing and desirable campaigns. These five themes provided key information in the development of Phase II (quantitative survey). They (Table CS23.2) could also inform relevant authorities and stakeholders about appropriate future actions that were necessary in this domain of health.

> **Theme one** focused on individual participant beliefs. These beliefs described the perceived intentions of participants towards cervical cancer and Pap smear testing. Four sub-themes emerged from theme one, namely perceived benefits, perceived severity, perceived susceptibility and perceived barriers. These sub-themes portray the participants' perceived intentions and feelings on having to attend cervical screening. Perceived barrier elements were the most frequently mentioned sub-themes compared with other categories.
>
> **Theme two** identified the outcome of the actions taken. Actions were those by the individual themselves or those cued by others. Sub-themes which emerged were based on participants' own awareness, their personal knowledge or the advice they received from the doctors or nurses that they met. Actions by individuals were also informed by the cues of the health providers during campaigns, to invite women to come and undergo their cervical check-ups.
>
> **Theme three** emerged from knowledge and experiences that participants had regarding cervical cancer and cervical screening. It was recognised that some knowledge and experiences differed from one participant to participant, depending on location, age and other social factors. These expressions were equally important as they highlighted what they knew, did not know or had confusion about on the particular subject matter. They

also shared their positive and negative experiences about their first screening, which was valuable as their first impression towards the overall screening process.

Theme four explains about improvements. These themes need further attention and understanding as they include the way the participants developed themselves through the knowledge and experiences that they had regarding cervical cancer and cervical screening, to finally come out with the ideas and suggestions to improve the attendance figures for cervical screening. They shared their ideas and they hope to be heard.

Theme five described the existing and desirable campaigns for the women to get screened for cervical cancer. From the experiences shared, there were a variety of campaigns used which included advertisements: on television, in newspapers, in magazines and at clinics, or from friends or the general public. In addition, many participants were not satisfied and thought that there was room for improvement, stating greater use of social media and other desired campaigns including letter of invitations and phone calls from clinics, tokens of appreciation, improved television adverts and greater involvement of health providers.

Table CS23.2 Summary of themes and sub-themes emerged from Phase I interviews

Themes	Sub-themes	Sub-sub-themes
Individual beliefs	Perceived barriers	Embarrassment
		Frightening
		Painful
		Time
		Religion/Beliefs
		Health practitioner's gender
		Support
		Lack of promotion
		Lack of education
		Lack of awareness
		Other difficulties
	Perceived benefits	Curiosity
		Act Fast
		Health urgencies
		Results oriented
	Perceived severity	Feeling impossible at first
		Seriousness
	Perceived susceptibility	Worries
		Family history
Action	Individual behaviours	Awareness
	Cues to action	Invitation from nurse
		Phone calls
		Tokens during campaign
		Free of charge screening
		Information sharing

(continued)

Table CS23.2 *(continued)*

Themes	Sub-themes	Sub-sub-themes
Knowledge and experience	Knowledge	Knowledge on screening
		Expectation from screening
		Understanding on cervical cancer
		Reasons for pap smear
	Experience	Post-test
		Treatment/service
		First time (when/experience)
		Experience on screening
Improvement	Suggestions	Instruments used (for screening)
		Increase awareness
		More promotion at rural areas
		Talks/meeting
		More exposure through TV
		Provide more pamphlets
		Enforcement
		Encouragement from health provider
		Threaten
		Tokens of appreciation
		Visit to residential areas
		Approaches by health provider
		Invitation from doctor/nurse
Campaigns		

Conclusion

In Malaysia, research on promoting cervical cancer awareness and prevention using health marketing strategies is still relatively new as most other related studies in this area explored from the medical perspective. Findings from this timely study have highlighted the benefits from deploying behavioural change marketing for cervical cancer awareness and prevention, as set out in the objectives. This platform study will also be used to address prevention of cervical cancer in Indian and Chinese ethnic groups in Malaysia, which have currently a higher incidence of this disease. Future linked quantitative studies should consider which behavioural change strategies are most effective among this cohort; do socio-demographic factors influence this population's beliefs about cervical screening; is there a relationship between socio-demographic factors and behavioural change strategies; and is there a relationship between individual beliefs and behavioural change strategies?

Case study questions

1. Explain how the Health Belief model formed the basis of Phase 1 research.
2. What are advantages and disadvantages of purposeful sampling approach? What other sampling strategies might have worked in this study?

3. Why were translation and back-translation conducted as part of this study? Explain how Brislin's Translation Model enhanced this process.

4. What is meant by the term 'bracketing'?

5. Other than Giorgi's framework, what other framework(s) for analysis might be considered appropriate for this study?

6. How would you use the findings from Phase 1 to undertake quantitative research, specifically a national survey for Phase 2?

References

Creswell, J.W. (2006) *Qualitative Inquiry And Research Design: Choosing Among Five Approaches.* London: Sage Publications.

De Castro, A. (2011) Introduction to Giorgi's existential phenomenological research method. *Psicología desde el Caribe.*

Dowling, M. (2006) 'Approaches to reflexivity in qualitative research', *Nurse Researcher*, 13(3): 7–21.

Ezat, W. and Aljunid, S. (2010) 'Cost-effectiveness of HPV vaccination in the prevention of cervical cancer in Malaysia', *Asian Pac J Cancer Prev*, 11(1): 79–90.

Flick, U. (2009) *An Introduction to Qualitative Research.* London: Sage Publications.

Gearing, R.E. (2004) 'Bracketing in research: A typology', *Qualitative Health Research*, 14(10): 1429–1452.

Giorgi, A. (2005) 'The phenomenological movement and research in the human sciences', *Nursing Science Quarterly*, 18(1): 75–82.

Gu, C., Chan, C.W., He, G.-P., Choi, K. and Yang, S.-B. (2013) 'Chinese women's motivation to receive future screening: The role of social-demographic factors, knowledge and risk perception of cervical cancer', *European Journal of Oncology Nursing*, 17(2): 154–161.

Gu, C., Chan, C.W., Twinn, S. and Choi, K.C. (2012) 'The influence of knowledge and perception of the risk of cervical cancer on screening behavior in mainland Chinese women', *Psycho-Oncology*, 21(12): 1299–1308.

Kumar, H. and Tanya, S. (2015) 'A study on knowledge and screening for cervical cancer among women in Mangalore city', *Annals of Medical and Health Sciences Research*, 4(5): 751–756.

Lopez, G., Figueroa, M., Connor S. and Maliski S. (2008) 'Translation barriers in conducting qualitative research with Spanish speakers', *Qualitative Health Research*, 18(12): 1729–1737.

Mander, R. (1992) 'Seeking approval for research access: The gatekeeper's role in facilitating a study of the care of the relinquishing mother', *Journal of Advanced Nursing*, 17(12): 1460–1464.

Mason, M. (2010) *Sample size and saturation in PhD studies using qualitative interviews.* Paper presented at the Forum Qualitative Sozialforschung/Forum: Qualitative Social Research.

McCaffery, K., Waller, J., Nazroo, J. and Wardle, J. (2006) 'Social and psychological impact of HPV testing in cervical screening: A qualitative study', *Sexually Transmitted Infections*, 82(2): 169–174.

National Cancer Society Malaysia, N. (2010) Types of Cancer. Online at: www.cancer.org.my/quick-facts/types-cancer/ (accessed 1 May 2016).

NCD (2010) National Strategic Plan For Non-Communicable Disease (D. C. D. Non-Communicable Disease Section (NCD), Trans.) (1st edition, p. 40). Putrajaya, Malaysia: Ministry of Health Malaysia.

NCR (2003) *The First Report of The National Cancer Registry Cancer Incidence in Malaysia* (M. o. H. M. National Cancer Registry, Trans.). In G.C.C. Li, Halimah Yahaya, T.O. Lim (eds) (p. 192). Kuala Lumpur: National Cancer Registry.

NCR (2003–2005) *Cancer Incidence in Peninsular Malaysia 2003–2005* (trans J.K. Awam). In D.S.R. Dr. Gerald Lim Chin Chye, Dato' Dr Halimah Yahaya (eds), (p. 92). Kuala Lumpur: Jabatan Kesihatan Awam, Ministry of Health Malaysia.

NCR (2011) *National Cancer Registry Report, Malaysia Cancer Satatistics - Data and Figures 2007.* In I.T.N.S.O Zainal Ariffin (ed.) (p. 126). Putrajaya, Malaysia: Ministry of Health, Malaysia.

Oon, S.W., Shuib, R., Ali, S.H., Hussain, N.H.N., Shaaban, J. and Yusoff, H.M. (2011) 'Factors Affecting Health Seeking Behaviour Among Kelantanese Women on Pap Smear Screening'. International Conference on Humanities, Society and Culture, IPEDR vol. 20. Singapore: IACSIT Press.

Othman, N.H. and Rebolj, M. (2009) 'Challenges to cervical cancer screening in a developing country: the case of Malaysia', *Asian Pacific Journal of Cancer Prevention*, 10: 747–752.

Rosenstock, I.M., Strecher, V.J. and Becker, M.H. (1988) 'Social learning theory and the health belief model', *Health Education & Behavior*, 15(2): 175–183.

Stretcher, V. and Rosenstock, I.M. (1997) The Health Belief Model. In Glanz, K., Lewis, F.M. and Rimer, B.K., (Eds.). *Health Behaviour and Health Education: Theory, Research and Practice*. San Francisco: Jossey-Bass.

Tavafian, S.S. (2012) *Predictors of Cervical Cancer Screening: An Application of Health Belief Model*. doi: 10.5772/27886.

Watson, R., McKenna, H., Cowman, S. and Keady, J. (2008) *Nursing Research Designs and Methods*. New York: Elsevier.

Whiting, L.S. (2002) 'Analysis of phenomenological data: Personal reflections on Giorgi's method', *Nurse Researcher*, 9(2): 60–74.

Wong, L., Wong, Y., Low, W., Khoo, E. and Shuib, R. (2008) 'Cervical cancer screening attitudes and beliefs of Malaysian women who have never had a pap smear: A qualitative study', *International Journal of Behavioral Medicine*, 15(4): 289–292.

24

Making India open-defecation-free

Lessons from the Swachh Bharat Mission – Gramin process evaluation

Anurudra Bhanot, Vinti Agarwal, Ashutosh Awasthi and Animesh Sharma

The Swachh Bharat Mission – Gramin (SBM–G) has been one of the most ambitious projects undertaken by the Government of India to achieve an open defecation free (ODF) status for its villages. It combines a twin approach of financing toilets with government administrative support to achieve this objective. A year after its launch, a process evaluation of the SBM–G was conducted by BBC Media Action. The results have been encouraging, albeit with some gaps that would need to be addressed to ensure the results of the campaign are sustainable post the initial stimulus provided by the intervention. This requires programme managers to focus on a total hygiene and sanitation approach in their social behavioural communications and remove any gender stereotyping on the use of toilets.

Introduction

With an expected growth rate of 7.6% in 2016–2017, India has emerged as one of the fastest-growing economies in the world (World Bank 2016). Despite this significant economic achievement, the country continues to grapple with poor sanitation. Open defecation is one of the major sanitation challenges that the country faces. Around 595 million people, nearly half the population of India, defecate in the open. That constitutes 90% of the people in South Asia and 59% of the 1.1 billion people in the world who practise open defecation (UNICEF n.d.). In rural areas of the country, only 45% of the households have a sanitary latrine (National Statistical Survey Organisation 2016). Different sanitation programmes over the past six decades have had limited success in promoting use of sanitary latrines and reducing open defecation in India (WaterAid 2008).

The unique challenge of achieving a status of complete freedom from open defecation lies in a combination of the unavailability of sanitary latrines as well as the cultural sentiments surrounding latrine usage. It has been found that mere availability of latrines is not enough to encourage use. In a recent survey of sanitation attitudes and practices in over 3,200 households in India, it was found that more than 40% of households with a working latrine had at least one member who still defecated in the open (Coffey *et al.* 2014). Therefore a policy of construction of latrines alone, accompanied without a change in attitudes and social norms surrounding open defecation, would not guarantee latrine use.

To accelerate the efforts for achieving universal sanitation coverage, the Prime Minister of India launched the Swachh Bharat Mission on 2 October 2014. Swachh Bharat Mission – Gramin (SBM–G) is the rural component of the mission that seeks to improve solid and liquid waste management activities in rural areas and make villages open-defecation-free (ODF) by 2019 (Ministry of Drinking Water and Sanitation n.d.). SBM-G guidelines recommend use of community-led and community-saturation approaches for motivating households to construct sanitary latrines, and community-based monitoring and vigilance activities to create peer pressure on the outliers to stop open defecation. For assisting households living below poverty line (BPL), the government provides a financial incentive of up to INR 12,000 per household for constructing a sanitary latrine (Ministry of Drinking Water and Sanitation 2014).

The Government of India and associated key stakeholders, with a view to assess the progress under SBM–G a year after launch, instituted a process evaluation in 2016. This was deemed necessary to identify approaches and processes that have been successful in reducing open defecation to subsequently enable replication across the country. The knowledge gleaned from this would also serve to inform decisions regarding social investment in sanitation in India.

Research approach

A process evaluation was conducted between March and April 2016 in 17 'champion districts' recognised by the Government of India's Ministry of Drinking Water and Sanitation, for using innovative approaches to implement SBM–G. These approaches showed promise in yielding the early results of programme achievements. Financial support for conducting the process evaluation was provided to BBC Media Action by the Bill and Melinda Gates Foundation (BMGF).

Table CS24.1 Districts assessed

Sr.	Districts studied	State	Number of districts
1.	Faridabad	Haryana	1
2.	Churu, Jalore and Udaipur	Rajasthan	3
3.	Indore and Harda	Madhya Pradesh	2
4.	Durg and Raigarh	Chattisgarh	2
5.	Khagaria, Vaishali and West Champaran	Bihar	3
6.	Angul and Gajapati	Odisha	2
7.	East Khasi and West Khasi Hills	Meghalaya	2
8.	Mandya and Koppal	Karnataka	2
Total number of districts studied			17

An independent research agency, Sambodhi Research and Communications Pvt. Ltd., was commissioned to hire, train, supervise and monitor field interviewers for gathering data from the study districts (see Table CS24.1).

The research used a mixed-methods approach using both qualitative and quantitative data for assessment purposes. This consisted of:

1. A quantitative survey of 1,700 households that had constructed latrines under the SBM–G programme (100 households were surveyed in each of the 17 districts).

2. An audit (physical inspection) of the latrines that had been constructed by the households surveyed.

3. A total of 85 in-depth interviews with key programme implementation staff (five interviews were conducted in each of the 17 districts, three with the officers at the district/block level, and two with the functionaries at the village level).

4. A total of 47 focus group discussions with community members in 85 villages. Discussions were conducted among males, females and community opinion leaders in villages that had been declared ODF by the district administration. A small sample of villages that had not yet become ODF was also included to understand the problems and barriers faced in eliminating open defecation.

Survey interviews were conducted with the head of each household, with certain interviews also carried out with a female member of the household based on her availability at the time of interview. The survey quantitative data were analysed using statistical packages of SPSS and STATA, while qualitative data were analysed using content analysis.

Research findings: common approaches

Overall, the 17 'champion districts' have performed well in putting SBM–G high on the development agenda, and have been successful in motivating households to construct and start using latrines to make villages open defecation free. Some of the overarching strategies/approaches that have worked well across the study districts include:

a. **High involvement of district leadership**: The District Collectors and Chief Executive Officers of Zilla Panchayats provided the impetus and direction for the implementation of the SBM–G programme. The district leadership was reported to have been instrumental in setting up the agenda for planning, creating resources, and leveraging the support of other departments like health, education, public health engineering and Panchayati Raj. It also enlisted corporate social responsibility (CSR) and non-governmental organisation (NGO) support for capacity strengthening of project implementation teams, and monitoring the progress on a regular basis. Day-to-day operations of the programme on the other hand were reported to be managed by the District Programme Coordinator (DPC) and the Block Development Officers (BDO) who worked with the village functionaries for implementation at the community level.

b. **Pivotal role played by local governance members and community motivators**: In implementing the programme at the village level, the village headman (*sarpanch*) across the champion districts emerged as the lynchpin in promoting the programme, and connecting the district administration and the village communities. The community motivators (*Swachhta Doot*, *Swachhta Prerak* and village functionaries) also reportedly played a key role as the interpersonal communicators responsible for mobilising and motivating individual households to construct and use sanitary latrines. Figure CS24.1 depicts the key players involved in the implementation of the SBM–G programme.

c. **Usage of community approaches to total sanitation (CATS)**:[1] All districts used some or the other form of community led total sanitation (CLTS)[2] to trigger demand for sanitary latrines at the village level. Districts that had received training and orientation in using CLTS seemed convinced of its effectiveness and also seemed to be

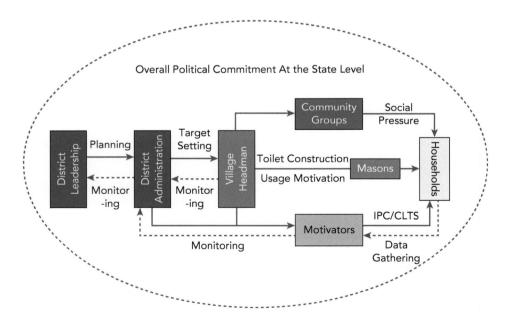

Figure CS24.1 Key players in the implementation of SBM-G

practising it more vigorously. The success of the CLTS implementation approach was aptly summed up in the words of the District Officer of Harda: "We were initially apprehensive that CLTS would not work, especially when the people facilitating CLTS were all newly trained and had no prior experience. However, to our amazement they were able to make a gram panchayat open defecation free within 15 days." Another official from Vaishali district in Bihar explained villagers' reaction when the district team facilitated social mapping in their village: "Most community members were shocked to notice two things – first the vast area within village that was being used for open defecation, and second the proximity of such areas to their residences and fields. This acted as a big spark for the entire village." Yet another district official's comment on the effectiveness of CLTS was "CLTS measures shake people to their core by conveying in no ambiguous terms that they are ingesting human faeces even if a single person in their village defecates in the open."

d. **Innovative promotional methods**: All the districts reported using a variety of promotional methods to create awareness about sanitation and the SBM–G programme. Nearly all districts used processions and sloganeering by schoolchildren, and *swachhta saptaha* (sanitation week) celebrations in schools and villages: among the many community-linked sanitation initiatives adopted, a very popular one is a march that is done by schoolchildren across the village on the theme of open defecation. Schoolchildren have the unique advantage of being more open to receiving and processing messaging related to the importance of a village being ODF and its impact on reducing disease especially among young children. Hence they become harbingers of change. Distribution of pamphlets, use of posters/wall-paintings, *nukkad natak* (street plays), and cultural programmes around sanitation were also important promotional tools. Some districts also reported using video films and radio jingles. Discussion findings also reveal that some of the information, education and communication (IEC) initiatives used in most districts had been tailored to the local situations. For instance, most districts created sub-campaigns within the umbrella SBM–G campaign with themes that resonated well with local issues and culture. Udaipur, for example, launched the 'Garvilo Mewar' campaign to invoke the Rajputana pride, while Indore launched the 'Lota Jalao' campaign to motivate people to reject the practice of open defecation. Angul district organised ministerial visits to villages that achieved ODF status, while Mandya organised 'Autorickshaw Campaigns' and half-marathons by inviting sports celebrities to villages to promote latrine use.

e. **Local campaigns**: The use of local campaigns by individual districts worked well to support the umbrella SBM–G campaign in raising general awareness about sanitation and the SBM–G programme. Community meetings organised by the village headman, *panchayat* members, and block and district officials as well as interpersonal communication by the community motivators, served to influence sanitation behaviour change at the community and household level by creating discussion around the benefits of the programme. Findings from the household survey show that 78% of respondents interviewed learnt about the sanitation programme from the village *sarpanch*, while 84% mentioned that they were counselled by a *panchayat* member on the benefits of using sanitary latrines. Fifty-eight per cent of the respondents mentioned learning about SBM–G through attendance of community meetings organised on the SBM–G programme and construction of latrines. More importantly, a significant number of study respondents indicated that most community members were inspired to sign up to the programme by fellow community members who had already signed up. Community discussions thus triggered a 'demonstration effect' wherein a large number of households get inspired by those who are among the first ones to sign up under a new programme. Further, data indicated that counselling by the village headman or a *panchayat* member is strongly associated with construction of latrines and stoppage of open defecation by the households.

f. **Use of community incentives and penalties**: Findings from the district assessments also included the use of constant vigils by community groups to ensure that all members in households that had constructed latrines used them. Villagers reported using a variety of strategies such as whistle blowing, naming and shaming and imposing fines of up to INR 500 on those caught defecating in the open. Some districts implemented more specific initiatives. The grounds used for open defecation in Indore district, for instance, were cleaned and planted with variety of plants considered holy (such as the Tulsi plant) to discourage open defecation, while in Churu district such grounds were turned into playgrounds for children. Harda is the only district that reported using a strategy to incentivise the ODF villages by getting the dairy companies to pay a slightly higher price for milk bought from villages recognised as ODF by the district administration. Other strategies included giving preference to ODF villages for official meetings, arranging *sarpanch* visits to nearby ODF villages to invoke healthy competition, and organising 'Rural Olympics' where only ODF villages could participate. Most districts also organised '*Gaurav Yatras*' (pride walks) in villages that had achieved open defecation status.

g. **Decision influencers in latrine construction**: The village headman and the mason emerged as key persons in consultative decisions relating to latrine size, pan type, pit size and number of pits when constructing sanitary latrines, by the majority of households. Data from the household survey indicated that about 50% of households had consulted the village headman for advice on the size of latrine, while advice on the pan type, pit type and pit size was mainly sought from the mason.

h. **Water availability**: This emerged as one of the important factors in households' decisions to construct and use sanitary latrines. Nearly half (45%) of the households did not have water for use inside or near the latrine. Water scarcity and its impact on sanitary latrine usage emerged as important factors in almost all interviews conducted across all the districts. This problem was particularly serious in the water-deficient states of Rajasthan, Madhya Pradesh, Chattisgarh, Odisha and Mehgalaya. In Odisha's Gajapati district for instance, some villages facing acute water shortage refused to build latrines until the district administration sanctioned funds for the construction of proper drinking water supply systems in those villages.

Research findings: specific strategies used by different districts

While there were overarching observations across the districts, a few activities/strategies varied widely across the 17 districts. The activity that varied most across districts was the nature of the involvement by the district administration in the construction of household latrines:

a. In districts like Faridabad, Churu and Jalore, the district administration and local village governance played only a facilitating role by providing basic guidelines and financial

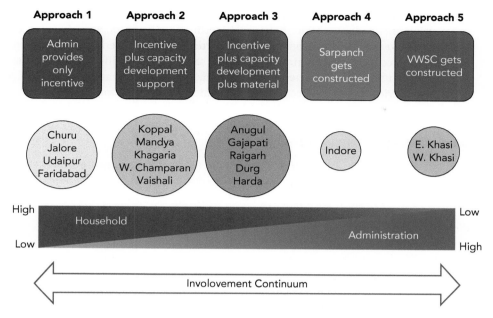

Figure CS24.2   Degrees of involvement

incentives to the households. On the other hand, latrine construction in the districts of East and West Khasi Hills in Meghalaya was managed completely by the Village Water and Sanitation Committee (VWSC). Somewhere in the middle of this continuum were districts like Angul and Gajapati which supported households constructing latrines by providing construction material and pans, and organising trained masons to meet the increased demand.

b. While most districts promoted financial incentives from the government to motivate households to construct sanitary latrines, Raigarh was the only district that delinked the financial incentive by motivating the households to use their own funds for constructing latrines. The district administration there completely relied on CLTS to trigger demand for latrines and behaviour change. It disbursed the incentive that was due to individual households as a collective fund, and encouraged the community to build or refurbish the community infrastructure such as community latrines or cement/concrete roads from that. It is expected that this approach is likely to have a higher chance of sustained latrine use, as the people who constructed these were motivated by the non-monetary benefits of latrine use.

c. The East and West Khasi Hills districts did not need to use any behaviour change communication strategy to motivate villagers to construct latrines as most people in the two districts were already using dry latrines (simple pit latrines). Dry latrines are not considered sanitary like the pour and flush latrines, but are less harmful than open defecation. The district administration used the incentive available under SBM–G to facilitate an upgrade of dry latrines into pour and flush sanitary latrines for individual households. The administration's strategy to strengthen and empower the Village

Water and Sanitation Committees to get latrines constructed ensured that latrine construction was consistent for all households in the village. It also increased cost effectiveness by the collective procurement of construction materials given the high transportation cost over mountains, and reduced the chances of pilfering or corruption by using community bargaining with raw material suppliers and masons. Some villages in the two districts opted for EcoSan latrines which are suitable for rocky soil and do not require water unlike pour and flush latrines.

Research findings: some pertinent issues

The findings also threw up certain aspects that may need to be re-examined, since they could become limiting factors in the way the programme is currently being implemented. Some of the key areas are:

a. Interviews with project staff and village communities suggest that some of the latrines being constructed may not be the two-pit sanitary latrine suitable for villages and recommended by international development organisations. Community focus groups and interviews with programme teams indicate that many latrines have single pits as deep as 12 to 28 feet (against the recommended 3.5 to 5.5 feet) (Ministry Of Drinking Water and Sanitation 2012). Some pits have been partitioned by placing a vertical slab. The main reason for digging deep pits is the belief that the pit will fill early if all members of the family use the latrine regularly. This increases the cost of construction, as people end up spending more for digging pits deeper than required. The majority of households (52%) consult the mason for the pit type and size. However, the masons may not provide correct advice due to ignorance or to increase their labour charges, since deeper pits take longer to dig and require more construction due to larger surface area. The average amount spent for latrine construction is INR 19,000 which is one and a half times the incentive offered by the government (INR 12,000). This reinforces the general perception that latrine construction is a 'costly affair' and demotivates the poorer households to construct latrines even with the availability of financial incentive as they may not be able to pay the remaining sum from their own sources.

b. Among households that are unable to construct very deep pits, the tendency is to let the women, children and the elderly use the latrine while the menfolk choose to continue defecating in the open. Survey results indicate between 4% to 8% households in certain districts have at least one family member who continues to defecate in the open even though there is a functional latrine at home.

c. There appear to be several reasons for open defecation by certain persons even when they have a functional latrine at home. While some large families find one latrine inadequate for use by all members, many prefer to defecate in the open believing that it is a healthier practice. In some communities, particularly in the northern states, women and girls find going outside for defecation a good opportunity to socially network with other women, as they tend to remained confined to their homes most of the time. Some people, particularly those in the older age group, are not habituated to the closed structure of the latrine.

d. The groups defecating in the open do create the perception that most people defecate in the open. This in turn reinforces the social norm that it is okay to defecate in the open, leading to the social acceptance of this behaviour. This often triggers the wheel in the opposite direction, pushing more people to go back to open defecation (see Figure CS24.3).

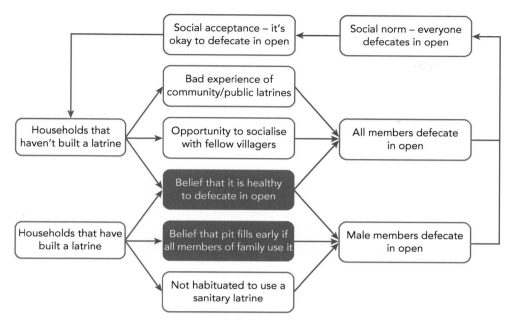

Figure CS24.3 The vicious cycle of open defecation

e. Making a village ODF (open defecation free) is an interdependent action that requires coordinated behavioural change among all households in the village. Unless everyone in the community shifts to consistent latrine usage, the benefits of disease and death reduction would not be realised. Any individual acting alone to build and use a latrine would incur a financial cost since the health benefits can be derived only if the entire village complies. It has been found that if all persons were to comply, the benefit to everyone in the village would be at its maximum (Mackie 2015; UNICEF 2015).

f. Two-thirds of households, particularly those from the northern states, reported constructing the latrines for the "safety and security" of women and girls. Interviews with community motivators and other village functionaries indicated that "safety of women and girls" is often used as a strong argument by them for promoting latrine construction among households. Using this strategy to promote latrines reinforces the perception that latrines are for use by women and girls only while men can continue to defecate in the open as they don't face any security and safety threat.

g. This strategy also exacerbates the gender stereotype among certain communities and religious groups by reinforcing the social norm that women and girls should remain confined within the home. While women and girls should certainly use sanitary latrines, they should be encouraged to use these for 'health' rather than 'gender' reasons. The health benefits of latrine usage must be emphasised since the health benefits cut across gender. This would be a stronger argument against open defecation.

h. Survey results indicate that about a quarter of the households continue to believe that open defecation is a healthier practice compared to usage of a sanitary latrine (see Figure CS24.4). Forty-five per cent of respondents did not practise handwashing with soap after defecation (see Figure CS24.5). Handwashing with soap before cooking and eating is also low at 10% and 29% respectively. This implies that while people in rural areas have constructed latrines under SBM–G, they may be unlikely to experience the benefits of sanitary practices given the continuation of an absence of handwashing with soap behaviour. Correspondingly if the incidence of diarrhoea and other infectious diseases does not reduce, people are unlikely to see the link between usage of sanitary latrines and the reduction in disease incidence. This poses the next challenge for SBM–G to take a more holistic approach in promoting sanitation and hygiene as an overarching goal rather than singular practices of only building latrines to achieve and sustain the goal of making villages completely open defecation free with a total sanitation-based approach.

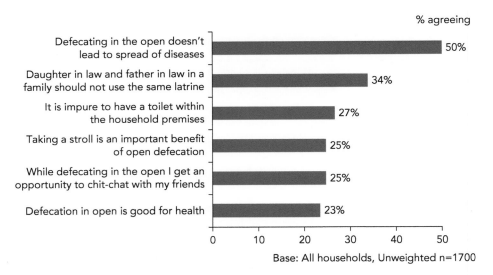

Figure CS24.4 Attitudes towards latrine use

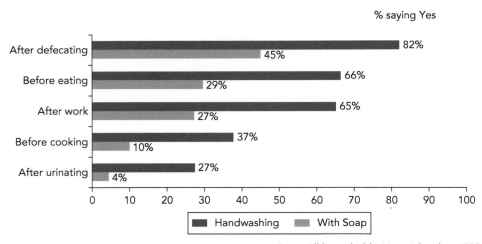

Figure CS24.5 Handwashing on specific occasions

i. Sustained use of sanitary latrines and handwashing are also likely to be influenced by the availability of water. An audit of latrines found that only about 55% of the households had water for use, while only 33% had soap near the handwashing area. The issue of water scarcity in certain districts of Rajasthan, Madhya Pradesh and Meghalaya was highlighted during community focus group discussions and interviews. This created a barrier for usage of sanitary latrines in these areas. Non-availability or scarcity of water was also one of the reasons cited by households that continued to have a family member defecating in the open.

Discussion and analysis

The findings of the study have indicated that the implementation of SBM–G across India will require a combination of 'push' and 'pull' strategies tailored to the specific needs and unique hydro-geological features of each district. The programme will also benefit from rigorous training of community motivators, *sarpanches*, masons and *panchayat* members on the use of CLTS for triggering demand for sanitary latrines. Further, masons and *sarpanches* would need to be educated on the recommended pit size and pit types, to ensure that people don't spend unnecessary amounts of money on deeper pits. Having too deep pits delays the decomposition of faecal sludge and may contaminate water tables thus affecting the realisation of the public health benefits of sanitation.

Interpersonal communication for promotion of latrine construction and usage must emphasise the health benefits of using sanitary latrines instead of the safety/security of women and girls. A gender-neutral approach that emphasises the health, hygiene, privacy, and dignity benefits of using sanitary latrines is likely to achieve more sustainable results.

The interdependence aspect of latrine usage also indicates that changing personal attitudes alone would not be sufficient for making villages ODF. The programme team must also work to change the social expectations of a sizeable number of community members that could culminate in a coordinated behavioural change among households in the village. An individual must be led to believe that compliance with the new norm is a legitimate expectation of the others that have chosen to comply, and non-compliance would invite punishment while compliance could imply rewards.

While elimination of open-defecation is the most critical outcome desired, CLTS interventions must also incorporate communication that seeks to address other personal hygiene behaviours relating to handwashing with soap after defecation and prior to cooking and feeding. Without a complete sanitation approach, the complete benefits of the SBMG programme may not accrue to communities.

Finally, sanitation programme implementation would benefit from a scientifically designed communication strategy to address the multiple barriers among different segments of households. Given the diversity of beliefs and barriers that affect sanitation behaviour, a 'one-size-fits-all' approach would be detrimental to the success of the programme. It would therefore be helpful to consider other non-uniform approaches, such as precision marketing of sanitation benefits. This approach, as the findings from the study clearly show, is more likely to help the programme address the multiple barriers across micro segments.

Case study questions

1. Would you describe the Government of India's rural sanitation campaign as a social marketing campaign? Explain your answer by discussing the marketing principles and processes used by the campaign.

2. The achievement of an open defecation free status by certain champion districts has required certain common strategies that have worked across districts. While some of them are native to India given its cultural context, which of these strategies could be replicated in other countries?

3. Certain districts also reported using a set of strategies that were customised according to local contexts. What were the local innovations and adaptations identified that could make sanitation campaigns more effective?

4. Social norms play an important part in the context of behaviour change at individual and societal levels. Explain how the rural sanitation campaign is addressing the prevalent social norms to achieve behaviour change in rural India.

5. Do you think the Government of India's strategy of supporting individual states to implement the campaign in a flexible way is a good strategy? Explain why you think so.

6. You are the creative head of an advertising agency hired by the Government of India to produce a public service advertisement for promoting the sanitation programme. What key message would you like to deliver through the advertisement?

7. The case has also highlighted some shortcomings and limitations of the sanitation campaigns. Which of these shortcomings would affect the sustainability of the total sanitation campaign?

Acknowledgements

All authors are from the Research and Learning Team at BBC Media Action, India. We acknowledge financing support for this study from the Bill and Melinda Gates Foundation (BGMF) and research data collection support from Sambodhi Research and Communications Pvt. Ltd.

Notes

1 CATS is an umbrella term used to describe a wide range of community-based activities that share the goal of eliminating open defecation, are rooted in community demand and leadership, focus on behaviour and social change, and are committed to local innovation. Source: www.communityledtotalsanitation.org/resource/unicef-community-approaches-sanitation-cats.

2 CLTS is an innovative methodology in which communities are facilitated to conduct their own appraisal and analysis of open defecation and take their own action to become open defecation free. Source: www.communityledtotalsanitation.org/page/clts-approach.

References

Coffey, D., Gupta, A., Hathi, P., Spears, D., Srivastav, N. and Vyas, S. (2014, December 14) 'Culture and the Health Transition: Understanding Sanitation Behaviour in Rural North India', Rice Institute Working Paper, 1–48. Online at: riceinstitute.org/wp-content/ . . . /download-pdf.php?pfile . . . /CultureSanitationIndia.pdf (accessed 10 October 2016).

Mackie, G.F. (2015) *What are Social Norms? How are They Measured?* Washington, DC: UNICEF. Online at: www.unicef.org/protection/files/4_09_30_Whole_What_are_Social_Norms.pdf (accessed 1 May 2016).

Ministry of Drinking Water and Sanitation, Government of India (n.d.) Online at http://sbm.gov. in/sbm/ (accessed 10 October 2016).

Ministry of Drinking Water and Sanitation (2012) *Handbook of Technical Options for On-site Sanitation.* New Delhi: Government of India. Online at: http://mdws.gov.in/sites/default/files/Final_ Handbook.pdf (accessed 10 October 2016).

Ministry of Drinking Water and Sanitation, Government of India (2014) *Swachh Bharat Mission-Gramin Guidelines.* Online at: http://sbm.gov.in/sbm/ (accessed 10 October 2016).

National Statistical Survey Organisation (2016) *Swachtha Status Report.* New Delhi: Government of India.

UNICEF (n.d.) *Eliminate Open Defecation.* Online at: http://unicef.in/Whatwedo/11/Eliminate-Open-Defecation (accessed 10 October 2016).

WaterAid (2008, November) *Feeling the Pulse, A Study of the Total Sanitation Campaign in Five States.*

World Bank (2016, June 20) *Manufacturing and Services, Urban Consumption Keep Indian Economy on Growth Path.* Online at: www.worldbank.org/en/news/press-release/2016/06/20/manufacturing-and-services-urban-consumption-keep-economy-on-growth-path (accessed 10 October 2016).

Index

AASM *see* Australian Association of Social Marketing
ABC *see* Act-Belong-Commit campaign
abolitionists 254–255
access rights 514–516, 522
accessibility 98
accountability 13, 244, 251, 460
Act-Belong-Commit (ABC) campaign 19, 113–114, 144, 482–491
action research 44, 122
'active' competition 13, 48, 201–204
addiction 375, 378
Adidas 189
Adkins, S. 242
advergames 239
advertising 16, 156, 158; Act-Belong-Commit campaign 482, 487; 'Black Ops' 239–240; bottled water 382; cervical screening 563; to children 234; drowning prevention 412, 413–415, 416–417; Facebook 236; Fife Project 366; native 237–239, 251; objectives 100; online 179, 237, 240; Porto Tap Water 388; promotion 105; regulation 207–208, 239; self-regulation 207; tobacco 88, 202, 208–209, 247n4, 463–464, 465–466; Walk to School 424–426
Advertising Standards Authority 239
advertorials 160–161
Agarwal, Vinti 567–579
agency 13, 42, 48, 182; building 43; collective 265; community social marketing 300; moral 153, 251, 256–259, 261–262, 265, 268, 273; social cognitive theory 61; structure and 37
agile marketing 354
Aguado Loi, Claudia X. 492–501

alcohol 5, 11; Alcoholics Anonymous 262–263; alcopops 202, 252; branding 173; commercial promotion of 7, 202–203, 221; community social marketing 297; competitive analysis 13, 191–192, 198, 199, 206; cooperation with industry 205–206; corporate social responsibility 207; health issues 252; regulation 207; research 140; as risk factor for drowning 406, 407, 413, 416; situation analysis 88, 89; social media 139; social norms campaign 62–63; *see also* drunk driving
Alden, D. 456
Alessi, Natalia 406–419
altruism 30–31, 256, 261
Amazon 223, 236
Ambassador School Programme 438–439
American Beverage Association 13
American Express 236
Amnesty International 243, 253, 254
Andrade, Marisa de 357–380
Andreasen, A.R. 6, 17, 39, 43, 56–57
Anholt, S. 388
Anker, T. 296–297
Anthropocene 2, 6
antibiotic prescriptions 311, 312–313, 314–325
antibiotic resistance (ABR) 18, 293, 310–312, 315, 319
Anwar-McHenry, Julia 482–491
Apple 43, 236
apps 139–140; Act-Belong-Commit campaign 487; drowning prevention 415–416; 'Moi(s) sans tabac' 446; Reduce Your Juice 165, 350; SIMPle 17, 320, 323–324; *Walk to School* 423; *see also* mobile technology

ARCBS *see* Australian Red Cross Blood Service
Arcelor Mittal 447
Arcila-Sierra, Jaime 462–467
Aristotle 489
Arwidson, Pierre 444–452
Asda 255
ASH 193, 299
aspirations 27, 60
asset-based approaches 104, 297, 357–358, 359
Attar, Farid ud-Din 250, 251, 264
Attenborough, David 113
attitudes: branding 383; Cycle Against Suicide 438; emotional connections 456; fear messages 166; Less Eyes than Belly Movement 455, 458–459; Making India Open Defecation Free 568, 576, 577; multiple interpretation of value 296; Porto Tap Water 383, 388; Sea for Society 330, 539; SME environmental behaviour in Pakistan 469; social change 460; speeding laws 526; waste management in Lebanon 394–395; Wheels, Skills and Thrills 529; *see also* beliefs
audience research 153, 158–165, 181; *see also* target audiences
Auletta, Ken 237–238
Auschwitz 263
Australia: Act-Belong-Commit campaign 19, 113, 482–489; drowning prevention 19, 406–419; fear campaigns 167, 169; International Tobacco Control Policy Evaluation Project 209; mental health 483, 484; Ningaloo Reef 20, 47, 271, 509–524; obesity 221; plain packaging 210; Reduce Your Juice 18, 346–356; road safety 10; textile waste 503; Walk to School 19, 420–431
Australian Association of Social Marketing (AASM) 15
Australian Red Cross Blood Service (ARCBS) 90–92
Ávila-García, Liliana Andrea 462–467
Ávila, Marian Lorena Ibarra 462–467
Awagu, C. 170–171
awareness raising 434, 436–437, 438, 440, 443
Awasthi, Ashutosh 567–579

Baggini, Julian 230
Bagozzi, R. 10, 71
Bajaj, Neha 502–508

Bakan, Joel 217, 224, 231
Baker, M.J. 231, 241
Bakewell, Joan 171
Bakonyi, Angelina 502–508
Balonas, Sara 103–104, 173, 381–389, 453–461
Bangladesh 7, 293, 476, 503, 505, 506
Bardus, Marco 390–405
Barry, Michael 478–481
Basil, D.Z. 170–171, 200, 201
Baum, Laura 492–501
beauty industry 226
behaviour change 4, 5–6, 12, 13, 17; Act-Belong-Commit campaign 486; barriers to 38; benefits of 455; branding 383; cervical screening 564; client orientation 27; collective orientation 38; costs of 109–110; Cycle Against Suicide 437, 438, 442; digital marketing 179; drowning prevention 407, 408, 412, 415–416, 417; emotions 153; ethical issues 279–281; fast fashion 506; fear messages 166; Food Dudes Programme 77; Less Eyes than Belly Movement 454, 456, 459; linked to social and systemic change 292; Making India Open Defecation Free 572, 575, 577; multi-layered engagement 417; outcome indicators 534; Porto Tap Water 383, 386–387, 388; product 106; Reduce Your Juice 351, 355; road safety 527, 532; SME environmental behaviour in Pakistan 474–475; social capital 66; social progress 297–298; stages of change theory 43, 53, 55–59, 78; stakeholder analysis 92; theory 53, 55, 76, 78; Walk to School 427, 428, 429; Wheels, Skills and Thrills 530; *see also* social change; systemic change
behavioural learning 351
behavioural reasoning theory (BRT) 78
behavioural repertoires 413, 416, 417
behavioural segmentation 94, 96
Belgium 331–332, 538
beliefs: Act-Belong-Commit campaign 486; behavioural norms 509; branding 383; cervical screening 562, 563, 564; co-evolution of 305; emotional connections 456; Health Belief Model 557–558; Making India Open Defecation Free 575, 576, 577; multiple interpretation of value 296; outcome indicators 534; SME environmental behaviour in Pakistan 469; social change 460; social movements 299; systems social marketing 303; values as 68; *see also* attitudes

belonging 483, 488–489
Bennett, Kathleen 310–328
Bhanot, Anurudra 567–579
'bigger picture' thinking 47
Biroscak, Brian J. 492–501
Bishop, D.B. 53
'Black Ops advertising' 239–240
Blair, Tony 46
blogs 176, 178, 179
Bloom, P.N. 14
Bogost, Ian 258
bottom-up approaches 178, 245, 299–300, 302, 305, 538
brand ambassadors 4
branding 13, 17, 154, 172–176, 224, 382–383; brand level competition 201; brand name 168; commercial 128–129; Cycle Against Suicide 437, 443; importance of 456; intervention mix 105; Less Eyes than Belly Movement 19, 459; logos 234; 'Moi(s) sans tabac' 19, 448; Olympic Games 235–236; point of sale marketing 464, 465, 466; Porto Tap Water 19, 173–174, 385, 388; relationship marketing 12; SIMPle 321, 322, 323; social 157; symbolic meaning 388; *Walk to School* 424; Wheels, Skills and Thrills 528
breastfeeding 41–42
Breen, Jim 434, 438
Brennan, Linda 76, 406–419
Brenner, Maria 555–566
Britton, Easkey 112
Broome, Benjamin J. 329–338
Browning, R. 192–193
BRT *see* behavioural reasoning theory
Bryant, Carol A. 492–501
Bryson, J. 90
Buchanan, D.R. 30–31
Bug Run School Days 319, 322
Bukowski, Charles 262, 263
Burger King 189, 190
business 221–223
butterfly effect 64
Buyer Behaviour and Decision Making Model 312
buyer power 194–198
Buzzfeed 240

Cacioppo, J.T. 172
Cadbury Schweppes 240

Cadwalladr, Carole 223
Callan, Aoife 310–328
Cameron, David 242
Camus, Albert 265, 273, 301
Canada 209
cancer: cervical screening 20, 96–97, 110, 135–136, 284, 555–566; colorectal cancer prevention 20, 298, 300, 304–305, 492–501; exposure to toxins 392; segmentation 99
Cancer Research UK (CRUK) 269, 272
Cannon, Amy 432–443
Cannon, T. 103
capitalism 217, 240–241, 259, 262
cardiovascular disease 478–479
Carling 191–192, 207
Carol, H. 362
cars 94, 109, 110, 202, 252
categorical imperative 285
Catholic Church 281
causal dynamics 302, 303, 305, 307
Cause Related Marketing 242
Cawley, Desmond 555–566
CBPM *see* Community Based Prevention Marketing
CBSM for Systems Change 20, 140, 298
celebrities 63–64, 443, 480; Cycle Against Suicide 436, 442; Fife Project 364; health communication in India 161, 545, 547, 548; Making India Open Defecation Free 158, 572
CEOs *see* chief executive officers
cervical screening 20, 96–97, 110, 135–136, 284, 555–566
Chase Manhattan 245
chief executive officers (CEOs) xxxii, 7, 8, 229
children: child labour 208, 254, 476, 503, 505; constriction of play 271; Convention on the Rights of the Child 266–267; dual influence between parents and 395; Fife Project 357–380; leather and tanning industry 476; Making India Open Defecation Free 571; marketing to 232–234; obesity interventions 257–258; point of sale tobacco marketing 466; reverse socialisation 414, 416; smoking 462, 463; *Walk to School* 420–431; waste management in Lebanon 395, 400–401, 402

Childs, Edith S. 291–292, 296, 299–300, 305
China 14–15
choice 28, 218, 251; 'choice architecture' 271, 286; Fife Project 363, 374; Nuffield Ladder of Interventions 268
Christian Aid 243, 244
Christmas 119, 120, 121
Churchman, C.W. 140, 293
citizenship 489
civic engagement 64
civic virtue 489
Civil Rights movement 84, 299
civil society 14, 39, 206
Clapp, J.D. 62–63
client orientation 27, 28, 29–33, 40–42, 47, 122; community social marketing 301–302; marketing mix 240; Porto Tap Water 386; relationship marketing 44; right to participation 269
climate change xxxii–xxxiii, 1–2, 17, 253; 'bigger picture' thinking 47; critical marketing 215, 245; moral agency 256, 262; Porto Tap Water 266; self-destructive collaboration as driver of 265; social ecological theory 64; social movements 299; systems social marketing 307; systems thinking 257; water 381; as 'wicked' problem 148
'clock' and 'cloud' problems 140
CLTS see Community Led Total Sanitation
co-creation 37, 43, 147, 153; branding 176; client orientation 122; colorectal cancer prevention 492, 499, 500; Cycle Against Suicide 440; digital marketing 176, 177, 178, 179; exchange theory 67; Fife Project 18; knowledge 306; Less Eyes than Belly Movement 456; Meals on Wheels 344; relationship marketing 47; right to participation 269; Sea for Society 330; theories 78; value triad 69
co-delivery 105, 111, 145, 269; community-based social marketing 432; marine interventions 540; Sea for Society 330; value triad 69
co-design 105, 111, 145, 269, 537; Cycle Against Suicide 441; Fife Project 104, 357–358, 360, 361, 364; marine interventions 540; Sea for Society 330; value triad 69
co-discovery 69, 105, 111, 145
co-evaluation 360, 361, 379

co-opetition 204
co-production xxxii, 104, 357–358, 359, 360, 361, 364
Coca-Cola 1–2, 14–15, 43, 128; advergames 239; advertising 16; branding 168, 172, 224; Christmas 120, 121; competitive analysis 189; marketing spend 225, 252; Olympic Games sponsorship 235–236, 261; shareholder value 240; WWF partnership 199, 200
Cochrane Collaboration 201
Codina, V. 271
collective agency 265
collective orientation 27–28, 36–38, 39, 40–42, 44, 48, 301–302
collusion 259
Colombia 19, 89, 221, 462–467
colorectal cancer (CRC) 20, 298, 300, 304–305, 492–501
coltan 254
commercial marketing 11, 14, 16, 21, 215, 300–301; client orientation 29; competition 13, 39; corporate power 7–8; digital 177–178; 4Ps 103; relationship marketing 12; role of 39–40; values 70–71, 73
commercialisation 220, 236
commitment 45, 46, 47, 127; Act-Belong-Commit campaign 483, 488–489; Cycle Against Suicide 436; long-term 460; partnerships 105; Sea for Society 306, 537, 538, 539; systems social marketing 306
common pool resources (CPRs) 510, 512–516, 517, 519–520, 522–523
commons problems 20, 90, 512, 522
communication 16, 155–166, 181, 224, 417; abolitionists 254; branding 172–176; drowning prevention 19, 412; effectiveness of 456; emotions 153–154, 171–172; fear messages 146, 154, 166–171, 181–182, 279, 282, 526; Fife Project 361, 362; health communication in India 20, 161, 542–554; Less Eyes than Belly Movement 459; Making India Open Defecation Free 572, 577; media channels 110; 'Moi(s) sans tabac' 450; objectives 100; partnerships 105; point of sale marketing 464, 465; Porto Tap Water 384, 386–387, 388; promotion 105; Reduce Your Juice 165, 349, 350; role of research

158–165; social change 460; target
audiences 98; *see also* media
community activism 455, 459
Community Based Prevention Marketing
(CBPM) 107–108, 493–499
Community Based Systems Dynamics 498
community incentives 572
community influences 60
Community Led Total Sanitation (CLTS)
570–571, 573, 577, 578n2
Community Readiness Model (CRM) 18,
36, 297, 339–344
community social marketing (CSM) 18,
294, 296–302, 307, 432–433; Act-Belong-
Commit campaign 19, 482; Cycle Against
Suicide 19, 435; Meals on Wheels
339–340, 343, 344; Reduce Your Juice
351; Walk to School 423; Wheels, Skills
and Thrills 20
competition 4, 16, 189–206, 210; 'active'
13, 48, 201–204; competitive strategy
92; Cycle Against Suicide 19; ethical
issues 279, 280, 281; levels of 200–201;
'passive' 13, 38, 48; Porter's competitive
forces 194–199; price 231; *Walk to School*
19; waste management in Lebanon
394, 396
competitive analysis 12–13, 86, 188,
189–206, 210; Act-Belong-Commit
campaign 484–485; colorectal cancer
prevention 497–498; Cycle Against
Suicide 434–436; drowning prevention
407–408; fast fashion 503–505;
health communication in India 543;
Less Eyes than Belly Movement 454;
'Moi(s) sans tabac' 446; Porto Tap Water
382; Reduce Your Juice 348; Sea for
Society 330–331; SME environmental
behaviour in Pakistan 469; Walk to
School 426
competitive orientation 27, 28, 38–40,
41–42, 44, 48
compromise 10, 30
conditioning 351
condoms 35, 36, 86, 108, 160;
embarrassment 109; ethical issues 276,
277, 281, 282; female 135; teenagers 101;
see also safe sex; sexual behaviour
Conservative Party 241–242
consumer satisfaction 43, 101–102, 127,
231, 240

consumption xxxiii, 2, 7, 8, 226, 253;
bottled water 382; children as 'consumers
of everything' 233, 234; containment 272;
corporate encouragement of 240, 241;
energy 347, 354; environmental issues 6;
fast fashion 502; inequalities 228; self-
harm 252; slow fashion 506; systemic
change 293
containment 272
content marketing 237
convenience 109, 384, 386
Convention on the Rights of the Child
(CRC) 266–267
Cooper, Karen 357–380
cooperation 6, 187–188, 204–206, 271,
301; business 221; exchange theory
67; inequalities 228; social capital 66;
systems social marketing 305
Corbett, C. 527
Cormican, Martin 310–328
corporate social responsibility (CSR)
13, 206–207, 216, 224, 242–244, 245;
consumer collusion 259; Good Samaritan
parable 260–261; health communication
in India 543, 545, 547, 553; Making India
Open Defecation Free 570; SMEs 19;
waste management in Lebanon 403
corporations 7–8, 217, 221, 222–225, 235,
245, 436; *see also* commercial marketing
corporatisation 181
cosmetics industry 226
Costa Rica 293
costs 104, 106, 109; clothing industry 504,
505; Making India Open Defecation Free
574; of mental health problems 483–484;
Reduce Your Juice 349; SIMPle 325; SME
environmental behaviour in Pakistan 469,
472, 473; waste management in Lebanon
397, 398, 402; whale shark tourism in
Ningaloo Reef 519, 521–522; *see also* price
counteraction 272
CPRs *see* common pool resources
CRC *see* Convention on the Rights of the Child
creative orientation 27, 33–36, 40–42, 44,
47, 84
credibility 43, 46, 110, 234, 416; branding
383; Cycle Against Suicide 442; digital
marketing 177; Porto Tap Water 387;
Wheels, Skills and Thrills 529
crime 95, 531
critical capacity 272

critical marketing 12, 18, 21, 38–39, 214–249, 264; business 221–223; corporate charm and power 223–225; corporate marketing methods 232–244; harm done by corporate marketing 225–227; individual responsibility 217–220; inequalities 228–229; need for regulation 244–245; salt intake reduction 19; selfishness 229–232; SMEs 19; tobacco control 19, 466

critical thinking 39, 77, 261, 265, 301; abolitionism 255; community social marketing 298; definition of 220; evaluation 144–145; Fife Project 359, 369–370, 378; individual responsibility 217; long-term 292

CRM see Community Readiness Model

CSM see community social marketing

CSR see corporate social responsibility

cultural capital 528, 530

cultural effects models 156

cultural symbolism 60, 172; see also symbolic meaning

culture: social norms 62; waste management in Lebanon 402

culture of desire 227

Cycle Against Suicide 19, 144, 300, 432–443

cyclical research 122

cycling 86

Daily Motion 179

Dalai Lama 227

Dante Alighieri xxxiii, 263–264, 265

Darnton, A. 112–113

data analysis: cervical screening 561; Reduce Your Juice 349–350; Walk to School 428

data collection: cervical screening 559–561; Reduce Your Juice 349–350; Sea for Society 332–333; SIMPle 323–324, 325; Walk to School 427; see also interviews; surveys

Davies, Jennifer 444–452

Day, Barry 168

De Bono, Edward 27

de Chernatony, L. 172

debt 252–253

deceit 16, 31

deferred gratification 196, 198

demand 241

Democratic Republic of Congo 254

demographic characteristics 94, 95, 96, 177

Denmark 489

denormalisation 61

dental health 74–75

deontological theory 285, 286

depression 488

deprivation 95, 526

Descartes, René 265

Devaney, Michelle 329–338

developmental research 145

Dewhirst, T. 40

Diageo 39, 180, 199, 202–203, 205, 224, 236, 252

dialogue 47, 105, 111, 177, 337

Dias, Ana Sofia 103–104, 173, 381–389

Dickens, Charles xxxii, 259

DiClemete, C.C. 55, 56–57, 59, 75

diet: branding 173; changing habits 484; client orientation 29; ethical issues 278; Food Dudes Programme 77–78; inequalities linked to 95; salt intake reduction 19, 478–481; segmentation 94; social norms 61; see also food

differentiation 195, 231, 242, 465

digital divide 181

digital marketing 157, 176–181; Cancer Research 269, 272; Reduce Your Juice 18, 347, 355; Walk to School 19, 424–426; see also online advertising

digital technology xxxiii, 37, 154, 265; Fife Project 360–361; online research 139–140; Reduce Your Juice 346, 349, 350, 354, 355; SIMPle 17; Walk to School 423; see also apps; mobile technology; social media; websites

dignity 262, 265, 273

Dillman, D. 538

diseases 5, 252, 265; Making India Open Defecation Free 576; waste management in Lebanon 392, 394

Disney Corporation 240

displays 463, 464–465, 466

distribution 13, 110, 224, 384, 387

Doll, R. 101

Domegan, Christine: cervical screening 555–566; critical perspective 39; Meals on Wheels 339–345; relationship marketing 46–47; Sea for Society 329–338, 534–541; SIMPle 310–328; social change 500; value co-creation 456, 499

Donnar, Glen 406–419

Donne, John 11
Donnelly, J. 268, 269
Donovan, Rob 46, 54, 76, 77, 113–114, 170, 482–491
downstream social marketing 89, 484
Doyle, P. 240–241
driver training 525, 527–532
drowning prevention 19, 162, 171, 406–419
drugs 110, 157; community social marketing 297; driving under the influence of 168, 169; ethical issues 278, 281, 284; harm minimisation 282; inequalities 228; NE Choices 44–45; process evaluation of programme implementation 143; as risk factor for drowning 406, 407
drunk driving 9, 10, 137, 168–169, 205–206, 284
Duane, Sinead 46, 310–328, 329–338
Dubner, S.J. 71
Dubois-Arber, F. 145–146
Duffy, Sarah 509–524
Dummett, Mark 254

early adopters 475
ecigarettes 32–33
ecocentrism 226
economic crisis 15, 222
education: colorectal cancer prevention 497; drowning prevention 412; drugs 143; Fife Project 357–380; health behaviour 60; India 244; inequalities 228; mental health 439; normative 61; road safety 526, 527; Scottish health education 173; social capital 64; waste management in Lebanon 393, 398–399, 400; see also schools
Einstein, Mara 239
Eisenhower, Dwight D. 222, 269
Eiser, Dick 35
El Harakeh, Amena 390–405
electronic cigarettes 32–33
Elliott, Barry 32
Elliott, R. 388
email 17, 423, 427, 428, 538
emotion xxxi–xxxii, 35, 153–154, 170, 456; abolitionists 254; behavioural science 77; branding 383, 388; communication 171–172, 181–182; digital marketing 179; empathy 123; Porto Tap Water 388; storytelling 178; values 68

empathy 26, 34, 36, 120, 123; client orientation 27, 29–30; communication 165–166; research 145, 147
empowerment 16, 43, 48, 154, 182, 455–456; branding 173; community-based social marketing 432–433; Fife Project 358, 361, 378; participation 111, 269; participatory research 132; relationships 537; Waves of Freedom 112
energy: community social marketing 297; competition in energy conservation 201; oil, gas and mining in Exmouth 511; Reduce Your Juice 18, 165, 346–356; Sea for Society 330, 331, 332, 333–337; waste management in Lebanon 398
engagement: corporate social responsibility 242; creative orientation 27; Cycle Against Suicide 437, 440–441, 442; Less Eyes than Belly Movement 459; Wheels, Skills and Thrills 529; workplace 424–426
environmental factors 59–60, 87–89
environmental issues 6, 39; behavioural reasoning theory 78; community social marketing 297; fast fashion 502; food waste 453, 458–459; India 244; marine environments 534, 535; moral agency 256; RARE Pride campaigns 296; resource degradation 514–516; Sea for Society 18, 20, 305, 306–307, 329–338, 536; Shell's pollution in Nigeria 243; SMEs in Pakistan 19, 468–477; social norms 61; waste management in Lebanon 394, 398; whale shark tourism in Ningaloo Reef 47, 511, 518, 521; wicked problems 509; see also climate change; pollution
equity 513, 521–522, 523
ESMA see European Social Marketing Association
ethics xxxii, 217, 276–290; fast fashion 20, 506; key challenges 279–284; Meals on Wheels 18; messages 170–171; online research 140; qualitative research 135; salt intake reduction 19; sustainable tourism 20; theories 285–287, 289
ethnicity 95
ethnography 35
European Commission 453
European Social Marketing Association (ESMA) 15
European Union (EU) 18, 20, 305, 329, 455, 483

evaluation: Act-Belong-Commit campaign 486, 487; co-evaluation 360, 361, 379; Cycle Against Suicide 442; developmental 107; engaging with young people 362; ethical issues 280; Fife Project 367, 379; importance of 388; Making India Open Defecation Free 20, 568–569; objectives 100; process 143, 324–325, 362, 379, 428, 429, 486, 487, 568–569; Reduce Your Juice 353–354; research 141, 144–146; Sea for Society 20, 537; SIMPle 323–325; SME environmental behaviour in Pakistan 473–474; strategic planning 86; system indicators 535–536; systems social marketing 303, 304; Walk to School 19, 427–428, 429

Everett, Edward 153

Ewing, Aldenise 492–501

exchange 9–10, 11, 15, 18, 30–31, 292, 302; communication 165–166; community social marketing 294; complex relational 46–47; ethical issues 282; exchange theory 53, 55, 67–74, 75–77, 78; mutually beneficial 27, 30, 48, 67–68, 75, 191, 225, 270; systems social marketing 303

exercise see physical activity

expectations 65, 180, 577

expenses 288–289

experiential view 122

Facebook 16, 236, 252, 295; Cycle Against Suicide 440, 441; digital marketing 176, 177, 180; drowning prevention 415; health communication in India 548; Less Eyes than Belly Movement 458; online research 139–140; Operation Transformation 59, 180; personalised content 362; Porto Tap Water 388; Walk to School 426

fairness 513, 521–522, 523

family influences 60

fast fashion 20, 72–73, 226, 502–508

Fatworld 257–259

fear 146, 154, 166–171, 181–182; ethical issues 279, 282; road safety 526

feedback: process evaluation 362, 379; research 141, 144; systems social marketing 303

feminism 299

fiduciary imperative 7–8, 207, 221, 272

Fife Project 18, 104, 298, 357–380

Fiji 489

financial services 241–242

Fitzgerald, Christine 339–345

Fitzgerald, Niall 207

flexible offerings 32–33

Florida Prevention Research Center (FPRC) 95, 107–108, 492–500

flu vaccinations 72, 73

fluoridation 278, 281, 282

focus 153

focus groups 135, 136, 137; ethical issues 284; fear messages 167–168; Making India Open Defecation Free 139, 569, 574; Meals on Wheels 36, 132, 343, 344; SIMPle 132–133, 312–313; waste management in Lebanon 395, 396–397

Foege, W.H. 5

food: branding 128; commercial promotion of unhealthy 7, 202, 203; competitive analysis 13; failure of new products 156; focus groups 136; food safety 46; health issues 252; inequalities 230; Less Eyes than Belly Movement 19, 453–461; Meals on Wheels 339–345; right to participation 269; Safefood campaigns 176–177; salt intake reduction 478–481; school dinners 194; Sea for Society 330, 331, 332; segmentation 95; social ecological theory 64; waste management in Lebanon 399, 402, 403; see also diet; obesity

Food Dudes Programme 77–78

Food Standards Agency 202

Foolspeed campaign 162, 164

Ford 245

Ford, Harrison 113

Ford, Henry 230

FOREST 220

formative evaluation indicators 535–536, 537

formative research 141, 142–143, 145, 159; colorectal cancer prevention 499; community social marketing 300; Reduce Your Juice 348; SIMPle 311–313, 317, 325; waste management in Lebanon 19, 395

formulating the offer 86, 102–114, 280

4Ps 4, 103; see also marketing mix

Foxhall, G. 232

FPRC see Florida Prevention Research Center

Framework Convention on Tobacco Control 462–463

framing 105, 112–113, 299
France: 'Moi(s) sans tabac' 19, 444–452; Sea for Society 331–332, 333–337, 538
free products 108–109
free riders 513, 514
Freedom Food 255
Freeman, Olivia 432–443
Freire, Paulo 132
French, J. 383, 456, 460, 500
Fujihira, Haruka 420–431
funding: salt intake reduction 480; SIMPle 317; Walk to School 423; waste management in Lebanon 394
FUSIONS project 455

Gallopel-Morvan, Karine 444–452
Galvin, Sandra 310–328
gambling 174–176, 299
games: advergames 239; obesity interventions 257–259; Reduce Your Juice 18, 165, 349, 350, 352–353, 354–355; SIMPle 17, 18
gamification 139–140, 352, 354–355
Gandhi, Mahatma 2
Geels, F.W. 6
gender 95, 244, 575, 577; see also women
General Electric 224
general practitioners (GPs) 311–325
geo-demographic characteristics 94, 95, 99
Gettysburg Address 152–153, 154, 182
Ghosh, Amitav 1, 2
Giorgi, A. 561
Gladwell, Malcolm 147
Glanz, K. 53
global warming see climate change
GMB see group model-building
goals 15, 60, 68, 122; see also objectives
Goldsmith, R.E. 232
Good Samaritan, parable of the 260–261
Goodwin, Fred 222, 247n5
Google 2, 140, 181, 236, 447
Gordon, R. 500, 536, 538
governance: local 570, 573; stakeholder analysis 92
GPs see general practitioners
Greece 331–332, 538
Green, L.W. 494
Grindle, M. 177, 178, 179
group interviews see focus groups
group model-building (GMB) 498–499
Guignard, Romain 444–452

Gulliver, A. 433
Gundlach, G.T. 14
Gurrieri, L. 536, 538

H&M 73, 504, 506
Hamilton, Ian 239
Hansen, W.B. 61
happiness 227, 244, 271, 285
Hardin, G. 6, 512
Hare, Dr 224
harm chain analysis 86, 200
harm reduction 33, 282
Harris, Fiona 138, 139
Hartman, Kellye 420–431
Hastings, Gerard: community activism 455, 459; research 120; segmentation and targeting 229; social change 500; social norms 61–62; systematic reviews 209; value co-creation 499; values 68; voices of the poor 7
hazard merchants 201–202, 204, 207, 210, 215, 217
HBM see Health Belief Model
Health Belief Model (HBM) 557–558
health issues 5, 7, 9, 10; advertorials 160–161; branding 173; cervical screening 20, 96–97, 110, 135–136, 284, 555–566; client orientation 29–30; colorectal cancer screening 20, 298, 300, 304–305, 492–501; community social marketing 297, 300, 301; competitive analysis 13; Convention on the Rights of the Child 266–267; critical marketing 18; CSR in India 244; definition of health 196; dental health 74–75; emotional communication 171–172; ethical issues 278, 285; exchange 30–31; fear campaigns 154; Fife Project 362–363, 374–376, 377–378; health communication in India 20, 161, 542–554; HIV/AIDS prevention 145–146; industrial epidemics 252; inequalities 228; leather and tanning industry 476; London cholera epidemic 218; Making India Open Defecation Free 20, 567–579; Meals on Wheels 18; Nuffield Ladder of Interventions 267, 268; prescription drugs 133–134; research 126–127; Safefood campaign 176–177; salt intake reduction 19, 478–481; Sea for Society 330, 331, 332; seasonal flu 71–72; segmentation 95, 98, 99; SIMPle

18, 41, 132–133, 310–328; social and relational contexts 361; social capital 64; thalidomide 126–127; vaccinations 72, 73; waste management in Lebanon 391–392, 398, 400; *see also* alcohol; cancer; mental health; obesity; smoking
health professionals 447, 450, 488; *see also* general practitioners
Health Sponsorship Council (HSC) 174–175
hedonism 69, 70
Heineken 181
Helman, S. 527–528
Henley, N. 46, 170
herd instinct 76
high blood pressure 478–479
Higham, Charles 245
Hilary, John 244
Hill, Ronald Paul 7, 119
Hilton, S. 385, 456
HIV/AIDS 17, 33, 35, 145–146, 283; community social marketing 297; competitive analysis 198; health communication in India 542–543, 549, 553; medications blocked by pharmaceutical industry 231–232
Hobbes, Thomas 67
Hoek, J. 40
Hogan, Michael 329–338
Homestay programme 440
Horrocks, Neil 346–356
Hovmand, Peter S. 492–501
HPV *see* Human Papillomavirus
HSC *see* Health Sponsorship Council
Hult, T. 343
human-centred design 107–108
human nature 269, 271
Human Papillomavirus (HPV) 555–566
human rights 14, 251, 265–269, 271, 273; ethical issues 286, 289; fast fashion 502, 503, 505
humanist research 125–126
humanity 263–264, 273
Hunger Project 231
Hunt, S.D. 45
Husserl, E. 558
Huxley, Aldous 234, 264, 265
Hyndman, D. 66

'I Know What I'm Doing' 19, 162, 171, 198, 406–419
IAM *see* Institute of Advanced Motoring

identity: corporate 242; 'responsible citizen' 397; smoking 197; social capital 65; youth 361
Idobro 547
IHBP *see* Improving Healthy Behaviors Programme
IM *see* Interactive Management
images 162–163, 165
Imlach, Hamish 33
implementation: Act-Belong-Commit campaign 486–487; ethical issues 280; Fife Project 379; research 141, 143–144; strategic planning 86; systems social marketing 304
Improving Healthy Behaviors Programme (IHBP) 542–554
India: clothing industry 504; corporate social responsibility 244; GDP 7; health communication 161, 542–554; Making India Open Defecation Free 20, 139, 154, 158, 298, 305, 567–579
indicators 20, 306–307, 534–540
indigenous people 218–219, 226–227, 269–271
individual responsibility xxxiii, 13–14, 217–220, 227, 245, 256, 378
individualism 8
industrial epidemics 252
inequalities xxxii, xxxiii, 6–7, 11, 17; austerity 199; corporate marketing 228–229; critical marketing 215, 216; digital divide 181; ethical issues 278, 280; food 230; health 95, 98, 286; lack of protest 259; role of big business 223; systems thinking 257; as 'wicked' problem 148
infant formula 243–244
informed consent 282, 286
infrastructure: common pool resources 512; community social marketing 300, 301; drowning prevention 413; Making India Open Defecation Free 573; SME environmental behaviour in Pakistan 469; systems social marketing 303
Instagram 139–140, 177, 180, 440
Institute for Social Marketing 35, 130, 202, 257, 278
Institute of Advanced Motoring (IAM) 528, 532
institutions 456
insurance 198, 531–532
integrated research 145–146

Interactive Management (IM) 332, 333, 335, 337
intermediaries 110–111
International Social Marketing Association (iSMA) 15
International Tobacco Control Policy Evaluation Project 209
'intervention mentality' 120–121
intervention mix 103–114, 159, 300, 388
interviews 132–137; cervical screening 558–562; colorectal cancer prevention 497; Fife Project 372–373, 374; GPs 312–313, 324; Making India Open Defecation Free 139, 569, 574; Meals on Wheels 36, 343, 344; SIMPle 132–133
intuition 147
iPhone 254
Ireland: cardiovascular disease 478; Cycle Against Suicide 19, 433–442; Meals on Wheels 18; Sea for Society 331–332, 538; SIMPle 18, 311–326
iSMA see International Social Marketing Association
Israel 538
Italy 331–332, 333–337, 538
ITT 245

Jacobs Douwe Egberts 255
Japan 489
Japan Tobacco 12
Jihadist radicalisation 489
Jobber, David 193, 207, 235
Jocz, K.E. 10
Joiner, T.E. 488–489
joint creation of value 30
Jones, J. 65–66
Jones, S. 40, 139
journalism 238–239, 251
Joyce, John 329–338
Jumper-Therman, P. 341

Kamayoqs 218–219
Kant, Immanuel 285, 289
Kapitan, Sommer 502–508
Kappel, K. 296–297
Katz, E. 156
Kelley, E. 15
Kelly, Samantha 178
Kelpsa, Laurynas 255
Kennedy, Ann-Marie 72, 502–508
Kenny, Patrick 61–62, 432–443

Key Informant Interviews (KII) 36, 132
key informants 340, 341–343
King, Martin Luther 83–84, 85, 114
Kiribati 292–293
Kirk, M. 112–113
Klein, Naomi 217
knowledge: cervical screening 562, 564; colorectal cancer prevention 498; community-based social marketing 432–433; energy efficiency 351, 354; Fife Project 378; outcome indicators 534; Sea for Society 306–307, 336, 536–537, 539; social epistemology theory 53, 63–64; waste management in Lebanon 394–395, 397, 398
Kotler, P. 9, 67, 74, 106, 110
Koushede, V. 483
Kreuter, M.W. 494
Krueger, Richard 124, 125
Kubacki, Krzysztof 179, 266, 420–431

La Boétie, Etienne de 259, 261
labelling 480
Layard, Richard 7, 67, 70, 100, 195
Layton, Roger A. 296, 302–303, 509–524
Lazarsfeld, P. 156
Lazer, E. 15
lean product development 107–108
learning 105, 128; behavioural approach 351; Interactive Management 337; participation 111; participatory research 132; research 120, 121–122; Sea for Society 306, 537, 538, 539; strategic planning 85–87; systems social marketing 306
Leathar, D.S. 171
leather and tanning industry 468–476
Lebanon 19, 390–405
Lee, Harper 123
Lee, W.B. 40
Lefebvre, R. Craig 31, 66, 67, 97, 171, 538
Less Eyes than Belly Movement 19, 67, 174, 453–461
Leventhal, H. 166
Levi, Primo 263–264, 265
Levitt, S. 71
Levitt, Theodore 192
Lewin, Kurt 54, 55, 122
lifestyles 43, 101, 179; bottled water 382; digital marketing 179; Malaysian Healthy Lifestyle Campaign 556; waste management in Lebanon 392

Lincoln, Abraham 152–153, 154, 182
linear sequential models 156–157
LinkedIn 139–140, 177
Linquivst, Sven 273
Little, Jo-Anne 346–356
lobbying 241–242
local campaigns 572
local governance 570, 573
localised meso systems 296
logic models 317, 353–354
logos 4, 234, 235, 369, 370; Less Eyes than Belly Movement 456, 457, 459; 'Moi(s) sans tabac' 448; Porto Tap Water 385
Lopez, G. 561
Lorenz, Edward 64
Louis C.K. 265
'low-hanging fruit' 475
Lowe, Jez 127–128, 129
Lowry, R. 68
loyalty schemes 12, 43, 252
Lu, S. 505

M&S 255
macro environment 87–88
macro-social marketing perspective 509
Madi, Farah 390–405
Maibach, E.W. 67–68
Making India Open Defecation Free 20, 139, 154, 158, 298, 305, 567–579
Malaysia 20, 555–566
Mandela, Nelson 123–124, 146
manipulation 16, 31, 156, 215, 224–225, 286
Maori 269–271
marine environment 18, 20, 329–338, 534, 535, 540
market research 86, 231; ABC Campaign 113–114; ethical issues 280; systems social marketing 303; *Walk to School* 427; *see also* research
marketing: to children 232–234; corporations 224; dark side of 6–7, 245; exchange process 9, 10, 11; Fife Project 364–367, 369; harm done by corporate 225–227; history of 231; moral maxims for 287; power of xxxiii, 2, 3–4, 8; social impact of 216–217; use of the term 16; *see also* advertising; commercial marketing; critical marketing; social marketing
marketing mix 103, 114, 202, 240–241, 272; ethical issues 279, 282; Fife Project 366; Porto Tap Water 19, 384, 387; SIMPle

314–323; waste management in Lebanon 19; *see also* intervention mix; place; price; product; promotion
Marlboro 2, 128, 168, 197
Marques, Susana 39, 46–47, 453–461
Marr, B. 341, 343
Martin, Micheál 40–41
materialism 2, 215, 226, 233, 244
maternal health 542–543, 545–550, 552–554
Mays, D. 177
Mazzonetto, Marzia 329–338
McAndrew, Ryan 346–356
McArdle, M. 39, 78
McConnell, Jack 40–41, 272
McDermott, Laura 16
McDermott, R. 144
McDonald's 2, 12, 128, 255; advergames 239; competitive analysis 189, 190–191, 193; Olympic Games sponsorship 235–236, 261
McGinnis, J.M. 5
McGonigal, Jane 180
McHugh, Patricia 39, 64, 90, 145, 306, 329–338, 534–541
McKenna, Frank 526
McKenzie-Mohr, D. 330
McMahon, E.M. 433
Meals on Wheels (MOW) 18, 36, 132, 339–345
measurability 100–101
media 110, 156; Act-Belong-Commit campaign 482; Cycle Against Suicide 435, 436, 440, 441, 442, 443; drowning prevention 412; health communication in India 547, 548; images of smoking 369–371; Less Eyes than Belly Movement 458; 'Moi(s) sans tabac' 447, 450; Porto Tap Water 387; regulation 238; Walk to School 423, 424–426; *see also* radio; social media; television
Medical Research Council (MRC) 126–127, 129, 323
mental health: Act-Belong-Commit campaign 19, 113–114, 144, 482–491; Cycle Against Suicide 19, 144, 432–443; inequalities 228
merchandising 464
Mercier, Anna 444–452
meso systems 296
message content 154, 157, 162, 168, 171, 362, 386

methodology 125, 129–140, 323, 332; *see also* data collection; research
Mill, John Stuart 289
Miller Brewing 205–206
Miller, M.C. 231
mission creep 283
MMR vaccine 43, 46
mobile phones 179, 180, 254, 265; Act-Belong-Commit campaign 487; drowning prevention app 415–416; health communication in India 547; SIMPle 323–324
mobile technology: drowning prevention 412; health communication in India 554; individual agency and empowerment 182; 'Moi(s) sans tabac' 446; Reduce Your Juice 350; Walk to School 424; *see also* apps
'Moi(s) sans tabac' 19, 66–67, 300–301, 444–452
Monahan, J.L. 171
Monbiot, George 253
Mongolia 489
monitoring: abolitionists 254; common pool resources 517, 523; ethical issues 280; Fife Project 379; importance of 388; research process 141; strategic planning 86; systems social marketing 302, 303, 304; tobacco control in Colombia 465–466; whale shark tourism in Ningaloo Reef 519–520, 521
Moore, E.S. 13, 216–217
Moore, Martin 240
morality 13, 261; moral agency 153, 251, 256–259, 261–262, 265, 268, 273; moral maxims 287; moral values 68–71, 72, 292, 296; systems social marketing 302, 303; *see also* ethics
Morgan, R.M. 45
Morocco 504
Morozov, Evgeny 258, 265
motivation 30, 68; Making India Open Defecation Free 573; operant conditioning 351; Reduce Your Juice 348; road safety 527; social movements 298
MRC *see* Medical Research Council
Mulcahy, Rory 346–356
Mullins, J.W. 112
multi-media campaigns 362
Murdoch, Rupert 238
Murphy, Andrew W. 310–328

Murphy, Maurice 478–481
mutuality 68–71, 72, 261, 292, 296, 302, 303
mutually beneficial exchange 27, 30, 48, 67–68, 75, 191, 225, 270

Nairn, A. 233–234
narrative reviews (NRs) 129–131
native advertising 237–239, 251
natural resources 6
navigational aid, research as a 120, 121, 147
Nazi Germany 156, 245, 263
NE Choices 44–45
needs 27
nested enterprises 517, 520
Nestlé 244, 255
Netflix 238
networks 17, 72; community social marketing 298; Cycle Against Suicide 437, 438, 442; exchange 71; Fife Project 362–363; importance of 76; Sea for Society 306–307, 536–538, 539, 540; social capital 65, 66; social movements 299, 300; systems social marketing 296, 305, 306–307; waste management in Lebanon 393
new entrants 194–195, 199, 200
new product development 13, 107–108, 224, 264
New York Times 238, 239
New Zealand 269–271
NGOs *see* non-governmental organisations
Nike 2, 128, 168, 189, 195
Ningaloo Reef 20, 47, 271, 509–524
Noble Foods 255
Noble, G. 200, 201
non-governmental organisations (NGOs) 10, 545; corporate social responsibility 245; Cycle Against Suicide 436; drowning prevention 411; health communication in India 547; Making India Open Defecation Free 570; salt intake reduction 479, 480; tobacco control 193; waste management in Lebanon 393, 394
NORAD *see* Norwegian Agency for Cooperation and Development
norms 72, 217; co-evolution of 305; energy use 348; ethical issues 285; informal 515; Making India Open Defecation Free 568, 574, 575, 577; social capital 65; social cognitive theory 60, 61; social

determinants of behaviour 28; social norms theory 53, 61–63, 75, 78; wicked problems 509; young people 362
Norway 489, 538
Norwegian Agency for Cooperation and Development (NORAD) 469, 470, 471
NRs *see* narrative reviews
'nudging' 286
Nuffield Ladder of Interventions 267, 268
nutrition 10, 19, 339–345; *see also* diet; food
NVivo 561

Obama, Barack 7, 291–292, 298, 299–300, 305
obedience 259, 265, 273
obesity 2, 5, 17, 28, 199; children 271, 420, 421; commercial promotion of 221; community social marketing 297; costs of 198; fast food industry 193; inequalities 228; promotion of 203; Safefood campaign 159, 177; social ecological theory 64; systematic reviews 209; systems thinking 257, 293; as 'wicked' problem 148; Zamzee and Fatworld interventions 257–259
objectives 86, 100–101, 114; abolitionists 254; Act-Belong-Commit campaign 485–486; cervical screening 557; colorectal cancer prevention 493–494; Cycle Against Suicide 436–438, 442; drowning prevention 408–412; ethical issues 280; fast fashion 505–506; Fife Project 359; Less Eyes than Belly Movement 454–455; Meals on Wheels 343; 'Moi(s) sans tabac' 447; point of sale tobacco marketing 464; Porto Tap Water 383; Reduce Your Juice 349; research 122, 144; Sea for Society 536; SIMPle 314; SME environmental behaviour in Pakistan 471; systems social marketing 303; Walk to School 422; waste management in Lebanon 398
Oetting, E.R. 341
Ogilvy, David 39
Ogoni people 243
Oil of Olay 226, 228, 231
Olins, Wally 172, 383, 456
Oliver, John 237, 238, 239
Olympic Games 234–236, 261
online advertising 179, 237, 240
online research 139–140

online surveys: Reduce Your Juice 350; Sea for Society 538; *Walk to School* 427–428
operant conditioning 351
Operation Transformation 59, 180
orientations 27–42, 44, 47–48
Orwell, George xxxi, 219, 220, 245, 271, 307
Oxfam xxxii, 7, 8, 222, 223, 241, 259

P&G 236
packaging 13, 224; food labelling 480; plain 209, 210, 446; point of sale displays 465, 466; Porto Tap Water 384, 385; waste management in Lebanon 403
Packard, Vance 156, 231
Pakistan 19, 468–477, 503
Pankhurst, Emmeline 245
Pap smear screening 20, 135–136, 555–566
Parker, Kathy 236
Parker, Lukas 406–419
participation 103, 105, 111–112, 153, 456; Act-Belong-Commit campaign 489; audience research 160; colorectal cancer prevention 498; communication 165–166; community social marketing 300; Cycle Against Suicide 435, 440–441; digital marketing 179; ethical issues 282; Fife Project 360, 361, 362–363; Interactive Management 337; networks 538; right to 268, 269, 286
participatory research 18, 36, 132, 485
partnerships 17, 18, 36, 103, 105, 112; academic-community 492, 493, 494, 498–499, 500; Act-Belong-Commit campaign 482, 485, 487; community social marketing 294, 298, 340; Cycle Against Suicide 300, 436, 437, 442, 443; digital marketing 177; drowning prevention 412; health communication in India 20, 542, 543–544, 545, 546–550, 552–554; Less Eyes than Belly Movement 459; Making India Open Defecation Free 20; 'Moi(s) sans tabac' 19, 445, 447; Porto Tap Water 387; Quechua Indians 218–219; relational thinking 47; right to participation 269; Sea for Society 540; systems social marketing 305, 307; Walk to School 423; waste management in Lebanon 19, 393, 394, 403
'passive' competition 13, 38, 48
peer influences 60, 360, 361

Pepsi 12, 189
Peretti, Jonah 240
personal influencers 348
personalised content 362
persuasion 166, 231, 464
Petty, R.E. 172
pharmaceutical industry 128, 129, 133–134, 231–232
phenomenology 558, 561
Philip Morris 12, 39, 199
physical activity 19, 96, 297, 420–429, 439
Pickett, Kate 228
Picketty, Thomas 259
Piercy, N. 201
Pingeot, Lou 8, 222
Piwowarczyk, Joanna 329–338
place 4, 84, 103, 105, 110–111, 157, 240; audience research 160; corporate stimulation of consumption 241; digital place analysis 140; ethical issues 280, 282; formulating the offer 86; 'Moi(s) sans tabac' 449; Porto Tap Water 104, 110, 384, 385–386; SIMPle 319–320, 321–322; SME environmental behaviour in Pakistan 472; waste management in Lebanon 399
planning: abolitionists 254; competition 189; Cycle Against Suicide 437; systems social marketing 302; see also strategic planning
point of sale (POS) 19, 76, 89, 208–209, 221, 463–466
Poizeau, Marion 112
Poland 331–332, 538
policy 14, 497, 521; see also regulation
pollution: community social marketing 297; marine 330; Porto Tap Water 266; Shell 243; SME environmental behaviour in Pakistan 469, 471, 473; systems thinking 293; waste management in Lebanon 391–392; water 381
Ponting, Clive 230
Pope Francis 271
Popper, Karl 140
populism xxxii, xxxiii
Porter, Michael 194–199, 201
Porto Tap Water 19, 103–104, 106, 110, 173–174, 266, 381–389
Portugal: food waste 19, 453–460; Porto Tap Water 381–389; Sea for Society 331–332, 538
POS see point of sale

positioning 103, 105, 112–114, 157, 385
positive affect 171
positivist research 125–126, 127, 153
Potter, Iain 174–176
poverty 7, 17, 31, 231; ethical issues 278; India 244; Porto Tap Water 266; right to participation 269; water 381
power 11, 48, 241–244; balance of 74; buyers 194–198; competitive analysis 188; corporate 7–8, 222, 223; elite 259; institutions 456; marketing relationships 225; social capital 66; stakeholder analysis 91–92; suppliers 194–195; tech superpowers 240; unequal power relations 266, 381
PPPs see public-private partnerships
PR see public relations
Practical Action 218–219
pre-testing 141, 142–143, 146
'precariat' 223
precautionary principle 210
prescription drugs 128, 129, 133–134, 310–328
price 4, 13, 84, 103, 104, 108–110, 240; audience research 160; competition 231; competitive orientation 27; corporate marketing 224; corporate stimulation of consumption 241; ethical issues 280; fast fashion 504, 505, 506; formulating the offer 86; 'Moi(s) sans tabac' 448; Porto Tap Water 104, 384; SIMPle 321–322, 323; SME environmental behaviour in Pakistan 472; tobacco 22; waste management in Lebanon 402
Primark 226
privacy 140, 251, 286
pro-social behaviour 456
problem definition 141, 142, 159–160; Act-Belong-Commit campaign 483–484; cervical screening 556–557; colorectal cancer prevention 493; Cycle Against Suicide 433; drowning prevention 407; fast fashion 503; Fife Project 358–359; health communication in India 543; Less Eyes than Belly Movement 454; Meals on Wheels 339–340; 'Moi(s) sans tabac' 445–446; point of sale tobacco marketing 463–464; Porto Tap Water 381–382; Reduce Your Juice 347; Sea for Society 330; SME environmental behaviour in Pakistan 469

process evaluation 143, 324–325, 362, 379; Act-Belong-Commit campaign 486, 487; Making India Open Defecation Free 568–569; Walk to School 428, 429
Prochaska, J.O. 55, 56–57, 75
product 4, 84, 103, 104–108, 240; audience research 160; competition 201; corporate stimulation of consumption 241; differentiation 231, 242, 465; ethical issues 279, 280, 282; formulating the offer 86; 'Moi(s) sans tabac' 448; Porto Tap Water 104, 384–385; SIMPle 314–319, 321–322; SME environmental behaviour in Pakistan 472; speed of adoption 475; stakeholder analysis 92; substitution 194–195, 198, 200; user-driven 157; waste management in Lebanon 398–399
product development 13, 107–108, 224, 264
profit motive 6, 222, 240, 272, 295–296
progressive learning 87, 121–122
projective techniques 134, 136
promotion 4, 13, 18, 103, 105, 111; audience research 160; communication 157; drowning prevention 412; ethical issues 280; formulating the offer 86; health communication in India 20; Making India Open Defecation Free 20, 571; 'Moi(s) sans tabac' 450; point of sale tobacco marketing 463, 464–465; Porto Tap Water 104, 384; SIMPle 321–322, 323; SME environmental behaviour in Pakistan 473; waste management in Lebanon 399
propaganda 234
PSA Group 447
psychographic characteristics 94, 95, 96
psychopaths, corporations as 224
public-private partnerships (PPPs) 542, 543–544, 546–550, 552–554
public relations (PR) 105, 224, 245; corporate social responsibility 242; drowning prevention 412, 415; Porto Tap Water 104, 387, 388; Walk to School 424
Pupavac, Vanessa 271
purchase behaviour 94
push marketing 109

qualitative research 35, 132–137, 139, 142, 147, 284, 323, 569; see also interviews
qualitative sampling 20

quality of life 8, 64
quantitative research 126, 137–139, 142, 147, 323, 569; see also surveys
Quechua Indians 218–219
Quelch, J.A. 10
questioning procedures 138–139
questionnaires 138–139; Act-Belong-Commit campaign 144, 487; mental health 486; see also surveys

radicalisation 489
radio: corporatisation 181; Cycle Against Suicide 440, 441, 443; Fife Project 358; health communication in India 546, 547, 548, 553; Less Eyes than Belly Movement 458; Making India Open Defecation Free 572; manipulative communication 156; 'Moi(s) sans tabac' 447; Safefood's obesity campaign 159; 'The Talk' campaign 415; *The War of the Worlds* 155
randomised controlled trials (RCTs) 126–127, 129, 131; colorectal cancer prevention 497; SIMPle 314, 324, 325
Rangun, Kash 109, 455
RARE Pride campaigns 296
Raza, Syed Aamir 244
RBS see Royal Bank of Scotland
RCTs see randomised controlled trials
rebellion 259, 265, 273, 301
reciprocity 537, 538–539
recklessness 525, 526, 530
recycling 9, 10, 78; competition 200–201; costs 109; fashion retailers 506; inequalities linked to 95; waste management in Lebanon 392, 393, 394, 395, 397, 403
reduce and reuse 19, 392, 397, 398–399, 400–403
Reduce Your Juice (RYJ) 18, 66, 165, 346–356
regional health authorities (RHAs) 445, 446
regulation 13, 207–210, 241, 244–245; advertising 239; common pool resources 522–523; containment 272; corporate social responsibility 544; financial 241–242; media 238; salt intake reduction 479; SME environmental behaviour in Pakistan 469, 474; smoking 62; stakeholder analysis 91; strategic 215; tobacco control 88, 247n4, 462–463, 464, 465, 466; waste management in Lebanon 391; whale shark tourism in Ningaloo Reef 521

Reichheld, F.F. 101–102

reinforcement 77

relationship marketing 12, 43–47, 102, 177, 259, 456

relationships: importance of 76; Sea for Society 536–537, 538, 539

relativity 105

Remafedi, G. 362

reputation 4, 108, 388; corporate social responsibility 242; digital marketing 177; stakeholder marketing 242; waste management in Lebanon 393

research 120–148; Act-Belong-Commit campaign 485, 486; cervical screening 20, 557–564; colorectal cancer prevention 498–499; communication 158–165, 181; community social marketing 300; Cycle Against Suicide 438; for decision-making 146–147; drowning prevention 413; ethical issues 279, 280, 281, 284; ethnographic 35; Fife Project 360–362; health communication in India 20; Less Eyes than Belly Movement 455; Making India Open Defecation Free 568–577; Meals on Wheels 36, 343–344; 'Moi(s) sans tabac' 448; as a navigational aid 120, 121, 147; online 139–140; participatory 18, 36, 132, 485; Porto Tap Water 382–383; positivist versus humanist 125–126; Reduce Your Juice 348, 349–350; research process 141, 142–146; Sea for Society 332–337, 538; secondary 129–132; SIMPle 311–313, 317, 325; SME environmental behaviour in Pakistan 473–474; storytelling 124–125, 148; systems social marketing 303; Walk to School 427; waste management in Lebanon 19, 395; see also data collection; market research; qualitative research; quantitative research

research and development (R&D) 92

resistance 17

resource boundaries 517, 519, 523

responsibility: individual xxxiii, 13–14, 217–220, 227, 245, 256, 378; modern slavery 256; 'responsible citizen' identity 397; rights and 251

responsivity 98–99

reusable bags 402, 403

reverse socialisation 414, 416

Revlon, Charles 73

rewards: common pool resources 513; digital marketing 179; Less Eyes than Belly Movement 459; Making India Open Defecation Free 577; message content 168; operant conditioning 351; Reduce Your Juice 349, 350

Rey-Pino, Juan Miguel 462–467

RHAs see regional health authorities

Rich, N. 201

rights: access 514–516, 522; common pool resources 517; ethical issues 286; whale shark tourism in Ningaloo Reef 520, 522; see also human rights

'risk proliferation' 283

RLSSA see Royal Life Saving Society – Australia

road safety 9, 10; fear campaigns 154, 167–169, 170, 526; Foolsspeed campaign 162, 164; seatbelts 109; social context 28; Walk to School 422; Wheels, Skills and Thrills 20, 34, 114, 300, 525–533

Roberts, Carter 200

Rogers, E.M. 475

Rogers, R.W. 166

role models 395, 531

Rowan, Neil 555–566

Roy, Arundhati 244, 270–271

Royal Bank of Scotland (RBS) 222, 247n5

Royal Life Saving Society – Australia (RLSSA) 406–407, 412, 413–415, 417

Ruiz, A. 388, 460

Rundle-Thiele, Sharyn 10, 130, 420–431

Russell-Bennett, Rebekah 37, 346–356

RYJ see Reduce Your Juice

safe sex 33, 35, 36, 101, 102; audience research 159–160, 162, 165; ethical issues 282, 283; marketing mix 103; Scottish health education 173; see also condoms; sexual behaviour

Safefood 46, 159, 163, 176–177, 180

Safta, Elodie 444–452

Sainsbury's 252, 255

salt intake 19, 478–481

sampling 20, 137–138, 559

Samson, Kay 357–380

Sands, Sean 502–508

sanitation 20, 139, 154, 158, 305, 567–579

Santé Publique France 444–451

Saren, M. 241

Saro-Wiwa, Ken 243

Save the Children UK 243–244
SBCC *see* social and behaviour change communication
SBM–G *see* Swachh Bharat Mission – Gramin
Scharf, Tom 339–345
Schneider, Tali 492–501
school dinners 194
schools: Cycle Against Suicide 436, 437, 438–439, 440; Fife Project 357–358, 359, 363–378; health communication in India 550, 552; Making India Open Defecation Free 571; suicide prevention programmes 434; Walk to School campaign 421–429; waste management in Lebanon 399, 400–401, 402, 403
Schwalbe, K. 341, 343
Schwartz, S.H. 70
Scotland: audience research 162; cancer screening 99; Fife Project 357–380; focus groups 136; health education 173; motives of non-smokers 257; smoke-free public places 40–41, 43, 62, 272; teenage anti-smoking campaign failure 134–135; underage smokers 283
Scottish Health Education Group (SHEG) 173
SCS *see* Smoking Cessation Service
SCT *see* social cognitive theory
Sea for Society 18, 140, 145, 298, 305, 329–338; indicators 20, 306–307, 534–541
Seabrook, Jeremy 227
seatbelts 109
secondary research 129–132
segmentation 84, 86, 93–99, 114, 302; colorectal cancer prevention 494–495; community social marketing 300; digital marketing 177; ethical issues 278, 281; Making India Open Defecation Free 577; Porto Tap Water 386; SIMPle 311; social cost of 228–229; system indicators 535; systems social marketing 303–304; waste management in Lebanon 394–395
self-efficacy 60, 95, 378
self-enhancement bias 526, 530
self-esteem 530
self-harm 252–253, 273, 433
self-image reinforcement 529
self-interest 68–71, 72, 222, 256, 296; balanced with mutuality and morality 261, 292; client power 195; critical marketing 216; systems social marketing 302, 303

self-regulation 206–207, 208
self-transcendence 264
selfishness 229–232
service quality 43
7Ps 103–114, 159; *see also* marketing mix
sexual behaviour 35, 36, 86; ethical issues 276–277, 279, 280, 281, 282, 284; marketing mix 103; qualitative research 135; social norms 61; teenagers 101, 102, 159–160; *see also* safe sex
shareholders 8, 231, 240
Sharma, Animesh 567–579
SHEG *see* Scottish Health Education Group
Shell 243
Simon, F. 527
SIMPle 17, 18, 41, 132–133, 310–328
Singapore 168, 195
situation analysis 86, 87–89, 200; abolitionists 254; colorectal cancer prevention 494; ethical issues 280; systems social marketing 302, 303; waste management in Lebanon 392–393
skills 60, 77
slavery 254–256
slow fashion 506
Smadja, Olivier 444–452
small and medium-sized enterprises (SMEs) 19, 195, 468–477
Smirnoff 202–203
Smith, Anne M. 468–477
Smith, Bill 27, 33–34
Smith, Marsha 111
Smith, R. 255
smoking 5, 9, 10, 17, 21–22, 156, 484; advertising 88; age at starting 219–220; benefits of quitting 196; branding 128, 172, 173; client orientation 29; co-opetition 204; commercial promotion of 7, 220–221; community social marketing 297, 300–301; competitive analysis 13, 193, 197, 198, 199, 201–202, 204; costs 109; ethical issues 279, 283, 284; fear messages 279; Fife Project 18, 104, 357–380; health issues 252; image values 68; inequalities linked to 95; insights into behaviour 102, 147; Mandela on 124; 'Moi(s) sans tabac' 19, 300–301, 444–452; motives of non-smokers 257; objectives 101; plain packaging 210; point of sale marketing 19, 76, 89, 208–209, 221, 463–466; product changes 32–33;

regulation 208–209, 244; relational thinking 102; right to protection from 269; Scottish health education 173; Singapore Pro-Quitting campaign 168, 195; smoke-free public places 40–41, 43, 62, 103, 272; social cognitive theory 61; social context 28; social epistemology theory 63; social norms 61, 62; stages of change theory 55, 56, 57–58; Stoptober 299, 445; symbolic value 171; taxation 283–284; teenage anti-smoking campaign failure 134–135; teenagers 38, 68, 106; tobacco control in Colombia 462–467; Truth Campaign xxxiii, 38, 204, 269, 272, 299, 300–301; see also tobacco industry
Smoking Cessation Service (SCS) 57, 59
Snapchat 139–140, 160, 177, 440
Snow, John 218, 219
social and behaviour change communication (SBCC) 542, 546, 549
social capital theory 53, 64–66, 78
social change xxxi, 13, 28, 48, 154, 257; behaviour change linked to 292; citizen-oriented 460; communication 460; community-based social marketing 432–433; community infrastructure 300; environmental protection 535; evaluation 144, 146; individual as motive force of 265; individual responsibility 227; popular engagement in 271; Porto Tap Water 388; positivist perspective 153; right to participation 268, 269, 286; Sea for Society 305, 539; SME environmental behaviour in Pakistan 468; values 500; see also behaviour change; systemic change
social class 21–22, 172, 177
social cognitive theory (SCT) 53, 55, 59–61, 75, 76, 78; ethical issues 283; role models 395; segmentation 95
social cohesion 6, 397
social contagion 67, 299, 451, 527
social context 27, 28, 53, 60, 215, 241, 361
social ecological theory (SET) 53, 64, 65, 75, 78
social epistemology theory 53, 63–64, 78
social franchising 482, 486–487
social justice 64
social marketing: definition of 9, 15–16, 21; emergence of 8–10; orientations 27–42, 44, 47–48; relational thinking 47; role of 217; 3Cs of 272

social mechanisms 301, 303
social media xxxi, 16–17, 154, 182; cervical screening 563; consumer collusion 259; Cycle Against Suicide 440, 441; digital marketing 176, 177, 179, 180; drowning prevention 412, 415; Fife Project 360–361; food safety 46; growth in marketing on 237; health communication in India 548; health promotion 362; 'Moi(s) sans tabac' 450; online research 139–140; Porto Tap Water 387, 388; promotion 105; Reduce Your Juice 349; SIMPle 17, 18; Walk to School 423, 424, 426, 427; see also Facebook; Twitter
social movements xxxiii, 19, 48, 298–301, 302
social networking sites 4, 139–140, 154, 177, 295, 362; see also social media
social norms theory (SNT) 53, 61–63, 75, 78; see also norms
social progress 251, 295, 296, 297–298, 302
social-systems approach 417
societal influence 348
'solutionism' 265
source credibility 43, 110, 177, 416
source effects 63–64
Spain 233, 331–332, 538
species extinction 253
speeding 526–527
spiritual dimensions xxxiii, 245, 250–275; collective agency 265; human rights 265–269; humanity 263–264; Maori hui 269–271; moral agency 256–259, 261–262; transcendence 264–265
sponsorship 235
SRs see systematic reviews
stages of change theory 43, 53, 55–59, 78
stakeholder analysis 86, 89–93, 302; Act-Belong-Commit campaign 485; cervical screening 557; Cycle Against Suicide 436; drowning prevention 408; ethical issues 280; health communication in India 544–545; Less Eyes than Belly Movement 454; Meals on Wheels 340–341; 'Moi(s) sans tabac' 446–447; Porto Tap Water 382; Reduce Your Juice 348–349; Sea for Society 331, 538; SME environmental behaviour in Pakistan 469–471; systems social marketing 303; Walk to School 426–427

stakeholder marketing 13, 193, 207, 242, 259, 272
stakeholders: abolitionists 254; Act-Belong-Commit campaign 485; cervical screening 557; colorectal cancer prevention 498, 499; community social marketing 294, 296, 298, 300, 307, 340–341; corporate marketing 224; Cycle Against Suicide 300, 436, 438, 442; definition of 89; drowning prevention 19, 408, 409–411, 412, 414, 415; environmental protection 535; ethical issues 283; health communication in India 544–545, 546; Interactive Management 337; Less Eyes than Belly Movement 454; Making India Open Defecation Free 568; mapping 93, 340, 341–343, 396, 409–411, 427; Meals on Wheels 339, 340–344; 'Moi(s) sans tabac' 446–447; Porto Tap Water 382, 386; problem definition 142; Reduce Your Juice 348–349; Sea for Society 18, 305, 331, 332–333, 337, 538; SME environmental behaviour in Pakistan 469–471; smoke-free public places 40–41; systems social marketing 303, 307; Walk to School 426–427; waste management in Lebanon 395, 396
Star Trek 221
Stead, M. 127, 144
Steinbeck, John 222
stigma 109, 281; Cycle Against Suicide 435, 438, 442; mental health 484, 486, 488
Stoptober 299, 445
stories 120, 124–125, 127, 146, 148, 178, 179, 374
strategic planning 84, 85–87, 101, 121, 147; abolitionists 254; competition 189; critical marketing 215, 232–234; Cycle Against Suicide 437
structuration theory 37, 61
Student Leader Ambassadors 438–439, 441, 442
Student Leaders' Congress 439–440, 441
Suanda, Julinawati 136, 555–566
substitution 194–195, 198, 200
suicide prevention 19, 300, 432–443, 488–489
summative evaluation indicators 535–536, 537, 539
summative research 145
Sunstein, C. 286

Super Kitchens 111
suppliers 194–195, 198–199, 201, 342, 343
surveys: Act-Belong-Commit campaign 487, 488; Making India Open Defecation Free 139, 569, 572, 573, 575–576; Reduce Your Juice 349–350; Sea for Society 538; *Walk to School* 427–428; *see also* questionnaires
sustainability 17, 18, 20, 47
Swachh Bharat Mission - Gramin (SBM-G) 567–579
Sweden: child wellbeing 233, 234; Sea for Society 331–332, 333–337, 538
Swinton, Tim 346–356
Switzerland 538
SWOT analysis 88, 89, 200, 393
symbolic meaning 388; *see also* cultural symbolism
symbolic needs 60
system dynamics modelling 20, 493, 498–499, 500
system indicators 535–540
systematic reviews (SRs) 129–131, 209–210
systemic change 148, 218, 219, 292, 293; mental health promotion 482; relational thinking 47; SME environmental behaviour in Pakistan 475–476; top-down and bottom-up 245; *see also* social change
systems analysis 302, 303
systems social marketing xxxiii, 294, 295–296, 302–307
systems thinking 16, 17, 257, 293–294, 295–296; colorectal cancer prevention 499, 500; Community Based Prevention Marketing 493; Interactive Management 337; macro-social marketing perspective 509; Ningaloo Reef 510
Szablewska, N. 266

The Taj Must Smile 20, 161, 545–550
Taleb, N.N. 35
'The Talk' campaign 162, 171, 198, 406–407, 413–417
Tanovic, Danis 244
Tapp, Alan 525–533
target audiences 98–99, 144; colorectal cancer prevention 494–496; communication 159, 417; community social marketing 297; Cycle Against Suicide 434, 435, 443; health communication in India 545; 'Moi(s) sans

tabac' 446; participation 111; Porto Tap Water 388; SME environmental behaviour in Pakistan 471, 472; waste management in Lebanon 394–395, 398, 399; Wheels, Skills and Thrills 528; see also audience research; segmentation

targeting xxxi–xxxii, 84, 86, 93–99, 114, 170, 302; community social marketing 300; digital marketing 177; ethical issues 278, 279, 280, 281; Porto Tap Water 19; social cost of 228–229; see also segmentation

tax dodging 223

tax on cigarettes 283–284

technology: black-box telematics 530, 532; NVivo software 561; obesity interventions 257–258; Reduce Your Juice 18; SIMPle 18; SME environmental behaviour in Pakistan 472, 473; see also apps; digital marketing; digital technology; mobile technology; social media

teenagers: cervical screening 555, 556; safe sex 101, 102, 109, 140, 159–160; smoking 38, 68, 106, 202, 361, 462; teenage pregnancy 282

teleological theory 285–286

television: cervical screening 563; corporatisation 181; Cycle Against Suicide 441, 443; health communication in India 546, 547, 548; Less Eyes than Belly Movement 458; manipulative communication 156; 'Moi(s) sans tabac' 447; Operation Transformation 180; Safefood's obesity campaign 159; 'The Talk' campaign 415

Tesco 43, 102, 252, 255

Thaler, R. 286

thalidomide 126–127

Thanh, Viêt Nguyen 444–452

theory 15, 19, 52–79; ethical issues 285–287, 289

Think! campaign 526

Thomas, Michael 222

Thoreau, Henry David 267–268

3Cs 272

thrill seeking 525, 526, 527

Tian, K.T. 504

Time magazine 238

tobacco industry xxxiii, 221, 300–301; advertising expenditure 22; competitive

analysis 197, 199, 446; competitive strategy 92; Fife Project 364–365; FOREST 220; point of sale marketing 463–466; product changes 32–33; regulation 208–209; relationships with politicians 193; right to protection from the 269; smoke-free public places 41; success of the 39; Truth Campaign 204; see also smoking

Tones, Keith 32, 96

tourism: Ningaloo Reef 20, 47, 271, 510, 511–512, 513–523; Sea for Society 330, 331, 332

trade 505

Traffic Light System (TLS) of food labelling 480

transcendence 264–265

transparency 286

Transtheoretical Model of Behavior Change (stages of change theory) 43, 53, 55–59, 78, 312

trust 43, 45–46, 47, 127, 301, 460; branding 383; digital marketing 177, 355; emotional communication 172; inequalities 228; multiple interpretation of value 296; online research 140; partnerships 105; Porto Tap Water 383, 385; Sea for Society 306, 537, 538, 539; social capital 65; systems social marketing 306; waste management in Lebanon 393; Wheels, Skills and Thrills 529

Truth Campaign xxxiii, 38, 204, 269, 272, 299, 300–301

Turkey 504

Twitter 16, 295; Cycle Against Suicide 440, 441; digital marketing 176, 177–178; drowning prevention 415; health communication in India 548; 'Moi(s) sans tabac' 447; online research 139–140; Operation Transformation 180; personalised content 362; Walk to School 426

two-step model 156

Tyson, Dinorah Martinez 492–501

ubiquity 215, 234–236

UNICEF see United Nations Children's Fund

Unilever 207

unintended effects 283–284

Uniqlo 506

United Kingdom: Act-Belong-Commit campaign 489; alcohol industry 88; child wellbeing 233, 234; common land in England 516; consumer debt 252–253; Fife Project 18; financial lobbying 241–242; health 98, 286; inequalities 95; International Tobacco Control Policy Evaluation Project 209; modern slavery 256; obesity 199, 221; salt intake reduction 19, 478–481; Sea for Society 538; Stoptober 299, 445; textile waste 503; tobacco advertising 88, 247n4; tobacco industry 22; Wheels, Skills and Thrills 20, 525–533; *see also* Scotland

United Nations 266, 269, 273

United Nations Children's Fund (UNICEF) 233, 234, 247n22

United States of America (USA): Act-Belong-Commit campaign 489; children's physical activity 420; colorectal cancer prevention 20, 492–501; fast fashion 504; food inequalities 230; International Tobacco Control Policy Evaluation Project 209; obesity 221; screen time 237; textile waste 503; tobacco advertising 88

Universal Declaration of Human Rights 251, 266

University of Minho 454–460

University of South Florida 304–305, 492–500

upstream social marketing 11, 89, 99, 271; ethical issues 283; mental health 484; salt intake reduction 19, 479

urinary tract infections (UTIs) 311–325

US Agency for International Development (USAID) 542, 543, 545, 546, 550

user-generated content 154

uses and gratifications approaches 156

utilitarianism 285–286

Uzbekistan 505

vaccinations: flu 72, 73; HPV 555–566; MMR vaccine 43, 46

value 68–71; branding 383; co-delivery 105, 111, 269; co-design 105, 111, 269; co-discovery 105, 111; corporate social responsibility 242; joint creation of 30; multiple interpretation of 296; Porto Tap Water 384; value creation and value destruction 71; *see also* co-creation

value action fields (VATs) 70–71, 72, 73, 111, 302

value-driven exchanges (VETs) 17, 71, 72, 73, 111, 302, 303, 307

values xxxii, 68–71, 78, 165; Act-Belong-Commit campaign 19; behavioural norms 509; behavioural science 77; change in 500; client orientation 27; community social marketing 298, 307; exchange theory 53, 72; humanitarian xxxiii; importance of 76; Less Eyes than Belly Movement 458–459; message content 171; 'Moi(s) sans tabac' 448; outcome indicators 534; partnerships 105; Sea for Society 330, 539; social capital 65; social movements 299; sponsorship 235; strategic regulation 215; systems social marketing 305; *see also* attitudes; beliefs

Vatican xxxii

VATs *see* value action fields

Vellinga, Akke 310–328

VETs *see* value-driven exchanges

viability 98

victim blaming 37, 61, 217, 218, 257

Victorian Health Promotion Foundation (VicHealth) 421–429

viral marketing 4

vision 83–84, 87, 254

volunteerism 489

VW 32, 33

Vyas, Sanjeev 161, 542–554

Wahga, Aqueel I. 468–477

Wal-Mart 236, 252

Walk to School 19, 39, 420–431

Wallace, David Foster 36–37, 215, 220, 226, 241, 244, 301

Wallack, Lawrence 11–12, 99

Walmart 43

Walsh, D.C. 33

The War of the Worlds 155

War on Want 244

Warfield, J. 332

waste 9, 10, 17; community social marketing 297; food 453–461; solid waste management in Lebanon 19, 390–405; textiles 503

water scarcity 573, 577

Wattanasuwan, K. 388

Waves of Freedom 112

Weber Shandwick PR 547

websites: Act-Belong-Commit campaign 487; drowning prevention 416–417;

'Moi(s) sans tabac' 447, 448; promotion 105; *Walk to School* 423, 427
Welles, Orson 155
West, Robert 57, 59
Wheels, Skills and Thrills 20, 34, 114, 300, 525–533
Whitbread, Jasmine 243–244
WHO *see* World Health Organisation
wicked problems 48, 90, 140, 148, 253; antibiotic resistance 310–311; community social marketing 298; environmental damage 509; fast fashion 20, 503, 505–506, 507; Interactive Management 337; marine environment 330; system indicators 539; systems social marketing 307; systems thinking 257, 293–294, 295, 302
Wiebe, G.D. 8–9, 73
Wilberforce, William 254
Wilkie, W.L. 13, 216–217
Wilkinson, Richard 228
win-wins 31, 47, 67, 92, 188, 292
wine 112, 113
women: cervical screening 96–97, 110, 135–136, 284, 555–566; clothing

industry 505; Making India Open Defecation Free 574, 575, 577
Wood, M. 71
working-class people 172
working conditions 505
workplace engagement 424–426
World Health Organisation (WHO) 5, 197, 209, 252; children's physical activity 420–421; definition of health 196; Framework Convention on Tobacco Control 463; hazard merchants 201, 202; leather and tanning industry 476; salt intake reduction 480
World Wildlife Fund (WWF) 199, 200
Wright, Annemarie 420–431
Wu, Timothy 181
WWF *see* World Wildlife Fund

Yahoo 179
YouTube 160, 177, 179; drowning prevention 415; health communication in India 548; personalised content 362

Zaltman, G. 9, 110
Zamzee 257–259
Zuckerberg, Mark 236